murach's HTML5 and CSS3

3RD EDITION

Anne Boehm

Zak Ruvalcaba

TRAINING & REFERENCE

murach's HTML5 and CSS3

3RD EDITION

Anne Boehm

Zak Ruvalcaba

MIKE MURACH & ASSOCIATES, INC.

4340 N. Knoll Ave. • Fresno, CA 93722

www.murach.com • murachbooks@murach.com

SHROFF PUBLISHERS & DISTRIBUTORS PVT. LTD.

Mumbai *Bangalore* *Kolkata* *New Delhi*

Editorial team

Authors: Anne Boehm
Zak Ruvalcaba

Editor: Mike Murach

Production: Maria Spera

Books for web developers

Murach's Dreamweaver CC 2014
Murach's JavaScript and jQuery
Murach's JavaScript
Murach's PHP and MySQL (2nd Edition)
Murach's Java Servlets and JSP (3rd Edition)
Murach's ASP.NET 4.5 Web Programming with C# 2012
Murach's ASP.NET 4.5 Web Programming with VB 2012

Books on Java, C#, and Visual Basic

Murach's Java Programming (4th Edition)
Murach's Android Programming
Murach's C# 2012
Murach's Visual Basic 2012

Books for database programmers

Murach's MySQL (2nd Edition)
Murach's SQL Server 2012 for Developers
Murach's Oracle SQL and PL/SQL for Developers (2nd Edition)

First Indian Reprint: March 2016
ISBN 13: 978-93-5213-324-6

Originally Printed in the United States of America
10 9 8 7 6 5 4 3 2 1 ISBN: 978-1-890774-83-7

Published by **Shroff Publishers and Distributors Pvt. Ltd.** C-103, MIDC, TTC Industrial Area, Pawane, Navi Mumbai 400 703, Tel: (91 22) 4158 4158, Fax: (91 22) 4158 4141, Web : www.shroffpublishers.com CIN : U22200MH1992PTC067760 Printed at Decora Book Prints Pvt. Ltd., Mumbai.

Content

Expanded contents

Section 1 A crash course in HTML and CSS

Chapter 3 How to use HTML to structure a web page

Chapter 4 How to use CSS to format the elements of a web page

Introduction

This 3rd edition of our best-selling book integrates all of the HTML5 and CSS3 skills that you need today with the proven instructional approach that made the first two editions of this book so popular. And now, this new edition includes Responsive Web Design, which has become an essential skill for professional web developers.

That's why this the right book if you're learning HTML and CSS for the first time. But this is also the right book if you're a web developer who wants to expand and update your skills. That includes web designers, JavaScript and jQuery programmers, and server-side programmers...because we all need a solid set of HTML5 and CSS3 skills and a great on-the-job reference.

What this book does

- To get you started right, the eight chapters in section 1 present a complete subset of HTML and CSS that shows you how to develop web pages at a professional level. In chapter 3, for example, you'll learn how to use the HTML5 semantic elements. Then, chapters 4 through 6 show you how to use CSS and CSS3 to format the HTML, including the CSS3 properties for text and border shadows, background gradients, and text columns.
- The last chapter in section 1 shows you how to build web pages with Responsive Web Design. That means that your pages will look good and work correctly on every type of screen from phone to tablet to desktop computer. This is an essential skill for a modern website, and that's why it's presented in section 1.
- When you finish the first 8 chapters, you will have the perspective and skills you need for developing professional web pages. Then, you can add to those skills by reading any of the chapters in the next 3 sections...and you don't have to read those sections or chapters in sequence. In other words, you can skip to any of the last three sections after you finish section 1.

- The chapters in section 2 let you learn new skills whenever you need them... like having a mentor right at your side, showing you how to do whatever you need to know next. If, for example, you want to learn how to use the HTML5 data validation features for forms, you can skip to chapter 11. If you want to learn how to use the HTML5 audio and video tags, you can skip to chapter 12. And if you want to learn how to use CSS3 transitions, transforms, animation, and filters, you can skip to chapter 14.
- Because most modern websites use some JavaScript, chapters 15 and 16 of section 3 show you how to use JavaScript, jQuery, jQuery UI, and jQuery plugins to add features like image swaps, carousels, accordions, and slide shows to a website. Then, chapter 17 shows you how to use jQuery Mobile to develop a separate website for mobile devices, which makes sense when it's impractical to convert an established website to Responsive Web Design.
- Finally, section 4 presents two related subjects that you can skip to whenever you're ready for them. In chapter 18, you can learn the basic principles for designing a website. In chapter 19, you can learn how to deploy a website and get it into the search engines.

Why you'll learn faster and better with this book

Like all our books, this one has features that you won't find in competing books. That's why we believe you'll learn faster and better with our book than with any other. Here are a few of those features.

- From the first page to the last, this book shows you how to use HTML and CSS the modern, professional way, with HTML for the structure and content of each page and CSS for the formatting and page layout. That way, your web pages and your websites will be easier to create and maintain.
- Because HTML5 and CSS3 are integrated throughout the book, you won't learn these features out of context, which is the way they're treated in most competing books. Instead, you'll learn exactly where these features fit into the overall context of website development.
- Because section 1 presents a complete subset of HTML and CSS, you are ready for productive work much sooner than you are when you use competing books. In many competing books, for example, you won't learn how to use CSS for page layout until late in the book, even though that's a critical part of web page development.
- If you page through this book, you'll see that all of the information is presented in "paired pages," with the essential syntax, guidelines, and examples on the right page and the perspective and extra explanation on the left page. This helps you learn faster by reading less...and this is the ideal reference format when you need to refresh your memory about how to do something.

- To show you how HTML and CSS work together, this book presents all the code for complete web pages that range from the simple to the complex. To see how that works, page through chapters 4, 5, and 6 to see the pages that they present. As we see it, studying complete examples like these is the best way to master HTML and CSS because they show the relationships between the segments of code. And yet, most competing books limit themselves to snippets of code that don't show these relationships.
- Of course, this book also presents dozens of short examples. So it's easy to find an example that shows you how to do whatever you need to do as you develop web pages. And our "paired pages" presentation method makes it much easier to find the example that you're looking for than it is with traditional presentations where the code is embedded in the text.

What software you need

To develop web pages with HTML and CSS, you can use any text editor that you like. However, a text editor that includes syntax coloring and auto-completion will help you develop applications more quickly and with fewer errors. That's why we recommend Aptana Studio 3 for both Windows and Mac OS users. Although Aptana is free, it provides many powerful features.

Then, to test a web page, you need multiple web browsers. Because the older versions of Internet Explorer deviated the most from the standards, you should always test your pages in IE. But we also recommend that you test your pages in browsers like Mozilla Firefox and Google's Chrome.

To help you install these products, Appendix A provides the website addresses and procedures that you'll need.

How our downloadable files can help you learn

If you go to our website at www.murach.com, you can download all the files that you need for getting the most from this book. These files include:

- the HTML and CSS files for all of the applications and examples in this book
- the HTML and CSS files that you will use as the starting points for the exercises in this book
- the HTML and CSS files for the solutions to the exercises in the book

These files let you test, review, and copy code. In addition, if you have any problems with the exercises, the solutions are there to help you over the learning blocks, which is an essential part of the learning process. Here again, appendix A shows you how to download and install these files.

Support materials for trainers and instructors

If you're a corporate trainer or a college instructor who would like to use this book for a course, we offer supporting materials that include: (1) a complete set of PowerPoint slides that you can use to review and reinforce the content of the book; (2) instructional objectives that describe the skills a student should have upon completion of each chapter; (3) test banks that measure mastery of those skills; (4) extra exercises beyond those in the book itself and projects that prove mastery; and (5) solutions to the extra exercises and projects.

To learn more about the instructor's materials and to find out how to get them, go to our website at www.murachforinstructors.com if you're an instructor. Or, if you're a trainer, go to www.murach.com and click on the Courseware for Trainers link. Another alternative is to call Kelly at 1-800-221-5528 or send an email to kelly@murach.com.

Please let us know how this book works for you

From the start of this project, we had three goals. First, we wanted to simplify and improve the second edition to help you learn even faster. Second, we wanted to add new material on Responsive Web Design because it is such an important part of modern website development. Third, we wanted to raise the level of expertise of the second edition so the new edition will work even better for professional developers.

Now, we hope we've succeeded. We thank you for buying this book. We wish you all the best with your web development. And if you have any comments, we would appreciate hearing from you.

Anne Boehm, Author
anne@murach.com

Zak Ruvalcaba
zak@modulemedia.com

Section 1

A crash course in HTML and CSS

The eight chapters in this section are designed to get you off to a fast start. First, chapter 1 presents the concepts and terms that you need for using HTML and CSS. Then, chapter 2 shows you how to enter, edit, test, and validate the HTML and CSS for the web pages of a website. These chapters provide all of the background that you need for learning the coding details of HTML and CSS.

Then, chapter 3 shows you how to code the HTML that defines the content and structure for a web page. Chapter 4 shows you how to code the CSS that does basic formatting to the HTML content. Chapter 5 shows you how to use the CSS box model for spacing, borders, and backgrounds. Chapter 6 shows you how to use CSS for page layout. And chapter 7 shows you how to work with links and lists.

Finally, chapter 8 shows you how to develop a website using Responsive Web Design. This is critical if you're developing a website that will be displayed on mobile devices such as smartphones and tablets as well as on PCs and Macs.

When you complete these chapters, you'll be able to develop web pages at a professional level. Then, you can expand your skills by reading the other chapters in this book.

Please note, however, that you don't have to read the chapters in the other sections in sequence. Instead, you can skip to the chapter that presents the skills that you want to learn next. In other words, the eight chapters in this section present the prerequisites for all of the other chapters, and all of the other chapters are written as independent learning modules. As a result, you can read any of those chapters whenever you need its skills.

1

Introduction to web development

This chapter introduces you to the concepts and terms that you need to work with HTML and CSS. When you're finished with this chapter, you'll have the background you need for learning how to build websites.

How web applications work

The *World Wide Web*, or web, consists of many components that work together to bring a web page to your desktop over the *Internet*. Before you start web pages of your own, you should have a basic understanding of how these components work together.

The components of a web application

The first diagram in figure 1-1 shows that web applications consist of *clients* and a *web server.* The clients are the computers, tablets, and mobile devices that use the web applications. They access the web pages through programs known as *web browsers*. The web server holds the files that make up a web application.

A *network* is a system that allows clients and servers to communicate. The Internet in turn is a large network that consists of many smaller networks. In a diagram like this, the "cloud" represents the network or Internet that connects the clients and servers.

In general, you don't need to know how the cloud works. But you should have a general idea of what's going on. That's why the second diagram in this figure gives you a conceptual view of the architecture of the Internet.

To start, networks can be categorized by size. A *local area network* (*LAN*) is a small network of computers that are near each other and can communicate with each other over short distances. Computers on a LAN are typically in the same building or in adjacent buildings. This type of network is often called an *intranet*, and it can be used to run web applications for use by employees only.

In contrast, a *wide area network* (*WAN*) consists of multiple LANs that have been connected together over long distances using *routers*. To pass information from one client to another, a router determines which network is closest to the destination and sends the information over that network. A WAN can be owned privately by one company or it can be shared by multiple companies.

An *Internet service provider* (*ISP*) is a company that owns a WAN that is connected to the Internet. An ISP leases access to its network to other companies that need to be connected to the Internet.

The Internet is a global network consisting of multiple WANs that have been connected together. ISPs connect their WANs at large routers called *Internet exchange points* (*IXP*). This allows anyone connected to the Internet to exchange information with anyone else.

This diagram shows an example of data crossing the Internet. Here, data is being sent from the client in the top left to the server in the bottom right. First, the data leaves the client's LAN and enters the WAN owned by the client's ISP. Next, the data is routed through IXPs to the WAN owned by the server's ISP. Then, it enters the server's LAN and finally reaches the server. All of this can happen in less than $1/10^{th}$ of a second.

The components of a web application

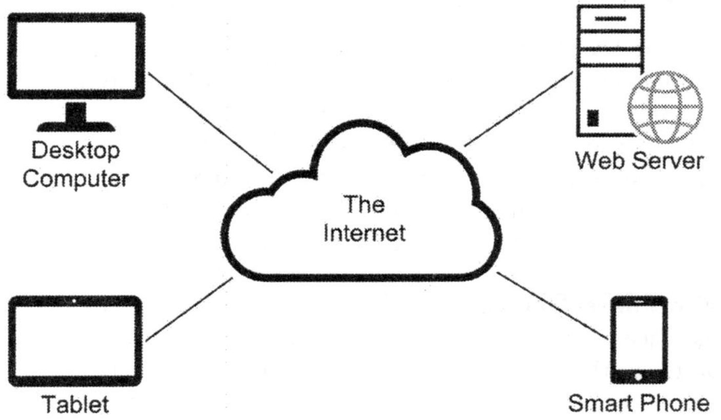

The architecture of the Internet

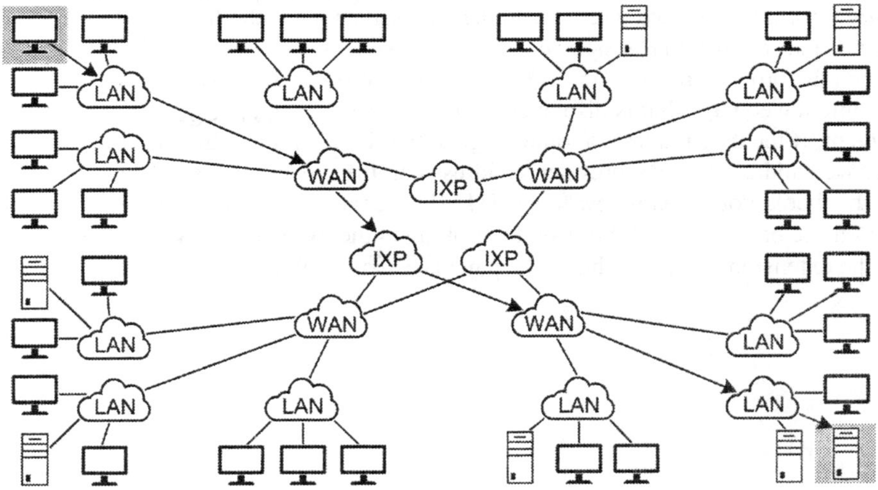

Description

- A web application consists of clients, a web server, and a network. The *clients* use programs known as *web browsers* to request web pages from the web server. The *web server* returns the pages that are requested to the browser.
- A *local area network* (LAN) directly connects computers that are near each other. This kind of network is often called an *intranet.*
- A *wide area network* (WAN) consists of two or more LANs that are connected by *routers.* The routers route information from one network to another.
- The *Internet* consists of many WANs that have been connected at *Internet exchange points* (IXP). There are several dozen IXPs located throughout the world.
- An *Internet service provider* (ISP) owns a WAN and leases access to its network. It connects its WAN to the rest of the Internet at one or more IXPs.

Figure 1-1 The components of a web application

How static web pages are processed

A *static web page* like the one at the top of figure 1-2 is a web page that only changes when the web developer changes it. This web page is sent directly from the web server to the web browser when the browser requests it.

The diagram in this figure shows how a web server processes a request for a static web page. This process begins when a client requests a web page in a web browser. To do that, the user can either type the address of the page into the browser's address bar or click a link in the current page that specifies the next page to load.

In either case, the web browser builds a request for the web page and sends it to the web server. This request, known as an *HTTP request*, is formatted using the *hypertext transfer protocol* (HTTP), which lets the web server know which file is being requested.

When the web server receives the HTTP request, it retrieves the requested file from the disk drive. This file contains the *HTML* (*HyperText Markup Language*) for the requested page. Then, the web server sends the file back to the browser as part of an *HTTP response*.

When the browser receives the HTTP response, it *renders* (translates) the HTML into a web page that is displayed in the browser. Then, the user can view the content. If the user requests another page, either by clicking a link or typing another web address into the browser's address bar, the process begins again.

In this book, you'll learn how to use HTML to create static web pages. You can spot these pages in a web browser by looking at the extension in the address bar. If the extension is .htm or .html, the page is a static web page.

A static web page at http://www.beachboardwalk.com

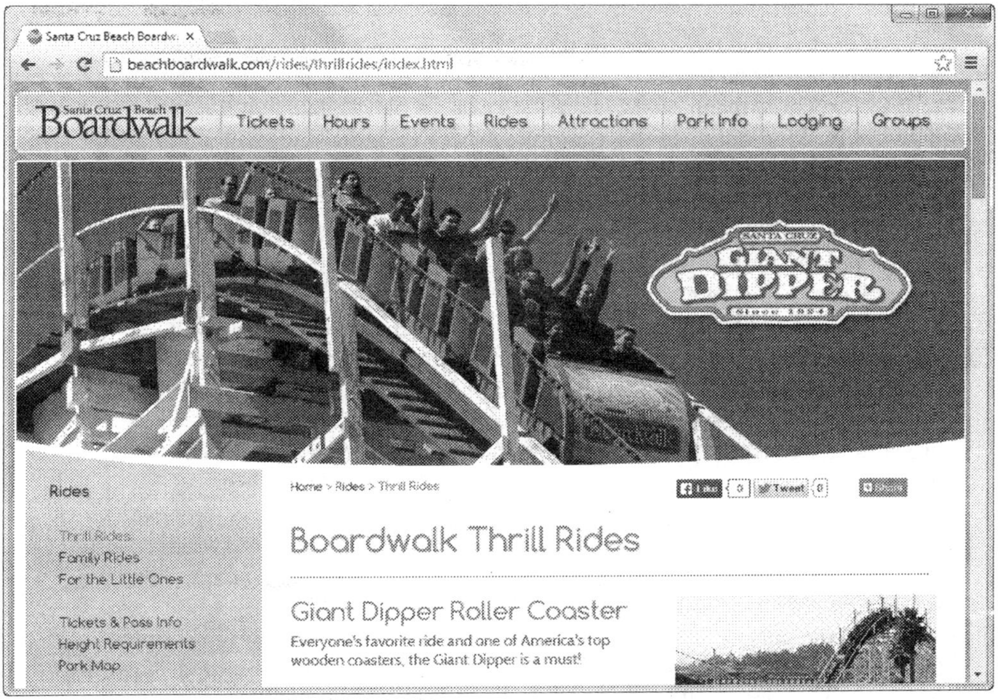

How a web server processes a static web page

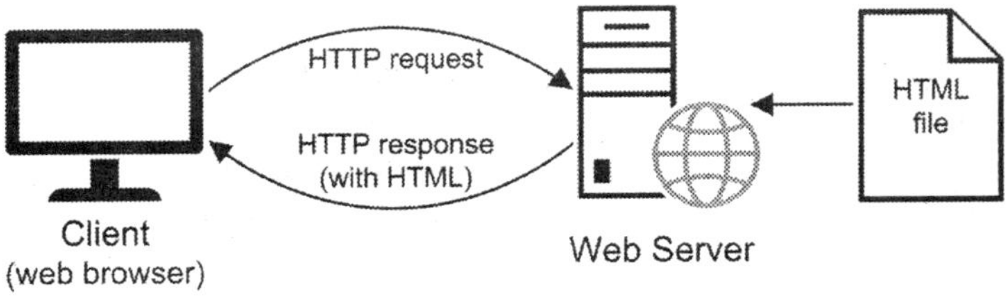

Description

- *Hypertext Markup Language* (*HTML*) is used to mark up web pages.
- A *static web page* is an HTML document that's stored on the web server and doesn't change. The filenames for static web pages have .htm or .html extensions.
- When the user requests a static web page, the browser sends an *HTTP request* to the web server that includes the name of the file that's being requested.
- When the web server receives the request, it retrieves the HTML for the web page and sends it back to the browser as part of an *HTTP response*.
- When the browser receives the HTTP response, it *renders* the HTML into a web page that is displayed in the browser.

Figure 1-2 How static web pages are processed

How dynamic web pages are processed

A *dynamic web page* like the one in figure 1-3 is a page that's created by a program or script on the web server each time it is requested. This program or script is executed by an *application server* based on the data that's sent along with the HTTP request. In this example, the HTTP request identified the book that's shown. Then, the program or script for the requested page retrieved the image and data for that book from a *database server*.

The diagram in this figure shows how a web server processes a dynamic web page. The process begins when the user requests a page in a web browser. To do that, the user can either type the URL of the page in the browser's address bar, click a link that specifies the dynamic page to load, or click a button that submits a form that contains the data that the dynamic page should process.

In each case, the web browser builds an HTTP request and sends it to the web server. This request includes whatever data the application needs for processing the request. If, for example, the user has entered data into a form, that data will be included in the HTTP request.

When the web server receives the HTTP request, the server examines the file extension of the requested web page to identify the application server that should process the request. The web server then forwards the request to the application server that processes that type of web page.

Next, the application server retrieves the appropriate program or script from the hard drive. It also loads any form data that the user submitted. Then, it executes the script. As the script executes, it generates the HTML for the web page. If necessary, the script will request data from a database server and use that data as part of the web page it is generating.

When the script is finished, the application server sends the dynamically generated HTML back to the web server. Then, the web server sends the HTML back to the browser in an HTTP response.

When the web browser receives the HTTP response, it renders the HTML and displays the web page. Note, however, that the web browser has no way to tell whether the HTML in the HTTP response was for a static page or a dynamic page. It just renders the HTML.

When the page is displayed, the user can view the content. Then, when the user requests another page, the process begins again. The process that begins with the user requesting a web page and ends with the server sending a response back to the client is called a *round trip*.

Dynamic web pages let you create interactive *web applications* that do all of the types of processing that you find on the Internet including eCommerce applications. Although you won't learn how to develop dynamic web pages in this book, you will learn how to create the HTML forms that send user data to the web server. Once you master HTML, you can learn how to use server-side languages like JSP, ASP, or PHP to create the dynamic pages that a website needs.

A dynamic web page at amazon.com

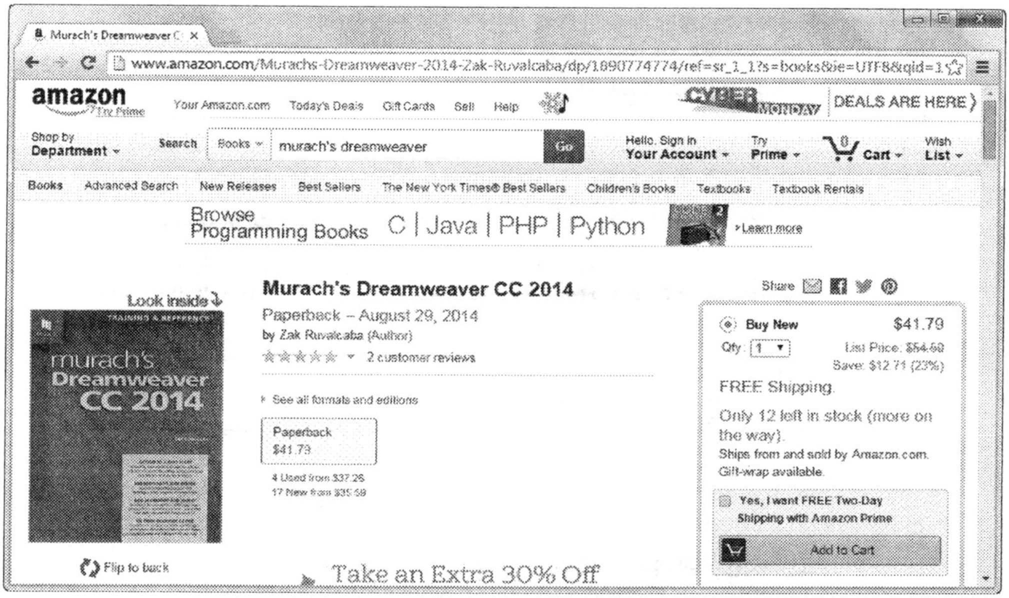

How a web server processes a dynamic web page

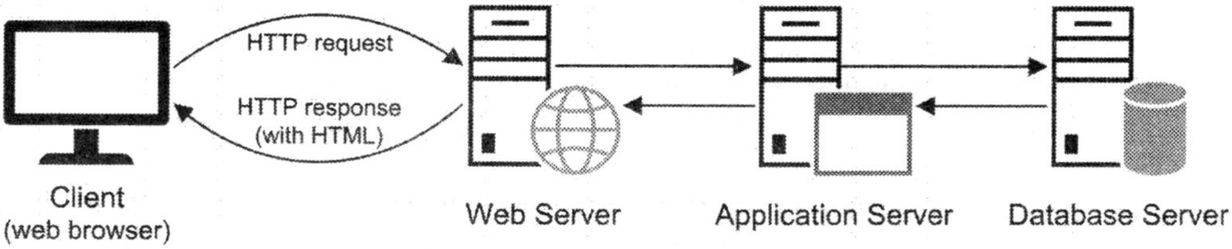

Description

- A *dynamic web page* is a web page that's generated by a server-side program or script.
- When a web server receives a request for a dynamic web page, it looks up the extension of the requested file to find out which *application server* should process the request.
- When the application server receives a request, it runs the specified script. Often, this script uses the data that it gets from the web browser to get the appropriate data from a *database server*. This script can also store the data that it receives in the database.
- When the application server finishes processing the data, it generates the HTML for a web page and returns it to the web server. Then, the web server returns the HTML to the web browser as part of an HTTP response.

Figure 1-3 How dynamic web pages are processed

A survey of web browsers and server-side scripting languages

Figure 1-4 summarizes the five web browsers that are used the most today. Google's Chrome is the most popular, even though it's a relatively recent addition to the choice of browsers. It has a clean, simple interface, it provides for searching directly from the address bar, and it has a large library of extensions and add-ons for developers. Plus, it's lightweight so it starts quickly and has a fast response time. Chrome is based on the WebKit rendering engine, and it's available for all major operating systems including Windows, Mac OS, and Linux.

Microsoft's Internet Explorer (IE) is the browser that comes with Windows. It was the most widely-used browser for many years, but Firefox has been catching up in recent years and Chrome has now surpassed it.

Like Chrome, Firefox is available for all major operating systems. Firefox was built using source code from the original Netscape Navigator web browser, and many web developers use it as their primary browser because they like its many features including its debugging features.

Safari and Opera are used by a smaller percentage of users. Safari is the default web browser on Mac OS, but it is also available for Windows. Opera is available for Windows, Mac OS, Linux, and other operating systems.

Next, this figure summarizes the most common *scripting languages* for web servers. These are the languages that let you develop dynamic web pages. For instance, ASP.NET is a Microsoft product. JSP is a free, open-source language that is commonly used with Java servlets. And PHP is another free, open-source language. To develop dynamic web pages, you need to choose the scripting language that you will use for *server-side processing*.

When you choose the scripting language, you also determine what web server you're going to need. For instance, JSP and PHP run on an *Apache web server*, which was developed by the Apache Software Foundation. It is an open-source software project that's available for free, and it runs on most operating systems, especially Linux systems. In contrast, ASP.NET runs on Microsoft's *Internet Information Services* (*IIS*), which isn't open source and runs on a Windows system.

Web browsers

Browser	Published by	Available on
Chrome	Google	All major operating systems
Internet Explorer	Microsoft	Windows
Firefox	Mozilla Corporation	All major operating systems
Safari	Apple	Macintosh and Windows
Opera	Opera Software	All major operating systems

Server-side scripting languages

Language	Description
ASP.NET	Runs on a Microsoft IIS web server. Its pages have the .aspx extension.
JSP	A free, open-source language that is commonly used with Java servlets. It runs on an Apache web server, and its pages have the .jsp extension.
PHP	A free, open-source language that is typically used with an Apache web server. Its pages have the .php extension.
ColdFusion	A commercial scripting language from Adobe that integrates well with Adobe Flash and Flex. Its pages have the .cfml file extension.
Ruby	A free, open-source language that is typically combined with the Rails framework to simplify development. Its pages have the .rb extension.
Perl	A free, open-source language that was originally designed for use at the UNIX command line to manipulate text. Its pages have the .pl extension.
Python	A free, open-source language that can be used to develop many types of applications besides web applications. Its pages have the .py extension.

Description

- When you develop a website for general use, you need to test it on all five of the web browsers listed above including all versions that are still in common use.
- To develop dynamic web pages, you use a *server-side scripting language* like ASP.NET, JSP, or PHP.
- The scripting languages are designed to run on specific web servers. The two most popular web servers are Microsoft IIS (Internet Information Services) and Apache.

Figure 1-4 A survey of web browsers and server-side scripting languages

How client-side JavaScript fits into web development

In contrast to the server-side processing that's done for dynamic web pages, *JavaScript* is a scripting language that provides for *client-side processing*. In the website in figure 1-5, for example, JavaScript is used to change the images that are shown without using server-side processing.

To make this work, all of the required images are loaded into the browser when the page is requested. Then, if the user clicks on one of the color swatches below a shirt, the shirt image is changed to the one with the right color. This is called an *image swap*. Similarly, if the user moves the mouse over a shirt, the image is replaced by a full-view image of the shirt. This is called an *image rollover*.

The diagram in this figure shows how JavaScript processing works. When a browser requests a web page, both the HTML and the related JavaScript are returned to the browser by the web server. Then, the JavaScript code is executed in the web browser by the browser's *JavaScript engine*. This takes some of the processing burden off the server and makes the application run faster. Often, JavaScript is used in conjunction with dynamic web pages, but it can also be used with static web pages.

Besides image swaps and rollovers, there are many other uses for JavaScript. For instance, another common use is to validate the data that the user enters into an HTML form before it is sent to the server for processing. This saves unnecessary trips to the server. Other common uses of JavaScript are to rotate headlines or products in one area of a web page and provide animation. In fact, whenever you see a portion of a web page cycle through a series of text blocks or images, that's probably being done by JavaScript.

In this book, you won't learn how to code JavaScript. However, you will learn how to use existing JavaScript routines in section 3 of this book. For instance, chapter 15 shows you how to use JavaScript and a JavaScript library known as jQuery to enhance your web pages with features like image swaps, image rollovers, and data validation. Then, chapter 16 shows you how to use the jQuery UI library and jQuery plugins to add features like accordions, pop-up dialog boxes, image galleries, and slide shows to your web pages.

A web page with image swaps and rollovers

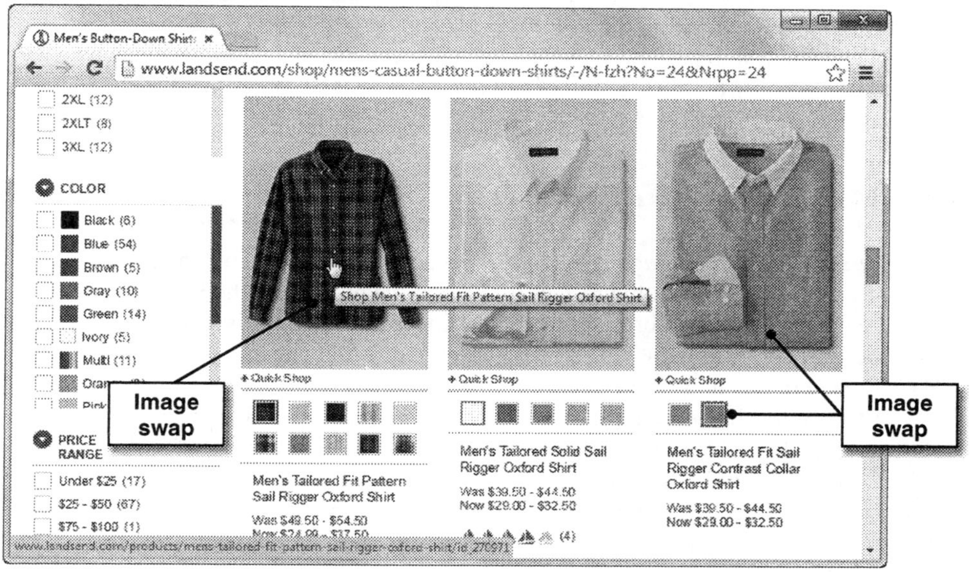

How JavaScript fits into this architecture

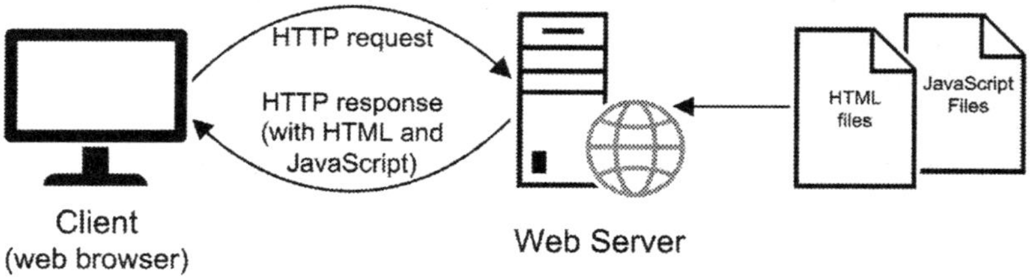

Three of the common uses of JavaScript

- Data validation
- Image swaps and rollovers
- Accordions

Description

- *JavaScript* is a *client-side scripting language* that is run by the *JavaScript engine* of a web browser.
- When the browser requests an HTML page that contains JavaScript or a link to a JavaScript file, both the HTML and the JavaScript are loaded into the browser.
- Because JavaScript runs on the client, not the server, it provides functions that don't require a trip back to the server. This can help an application run more efficiently.

Figure 1-5 How client-side JavaScript fits into web development

An introduction to HTML and CSS

To develop a web page, you use HTML to define the content and structure of the page. Then, you use CSS to format that content. The topics that follow introduce you to HTML and CSS.

The HTML for a web page

HyperText Markup Language (*HTML*) is used to define the content and structure of a web page. In figure 1-6, for example, you can see the HTML for a web page followed by a browser that shows how that page is displayed in the Chrome browser. Although you're going to learn how to code every aspect of an HTML page in this book, here's a brief introduction to what's going on.

The code for the entire page is called an *HTML document*. This document starts with a *DOCTYPE declaration* that is followed by *tags* that identify the *HTML elements* within the document. The *opening tag* for each element consists of the element name surrounded by angle brackets, as in <html>. And the *closing tag* consists of a left angle bracket, a forward slash, the element name, and the right angle bracket, as in </html>.

The basic structure of an HTML document consists of head and body elements that are coded within the html element. The head section contains elements that provide information about the document. The body section contains the elements that will be displayed in the web browser. For instance, the title element in the head section provides the title that's shown in the tab for the page in the web browser, while the h1 element in the body section provides the heading that's displayed in the browser window.

Many elements can be coded with *attributes* that identify the element and define the way the content in the element is displayed. These attributes are coded within the opening tag, and each attribute consists of an attribute name, an equals sign, and the attribute value. For instance, the <img> tag in this example has two attributes named src and alt. In this case, the src attribute provides the name of the image file that should be displayed and the alt attribute provides the text that should be displayed if the image can't be found.

The code for an HTML file named dreamweaver_book.html

```
<!doctype html>
<html lang="en">
    <head>
        <meta charset="utf-8">
        <title>Dreamweaver book</title>
    </head>
    <body>
        <h1>Dreamweaver CC 2014</h1>
        <img src="dreamweaverbook.jpg" alt="Dreamweaver Book">
        <p>Since 1996, Dreamweaver has been the leading product for web
           developers who want to build web pages by using a visual
           interface. Now, Dreamweaver CC 2014 takes that to a new level,
           with tools that make it easier than ever to take advantage of
           today's best web design practices.</p>
        <p>The trick to mastering Dreamweaver is learning how to use all of
           its windows, panels, toolbars, and web technologies. To find
           out how this book teaches you the skills you need, <a href="">
           read more...</a></p>
    </body>
</html>
```

The HTML displayed in a web browser

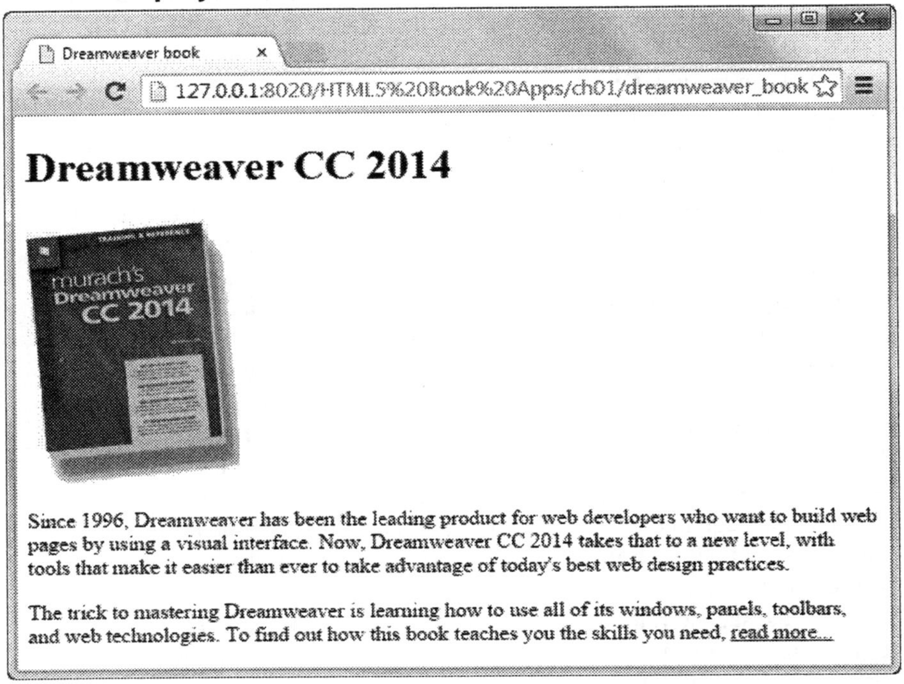

Description

- *HTML (HyperText Markup Language)* is used to define the structure and content of a web page.

Figure 1-6 The HTML for a web page

The CSS for a web page

Not long ago, HTML documents were coded so the HTML not only defined the content and structure of the web page but also the formatting of that content. However, this mix of structural and formatting elements made it hard to edit, maintain, and reformat the web pages.

Today, however, *Cascading Style Sheets* (*CSS*) let you separate the formatting from the content and structure of a web page. As a result, the formatting that was once done with HTML should now be done with CSS.

In most cases, the best way to apply a *style sheet* to an HTML document is to code the styles in a separate file called an *external style sheet*. Then, to apply the style sheet, you code a link element in the head section of the HTML document as shown at the top of figure 1-7. Here, the href attribute of the tag says that the style sheet in the file named book.css should be applied to the HTML document.

After this link element, you can see the CSS that's in the book.css file. This is followed by a browser that shows how the web page is displayed after the style sheet has been applied to it. If you compare this to the browser in the previous figure, you can see that the page is now centered with a border around it, the font for the text has been changed, there's less spacing between paragraphs, and the text is displayed to the right of the book image. This gives you a quick idea of how much you can do with CSS.

Although you're going to learn how to code CSS in chapters 4, 5, and 6, here's a brief introduction to how the CSS works. First, this CSS file consists of four *rule sets*. Each of these rule sets consists of a *selector* and a *declaration block*. The selector identifies an HTML element, and the declaration block specifies the formatting for the element. Within the declaration block are one or more *declarations* (or *rules*) that specify the formatting for the element.

For instance, the first rule set applies to the body element. Its first rule says that the font family for the content should be Arial, Helvetica, or the default sans-serif type, in that order of preference. Then, the second rule says that the font-size should be 100% of the browser's default font size. These rules set the base font and font size for the elements that are coded within the body.

The third rule for the body sets its width to 550 pixels. Then, the fourth rule sets the top and bottom margins to zero and the left and right margins to auto, which centers the page in the browser window. Finally, the fifth rule sets the padding within the body to 1 em (a unit that you'll learn about in chapter 4), and the sixth rule adds a solid, navy border to the body.

Similarly, the second rule set formats the h1 element in the HTML with a larger font size and the navy color. The third rule set formats the image by floating it to the left so the <p> elements are displayed to its right. And the fourth rule set changes the spacing between <p> elements.

You will of course learn all of the details for coding rule sets in this book, but this should give you an idea of what's going on. In short, the HTML defines the content and structure of the document, and the CSS defines the formatting of the content. This separates the content from the formatting, which makes it easier to create and maintain web pages.

The element in the head section of the HTML file that links it to the CSS file

```
<link rel="stylesheet" href="book.css">
```

The code for the CSS file named book.css

```
body {
    font-family: Arial, Helvetica, sans-serif;
    font-size: 100%;
    width: 550px;
    margin: 0 auto;
    padding: 1em;
    border: 1px solid navy;
}
h1 {
    margin: 0;
    padding: .25em;
    font-size: 200%;
    color: navy;
}
img  {
    float: left;
    margin: 0 1em 1 em 1em;
}
p {
    margin: 0;
    padding-bottom: .5em;
}
```

The web page displayed in a web browser

Description

- *Cascading Style Sheets* (*CSS*) are used to control how web pages are displayed by specifying the fonts, colors, borders, spacing, and layout of the pages.

Figure 1-7 The CSS for a web page

A short history of the HTML and CSS standards

As figure 1-8 shows, HTML is a standardized language that has been around since the early 1990's. During the 90's, three different versions of HTML were adopted. Then, XHTML 1.0 was adopted in January 2000.

XHTML (*eXtensible HTML*) is a modified version of HTML that supports the same elements as HTML 4.01, but uses the syntax of XML. This is a stricter syntax that allows XHTML to be read and manipulated by automated tools. This also allows XHTML editors to identify errors in the document structure more easily.

Today, HTML 5 along with its first revision, HTML 5.1, is a specification that provides many new features and replaces the old HTML and XHTML standards with a single standard. Although this standard hasn't been officially adopted, all current browsers support most of its features. Because these features improve the way that web pages are developed, you should start using them right now.

As this figure also shows, CSS is a standardized language that goes back to 1996. However, it wasn't widely used as the right way to format HTML pages until the 2000's. Today, CSS 3.0 is the latest draft standard, and most of its features are supported by all modern browsers. Here again, these features improve the way web pages are developed so it makes sense to start using them right now.

In this book, you're going to learn how to use HTML 5 and CSS 3 to develop web pages. That means that you're going to learn the HTML and CSS that hasn't changed because that's still essential for developing web pages. But you're also going to learn the new features of HTML 5.1 and CSS 3 that are currently supported by all modern browsers, plus the new features that are most likely to be supported in the next couple of years. That way, you'll be developing web pages that take advantage of the best features of HTML 5.1 and CSS 3.

What about browsers that don't support the new features? This book will also show you how to get your web pages to work in those browsers. Often, though, you won't have to do anything because the new features will just be ignored by those browsers with no harm done. If, for example, you use CSS 3 to provide for rounded corners or shadows on HTML boxes, these features will improve the graphics in some browsers but be ignored in other browsers.

This figure also presents two websites that you ought to become familiar with. The first is for the *World Wide Web Consortium*, which is commonly referred to as *W3C*. This is the group that develops the standards, and this site should be one of your primary sources for HTML and CSS information.

The second website is for the *Web Hypertext Application Technology Working Group* (*WHATWG*). This is a community of people interested in evolving HTML and related technologies, and this site should be another primary source for HTML and CSS information.

Incidentally, from this point forward, we'll refer to HTML 5 and CSS 3 as *HTML5* and *CSS3*. In particular, we'll use these terms to identify the new features of HTML5 and CSS3 so you won't miss them.

Highlights in the development of the HTML standards

Version	Description
HTML 1.0	A draft specification released in January 1993 that was never adopted as a standard.
HTML 2.0	Adopted in November 1995.
HTML 4.0	Adopted in December 1997. It formalized new features that were used by web browsers and deprecated older features.
HTML 4.01	Adopted in December 1999 and updated through May 2001.
XHTML 1.0	Adopted in January 2000 and revised in August 2002. It reformulates HTML 4 using the syntax of XML, which makes it easier to parse the web page. This allows automated tools to find errors in a web page.
XHTML 1.1	Adopted in May 2001. The control of the presentation of content is now done through CSS.
HTML 5	Released as a working draft in January 2008. Originally, it defined an HTML version called HTML 5 and an XHTML version called XHTML 5. Today, the draft has been enhanced into a new HTML specification that replaces both HTML 4 and XHTML 1.
HTML 5.1	Released as the first minor revision of HTML 5 in April of 2013. It added the main element and removed the hgroup element.

Highlights in the development of the CSS standards

Version	Description
1.0	Adopted in December 1996.
2.0	Adopted in May 1998.
2.1	First released as a candidate standard in February 2004, it returned to working draft status in June 2005. It became a candidate standard again in July 2007.
3.0	A modularized version of CSS with the earliest drafts in June 1999.

Two websites that you should become familiar with

- The *World Wide Web Consortium* (*W3C*) is an international community in which member organizations, a full-time staff, and the public work together to develop Web standards. Its website address is: www.w3.org.
- The *Web Hypertext Application Technology Working Group* (*WHATWG*) is a community of people interested in evolving HTML and related technologies. Its website address is: www.whatwg.org.

Description

- Today, HTML 5 is an HTML specification that replaces both HTML 4 and XHTML 1.
- At this writing in 2015, the HTML5 and CSS3 standards still haven't been accepted, but it's possible they will be in the next year or two.
- Nevertheless, all modern browsers support the best features of HTML5 and CSS3. Those are the features that this book emphasizes, and those are the features that you should start implementing right now.

Figure 1-8 A short history of the HTML and CSS standards

Tools for web development

To create and edit the HTML and CSS files for a website, you need either a text editor or an IDE for web development. To deploy a website on the Internet, you also need an FTP program to upload the files from your computer or network server to the web server. You'll learn about these tools next.

Text editors for HTML and CSS

Although you can use any text editor to enter and edit HTML and CSS files, a better editor can speed development time and reduce coding errors. For that reason, we recommend Aptana Studio 3. It is a free editor that runs on both Windows and Mac OS systems, and it has many excellent features. For instance, Aptana provides syntax highlighting and auto-completion lists that let you select an item after you enter the first characters.

Aptana's auto-completion feature is illustrated in figure 1-9. Here, the developer has entered the first letter of an <img> tag, and the auto-completion list shows the words that start with that letter. At that point, the developer can move the cursor to the right word in the list and press the Tab key to enter that word into the code. Then, Aptana finishes the opening tag and adds the ending tag so the developer can type the content between the two tags.

In the next chapter, you'll learn how to use Aptana Studio 3 to develop your web pages. That will help you appreciate the many features that it provides. Please note, however, that you can use any text editor that you like for developing your web pages. Or, you can use an IDE like one of those in the next figure.

Aptana Studio 3 with open HTML and CSS files

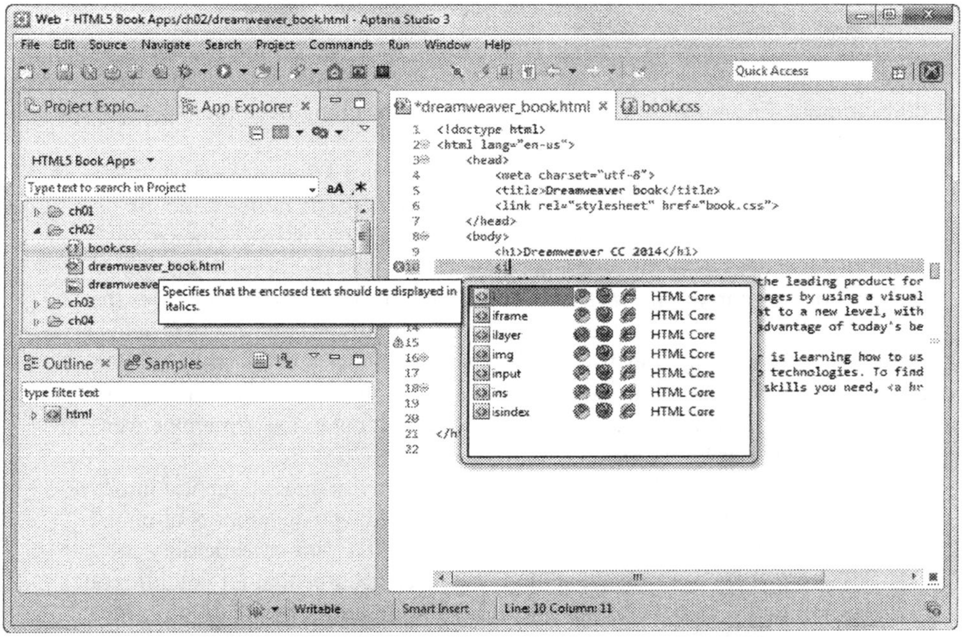

Four free text editors that you can use with this book

Editor	Runs on
Aptana Studio 3	Windows, Macintosh, Linux
Brackets 1.0	Windows, Macintosh, Linux
Notepad++	Windows
TextMate	Macintosh

Description

- A text editor lets you enter and edit the HTML and CSS files for a web application.
- Some common features of a text editor for HTML and CSS are syntax highlighting and auto-completion.
- Today, there are many text editors for developing web applications with HTML and CSS. Most of them are either free or inexpensive.
- For this book, we use Aptana Studio 3 because it's free; it runs on Windows, Macintosh, and Linux; and it has many excellent features. Brackets 1.0 is another excellent option.
- In chapter 2, you'll learn how to use Aptana Studio 3, but you don't have to use it to do the exercises for this book.

Figure 1-9 Text editors for HTML and CSS

IDEs for web development

After you get some experience with a text editor like Aptana Studio 3, you may be interested in an *Integrated Development Environment* (*IDE*) for web development. For instance, Adobe Dreamweaver has long been the most popular commercial IDE for web development.

As you can see in figure 1-10, the latest release of Dreamweaver, Dreamweaver CC 2014, lets you edit HTML or CSS code in one panel of its window while it shows you how the web page will look in another panel. Dreamweaver also lets you generate code instead of entering it by dragging the symbols for common elements onto the HTML document. It provides the starting code for an HTML document whenever you start a new file. It helps you manage the folders and files for the website. It provides an FTP program that uploads the pages from your development server to your Internet server. And it has many other features. For more information on how to use Dreamweaver CC, we recommend our book, *Murach's Dreamweaver CC 2014*.

In general, an IDE like Dreamweaver can help you make dramatic improvements in your productivity. That's why professional web developers often use IDEs for web development. Note, however, that IDEs vary considerably in features and price. For instance, some IDEs offer features that let you integrate your HTML and CSS development with JavaScript and server-side scripting languages like PHP, Perl, and Python. So before you buy an IDE, you need to find the IDE that best suits your requirements and budget.

At the highest level, an IDE for web development can include all of the programs that are required for developing a website. IDEs like this are often referred to as *suites*. For example, a suite of Adobe Creative Cloud products might include Photoshop CC for editing photos and images, Illustrator CC for creating and editing illustrations, Flash Professional CC for adding animation and interactivity to web pages, and several other programs that are related to web development.

Adobe Dreamweaver CC

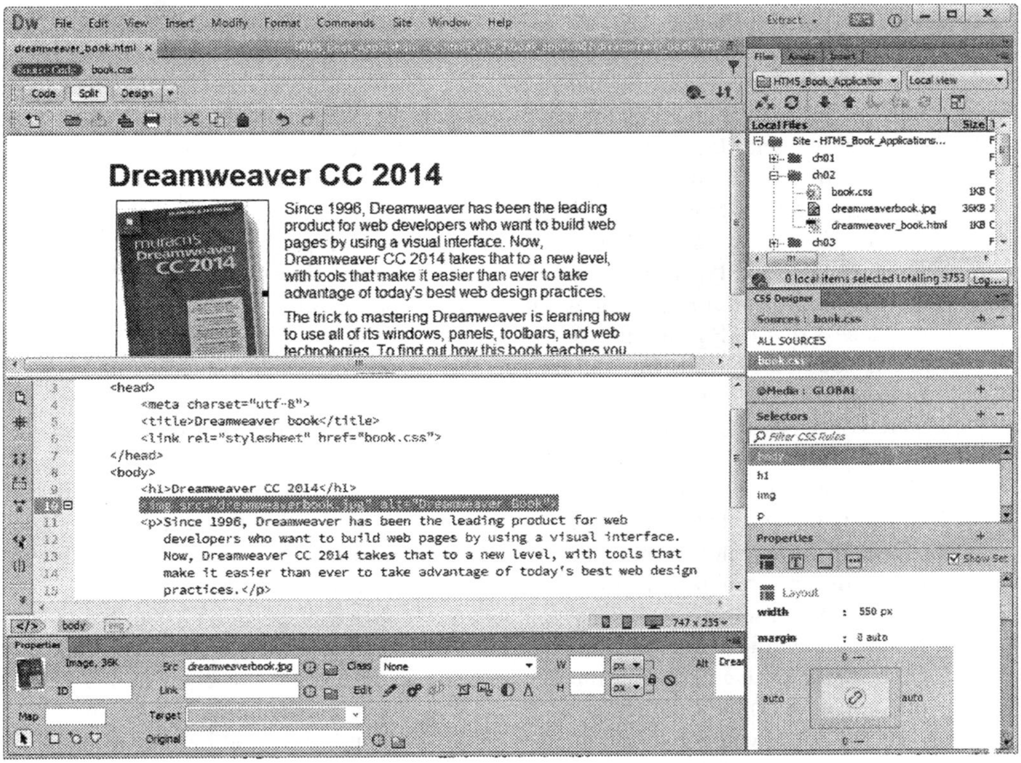

Popular IDEs for web development

IDE	Runs on
Adobe Dreamweaver CC	Windows and Macintosh
Microsoft Visual Studio	Windows
JetBrains	Windows, Macintosh, and Linux
Eclipse	Windows, Macintosh, and Linux
NetBeans	Windows, Macintosh, Linux, and more

Description

- An *Integrated Development Environment* (*IDE*) goes beyond text editing to provide other features for the development of websites.

Figure 1-10 IDEs for web development

FTP programs for uploading files to the web server

If you want to *deploy* (or *publish*) your website on the Internet, you need to transfer the folders and files for your website from your computer or network to a web server with Internet access. To do that, you use an *FTP program* like one of those listed in figure 1-11. This type of program uses *File Transfer Protocol* to transfer files to or from the web server.

Some text editors like Aptana Studio 3 include FTP programs, and IDEs like Dreamweaver CC typically include them. If your text editor doesn't provide an FTP program, you may be able to find a *plugin* for an FTP program. Then, you can access that FTP program from your text editor.

If you don't already have an Internet web server, one option is to find an *Internet Service Provider* (*ISP*) that provides *web hosting*. If you search the web, you'll be able to find many ISPs that provide web hosting, often for a small monthly fee.

If you're going to use dynamic web pages on your website, you need to find an ISP that supports the server-side language and the database that you're going to use. If, for example, you're going to use PHP with a MySQL database, which is a common combination, you need to find an ISP that supports that.

When you select a web host, you get an *IP address* like 64.71.179.86 that uniquely identifies your website (IP stands for Internet Protocol). Then, you can get a *domain name* like www.murach.com. To do that, you can use any number of companies on the Internet, and sometimes you can get the domain name from your ISP. Until you get your domain name, you can use the IP address to access your site.

After you get a web host, you use your FTP program to upload the files for your website to the web server of the web host. Then, you can test your website on the Internet. When you're through testing, you can announce your website to the world and let it go live.

FileZilla as it is used to upload files to the web server

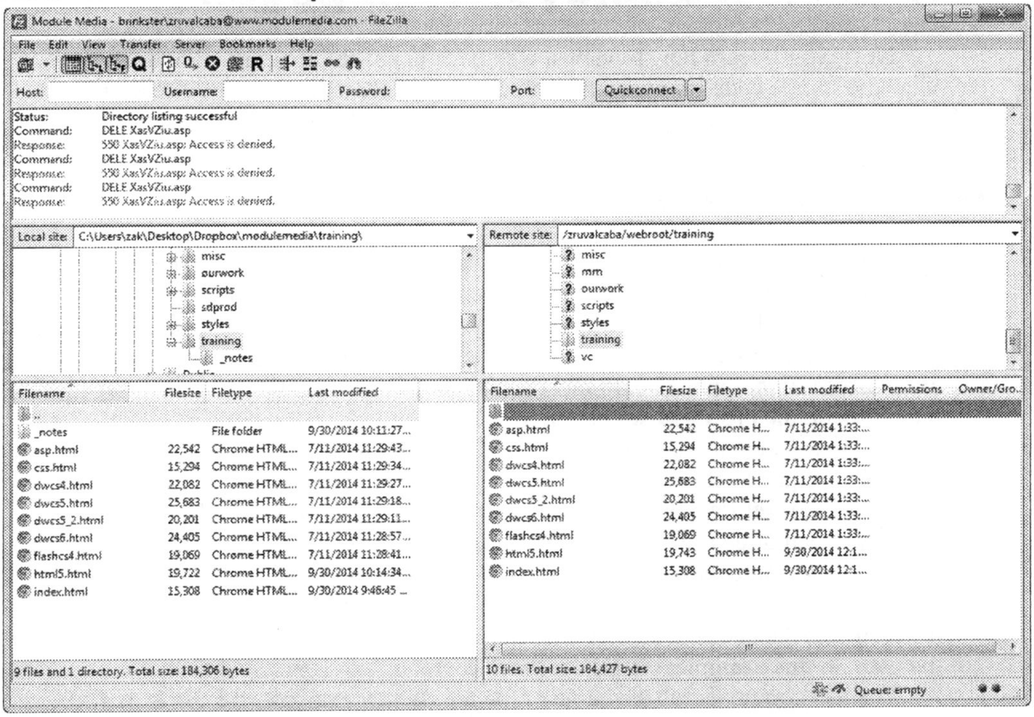

Some popular FTP programs

Program	Description
FileZilla	A free program for Windows, Macintosh, and Linux.
FTP Voyager	An inexpensive program for Windows.
CuteFTP	An inexpensive program for Windows and Macintosh.
Fetch	An inexpensive program for Macintosh.

Description

- To *deploy* (or *publish*) a website on the Internet, you need to transfer the folders and files for the website from your computer or network to a web server on the Internet. To do that, you use an *FTP program* that uses *File Transfer Protocol.*
- An FTP program not only lets you transfer files from a client to a web server but also from a web server to a client.
- Most IDEs and some text editors have built-in FTP programs. For instance, both Dreamweaver CC and Aptana Studio 3 provide FTP.
- If you're using some text editors, you may have to use a separate FTP program or add a plugin FTP program to your editor.
- For more information on deploying an application to a web server, please see chapter 19.

Figure 1-11 FTP programs for uploading files to the web server

How to view deployed web pages

Next, you'll learn how to view a web page in a web browser and how to view the source code for a web page that's displayed in the browser. These are valuable skills as you test your own web pages or study the pages on other sites.

How to view a web page

Figure 1-12 shows you how to view a web page on the Internet. One way is to enter a *uniform resource locator* (*URL*) into the address bar of your browser. The other is to click on a link on a web page that requests another page.

As the diagram at the start of this figure shows, the URL for an Internet page consists of four components. In most cases, the *protocol* is HTTP. If you omit the protocol, the browser uses HTTP as the default.

The second component is the *domain name* that identifies the web server that the HTTP request will be sent to. The web browser uses this name to look up the address of the web server for the domain. Although you can't omit the domain name, you can often omit the "www." from the domain name.

The third component is the *path* where the file resides on the server. The path lists the folders that contain the file. Forward slashes are used to separate the names in the path and to represent the server's top-level folder at the start of the path. In this example, the path is "/ourwork/".

The last component is the name of the file. In this example, the file is named index.html. If you omit the filename, the web server will search for a default document in the path. Depending on the web server, this file will be named index.html, default.htm, or some variation of the two.

If you want to view an HTML page that's on your own computer or an intranet, you can use the Open command (IE) or Open File command (Firefox) in the File menu of the browser. Or, in Chrome, you can use the file explorer to locate the HTML file and then drag the file into the browser window. However, it's easier to use your text editor or IDE, and you'll learn more about that in the next chapter.

At the bottom of this figure, you can see our naming recommendations for your folders and files. In general, we recommend that folder and filenames should only contain lowercase letters, numbers, underscores or hyphens, and the period. In the examples in this book, you'll see the author's preference, which is to use underscores instead of hyphens to separate the words in a name. But some developers use hyphens instead of underscores.

The other recommendation is to create names that clearly indicate the contents of your folders and web pages. This can improve search engine optimization (SEO), which you'll learn more about in a moment.

Incidentally, Linux/Apache web servers are case-sensitive. Then, if a URL specifies a folder named "Images", but the folder on the server is actually named "images", the web server will report that it cannot find the file. By using lowercase letters only, you avoid this problem.

The components of an HTTP URL

```
http://www.modulemedia.com/ourwork/index.html
```

protocol | domain name | path | filename

The web page at http://www.modulemedia.com/ourwork/index.html

What happens if you omit parts of a URL

- If you omit the protocol, the default of http:// will be used.
- If you omit the filename, the default document name for the web server will be used. This is typically index.html, default.htm, or some variation.

Two ways to access a web page on the Internet

- Enter the URL of a web page into the browser's address bar.
- Click on a link in the current web page to load the next web page.

Two ways to access a web page on your own server or computer

- Use the File→Open command with Internet Explorer or the File→Open File command with Firefox. With Chrome, use your file explorer to locate the file and then drag it into the browser window.
- Use the features of your text editor or IDE.

Naming recommendations for your own folders and files

- Create names for folders and files that consist of lowercase letters, numbers, underscores or hyphens, and the period.
- Use filenames that clearly indicate what a page contains. This is good for search engine optimization (see figure 1-18).

Figure 1-12 How to view a web page

How to view the source code for a web page

When a web page is displayed by a browser, you can use the techniques in figure 1-13 to view the HTML code for the page in a separate window. If, for example, you're using the Chrome browser, you can click the Menu icon to the right of the address bar and then select the More Tools→View Source command to see the HTML code. In this example, the HTML code for the page in the previous figure is shown.

Viewing the source code can be useful when you're testing an application. But you can also use this technique to view the HTML for the pages of other sites on the Internet. This can be a good way to learn how other sites work. Although some sites use various techniques to hide their code, a lot of the code for Internet sites is available.

If the CSS for an HTML page is stored in an external file, you can sometimes use the Chrome or Firefox browser to open that file by clicking on the path in the HTML code. In the code in this figure, for example, you can click on styles/core.css to access the first of the three css files that this site uses. This lets you analyze how the CSS code works.

If you're using Internet Explorer, you can view the CSS code in an external file by entering the URL for the CSS file in the browser's address bar. For instance, for the first CSS file that's identified by the link element in the HTML code in this figure, you can enter this address into the browser:

```
http://www.modulemedia.com/styles/core.css
```

Then, when you press the Enter key, the file is opened in another browser window. In chapter 3, you'll learn more about the relative addresses that are used in HTML code so you'll be able to determine what their URLs are.

When you view the HTML code for a web page, keep in mind that it may include embedded CSS code or JavaScript code. Beyond that, you'll find that all but the simplest sites are quite complicated. Once you finish this book, though, you should be able to figure out how the HTML and CSS for most sites work. And you'll learn a lot by studying how the best sites are coded.

The HTML source code for the page in figure 1-12

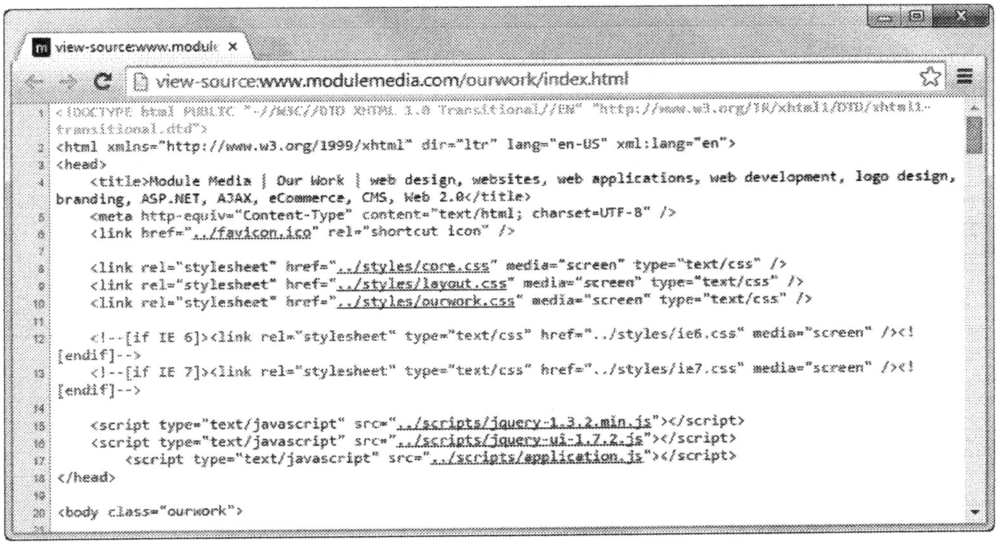

How to view the HTML source code for a web page

- In Chrome, click the Menu icon to the right of the address bar and select the More Tools→View Source command.
- In Firefox, choose Tools→Web Developer→Page Source or click the Menu icon to the right of the address bar, click the Developer icon, and select the Page Source command.
- In Internet Explorer, choose the View→Source command.
- You can also display the source code by right-clicking on the page and selecting the View Source or View Page Source command.

How to view the CSS code in an external CSS file

- In Chrome or Firefox, click on the link element that refers to it.
- In Internet Explorer, enter the URL for the CSS file in the address bar of your web browser.

Description

- When you view the source code for a web page in a web browser, the HTML code is opened in a separate window.
- If the CSS is stored in the HTML file, you'll be able to see both the HTML and CSS code in the one file.
- If the CSS for the page is stored in an external file, you can often view that file by using the techniques above.

Figure 1-13 How to view the source code for a web page

Five critical web development issues

Whenever you develop a web application, you should be aware of the issues that are presented in the next five figures. Then, as you progress through this book, you will be given guidelines for coding the tags and attributes that help provide for cross-browser compatibility, user accessibility, and search engine optimization.

Users and usability

Before you design a website, you need to think about who your users are going to be and what they are going to expect. After all, it is your users who are going to determine the success of your website.

What do users want when they reach a website? They want to find what they're looking for as quickly and easily as possible. And when they find it, they want to extract the information or do the task as quickly and easily as possible.

How do users use a web page? They don't read it in an orderly way, and they don't like to scroll any more than they have to. Instead, they scan the page to see if they can find what they're looking for or a link to what they're looking for. Often, they click quickly on a link to see if it gives them what they want, and if it doesn't, they click on the Back button to return to where they were. In fact, users click on the Back button more than 30% of the time when they reach a new page.

If the users can't find what they're looking for or get too frustrated, they leave the site. It's that simple. For some websites, more than 50% of first-time visitors to the home page leave without ever going to another page.

In web development terms, what the users want is *usability*. This term refers to how easy it is to use a website, and usability is one of the key factors that determines the effectiveness of a website. If a site is easy to use, it has a chance to be effective. If it isn't easy to use, it probably won't be effective.

Figure 1-14 presents one page of a website that has a high degree of usability, and it presents four guidelines for improving usability. First, you should try to present the essential information "above the fold." This term refers to what's shown on the screen when a new page is displayed, which is analogous to the top half of a newspaper. This reduces the need for scrolling, and it gives the page a better chance for success.

Second, you should try to group related items and limit the number of groups on each page. That will make the page look more manageable and will help people find what they're looking for.

Third, you should adhere to the current conventions for the header. For instance, the header should include a logo and tagline that identify the website. It should also include a navigation bar and links to utilities. If your site requires a search function, it should also be in the header.

Fourth, you should adhere to the current conventions for navigation. For instance, the home page should be displayed when the user clicks on the logo, and the shopping cart should be displayed when the user clicks the cart icon. In addition, it should be clear what other items on the page are clickable.

A website that is easy to use

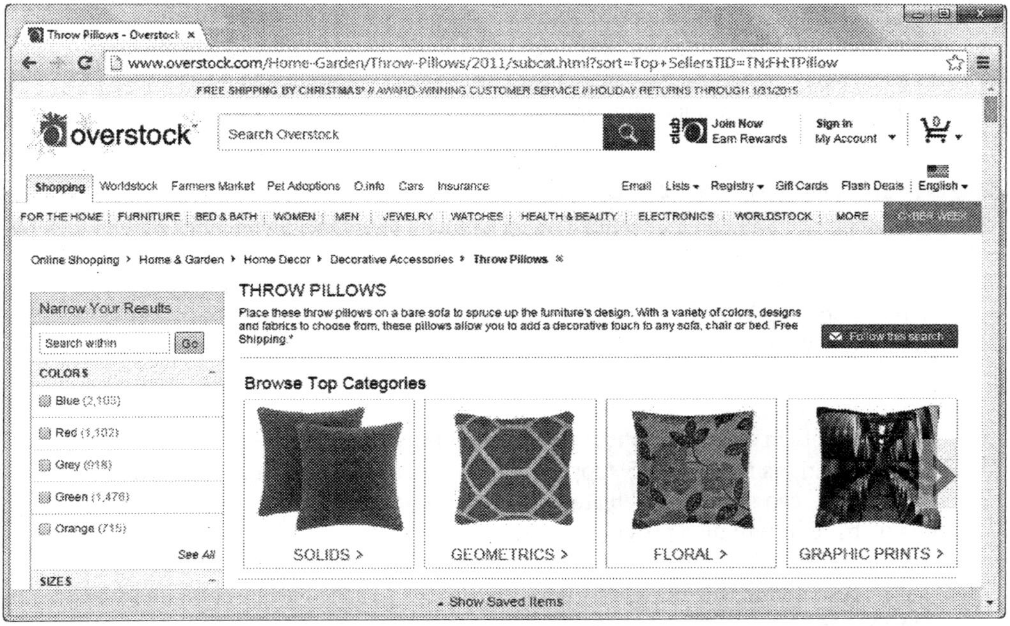

What website users want

- To find what they're looking for as quickly and easily as possible
- To get information or do a task as quickly and easily as possible

How website users use a web page

- They scan the page to find what they're looking for or a link to what they're looking for, and they don't like to scroll. If they get frustrated, they leave.
- They often click on links and buttons with the hope of finding what they're looking for, and they frequently click on the Back button when they don't find it.

Four guidelines for improving usability

- Present as much critical information as possible "above the fold" so the user has to scroll less.
- Group related items and limit the number of groups on each page.
- Include a header that identifies the site and provides a navigation bar and links to utilities.
- Use current navigation conventions, like including a logo that goes to your home page when clicked and a cart icon that goes to your shopping cart when clicked.

Description

- *Usability* refers to how easy it is to use a website, and usability is a critical requirement for an effective website.

Figure 1-14 The issue of usability

If you look at the website in figure 1-14, you can see that it has implemented these guidelines. All of the critical information is presented above the fold. The page is divided into a header and three other well-defined groups. It's also easy to tell where to click on the page. That's true even though this is a large website with hundreds of product categories and thousands of products.

Cross-browser compatibility

If you want your website to be used by as many visitors as possible, you need to make sure that your web pages are compatible with as many browsers as possible. That's known as *cross-browser compatibility*. That means you should test your applications on as many browsers as possible, including the five browsers summarized in figure 1-15 as well as older versions of Internet Explorer.

The table in this figure shows the current release numbers of these browsers and their ratings for HTML5 support. To get an updated version of this information, you can go to the website at www.html5test.com. When you access this website, it will also provide details of how the browser that you're using supports HTML5. If a browser doesn't support an HTML5 or CSS3 feature that's presented in this book, this book will show you the workaround that you need to use.

In general, Internet Explorer gives web developers the most problems because it's the least standard. In contrast, the other four browsers generally support the same features so if a web page runs on one of them, it will also run on the others. The other four browsers also provide for automatic updates, but IE hasn't always done that. As a result, the other four browsers should always be up-to-date, which means you shouldn't have to test your web pages in older versions of these browsers.

In the past, it's been difficult to test web pages in older versions of Internet Explorer because (1) you couldn't get them anymore and (2) you couldn't put more than one version on a single system even if you could get them. Fortunately, newer versions of IE have made it easier to test in older versions by providing tools that let you emulate those versions. To use these tools, you press F12 from the browser window to display the Developer Tools window. Then, you press Ctrl+8 or click the Emulation icon at the left side of the window to display the emulation options. Finally, you select the version of IE you want to use from the Document Mode drop-down list.

If you're a student, you probably won't need to test your web pages in old versions of Internet Explorer. But for production applications, that type of testing is essential.

To do the exercises in this book, you can get by with just the current versions of IE, Firefox, and Chrome. That's why the appendix shows you how to install those browsers. But if you're using a Mac OS system, you won't be able to install IE so you can skip any steps that require it or substitute Safari for IE references. For a production system, of course, you need to install all five browsers and make sure your web pages work on all of them.

The current browsers and their HTML5 ratings (perfect score is 555)

Browser	Release	HTML5 Test Rating
Google Chrome	39	501
Opera	26	497
Mozilla Firefox	35	449
Apple Safari	8	396
Internet Explorer	11	336

The website for these ratings

`http://www.html5test.com`

Guidelines for cross-browser compatibility

- Test your web pages on all of the major browsers, including older versions of Internet Explorer that are still in common use.
- Use the HTML5 and CSS3 features that are supported by most modern browsers, which are the features that are presented in this book. But use the workarounds so those features will work in all browsers still in use.

How to test your web pages in older versions of Internet Explorer

- One of the problems in testing different versions of Internet Explorer is that you can't install more than one version on a system at the same time.
- The solution is to use the emulation tools that became available with Internet Explorer 9. These tools let you emulate several older versions of Internet Explorer.

Description

- As a web developer, you want your web pages to work on as many different web browsers as possible. This is referred to as *cross-browser compatibility*.
- When you develop a website for general use, you need to test it on the current release of all five of the web browsers listed above plus older versions of Internet Explorer that are still in common use.
- Although Internet Explorer is still a commonly-used browser, it gives web developers the most problems because it is the least standard and because it hasn't always provided for automatic updates.
- In this book, you'll be alerted to cross-browser compatibility problems, and you'll learn to use the workarounds that you need for these browsers.
- Eventually, all browsers will support HTML5 and CSS3 so the workarounds won't be necessary.
- When you access www.html5test.com, it will automatically rate the browser you're using.

Figure 1-15 The issue of cross-browser compatibility

User accessibility

The third major issue is *user accessibility*, or just *accessibility*. This refers to the qualities that make a website accessible to as many users as possible, especially disabled users.

For instance, visually-impaired users may not be able to read text that's in images so you need to provide other alternatives for them. Similarly, users with motor disabilities may not be able to use the mouse, so you need to make sure that all of the content and features of your website can be accessed through the keyboard.

To a large extent, this means that you should develop your websites so the content is still usable if images, CSS, and JavaScript are disabled. A side benefit of doing that is that your site will also be more accessible to search engines, which rely primarily on the text portions of your pages.

In this book, you will be given guidelines for providing accessibility as you learn the related HTML. However, there's a lot more to accessibility than that. As a result, we recommend that you learn more on your own by going to the sites that are identified in this figure.

Articles on Web accessibility on the WebAIM site

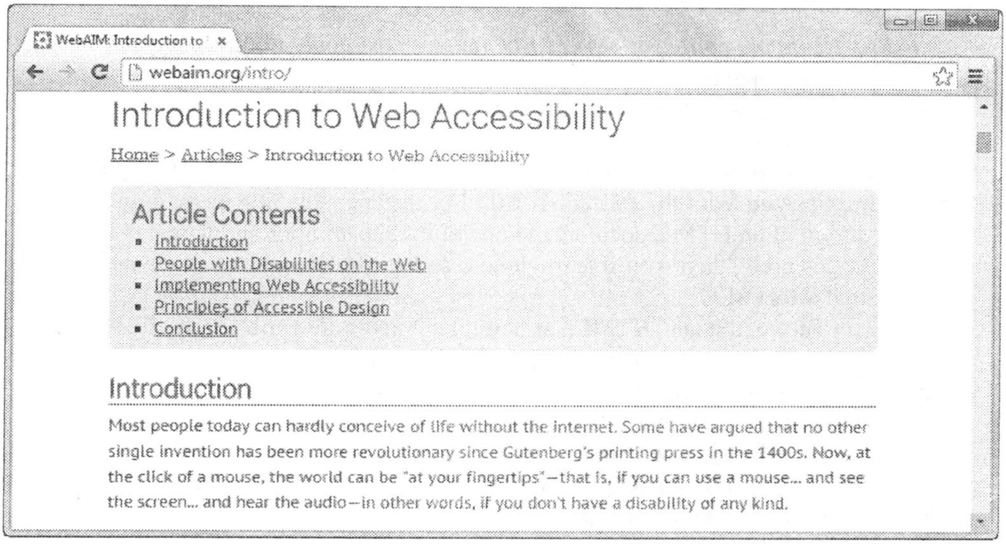

Accessibility laws that you should be aware of

- The Americans with Disabilities Act (ADA).
- Sections 504 and 508 of the federal Rehabilitation Act.
- Section 255 of the Telecommunications Act of 1996.

Types of disabilities

- Visual
- Hearing
- Motor
- Cognitive

Information sources

- The WebAIM website provides a good starting point for learning about accessibility at http://www.webaim.org.
- The World Wide Web Consortium (W3C) provides a full set of accessibility guidelines at http://www.w3.org/TR/WCAG.
- W3C also provides a specification called WAI-ARIA (Web Accessibility Initiative—Accessible Rich Internet Applications) that shows how to make rich internet applications more accessible to the disabled at http://www.w3.org/TR/wai-aria.

Description

- *Accessibility* refers to the qualities that make a website accessible to users, especially disabled users.
- As you go through this book, you'll be given guidelines for coding the elements and attributes that provide accessibility. However, there's a lot more to accessibility than that.

Figure 1-16 The issue of user accessibility

Search engine optimization

Search engine optimization, or *SEO*, refers to the goal of optimizing your website so your pages rank higher in search engines like Google, Bing, and Yahoo. In figure 1-17, for example, what causes the links that are shown to be returned by Google?

Since SEO is critical to the success of a website, this book presents SEO guidelines as you learn the related HTML. For instance, the title element in the head section of an HTML document is one of the most important elements for SEO. In this book, then, you'll learn how to code this element and all elements like it that affect SEO.

In the future, the new HTML5 structural elements are expected to affect the way that search engines rank pages. In particular, these elements should help the search engines find pages that are more relevant to the search term. That's one of the reasons for starting to implement these elements right away, and this book will show you the right way to do that.

Note, however, that SEO goes way beyond the way HTML pages are coded. So here again, you need to do some independent research. To start, you can search the Internet for information on SEO, but you might also want to buy a book or two on the subject.

The Google search results for "HTML5 documentation"

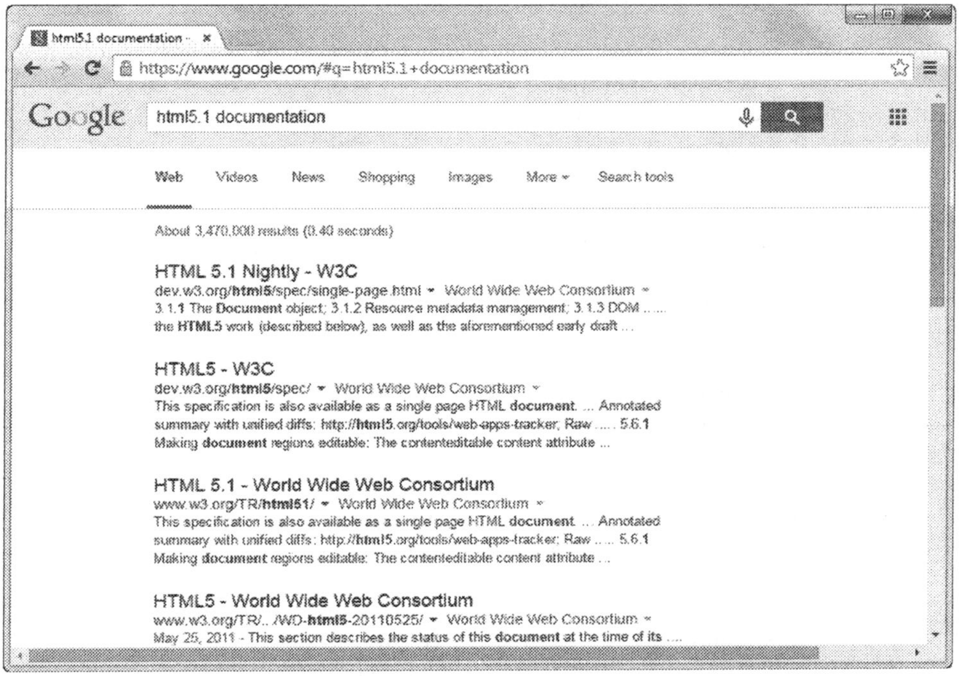

The most popular search engines

- Google
- Yahoo
- Bing

Description

- *Search engine optimization* (*SEO*) refers to the goal of optimizing your website so its pages will rank high in the search engines that are used to access them.
- Although the search algorithms that are used by the search engines are changed frequently, there are some common coding techniques that will help your pages do better in the search engines.
- HTML5 has some elements that are designed to help search engines deliver results that are more relevant.
- As you go through this book, you'll be given guidelines for coding the elements and attributes that will help your websites place better in the search engine results. However, there's a lot more to SEO than that.

Figure 1-17 The issue of search engine optimization

Responsive Web Design

The term *Responsive Web Design*, or *RWD*, was first coined by Ethan Marcotte in an article in the May 2010 issue of *A List Apart Magazine*. It refers to the theory and practice of creating websites that adapt gracefully to all viewing mediums, from desktop computers to mobile phones. The idea is to provide a website that is easy to read and navigate and that requires a minimum amount of resizing and scrolling.

According to Marcotte, the layout of a website that's designed with RWD in mind should adapt to the viewing environment by using fluid, proportion-based grids, flexible images, and CSS3 media queries. His idea for RWD has now become one of the hottest trends in web development. In fact, it has been touted as a cost-effective alternative to the development of mobile applications for specific platforms like iOS and Android, called *native mobile applications*. In addition, several popular open-source web design frameworks such as Skeleton, Foundation, Gumby, and Twitter Bootstrap incorporate RWD principles as a base for developing responsive websites.

So why should you consider using Responsive Web Design as you develop your websites? Most importantly, because statistics prove that mobile devices are being used more every day to access the Web. Some of these statistics are listed in figure 1-18. Consider, for example, that 80% of all consumers do some shopping on smartphones. Also consider that by 2017, it's estimated that 87% of devices that are connected to the Internet will be smartphones and tablets, with 70.5% of those being smartphones.

The increase in smartphone sales is due in part to the increase in the screen size of some phones. That includes the iPhone 6 Plus with a 5.5 inch display, the Galaxy Note 4 with a 5.7 inch display, the Nexus 6 with a 5.96 inch display, and the Nokia Lumia 1520 with a 6 inch display. These phones are sometimes referred to as "phablets" because they're so large, and their sales have started cutting into the tablet market.

This figure also illustrates how a site that uses RWD adapts to the size and orientation of the screen. Here, you can see the home page of the Murach Books website in a desktop browser. Because it uses RWD, the layout of the page changes when it's displayed on a device with a smaller screen size. In this figure, for example, you can see how the page appears in an iPhone 6 in both portrait and landscape orientation. Note that the basic look-and-feel of the page remains the same across the different screen sizes. That way, users won't feel that they're visiting completely different sites from different devices. That's the beauty of Responsive Web Design!

The Murach Books website displayed on a desktop and a smartphone

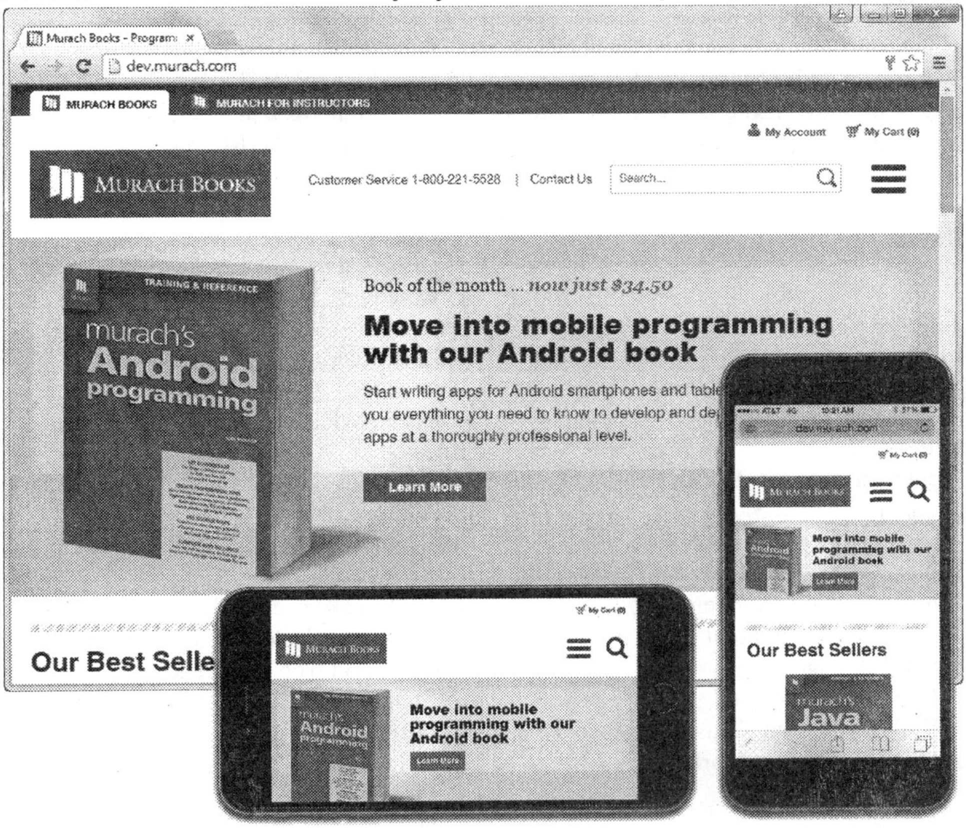

Statistics that prove the need for Responsive Web Design

- More people in the world own smartphones than toothbrushes.
- 80% of all consumers do some shopping on smartphones.
- 70% of all mobile searches lead to some type of action within an hour.
- 40% of users will choose a different search result if the first one isn't mobile friendly.
- 45% of mobile users ages 18 to 29 use their smartphones for searches every day.
- By 2017, 87% of connected devices will be smartphones and tablets.

Description

- *Responsive Web Design* refers to websites that are designed to adapt gracefully to the screen size.
- Typically, the overall look-and-feel of a website will remain consistent from one screen size to the next.
- Media queries, scalable images, and flexible layouts are the backbone of Responsive Web Design.

Figure 1-18 The issue of Responsive Web Design

Perspective

Now that you know the concepts and terms that you need for developing websites with HTML and CSS, you're ready to learn how to develop a web page. So in the next chapter, you'll learn how to enter, edit, test, and validate a web page. After that, you'll be ready to learn all the details of HTML and CSS that you need for developing the pages of a website.

Terms

World Wide Web
Internet
client
web browser
web server
network
local area network (LAN)
intranet
wide area network (WAN)
router
Internet service provider (ISP)
Internet exchange point (IXP)
static web page
HTTP request
HTTP (HyperText Transfer Protocol)
HTML (HyperText Markup Language)
HTTP response
render a web page
dynamic web page
application server
database server
round trip
web application
scripting language
server-side processing
Apache web server
IIS (Internet Information Services)
JavaScript
client-side processing
image swap
image rollover
JavaScript engine
HTML document
DOCTYPE declaration
HTML element
tag
opening tag
closing tag
attribute
CSS (Cascading Style Sheets)
style sheet
external style sheet
rule set
selector
declarative block
declaration
rule
XHTML (eXtensible HTML)
W3C (World Wide Web Consortium)
WHATWG (Web Hypertext Application Technology Working Group)
IDE (Integrated Development Environment)
suite
deploy
publish
FTP program
FTP (File Transfer Protocol)
FTP plugin
ISP (Internet Service Provider)
web hosting
IP address
domain name
URL (Uniform Resource Locator)
protocol
domain name
path
usability
cross-browser compatibility
user accessibility
SEO (Search Engine Optimization)
RWD (Responsive Web Design)
native mobile applications

Summary

- A web application consists of clients, a web server, and a network. *Clients* use *web browsers* to request web pages from the web server. The *web server* returns the requested pages.
- A *local area network* (*LAN*) connects computers that are near to each other. This is often called an *intranet*. In contrast, a *wide area network* (*WAN*) uses *routers* to connect two or more LANs. The *Internet* consists of many WANs.
- To request a web page, the web browser sends an *HTTP request* to the web server. Then, the web server retrieves the HTML for the requested page and sends it back to the browser in an *HTTP response*. Last, the browser *renders* the HTML into a web page.
- A *static web page* is a page that is the same each time it's retrieved. The file for a static page has .html or.htm as its extension, and its HTML doesn't change.
- The HTML for a *dynamic web page* is generated by a server-side program or script, so its HTML can change from one request to another.
- *JavaScript* is a *scripting language* that is run by the *JavaScript engine* of a web browser. It provides for *client-side processing*.
- *HTML* (*HyperText Markup Language*) is the language that defines the structure and contents of a web page. *CSS* (*Cascading Style Sheets*) are used to control how the web pages are formatted.
- To develop web pages, you can use a text editor like Aptana Studio 3 or an *Integrated Development Environment* (*IDE*) like Adobe Dreamweaver CC.
- To *deploy* (or *publish*) a website on the Internet, you need to transfer the folders and files for your site from your computer to a web server with Internet access. To do that, you use an *FTP program* that uses *File Transfer Protocol*.
- To view a web page on the Internet, you can enter the *URL* (*Uniform Resource Locator*) into a browser's address bar. A URL consists of the *protocol*, *domain name*, *path*, and filename.
- To view a web page that's on your own computer or server, you can use the browser's File→Open (IE) or File→Open File (Firefox) command. With Chrome, you can use your file explorer to locate the file for the page and then drag it into the browser window.
- To view the HTML for a web page, right-click on the page and select View Source or View Page Source. Then, to view the CSS for a page, you can click on its link in the source code or enter its URL in the address bar.
- Five critical issues for web development are *usability*, *cross-browser compatibility*, *user accessibility*, *search engine optimization* (*SEO*), and *Responsive Web Design* (*RWD*). In this book, you'll learn the HTML and CSS techniques that are related to these issues.

Before you do the exercises for this book...

Before you do the exercises for this book, you should download and install the Firefox and Chrome browsers. You should also download and install the applications for this book. The procedures for installing the software and applications for this book are described in appendix A.

Exercise 1-1 Visit some Internet websites

In this exercise, you'll visit some Internet websites and view the source code for those sites.

Visit the author's website with Chrome

1. Start Chrome.
2. Enter www.modulemedia.com into the address bar and press the Enter key. That should display the home page for this website. Here, JavaScript is used to rotate the images at the top of the page.
3. If you're using a Windows system, enter "modulemedia" into the address bar, hold down the Ctrl key, and press the Enter key. If this works, it will add www. and .com to your entry. This is a quick way to enter the URL for a .com address.
4. Use one of the techniques in figure 1-13 to view the source code for the home page. Here, the three link elements identify the CSS files that do the formatting for the page. This is followed by three script elements that identify JavaScript files.
5. If you scroll through this code, it probably looks overwhelming, even though this site is relatively simple. By the time you complete this book, though, you should understand the HTML and CSS that it uses.
6. Click on the underlined value of the href attribute in the first link element. That should open the first CSS file for this page. This shows how easy it is to access the HTML and CSS code for many (but not all) sites.

Visit other websites

7. Go to www.landsend.com, find a page like the one in figure 1-5, and experiment with the image swaps and rollovers. Those are done by JavaScript after all of the images are loaded with the page.
8. Use Chrome to visit other websites and view the source code for those sites. When you're through experimenting, go to the next exercise.

Exercise 1-2 View the application for this chapter

In this exercise, you'll visit the book page that was used as an example in figures 1-6 and 1-7.

Open the book page in Firefox

1. Start Firefox if it isn't already open.
2. Use the File→Open File command to open this HTML file:
   `c:\murach\html5_css3_2\book_apps\ch01\dreamweaver_book.html`
3. Right-click on the page and choose View Page Source to display the source code for this page.
4. Click on book.css in the link element in the HTML code to display the CSS file for this page.

Open the book page in IE (if you're using a Windows system)

5. Start Internet Explorer if it isn't already open.
6. Use the File→Open command to open the same HTML file as in step 2.
7. Use the View→Source command to display the source code for this page.
8. Click on book.css in the link element in the source code to try to display the CSS file for this page. Note that this doesn't work with IE.

Exercise 1-3 View other applications and examples

1. Start Chrome if it isn't already open.
2. Use your file explorer to locate this file:
   `c:\murach\html5_css3_2\book_apps\ch07\town_hall\index.html`
   Then, drag the index.html file to the browser window to display the web page.
3. Click on the link for Scott Sampson to see that page. This is the website that's presented at the end of chapter 7, and this gives you some idea of what you'll be able to do when you complete that chapter. Note, however, that only the Scott Sampson link has been implemented for this website.
4. Open this file in the Chrome browser:
   `c:\murach\html5_css3_2\book_examples\ch05\12_gradients.html`
   This is the example for figure 5-12 in chapter 5. Here, the 12 in the filename refers to the figure number. As you do the exercises for this book, you may want to copy code from the examples to your exercise solution.
5. Open this file in the Chrome browser.
   `c:\murach\html5_css3_2\book_examples\ch15\05_print_page\index.html`
   This is the example for figure 15-5 in chapter 15. Note that the figure number is in the folder name this time. This is true for all of the examples that require more than one file.

Exercise 1-4 Learn more about HTML5, accessibility, SEO, and RWD

1. Go to www.w3.org. This is the website for the group that develops the HTML5 and CSS3 standards. It provides all sorts of useful information including HTML5 documentation.
2. Go to www.whatwg.org. This is the website for a community that is interested in evolving HTML and its related technologies. It also provides all sorts of useful information including HTML5 documentation.
3. Go to www.html5test.com, and view the HTML5 rating for your browser. Then, review the other browser data that this site provides.
4. Go to www.webaim.org. Then, review the information about accessibility that this site provides.
5. Use Google to search for "search engine optimization". Then, click on the first google.com link for this subject to get more information about it. You may also want to download and print the PDF on SEO that Google offers.
6. Use Google to search for "responsive web design". Then, click on one or more of the links to see what type of information is available.

2

How to code, test, and validate a web page

In this chapter, you'll learn how to create and edit HTML and CSS files. Then, you'll learn how to test those files to make sure they work correctly. Last, you'll learn how to validate the code in HTML and CSS files to make sure that it doesn't have any errors. When you're through with this chapter, you'll be ready to learn all the details of HTML and CSS coding.

The HTML syntax

When you code an HTML document, you need to adhere to the rules for creating the HTML elements. These rules are referred to as the *syntax* of the language. In the four topics that follow, you'll learn the HTML syntax.

The basic structure of an HTML document

Figure 2-1 presents the basic structure of an *HTML document*. As you can see, every HTML document consists of two parts: the DOCTYPE declaration and the document tree.

When you use HTML5, you code the *DOCTYPE declaration* exactly as it's shown in this figure. It will be the first line of code in every HTML document that you create, and it tells the browser that the document is using HTML5. If you've developed web pages with earlier versions of HTML or XHTML, you will be pleased to see how much this declaration has been simplified.

The *document tree* starts right after the DOCTYPE declaration. This tree consists of the *HTML elements* that define the content and structure of the web page. The first of these elements is the html element itself, which contains all of the other elements. This element can be referred to as the *root element* of the tree.

Within the html element, you should always code a head element and a body element. The head element contains elements that provide information about the page itself, while the body element contains the elements that provide the structure and content for the page. You'll learn how to code these elements in the next chapter.

You'll use the elements shown in this figure in every HTML document that you create. As a result, it's a good practice to start every HTML document from a template that contains this code or from another HTML document that's similar to the one you're going to create. Later in this chapter, you'll learn how you can use Aptana to do that.

When you use HTML5, you can code elements using lowercase, uppercase, or mixed case. For consistency, though, we recommend that you use lowercase unless uppercase is required. The one exception we make is in the DOCTYPE declaration because DOCTYPE has historically been capitalized (although lowercase works too). You will see this use of capitalization in all of the examples and applications in this book.

The basic structure of an HTML5 document

```
<!DOCTYPE html> ——————— DOCTYPE declaration

<html>          ─┐
    <head>  ┐    │
       .    ├ head element
       .    │    │
    </head> ┘    │
                 ├ document tree
    <body>  ┐    │
       .    ├ head element
       .    │    │
    </body> ┘    │
</html>         ─┘
```

A simple HTML5 document

```
<!DOCTYPE html>
<html lang="en">
    <head>
        <meta charset="utf-8">
        <title>San Joaquin Valley Town Hall</title>
    </head>
    <body>
        <h1>San Joaquin Valley Town Hall</h1>
        <p>Welcome to San Joaquin Valley Town Hall.</p>
        <p>We have some amazing speakers in store for you this season!</p>
        <p><a href="speakers.html">Speaker information</a></p>
    </body>
</html>
```

General coding recommendations for HTML5

- Although you can code the HTML using lowercase, uppercase, or mixed case, we recommend that you do all coding in lowercase because it's easier to read.

Description

- An *HTML document* contains *HTML elements* that define the content and structure of a web page.
- Each HTML5 document consists of two parts: the DOCTYPE declaration and the document tree.
- The *DOCTYPE declaration* shown above indicates that the document is going to use HTML5. You'll code this declaration at the start of every HTML document.
- The *document tree* starts with the html element, which marks the beginning and end of the HTML code. This element can be referred to as the *root element* of the document.
- The html element always contains one head element that provides information about the document and one body element that provides the structure and content of the document.

Figure 2-1 The basic structure of an HTML document

How to code elements and tags

Figure 2-2 shows you how to code elements and tags. As you have already seen, most HTML elements start with an *opening tag* and end with a *closing tag* that is like the opening tag but has a slash within it. Thus, <h1> is the opening tag for a level-1 heading, and </h1> is the closing tag. Between those tags, you code the *content* of the element.

Some elements, however, have no content or closing tag. These tags are referred to as *empty tags*. For instance, the <br> tag is an empty tag that starts a new line, and the <img> tag is an empty tag that identifies an image that should be displayed.

The third set of examples in this figure shows the right way and the wrong way to code tags when one element is *nested* within another. In short, the tags for one element shouldn't overlap with the tags for another element. That is, you can't close the outer element before you close the inner element.

From this point on in this book, we will refer to elements by the code used in the opening tag. For instance, we will refer to head elements, h1 elements, and img elements. To prevent misreading, though, we will enclose single-letter element names in brackets. As a result, we will refer to <a> elements and <p> elements. We will also use brackets wherever else we think they will help prevent misreading.

Two elements with opening and closing tags

```
<h1>San Joaquin Valley Town Hall</h1>
<p>Here is a list of links:</p>
```

Two empty tags

```
<br>
<img src="logo.gif" alt="Murach Logo">
```

Correct and incorrect nesting of tags

Correct nesting

```
<p>Order your copy <i>today!</i></p>
```

Incorrect nesting

```
<p>Order your copy <i>today!</p></i>
```

Description

- Most HTML elements have an opening tag, content, and a closing tag. Each tag is coded within a set of brackets (<>).
- An element's *opening tag* includes the tag name. The *closing tag* includes the tag name preceded by a slash. And the *content* includes everything that appears between the opening and closing tags.
- Some HTML elements have no content. For example, the <br> element, which forces a line break, consists of just one tag. This type of tag is called an *empty tag*.
- HTML elements are commonly *nested*. To nest elements correctly, though, you must close an inner set of tags before closing the outer set of tags.

Figure 2-2 How to code elements and tags

How to code attributes

Figure 2-3 shows how to code the *attributes* for an HTML element. These attributes are coded within the opening tag of an element or within an empty tag. For each attribute, you code the attribute name, an equal sign, and the attribute value.

When you use HTML5, the attribute value doesn't have to be coded within quotation marks unless the value contains a space, but we recommend that you use quotation marks to enclose all values. Also, although you can use either double or single quotes, we recommend that you always use double quotes. That way, your code will have a consistent appearance that will help you avoid coding errors.

In the examples in this figure, you can see how one or more attributes can be coded. For instance, the second example is an opening tag with three attributes. In contrast, the third example is an empty img element that contains a src attribute that gives the name of the image file that should be displayed plus an alt attribute that gives the text that should be displayed if the image file can't be found.

The next example illustrates the use of a *Boolean attribute*. A Boolean attribute can have just two values, which represent either on or off. To turn a Boolean attribute on, you code just the name of the attribute. In this example, the checked attribute turns that attribute on, which causes the related check box to be checked when it is rendered by the browser. If you want the attribute to be off when the page is rendered, you don't code the attribute.

The next set of examples illustrates the use of two attributes that are commonly used to identify HTML elements. The id attribute is used to uniquely identify just one element, so each id attribute must have a unique value. In contrast, the class attribute can be used to mark one or more elements, so the same value can be used for more than one class attribute. You'll see these attributes in a complete example in figure 2-6.

How to code an opening tag with attributes

An opening tag with one attribute

```
<a href="contact.html">
```

An opening tag with three attributes

```
<a href="contact.html" title="Click to Contact Us" class="nav_link">
```

How to code an empty tag with attributes

```
<img src="logo.gif" alt="Murach Logo">
```

How to code a Boolean attribute

```
<input type="checkbox" name="mailList" checked>
```

Two common attributes for identifying HTML elements

An opening tag with an id attribute

```
<div id="page">
```

An opening tag with a class attribute

```
<a href="contact.html" title="Click to Contact Us" class="nav_link">
```

Coding rules

- An attribute consists of the attribute name, an equal sign (=), and the value for the attribute.
- Attribute values don't have to be enclosed in quotes if they don't contain spaces.
- Attribute values must be enclosed in single or double quotes if they contain one or more spaces, but you can't mix the type of quotation mark used for a single value.
- Boolean attributes can be coded as just the attribute name. They don't have to include the equal sign and a value that's the same as the attribute name.
- To code multiple attributes, separate each attribute with a space.

Our coding recommendation

- For consistency, enclose all attribute values in double quotes.

Description

- *Attributes* can be coded within opening or empty tags to supply optional values.
- A *Boolean attribute* represents either an on or off value.
- The id attribute is used to identify a single HTML element, so its value can be used for just one HTML element.
- A class attribute with the same value can be used for more than one HTML element.

Figure 2-3 How to code attributes

How to code comments and whitespace

Figure 2-4 shows you how to code *comments*. Here, the starting and ending characters for the two comments are highlighted. Then, everything within those characters is ignored when the page is rendered.

One common use of comments is to describe or explain portions of code. That is illustrated by the first comment.

Another common use of comments is to *comment out* a portion of the code. This is illustrated by the second comment. This is useful when you're testing a web page and you want to temporarily disable a portion of code that you're having trouble with. Then, after you test the rest of the code, you can remove the comments and test that portion of the code.

This figure also illustrates the use of *whitespace*, which consists of characters like tab characters, return characters, and extra spaces. For instance, the return character after the opening body tag and all of the spaces between that tag and the next tag are whitespace.

Since whitespace is ignored when an HTML document is rendered, you can use the whitespace characters to format your HTML so it is easier to read. In this figure, for example, you can see how whitespace has been used to indent and align the HTML elements.

That of course is a good coding practice, and you'll see that in all of the examples in this book. Note, however, that the code will work the same if all of the whitespace is removed. In fact, you could code all of the HTML for a document in a single line.

Although whitespace doesn't affect the way an HTML document is rendered, it does take up space in the HTML file. As a result, you shouldn't overdo your use of it. Just use enough to make your code easy to read.

An HTML document with comments and whitespace

```
<!DOCTYPE html>
<!--
    This document displays the home page
    for the website.
-->

<html>
    <head>
        <title>San Joaquin Valley Town Hall</title>
    </head>

    <body>
        <h1>San Joaquin Valley Town Hall</h1>
        <h2>Bringing cutting-edge speakers to the valley</h2>
    <!-- This comments out all of the HTML code in the unordered list
        <ul>
            <li>October 19, 2011: Jeffrey Toobin</li>
            <li>November 16, 2011: Andrew Ross Sorkin</li>
            <li>January 18, 2012: Amy Chua</li>
            <li>February 15, 2012: Scott Sampson</li>
            <li>March 21, 2012: Carlos Eire</li>
            <li>April 18, 2012: Ronan Tynan</li>
        </ul>
    The code after the end of this comment is active -->
        <p>Contact us by phone at (559) 444-2180 for ticket information.</p>
    </body>
</html>
```

Our coding recommendations

- Use whitespace to indent lines of code and make them easier to read.
- Don't overdo your use of whitespace, because it does add to the size of the file.

Description

- An HTML *comment* is text that appears between the <!-- and --> characters. Since web browsers ignore comments, you can use them to describe or explain portions of your HTML code that might otherwise be confusing.
- You can also use comments to *comment out* elements that you don't want the browser to display. This can be useful when you're testing a web page.
- An HTML comment can be coded on a single line or it can span two or more lines.
- *Whitespace* consists of characters like tab characters, line return characters, and extra spaces.
- Since whitespace is ignored by browsers, you can use it to indent lines of code and separate elements from one another by putting them on separate lines. This is a good coding practice because it makes your code easier to read.

Figure 2-4 How to code comments and whitespace

The CSS syntax

Like HTML, CSS has a syntax that must be adhered to when you create a CSS file. This syntax is presented next.

How to code CSS rule sets and comments

A CSS file consists of *rule sets*. As the diagram in figure 2-5 shows, a rule set consists of a *selector* followed by a set of braces. Within the braces are one or more *declarations*, and each declaration consists of a *property* and a *value*. Note that the property is followed by a colon and the value is followed by a semicolon.

In this diagram, the selector is h1 so it applies to all h1 elements. Then, the rule set consists of a single property named color that is set to the color navy. The result is that the content of all h1 elements will be displayed in navy blue.

In the CSS code that follows, you can see four other rule sets. Three of these contain only one declaration (or *rule*), but the third example is a rule set that consists of two rules: one for the font-style property, and one for the border-bottom property.

Within a CSS file, you can also code comments that describe or explain what the CSS code is doing. For each comment, you start with /* and end with */, and anything between those characters is ignored. In the example in this figure, you can see how CSS comments can be coded on separate lines or after the lines that make up a rule set.

You can also use comments to comment out portions of code that you want disabled. This can be useful when you're testing your CSS code just as it is when you're testing your HTML code.

The parts of a CSS rule set

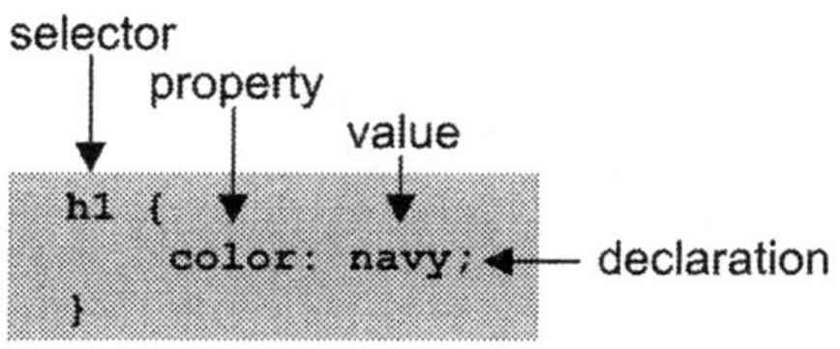

A simple CSS document with comments

```
/*********************************************************
* Description: Primary style sheet for valleytownhall.com
* Author:      Anne Boehm
*********************************************************/
/* Adjust the styles for the body */
body {
    background-color: #FACD8A;         /* This is a shade of orange. */
}

/* Adjust the styles for the headings */
h1 {
    color: #363636;
}
h2 {
    font-style: italic;
    border-bottom: 3px solid #EF9C00;  /* Adds a line below h2 headings */
}

/* Adjust the styles for the unordered list */
ul {
    list-style-type: square;           /* Changes the bullets to squares */
}
```

Description

- A CSS *rule set* consists of a selector and a declaration block.
- A CSS *selector* consists of the identifiers that are coded at the beginning of the rule set.
- A CSS *declaration block* consists of an opening brace, zero or more declarations, and a closing brace.
- A CSS *declaration* (or *rule*) consists of a *property*, a colon, a *value*, and a semicolon.
- To make your code easier to read, you can use spaces, indentation, and blank lines within a rule set.
- CSS *comments* begin with the characters /* and end with the characters */. A CSS comment can be coded on a single line, or it can span multiple lines.

Figure 2-5 How to code CSS rule sets and comments

How to code basic selectors

The selector of a rule set identifies the HTML element or elements that the rules should be applied to. To give you a better idea of how this works, figure 2-6 shows how to use the three basic selectors for CSS rule sets. Then, in chapter 4, you'll learn how to code all types of selectors.

The first type of selector identifies HTML elements like body, h1, or <p> elements. For instance, the selectors in the first two examples apply to the body and h1 elements. These selectors are called *type selectors*.

The second type of selector starts with the pound sign (#) and applies to the single HTML element that's identified by the id attribute. For instance, #copyright applies to the HTML element that has an id attribute with a value of copyright. As you can see, that's the last <p> element in the HTML code.

The third type of selector starts with a period (.) and applies to all of the HTML elements that are identified by the class attribute with the named value. For instance, .base_color applies to all elements with class attributes that have a value of base_color. In the HTML code, this includes the h1 element and the last <p> element.

Starting with chapter 4, you'll learn all of the coding details for rule sets. But to give you an idea of what's going on in this example, here's a quick review of the code.

In the rule set for the body element, the font-family is set either to Arial (if the browser has access to that font) or the sans-serif type that is the default for the browser. This font is then used for all text that's displayed within the body element, unless it's overridden later on by some other rule set. So in this example, all of the text will be Arial or sans-serif, and you can see that font in the browser display.

The rule set for the body element also sets the font-size to 100% of the default size. Although this is the default, this selector is often coded for completeness. Next, the width of the body is set to 300 pixels, and the padding between the contents and the border is set to 1 em, which is the height of the default font.

In the rule set for the h1 element, the font-size is set to 180% of the default font size for the document (the size set by the selector for the body element). Then, in the rule set for the second <p> element (#copyright), the font size is set to 75% of the default font size, and the text is right-aligned. Here again, you can see how these rule sets are applied in the browser display.

Last, in the rule set for the class named base_color, the color is set to blue. This means that both of the HTML elements that have that class name (the h1 element and the second <p> element) are displayed in blue.

This example shows how easy it is to identify the elements that you want to apply CSS formatting to. This also shows how the use of CSS separates the formatting from the content and structure that is defined by the HTML.

HTML elements that can be selected by element type, id, or class

```
<body>
    <h1 class="base_color">Student materials</h1>
    <p>Here are the links for the downloads:</p>
    <ul id="links">
        <li><a href="exercises.html">Exercises</a></li>
        <li><a href="solutions.html">Solutions</a></li>
    </ul>
    <p id="copyright" class="base_color">Copyright 2012</p>
</body>
```

CSS rule sets that select by element type, id, and class

Type

```
body {
    font-family: Arial, sans-serif;
    font-size: 100%;
    width: 300px;
    padding: 1em;
}
h1 {
    font-size: 180%;
}
```

ID

```
#copyright {
    font-size: 75%;
    text-align: right;
}
```

Class

```
.base_color {
    color: blue;
}
```

The elements in a browser

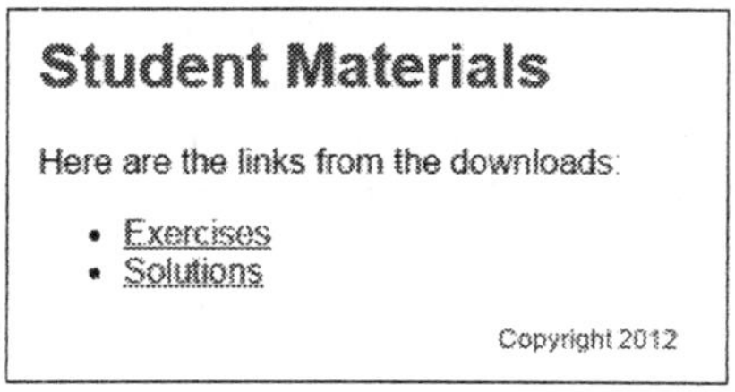

Description

- To code a selector for an HTML element, you simply name the element. This is referred to as a *type selector*.
- If an element is coded with an id attribute, you can code a selector for that id by coding a pound sign (#) followed by the id value, as in #copyright.
- If an element is coded with a class attribute, you can code a selector for that class by coding a period followed by the class name, as in .base_color.

Figure 2-6 How to code basic selectors

How to use Aptana to work with HTML and CSS files

In chapter 1, you were introduced to text editors like Aptana Studio 3. This is the text editor that we recommend because it's free; it runs on Windows, Mac OS, and Linux; and it has some excellent features. In the topics that follow, you'll learn how to use Aptana for common development functions.

If you're going to use a different editor as you work with the applications for this book, you may still want to browse these topics because they will give you a good idea of what an editor should be able to do. They may also encourage you to give Aptana a try.

How to create a project

In Aptana, a *project* consists of the folders and files for a complete web application. Once you create a project, it's easier to work with its folders and files, to create new files for the project, and so forth.

The technique you use to create a projects depends on whether the project is for a new website or an existing website. To create a project for a new website, you can use the first procedure in figure 2-7. With this procedure, you use the New Web Project dialog to choose a template and specify a name and location for the project. In most cases, you'll use the Default Template, which creates a project with no files. Then, you can add new HTML and CSS files as described later in this chapter.

To create a project for an existing website, you use the second procedure in this figure. In this case, you import the folder that contains the files for the website as a new project. Then, you can work with these files just as if you had created them in Aptana.

To make it easier to work with the applications for this book, we recommend that you create an Aptana project that includes all of them. To do that, you can create a project named HTML5 Book Apps that starts with the path shown in this figure. The first dialog box for doing this with Aptana 3.0 is displayed in this figure.

The first dialog box for creating an Aptana project for an existing website

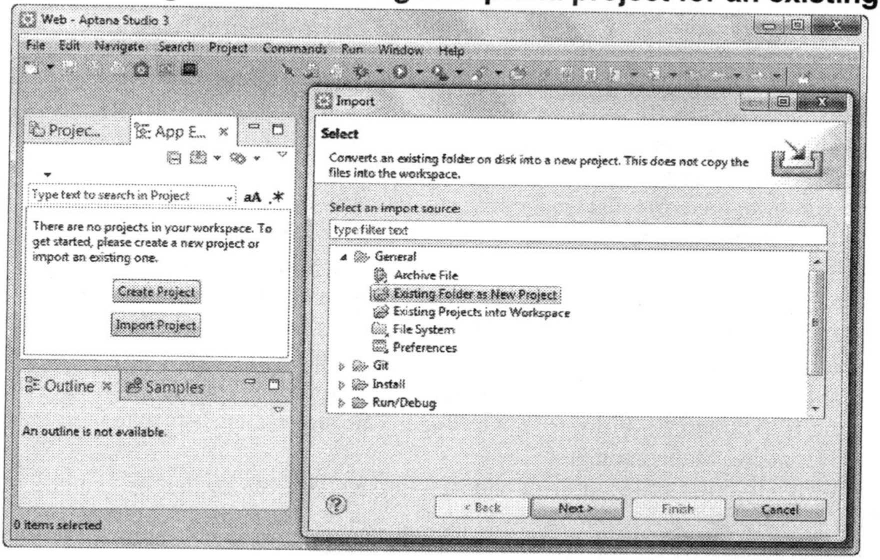

The folder that contains the folders for all of the book applications

```
C:\html5_css3_2\book_apps
```

How to create a project for a new website

- Use the File→New→Web Project command to display the New Web Project dialog box. Or, in the App Explorer window, click the Create Project button, select Web Project in the dialog box that's displayed, and click the Next button to display the New Web Project dialog box.
- In the New Web Project dialog box, choose a template, click the Next button, enter a project name, and click the Finish button.

How to create a project for an existing website

- Use the File→Import command or click the Import Project button in the App Explorer window to display the Import dialog box that's shown above. Then, expand the General category, select Existing Folder as New Project, and click the Next button to display the Promote to Project dialog box.
- Browse to the folder for the project, enter a project name, and click on the Finish button.

Description

- Aptana works the best when you set up projects for the web applications that you're developing and maintaining.
- In general, each Aptana *project* should contain the folders and files for one web application. For the purposes of this book, however, you can set up one project for all of the book applications and another project for all of the exercises.

Figure 2-7 How to create a project in Aptana

How to open an HTML file

Figure 2-8 shows how to open an HTML file after you've created a project. Here, the HTML5 Book Apps project is shown in the App Explorer window on the left side of Aptana. If you have created more than one project, you can switch from one to another by using the drop-down project list that's at the top of the App Explorer window.

Once you have the correct project open, you can drill down to the file that you want to open by clicking on the ◢ symbols for the folders. In this example, the ch02 folder has been expanded so you can see the three files for the application for chapter 2. Then, to open a file, you just double-click on it.

When you open an HTML file in Aptana, it is opened in a new tab. This means that you can have several files open at the same time and move from one to another by clicking on a tab. This makes it easy to switch back and forth between the HTML and CSS files for a web page. This also makes it easy to copy code from one file to another.

If you want to open a file that isn't part of a project, you can do that by using one of the methods shown in this figure. First, you can use the Project Explorer window to locate the file on your computer and then double-click on it. Second, you can use the File→Open File command to open a file. (Incidentally, this notation means to drop-down the File menu and select the Open File command, and this notation will be used throughout this book.)

When a file is open and selected, its outline is displayed in the Outline window in the lower left corner of Aptana. Then, you can drill down to see all of the elements in the HTML document. When you select one of them in the outline, it is also selected in the HTML.

Aptana with a project in the App Explorer and an HTML file in the first tab

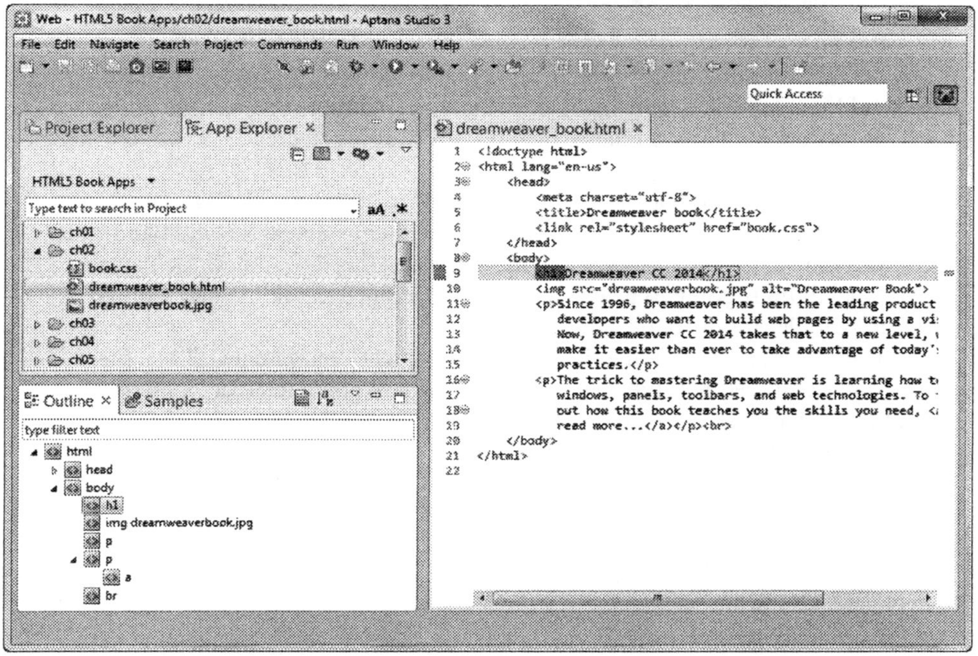

How to open an HTML file within a project

- Use the drop-down list in Aptana's App Explorer to select the project. Then, locate the file and double-click on it.

Two ways to open an HTML file that isn't in a project

- Use Aptana's Project Explorer to locate the file. Then, double-click on it.
- Use the File→Open File command.

Description

- When you open an HTML file, the file is opened in a new tab and its outline is displayed in the Outline window.

Figure 2-8 How to open an HTML file in Aptana

How to start a new HTML file

Because all HTML documents contain the same DOCTYPE declaration and the same starting tags for the document tree, it makes sense to start each new HTML file from a *template* that includes the starting code or from an HTML document that's similar to the one you're going to create. If you're using projects, Aptana makes that easy to do.

The first procedure in figure 2-9 shows how to start a new HTML file from your own template. To do that, you can use the File→New→File command, and complete the dialog box as shown in this figure. In this case, a new file named php_book.html is going to be created from the template.html file that's stored in the ch02 folder for the book applications.

The second procedure in this figure shows how to start a new HTML file from an existing HTML file. If, for example, you're going to create a second book page that's similar to an existing book page, it makes sense to start the new file from the old file. To do that, you just open the old file and save it with a new name. Then, you can delete the parts of the old file that the new page doesn't need and add the new parts.

Another option is to start a new HTML file from Aptana's HTML5 template. However, this template contains code and comments that you're going to want to delete. As a result, you're better off using a template that is designed for the application that you're working on. In fact, for most websites, you should have one template for each type of page that you're developing.

As you become more familiar with HTML, you can create your own templates. If, for example, you're going to develop several pages that have the same general content, you can create an HTML template for those pages. That will make it easier for you to develop those pages.

If you're using a text editor that doesn't provide for the use of templates, you can get the same result by opening a file that contains a template and then saving it right away with a new name before you modify the file. That way, the original template file remains unchanged. The main problem with this is that you're likely to forget to save the template with a new name and modify its code before you realize it.

Aptana's dialog box for creating a new HTML file from a template

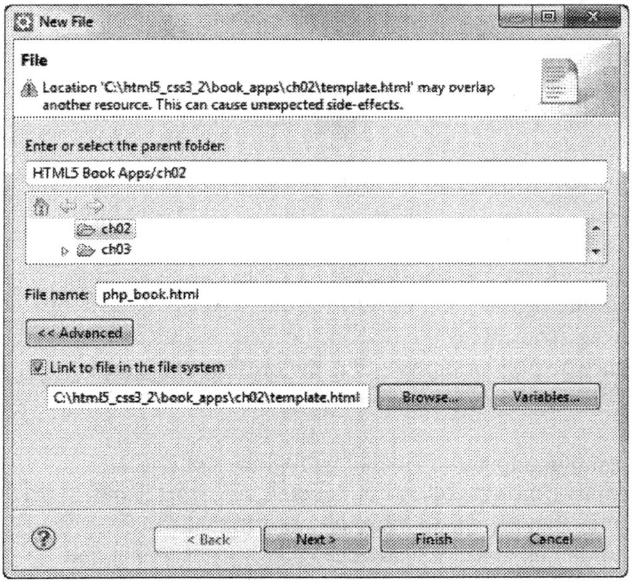

How to start a new HTML file from any template

- Select the File→New→File command. In the New File dialog box that's displayed, select the folder that the new file should be stored in and enter a filename for the new file including its .html extension.
- Still in the New File dialog box, click the Advanced button, check the Link to File in the File System box, click the Browse button, and select the template that you want to start the new file from. Then, click the Finish button.

How to start a new HTML file from another HTML file

- Open the file that you want to base the new file on. Then, use the File→Save As command to save the file with a new name.

Description

- Because all HTML files require the same starting elements, it's a good practice to start a new file from a *template* that contains those elements. When you use projects, Aptana makes that easy to do.
- If you're going to create a new file that's similar to an existing file, you can open the existing file and save it with a new name.
- Although you can use the File→New From Template→HTML→HTML 5 Template command to start a new file from the Aptana HTML5 template, it's usually better to start your files from a template that's specifically designed for your HTML documents.

Figure 2-9 How to start a new HTML file in Aptana

How to edit an HTML file

Figure 2-10 shows how to edit an HTML file. When you open a file with an html extension, Aptana knows what type of file you're working with so it can use color to highlight the syntax components. That makes it easier to spot errors in your code.

As you enter new code, the auto-completion feature presents lists of words that you can enter into your code. If you enter the bracket at the beginning of a tag, for instance, a list of all of the elements you can enter is displayed. Then, you can select an element and press the Tab key to insert it into your code. This causes Aptana to close the opening tag and add the closing tag so all you have to do is enter the content for the tag. You can also enter one or more letters after the bracket to filter the list so it only displays elements that start with those letters. In the example in this figure, I entered the letter *i* so only the words that start with that letter are displayed.

You can use a similar technique to enter attributes within an opening tag. To do that, enter a space and one or more letters after the element name. That displays a list of all the attributes that start with those letters and that can be used with that element. Then, you can select the attribute you want to select and press the Tab key. When you do, Aptana inserts the attribute along with an equal sign and double quotes, and you can enter the value of the attribute between the quotes.

This figure also lists some common coding errors. Often, the color coding will help you spot the first three types of errors. If, for example, you misspell an attribute name or if you forget to code a closing quotation mark, the color coding will indicate that the code isn't correct.

Beyond that, Aptana provides error markers and warning markers that help you find and correct errors. In this figure, for example, you can see one error marker and one warning marker. Then, to get the description of the error or warning, you can hover the mouse over the marker.

On the other hand, Aptana has no way of knowing what the correct code should be for file references in link, img, or <a> elements. As a result, you must discover those errors when you test the web page. If, for example, the file reference for a style sheet in a link element is incorrect, the CSS won't be applied. If the file reference in an img element is incorrect, the image won't be displayed and the value of the alt attribute will be displayed. And if the file reference for an <a> element is incorrect, the browser won't access the correct page.

Please note that this figure also shows how to change the colors that are used to highlight the syntax. If you find that the default colors are hard to read, this is something that you may want to do.

Aptana with an auto-completion list for an HTML file

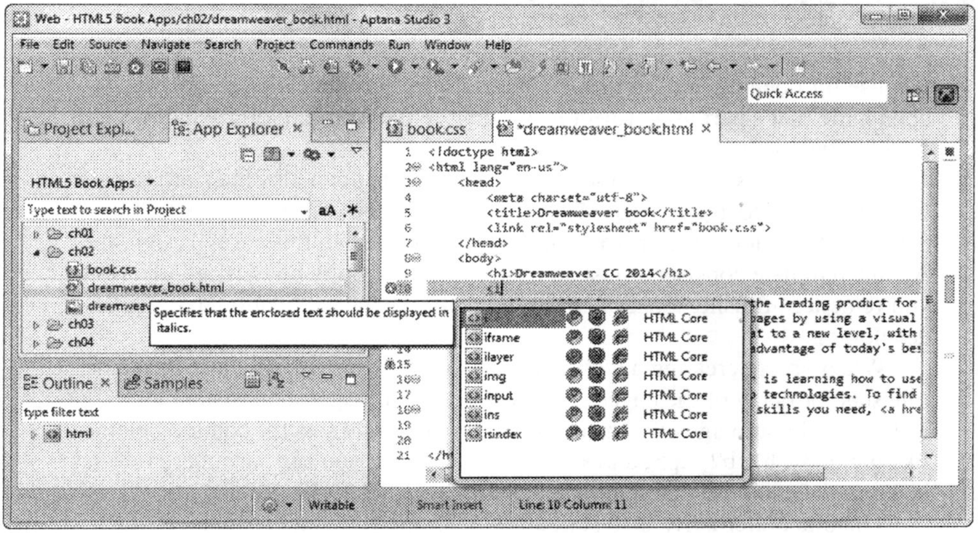

Common coding errors

- An opening tag without a closing tag.
- Misspelled tag or attribute names.
- Quotation marks that aren't paired.
- Incorrect file references in link, img, or <a> elements.

How to set the colors that are used to highlight the syntax

- Use the Window→Preferences command to open the Preferences dialog box. Then, click on Aptana Studio, click on Themes, and choose a theme from the drop-down list. (In this book, we use the Dreamweaver theme.)

Description

- Aptana displays the different parts of a file in different colors so they're easy to recognize. This helps you spot some of the common errors. For this to work, the file must have the html extension.
- The auto-completion feature displays a list of elements that start with what you've typed. To insert one of those terms, double-click on it or use the arrow keys to highlight it and press the Tab key. Aptana automatically adds the closing tag or /> for an empty tag (although our coding recommendation is to change the /> to just > for an empty tag).
- An error marker is a red circle that contains a white X at the start of a line. A warning marker is a yellow triangle that contains an exclamation mark. These markers are displayed as you enter and edit code.
- To get a description of the error or warning, hover the mouse over the marker.

Figure 2-10 How to edit an HTML file in Aptana

How to open or start a CSS file

In general, you use the same methods for opening and starting CSS files that you use for opening and starting HTML files. For instance, the easiest way to open a file that's part of a project is to find it in the App Explorer window and double-click on it.

Similarly, to start a CSS file from a template that contains the starting code, you use the procedure in figure 2-11. Here again, you can start a new CSS file from your own template or from the Aptana template. In this case, though, the Aptana template consists of just an empty rule set for the body type. As a result, you're better off using a template that's specific to the application that you're developing.

When you're creating a website, for example, you will often use the same rule sets for many of the pages. That will give your pages a consistent look. For instance, all your pages are likely to use the same rule sets for common elements like the body, h1, h2, <p>, and <a> elements. Then, you can save these rule sets in a template and use that template to start new CSS files.

The other alternative is to start a new CSS file from an existing CSS file. To do that, you just open the file in Aptana and save it with a new name. This makes sense when the new file will use many of the same styles as the old file. Then, you just delete the styles that you don't need and add the files that you do need.

Aptana's dialog box for creating a new CSS file from a template

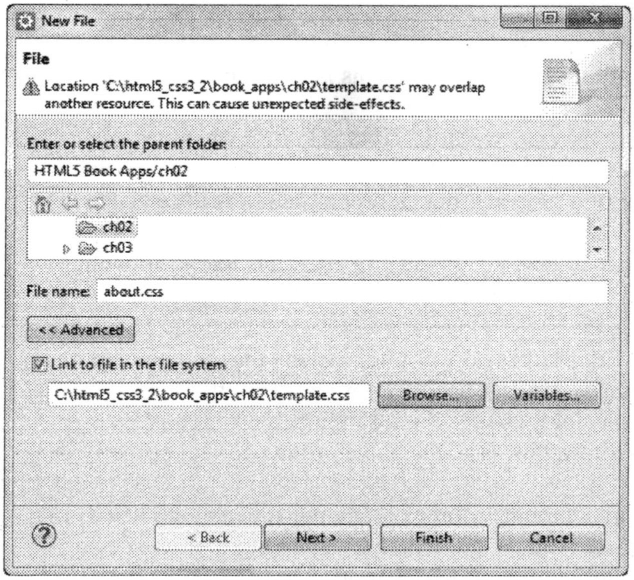

How to start a new CSS file for a project from any template

- Select the File→New→File command. In the New File dialog box that's displayed, select the folder that the new file should be stored in, and enter a filename for the new file, including its .css extension.
- Still in the New File dialog box, click the Advanced button, check the Link to File in the File System box, click the Browse button, and select the template that you want to start the new file from. Then, click the Finish button.

How to start a new CSS file from another CSS file

- Open the file that you want to base the new file on. Then, use the File→Save As command to save the file with a new name.

Description

- Because all CSS files require some of the same elements, it's good to start a new file from a template that contains those elements. Aptana makes that easy to do.
- If you're going to create a new file that's similar to an existing file, you can open the existing file and save it with a new name.
- Although you can use the File→New From Template→CSS→CSS Template command to start a new file from the Aptana CSS template, it's better to use your own templates.

Figure 2-11 How to start a new CSS file from a template in Aptana

How to edit a CSS file

In general, when you use Aptana to edit a CSS file, you use the same techniques that you use for editing an HTML file. This is summarized in figure 2-12.

When you open a file with the css extension, Aptana knows what type of file you're working with so it can use color to highlight the syntax components. When you type the first letter of a property, the auto-completion feature displays a list of properties that start with that letter. Then, you can select the property you want and press the Tab key to insert it. When you enter the colon following the property, Aptana displays another list that you can use to select the value of the property in some cases.

Beyond that, Aptana provides error and warning markers that help you spot errors. In this figure, for example, you can see an error marker at the start of one of the coding lines. In addition, color coding is used to indicate which property within this line caused the error. In this case, the name of the padding property is spelled wrong.

These features help you avoid the first three common errors that are listed in this figure. On the other hand, Aptana has no way of knowing if you code an id or class name incorrectly. Instead, you'll find that out during testing when you notice that the rule sets that you've specified for the elements haven't been applied.

Aptana with an auto-completion list for a CSS file

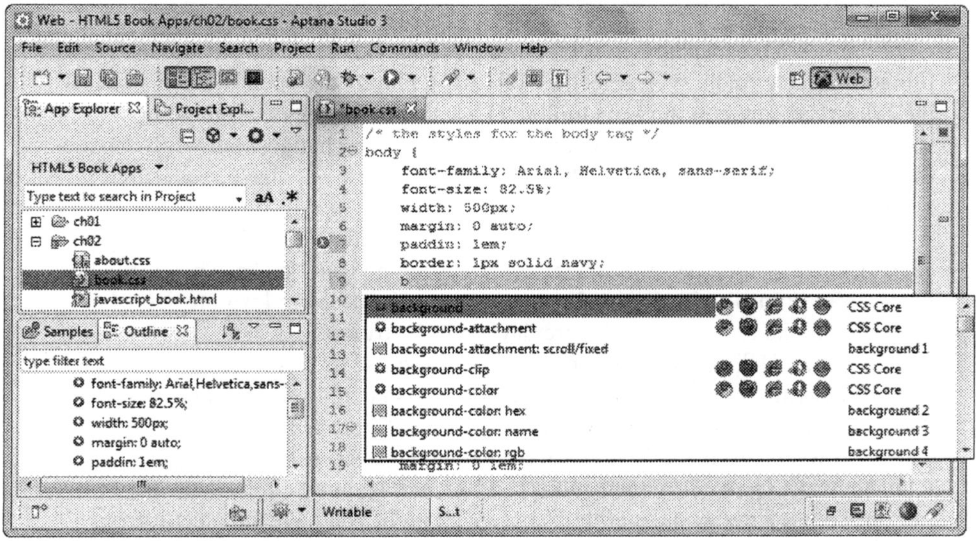

Common coding errors

- Braces that aren't paired correctly.
- Missing semicolons.
- Misspelled property names.
- Id or class names that don't match the names used in the HTML.

Description

- To edit a CSS file, you can use the same techniques you use to edit an HTML file. Here again, the color coding and the error markers will help you spot syntax errors. For this to work, the file must have the css extension.
- The auto-completion feature displays a list of properties that start with what you've typed. To insert one of those properties, double-click on it or use the arrow keys to highlight it and press the Tab key. Aptana automatically adds the colon after the property name.
- When you type the left brace after a selector, Aptana automatically adds the right brace. Then, you can enter the rules between the braces.

Figure 2-12 How to edit a CSS file in Aptana

How to preview and run an HTML file

Figure 2-13 shows how to preview and run an HTML file from Aptana. To preview the document, you select the tab that contains the open file and click on the Show Preview button in the toolbar. That shows the preview in another tab of the editor window. This is a quick way to see how the changes that you've made to an HTML or CSS file are displayed, but the preview may have rendering errors that you won't find in browsers.

To run an HTML file in the browser that you used most recently, you again select the tab of the open file. Then, you click on the Run button. This opens the browser and runs the file in that browser. This is the preferred way to see what a web page looks like because the preview can't be trusted.

To run an HTML file in another browser, you use the drop-down list to the right of the Run button. In this figure, this list has been dropped down, and it shows that three browsers are available: Chrome, Firefox, and Internet Explorer. These browsers are listed in the sequence they were last used. In this case, Chrome was used most recently so it can be used again by clicking the Run button. To use Firefox or Internet Explorer, though, you have to select it from this list.

You should also know that you can add browsers to this list. In fact, when I first installed Aptana, Chrome wasn't included in this list. To add it, I selected Run Configurations from the drop-down menu to display the Run Configurations dialog box. Then, I clicked the New button at the left side of the toolbar, clicked the Browse button to locate the executable file for the browser, and entered a name for the new configuration in the Web Browser category at the left side of the dialog box.

Incidentally, if you click on the Show Preview or Run button when an HTML file isn't selected, nothing happens. Also, you need to save any changes to an HTML file and its related CSS file before you can preview and run it. To do that, you can click on the Save or Save All button in the toolbar. But if you forget to do that, Aptana will warn you.

The Show Preview and Run buttons

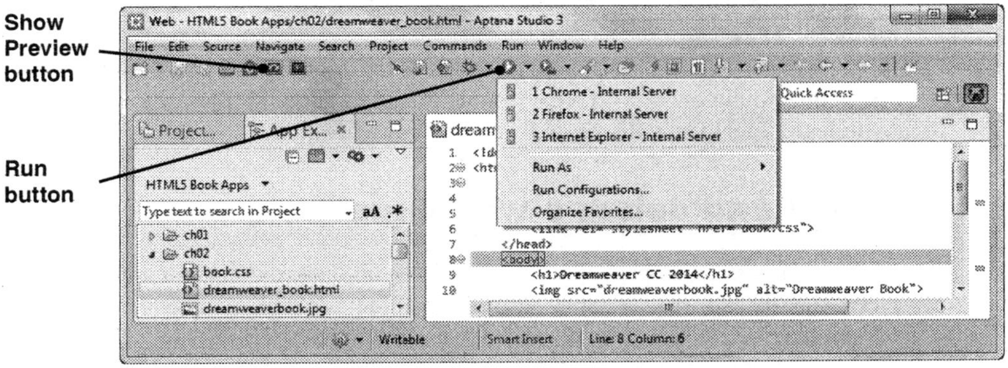

The preview of the dreamweaver_book.html file

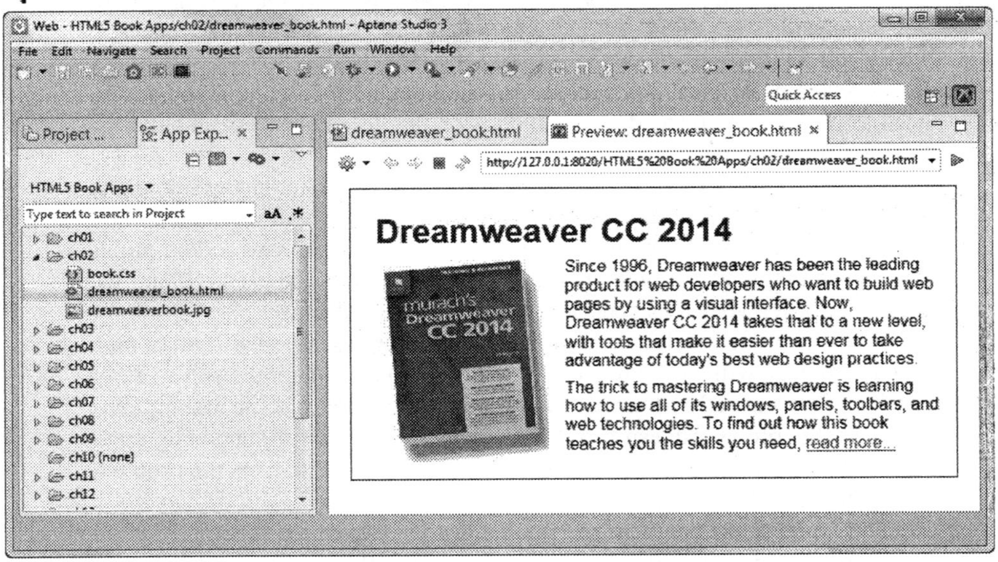

Description

- To preview an HTML file in an Aptana tab, open the HTML file, select its tab, and click on the Show Preview button.
- To run an HTML file in the most recently used browser, open the file, select its tab, and click on the Run button.
- To run an HTML file in another browser, click the down-arrow to the right of the Run button and select the browser.
- Before you preview or run a file, you should save any changes that you've made to it or its related CSS file. To do that, you can click on the Save or Save All button in the toolbar. But if you forget to save the files, Aptana will warn you.

Figure 2-13 How to preview and run an HTML file from Aptana

How to test, debug, and validate HTML and CSS files

Now that you know how to create and edit HTML and CSS files, you're ready to learn how to test, debug, and validate those files.

How to test and debug a web page

When you *test* a web page, you run the file on all the browsers that are likely to access the file and try to identify all of the problems. When you *debug* a web page, you find the causes of the problems, fix them, and test again.

To run a web page, you can use one of the techniques in figure 2-14. If you're using Aptana, though, you can just click on the Run button. Once the page is displayed in the browser, you study it to make sure that it looks the way you want it to. You should also make sure that all of the links work.

If you find errors, you need to change the HTML, the CSS, or both, and test the page again. When you test a page for the second time, though, you don't need to run it again. Instead, you can click on the Reload or Refresh button in the browser's toolbar.

Often, the changes you make as you test a web page are just minor adjustments or improvements. But sometimes, the web page doesn't look at all the way you expected it to. Often, these errors are caused by trivial coding problems like missing tags, quotation marks, and braces, but finding these problems can be hard to do when your files consist of dozens of lines of code.

When you test a web page on more than one browser, you will often find that a web page will work on one browser, only to find that it doesn't work on another. That's usually because one of the browsers makes some assumptions that the other browser doesn't. If, for example, you have a slight coding error in an HTML file, one browser might make an assumption that fixes the problem, while the other doesn't.

To fix problems like these, it often helps to validate the HTML or CSS file. That should clearly identify the coding errors. You'll learn how to do that in the next two figures.

The HTML file displayed in the Chrome browser

Three ways to run a web page that's on an intranet or your own computer

- Start your browser, and use the File→Open or Open File command to open the file. Or, type the complete path and filename into the address bar, and press Enter.
- Use the file explorer on your system to find the HTML file, and double-click on it.
- If you're using Aptana, select the HTML file in the App Explorer and click the Run button to open the file in the most recently used browser. If you're using another text editor or IDE, look for a similar button or command.

How to rerun a web page from a browser after you change its source code

- Click the Reload or Refresh button in the browser.

How to test a web page

- Run the page in all of the browsers that are likely to access your site.
- Check the contents and appearance of the page to make sure it's correct in all browsers.
- Click on all of the links to make sure they work properly.

How to debug a web page

- Find the causes of the errors in the HTML or CSS code, make the corrections, and test again.

Description

- When you *test* a web page, you try to find all of the errors.
- When you *debug* a web page, you find the causes of the errors in the HTML or CSS code, correct them, and test the page again.

Figure 2-14 How to test and debug the HTML and CSS for a web page

How to validate an HTML file

To *validate* an HTML document, you use a program or website for that purpose. One of the most popular websites for validating HTML is the one for the W3C Markup Validation Service that's shown in figure 2-15.

When you use this website, you can provide the HTML document that you want to validate in three ways. You can provide the URL for the page. You can upload the document. And you can copy and paste the document into the Validate by Direct Input tab.

In this figure, the Validate by File Upload tab is shown. Then, you click the Browse button to find the file that you want to validate. Once that's done, you click the Check button to validate the document.

Another way to validate an HTML document is to use the Aptana command for doing that, which is explained in this figure. Then, the results of the validation are displayed in one tab of the editor window, as shown in the next figure. This makes it much easier to validate a document, which is another reason for using Aptana. At this writing, however, this command causes an error to occur so the validation isn't done. This is a known bug that should be corrected in the near future.

The home page for the W3C validator

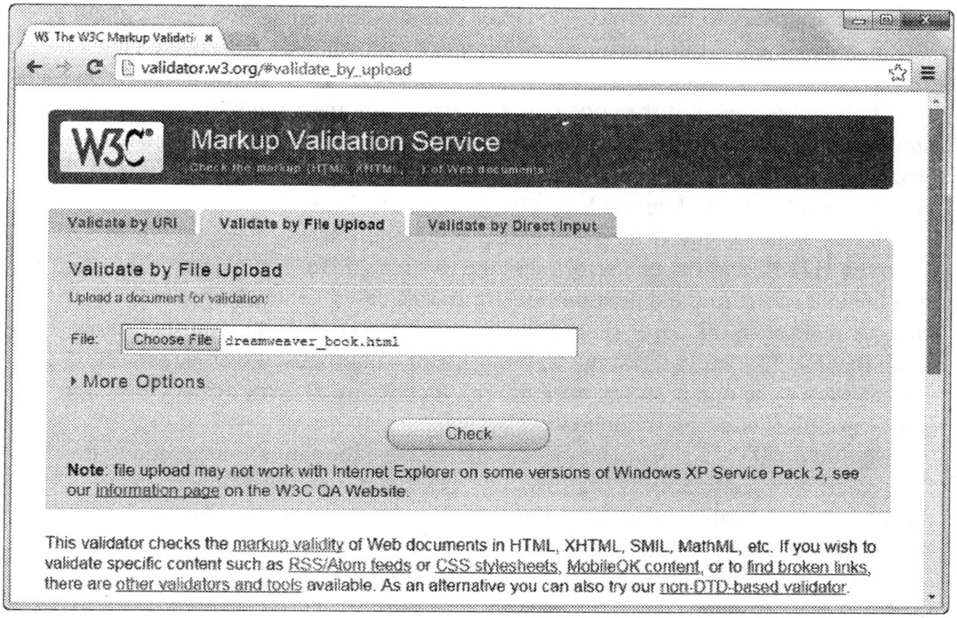

How to use the W3C Markup Validation Service

- Go to the URL that follows, identify the file to be validated, and click the Check button:

  `http://validator.w3.org/`

How to validate an HTML file from Aptana

- Open the file and choose Commands→HTML→Validate Syntax (W3C).
- At this writing, this command causes an error to occur due to a known bug. This should be corrected in the near future.

Description

- To *validate* the HTML for a page, you can use a program or website for that purpose. One of the most popular websites is the W3C Markup Validation Service.
- When you use the W3C Markup Validation Service, if the file you want to validate has already been uploaded to a web server, you can validate it by entering its URL on the Validate by URI tab. If the file you want to validate hasn't been uploaded to a web server, you can validate it by locating it on the Validate by File Upload tab.
- With the W3C Markup Validation Service, you can also validate HTML by copying and pasting it into the Validate by Direct Input tab.
- If you're using Aptana, you can validate an HTML file by using the command above. However, you may get slightly different results because Aptana uses the HTML Tidy validator and W3 uses its own validator.

Figure 2-15 How to validate an HTML file (part 1 of 2)

If the HTML code is valid when a document is validated, the validator displays a message to that effect. However, it may still display one or more warning messages. At this writing, one warning is displayed for the web pages in this book.

On the other hand, if the code contains errors, the message will indicate the number of errors that were detected. Then, you can scroll down to a list of the errors like the one in the second part of this figure. Here, the validation results are shown at the W3C Markup Validation Service website.

In this example, the two error messages and one warning message for line 11 in the HTML and the one error message for line 15 were caused by a missing > at the end of the img element on line 10. In this case, Aptana would display an error marker so this error shouldn't slip by you. And if it did, you should catch that error when you test the web page. But sometimes, a web page will be displayed okay in one browser, even though it contains an error or two, although it may not display correctly in another browser.

Should all HTML documents be validated, even though it's estimated that 99% of all web pages aren't? We say, yes! As we see it, validation is a useful practice that will solve some testing problems, and programs like Aptana and Dreamweaver make validation so easy that it's well worth doing. Besides that, validation may help your SEO results because clean code gets better results.

The errors and warning for an HTML file with a missing > at the end of the img element

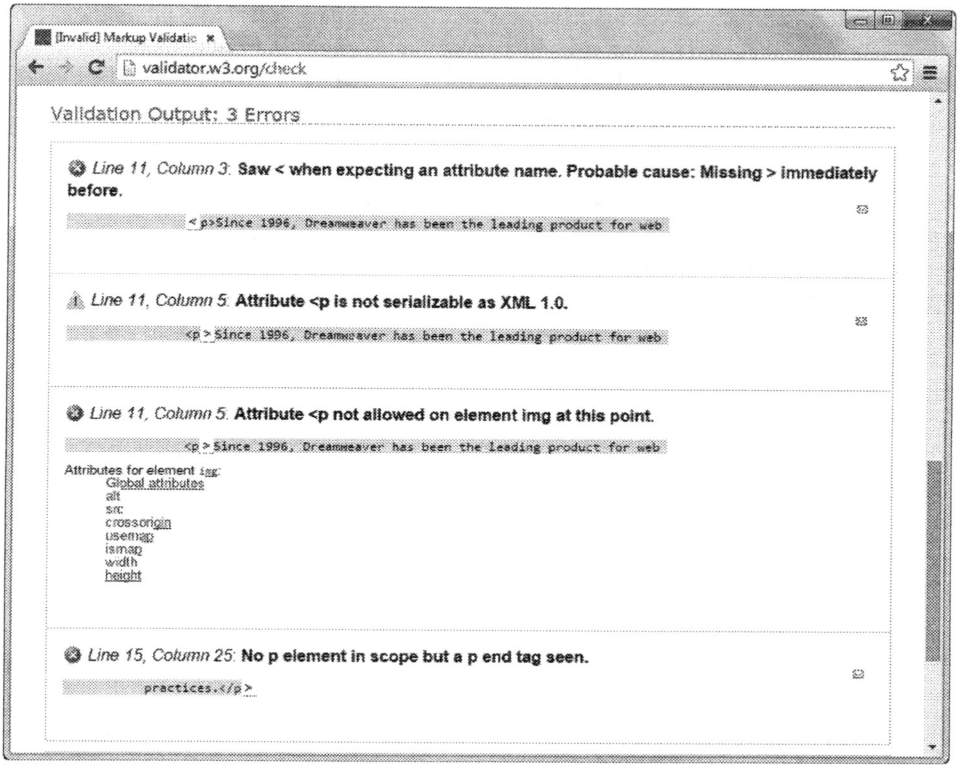

Description

- If the HTML document is valid, the validator will indicate that the document passed the validation. However, one or more warnings may still be displayed.
- If the HTML document isn't valid, the validator will indicate the number of errors that were detected. Then, you can scroll down to a description of the errors.

Figure 2-15 How to validate an HTML file (part 2 of 2)

How to validate a CSS file

You can validate a CSS file the same way you validate an HTML file, either with a validation program that may be part of a text editor or an IDE, or with a website service like the W3C CSS Validation Service. If you use the W3C Validation Service, the opening page looks like the one for markup validation. Then, you can use any one of the three tabs to validate a CSS file.

If the file contains errors, the validation service will display a screen like the one in figure 2-16. Here, the error was caused by a missing semicolon at the end of a rule. Although you would normally catch this type of error with Aptana's error markers and color coding, CSS validation is useful when the file is large, the CSS isn't working right, and you can't spot any errors. CSS validation may also mean that your CSS will work on an infrequently-used browser that isn't one of the browsers that you're using for testing.

The CSS Validation Service with errors displayed

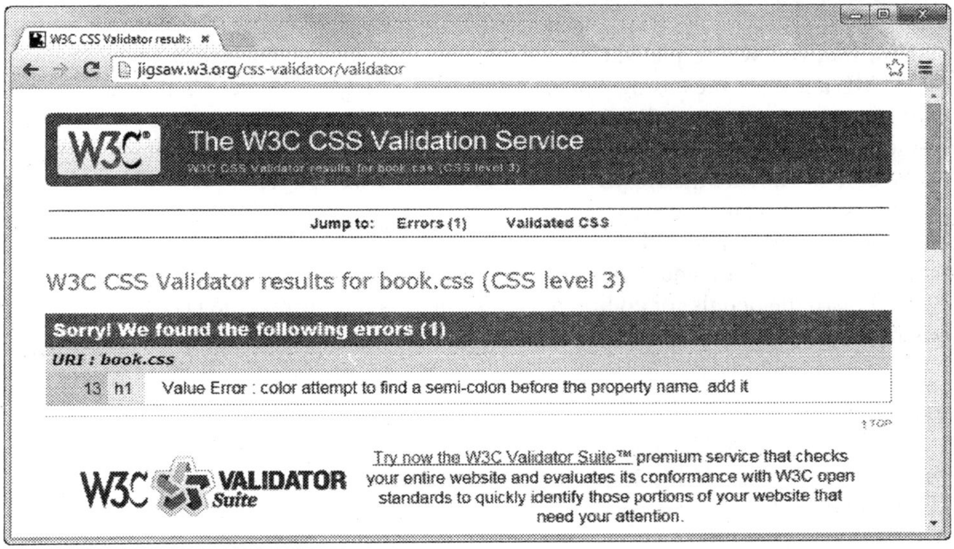

How to use the W3C CSS Validation Service

- Go to the URL that follows, identify the file to be validated, and click the Check button:
  `http://jigsaw.w3.org/css-validator/`

How to validate a CSS file from Aptana

- Open the file. Then, issue the Commands→CSS→Validate Selected CSS (W3C) command.

Description

- To validate the CSS for a page, you can use a program or website for that purpose. One of the most popular websites is the W3C CSS Validation Service. This website works the same as the W3C Markup Validation Service.
- If the CSS for a page is valid, the CSS Validation Service displays a message that indicates that no errors were found.
- If you're using Aptana, you can validate a CSS file by using the command above. However, you may get slightly different results because Aptana uses the CSS Tidy validator and W3 uses its own validator.

Figure 2-16 How to validate a CSS file

Perspective

Now that you've completed this chapter, you should be able to create and edit HTML and CSS files using Aptana or the editor of your choice. Then, you should be able to test those files by displaying their web pages in your web browser and in any other web browsers that your users might use. You should also be able to validate the HTML and CSS files for a web page.

At this point, you're ready to learn the coding details for HTML and CSS. So, in the next chapter, you'll learn the details for coding the HTML elements that define the structure and content for a web page. And in chapters 4, 5, and 6, you'll learn the details for coding the CSS rule sets that format the HTML content.

Terms

syntax
HTML document
DOCTYPE declaration
document tree
HTML element
root element
opening tag
closing tag
content of an element
empty tag
nested elements
attribute
Boolean attribute
comment
comment out
whitespace
rule set
selector
declaration block
declaration
rule
property
value
type selector
template
Aptana project
testing
debugging
HTML validation
CSS validation

Summary

- An *HTML document* consists of a *DOCTYPE declaration* that indicates what version of HTML is being used and a *document tree* that contains the *HTML elements* that define the content and structure of a web page.
- The *root element* in a document tree is the html element, which always contains a head element and a body element. The head element provides information about the page, and the body element provides the structure and content for the page.
- Most HTML elements consist of an *opening tag* and a *closing tag* with *content* between these tags. When you *nest* elements with HTML, the inner set of tags must be closed before the outer set.
- *Attributes* can be coded in an opening tag to supply optional values. An attribute consists of the name of the attribute, an equal sign, and the attribute value. To code multiple attributes, you separate them with spaces.
- An *HTML comment* can be used to describe or explain a portion of code. Because comments are ignored, you can also use comments to *comment out* a portion of HTML code so it isn't rendered by the browser. This can be helpful when you're testing your HTML code.
- *Whitespace* consists of characters like tab characters, line return characters, and extra spaces that are ignored by browsers. As a result, you can use whitespace to indent and align your code.
- A *CSS rule set* consists of a selector and a declaration block. The *selector* identifies the HTML elements that are going to be formatted. Three of the common CSS selectors select by element (called a *type selector*), ID, and class.
- The *declaration block* in a CSS rule set contains one or more *declarations* that do the formatting. Each declaration (or *rule*) consists of a *property*, a colon, a *value*, and a semicolon.
- *CSS comments* work like HTML comments. However, CSS comments start with /* and end with */, and HTML comments start with <!-- and end with -->.
- Aptana is a text editor that can be used to edit HTML or CSS code. To help you read the code, Aptana displays the syntax components with different colors. It also provides auto-completion lists and error checking that detects common entry errors.
- When you start a new HTML or CSS file, it's best to start from a *template* or an old file that's similar to the new file that you're going to create.
- To *test* an HTML file, you run it on all of the browsers that your clients may use. Then, if you discover problems, you need to *debug* the code and test it again.
- To *validate* an HTML or CSS file, you can use a program or website for that purpose. Often, a validation program will detect errors in a file, even though the web page displays the way you want it to on all browsers.

Before you do the exercises for this book...

If you haven't already done it, you should install the Chrome and Firefox browsers and the applications, examples, and exercises for this book. If you're going to use Aptana Studio 3 as your text editor, you should also download and install that product. The procedures for doing all three are in appendix A.

Exercise 2-1 Get started right with Aptana

This exercise is for readers who are going to use Aptana Studio 3 with this book. It guides you through the process of creating projects that provide easy access to the book applications, examples, and exercise starts that you've downloaded.

Create the projects

1. Use the procedure in figure 2-7 to create a project for the book applications that are stored in this folder:
   ```
   c:\murach\html5_css3_2\book_apps
   ```
   This project should be named HTML5 Book Apps.
2. Use the same procedure to create a project named HTML5 Examples for the book examples that are stored in this folder:
   ```
   c:\murach\html5_css3_2\book_examples
   ```
3. Use the same procedure to create a project named HTML5 Exercises for the exercises that are stored in this folder:
   ```
   c:\html5_css3_2\exercises
   ```

Use the projects that you've created

4. Use the drop-down list in the App Explorer to select the HTML5 Book Apps project. This provides access to all of the applications that are in this book.
5. Click on the ◢ symbol before ch02 to display the files in this folder. Then, double-click on the file named dreamweaver_book.html to open that file.
6. Delete the l in the opening tag for the h1 element and note how Aptana highlights this error. Then, undo this change. (To use the keyboard to undo a change, press Ctrl+Z.)
7. Start a new element after the h1 element and note how Aptana provides auto-completion. Then, undo this change and save the file if necessary.
8. Click on the Show Preview button shown in figure 2-13 to preview the file in Aptana. Then, click on the tab for the HTML file and click on the Run button shown in figure 2-13 to run the file in your default browser.
9. Use the drop-down list in the App Explorer to select the HTML5 Exercises project. This provides access to all of the starting files for the exercises.
10. Right-click on one of the tabs in the editor window, and select Close All to close all of the tabs. Then, experiment on your own if you like.

Exercise 2-2 Edit and test the book page

In this exercise, you'll edit and test the book page that is shown in figure 2-14. You should do this exercise whether you're using Aptana or another text editor.

Open the HTML and CSS files for the book page

1. Start your text editor.
2. Open this HTML file in your text editor:
   ```
   c:\html5_css3_2\exercises\ch02\dreamweaver_book.html
   ```
   For Aptana users, this will be in the project named HTML5 Exercises.
3. Open the CSS file named book.css that's in the same folder. This should open in a new tab.

Test the book page in Firefox and Chrome

4. Run the HTML file in Firefox.
5. Run the HTML file in Chrome. Is there a difference in the pages? If so, this illustrates why you need to test a web page in more than one browser.

Modify the HTML and CSS code and test again

6. Go back to your text editor and click on the tab for the book.css file. Then, change the float property for the img element from left to right, and save the file. Now, test this change in both browsers.
7. Go back to the book.css file, and change the color for the h1 element to "red" and change the font-size to 180%. Then, save the file, and test the change in one or both browsers.
8. Go back to the dreamweaver_book.html file, and add a <p> element at the bottom of the page that has this content:
   ```
   For customer service, call us at 1-555-555-5555.
   ```
   Then, save the file and test this change in both browsers. When you do, you will notice that this paragraph displays differently in the two browsers.
9. Go to the dreamweaver_book.html file and add an id attribute with the value "service" to the <p> element that you just entered. Then, go to the book.css file and enter a rule set for the <p> element with that id. This rule set should use the color property to change the text to red, and it should use the clear property with a value of both to stop the floating before the paragraph. If you need help doing this, refer to figures 2-5 and 2-6. Now, save both the html and css files, and test these changes.

Validate the HTML and CSS files

10. In the HTML file, delete the ending > for the img tag, and save the file. Then, go to the site in figure 2-15, and use the Validate by File Upload tab to validate the file. If you scroll down the page when the validation is done, you'll see 3 error messages, even though the file contains just one error.

11. In the CSS file, delete the semicolon for the color rule in the h1 rule set, and save the file. Then, go to the site in figure 2-16, and use the Validate by File Upload tab to validate the file. This time, you'll see 1 error message.
12. If you're using Aptana, note the error marker in the HTML file. Then, validate the HTML file by using the command in figure 2-15. This shows how much easier it is to validate files within the text editor or IDE that you're using.
13. If you're using Aptana, note the error marker in the CSS file. Then, validate the CSS file by using the command in figure 2-16. Note here that the validation found no errors, which differs from the results for step 11.
14. Now, undo the errors in the files, save the files, and validate the HTML page again. This time, it should pass with one warning. Then, test the web page one last time.

Exercise 2-3 Start a new web page

In this exercise, you'll start HTML and CSS files from templates in this folder:

```
c:\html5_css3_2\exercises\ch02
```

For Aptana users, this will be in the project named HTML5 Exercises.

Start your files from templates

1. Create a new HTML file named testpage.html from the template named template.html. If you're using Aptana, you can use the first procedure in figure 2-9. Otherwise, you can use the second procedure in this figure.
2. Create a new CSS file named testpage.css from the template named template.css. If you're using Aptana, you can use the first procedure in figure 2-11. Otherwise, you can use the second procedure in this figure.

Add some content to the HTML file and test it

3. In the title element, change the content to "Test page".
4. In the link element, enter "testpage.css" for the value of the href attribute.
5. Add an h1 element to the body of the HTML file that says: "This is a test page." Then, save the file, and test the page by running it in Chrome, Firefox, or IE.
6. This illustrates how fast you can get started with a new web page when you start the html and css files from templates. Now, if you want to add more elements to the HTML or more rules or rule sets to the CSS, give it a try.
7. When you're through experimenting, close the files in your editor.

3

How to use HTML to structure a web page

In chapter 2, you saw the basic structure of an HTML document, you learned the basic techniques for coding the elements that make up a document, and you learned that these elements specify the structure and content of a page when it's displayed in a browser. Now, in this chapter, you'll learn how to code the HTML elements that you'll use in most of the documents you create. Then, in the next three chapters, you'll learn how to use CSS to format those HTML elements.

How to code the head section

The head section of an HTML document contains elements that provide information about the web page rather than the content of the page. In chapter 1, for example, you learned that the title element sets the text that's displayed in the tab for the page in the web browser. Now, you'll learn more about this element as well as some other elements that you can code in the head section.

How to code the title element

The head section of every page should include a unique title element that describes the content of the page. In the HTML shown in figure 3-1, for example, you can see that this element gives the name of the organization followed by the keywords *speakers* and *luncheons*. This title is used by search engines for search engine optimization, and it appears in the results of a search to help the users decide whether they want to go to that page. That's why you should follow the SEO guidelines in this figure when you code this element.

The content of the title element is also displayed in the browser's tab for the page. As you can see in this figure, though, only the portion of the title that fits in the tab is displayed. But if you hover the mouse over the tab, the entire title will be displayed in a tooltip.

How to link to a favicon

The link element is an optional element that you can use to specify a file that should be linked to the web page. In figure 3-1, the link element is used to link a custom icon, called a *favicon*, to the web page. This causes the icon to be displayed to the left of the title in the tab for the page. Note that you typically name this icon favicon.ico as shown in this figure.

When you code the link element, you typically include two attributes. The rel attribute indicates the relationship of the linked resource to the document. For a favicon, you use the value "shortcut icon".

The href attribute provides the URL of the resource. In this example, the favicon is in the same folder as the HTML file, so the URL is just the filename. If the file is in a different location, though, you can use an absolute or relative URL to identify that location. You'll learn how to code absolute and relative URLs later in this chapter.

If you're using an older version of Internet Explorer, you should realize that it won't display a favicon if the page is displayed from your local file system. To test a favicon in this browser, then, you need to upload the page to a server and display it from that server.

A browser that shows the title and favicon

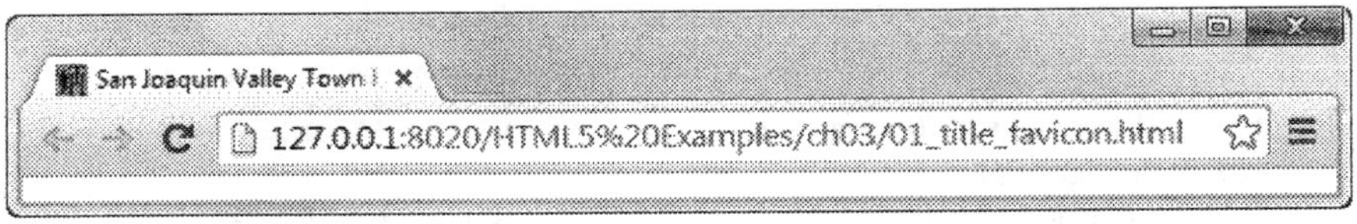

A head section that specifies a title and links to a favicon

```
<head>
    <title>San Joaquin Valley Town Hall | speakers and luncheons</title>
    <link rel="shortcut icon" href="favicon.ico">
</head>
```

SEO guidelines for the title tag

- Always code a title tag in the head section.
- The title should accurately describe the page's content, and it should include the one or two keywords that you want the page ranked for.
- The title should be interesting enough to entice the reader to click on it when it's shown in the search results for a search engine.
- The title should be unique for each page in your website.
- Limit the length of your titles to around 65 characters because most search engines don't display more than that in their results.

Description

- The title element specifies the text that's displayed in the browser's tab for the web page.
- The title is also used as the name of a favorite or bookmark for the page.
- A custom icon, called a *favicon*, is typically named favicon and must have the extension .ico to work correctly with Internet Explorer. A favicon typically appears to the left of the title in the browser's tab for the page. It may also appear to the left of the URL in the browser's address bar, and it may be used in a favorite or bookmark.
- To specify a favicon for a page, you use a link tag exactly like the one shown above.
- To create an ico file, you can use an icon editor, a program that converts an image to an ico file, or a web-based converter. You may also be able to find an icon on the Internet by searching for "web icons". For more information, see chapter 9.

Internet Explorer note

- A favicon isn't displayed in older versions of Internet Explorer if the page is served from your local file system. It is only displayed if the page is served from the web server.

Figure 3-1 How to code the title element and link to a favicon

How to include metadata

The meta element is another optional element that you can code within the head element. You use it to specify *metadata*, which provides information about the content of the document.

The head element in figure 3-2 includes three meta elements. The first one specifies the character encoding used for the page, and UTF-8 is the encoding that's commonly used for the World Wide Web. Since this element is required for HTML5 validation, you should include it in the head section of every HTML document, and it should be one of the first elements in the head section.

The next two meta elements in this figure provide metadata that can be used by search engines to index the page. Here, the first element uses the name attribute with the value "description" to indicate that the content attribute that follows contains a description of the web page. This can be a longer description than the one in the title element, and it should also be unique for each page in your website.

The second meta element uses the name attribute with the value "keywords" to indicate that the content attribute contains a list of keywords related to the page. At one time, the keywords were an important factor for search engine optimization, but they have been de-emphasized in recent years, partly because some web masters used keywords to misrepresent what a page contained.

At present, there is some debate about how search engines use the description and keywords metadata. In fact, the algorithms that search engines use are frequently changed, so it's hard to know what the best use of metadata is. There is also the danger that you might change the content of a page and forget to change the metadata. In that case, a search engine might index the page incorrectly. Nevertheless, it's still a good practice to provide the description and keywords metadata for at least the important pages of a website. Just make sure that your descriptions and keywords accurately represent the contents of your pages.

A head section that includes metadata

```
<head>
    <title>San Joaquin Valley Town Hall | speakers and luncheons</title>
    <meta charset="utf-8">
    <meta name="description" content="A yearly lecture series with speakers
        that present new information on a wide range of subjects">
    <meta name="keywords" content="san joaquin, town hall, speakers,
        lectures, luncheons">
</head>
```

Three attributes of the <meta> tag

Attribute	Description
`charset`	A required tag in HTML5 that specifies the type of character encoding to be used for the page. UTF-8 is the encoding that's commonly used for the World Wide Web.
`name`	Specifies the type of metadata being added to the document. The values "description" and "keywords" can be used to specify content that's used by some search engines.
`content`	Specifies the value to be used for the item specified by the name attribute.

SEO guidelines

- Code the description metadata for each page of your website. It should summarize the contents of the page, it should be unique for each page, and it can be longer than the title tag. When it is displayed in the search-engine results, it should encourage users to click on your link.
- Code the keywords metadata for each page of your website. It should consist of no more than 10 keywords or phrases, and it should be unique for each page.

Description

- The meta element provides information about the HTML document that's called *metadata*.
- The charset metadata is required for HTML5 validation.
- All or part of the description metadata may be displayed in the search results of some search engines.
- Although the keywords metadata has been de-emphasized by some search engines, it's still a good practice to include this data.

Figure 3-2 How to include metadata

How to code text elements

Within the body of a document, you can code two types of elements: block elements and inline elements. In the topics that follow, you'll learn how to code a variety of block and inline elements that define the text for a document.

How to code headings and paragraphs

Headings and paragraphs are the most common content of a web page. These are defined by the HTML elements shown in figure 3-3. These elements are called *block elements*, and each one begins on a new line when it is displayed.

If you review the example in this figure, you shouldn't have any trouble understanding how these elements work. Here, the HTML uses the h1, h2, and <p> elements to generate the text that's shown. When these elements are displayed by a browser, each element has a default font and size that's determined by the base font of the browser. This base font is typically Times New Roman in 16 pixels.

When you use the h1 through h6 elements, you should use them to provide a logical structure for your document, not to format the text. That means that the most important heading on a page should always be an h1 element, and you should only code one h1 element on each page. That also means you should only go down one level at a time, not jump down two or more levels to indicate less importance. In other words, the first heading level after an h2 should be an h3, not an h4.

For example, the h1 element in this figure is used to mark the most important heading on the page, and the h2 elements are used to mark the next level of importance. Then, if the first h2 element required two subheadings below it, they would both be coded at the h3 level. This structure helps search engines index your site properly, and it makes your pages more accessible to devices like screen readers. Then, you can use CSS to size and format the text in these elements, as shown in the next chapter.

Common block elements for headings and paragraphs

Element	Description
h1	Creates a level-1 heading with content in bold at 200% of the base font size.
h2	Creates a level-2 heading with content in bold at 150% of the base font size.
h3	Creates a level-3 heading with content in bold at 117% of the base font size.
h4	Creates a level-4 heading with content in bold at 100% of the base font size.
h5	Creates a level-5 heading with content in bold at 83% of the base font size.
h6	Creates a level-6 heading with content in bold at 67% of the base font size.
p	Creates a paragraph of text at 100% of the base font size.

HTML that uses the block elements

```
<h1>San Joaquin Valley Town Hall Programs</h1>
<h2>Pre-lecture coffee at the Saroyan</h2>
<p>Join us for a complimentary coffee hour, 9:15 to 10:15 a.m. on the day
   of each lecture. The speakers usually attend this very special event.</p>

<h2>Post-lecture luncheon at the Saroyan</h2>
<p>Extend the excitement of Town Hall by purchasing tickets to the
   luncheons</p>
```

The block elements in a web browser

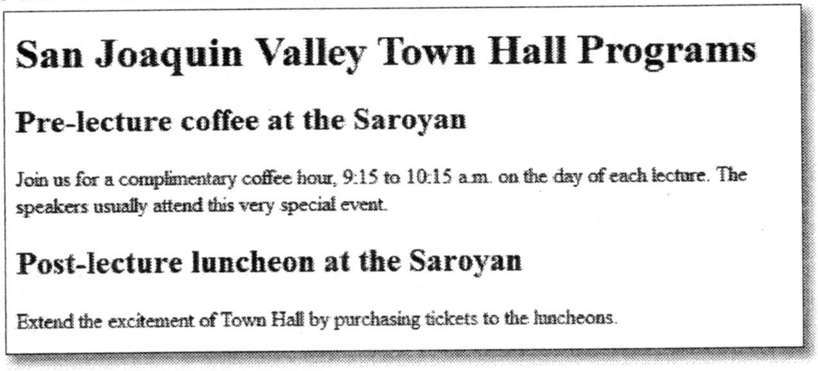

SEO guidelines

- Use the heading tags to show the structure and importance of the content on a page. Always use the h1 tag to identify the most important information on the page, and only code a single h1 tag on each page. Then, decrease one level at a time to show subsequent levels of importance.
- Don't use heading levels as a way to size text. Instead, use CSS to size the headings.

Description

- *Block elements* are the main building blocks of a website and can contain other elements. Each block element begins on a new line.
- The base font size and the spacing above and below headings and paragraphs are determined by the browser, but you can change these values by using CSS.

Figure 3-3 How to code headings and paragraphs

How to code special blocks of text

In addition to the elements for headings and paragraphs, HTML provides some elements that you can use to code special blocks of text. For instance, three of the most common elements are described in figure 3-4.

You typically use the pre element to display preformatted blocks of code. When you use this element, any whitespace or line breaks that appear in the content is maintained. In addition, the content is displayed in a monospaced font. In this figure, the pre element is used to display two lines of JavaScript code.

You typically use the blockquote element to display an actual quote like the one shown in this figure. Depending on the browser, this element may cause the content to be indented from the left side of the block element that contains it or from both the left and right sides. But note that this doesn't add quotation marks to the text.

You can use the address element to display contact information for the developer or owner of a website. In this figure, the address element is used to display a phone number and an email address. As you can see, the browser displays this information in italics.

Although these elements provide some default HTML formatting, you shouldn't think of these elements that way. Instead, you should use these elements to identify specific types of content. Then, you can use CSS to format these elements so they look the way you want them to.

Block elements for special types of text

Element	Description
pre	Used for portions of code that are formatted with line breaks and spaces. Creates a block of preformatted text that preserves whitespace and is displayed in a monospaced font.
blockquote	Used for quotations. Can be used with the cite and <q> elements of figure 3-5.
address	Used for contact information for the developer or owner of a website.

HTML that uses the block elements

```
<p>How to use JavaScript to display the year:</p>
<pre>
        var today = new Date();
        document.writeln( today.getFullYear() );
</pre>

<p>Ernest Hemingway wrote:</p>
<blockquote>Cowardice, as distinguished from panic, is almost always
    simply a lack of ability to suspend the functioning of the imagination.
</blockquote>

<p>How to contact Mike Murach &amp; Associates:</p>
<address>1-800-221-5528<br>
    <a href="emailto:murachbooks@murach.com">murachbooks@murach.com</a>
</address>
```

The block elements in a web browser

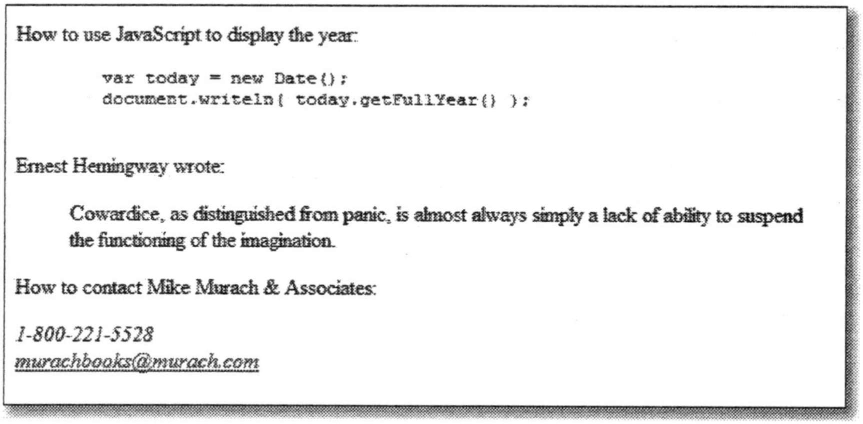

Description

- These block elements identify the type of content that they contain. That's consistent with the way the HTML5 semantic elements are used (see figures 3-8 and 3-9).

How to code inline elements for formatting and identifying text

In contrast to a block element, an *inline element* doesn't start on a new line. Instead, an inline element is coded within a block element. In this topic, you'll learn how to code some of the most common inline elements for identifying and formatting.

The first table in figure 3-5 presents five elements for formatting text. for instance, the <i> element is used to italicize text, and the <b> element is used to boldface text. With the exception of the <br> element, each element must have both an opening and a closing tag. Then, the appropriate formatting is applied to the content between these tags.

In contrast, the <br> element starts a new line of text. You can use this element to start a new line within another element, but you shouldn't use it to provide space between block elements. Instead, you should use CSS to control the space between block elements, which you'll learn how to do in chapter 5.

The second table in this figure presents elements that are used for identifying inline content. For instance, you can use the abbr element to identify an abbreviation, the <q> element to identify a quotation, and the cite element to identify the source of a block element like a quotation.

Unlike the blockquote element, which is a block element, the browser adds quotation marks to a <q> element. Also, these quotation marks are curly instead of straight. In the examples, you can see that a <q> element is used for a quotation within a paragraph, but this inline element could also be used within a blockquote element to add the quotation marks.

In general, you should use the elements in the second table to identify the type of text whenever some meaning is implied. Then, you can use CSS to format those elements. In contrast, you should only use the elements in the first table to format text when no meaning is implied.

This is different from the way the <i> and <b> elements were used before CSS become available. Previously, these elements were commonly used to apply formatting. Now, it's more common to use em and strong and to use CSS to apply the appropriate formatting.

Inline elements for formatting text

Element	Description
`i`	Displays the content in italics.
`b`	Displays the content in bold.
`sub`	Displays the content as a subscript.
`sup`	Displays the content as a superscript.
`br`	An empty element that starts a new line of text.

Inline elements for identifying content

Element	Description
`abbr`	Used for abbreviations.
`cite`	Used to indicate a bibliographic citation like a book title.
`code`	Used for computer code, which is displayed in a monospaced font.
`dfn`	Used for special terms that can be defined elsewhere (definitions).
`em`	Indicates that the content should be emphasized, which is displayed in italics.
`kbd`	Used for keyboard entries, which is displayed in a monospaced font.
`q`	Used for quotations, which are displayed within quotation marks.
`samp`	Used to mark a sequence of characters (sample) that has no other meaning.
`strong`	Indicates that the content should be strongly emphasized, which is displayed in bold.
`var`	Used for computer variables, which are displayed in a monospaced font.

HTML that uses some of the inline elements

```
<p>If you don't get 78% or more on your final, <em>you won't pass.</em></p>
<p>Save a bundle at our <strong>big yearend sale</strong>.</p>
<p>When the dialog box is displayed, enter <kbd>brock21</kbd>.</p>
<p>The chemical symbol for water is H<sub>2</sub>O.</p>
<p><q>To sleep, perchance to dream-ay, there's the rub.</q></p>
```

The inline elements in a web browser

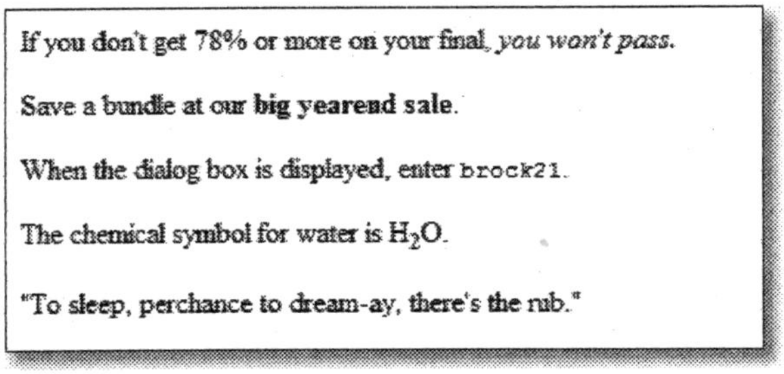

Description

- An *inline element* is coded within a block element and doesn't begin on a new line.
- The formatting elements should be used when no special meaning is implied.
- The content elements should be used to convey meaning. Then, you can use CSS to format them.

Figure 3-5 How to code inline elements for formatting and identifying text

How to code character entities

Many of the web pages you develop will require special characters such as a copyright symbol and opening and closing “curly” quotes. To display these special characters, you use *character entities*. Figure 3-6 presents the most common of these entities.

As you can see, all character entities start with an ampersand (&) and end with a semicolon (;). Then, the rest of the entity identifies the character it represents. To insert the copyright symbol (©), for example, you use the © character entity.

Because the & character marks the start of each character entity, you shouldn’t use this character within an HTML document to represent an ampersand. Instead, you should use the & entity. Similarly, because the left bracket (<) and right bracket (>) are used to identify HTML tags, you shouldn’t use those characters within an HTML document to represent less-than and greater-than signs. Instead, you should use the < and > entities.

Besides the entities for characters, you may sometimes need to insert a non-breaking space to force a browser to display a space. To do that, you use the   character entity. In the third paragraph in this figure, for example, this character entity is used to indent the first line of the paragraph four spaces. However, because you can accomplish the same thing with CSS, you probably won’t use the   character entity this way.

Common HTML character entities

Entity	Character	Entity	Character
&	&	°	°
<	<	±	±
>	>	‘	‘ (opening single quote)
©	©	’	’ (closing single quote or apostrophe)
®	®	“	“ (opening double quote)
™	™	”	” (closing double quote)
¢	¢		non-breaking space

Examples of character entities

```
<p>It&rsquo;s time to start your Christmas shopping!</p>

<p>President John F. Kennedy said, &ldquo;And so, my fellow Americans,
ask not what your country can do for you; ask what you can do for
your country.&rdquo;</p>

<p>    Turning fear into hope, medical futurist
Dr. Alan J. Russell will discuss the science of regenerating damaged
or diseased human body parts, while offering real hope for the future
of human health.</p>

<p>&copy; 2015 Mike Murach &amp; Associates, Inc.</p>
```

The character entities in a web browser

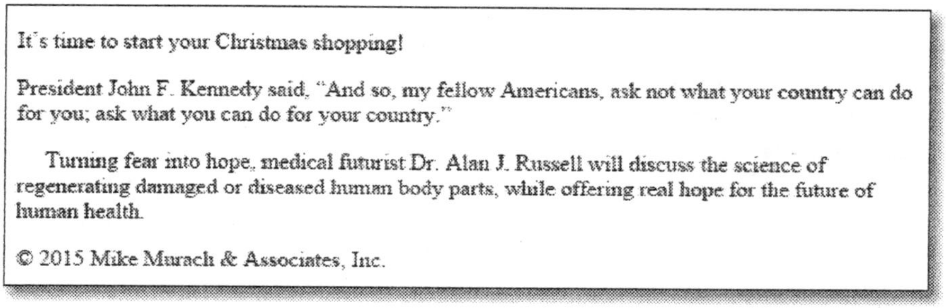
It’s time to start your Christmas shopping!

President John F. Kennedy said, “And so, my fellow Americans, ask not what your country can do for you; ask what you can do for your country.”

Turning fear into hope, medical futurist Dr. Alan J. Russell will discuss the science of regenerating damaged or diseased human body parts, while offering real hope for the future of human health.

© 2015 Mike Murach & Associates, Inc.

Description

- *Character entities* can be used to display special characters in an HTML document.
- HTML5 provides a variety of character entities in addition to the ones above. For a complete list of character entities, see
  http://www.w3.org/TR/html5/syntax.html#named-character-references

How to code the core attributes

Besides the attributes you've learned about so far, HTML provides some core attributes that you can use with most elements. In figure 3-7, you can see the core attributes that you're most likely to use.

You use the id attribute to uniquely identify an HTML element. Then, you can use CSS to work with the element.

The class attribute is similar, except it doesn't have to be unique. That lets you assign more than one element to the same class. Then, you can use CSS to apply the same formatting to all the elements in the class. When you use the class attribute, you can also assign more than one class to a single element.

In the example in this figure, you can see that the first input element has an id attribute with the value "email". As you'll see in the next chapter, CSS can be used to apply unique formatting to elements with id attributes.

In this example, you can also see that a class attribute is used to assign a class named "first" to the first <p> element. Then, another class attribute is used to assign two classes to the second <p> element. These classes are "first" and "field". Later, you can use CSS to apply formatting to the elements in each class.

You can use the title attribute to provide additional information for an element. In the example in this figure, this attribute is used to provide a tooltip for an input field that lets the user enter an email address (you'll learn more about input fields in chapter 11). Then, when the cursor is moved over this field in the browser, the tooltip is displayed. For some elements, though, a tooltip isn't displayed so the title attribute has no purpose.

The lang attribute lets you specify the language used by a document. For instance, we recommend that you code this attribute on the html element to specify the language for the entire document. For English-speaking countries, you typically code this attribute like this:

```
<html lang="en">
```

This can help a screen reader pronounce words correctly. However, you can also code this attribute for individual elements. If a sentence on a web page is written in French, for example, you can code this attribute for the element that contains the sentence.

Core HTML attributes

Attribute	Description
`id`	Specifies a unique identifier for an element that can be referred to by CSS.
`class`	Specifies one or more class names that can be referred to by CSS, and the same name can be used for more than one element. To code more than one class name, separate the class names with spaces.
`title`	Specifies additional information about an element. For some elements, the title appears in a tooltip when the user hovers the mouse over the element.
`lang`	Identifies the language that the content of the element is written in.

HTML that uses these attributes

```
<html lang="en">
<body>
    <h1>San Joaquin Valley Town Hall</h1>
    <p class="first">Welcome to San Joaquin Valley Town Hall.</p>
    <form action="subscribe.php" method="post">
        <p>Please enter your e-mail address to subscribe to our
           newsletter.</p>
        <p class="first field">E-Mail:
        <input type="text" name="email" id="email"
               title="Enter e-mail here."></p>
        <p><input type="submit" value="Subscribe"></p>
    </form>
</body>
</html>
```

The HTML in a web browser with a tooltip displayed

Accessibility guideline

- Always code the lang attribute on the html element to identify the language for the page.

Description

- The core attributes can be coded for most HTML elements.
- ID and class names are case sensitive, should start with a letter, and can include letters, numbers, underscores, hyphens, colons, and periods.
- The lang attribute is typically used to assist screen readers to read content correctly and to provide for searches that are restricted by language.

Figure 3-7 How to code the core attributes

How to structure the content of a page

One of the key features of HTML5 is the addition of the new structural elements. After I present these elements, I'll show you how pages were traditionally structured before the release of HTML5.

How to use the primary HTML5 semantic elements

Figure 3-8 presents the HTML5 *semantic elements* that improve the way you can structure a page. For instance, the example in this figure shows how the header, main, and footer elements can be used to divide a document into three parts. This makes it easy to see the structure of the page by looking at the HTML tags. This also makes it easy to code the selectors that you need for formatting these elements.

The use of these structural elements is often referred to as *HTML5 semantics*. The implication is that you do a better job of creating meaning when you use these elements. In the long run, using HTML5 semantics may mean that search engines will be able to do a better job of coming up with relevant pages. For that reason, you should start using the semantic elements right away.

Although this figure only illustrates the use of three of the seven elements in the table, you'll see the nav element used in the web page at the end of this chapter. Then, in chapter 6, you'll see how the aside element is used for a sidebar within the main element, and you'll see how the section element is used for other content within the main element. In addition, you'll see how the article element is used for an article about a speaker.

If you review the HTML5 semantic elements in this figure, you'll see that the section element is the only one that doesn't indicate the specific type of content it contains. Because of that, we'll use section elements in this book whenever there isn't another appropriate HTML5 element for a grouping. The main point of HTML5 semantics, though, is to use the other HTML5 elements whenever they provide the appropriate meaning. That way, you'll get the benefits of HTML5.

The primary HTML5 semantic elements

Element	Contents
`header`	The header for a page.
`main`	The main content for a page.
`section`	A generic section of a document that doesn't indicate the type of content.
`article`	A composition like an article in the paper.
`nav`	A section of a page that contains links to other pages or placeholders.
`aside`	A section of a page like a sidebar that is related to the content that's near it.
`footer`	The footer for a page.

A page that's structured with header, main, and footer elements

```
<body>
    <header>
        <h1>San Joaquin Valley Town Hall</h1>
    </header>
    <main>
        <p>Welcome to San Joaquin Valley Town Hall. We have some
           fascinating speakers for you this season!</p>
    </main>
    <footer>
        <p>&copy; Copyright 2015 San Joaquin Valley Town Hall.</p>
    </footer>
</body>
```

The page displayed in a web browser

Accessibility and SEO guideline

- Use the HTML5 semantic elements to indicate the structure of your pages.

Description

- HTML5 provides *semantic elements* that you should use to structure the contents of a web page. The use of these elements can be referred to as *HTML5 semantics*.
- All of the HTML5 elements in this figure are supported by the modern browsers.

Figure 3-8 How to use the primary HTML5 semantic elements

How to use some of the other HTML5 semantic elements

Figure 3-9 presents some of the other HTML5 semantic elements that are currently supported by modern browsers. For instance, the time element provides a date or date and time in a standard format that can be parsed by a browser. This is illustrated by the first example. Here, the <p> element says that next year's conference will be on May 31st. But the time element makes it clear that this is May 31st of 2015. If the time element is used within an article, you can also use the pubdate attribute to make it clear that the date is the publication date for the article.

The second and third semantic elements in this figure apply to the use of figures within web pages. A figure can be a block of text, an image, a diagram, or anything that is referred to from the text outside of the figure. Within the figure element that contains the figure, the figcaption element can be used to provide a caption for the figure. This is illustrated by the second example, which treats two lines of JavaScript code as a figure. Then, in chapters 9 and 10, you can see how these elements can be used to treat images and tables as figures.

Here again, these elements are designed to provide more meaning. That way, search engines can do a better job of ranking your pages and screen readers can do a better job of reading your pages. In addition, using these elements makes it easier for you to code and format your pages.

Other HTML5 semantic elements

Element	Contents
`time`	A date or date and time that can be parsed by a browser.
`figure`	An illustration, diagram, photo, code listing or the like that is referred to from the main content of the document.
`figcaption`	The caption that identifies a figure.

The attributes of the time element

Attribute	Description
`datetime`	A date and time in a standard format that can be parsed by a browser.
`pubdate`	A Boolean attribute that indicates that the date is the publication date for the article that contains the time element.

A time element

```
<p>Next year's conference will be on
    <time datetime="2015-05-31">May 31st</time>.</p>
```

The figure and figcaption elements

```
<figure>
    <code>
        var today = new Date();<br>
        document.writeln( today.getFullYear() );<br><br>
    </code>
    <figcaption>
        JavaScript code for getting the year
    </figcaption>
</figure>
```

The code displayed in a browser

```
var today = new Date();
document.writeln( today.getFullYear() );

JavaScript code for getting the year
```

Accessibility and SEO guideline

- Use the HTML5 semantic elements to indicate the structure of your pages.

Description

- Although there are other HTML5 semantic elements, these are the most useful ones that are currently supported by modern browsers.

Note

- The hgroup element that was originally included in the HTML5 specifications has now been dropped. Because of that, you shouldn't use this element in new web development.

Figure 3-9 How to use some of the other HTML5 semantic elements

When and how to code div and span elements

Figure 3-10 shows how to code the div and span elements that have traditionally been used to structure a page and to format portions of inline content. You need to know how these elements are used because you're sure to see them in the HTML for pages that haven't yet been converted to HTML5. For new pages, though, you should use the HTML5 semantic elements.

The div element is a block element that you can use to divide an HTML document into divisions. In the example in this figure, you can see that the content of the document is divided into three divisions. The first division contains the header for the page, the second division contains the main content of the page, and the third division is for the footer. If you look at this web page as it's displayed in the browser, you can see that these div elements don't affect the appearance of the page.

For each div element, the id attribute is used to indicate the contents of the division. As you'll see in the next chapter, this id can be used as the selector that's used to apply CSS formatting to each division. If you refer back to figure 3-8, though, you'll see how this can be done more easily by using the HTML5 structural tags.

Does this mean that you shouldn't ever use div elements? The quick answer is, no. In general, you should only use div elements as a last resort, but there will be situations where it doesn't make sense to use section elements to define a grouping of elements. Just keep in mind that div elements should be used sparingly and only when an HTML5 semantic element doesn't apply.

The other element that's presented in this figure is the span element. This inline element has traditionally been used to identify content so CSS can be used to format it. For instance, the <p> element in the main division in this figure contains an inline span element. Here again, the span element doesn't affect the appearance of the page, but its id attribute can be used as the selector for CSS formatting.

For modern websites, span elements should only be used when more specific tags don't apply. Instead of span elements, you should use the block elements of figure 3-4 and the inline elements of figure 3-5 to identify the content types. By using these elements instead of span elements, you not only improve accessibility but also SEO.

A block element for structuring a web page

Element	Description
div	Lets you divide a page into divisions that can be formatted and positioned with CSS.

An inline element for formatting text

Element	Description
span	Lets you identify text that can be formatted with CSS.

A page that's structured with div and span elements

```
<body>
    <div id="header">
        <h1>San Joaquin Valley Town Hall</h1>
    </div>
    <div id="main">
        <p><span id="welcome">Welcome to San Joaquin Valley Town
            Hall.</span>
            We have some fascinating speakers for you this season!</p>
    </div>
    <div id="footer">
        <p>&copy; Copyright 2015 San Joaquin Valley Town Hall.</p>
    </div>
</body>
```

The page displayed in a web browser

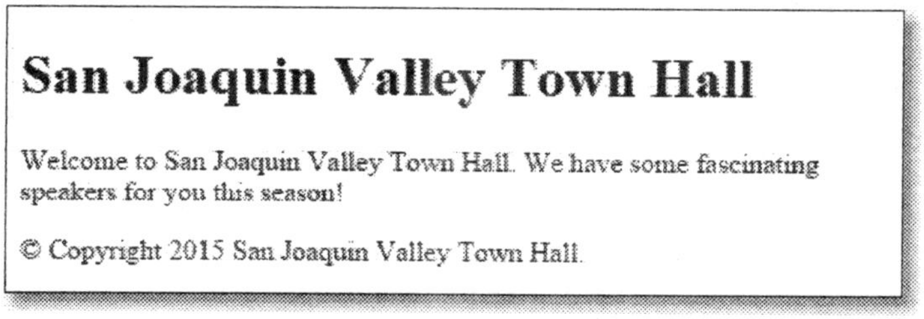

Accessibility and SEO guidelines

- Use div tags only when the HTML5 semantic elements don't apply.
- Use span tags only when the tags for identifying content don't apply.

Description

- Before HTML5, div elements were used to define divisions within the body of a document. Now, the HTML5 semantic elements will be replacing div elements.
- Before HTML5, span elements were used to identify portions of text that you could apply formatting to. Today, a better practice is to use the elements in figures 3-4 and 3-5 to identify content and to use CSS to format that content.

Figure 3-10 When and how to code the div and span elements

How to code links, lists, and images

Because you'll use links, lists, and images in most of the web pages that you develop, the topics that follow introduce you to these elements. But first, you need to know how to code absolute and relative URLs so you can use them with your links and images.

How to code absolute and relative URLs

Figure 3-11 presents some examples of absolute and relative URLs. To help you understand how these examples work, the diagram at the top of this figure shows the folder structure for the website used in the examples. As you can see, the folders for this website are organized into three levels. The root folder for the site contains five subfolders, including the folders that contain the images and styles for the site. Then, the books folder contains subfolders of its own.

In chapter 1, you learned about the basic components of a URL. The URL you saw in that chapter was an *absolute URL*, which includes the domain name of the website. This is illustrated by the first group of examples in this figure. Here, both URLs refer to pages at www.murach.com. The first URL points to the index.html file in the root folder of this website, and the second URL points to the toc.html file in the root/books/php folder.

When used within the code for the web pages of a site, an absolute URL is used to refer to a file in another website. In contrast, a *relative URL* is used to refer to a file within the same website. As this figure shows, there are two types of relative URLs.

In a *root-relative path*, the path is relative to the root folder of the website. This is illustrated by the second group of examples. Here, the leading slash indicates the root folder for the site. As a result, the first path refers to the login.html file in the root folder, and the second path refers to the logo.gif file in the images folder.

In a *document-relative path*, the path is relative to the current document. This is illustrated by the third group of examples. Here, the assumption is that the paths are coded in a file that is in the root folder for a website. Then, the first path refers to a file in the images subfolder of the root folder, and the second path refers to a file in the php subfolder of the books subfolder. This illustrates paths that navigate down the levels of the folder structure.

But you can also navigate up the levels with a document-relative path. This is illustrated by the fourth group of examples. Here, the assumption is that the current document is in the root/books folder. Then, the first path goes up one level for the index.html file in the root folder. The second path also goes up one level to the root folder and then down one level for the logo.gif file in the images folder.

This shows that there's more than one way to code the path for a file. If, for example, you're coding an HTML file in the root/books folder, you can use either a root-relative path or a document-relative path to get to the images subfolder. If this is confusing right now, you'll quickly get used to it once you start coding your own pages.

A simple website folder structure

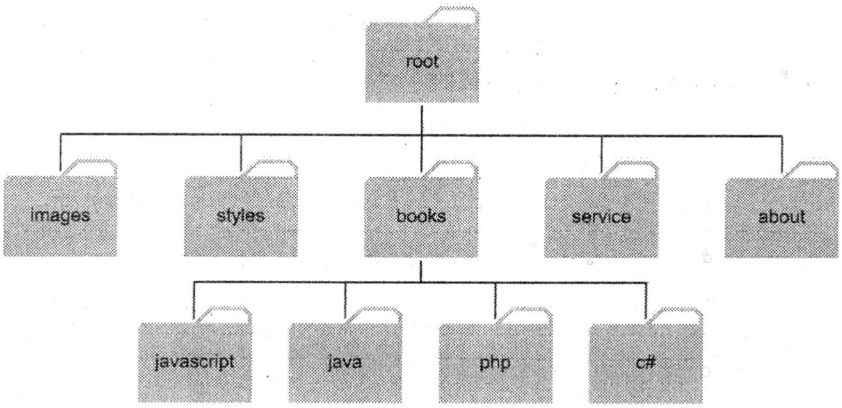

Examples of absolute and relative URLs

Absolute URLs

```
http://www.murach.com/index.html
http://www.murach.com/books/php/toc.html
```

Root-relative paths

```
/login.html                (refers to root/login.html)
/images/logo.gif           (refers to root/images/logo.gif)
```

Document-relative paths that navigate down from the root folder

```
images/logo.gif            (refers to root/images/logo.gif)
books/php/overview.html    (refers to root/books/php/overview.html)
```

Document-relative paths that navigate up from the root/books folder

```
../index.html              (refers to root/index.html)
../images/logo.gif         (refers to root/images/logo.gif)
```

Description

- When you code an *absolute URL*, you code the complete URL including the domain name for the site. Absolute URLs let you display pages at other websites.
- When you code a *relative URL*, you base it on the current folder, which is the folder that contains the current page.
- A *root-relative path* is relative to the root folder of the website. It always starts with a slash. Then, to go down one subfolder, you code the subfolder name and a slash. To go down two subfolders, you code a second subfolder name and another slash. And so on.
- A *document-relative path* is relative to the folder the current document is in. Then, to go down one subfolder, you code the subfolder name followed by a slash. To go down two subfolders, you code a second subfolder name followed by another slash. And so on.
- You can also go up in a document-relative path. To go up one level from the current folder, you code two periods and a slash. To go up two levels, you code two periods and a slash followed by two more periods and a slash. And so on.

Figure 3-11 How to code absolute and relative URLs

How to code links

Most web pages contain *links* that go to other web pages or web resources. To code a link, you use the <a> element (or anchor element) as shown in figure 3-12. Because this element is an inline element, you usually code it within a block element like a <p> element.

In most cases, you'll code only the href attribute for the <a> element. This attribute specifies the URL for the resource you want to link to. The examples in this figure illustrate how this works.

The first example uses a relative URL to link to a page in the same folder as the current page. The second example uses a relative URL to link to a page in a subfolder of the parent folder. The third example uses a relative URL to link to a page based on the root folder. And the last example uses an absolute URL to link to a page at another website.

By default, links are underlined when they're displayed in a browser to indicate that they're clickable. As a result, most web users have been conditioned to associate underlined text with links. Because of that, you should avoid underlining any other text.

When a link is displayed, it has a default color depending on its state. For instance, a link that hasn't been visited is displayed in blue, and a link that has been visited is displayed in purple. Note, however, that you can use CSS as described in the next chapter to change these settings.

When you create a link that contains text, the text should clearly indicate the function of the link. For example, you shouldn't use text like "click here" because it doesn't indicate what the link does. Instead, you should use text like that in the examples in this figure. In short, if you can't tell what a link does by reading its text, you should rewrite the text. This improves the accessibility of your site, and it helps search engines index your site.

Basic attribute of the <a> element

Attribute	Description
`href`	Specifies a relative or absolute URL for a link.

A link to a web page in the same folder

```
<p>Go view our <a href="products.html">product list</a>.</p>
```

A link to a web page in a subfolder of the parent folder

```
<p>Read about the <a href="../company/services.html">services we
provide</a>.</p>
```

A link to a web page based on the root folder

```
<p>View your <a href="/orders/cart.html">shopping cart</a>.</p>
```

A link to a web page at another website

```
<p>To learn more about JavaScript, visit the
<a href="http://www.javascript.com/">official JavaScript website</a>.</p>
```

The links in a web browser

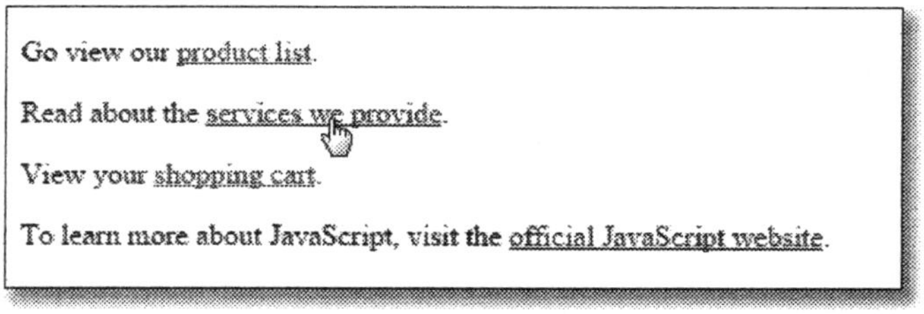

SEO and accessibility guideline

- The content of a link should be text that clearly indicates where the link is going.

Description

- The <a> element is an inline element that creates a *link* that loads another web page. The href attribute of this element identifies the page to be loaded.
- The text content of a link is underlined by default to indicate that it's clickable.
- If a link hasn't been visited, it's displayed in blue. If it has been visited, it's displayed in purple. You can change these values using CSS.
- If the mouse hovers over a link, the cursor is changed to a hand with the finger pointed as shown above.
- See chapters 4 and 7 for more information on formatting and coding the <a> element.

Figure 3-12 How to code links

How to code lists

Figure 3-13 shows how to code the two basic types of lists: ordered lists and unordered lists. To create an *unordered list*, you use the ul element. Then, within this element, you code one li (list item) element for each item in the list. The content of each li element is the text that's displayed in the list. By default, when a list is displayed in a browser, each item in an unordered list is preceded by a bullet. However, you can change that bullet with CSS.

To create an *ordered list*, you use the ol element, along with one li element for each item in the list. This works like the ul element, except that the items are preceded by numbers rather than bullets when they're displayed in a browser. In this case, you can change the type of numbers that are used with CSS.

The two lists shown in this figure illustrate how this works. Here, the first list simply displays the names of several programming languages, so these items don't need to reflect any order. In contrast, the second list identifies three steps for completing an order. Because these steps must be completed in a prescribed sequence, they're displayed in an ordered list.

When you work with the li element, you should be aware that it can contain text, inline elements, or block elements. For example, an li element can contain an <a> element that defines a link. In fact, it's a best practice to code a series of links within an unordered list. You'll see an example of that later in this chapter, and you'll learn all about this in chapter 7.

Elements that create ordered and unordered lists

Element	Description
<ul>	Creates an unordered list.
<ol>	Creates an ordered list.
<li>	Creates a list item for an unordered or ordered list.

HTML that creates two lists

```
<p>We have books on a variety of languages, including</p>
<ul>
    <li>JavaScript</li>
    <li>PHP and MySQL</li>
    <li>Servlets and JSP</li>
    <li>ASP.NET</li>
</ul>

<p>You will need to complete the following steps:</p>
<ol>
    <li>Enter your billing information.</li>
    <li>Enter your shipping information.</li>
    <li>Confirm your order.</li>
</ol>
```

The lists in a web browser

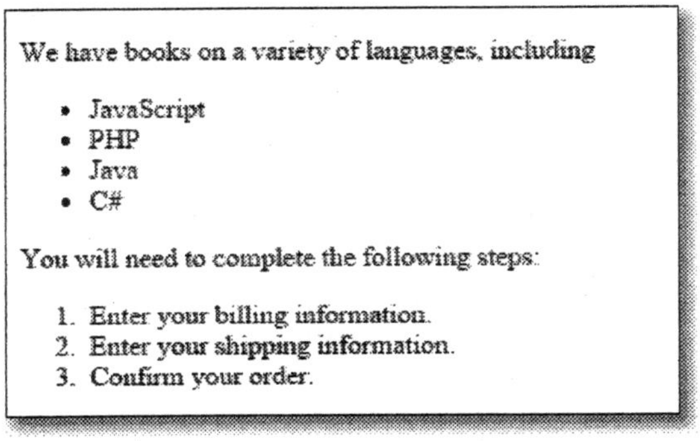

Description

- The two basic types of lists are *unordered lists* and *ordered lists*. By default, an unordered list is displayed as a bulleted list and an ordered list is displayed as a numbered list.
- See chapters 4 and 7 for more information on formatting and coding lists.

Figure 3-13 How to code lists

How to include images

Images are an important part of most web pages. To display an image, you use the img element shown in figure 3-14. This is an inline element that's coded as an empty tag. In the example in this figure, this tag is coded before an h1 element. The h1 element is displayed after it, though, because it's a block element that starts on a new line.

The src (source) attribute of an img element specifies the URL of the image you want to display, and it is required. For instance, the src attribute for the image in the example indicates that the image named murachlogo.gif can be found in the images subfolder of the current folder.

The alt attribute should also be coded for img elements. You typically use this attribute to provide information about the image in case it can't be displayed or the page is being accessed using a screen reader. This is essential for visually-impaired users.

For instance, because the image in this figure is our company's logo, the value of the alt attribute is set to "Murach Logo". If an image doesn't provide any meaning, however, you can code the value of the alt attribute as an empty string (""). You should do that, for example, when an image is only used for decoration.

The images that you include in a web page need to be in one of the formats that modern web browsers support. Currently, most web browsers support the JPEG, GIF, and PNG formats. Typically, a web designer uses imaging software such as Adobe Photoshop to create and maintain these files for a website. In particular, you use imaging software to create images that are the right size for your web pages.

Then, you can use the height and width attributes of an img element to tell the browser what the size of an image is. That can help the browser lay out the page as the image is being loaded. Although you can also use the height and width attributes to render an image larger (known as "stretching") or smaller than the original image, it's better to use your image editor to make the image the right size. You'll learn more about working with images in chapter 9.

Attributes of the <img> element

Attribute	Description
`src`	Specifies the relative or absolute URL of the image to display. It is a required attribute.
`alt`	Specifies alternate text to display in place of the image. This text is read aloud by screen readers for users with disabilities. It is required.
`height`	Specifies the height of the image in pixels.
`width`	Specifies the width of the image in pixels.

An img element

```
<img src="images/murachlogo.gif" alt="Murach Logo" height="75">
<h1>Mike Murach &amp; Associates, Inc.</h1>
```

The image in a web browser

The image formats that are supported by most browsers

- JPEG (Joint Photographic Experts Group)
- GIF (Graphic Interchange Format)
- PNG (Portable Network Graphics)

Accessibility guidelines

- For images with useful content, always code an alt attribute that describes the image.
- For images that are used for decoration, code the alt attribute with no value ("").

Description

- The img element is an inline element that is used to display an image that's identified by the src attribute.
- The height and width attributes can be used to indicate the size of an image so the browser can allocate the correct amount of space on the page. These attributes can also be used to size an image, but it's usually better to use an image editor to do that.
- JPEG files commonly use the JPG extension and are typically used for photographs and scans. GIF files are typically used for small illustrations and logos. And PNG files combine aspects of JPEG and GIF files.
- See chapters 4 and 9 for more information on formatting and coding img elements.

Figure 3-14 How to include images

A structured web page

Now that you've seen the HTML elements for structuring a web page, you're ready to see a simple web page that uses these elements.

The page layout

The web page shown in figure 3-15 uses many of the HTML elements you learned about in this chapter. The purpose of this web page is to display information about a series of lectures being presented by a non-profit organization.

This figure shows the default formatting for the HTML that's used for this page. In other words, CSS hasn't been used to improve the formatting. In the next chapter, though, you'll learn how to use CSS to improve the formatting of this page.

When you review the HTML code for this page in the next figure, you'll see that the first heading in the header of this page is an h2 element and the second heading is an h3 element. Then, the heading in the main content of the page is an h1 element. That's because this heading identifies the most important information on the page, and this is important for SEO. Then, you can use CSS to format all three headings the way you want them to look in the browser.

A web page that uses some of the HTML presented in this chapter

Description

- This web page provides information for a non-profit organization that arranges lectures by renowned speakers.
- This web page contains HTML5 semantic elements that define a header, the main content, and a footer.
- The header element contains an image and h2 and h3 elements.
- The main element contains an h1 element, a nav element that contains an unordered list that contains <a> elements, and a <p> element.
- The footer element contains a <p> element that uses a character entity to include the copyright symbol.
- This page includes a favicon that's displayed to the left of the page title in the browser's tab.
- This illustrates the default formatting for the HTML elements. In the next chapter, you'll learn how to use CSS to format the HTML so it looks more appealing.

Figure 3-15 The page layout for a structured web page

The HTML file

Figure 3-16 presents the HTML file for the web page. To start, the DOCTYPE declaration, the html element, and head element illustrate the way these items should be coded in every document that you create.

In the html element, you can see the use of the lang attribute. In the head element, you can see the coding for the charset meta element and the title element. Although the link element for the favicon is optional, most websites use one. Beyond that, you should include meta elements for description and keywords in most web pages, although they aren't used in the examples in this book.

What's most important, though, is the use of the HTML5 semantic elements. Here, the header element contains one h2 and one h3 element. Then, the main element contains one h1 element, a nav element, and a <p> element. Last, the footer element contains one <p> element.

Within the nav element is an unordered list that contains six li elements. Then, each li element contains an <a> element. This is consistent with HTML5 semantics because a nav element should contain a series of links. It is also a best practice to code the <a> elements within an unordered list.

You can also see the use of an <em> element that italicizes the first four words in the second last paragraph and a character entity that inserts the copyright symbol into the last paragraph. But above all, the new HTML5 semantic elements make the structure of this page obvious.

The HTML file for the web page

```
<!DOCTYPE html>

<html lang="en">
    <head>
        <meta charset="utf-8">
        <title>San Joaquin Valley Town Hall</title>
        <link rel="shortcut icon" href="images/favicon.ico">
    </head>

    <body>
        <header>
            <img src="images/logo.jpg" alt="Town Hall Logo" width="50">
            <h2>San Joaquin Valley Town Hall</h2>
            <h3>Bringing cutting-edge speakers to the valley</h3>
        </header>

        <main>
            <h1>This season's guest speakers</h1>
            <nav>
                <ul>
                    <li>October: <a href="speakers/toobin.html">
                        Jeffrey Toobin</a></li>
                    <li>November: <a href="speakers/sorkin.html">
                        Andrew Ross Sorkin</a></li>
                    <li>January: <a href="speakers/chua.html">
                        Amy Chua</a></li>
                    <li>February: <a href="speakers/sampson.html">
                        Scott Sampson</a></li>
                    <li>March: <a href="speakers/eire.html">
                        Carlos Eire</a></li>
                    <li>April: <a href="speakers/tynan.html">
                        Ronan Tynan</a></li>
                </ul>
            </nav>

            <p><em>Contact us by phone</em> at (559) 555-1212 for ticket
               information.</p>
        </main>

        <footer>
            <p>&copy; Copyright 2015 San Joaquin Valley Town Hall.</p>
        </footer>
    </body>
</html>
```

Figure 3-16 The HTML file for a structured web page

Perspective

This chapter has presented many of the HTML elements that you need for developing web pages. In particular, it has presented the main block and inline elements that you need for creating and identifying the content for a page. It has also presented the HTML5 elements that you need for structuring a page.

With these skills, you can create web pages with the default formatting of the browser. As I've mentioned throughout this chapter, though, the right way to format and lay out your web pages is to use CSS. That's why the next three chapters show you how to do that.

Terms

favicon
metadata
block element
inline element
character entity
semantic elements
HTML5 semantics
absolute URL
relative URL
root-relative path
document-relative path
link
ordered list
unordered list
JPEG (Joint Photographic Experts Group)
GIF (Graphic Interchange Format)
PNG (Portable Network Graphics)

Summary

- In the head section of an HTML document, the title element provides the text that's displayed in the browser's title bar. This is an important element for search engine optimization.
- One common use of the link element in the head section is to identify a custom icon called a *favicon* that appears in the browser's tab for the page. This icon may also appear in the browser's address bar or as part of a bookmark.
- The meta elements in the head section provide *metadata* that is related to the page. Here, the charset metadata is required for HTML5 validation, and the description and keywords metadata should be coded because they can affect search engine optimization.

- *Block elements* are the primary content elements of a website, and each block element starts on a new line when it is rendered by a browser. Headings and paragraphs are common block elements.
- *Inline elements* are coded within block elements, and they don't start on new lines when they are rendered. Some common inline elements like <i> (for italics) and <b> (for bold) can be used to format text without implying any meaning. Whenever possible, though, you should use the inline elements that imply meaning.
- *Character entities* are used to display special characters like the ampersand and copyright symbols in an HTML document. In code, character entities start with an ampersand and end with a semicolon as in   (a non-breaking space).
- The core attributes that are commonly used for HTML elements are the id, class, and title attributes. The id attribute uniquely identifies one element. The class attribute can be used to identify one or more elements. And the title attribute can provide other information about an element like its tooltip text.
- The HTML5 *semantic elements* provide a new way to structure the content within an HTML document. This makes it easy to code and format elements. In the long run, it may also improve the way search engines rank your pages.
- Historically, the div element has been used to divide the code for an HTML document into divisions, and the span element has been used to identify portions of text so formatting can be applied to them.
- When you code an *absolute URL*, you code the complete URL including the domain name. When you code a *relative URL*, you can use a *root-relative path* to start the path from the root folder for the website or a *document-relative path* to start the path from the current document.
- The <a> element (or anchor element) is an inline element that creates a link that usually loads another page. By default, the text of an <a> element is underlined. Also, an unvisited link is displayed in blue and a visited link in purple.
- Lists are block elements that can be used to display both *unordered lists* and *ordered lists*. By default, these lists are indented with bullets before the items in an unordered list and numbers before the items in an ordered list.
- The img element is used to display an image file. The three common formats for images are *JPEG* (for photographs and scans), *GIF* (for small illustrations and logos), and *PNG*, which combines aspects of JPEG and GIF.

About the exercises

In the exercises for chapters 3 through 8, you'll develop a new version of the Town Hall website. This version will be like the one in the text, but it will have different content, different formatting, and different page layouts. Developing this site will give you plenty of practice, and it will also show you how similar content can be presented in two different ways.

As you develop this site, you will use this folder structure:

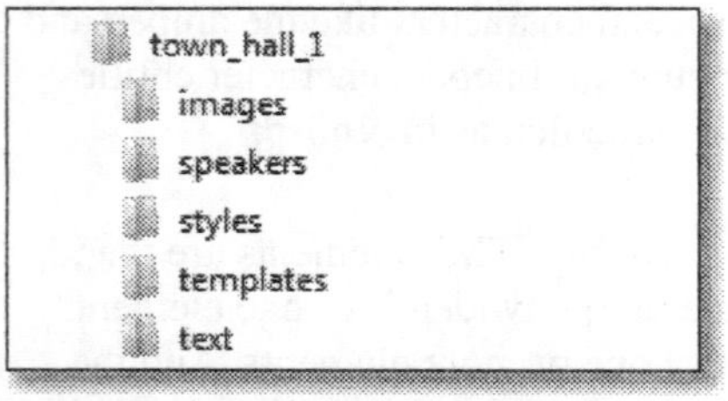

This is a realistic structure with images in the images folder, speaker HTML pages in the speakers folder, CSS files in the styles folder, and template files in the templates folder. In addition, the text folder contains text files that will provide all of the content you need for your pages. That too is realistic because a web developer often works with text that has been written by someone else.

Exercise 3-1 Enter the HTML for the home page

In this exercise, you'll code the HTML for the home page. When you're through, the page should look like the one on the facing page, but with three speakers.

Open the starting page and get the contents for it

1. Use your text editor to open this HTML file:
   `c:\html5_css3_2\exercises\town_hall_1\index.html`
   Note that it contains the head section for this web page as well as a body section that contains header, main, and footer tags.
2. Use your text editor to open this text file:
   `c:\html5_css3_2\exercises\town_hall_1\text\c3_content.txt`
   Note that it includes all of the text that you need for this web page.

Enter the header

3. Code the img element that gets the image at the top of the page from the images directory. To locate the image file, use this document-relative path: images/town_hall_logo.gif. Be sure to include the alt attribute, and set the height attribute of the image to 80.
4. Copy the text for the first two headings from the txt file in the text folder into the header of the HTML file. Next, apply the h2 and h3 elements.
5. Test this page in Chrome. If necessary, correct the HTML and test again.

What the home page should look like

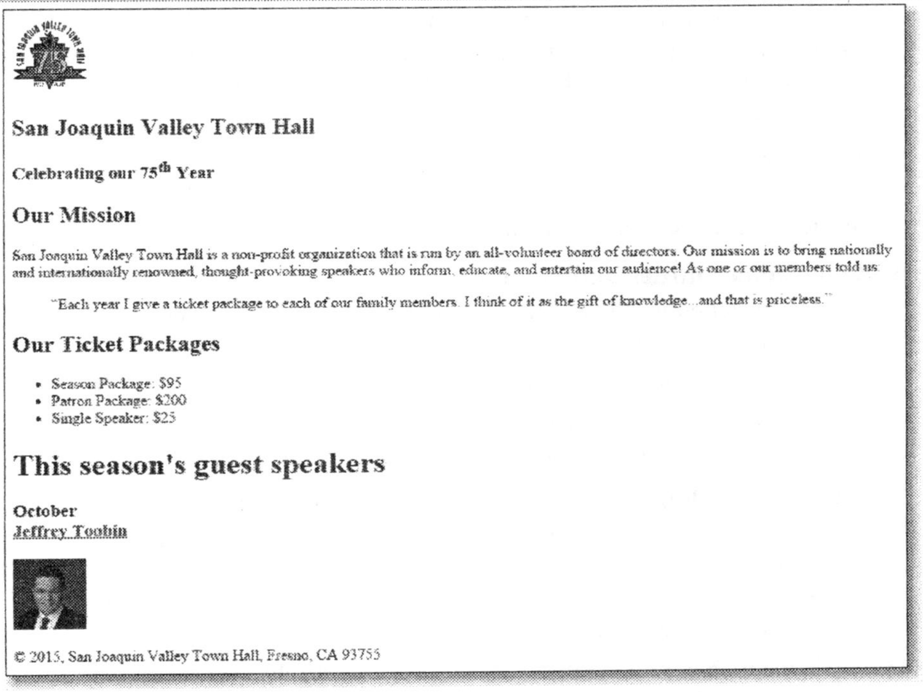

Enter the content for the main element

6. Copy all of the content for the main element from the txt file into the HTML file. Then, add an h1 tag to the heading "This season's guest speakers", and add h2 tags to these headings "Our Mission" and "Our Ticket Packages".
7. Add <p> tags to the first block of text after the "Our Mission" heading, and add blockquote tags to the second block of text as shown above.
8. Add the ul and li tags that are needed for the three items after the "Our Ticket Packages" heading. Then, test these changes and make any adjustments.
9. Format the name and month for the first speaker after the "This season's guest speakers" heading as one h2 element with a <br> in the middle that rolls the speaker's name over to a second line. Then, test and adjust.
10. When that works, do the same for the next two speakers.
11. Enclose the name for each speaker in an <a> tag. The href attribute for each tag should refer to a file in the speakers subfolder that has the speaker's last name as the filename and html as the file extension. In other words, the reference for the first speaker should be:

```
speakers/toobin.html
```

12. After the h2 element for each speaker, code an img element that displays the image for the speaker, and be sure to include the alt attribute. The images are in the images subfolder, and the filename for each is the speaker's last name, followed by 75 (to indicate the image size), with jpg as the extension. So to refer to the first speaker's file, you need to use a document-relative path like this: images/toobin75.jpg. Now, test and adjust.

Enter the footer

13. Copy the last paragraph in the txt file into the footer of the HTML file. Then, enclose the text in a <p> element.

Add character entities and formatting tags

14. Use character entities to add the quotation marks at the start and end of the text in the blockquote element.
15. Use a character entity to add the copyright symbol to the start of the footer.
16. Add the sup tags that you need for raising the *th* in the second line of the header (as in 75th). Then, test these enhancements.

Test the links, validate the HTML, and test in Firefox and IE

17. Click on the link for the speaker page. This should display a page that gives the speaker's name and says "This page is under construction". If this doesn't work, fix the href attribute in the link and test again. To return to the first page, you can click the browser's Back button.
18. Open the toobin.html file that's in the speakers subfolder. Then, add a link within a <p> element that says "Return to index page." To refer to the index.html file, you'll have to go up one level in the folder structure with a document-relative path like this: ../index.html. Now, test this link.
19. Validate the HTML for the index page as shown in figure 2-15 of chapter 2. This should indicate one warning but no errors. If any errors are detected, fix them and validate the HTML again.
20. Test the index page in the Firefox browser. If necessary, fix any problems and test again in both Chrome and Firefox.
21. Test the index page in the IE browser. If necessary, fix any problems and test again in all three browsers.

4

How to use CSS to format the elements of a web page

After you code the HTML that defines the structure of a web page, you're ready to code the CSS rule sets that determine how the page is formatted. To do that, you need to learn how to code selectors, and you need to learn how to code the properties and values for rule sets.

In this chapter, you'll learn how to code all types of selectors, and you'll learn how to apply the CSS properties for formatting text. Then, in the next chapter, you'll learn how to use the CSS box model for doing other types of formatting.

An introduction to CSS

Before you code the CSS for a web page, you need to know how to provide the CSS for a web page. You also need to know how to make the HTML5 semantic elements work in older browsers and how to make sure that the elements of a page are rendered the same in every browser.

Three ways to provide CSS styles for a web page

Figure 4-1 shows three ways to provide CSS styles for a web page. First, you can code a link element that refers to an *external style sheet*. That's a separate file that contains the CSS for the page. This separates the content from the formatting and makes it easy to use the same styles for more than one page.

The attributes for a link element that links to an external file are the rel (relationship) attribute with a value of "stylesheet", and the href attribute that locates the file. As you learned in the last chapter, href attributes are usually coded with a URL that is relative to the current file. As a result, the relative URL in the first example goes down one folder to the styles folder and locates a file named main.css.

Second, you can embed a CSS style sheet in the HTML for a page. This is referred to as an *embedded style sheet*. When you embed a style sheet, the CSS rule sets are coded in a style element in the head section of the HTML. For instance, the embedded style sheet in the first group contains one rule set for the body element and another for the h1 element. This works okay if the styles are only going to be used for that one document, but otherwise it's better to use an external style sheet.

Third, you can use *inline styles* within an HTML document as shown by the third example. When you use an inline style, you code a style attribute for the HTML element with a value that contains all the CSS rules that apply to the element. For instance, the inline style in this example applies two CSS rules to the h1 element. Unfortunately, this type of formatting means that the content and formatting are tightly linked, so this can quickly get out of control.

If you use more than one way to provide styles for a page, the styles that are applied last override the styles that are applied earlier. This is illustrated by the example in this figure. Here, an inline style sets the font size for h1 elements, and that will override the embedded style that sets the font size for h1 elements.

The next example in this figure shows that you can include more than one style sheet in a single document. Then, the styles are applied from the first external style sheet to the last. Here again, a style in the last style sheet will override a style for the same element in an earlier style sheet.

Three ways to provide styles

Use an external style sheet by coding a link element in the head section

```
<link rel="stylesheet" href="styles/main.css">
```

Embed the styles in the head section

```
<style>
    body {
        font-family: Arial, Helvetica, sans-serif;
        font-size: 100%; }
    h1 { font-size: 250%; }
</style>
```

Use the style attribute to apply styles to a single element

```
<h1 style="font-size: 500%; color: red;">Valley Town Hall</h1>
```

The sequence in which styles are applied

- Styles from an external style sheet
- Embedded styles
- Inline styles

A head element that includes two style sheets

```
<head>
    <title>San Joaquin Valley Town Hall</title>
    <link rel="stylesheet" href="../styles/main.css">
    <link rel="stylesheet" href="../styles/speaker.css">
</head>
```

The sequence in which styles are applied

- From the first external style sheet to the last

Description

- When you use *external style sheets*, you separate content (HTML) from formatting (CSS). That makes it easy to use the same styles for two or more documents.
- If you use *embedded styles*, you have to copy the styles to other documents before you can use them a second time.
- If you use *inline styles* to apply styles, the formatting is likely to get out of control.
- If more than one rule for the same property is applied to the same element, the last rule overrides the earlier rules.
- When you specify a relative URL for an external CSS file, the URL is relative to the current file.

Figure 4-1 Three ways to provide CSS styles for a web page

Two ways to provide for browser compatibility

To provide for cross-browser compatibility, you first need to make sure that the HTML5 semantic elements will work in older browsers because they ignore them. As a result, you won't be able to format them with CSS. However, figure 4-2 provides an easy way to fix this problem.

To do that, you simply add the script element shown at the top of this figure to the head element of each HTML document that uses HTML5 elements. This script element points to a JavaScript file known as a *shiv* (or *shim*). Then, when the page is loaded, the JavaScript file is loaded and executed.

When the shiv is executed, it forces the browser to recognize the HTML5 semantic elements. This shiv also adds a CSS rule set to the page that tells older browsers that these elements are block elements, not inline elements. Otherwise, older browsers assume that they're inline elements.

Today, the only browsers that don't already support the HTML5 semantic elements are versions of Internet Explorer before version 9. So, unless you know that your users will be using these older browsers, you don't need to use the JavaScript shiv. That's why none of the examples in the book use the shiv.

The other problem that faces web developers today is that the five modern browsers render some elements of a web page differently. One example is the inline abbr element that's used to define abbreviations.

In Firefox, the textual content for this element is displayed with a dotted line below it. Then, when the user points to the element with the mouse, a tooltip that defines the abbreviation is displayed. In contrast, a dotted line isn't displayed under the abbreviation in Chrome or Internet Explorer. Because of that, the user won't know that there is an abbreviation on the page unless he happens to point to it. Then, a tooltip appears just as it does in Firefox.

To standardize how elements like this are displayed, you can use the normalize.css style sheet that's described in this figure. This style sheet applies styles to elements like the abbr element so they appear exactly the same in all browsers. This can save you a lot of time dealing with small rendering issues near the end of a web development project.

The normalize.css style sheet also sets the margins for the body of the document to zero. That means that there's no space between the body and the edge of the browser window. This is important because different browsers provide for different margins for the body. You'll learn more about working with the margins for the body as well as other elements in chapter 5.

A third example of what the normalize.css style sheet does is that it sets the default font family for the document to sans-serif. You'll learn more about font families later in this chapter. When you do, you'll learn that sans-serif fonts are easiest to read in a browser. Even so, the default font for all of the major browsers is a serif font. If you use the normalize.css style sheet, then, you only need to set the font family if you want to use a specific sans-serif font.

For reasons like these, many web developers use the normalize.css style sheet for all of their pages. That's also why this style sheet is used in all of the web applications for this book.

The JavaScript shiv for using HTML5 semantics with IE 7 and 8

```
<head>
    <script src="http://html5shiv.googlecode.com/svn/trunk/html5.js">
    </script>
</head>
```

What the shiv does

- A JavaScript *shiv* (or *shim*) forces older browsers, like Internet Explorer 7 and 8, to recognize the HTML5 semantic elements and let you apply CSS to these elements.
- The effect of the shiv is to add the HTML5 semantic elements to the DOM in the browser and also to add a CSS rule set that tells the browser to treat the HTML5 elements as block elements instead of inline elements.
- Because the use of the older IE browsers accounts for a small percentage of browser usage, none of the examples in this book use the shiv.

The URL for downloading the normalize.css style sheet

- http://necolas.github.io/normalize.css/

How to download normalize.css and save it to your website

- Open a browser, browse to the URL shown above, and click the Download button.
- If CSS files are associated with a program that's installed on your computer, the normalize.css file will be opened in that program. Then, you can use that program to save the file to your website.
- If CSS files aren't associated with a program on your computer, the normalize.css file will be displayed on a page within the browser. Then, you can right-click the page, choose Save As, and use the dialog box that's displayed to save the normalize.css file to your website.
- Once you save the normalize.css file to your website, you can code a link element for it in each page. This element must be coded before the link elements for other style sheets.

What the normalize.css style sheet does

- Normalize.css is a style sheet that makes minor adjustments to browser defaults so all browsers render HTML elements the same way.
- For instance, the normalize.css style sheet sets the margins for the body of the document to zero so there's no space between the body and the edge of the browser window. See chapter 5 for more information on margins.
- The normalize.css style sheet also sets the default font family for the document to sans-serif. See figure 4-11 in this chapter for more information on working with font families.
- Because the normalize.css style sheet resolves minor browser variations, all of the web pages from this point on in this book will use it.

Figure 4-2 Two ways to provide for browser compatibility

How to specify measurements and colors

For many of the properties of a rule set, you will need to know how to specify measurements and colors. So let's start there.

How to specify measurements

Figure 4-3 shows the four units of measure that are commonly used with CSS: pixels, points, ems, and percent. Here, the first two are *absolute units of measure*, and the second two are *relative units of measure*. Other absolute units are inches and picas, but they aren't used as often.

When you use relative units of measure like ems or a percent, the measurement will change if the user changes the browser's font size. If, for example, you set the size of a font to 80 percent of the browser's default font size, that element will change if the user changes the font size in the browser. Because this lets the users adjust the font sizes to their own preferences, we recommend that you use relative measurements for font sizes.

In contrast, when you use an absolute unit of measure like pixels or points, the measurement won't change even if the user changes the font size in the browser. If, for example, you set the width of an element in pixels and the font size in points, the width and font size won't change.

When you use pixels, though, the size will change if the screen resolution changes. That's because the screen resolution determines the number of pixels that are displayed on the monitor. For instance, the pixels on a monitor with a screen resolution of 1280 x 1024 are closer together than the pixels on the same monitor with a screen resolution of 1152 x 864. That means that a measurement of 10 pixels will be smaller on the screen with the higher resolution. In contrast, a point is $1/72^{nd}$ of an inch no matter what the screen resolution is.

The examples in this figure show how you can use pixels and relative measurements in your CSS. Here, the bottom border for the header is set to 3 pixels. In contrast, the font sizes are set as percentages, and the margins and padding are set as ems. This is a typical way to use these measurements.

To start, a font size of 100% is applied to the body element. This means that the font will be set to 100% of the default font size for the browser, which is usually 16 pixels. Although you can get the same result by omitting the font-size property, this property is typically included to make it clear that the default font size for the browser will be used.

Left and right margins of 2 ems are also applied to the body element. Because an em is equal to the current font size, the body element is indented 32 pixels (2 times 16 pixels). These properties are included because the normalize.css style sheet that's used with this page sets these margins to zero. Note, however, that it's not necessary to set the top and bottom margins for the body. That's because the h1 element has a default top margin and the <p> element has a default bottom margin.

Common units of measure

Symbol	Name	Type	Description
`px`	pixels	absolute	A pixel represents a single dot on a monitor. The number of dots per inch depends on the resolution of the monitor.
`pt`	points	absolute	A point is 1/72 of an inch.
`em`	ems	relative	One em is equal to the font size for the current font.
`%`	percent	relative	A percent specifies a value relative to the current value.

The HTML for a web page

```
<body>
    <header>
        <h1>San Joaquin Valley Town Hall</h1>
    </header>
    <main>
        <p>Welcome to San Joaquin Valley Town Hall. We have some
           fascinating speakers for you this season!</p>
    </main>
</body>
```

CSS that uses relative units of measure with a fixed border

```
body {
    font-size: 100%;
    margin-left: 2em;
    margin-right: 2em; }
header {
    padding-bottom: .75em;
    border-bottom: 3px solid black;
    margin-bottom: 0; }
h1 {
    font-size: 200%;
    margin-bottom: 0; }
```

The web page in a web browser

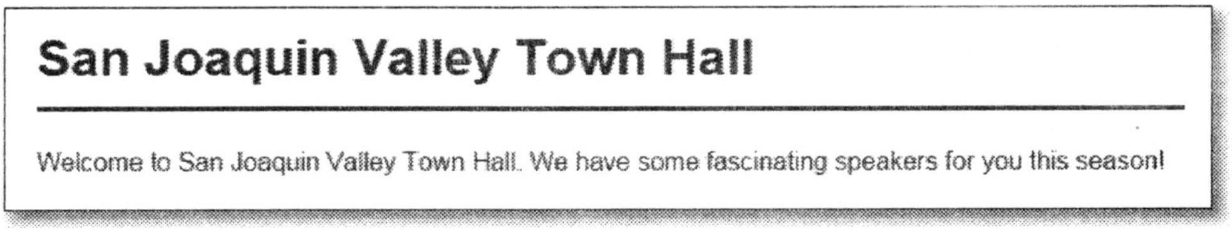

Description

- You use the units of measure to specify a variety of CSS properties, including font-size, line-height, width, height, margin, and padding.
- To specify an *absolute measurement*, you can use pixels or points.
- To specify a *relative measurement*, you can use ems or percents. This type of measurement is relative to the size of another element.

Figure 4-3 How to specify measurements

Next, the padding below the header element is set to .75 em, or 12 pixels (16 times .75). Then, a solid black border that's 3 pixels wide is added below the padding, and the margin below the border is set to 0. For the margin bottom, no unit of measure is specified because it doesn't matter what the unit of measure is when the value is zero.

The last rule set indicates that the h1 element should be 200% of the base font, which was set in the rule set for the body element. Also, the margin below the heading should be zero.

How to specify colors

Figure 4-4 shows three ways to specify colors. The easiest way is to specify a color name, and this figure lists the names for 16 colors that are supported by all browsers. In addition to these names, though, most browsers support the color names in the draft CSS3 Color specification. To find a complete list of these color names, you can go to the website listed in the next figure.

Another way to specify a color is to use an *RGB* (red, green, blue) *value*. One way to do that is to specify the percent of red, green, and blue that make up the color. For instance, the example in this figure specifies 100% red, 40% green, and 20% blue. When you use this method, you can also use any values from 0 through 255 instead of percents. Then, 0 is equivalent to 0% and 255 is equivalent to 100%. This gives you more precision over the resulting colors.

The third way to specify a color is to use *hexadecimal*, or *hex*, *values* for the red, green, and blue values, and this is the method that has been preferred by most web designers. In hex, a value of "000000" results in black, and a value of "FFFFFF" results in white. The simple conversion of percentages to hex is 0% is 00, 20% is 33, 40% is 66, 60% is 99, 80% is CC, and 100% is FF. When you use this technique, the entire value must be preceded by the pound sign (#).

When you use complex values for colors, you usually get the hex value that you want from a chart or palette that shows all of the colors along with their hex values. For instance, you can get a complete list of the hex values for colors by going to the website listed in this figure. Or, if you're using an IDE like Dreamweaver CC, you may also be able to choose a color from a palette and then have the IDE insert the hex value for that color into your code. A third alternative is to get the right hex values from printed color charts, which are commonly found in graphics design books.

Before I go on, you should realize that the color property determines the foreground color, which is the color of the text. In the CSS in this figure, for example, the color of the h1 element is set to blue (#00F or #0000FF), and the background color of the body is set to a light yellow (#FFFFCC or #FFC). You'll learn more about setting background colors in the next chapter.

You should also realize that the color property for an element is *inherited* by any child elements. If, for example, you set the color property of the body element to navy, that color will be inherited by all of the elements in the body of the document. However, you can override an inherited property by coding a rule set with a different value for that property. Throughout this chapter and book, I'll point out the properties that are inherited as well as those that aren't.

16 descriptive color names

black	silver	white	aqua	gray	fuchsia
red	lime	green	maroon	blue	navy
yellow	olive	purple	teal		

Three ways to specify colors

With a color name

```
color: silver;
```

With an RGB (red-green-blue) value

```
color: rgb(100%, 40%, 20%);
color: rgb(255, 102, 51);    /* Using multiples of 51 from 0 to 255 */
```

With an RGB value that uses hexadecimal numbers

```
color: #ffffff;              /* This color is white */
color: #000000;              /* This color is black */
color: #ff0000;              /* This color is red */
```

CSS that uses hexadecimal values to specify colors

```
body {
    font-size: 100%;
    margin-left: 2em;
    background-color: #FFFFCC; }    /* This could also be coded as #FFC */
h1 {
    font-size: 200%;
    color: #00F; }                  /* This could also be coded as #0000FF */
```

The HTML in a web browser

Accessibility guideline

- Remember the visually-impaired. Dark text on a light background is easier to read, and black type on a white background is easiest to read.

Description

- All browsers support the 16 color names shown above, and most browsers support many more. These are okay for getting started with the use of colors.
- Most graphic designers use *hexadecimal*, or *hex*, *values* to specify an *RGB value* because that lets them choose from over 16 million colors. You can find a list of color names and their corresponding hex values at http://www.w3.org/TR/css3-color.
- With IDEs like Dreamweaver CC, you can select a color from a palette of colors and let the IDE insert the right color codes into your rule sets in either RGB or hex format.

Figure 4-4 How to specify colors

Whenever you're using colors, please keep the visually-impaired in mind. For anyone, dark text on a light background is easier to read, and black on white is easiest to read. In general, if your pages are hard to read when they're displayed or printed in black and white, they aren't good for the visually-impaired. On that basis, the example in this figure could be improved.

How to use the CSS3 color specifications

To provide even more color options for web designers, CSS3 lets you code color specifications in three more ways. These are summarized in figure 4-5.

First, you can use *RGBA values*. This works like RGB values, but with a fourth parameter that provides an opacity value. If, for example, you set this value to 0, the color is fully transparent so anything behind it will show through. Or, if you sent this value to 1, nothing will show through.

Second, you can use *HSL values*. To do that, you provide a number from 1 through 359 that represents the hue that you want. The hue is one of the main properties of a color. Then, you can provide a number from 0 through 100 that represents the saturation percent with 100 being the full hue. Last, you can provide a number from 0 through 100 that represents the lightness percent with 50 being normal, 100 being white, and 0 being black.

Third, you can use *HSLA values*. This is just like HSL values, but with a fourth parameter that provides an opacity value between 0 and 1.

The examples in this figure give you some idea of how these values work, especially if you see them in color in the eBook or in the examples you can download for this book. Note here that the second and third examples are the same hue, but the saturation and lightness percents make them look quite different. This should give you some idea of the many color variations that CSS3 offers. But here again, please keep accessibility in mind whenever you're using colors.

Besides providing for RGBA, HSL, and HSLA values, CSS3 also provides 147 more keywords for colors that are generally supported by modern browsers. For a complete listing, you can go to the URL in this figure.

Three ways to code CSS3 colors

The syntax for RGBA colors

```
rgba(red%, green%, blue%, opacity-value)
```

The syntax for HSL and HSLA colors

```
hsl(hue-degrees, saturation%, lightness%)
hsla(hue-degrees, saturation%, lightness%, opacity-value)
```

Values	Description
`opacity-value`	A number from 0 to 1 with 0 being fully transparent and 1 being fully opaque.
`hue-degrees`	A number of degrees ranging from 0 to 359 that represents the color.
`saturation%`	A percentage from 0 to 100 with 0 causing the hue to be ignored and 100 being the full hue.
`lightness%`	A percentage from 0 to 100 with 50 being normal lightness, 0 being black, and 100 being white.

Examples

```
h1 { color: rgba(0, 0, 255, .2)          /* transparent blue */ }
h1 { color: hsl(120, 100%, 25%)          /* dark green */ }
h1 { color: hsl(120, 75%, 75%)           /* pastel green */ }
h1 { color: hsla(240, 100%, 50%, 0.5)    /* semi-transparent solid blue */ }
```

The colors in a browser

Description

- *RGBA* enhances the RGB specification by providing a fourth value for opacity.
- With *HSL* (Hue, Saturation, and Lightness) and *HSLA*, you specify the number of hue degrees for a color. Then, you can enhance the hue by providing for both saturation and lightness percentages. HLSA also offers a fourth value for opacity.
- CSS3 also provides 147 more keywords for colors that are generally supported by modern browsers. For a complete listing, go to:
  `http://www.w3.org/TR/SVG/types.html#ColorKeywords`
- With an IDE like Dreamweaver, you can select the type of color specification you want to use (RGBA, HSL, or HSLA). Then, you can select the color or hue, saturation, lightness, and opacity.

Figure 4-5 How to use the CSS3 color specifications

How to code selectors

Now, you're ready to learn how to code selectors. Once you understand that, you will be able to apply CSS formatting to any elements in a web page.

How to code selectors for all elements, element types, ids, and classes

Figure 4-6 presents the four types of selectors that you'll use the most. To start, this figure shows the body of an HTML document that contains a main and a footer element. Here, the two <p> elements in the main element have class attributes with the value "blue". Also, the <p> element in the footer has been assigned an id of "copyright", and it has a class attribute with two values: "blue" and "right". This means that this element is assigned to two classes.

Next, this figure shows the CSS rule sets that are used to format the HTML. Here, the rule set in the first example uses the *universal selector* (*) so it applies to all HTML elements. This sets the top and bottom margins for all elements to .5em and the left and right margins to 1em. The exception is if the normalize.css style sheet is linked to the document. Then, the margins specified by the universal selector don't override the margins that are set for any specific elements in normalize.css. Because of that, you probably won't use the universal selector often.

The two rule sets in the second group of examples select elements by type. These are referred to as *type selectors*. To code a type selector, you just code the name of the element. As a result, the first rule set in this group selects the main element, the second rule set selects all h1 elements, and the third rule set selects all p elements. These rule sets set the border and padding for the main element, the font family for the h1 elements, and the left margin for all <p> elements.

The rule set in the third group of examples selects an element by its id. To do that, the selector is a pound sign (#) followed by an id value that uniquely identifies an element. As a result, this rule set selects the <p> element that has an id of "copyright". Then, its rule set sets the font size for the paragraph to 80% of the font size for the page.

The two rule sets in the last group of examples select HTML elements by class. To do that, the selector is a period (.) followed by the class name. As a result, the first rule set selects all elements that have been assigned to the "blue" class, which are all three <p> elements. The second rule set selects any elements that have been assigned to the "right" class. That is the paragraph in the footer. Then, the first rule set sets the color of the font to blue and the second rule set aligns the paragraph on the right.

One of the key points here is that a class attribute can have the same value for more than one element on a page. Then, if you code a selector for that class, it will be used to format all the elements in that class. In contrast, since the id for an element must be unique, an id selector can only be used to format a single element.

HTML that can be selected by element type, id, or class

```
<main>
    <h1>This Season's Speaker Lineup</h1>
    <p class="blue">October: Jeffrey Toobin</p>
    <p class="blue">November: Andrew Ross Sorkin</p>
</main>
<footer>
    <p id="copyright" class="blue right">Copyright 2015</p>
</footer>
```

CSS rule sets that select by element type, id, and class

All elements

```
* { margin: .5em 1em; }
```

Elements by type

```
main {
    border: 2px solid black;
    padding: 1em; }
h1 { font-family: Arial, sans-serif; }
p { margin-left: 3em; }
```

One element by ID

```
#copyright { font-size: 80%; }
```

Elements by class

```
.blue { color: blue; }
.right { text-align: right; }
```

The elements displayed in a browser

Description

- You code a selector for all elements by coding the *universal selector* (*).
- You code a selector for all elements of a specific type by naming the element. This is referred to as a *type selector*.
- You code a selector for an element with an id attribute by coding a pound sign (#) followed by the id value.
- You code a selector for an element with a class attribute by coding a period followed by the class name. Then, the rule set applies to all elements with that class name.

Figure 4-6 How to code selectors for all elements, element types, ids, and classes

Incidentally, the margin-left property for the <p> elements overrides the margin setting for all elements, which of course includes all <p> elements. That's why the two paragraphs in the section are indented.

How to code relational selectors

Figure 4-7 shows how to code *relational selectors*. As you read about these selectors, keep in mind that terms like *parent*, *child*, *sibling*, and *descendent* are used in the same way that they are in a family tree. Child elements are at the first level below a parent element. Sibling elements are at the same level. And descendent elements can be one or more levels below a parent element.

That means a *descendant selector* selects all the elements that are contained within another element. For instance, all of the elements in the HTML in this figure are descendents of the main element, the li elements are also descendents of the ul element, and the <a> elements are descendents of the li, ul, and main elements.

To code a descendant selector, you code a selector for the parent element, followed by a space and a selector for the descendent element. This is illustrated by the first group of examples. Here, the first selector selects all li elements within the main element. Then, the second descendant selector selects all the <a> elements that are descendants of the ul element.

The next group of examples shows how to use an *adjacent sibling selector* to select an element that's coded at the same level as another element and is also coded right next to it. For instance, the h1, ul, h2, and <p> elements in the HTML are all siblings, and the h1 and ul elements are adjacent siblings. In contrast, the h1 element and the <p> elements aren't adjacent siblings, but the h2 element and the first <p> element are adjacent siblings.

To code an adjacent sibling selector, you code a selector for the first element, followed by a plus sign and a selector for the sibling element. In the example in this group, the selector will select any <p> elements that are adjacent to h2 elements. That means it will select the first <p> element that follows the h2 element.

If you want to select elements only when they're child elements of a parent element, you can code a *child selector*. To do that, you separate the parent and child selector with a greater than (>) sign. In this figure, for example, the first child selector selects the <p> elements that are children of the main element, and the second selector selects the <a> elements that are children of the li elements.

Unlike the adjacent sibling selector, a *general sibling selector* selects any sibling element whether or not the elements are adjacent. To code this type of selector, you separate the selector for the first element and the selector for the sibling element by a tilde (~). In this figure, the general sibling selector selects all the <p> elements that follow any h2 element.

HTML that can be selected by relationships

```
<main>
    <h1>This Season's Town Hall speakers</h1>
    <ul class="speakers">
        <li>January: <a href="speakers/brancaccio.html">
            David Brancaccio</a></li>
        <li>February: <a href="speakers/fitzpatrick.html">
            Robert Fitzpatrick</a></li>
        <li>March: <a href="speakers/williams.html">
            Juan Williams</a></li>
    </ul>
    <h2>Post-lecture luncheons</h2>
    <p>Extend the excitement by going to the luncheon</p>
    <p>A limited number of tickets are available.</p>
    <p><em>Contact us by phone</em> at (559) 555-1212.</p>
</main>
```

CSS rule sets with relational selectors

Descendant

```
main li { font-size: 90%; }
ul a { color: green; }
```

Adjacent sibling

```
h2+p { margin-top: .5em; }
```

Child

```
main>p { font-size: 80%; }
li>a { color: green; }
```

General sibling (a new feature of CSS3)

```
h2~p { margin-left: 2em; }
```

Description

- When you use relational selectors, you can often avoid the need for id or class attributes.
- To select elements only when they are descendants of a higher-level element, use a *descendant selector* that consists of the higher element, a space, and the descendent element.
- To select a sibling element that's adjacent to another element, use an *adjacent sibling selector* that consists of the first element, a plus sign (+), and the sibling element.
- To select elements only when they are child elements of the parent element, you can use a *child selector* that consists of the parent element, the greater than sign (>), and the child element.
- To select any elements that are siblings to another element, you can use a *general sibling selector* that consists of the first element, a tilde (~), and the sibling element, but this can only be used by browsers that support CSS3.

Figure 4-7 How to code relational selectors

How to code combinations of selectors

The first group of examples in figure 4-8 shows how to code selector combinations. To select an element type by class name, for example, you code the element name, followed by a period and the class name. Here, the first rule set selects ul elements that have a class of "speakers".

You can also code multiple selectors for the same rule set. To do that, you separate the selectors with commas as shown in the next group of examples. Here, the first rule set uses multiple selectors to apply its rules to all h1, h2, and h3 elements. Then, the second rule set uses multiple selectors to apply its rules to all <p> elements and to li elements that are descendents of the ul elements that are assigned to the speakers class.

How to code attribute selectors

An *attribute selector* selects elements based on an attribute or attribute value. This is illustrated by the second group of examples in figure 4-8. Although you may never need to code attribute selectors for your HTML code, these selectors are often used by JavaScript.

To code an attribute selector that selects elements that have an attribute, you code an element selector followed by the name of the attribute in brackets [ ]. For instance, the first attribute example uses the universal selector to select all elements that have an href attribute. Note, however, that you can also omit the universal selector and code just the attribute in brackets to select all elements with that attribute. In contrast, the second attribute selector selects all of the <a> elements that have an href attribute.

To code an attribute selector that selects elements with the specified attribute value, you follow the attribute name with an equals sign and the value enclosed in quotation marks. This is illustrated in the third example. This selector will select all input elements with a type attribute whose value is set to "submit".

Combinations of selectors

A selector for a class within an element

```
ul.speakers { list-style-type: square; }
```

Multiple selectors

```
h1, h2, h3 { color: blue; }
p, ul.speakers li { font-family: "Times New Roman", serif; }
```

Attribute selectors

All elements with href attributes

```
*[href] { font-size: 95%; }
```

All <a> elements with href attributes

```
a[href] { font-family: Arial, sans-serif; }
```

All input elements with type attributes that have a value of "submit"

```
input[type="submit"] {
    border: 1px solid black;
    color: #ef9c00;
    background-color: #facd8a; }
```

Description

- To code a selector for an element and class, code the element name, a period, and the class name.
- To code multiple selectors for the same rule set, use commas to separate the selectors.
- To select all elements with a specific attribute, you can use an *attribute selector* that consists of the universal selector followed by the attribute name in brackets. You can also omit the universal selector when you code this type of selector.
- To select elements with a specific attribute, you can use an attribute selector that consists of the element followed by the attribute name within brackets.
- To select an element with a specific attribute value, you can use an attribute selector that consists of the element followed by the attribute name, an equal sign, and a value within quotation marks.
- When you're coding the CSS for an HTML page, you usually don't need attribute selectors. They're more useful when you're using JavaScript.

Figure 4-8 How to code combinations and attribute selectors

How to code pseudo-class and pseudo-element selectors

Figure 4-9 shows how to code *pseudo-class* and *pseudo-element* selectors. To code pseudo-class selectors, you use the classes in the first two tables of this figure. These classes represent conditions that apply to the elements on a page. For example, you can use the :link pseudo-class to refer to a link that hasn't been visited, the :hover pseudo-class to refer to the element that has the mouse hovering over it, and the :focus pseudo-class to refer to the element that has the focus.

You can also use the CSS3 pseudo-classes to refer to specific relationships. For example, the :first-child class refers to the first child of an element, and the :only-child class refers to the only child for an element that has only one. Although some older browsers don't support these classes, that's okay if these selectors are only used for graphics.

The third table in this figure presents CSS3 pseudo-elements that you can use to select portions of text. For instance, you can use the ::first-line element to refer to the first line in a paragraph that consists of more than one line. Although these pseudo-elements were available in earlier versions of CSS, they were coded with a single colon just like the pseudo-classes. With CSS3, the pseudo-elements were redefined with double colons to help distinguish them from the pseudo-classes. Because of that, it's best to code the pseudo-elements with two colons as shown in the fourth example in this figure. The exception is if the formatting needs to work in older browsers like versions of IE before IE9.

In the examples, the first pseudo-class selector causes all links to be displayed in green. Then, the second selector is a combination selector that applies to any link that has the mouse hovering over it or the focus on it. As the accessibility guideline in this figure indicates, you should always code the hover and focus pseudo-classes for links in combination so the formatting is the same whether the user hovers the mouse over a link or tabs to it.

The third example uses a pseudo-class selector that causes the text in the first <p> element in the section to be boldfaced. You can see how this works in the browser display. Note here that the second <p> element isn't boldfaced because it isn't the first child in the main element.

The fourth example takes this one step further by combining a pseudo-class and a pseudo-element in a selector. As a result, the first letter of the first child in the main element is larger than the other letters in the paragraph.

Although the pseudo-class and pseudo-element selectors in this figure are the ones you'll use most often, there are others that can be useful. In chapter 7, for example, you'll learn how to use the ::after pseudo-element to format a multi-tier navigation menu. And in chapter 10, you'll be introduced to some CSS3 pseudo-classes that apply to tables. For a complete list of these classes and elements, you can go to the W3C documentation on the web.

Common CSS pseudo-classes

`:link`	A link that hasn't been visited. By default, blue, underlined text.
`:visited`	A link that has been visited. By default, purple, underlined text.
`:active`	The active link (mouse button down but not released). By default, red, underlined text.
`:hover`	An element with the mouse hovering over it. Code this after :link and :visited.
`:focus`	An element like a link or form control that has the focus.

Common CSS3 pseudo-classes

`:first-child`	The first child of an element.
`:last-child`	The last child of an element.
`:only-child`	The only child of an element.

Common CSS3 pseudo-elements

`::first-letter`	The first letter of an element.
`::first-line`	The first line of an element.

HTML that can be used by pseudo-class and pseudo-element selectors

```
<main>
    <p>Welcome to San Joaquin Valley Town Hall.</p>
    <p>We have some fascinating speakers for you this season!</p>
    <ul>
        <li><a href="toobin.html">Jeffrey Toobin</a></li>
        <li><a href="sorkin.html">Andrew Ross Sorkin</a></li>
        <li><a href="chua.html">Amy Chua</a></li></ul>
</main>
```

The CSS for pseudo-class and pseudo-element selectors

```
a:link { color: green; }
a:hover, a:focus { color: fuchsia }
main p:first-child { font-weight: bold; }
main p:first-child::first-letter { font-size: 150% }
```

The pseudo-class and pseudo-element selectors in a browser

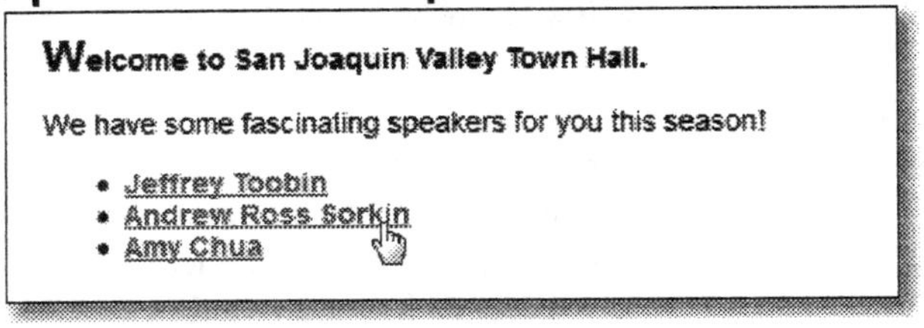

Accessibility guideline

- Apply the same formatting to the :hover and :focus pseudo-classes for an element. That way, those who can't use the mouse will have the same experience as those who can.

Description

- *Pseudo-classes* are predefined classes that apply to specific conditions. In contrast, *pseudo-elements* let you select a portion of text.

Figure 4-9 How to code pseudo-class and pseudo-element selectors

How to work with Cascading Style Sheets

The term *Cascading Style Sheets* refers to the fact that more than one style sheet can be applied to a single web page. Then, if two or more rules for the same property are applied to the same element, the cascade order and other rules determine which rule takes precedence.

How the cascade rules work

The term *Cascading Style Sheets* refers to the fact that more than one style sheet can be applied to a single web page. Then, if two or more rules for the same property are applied to the same element, the cascade order and other rules in figure 4-10 determine which rule takes precedence.

Before you can understand the cascade rules, though, you need to know that a user can create a *user style sheet* that provides default rule sets for web pages. Because most users don't create user style sheets, this usually isn't an issue. But some users do. For instance, users with poor vision often create user style sheets that provide for large font sizes. In that case, you need to consider how the user style sheets could affect your web pages.

You should also know how to identify one of your rules as important so it has precedence over other rules. To do that, you code "!important" as part of the rule. This is shown by the example in this figure.

With that as background, this figure lists the five levels of the *cascade order* from highest to lowest. As you can see, the important rules in a user style sheet override the important rules in a web page, but the normal rules in a web page override the normal rules in a user style sheet. Below these rules are the default rules in the web browser.

What happens if an element has more than one rule applied to it at the same level? To start, the rule with the highest specificity takes precedence, and this figure shows you which parts of a selector are more specific. For instance, the .speakers selector is more specific than the li selector because a class is more specific than an element.

If a selector contains multiple parts, the additional parts add to that selector's specificity. This means that a selector with an element and a class is more specific than a selector with just a class. For instance, the p.highlight selector is more specific than the .highlight selector. As a result, p.highlight takes precedence.

If that doesn't settle the conflict, the rule that's specified last is applied. Earlier in this chapter, for example, you learned that if you provide two or more external style sheets for a document, the rule sets in each style sheet will override the rule sets in the preceding style sheets. This notion also applies if you accidentally code two rule sets for the same element in a single style sheet. Then, the one that is last takes precedence. In addition, inline styles take precedence over the styles in an embedded style sheet, and embedded styles take precedence over the styles in an external style sheet.

How to identify a rule as important

```
.highlight {
    font-weight: bold !important;
}
```

The cascade order for applying CSS rule sets

Search for the rule sets that apply to an element in the sequence that follows and apply the rule set from the first group in which it's found:

- !important rules in a user style sheet
- !important rules in a web page
- Normal rules in a web page
- Normal rules in a user style sheet
- Default rules in the web browser

If more than one rule set at a cascade level is applied to an element...

- Use the rule set with the highest specificity. For example, the p.highlight selector is more specific than the .highlight selector.
- If the specificity is the same for two or more rule sets in a group, use the rule set that's specified last.

How to determine the specificity of a selector

- An id is the most specific.
- A class, attribute selector, or pseudo-class selector is less specific.
- An element or pseudo-element selector is least specific.

Description

- When two or more rule sets are applied to an HTML element, CSS uses the *cascade order* and rules shown above to determine which rule set to apply.
- A user can create a *user style sheet* that provides a default set of rules for web pages. Users with poor vision often do this so the type for a page is displayed in a large font.
- Since most users don't create user style sheets, you usually can control the way the rules are applied for your websites. But you should keep in mind how your web pages could be affected by user style sheets.
- If you want to create or remove a user style sheet for a browser, you can search the Internet for the procedures that your browser requires.

Figure 4-10 How the cascade rules work

How to use the developer tools to inspect the styles that have been applied

If you have problems wih cascading styles when you're testing a web page, you can use the developer tools for your browser to find out exactly what's happening as shown in figure 4-11. If you're using Chrome, Internet Explorer, or Firefox, you can access these tools by pressing the F12 key. You can also access the developer tools from these browsers as well as from Opera and Safari by right-clicking on a page and selecting Inspect Element.

In this figure, the developer tools are displayed in a panel below the web page in a Chrome browser. This is the same page that's shown in figure 4-17, which you'll study at the end of this chapter.

In the left pane of the developer tools panel, you can see all of the HTML elements of the page. To expand or collapse a group of elements, you click on the symbol before the element. In this example, you can see that the html, body, and main elements have been expanded.

To inspect the styles for an element, you click on the element in the Elements pane. Or, you can click on the inspect icon at the left of the toolbar for the developer tools (the one with the magnifying glass on it), and then click on the element in the web page. In this case, the user has clicked on the h1 element in the Elements pane.

When an element is selected, its styles are shown in the Styles pane at the right side of the developer tools panel. This pane shows all of the styles that have been applied to the element, from the first styles at the bottom of the pane to the last styles at the top. In this example, the bottom of the pane shows the styles that are inherited from the body element. Here, the font-size style has been crossed out because it has been overridden. Next, the shaded group shows the styles that are applied by the user agent style sheet, which is the one provided by the browser. Here again, the font-size style has been overridden.

The last two groups are for the normalize style sheet and the main style sheet. This shows that the main style sheet sets the final value of the font-size property to 170%. This overrides the value for this property set by the preceding groups. However, the margin property for this element in the normalize style sheet hasn't been overridden, so a top and bottom margin of .67em is retained.

If you scroll to the bottom of the Styles pane, you can see a graphic representation of this element that shows the exact size of these margins. This graphic also shows the width and height of the element, as well as any padding and border that's been applied to it. You'll learn about these properties in the next chapter. For now, just realize that the developer tools can be a valuable resource for identifying problems with the styles for these properties as well as any other properties in the style sheets for a page.

You should also realize that you can do more than just inspect styles using the developer tools. For instance, you can also change the generated HTML to see how that affects the page. And you can edit the styles that are applied to a page. For more information on these and other features of the developer tools, please see the help information for your browser.

How Chrome's developer tools show the effects of cascading styles

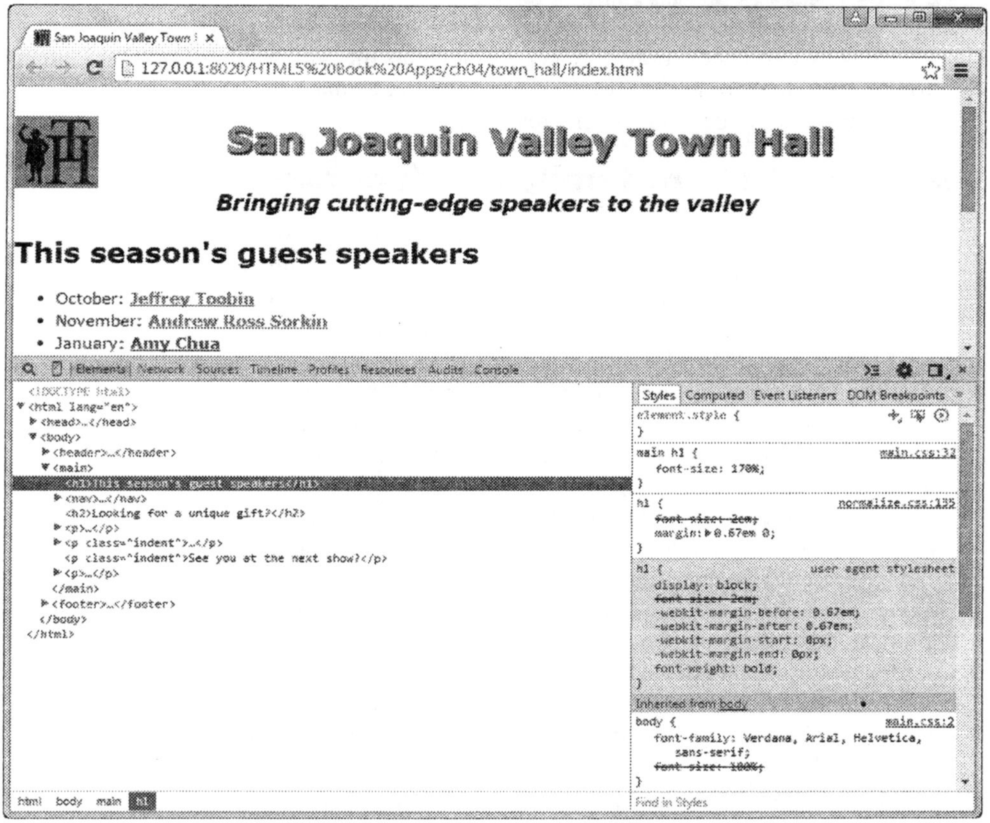

How to use Chrome's developer tools

- To display the panel for the tools, press the F12 key.
- To inspect the styles that have been applied to an element, click on the element in the Elements pane at the left side of the developer tools panel. Or, click on the inspect icon at the left of the toolbar for this panel, and then click on an element in the web page.
- The styles that have been applied to the selected element are displayed in the Styles pane at the right side of the developer tools panel.

Description

- Most modern browsers provide developer tools that can be accessed by pressing the F12 key or by right-clicking on the page and selecting Inspect Element.
- One of the primary uses of the developer tools is to inspect the styles that have been applied to an element, including how the styles in one style sheet have overridden inherited styles or the styles in another style sheet.

Figure 4-11 How to use the developer tools to inspect styles

How to work with text

Now that you know how to select the elements that you want to format, you're ready to learn how to use CSS to apply that formatting. To start, you'll learn how to style fonts and format text.

How to set the font family and font size

Figure 4-12 shows how to set the *font family* and font size for text elements. The table at the top of this figure lists the five generic font families, and the examples below that table show what typical fonts in these families look like.

When you develop a website, your primary font family should be a sans-serif font family. That's because sans-serif fonts are easier to read in a browser than the other types of fonts, including serif fonts, even though serif fonts have long been considered the best for printed text. You can also use serif and monospace fonts for special purposes, but you should avoid the use of cursive and fantasy fonts.

When you code the values for the font-family property, you code a list of the fonts that you want to use. For instance, the first example in this figure lists Arial, Helvetica, and sans-serif as the fonts, and sans-serif is a generic font name. Then, the browser will use the first font in the list that is available to it. But if none of the fonts are available, the browser will substitute its default font for the generic font that's coded last in the list.

If the name of a font family contains spaces, like "Times New Roman", you need to enclose the name in quotation marks when you code the list. This is illustrated by the second and third examples in the first group.

To set the font size for a font, you use the font-size property as illustrated by the second group of examples. For this property, we recommend relative measurements so the users will be able to change the font sizes in their browsers.

When you use a relative measurement, it's relative to the parent element. For example, the second rule in the second set of examples will cause the font to be 150% larger than its parent element. So if the parent element is 16 points, this element will be 24 points. Similarly, the third rule specifies 1.5 ems so it will also be 150% of the parent font.

The next example shows how the font family and font size can be set in the body element. Here, the default font family for the browser is changed to a sans-serif font. This overrides the Times New Roman font that's used by most browsers. In addition, the default font size is set to 100% of the browser's default size. Although this doesn't change the font size, it does make the size relative to the browser's default size, which is usually 16 pixels. Then, if the user changes the browser's font size, that change is reflected in the web page.

Like colors, the font properties that you set in an element are inherited by all of its descendents. Note, however, that it's not the relative value that's inherited when you use a relative measurement for the font size. Instead, it's the actual size that's calculated for the font. If, for example, the default font size is 16 pixels and you set the font-size property to 125%, the size of the element and any descendents will be 20 pixels.

The five generic font families

Name	Description
`serif`	Fonts with tapered, flared, or slab stroke ends.
`sans-serif`	Fonts with plain stroke ends.
`monospace`	Fonts that use the same width for each character.
`cursive`	Fonts with connected, flowing letters that look like handwriting.
`fantasy`	Fonts with decorative styling.

Examples of the five generic font families

Times New Roman is a serif font. It is the default for most web browsers.

Arial is a sans-serif font that is widely used, and sans-serif fonts are best for web pages.

Courier New is a monospace font that is used for code examples.

Lucida Handwriting is a cursive font that is not frequently used.

Impact is a fantasy font that is rarely used.

How to specify a font family

```
font-family: Arial, Helvetica, sans-serif;
font-family: "Times New Roman", Times, serif;
font-family: "Courier New", Courier, monospace;
```

How to specify the font size

```
font-size: 12pt;          /* in points */
font-size: 150%;          /* as a percent of the parent element */
font-size: 1.5em;         /* same as 150% */
```

A font-family rule in the body element that is inherited by all descendants

```
body {
    font-family: Arial, Helvetica, sans-serif;
    font-size: 100%; }
```

A font-family rule in a descendent that overrides the inherited font family

```
p { font-family: "Times New Roman", Times, serif; }
```

Description

- The fonts specified for the font-family property are searched in the order listed. If you include a font name that contains spaces, the name must be enclosed in quotes.
- If you specify a generic font last and the web browser can't find any of the other fonts in the list, it will use its default font for the generic font that you specified.
- The font properties that you set for an element are inherited by all of its descendants.
- If you use relative font sizes, the users will be able to vary the sizes by using their browsers. If you use pixels, the font size will vary based on the screen resolution.

Figure 4-12 How to set the font family and font size

How to set the other properties for styling fonts

The table in figure 4-13 summarizes the other properties that you can use for styling a font. Like the font-family and font-size properties, these properties are also inherited by their descendents.

In this figure, the first group of examples shows how italics and small caps can be applied to a font by using the font-style and font-variant properties. Then, the second group of examples shows how font weights can be applied to a font. In most cases, you'll use the bold keyword to boldface a font. But if you want to use varying degrees of boldness, you can use multiples of 100. You can also specify the boldness of a font relative to the boldness of the parent font by using the lighter or bolder keyword as shown in the last example.

The third group of examples shows how to set the line height for a font. This property lets you increase or decrease the amount of vertical space that's used for a font. If, for example, you set the line height to 14 points for a font that is set to 12 points, there will be two extra points of space for the font. This space will be divided equally above and below the font. This provides extra spacing for block elements that are displayed on more than one line.

Like the font-size property, it's usually better to set the line-height property with a relative measurement like a percent or ems. That way, all modern browsers will be able to adjust the line height relative to the font size. The first three examples illustrate that. The fourth example is similar, but it specifies a number that is used to calculate the line height.

Note that when you use a percent or ems as in the second and third examples, the actual line height will be inherited by descendent elements. When you use a number, however, the number itself will be inherited. If a descendent element has a smaller font size, then, the line height will also be smaller, which is usually what you want.

Often, you code each of the font properties that you've just learned about in a separate rule. However, you can also use the *shorthand property* for fonts that's shown in this figure. If you look at the syntax for this property, you can see that it provides for all six font properties. In this syntax summary, the properties in brackets [ ] are optional, which means that only the font-size and font-family are required.

When you use this property, you code the font properties separated by spaces without coding the property names. You combine the font-size and line-height properties separated by a slash. And you separate the list of fonts for the font-family property with commas. This is illustrated by the three examples after the syntax summary.

Here, the first rule includes all the font properties except for font-variant. The second rule includes the font-variant, font-size, and font-family properties. And the third rule includes the font-size, line-height, and font-family properties.

Other properties for styling fonts

Property	Description
font-style	A keyword that determines how the font is slanted: normal, italic, and oblique.
font-weight	A keyword or number that determines the boldness of the font: normal, bold, bolder, lighter, or multiples of 100 from 100 through 900, with 400 equivalent to normal. Bolder and lighter are relative to the parent element.
font-variant	A keyword that specifies whether small caps will be used: normal and small-caps.
line-height	A relative or absolute value or a number that specifies the amount of vertical space for each line. The excess space is divided equally above and below the font.

How to specify font styles and variants

```
font-style: italic;
font-style: normal;          /* remove style */
font-variant: small-caps;
```

How to specify font weights;

```
font-weight: 700;
font-weight: bold;           /* same as 700 */
font-weight: normal;         /* same as 400 */
font-weight: lighter;        /* relative to the parent element */
```

How to specify line height

```
line-height: 14pt;
line-height: 140%;
line-height: 1.4em;          /* same as 140% */
line-height: 1.4;            /* same as 140% and 1.4em */
```

The syntax for the shorthand font property

```
font: [style] [weight] [variant] size[/line-height] family;
```

How to use the shorthand font property

```
font: italic bold 14px/19px Arial, sans-serif;
font: small-caps 150% "Times New Roman", Times, serif;
font: 90%/120% "Comic Sans MS", Impact, sans-serif;
```

Description

- You can set the font-style, font-weight, and font-variant properties to a value of "normal" to remove any formatting that has been applied to these properties.
- The line-height property determines the spacing between lines within a block element.
- If you specify just a number for the line-height property, the font size is multiplied by that value to determine the line height, and the multiplier is inherited by child elements. If you specify an absolute or relative size for the line-height property, the actual line height is inherited by child elements.
- You can use the shorthand property for a font to set all six font properties with a single rule. When you use this property, the font-size and font-family properties are required.

Figure 4-13 How to set the other properties for styling fonts

How to set properties for formatting text

Figure 4-14 presents four of the properties for formatting text. You can use the text-indent property to indent the first line of text in a paragraph. When you set this property, it usually makes sense to use a relative unit of measure such as ems. That way, if the size of the current font changes, the indentation will also change.

To align text horizontally, you can use the text-align property. By default, most elements are left-aligned, but you can use the "center", "right", or "justify" values to change that. Note, however, that when you justify text, the spacing between words is adjusted so the text is aligned on both the left and right sides. Since this makes the text more difficult to read, justified text should be avoided.

You can also align inline elements vertically. To illustrate, suppose that you code a span element within a paragraph, and you code a style rule that sets the font size for the text in the span element so it's smaller than the text in the paragraph. Then, the vertical-align property determines how the span element is aligned relative to its parent element. If, for example, you set the vertical-align property to "text-bottom", the bottom of the text in the span element will be aligned with the bottom of the text in the paragraph. Another alternative is to specify a relative or absolute value for this property to determine how far above or below its normal position the element should be displayed.

The example in this figure shows how to use the text-indent and text-align properties. Here, the paragraph below the heading is indented by 2 ems, and the paragraph that contains the copyright information is right-aligned.

You can use the text-decoration property to display a line under, over, or through text. However, this property has limited value for two reasons. First, you usually shouldn't underline words that aren't links. Second, you can use borders as shown in the next chapter to put lines over and under a block element, and that gives you more control over the lines.

If you want to remove any text decorations that have been applied to an element, you can specify a value of "none" for these properties. For example, the text-decoration property of an <a> element is set to "underline" by default. If that's not what you want, you can set this property to "none". You'll see how this works in chapter 7.

Properties for indenting, aligning, and decorating text

Property	Description
`text-indent`	A relative or absolute value that determines the indentation for the first line of text. This property is inherited.
`text-align`	A keyword that determines the horizontal alignment of text. Possible values are left, center, right, and justify. This property is inherited.
`vertical-align`	A relative or absolute value or a keyword that determines the vertical alignment of text. Possible keywords are baseline, bottom, middle, top, text-bottom, text-top, sub, and super.
`text-decoration`	A keyword that determines special decorations that are applied to text. Possible values are underline, overline, line-through, and none.

The HTML for a web page

```
<header>
    <h1>San Joaquin Valley Town Hall</h1>
</header>
<main>
    <p>Welcome to San Joaquin Valley Town Hall. We have some
       fascinating speakers for you this season!</p>
</main>
<footer>
    <p>&copy; Copyright 2012 San Joaquin Valley Town Hall.</p>
</footer>
```

CSS that specifies a text indent and horizontal alignment

```
body {
    font-size: 100%;
    margin: 2em; }
h1 { font-size: 180%; }
main p { text-indent: 2em; }
footer p {
    font-size: 80%;
    text-align: right; }
```

The HTML in a web browser

Description

- The text-indent and text-align properties are often used with text, and the vertical-align property is often used with tables.
- The text-decoration property is often set to "none" to remove the underlines from links.

Figure 4-14 How to set properties for formatting text

How to use CSS3 to add shadows to text

Before CSS3, you had to use an image to display text with shadows. But now, CSS3 offers the text-shadow property for this purpose. That makes it much easier to provide shadows.

Figure 4-15 shows how to use this property. As the syntax shows, you can set four parameters for it. The first one specifies how much the shadow should be offset to the right (a positive value) or left (a negative value). The second one specifies how much the shadow should be offset down (a positive value) or up (a negative value). The third one specifies how big the blur radius for the shadow should be. And the fourth one specifies the color for the shadow.

The first example shows text with a shadow that is 4 pixels to the right and down, with no blur and with the shadow the same color as the text. The result is shown in the browser.

In contrast, the shadow for the heading in the second example is offset to the left and up by 2 pixels, with a blur radius of 4 pixels and with the shadow in red. Since the heading is in blue, this provides an interesting effect.

As this figure shows, this property is supported by all modern browsers. But if a browser doesn't support this property, it is simply ignored so no harm is done: the heading is just displayed without the shadow. That's why you can start using this property right away.

When you use this property, though, remember the visually-impaired. If the offsets or blur are too large, the shadow can make the text more difficult to read. On that basis, both examples in this figure should probably be toned down so they're easier to read.

The syntax of the text-shadow property

```
text-shadow: horizontalOffset, verticalOffset, blurRadius, shadowColor;
```

Two examples

The h1 element

```
<h1>San Joaquin Valley Town Hall</h1>
```

The CSS

```
h1 {
    color: #ef9c00;
    text-shadow: 4px 4px; }
```

The heading in a browser

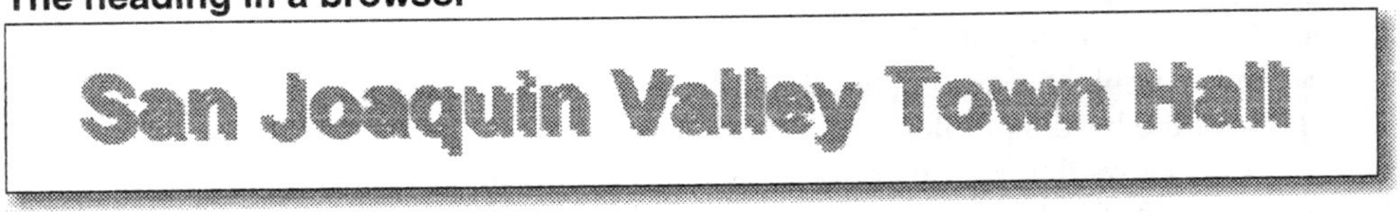

Different CSS for the same h1 element

```
h1 {
    color: blue;
    text-shadow: -2px -2px 4px red; }
```

The heading in a browser

Accessibility guideline

- Remember the visually-impaired. Too much shadow or blur makes text harder to read.

Description

- Positive values offset the shadow to the right or down. Negative values offset the shadow to the left or up.
- The blur radius determines how much the shadow is blurred.
- The text-shadow property is supported by all modern browsers.
- If this property isn't supported by a browser, it is ignored so there's no shadow, which is usually okay.

Figure 4-15 How to use CSS3 to add shadows to text

How to float an image so text flows around it

In chapters 5 and 6, you'll learn everything you need to know about setting margins and floating an image so the text flows around it. But just to get you started with this, figure 4-16 shows how you can float the logo for a header to the left so the headings flow to its right.

In the HTML for the example, you can see an img element, an h1 element, and an h2 element. Then, in the CSS for the img element, the float property is set to left and the right-margin property is set to 1em. The result is that the two headings flow to the right of the image as shown in the first browser example.

You should know, however, that this depends on the size of the image. Because the width of the image is set to 80 pixels for the first example, both headings flow to its right. But if the width is reduced to 40 pixels as in the second example, the second heading is under the image because the image is too short for the heading to flow to its right.

This shows that you're going to have to fiddle with the image size to get this to work right for the time being. But in the next two chapters, you'll learn the right ways to get this result.

If you want to stop elements from flowing to the right of a floated element, you can use the clear property that's shown in this figure. Here, the clear property is used for the main element, and it stops the flow around an element that has been floated to its left. If the main element follows a header, the flow of the text will stop before any of the elements within the main element are displayed.

An image that has been floated to the left of the headings that follow

The HTML

```
<img src="images/logo.gif" alt="Town Hall Logo" width="80">
<h1>San Joaquin Valley Town Hall</h1>
<h2>Bringing cutting-edge speakers to the valley</h2>
```

The CSS

```
img {
    float: left;
    margin-right: 1em;
}
```

The page if the width of the image is reduced to 40

The property that will stop the floating before a subsequent element

```
main { clear: left; }
```

Description

- To float an image, you use the float property, and to set the margins around it, you use the margin property.
- In chapters 5 and 6, you'll learn how to set margins and float elements, but this will give you an idea of how you can use an image in a header.
- When you float an image to the left, the block elements that follow it fill the space to the right of it. When the elements that follow get past the height of the image and its top and bottom margins, they flow into the space below the element.
- You can use the clear property to stop an element from flowing into the space alongside a floated element.
- For now, you can experiment with the size of the image to get the effect that you want, but in the next two chapters you'll learn the right ways to get the same results.

Figure 4-16 How to float an image so text flows around it

A web page that uses external style sheets

Now that you've learned how to code selectors and how to format text, you're ready to see a web page that uses these skills.

The page layout

Figure 4-17 presents a web page that uses two external style sheets. First, it uses the normalize.css style sheet that you learned about earlier in this chapter. Second, it uses a style sheet with styles that are specific to this page.

If you study this web page, you can see that the CSS in the style sheets has been used to change the default font to a sans-serif font, to apply colors to some of the headings and text, to center the headings, to apply shadows to the text in the first heading, to add line height to the items in the unordered list, to apply boldfacing to portions of text, and to right-align the footer. Overall, this formatting makes the page look pretty good.

In terms of typography, though, this web page needs to be improved. For instance, there should be less space after "San Joaquin Valley Town Hall", less space after "This season's guest speakers", less space after "Looking for a unique gift?", and less space between the first three paragraphs. There should also be space at the left and right sides of the page. To make these adjustments, though, you need to know how to use the margin and padding properties that are part of the CSS box model. So that's what you'll learn first in the next chapter. Once you learn how to use those properties, you'll be able to get the typography just the way you want it.

A web page that uses some of the styles presented in this chapter

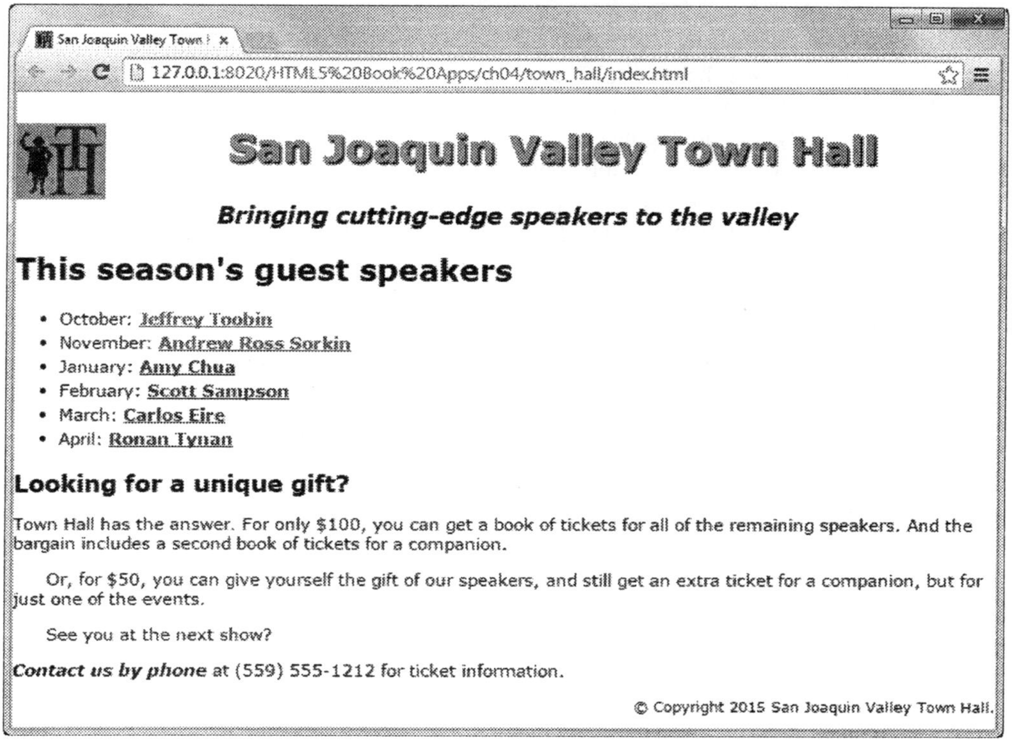

Description

- This web page uses an external style sheet to apply the styles that are illustrated.
- A sans-serif font has been applied to all of the text in this document because that's the most readable type of font for web pages. Also, relative font sizes have been applied to the elements on the page.
- Italics and boldfacing have been applied to portions of the text, the copyright information has been right-aligned, and colors have been applied to two of the headings.
- Colors have also been applied to the <a> tags in the unordered list. Because the first two lectures have passed, the first two links in the list have the color gray applied to them.

What's wrong with the typography in this web page

- The spacing above and below the block elements and around the body of the page should be improved. In the next chapter, you'll learn how to do that by using the margin and padding properties.

Figure 4-17 The page layout for a web page that uses an external style sheet

The HTML file

Figure 4-18 presents the HTML for the web page in figure 4-17. In the head section, you can see the two link elements that refer to the external style sheets that are used for formatting this web page. They are both in the styles folder.

In the body section, the header and the first part of the main element are the same as they were in the example at the end of the last chapter with one exception. That is, the <a> elements in the first and second <li> elements have class attributes that assign them to the "date_passed" class. This class name will be used to apply the color gray to those items because this example assumes that the dates for those events have already passed, and the gray color is intended to indicate that to the user.

After the nav element, this HTML includes another h2 element and three new <p> elements. The second and third <p> elements have their class attributes set to "indent". Then, this class will be used as the CSS selector for indenting these paragraphs.

The HTML file for the web page

```
<!DOCTYPE HTML>

<html lang="en">
<head>
    <title>San Joaquin Valley Town Hall</title>
    <meta charset="utf-8">
    <link rel="shortcut icon" href="images/favicon.ico">
    <link rel="stylesheet" href="styles/normalize.css">
    <link rel="stylesheet" href="styles/main.css">
</head>

<body>
    <header>
        <img src="images/logo.gif" alt="Town Hall Logo" width="80">
        <h2>San Joaquin Valley Town Hall</h2>
        <h3>Bringing cutting-edge speakers to the valley</h3>
    </header>
    <main>
        <h1>This season's guest speakers</h1>
        <nav>
            <ul>
              <li>October: <a class="date_passed"
                  href="speakers/toobin.html">Jeffrey Toobin</a></li>
              <li>November: <a class="date_passed"
                  href="speakers/sorkin.html">Andrew Ross Sorkin</a></li>
              <li>January: <a href="speakers/chua.html">
                  Amy Chua</a></li>
              <li>February: <a href="speakers/sampson.html">
                  Scott Sampson</a></li>
              <li>March: <a href="speakers/eire.html">
                  Carlos Eire</a></li>
              <li>April: <a href="speakers/tynan.html">
                  Ronan Tynan</a></li>
            </ul>
        </nav>

        <h2>Looking for a unique gift?</h2>
        <p>Town Hall has the answer. For only $100, you can get a book of
           tickets for all of the remaining speakers. And the bargain
           includes a second book of tickets for a companion.</p>
        <p class="indent">Or, for $50, you can give yourself the gift of
           our speakers, and still get an extra ticket for a companion, but
           for just one of the events.</p>
        <p class="indent">See you at the next show?</p>

        <p><em>Contact us by phone</em> at (559) 555-1212 for ticket
           information.</p>
    </main>
    <footer>
        <p>&copy; Copyright 2015 San Joaquin Valley Town Hall.</p>
    </footer>
</body>
</html>
```

Figure 4-18 The HTML file for the web page

The CSS file

Figure 4-19 shows the CSS file for the web page. To start, notice the way that the code in this file is structured. First, the rule sets for specific elements are presented. In effect, this sets the default formatting for these elements. Then, these rule sets are followed by rule sets that are specific to the header, main, and footer elements. The rules in these rule sets override the ones for the elements because they're more specific. For instance, the font size for the main h1 selector overrides the font size for the body selector.

You might also note that many of the rule sets that contain a single rule are coded on a single line. This of course is a valid way to code these rule sets because white space is ignored. For rule sets that require more than one rule, though, each rule is coded on a single line to make the rules easier to read.

In the rule set for the body element, the two properties specify the font-family and font-size. Because these properties are inherited, they become the defaults for the document. Notice too that the font size is specified as 100 percent. That means the actual font size will be determined by the default font size for the browser. The font sizes for the headings are also specified as percents, so they will be based on the size that's calculated for the body element.

In the rule sets for the <a> element, the hover and focus pseudo-classes are set to the same color. Then, in the rule set for the unordered list, the line-height property is specified to increase the spacing between the items. Similarly, the font weight is specified for the em element so it is boldfaced. However, this element will also be italicized because that's its normal behavior. To remove the italics, you would have to code a font-style property with normal as its value.

In the rule sets for the header, you can see that the image is floated to the left so the elements that follow will appear to the right. If you look back at the web page in figure 4-17, though, you'll see that only the h2 heading flows to the right of the image. That's because the image is too short for the h3 element to flow to its right. Then, although both the h2 and h3 elements are centered, the h2 element appears centered in the header but the h3 element appears centered on the page. You can also see that the h2 heading has a 2 pixel, black shadow to its right and down with 2 pixels of blur.

In the rule sets for the main element, you can see that the clear property is used to stop the flow of the text around the image that has been floated left. You can also see that the elements in the "indent" class will be indented 2 ems, and the elements in the "date_passed" class will be gray.

Of course, you can code the CSS in other ways and get the same results. For instance, you could code this rule set for the h2 and h3 elements in the header:

```
header h2, header h3 { text-align: center; }
```

Then, you could drop the text-align properties from the header h2 and header h3 rule sets that follow. You could also code the selectors for the date_passed and indent classes so they're less specific since they aren't used outside the main element. If you code the selectors so they're more specific, though, they're less likely to cause problems if you add rule sets later on.

The CSS file for the web page

```
/* the styles for the elements */
body {
    font-family: Verdana, Arial, Helvetica, sans-serif;
    font-size: 100%;
}

a { font-weight: bold; }
a:link { color: #931420; }
a:visited { color: #f2972e;}
a:hover, a:focus { color: blue; }

ul { line-height: 1.5; }
li, p { font-size: 95%; }
em { font-weight: bold; }

/* the styles for the header */
header img { float: left; }
header h2 {
    font-size: 220%;
    color: #f2972e;
    text-align: center;
    text-shadow: 2px 2px 2px black;
}
header h3 {
    font-size: 130%;
    font-style: italic;
    text-align: center;
}

/* the styles for the main content */
main { clear: left; }
main h1 { font-size: 170%; }
main h2 { font-size: 130%; }

main p.indent { text-indent: 2em; }
main a.date_passed { color: gray; }

/* the styles for the footer */
footer p {
    font-size: 80%;
    text-align: right;
}
```

Figure 4-19 The CSS file for the web page

Perspective

At this point, you should know how to code all types of selectors, and you should know how to code the CSS properties for formatting text. That gets you off to a good start with CSS, but there's still a lot to learn.

So, in the next chapter, you'll learn how to use the CSS box model. You use that model to set the margins, padding, and borders for the elements in your pages so your typography looks the way you want it to. Then, in chapter 6, you'll learn how to use CSS for page layout.

Terms

external style sheet
embedded style sheet
inline style
shiv
shim
absolute unit of measure
relative unit of measure
absolute measurement
relative measurement
RGB value
hexadecimal (hex) value
inherited property
RGBA value
HSL value
HSLA value
universal selector
type selector
id selector
class selector
relational selector
descendant selector
adjacent sibling selector
child selector
general sibling selector
attribute selector
pseudo-class selector
pseudo-element selector
cascade order
user style sheet
font family
shorthand property

Summary

- If you're going to use a style sheet for more than one HTML document, it's usually best to use an *external style sheet*. However, you can also apply CSS by embedding a style sheet in the HTML or by using the style attribute of an element.
- To provide cross-browser compatibility with older versions of Internet Explorer when you use the HTML5 semantic elements, you can add a script element that accesses a JavaScript *shiv* to the head element of each HTML document.
- To make sure that all HTML elements are rendered the same in all modern browsers, you can include the normalize.css style sheet in your web pages.
- You can use *absolute measurements* like pixels or *relative measurements* like ems or percents to specify the CSS properties for sizes. For fonts, it's better to use relative measurements so the user can change the font sizes by changing the browser's default font size.

- Most graphic designers use *hex* for the *RGB values* that represent the colors that they want because that gives them the most control. However, most browsers also support 16 standard color names like red and blue.
- CSS3 lets you use *RGBA*, *HSL*, and *HLSA* values to specify colors. This gives the web designer more control over colors and transparency. CSS also provides 147 more keywords for colors.
- You can code CSS selectors for element types, ids, classes, relations, and attributes. You can also code selectors for combinations of these items.
- A *pseudo-class selector* can be used to apply CSS formatting when certain conditions occur or have occurred, like when the mouse hovers over an element or the focus is on an element. A *pseudo-element selector* lets you select a portion of text.
- If more than one style sheet is applied to an HTML document and two or more rule sets apply to the same element, the *cascade order* determines which rule set takes precedence. The first four levels of this order are: the important rules in a *user style sheet* for the browser; the important rules in a web page; the normal rules in a web page; and the normal rules in a user style sheet.
- If more than one rule set in a cascade level is applied to an element, the rule set with the highest specificity is used. But if the specificity is the same for two or more rule sets in a cascade level, the rule set that's specified last is used.
- The developer tools for a modern browser let you inspect all of the styles that have been applied to an element, including the styles that have been overridden.
- The default font for most browsers is a 16-pixel, serif font. However, because sans-serif fonts are easier to read in a browser, you normally change the font family. It's also good to change the font size to a relative measurement like a percent of the default font size.
- The colors and font properties of a parent element are *inherited* by the child elements. But those properties can be overridden by the rule sets for the children.
- The *shorthand property* for fonts can be used to apply all six of the font properties to an element: font-family, font-size, font-style, font-weight, font-variant, and line-height.
- Text properties can be used to indent, align, and decorate the text in a block element like a heading or paragraph. CSS3 also provides for adding shadows to text.
- You can use the float property of an image to float the image to the left. Then, the block elements that follow in the HTML flow to its right. To stop the flow, you can code the clear property for an element.

Exercise 4-1 Format the Town Hall home page

In this exercise, you'll format the home page that you built in exercise 3-1 by using the skills that you've learned in this chapter. When you're through, the page should look like this.

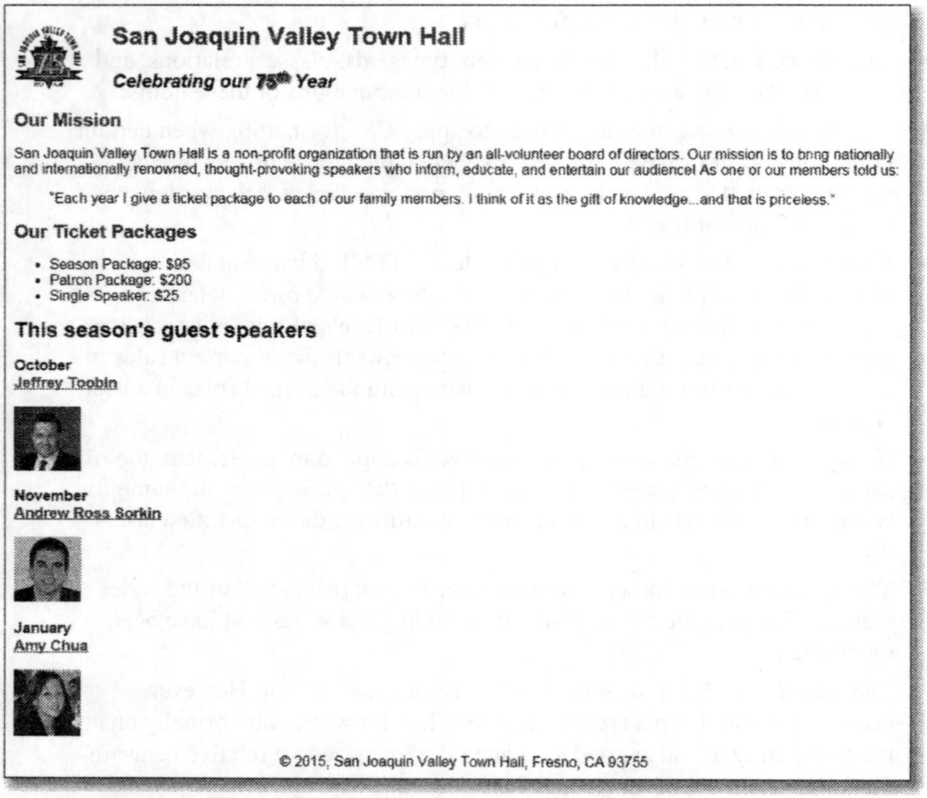

Open the index.html page and update the head section

1. Use your text editor to open the HTML file that you created for exercise 3-1:
   c:\html5_css3_2\exercises\town_hall_1\index.html
2. Use your text editor to open this HTML template file:
   c:\html5_css3_2\exercises\town_hall_1\templates\basic.html
   Then, copy the second and third link elements from the head section to the clipboard, switch to the index.html file, and paste these elements at the end of the head section.
3. Note that the first link element you just copied into the head is for the normalize.css style sheet in the styles subfolder. Next, complete the href attribute in the second link element so it refers to the main.css file in the styles subfolder. Then, close the template.

Open the main.css file and format the header

4. Use your text editor to open this CSS file:

   ```
   c:\html5_css3_2\exercises\town_hall_1\styles\main.css
   ```

   Note that this file contains some of the CSS code that you'll need, including the rule set that specifies the font family and font size for the body, the rule set that floats the image in the header, and the rule set that clears the floating in the main element.

5. Add two rule sets for the header to the style sheet. The first one should be for the h2 element, and it should set the font size to 170%, set the color to #800000, and indent the heading 30 pixels. The second one should be for the h3 element, and it should set the font size to 130%, set the font style to italic, and indent the heading 30 pixels.

6. Test the HTML page in Chrome to make sure that the style sheets have been linked properly, the image has been floated, and the headings have been formatted correctly. If necessary, make corrections and test again.

Format the main element and the footer

From now on, test each change right after you make it.

7. Add a rule set for the h1 elements within the main element that sets the font size to 150%.

8. Add a rule set for the h2 elements within the main element that sets the font size to 130% and the color to #800000.

9. Add a rule set for the h3 elements within the main element that sets the font size to 105%.

10. Add a rule set that italicizes any link that has the focus or has the mouse hovering over it.

11. Add a rule set that centers the <p> tag in the footer.

Use the developer tools to review the styles for the page

12. Display the page in Chrome, and then press the F12 key to display the developer tools. Next, expand the main element in the Elements pane and click on one of the h2 elements.

13. Review the styles for the h2 element in the Styles pane, and notice how the font-family style for the html element in the normalize style sheet is overridden by the font-family style for the body element in the main style sheet. Also notice how the font-size style for the body element in the main style sheet and the h2 element in the user agent style sheet are overridden by the font-size style for the main h2 element in the main style sheet.

14. Click the icon in the developer tools toolbar that has a magnifying glass on it, and then click on the h2 element in the header to see that it's now selected in the Elements pane.

15. Review the styles for this h2 element to see that they're similar to the styles for the main h2 element. However, the font size for this element is smaller and it has a text indent.

16. When you're done with the developer tools, close the panel by clicking the icon with an "X" on it in the upper right corner.

Add the finishing touches and test in IE

17. Add a text shadow to the *75th* in the second heading in the header. To do that, enclose the *75th* in the HTML in an em or span element and give that element a class attribute with a value of "shadow". Then, create a rule set that uses a class selector (.shadow) for that class, and code a rule that adds a shadow to the text with #800000 as the color of the shadow.
18. Test the page in IE. There the text shadow won't work if you're using a version before version 10. But if you see any other formatting problems, make the corrections and test again in both Chrome and IE.

5

How to use the CSS box model for spacing, borders, and backgrounds

In the last chapter, you learned some basic CSS properties for formatting text. Now, you'll learn the properties for controlling the spacing between elements and for displaying borders and backgrounds. Specifically, you'll learn how to use the CSS box model for those purposes.

An introduction to the box model

When a browser displays a web page, it places each HTML block element in a box. That makes it easy to control the spacing, borders, and other formatting for elements like headers, sections, footers, headings, and paragraphs. Some inline elements like images are placed in a box as well. To work with boxes, you use the CSS *box model*.

How the box model works

Figure 5-1 presents a diagram that shows how the box model works. By default, the box for a block element is as wide as the block that contains it and as tall as it needs to be based on its content. However, you can explicitly specify the size of the content area for a block element by using the height and width properties. You can also use other properties to set the borders, margins, and padding for a block element.

If you look at the diagram in this figure, you can see that *padding* is the space between the content area and a border. Similarly, a *margin* is the space between the border and the outside of the box.

If you need to calculate the overall height of a box, you can use the formula in this figure. Here, you start by adding the values for the margin, border width, and padding for the top of the box. Then, you add the height of the content area. Last, you add the values for the padding, border width, and margin for the bottom of the box. The formula for calculating the overall width of a box is similar.

When you set the height and width properties for a block element, you can use any of the units that you learned about in the last chapter. For now, though, we'll use pixels so the sizes are fixed. That way, the size of the page won't change if the user changes the size of the browser window. This is referred to as a *fixed layout*.

When you use a fixed layout, you can use either absolute or relative units of measure for margins and padding. If you use a relative unit such as ems, the margins and padding will be adjusted if the font size changes. If you use an absolute unit, the margins and padding will stay the same.

The CSS box model

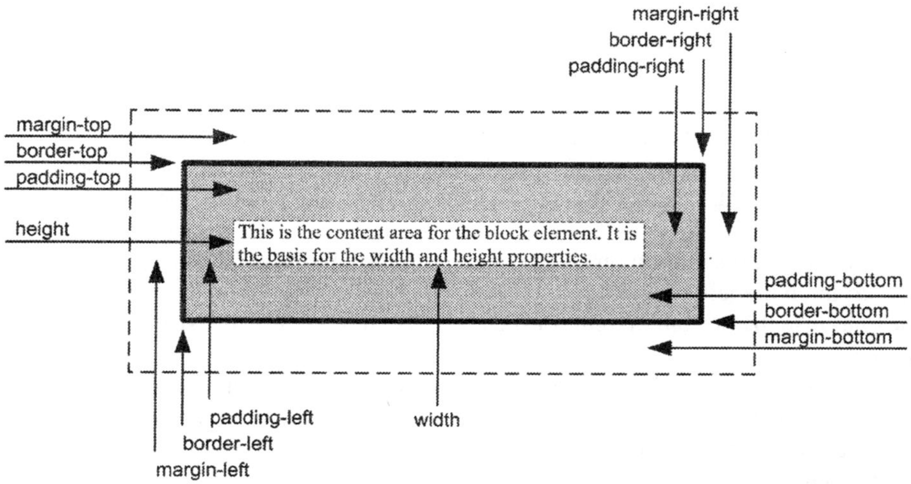

The formula for calculating the height of a box

```
top margin + top border + top padding +
height +
bottom padding + bottom border + bottom margin
```

The formula for calculating the width of a box

```
left margin + left border + left padding +
width +
right padding + right border + right margin
```

Description

- The CSS *box model* lets you work with the boxes that a browser places around each block element as well as some inline elements. This lets you add formatting such as margins, padding, and borders.
- By default, the box for a block element is as wide as the block that contains it and as tall as it needs to be based on its content.
- You can use the height and width properties to specify the size of the content area for a block element explicitly.
- You can use other properties to control the margins, padding, and borders for a block element. Then, these properties are added to the height and width of the content area to determine the height and width of the box.

Figure 5-1 How the box model works

A web page that illustrates the box model

To help you understand how the box model works, figure 5-2 presents the HTML for a simple web page. Then, the CSS adds borders to the four types of elements in the HTML: a dotted 3-pixel border to the body, a solid 2-pixel border to the main element, and dashed 1-pixel borders to the h1 and <p> elements. If you look at the web page in the browser, you can see how these four borders are rendered. You can also see how the margins and padding for these boxes work.

For the body, the margin on all four sides is set to 10 pixels. You can see that margin on the left, top, and right of the body border, but not on the bottom. That's because the bottom margin for the body is determined by the size of the window.

For the main element, the width is set to 500 pixels, and the margins on all four sides of the box are set to 20 pixels. You can see these margins on the left, top, and bottom of the main box, but not on the right because the width of the section is set to 500 pixels.

The next rule set sets properties for both the h1 and <p> elements. In this case, the properties set the border and the padding for these elements. Then, the next two rule sets set additional properties for each of these elements.

The rule set for the h1 element sets the top margin to .5em, the right and left margins to 0, and the bottom margin to .25em. As a result, there is more space above the h1 element than below it. This rule set also sets the padding on the left side of the element to 15 pixels so space is added between the border of the box and the text.

The rule set for the <p> element starts by setting all the margins to 0. As a result, all of the space between the h1 and <p> elements is due to the bottom margin of the h1 element. In addition, the padding on the left side of the element is set to 15 pixels so the text for the h1 and <p> elements is aligned.

Please note that if I had used relative measures for the padding on the left of the h1 and <p> elements, they wouldn't be aligned because the font sizes for these elements are different. One more thing to notice is that the padding-left properties in the rule sets for the h1 and <p> elements override the left padding specified by the rule set for both of these elements.

This should help you understand how the box model works. Now, it's on to the details for setting the properties for the box model.

The HTML for a page that uses the box model

```
<body>
    <main>
        <h1>San Joaquin Valley Town Hall</h1>
        <p>Welcome to San Joaquin Valley Town Hall.
        We have some fascinating speakers for you this season!</p>
    </main>
</body>
```

The CSS for the page

```
body {
    border: 3px dotted black;
    margin: 10px;
}
main {
    border:  2px solid black;
    width:   500px;
    margin:  20px;          /* all four sides */
    padding: 10px;          /* all four sides */
}
h1, p {
    border: 1px dashed black;
    padding: 10px;
}
h1 {
    margin: .5em 0 .25em;   /* .5em top, 0 right and left, .25em bottom */
    padding-left: 15px;
}
p {
    margin: 0;              /* all four sides */
    padding-left: 15px;
}
```

The web page in a browser

Figure 5-2 A web page that illustrates the box model

How to size and space elements

As you saw in the last figure, you can use several different properties to determine the size of an element and the spacing between the elements on a page. In the topics that follow, you'll learn the details of coding these properties.

How to set heights and widths

Figure 5-3 presents the properties for setting heights and widths. The two properties you'll use most often are width and height. By default, these properties are set to a value of "auto". As a result, the size of the content area for the element is automatically adjusted so it's as wide as the element that contains it and as tall as the content it contains. To change that, you can use the height and width properties.

The first two sets of examples in this figure illustrate how this works. Here, the first example in each set specifies an absolute value using pixels. Then, the second example specifies a relative value using percents. As a result, the width is set to 75% of the *containing block.*

Finally, the third example in each set uses the keyword "auto". That sets the width based on the size of the containing element and the height based on the content of the element. Because the default width and height is "auto", you usually won't need to use that value.

In addition to the width and height properties, you can use the min-width, max-width, min-height, and max-height properties to specify the minimum and maximum width and height of the content area. Like the width and height properties, you can specify either a relative or an absolute value for these properties. For instance, the last set of examples in this figure sets the values of these properties using pixels.

Properties for setting heights and widths

Property	Description
width	A relative or absolute value that specifies the width of the content area for a block element. You can also specify auto if you want the width of the box calculated for you based on the width of its containing block. This is the default.
height	A relative or absolute value that specifies the height of the content area for a block element. You can also specify auto if you want the height of the area calculated for you based on its content. This is the default.
min-width	A relative or absolute value that specifies the minimum width of the content area for a block element. The area will always be at least this wide regardless of its content.
max-width	A relative or absolute value that specifies the maximum width of the content area for a block element. You can also specify none to indicate that there is no maximum width.
min-height	A relative or absolute value that specifies the minimum height of the content area for a block element. The area will always be at least this tall regardless of its content.
max-height	A relative or absolute value that specifies the maximum height of the content area for a block element. You can also specify none to indicate that there is no maximum height.

How to set the width of the content area

```
width: 450px;          /* an absolute width */
width: 75%;            /* a relative width */
width: auto;           /* width based on its containing block (the default) */
```

How to set the height of the content area

```
height: 125px;
height: 50%;
height: auto;          /* height based on its content (the default) */
```

How to set the minimum and maximum width and height

```
min-width: 450px;
max-width: 600px;
min-height: 120px;
max-height: 160px;
```

Description

- If you specify a percent for the width property, the width of the content area for the block element is based on the width of the block that contains it, called the *containing block*. In that case, the width of the containing block must be specified explicitly.
- If you specify a percent for the height property, the height of the content area for the block element is based on the height of the containing block. In that case, the height of the containing block must be specified explicitly. Otherwise, "auto" is substituted for the percent.
- The min-width, max-width, min-height, and max-height properties are typically used to accommodate a change in font size.

Figure 5-3 How to set heights and widths

How to set margins

Figure 5-4 presents the properties for setting margins. As you can see, you can use individual properties like margin-top or margin-left to set individual margins. This is illustrated in the first set of examples in this figure.

Instead of setting individual margins, though, you can use the margin property to set the margins for all four sides of a box. When you use a *shorthand property* like this, you can specify one, two, three, or four values. If you specify all four values, they are applied to the sides of the box in a clockwise order: top, right, bottom, and left. To remember this order, you can think of the word *trouble*.

If you specify fewer than four values, this property still sets the margins for all four sides of the box. If, for example, you only specify one value, each margin is set to that value. If you specify two values, the top and bottom margins are set to the first value, and the left and right margins are set to the second value. And if you specify three values, the top margin is set to the first value, the left and right margins are set to the second value, and the bottom margin is set to the third value. This is illustrated in the second set of examples in this figure.

Although it isn't shown here, you can also specify the keyword "auto" for any margin. In most cases, you'll use this keyword to center a page in the browser window or a block element within its containing block. To do that, you specify auto for both the left and right margins. For this to work, you must also set the width of the element. You'll see an example of how this works in figure 5-6.

One more thing you should know about margins is that different browsers have different default margins for the block elements. Because of that, it's a good practice to explicitly set the top and bottom margins of the elements that you're using. That way, you can control the space between elements like headings and paragraphs.

Finally, if you specify a bottom margin for one element and a top margin for the element that follows it, the margins are *collapsed*. That means the smaller margin is ignored, and only the larger margin is applied. In that case, there may not be as much space between the two elements as you expected. One solution to this problem is to set the margins to zero and use padding for the spacing.

Properties for setting margins

Property	Description
`margin-top`	A relative or absolute value that defines the space between the top border of an element and the top of the containing block or the bottom of the element above it.
`margin-right`	A relative or absolute value that defines the space between the right border of an element and the right side of the containing block or the left side of the element to its right.
`margin-bottom`	A relative or absolute value that defines the space between the bottom border of an element and the bottom of the containing block or the top of the element below it.
`margin-left`	A relative or absolute value that defines the space between the left border of an element and the left side of the containing block or the right side of the element to its left.
`margin`	One to four relative or absolute values that specify the size of the margins for a box. One value is applied to all four margins. Two values are applied to the top and bottom and right and left margins. Three values are applied to the top, right and left, and bottom margins. And four values are applied to the top, right, bottom, and left margins (think trouble).

How to set the margin on a single side of an element

```
margin-top: .5em;
margin-right: 1em;
margin-bottom: 2em;
margin-left: 1em;
```

How to set the margins on multiple sides of an element

```
margin: 1em;             /* all four sides */
margin: 0 1em;           /* top and bottom 0, right and left 1em */
margin: .5em 1em 2em;    /* top .5em, right and left 1em, bottom 2em */
margin: .5em 1em 2em 1em; /* top .5em, right 1em, bottom 2em, left 1em */
```

Description

- If you specify a bottom margin for one element and a top margin for the element that follows in the HTML, the margins are *collapsed*, which means that only the larger margin is applied.
- You typically use the "auto" keyword to center an element in its *containing block*. To do that, you must also specify the width of the element.
- Because different browsers have different default margins for block elements, you often need to set these margins explicitly.

Figure 5-4 How to set margins

How to set padding

The properties for setting padding are similar to the properties for setting margins. These properties are presented in figure 5-5. As you can see, you can set the padding for the sides of a box individually, or you can set the padding for all four sides of a box at once using a shorthand property.

Properties for setting padding

Property	Description
`padding-top`	A relative or absolute value that defines the space between the top of an element and its top border.
`padding-right`	A relative or absolute value that defines the space between the right side of an element and its right border.
`padding-bottom`	A relative or absolute value that defines the space between the bottom of an element and its bottom border.
`padding-left`	A relative or absolute value that defines the space between the left side of an element and its left border.
`padding`	One to four relative or absolute values that specify the padding on multiple sides of an element. One value is applied to all four sides. Two values are applied to the top and bottom and right and left. Three values are applied to the top, right and left, and bottom. And four values are applied to the top, right, bottom, and left (think trouble).

How to set the padding on a single side of an element

```
padding-top: 0;
padding-right: 1em;
padding-bottom: .5em;
padding-left: 1em;
```

How to set the padding on multiple sides of an element

```
padding: 1em;              /* all four sides */
padding: 0 1em;            /* top and bottom 0, right and left 1em */
padding: 0 1em .5em;       /* top 0, right and left 1em, bottom .5em */
padding: 0 1em .5em 1em;   /* top 0, right 1em, bottom .5em, left 1em */
```

Description

- If you set the top and bottom margins for elements to zero, you can use padding to set the spacing between the elements.

Figure 5-5 How to set padding

A web page that illustrates sizing and spacing

To illustrate the use of the properties for sizing and spacing, figure 5-6 presents a web page that uses many of these properties. This web page is similar to the one at the end of the last chapter. However, the page has been centered in the browser window, the spacing between the elements has been improved, and the second and third paragraphs aren't indented.

The HTML for the web page

The HTML for this web page is the same as in the application at the end of the last chapter, with two exceptions. First, the last paragraph in the main element has an id attribute of "contact_us". Second, the second and third paragraphs in the main element don't have a class attribute that's used to indent them.

If you want to review this HTML before you look at the CSS for this page, you can refer back to the last chapter. Or, you can open this page in your text editor. You shouldn't need to do that, though, because the focus here is on margins, padding, and the use of the box model.

A web page that uses widths, margins, and padding

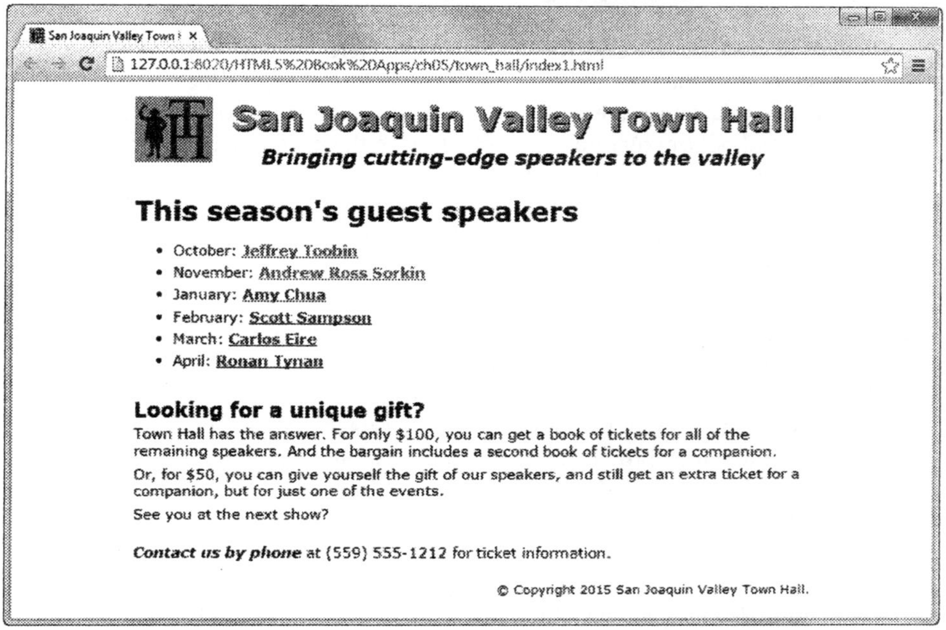

Description

- This page is centered in the browser window and uses margins and padding to improve the spacing before and after headings, between list items, and between paragraphs.

Figure 5-6 A web page that illustrates the use of margins and padding

The CSS for the web page

Figure 5-7 presents the CSS for the web page. Here, I've highlighted all the style rules that affect the size and spacing of the elements on the page.

To start, the rule set for the body sets the width of the page to 700 pixels. Then, the top and bottom margins are set to 1em so there's space between the body and the top of the browser window. In addition, the left and right margins are set to "auto". Because a width is specified for the body, this causes the left and right margins to be calculated automatically so the page is centered in the browser window.

The next highlighted rule set is for the h1, h2, h3, and <p> elements. This sets the margins and padding for these elements to 0. This prevents margin collapse when these items are next to each other. Then, the rule sets that follow can provide the right margins and padding for these elements.

For instance, the rule set for the <p> element sets the top and bottom padding to .25em, which provides the spacing between the paragraphs. Also, the rule set for the h2 element in the header sets the margin bottom to .25em, and the rule set for the h1 element in the main element sets the margin top to 1em and the margin bottom to .35em. This provides the proper spacing before and after the headings.

In the rule set for the ul element, you can see that the bottom margin is set to 1.5em, and the other margins are set to zero. This reduces the space before the unordered list and increases the space after. Similarly, the bottom padding for the li elements is set to .35em. That provides the spacing after the list items, which means that you don't have to set the line height for the list.

Last, in the rule set for the element with "contact_us" as its id, you can see that the top margin is set to 1em, which provides the spacing before it. And the rule set for the footer sets the top margin to 1em, which provides more space between it and the last paragraph in the section.

If you study all of this code, you can see that it avoids the problems of collapsing margins. It does that by first setting the margins for the elements to zero and then overriding those margins or using padding to provide the spacing before and after elements.

The CSS for the web page

```
/* the styles for the elements */
body {
    font-family: Verdana, Arial, Helvetica, sans-serif;
    font-size: 100%;
    width: 700px;
    margin: 1em auto; }

h1, h2, h3, p {
    margin: 0;
    padding: 0; }

a { font-weight: bold; }
a:link { color: #931420; }
a:visited { color: #f2972e; }
a:hover, a:focus { color: blue; }

ul { margin: 0 0 1.5em; }
li {
    font-size: 95%;
    padding-bottom: .35em; }

p {
    font-size: 95%;
    padding: .25em 0; }
em { font-weight: bold; }

/* the styles for the header */
header img { float: left; }
header h2 {
    font-size: 220%;
    color: #f2972e;
    text-align: center;
    text-shadow: 2px 2px 0 black;
    margin-bottom: .25em; }
header h3 {
    font-size: 130%;
    font-style: italic;
    text-align: center; }

/* the styles for the main content */
main { clear: left; }
main h1 {
    font-size: 175%;
    margin: 1em 0 .35em;
}
main h2 { font-size: 130%; }
#contact_us { margin-top: 1em; }
a.date_passed  { color: gray; }

/* the styles for the footer */
footer { margin-top: 1em; }
footer p {
    font-size: 80%;
    text-align: right; }
```

Figure 5-7 The CSS for the web page

A version of the CSS that uses a reset selector

In figure 5-8, you can see another version of the CSS for this application. This time, the CSS uses a *reset selector*. That refers to the use of a universal selector that sets the margins and padding for all of the elements to zero. After you code the reset selector, you can get the spacing that you want by applying margins and padding to specific elements, which overrides the settings of the reset selector.

In the CSS for this figure, only the rule sets that provide margins or padding are listed. This works pretty much the way the code in the previous figure works, except for the ul and li elements. Because the reset selector set the margins and padding for these elements to zero, you need to provide margins and padding for these elements.

To bring the ul element in line with the heading above it, you need to set its left margin. In this example, the left margin is set to 1.25em. You also need to provide left padding for the li elements to provide space between the bullets and the text. In this example, that space is set to .25em.

Because of these CSS differences, the formatting of the web page in this figure is slightly different than the formatting in figure 5-6. Specifically, the bulleted list isn't indented, and there's more space between the bullets and text in the list items. Of course, you could make them the same by changing the settings for the ul and li elements, but this shows the options that you have when you use a reset selector. In chapter 7, you'll learn more about formatting lists.

One other thing you should notice is that no top margin is applied to the main h1 element like it was in the previous example. Because of that, you might expect this element to have no top margin. Remember, though, that the universal selector doesn't override a style that's set for a specific element in the normalize.css file that's linked to this document. In this case, the normalize.css file sets the top margin for h1 elements to .67 ems, so that's the margin that's used for this element. If you wanted to override that margin, you'd have to set it explicitly for the h1 element as shown in the previous figure. When you use the reset selector, then, you need to be aware of what margins and padding are set in the normalize.css style sheet so you can override them if you need to.

A slightly modified version of the page that uses a reset selector

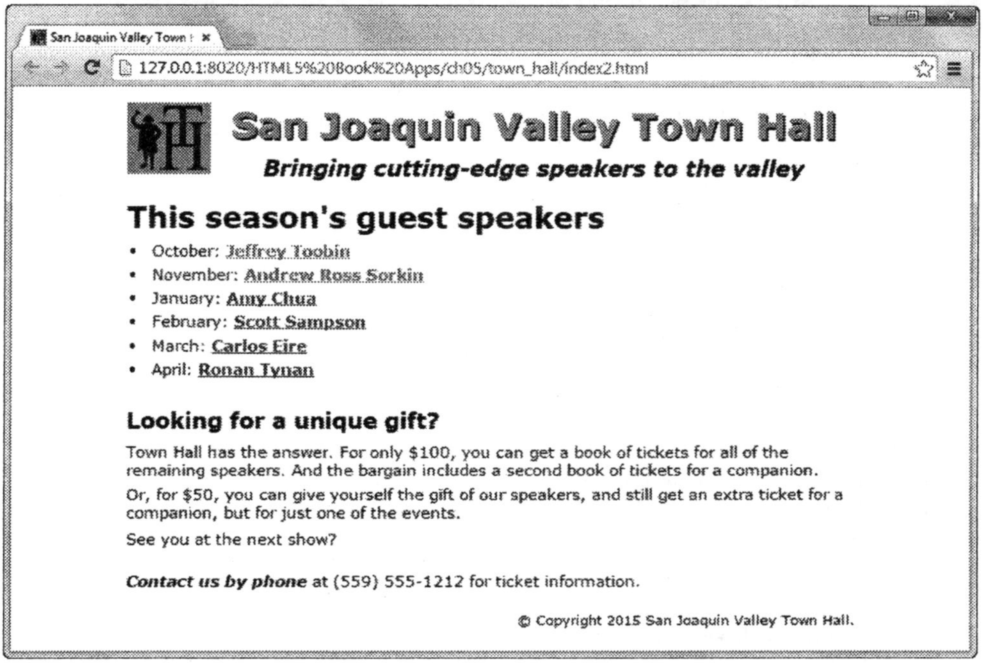

The CSS for this version of the page

```
/* the reset selector */
* {
    margin: 0;
    padding: 0; }

/* just the styles for the elements that provide margins or padding */
body {
    font-family: Verdana, Arial, Helvetica, sans-serif;
    font-size: 100%;
    width: 700px;
    margin: 15px auto; }
h1, h2, h3 { margin-bottom: .25em; }
ul { margin: 0 0 1.5em 1.25em; }
li {
    font-size: 95%;
    padding-bottom: .35em;
    padding-left: .25em; }
p {
    font-size: 95%;
    padding: .25em 0; }
main h1 { font-size: 175%; }
#contact_us { margin-top: 1em; }
footer { margin-top: 1em; }
```

Figure 5-8 A version of the CSS that uses a reset selector

How to set borders and backgrounds

Now that you know how to size and space elements using the box model, you're ready to learn how to apply other formatting to boxes. That includes adding borders and setting background colors and images.

How to set borders

Figure 5-9 presents the properties for setting *borders* and illustrates how they work. To start, if you want the same border on all four sides of a box, you can use the shorthand border property. This property lets you set the width, style, and color for the borders. This is illustrated in the first set of examples in this figure.

Here, the first rule creates a thin, solid, green border. Note that different browsers interpret the thin keyword, as well as the other keywords for width, differently. Because of that, you'll typically set the width of a border to an absolute value as shown in the second and third rules. Notice that the third rule doesn't specify a color. In that case, the border will be the same color as the element's text.

To set the border for just one side of a box, you can use the shorthand property for a border side. This is illustrated by the second set of examples. Here, the first rule sets the top border and the second rule sets the right border.

Most of the time, you'll use the shorthand properties to set all four borders or just one border of a box. However, you can use the other properties in this figure to set the width, styles, and colors for the sides of a border. This is illustrated by the last four groups of examples in this figure. You may want to use these properties to override another border setting for an element.

For instance, to set the width for each side of a border, you can use the border-width property as shown in the third set of examples. Here, you can specify one, two, three, or four values. This works just like the shorthand margin and padding properties you learned about earlier in this chapter. That means that the values are applied to the top, right, bottom, and left sides of the border.

The border-style and border-color properties are similar. You can use them to set the style and color for each side of a border by specifying one to four values. This is illustrated in the fourth and fifth sets of examples in this figure. Notice in the last example for the border-style property that the left and right borders are set to "none". That way, only the top and bottom borders will be displayed.

Properties for setting borders

Property	Description
border	A border width, border style, and border color. The values are applied to all sides of the border.
border-side	Border width, style, and color values for the specified side of a border.
border-width	One to four relative or absolute values (excluding a percent) or keywords that specify the widths for each side of a border. Possible keywords are thin, medium, and thick.
border-style	One to four keywords that specify the styles for each side of a border. Possible values are dotted, dashed, solid, double, groove, ridge, inset, outset, and none. The default is none.
border-color	One to four color values or keywords that specify the color for each side of a border. The default is the color of the element.
border-side-width	A relative or absolute value (excluding a percent) or a keyword that specifies the width of the indicated side of a border.
border-side-style	A keyword that specifies the style for the indicated side of a border.
border-side-color	A color value or keyword that specifies the color of the indicated side of a border.

The syntax for the shorthand border and border-*side* properties

```
border: [width] [style] [color];
border-side: [width] [style] [color];
```

How to set border properties

```
border: thin solid green;
border: 2px dashed #808080;
border: 1px inset;              /* uses the element's color property */
```

How to set side borders

```
border-top: 2px solid black;
border-right: 4px double blue;
```

How to set the widths of borders

```
border-width: 1px;              /* all four sides */
border-width: 1px 2px;          /* top and bottom 1px, right and left 2px */
border-width: 1px 2px 2px;      /* top 1px, right and left 2px, bottom 2px */
border-width: 1px 2px 2px 3px;  /* top 1px, right 2px, bottom 2px, left 3px */
```

How to set the style of borders

```
border-style: dashed;      /* dashed line all sides */
border-style: solid none;  /* solid top and bottom, no border right and left */
```

How to set the color of borders

```
border-color: #808080;
border-color: black gray;  /* black top and bottom, gray right and left */
```

How to set the width, style, and color of border sides

```
border-bottom-width: 4px;
border-right-style: dashed;
border-left-color: gray;
```

Figure 5-9 How to set borders

How to use CSS3 to add rounded corners and shadows to borders

Figure 5-10 shows how to use the CSS3 features for adding *rounded corners* and *shadows* to borders. This lets you supply these graphic effects without using images. These features are currently supported by all modern browsers. But if an older browser doesn't support them, it just ignores them, which is usually okay. That's why you can start using these features right away.

To round the corners, you use the border-radius property that's summarized in this figure. If you supply one value for it, it applies to all four corners of the border. But if you supply four values as in the example, you can apply specific rounding to each corner. Here, the upper-left corner has a 10 pixel radius, the upper-right corner has a 20 pixel radius, the lower-right corner has a zero radius so it isn't rounded, and the lower-left corner has a 20 pixel radius.

To add shadows to a border, you use the box-shadow property. This works much like the text-shadow property that you learned about in the last chapter. With the first two values, you specify the offset for the shadow. With the third value, you can specify the blur radius. With the fourth value, you specify how far the blur is spread. And with the fifth value, you can specify a different color for the shadow than the one for the border. To get the effects that you want, you usually need to experiment with these values, but this is easier than using an image to get those effects.

Incidentally, there are some options for these features that aren't presented in this figure. For instance, you can use a separate property like border-top-left- radius for each corner. You can also set the curvature of a corner by supplying two values for a single corner like this:

```
border-top-left-radius: 50px 20px;
```

So, if you want to go beyond what this figure offers, please refer to the W3C documentation.

The syntax for the border-radius and box-shadow properties

```
border-radius: radius;  /* applies to all four corners */
border-radius: topLeft topRight lowerRight lowerLeft;
box-shadow: horizontalOffset verticalOffset blurRadius spread color;
```

The HTML for a section

```
<section>
    <a href="ebooks_index.html">$10 Ebooks!</a>
</section>
```

The CSS for the section

```
section {
    padding: 20px;
    width: 160px;
    border: 5px double blue;
    color: blue;
    font-size: 200%;
    text-align: center;
    font-weight: bold;
    border-radius: 10px 20px 0 20px;
    box-shadow: 3px 3px 4px 4px red;
}
```

The section in a browser

Description

- When you code the border-radius property, you can assign one rounding radius to all four corners or a different radius to each corner.
- When you code the box-shadow property, positive values offset the shadow to the right or down, and negative values offset the shadow to the left or up.
- The third value in the box-shadow property determines how much the shadow is blurred, and the fourth value determines how far the blur is spread.
- The fifth value in the box-shadow property specifies the color of the shadow. If this is omitted, it is the same color as the border.
- These properties are supported by all modern browsers. If they aren't supported by a browser, they are ignored, which is usually okay.

Figure 5-10 How to use CSS3 to add rounded corners and shadows to borders

How to set background colors and images

Figure 5-11 presents the properties you can use to set the *background* for a box. When you set a background, it's displayed behind the content, padding, and border for the box, but it isn't displayed behind the margin.

When you specify a background, you can set a background color, a background image, or both. If you set both, the browser displays the background color behind the image. As a result, you can only see the background color if the image has areas that are transparent or the image doesn't repeat.

As this figure shows, you can set all five properties of a background by using the shorthand background property. When you use this property, you don't have to specify the individual properties in a specific order, but it usually makes sense to use the order that's shown. If you omit one or more properties, the browser uses their default values.

The first set of examples illustrates how this works. Here, the first rule sets the background color to blue, the second rule sets the background color and specifies the URL for an image, and the third rule specifies all five background properties. You can also code each of these properties individually.

By default, the background color for a box is transparent. As a result, you can see through the box to the color that's behind it, which is usually what you want. Otherwise, you need to set the color. The first rule in the second set of examples shows how to do that using the background-color property.

If you want to display a background image, you need to specify a URL that points to the file for the image. You can do that using the background-image property as shown in the second rule in the second set of examples.

If you add a background image to a box, it will repeat horizontally and vertically to fill the box by default. This works well for small images that are intended to be tiled across or down a box. If you want to change this behavior, you can set the background-repeat property so the image is only repeated horizontally, so it's only repeated vertically, or so it isn't repeated at all. This is illustrated by the first four rules in the last set of examples.

If an image doesn't repeat horizontally and vertically, you may need to set additional properties to determine where the image is positioned and whether it scrolls with the page. By default, an image is positioned in the top left corner of the box. To change that, you use the background-position property. This property lets you specify both a horizontal and a vertical position.

The next three rules illustrate how this works. The first rule positions the image at the top left corner of the box, which is the default. The second rule centers the image at the top of the box. And the third rule positions the image starting 90% of the way from the left side to the right side of the box and 90% of the way from the top to the bottom of the box.

In most cases, you'll want a background image to scroll as you scroll the box that contains it. For example, if you use a background image for an entire page and the page is larger than the browser window, you'll usually want the image to scroll as you scroll through the page. If not, you can set the background-attachment property to "fixed".

The properties for setting the background color and image

Property	Description
`background`	Background color, image, repeat, attachment, and position values.
`background-color`	A color value or keyword that specifies the color of an element's background. You can also specify the transparent keyword if you want elements behind the element to be visible. This is the default.
`background-image`	A relative or absolute URL that points to the image. You can also specify the keyword none if you don't want to display an image. This is the default.
`background-repeat`	A keyword that specifies if and how an image is repeated. Possible values are repeat, repeat-x, repeat-y, and no-repeat. The default is repeat, which causes the image to be repeated both horizontally and vertically to fill the background.
`background-attachment`	A keyword that specifies whether an image scrolls with the document or remains in a fixed position. Possible values are scroll and fixed. The default is scroll.
`background-position`	One or two relative or absolute values or keywords that specify the initial horizontal and vertical positions of an image. Keywords are left, center, and right; top, center, and bottom. If a vertical position isn't specified, center is the default. If no position is specified, the default is to place the image at the top-left corner of the element.

The syntax for the shorthand background property

```
background: [color] [image] [repeat] [attachment] [position];
```

How to use the shorthand property

```
background: blue;
background: blue url("../images/texture.gif");
background: #808080 url("../images/header.jpg") repeat-y scroll center top;
```

How to set the background color and image with separate properties

```
background-color: blue;
background-image: url("../images/texture.gif");
```

How to control image repetition, position, and scrolling

```
background-repeat: repeat;          /* repeats both directions */
background-repeat: repeat-x;        /* repeats horizontally */
background-repeat: repeat-y;        /* repeats vertically */
background-repeat: no-repeat;       /* doesn't repeat */

background-position: left top;      /* 0% from left, 0% from top */
background-position: center top;    /* centered horizontally, 0% from top */
background-position: 90% 90%;       /* 90% from left, 90% from top */

background-attachment: scroll;      /* image moves as you scroll */
background-attachment: fixed;       /* image does not move as you scroll */
```

Accessibility guideline

- Don't use a background color or image that makes the text that's over it difficult to read.

Figure 5-11 How to set background colors and images

How to use CSS3 to set background gradients

Figure 5-12 shows the basics of how to use the CSS3 feature for *linear gradients*. Here again, this feature lets you provide interesting backgrounds without using images. And if a browser doesn't support this feature, it just ignores it, which is usually okay.

At present, all modern browsers provide at least basic support for this feature. Except for Internet Explorer, though, the browsers support this feature with properties that are prefixed by -webkit- for Safari and Chrome, -moz- for Firefox, and -o- for Opera. Eventually, though, these prefixes will be dropped. For simplicity, the examples in this figure only use the -webkit- prefix.

If you study the examples in this figure, you'll start to see how this feature works. In the first example, the color goes from left to right; the first color is white starting at the far left (0%), and the second color is red ending at the far right (100%). Then, CSS provides the gradient from left to right when the page is rendered.

In the second example, the direction is 45 degrees and there are three color groups. Red starts at the far left (0%). White is in the middle (50%). And blue is on the right (100%). Then, CSS provides the gradients when the page is rendered.

In the third coding example, after the browser display, you can see how to code solid stripes. Here, both a starting and ending point is given for each color. The result is three solid stripes of red, white, and blue at a 45 degree angle.

If you experiment with this feature, you'll see the interesting effects that you can get with it. But you can take this feature even further. For complete details, please refer to the W3C documentation.

The syntax for using a linear gradient in the background-image property

```
background-image:
    linear-gradient(direction, color %, color %, ... );
```

The HTML for two divisions

```
<div id="eg1"></div>
<div id="eg2"></div>
```

The CSS for the two divisions using Chrome prefixes (-webkit-)

```
#eg1 {
    background-image: -webkit-linear-gradient(
        to right, white 0%, red 100%); }
#eg2 {
    background-image: -webkit-linear-gradient(
        45deg, red 0%, white 50%, blue 100%); }
```

The linear gradients in a browser

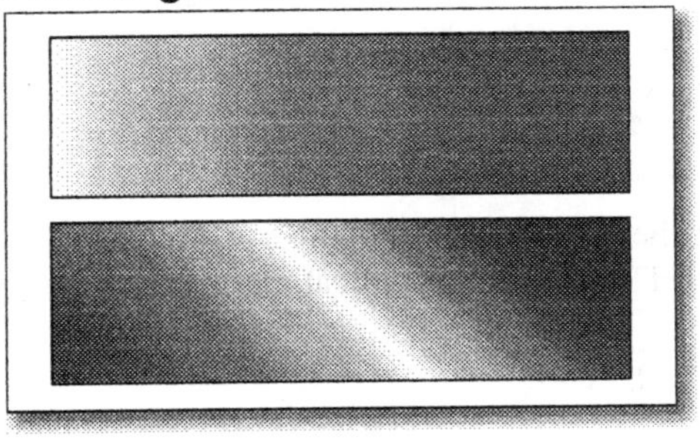

A background-image property that creates red, white, and blue stripes

```
background-image:
   -webkit-linear-gradient(45deg, red 0%, red 33%, white 33%, white 66%,
                           blue 66%, blue 100%);
```

Discussion

- The CSS3 for *linear gradients* lets you create gradients for backgrounds without using images.
- Today, all of the modern browsers provide some support for linear gradients. Except for Internet Explorer, though, they implement them with their own prefixes: -webkit- for WebKit browsers like Chrome and Safari, -moz- for Mozilla Firefox, and -o- for Opera. Later, when the final CSS3 specification is set, these prefixes will be removed.
- The first parameter of a linear gradient indicates the direction the gradient will go: "to right" for left to right, "to bottom" for top to bottom, "to left" for right to left, "to top" for bottom to top, and a number of degrees if the gradient should be on an angle.
- The direction is followed by two or more parameters that consist of a color and a percent. The first percent indicates where the first color should start, the last percent indicates where the last color should end, and the percents in between indicate the points at which one gradient stops and the next one starts.

Figure 5-12 How to use CSS3 to set background gradients

A web page that uses borders and backgrounds

Figure 5-13 presents a web page that's similar to the one in figure 5-6. In fact, the HTML for these two pages is identical. However, the page in this figure has some additional formatting.

First, this page uses a gradient for the background behind the body. It also uses white as the background color for the body. That way, the gradient doesn't show behind the body content.

Second, this page has a border around the body with rounded corners and shadows. Also, the header has a border below it, and the footer has a border above it.

Third, the shadow for the text in the h1 element of the heading has been adjusted so the shadow is black and there is no blur. This makes this heading easier to read.

The HTML for the web page

The HTML is identical to the HTML for the page shown in figure 5-6. If you want to review this HTML, you can open the HTML for this application in your text editor.

A web page that uses borders and a background gradient

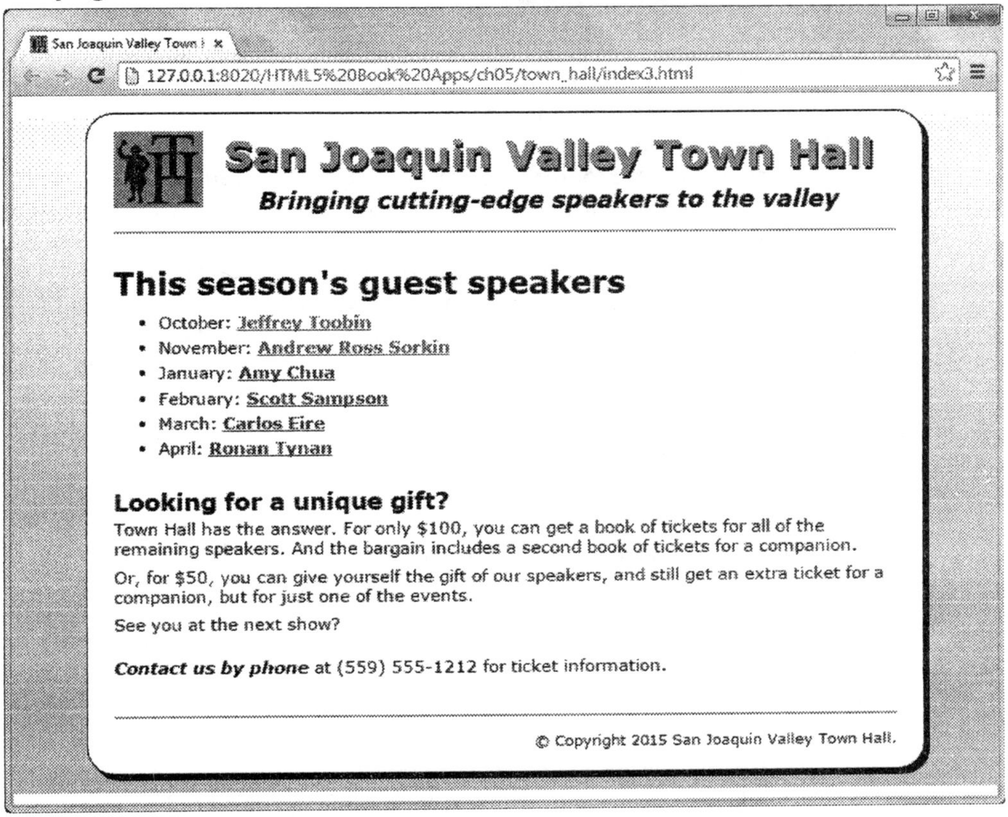

Description

- The HTML for this web page is the same as for figure 5-6.
- The styles for this web page include a border around the page content, a border below the header, and a border above the footer. The border around the body of the page has rounded corners and a drop shadow.
- The background behind the body is a linear gradient. If you use a browser that doesn't support linear gradients, it will be ignored.

Figure 5-13 A web page that uses borders and a linear gradient for the background

The CSS for the web page

Figure 5-14 presents the CSS for the web page in figure 5-13. In this case, I've highlighted the rules that are different from the ones in figure 5-7. Although you should be able to understand this code without any help, here are some points that you should note.

First, a gradient is used for the background image of the html element. This is the gradient that you see on the top, bottom, and sides of the body element. To make this work in all browsers, the gradient is coded four times: one time each for the -webkit-, -moz-, and -o- prefixes, and one time without a prefix. When this rule set is rendered by a browser, the browser will ignore any rules that it doesn't recognize and render the first rule that it does recognize. When all of the browsers drop their prefixes, the last rule is the one that the browsers will execute.

Second, the background color of the body of the document is set to white. That way, the contents of the page will be displayed on a white background. Also, the top and bottom margins for the body are set to 1 em, which lets the gradient show above and below the body, and the right and left margins are set to auto, which centers the body in the browser window. Next, the top and bottom padding for the body is set to 1 em and the left and right padding is set to 1.5 ems. Then, a border with rounded corners and a shadow is added to the body.

Third, a border has been added below the header and above the footer. For the footer, the top margin is 2 ems, which is the space above the border, and top padding is .7 ems, which is the space between the border and the paragraph below it.

Last, the text-shadow property for the header h2 selector has been changed so there is no blur and the shadow is black. If you compare this heading in figure 5-13 with the one in figure 5-6, I think you'll agree that it's easier to read.

The CSS for the web page

```
/* the styles that provide the background behind the body */
html {
    background-image: -webkit-linear-gradient(
        to bottom, white 0%, #facd8a 100%);
    background-image: -moz-linear-gradient(to bottom, white 0%, #facd8a 100%);
    background-image: -o-linear-gradient(to bottom, white 0%, #facd8a 100%);
    background-image: linear-gradient(to bottom, white 0%, #facd8a 100%);
}
body {
    font-family: Verdana, Arial, Helvetica, sans-serif;
    font-size: 100%;
    width: 700px;
    background-color: white;
    margin: 15px auto;
    padding: 15px 1.5em;
    border: 1px solid black;
    border-radius: 25px;
    box-shadow: 5px 5px 0 0;
}

/* the styles for the other type selectors are the same as in figure 5-7 */

/* the styles for the header */
header {
    padding-bottom: 1em;
    border-bottom: 2px solid #f2972e; }
header img { float: left; }
header h2 {
    font-size: 220%;
    color: #f2972e;
    text-align: center;
    text-shadow: 2px 3px 0 black;
    margin-bottom: .25em; }
header h3 {
    font-size: 130%;
    font-style: italic;
    text-align: center; }

/* the styles for the main content */
main { clear: left; }
main h1 {
    font-size: 175%;
    margin: 1em 0 .35em; }
main h2 { font-size: 130%; }

#contact_us { margin-top: 1em; }
a.date_passed  { color: gray; }

/* the styles for the footer */
footer {
    margin-top: 2em;
    border-top: 2px solid #f2972e;
    padding-top: .7em; }
footer p {
    font-size: 80%;
    text-align: right; }
```

Figure 5-14 The CSS for the web page

Perspective

Now that you've completed this chapter, you should understand how the box model is used for margins, padding, borders, backgrounds, and background images. As a result, you should be able to get the spacing, borders, and backgrounds for your web pages just the way you want them. Then, in the next chapter, you'll learn how to use CSS for laying out the elements on a page in two- and three-column arrangements with both headers and footers.

Terms

box model
padding
margin
fixed layout
containing block
shorthand property
collapsed margins
reset selector
border
background
rounded corners
shadows
linear gradient

Summary

- The CSS *box model* refers to the box that a browser places around each block element as well as some inline elements. Each box includes the content of the element, plus optional padding, borders, and margins.
- To set the height and width of a content area, you can use absolute measurements like pixels or relative measurements like percents. If you use a percent, the percent applies to the block that contains the box you're formatting.
- You can set the *margins* for all four sides of a box. Because different browsers have different default values for margins, it's good to set the margins explicitly.
- If you specify a bottom margin for one element and a top margin for the element that follows, the margins are *collapsed* to the size of the largest margin.
- Like margins, you can set the *padding* for all four sides of a box. One way to avoid margin collapse is to set the margins to zero and use padding for the spacing.
- A *border* can be placed on any of the sides of a box. That border goes on the outside of the padding for the box and inside any margins, and you can set the width, style, and color for a border.
- When you set the *background* for a box, it is displayed behind the content, padding, and border for the box, but not behind the margins. The background can consist of a color, an image, or both.
- You can use CSS3 to *round corners* and add *shadows* to borders. You can also use CSS3 to provide *linear gradients* as backgrounds.

Exercise 5-1 Enhance the Town Hall home page

In this exercise, you'll enhance the formatting of the Town Hall home page that you formatted in exercise 4-1. When you're through, the page should look like this:

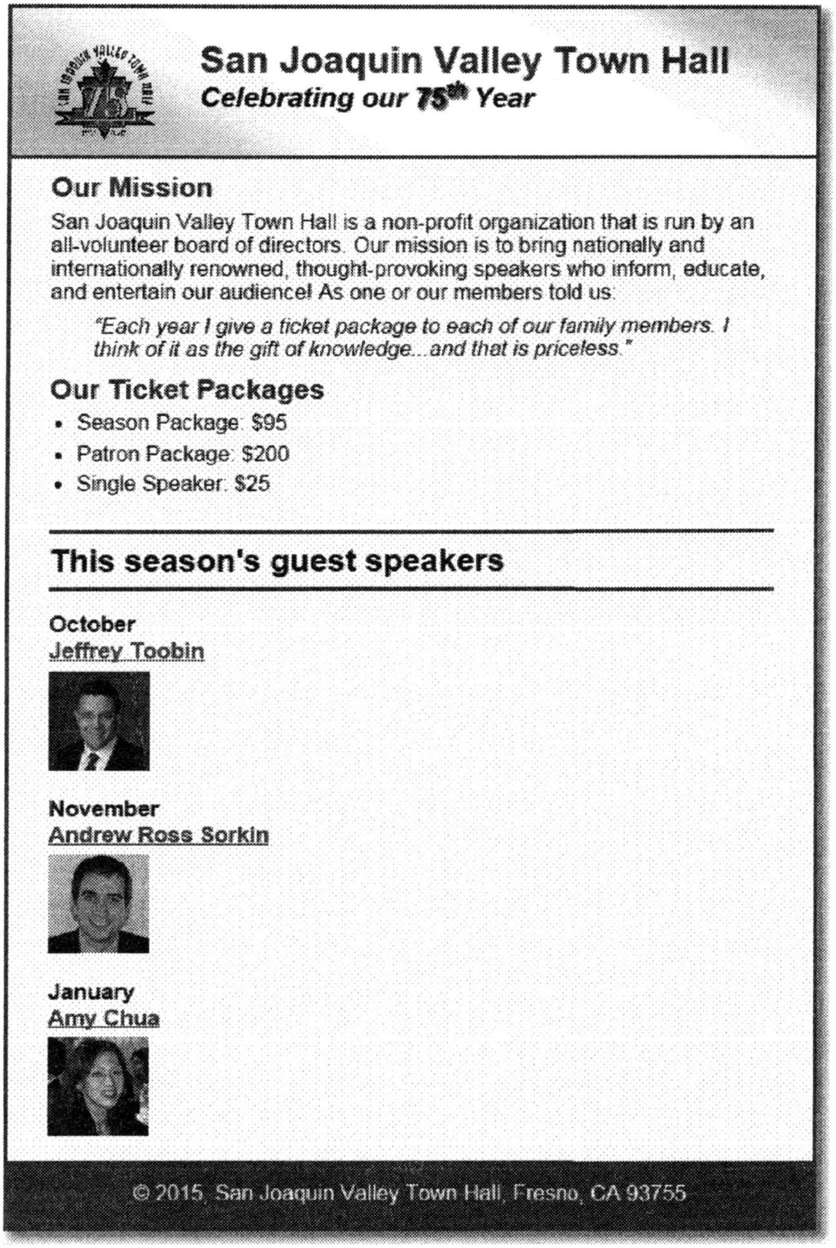

Open the HTML and CSS files and start enhancing the CSS

1. Use your text editor to open the HTML and CSS files that you created for exercise 4-1:

   ```
   c:\html5_css3_2\exercises\town_hall_1\index.html
   c:\html5_css3_2\exercises\town_hall_1\styles\main.css
   ```

2. Enhance the rule set for the body, by setting the width to 600 pixels, setting the top and bottom margins to 0 and the right and left margins to auto, and adding a 3-pixel, solid border with #931420 as its color. Then, test this change in Chrome. If the page isn't centered with a border, make the required corrections.
3. Add one more rule to the body that sets the background color to #fffded. Then, test this change, and note that the entire window is set to the background color, not just the body.
4. To fix this, code a rule set for the html element that sets the background color to white. Then, test to make sure that worked.

Add the other borders and another background color

From this point on, test each change right after you make it. If you have any problems, use the developer tools as shown in figure 8-11 to help you debug them.

5. Add a bottom border to the header that's the same as the border around the body.
6. Add top and bottom borders to the h1 heading in the main element. Both borders should be the same as the borders for the header and footer.
7. Set the background color of the footer to the same color as the borders, and then set the font color for the paragraph in the footer to white so it's easier to read.

Get the padding right for the header, section, and footer

At this point, you have all of the borders and colors the way they should be, so you just need to set the margins and padding. In the steps that follow, you'll start by adding a reset selector to the CSS file. Then, with one exception, you'll use padding to get the spacing right.

8. Add a reset selector like the one in figure 5-8 to the CSS file. When you test this change, the page won't look good at all because the default margins and padding for all of the elements have been removed.
9. For the header, add 1.5 ems of padding at the top and 2 ems of padding at the bottom. Then, delete the text-indent rules for the h2 and h3 elements in the header, and add 30 pixels of padding to the right and left of the image in the header. When you test these changes, you'll see that the heading looks much better.
10. For the main element, add 30 pixels of padding to the right and left.

Get the padding right for the headings and text

11. In the main element, set the padding for the headings and text as follows:

Element	Padding
h1	.3em top and bottom
h2	.5em top, .25em bottom
h3	.25em bottom
img	1em bottom
p	.5em bottom
blockquote	2em right and left
ul	.25em bottom, 1.25em left
li	.35em bottom

12. Set the padding for the top and bottom of the paragraph in the footer to 1em.
13. Test these changes. At this point, all of the spacing should look right.

Add the finishing touches and test in IE

14. Italicize the blockquote element to make it stand out.
15. Add a linear gradient as the background for the header. The one that's shown uses #f6bb73 at 0%, #f6bb73 at 30%, white at 50%, #f6bb73 at 80%, and #f6bb73 at 100% as its five colors at a 30 degree angle. But experiment with this until you get it the way you want it.
16. Do one final test to make sure that the page looks like the one at the start of this exercise. Then, experiment on your own to see if you can improve the formatting. For instance, you may want to add some space between the author names and their images.
17. When you're through experimenting, test the page in IE. If you see any problems, fix them and test again in both Chrome and IE.

Exercise 5-2 Add rounded corners and box shadows to the Speakers heading

Use CSS to add a double border with rounded corners and box shadows to the Speakers heading so it looks like this:

This should work in both Chrome and IE.

6

How to use CSS for page layout

In this chapter, you'll learn how to use CSS to control the layout of a page. That means that you can control where each of the HTML elements appear on the page. When you finish this chapter, you should be able to implement sophisticated 2- and 3-column page layouts.

How to float elements in 2- and 3-column layouts

To create a page layout with two or three columns, you usually float the elements that make up the columns of the page. You'll learn how to do that in the topics that follow.

How to float and clear elements

By default, the block elements defined in an HTML document flow from the top of the page to the bottom of the page, and inline elements flow from the left side of the block elements that contain them to the right side. When you *float* an element, though, it's taken out of the flow of the document. Because of that, any elements that follow the floated element flow into the space that's left by the floated element.

Figure 6-1 presents the basic skills for floating an element on a web page. To do that, you use the float property to specify whether you want the element floated to the left or to the right. You also have to set the width of the floated element. In the example, the aside is 150 pixels wide, and it is floated to the right. As a result, the main element that follows flows into the space to the left of the aside.

Although you can use the float property with any block element, you can also use it with some inline elements. In chapter 4, for example, you learned how to float an image in the header of a document. When you float an img element, you don't have to set the width property because an image always has a default size.

By default, any content that follows a floated element in an HTML document will fill in the space to the side of the floated element. That includes block elements as well as inline elements.

However, if you want to stop the flow of elements into the space beside a floated element, you can use the clear property. In this example, this property is used to stop the footer from flowing into the space next to the aside. The value for this property can be left, right, or both, and either right or both will work if the element ahead of it is floated to the right. Similarly, left or both will work if the element ahead of it is floated to the left.

The properties for floating and clearing elements

Property	Description
float	A keyword that determines how an element is floated. Possible values are left, right, and none. None is the default.
clear	Determines whether an element is cleared from flowing into the space left by a floated element. Possible values are left, right, both, and none (the default).

The HTML for a web page with a sidebar

```
<body>
    <aside>
        <p>The luncheon starts 15 minutes after the lecture ends</p>
    </aside>
    <main>
        <p>Welcome to San Joaquin Valley Town Hall. We have some fascinating
           speakers for you this season!</p>
    </main>
    <footer>
        <p>Please call today at (559) 555-1212 to get your tickets!</p>
    </footer>
</body>
```

The CSS for the web page for floating the sidebar

```
body { width: 500px; }
main, aside, footer {
    margin: 0;
    padding: 0px 20px; }
aside {
    margin: 0 20px 10px;
    width: 150px;
    float: right;
    border: 1px solid black; }
footer { clear: both; }
```

The web page in a browser

Description

- When you *float* an element to the right or left, the content that follows flows around it.
- When you use the float property for an element, you also need to set its width.
- To stop the floating before an element, use the clear property.
- In the example above, if the clear property for the footer isn't set, its content will flow into the space beside the floated element.

Figure 6-1 How to float and clear elements

How to use floating in a 2-column, fixed-width layout

Figure 6-2 shows how floating can be used to create a 2-column, fixed-width page layout. Here, the HTML consists of four elements: header, main, aside, and footer.

In the CSS, you can see that the width is set for the body, main, and aside elements. Here, the width of the body must be the sum of the widths of the main and aside elements, plus the widths of any margins, padding, or borders for the main and aside elements. Since the right border for the main element is 2 pixels and neither the main nor aside elements have margins or padding, the width of the body is 962 pixels (360 + 600 + 2).

After you set up the widths for the body and columns, you create the columns by floating the main element to the left and the aside element to the right. This will work whether the main or aside element is coded first in the HTML.

Another alternative is to float both the main and aside elements to the left. But then, the main element must come first in the HTML. In that case, though, the aside doesn't need to be floated at all. That's because the natural behavior of the aside is to flow into the space left by the floated main element that's ahead of it in the HTML.

A 2-column web page with fixed-width columns

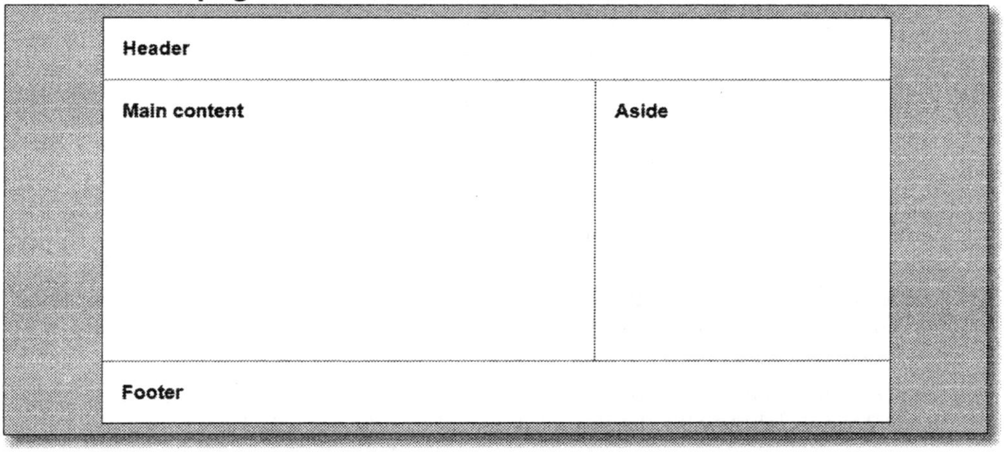

The HTML for the page

```
<body>
    <header><h2>Header</h2></header>
    <main><h2>Main content</h2></main>
    <aside><h2>Aside</h2></aside>
    <footer><h2>Footer</h2></footer>
</body>
```

The CSS for the page

```
* { margin: 0; padding: 0; }
body {
    width: 962px;
    background-color: white;
    margin: 15px auto;
    border: 1px solid black; }
h2 { padding: 1em; }

header { border-bottom: 2px solid #ef9c00; }
main {
    height: 350px;      /* to give the sidebar some height for its border */
    width: 600px;
    float: left;
    border-right: 2px solid #ef9c00; }
aside {
    width: 360px;
    float: right; }
footer {
    clear: both;
    border-top: 2px solid #ef9c00; }
```

Description

- The main element is floated to the left and the aside is floated to the right. Then, it doesn't matter whether the aside comes before or after the main element in the HTML.
- Another alternative is to float both the main element and the aside to the left, but then the main element has to be coded before the aside in the HTML.

Figure 6-2 How to use floating in a 2-column, fixed-width layout

How to use floating in a 2-column, fluid layout

Instead of creating a *fixed layout* like the one in figure 6-2, you can create a *fluid layout*. With a fluid layout, the width of the page changes as the user changes the width of the browser window. Also, the width of one or more columns within the page changes.

The key to creating a liquid layout is using percents to specify the widths. This is illustrated by figure 6-3. In both of these examples, the width of the page is set to 90%. That means that the page will always occupy 90% of the browser window, no matter how wide the window is. Of course, you can omit the width property entirely if you want the page to occupy 100% of the browser window.

In the first example, the widths of the main and aside elements are set to percents. This means that the widths of both columns will change if the user changes the width of the browser window. In this case, since the main element has a 2-pixel right border, the sum of the widths of the main and aside elements is 99%, not 100%. However, if there wasn't a border, the sum could be 100%.

In the second example, the width of the aside element is set to 360 pixels and no width is specified for the main element. This means that only the width of the main element will change if the user changes the width of the browser window. In this case, the border is applied to the left of the aside element rather than to the right of the main element because it's the width of the aside element that's fixed.

As you decide whether to use a fixed or a fluid layout, your main consideration should be the content of the page. If the page consists of a lot of text, you probably won't want to use a fluid layout. That's because a page becomes more difficult to read as the length of a line of text gets longer. On the other hand, if you want the users to be able to use their browsers to increase the size of the text on a page, you might want to use a fluid layout. Then, the users can adjust the size of their browser windows to get the optimal line length for reading.

You may also want to use a fluid layout if you're designing a website for use on mobile devices. That way, the width of the page will change automatically depending on the screen width of the device. Keep in mind, though that this is just one part of developing pages for mobile sites. In chapter 8, you'll learn all the skills you need to develop responsive sites using a technique called Responsive Web Design.

A 2-column web page with fluid widths for both columns

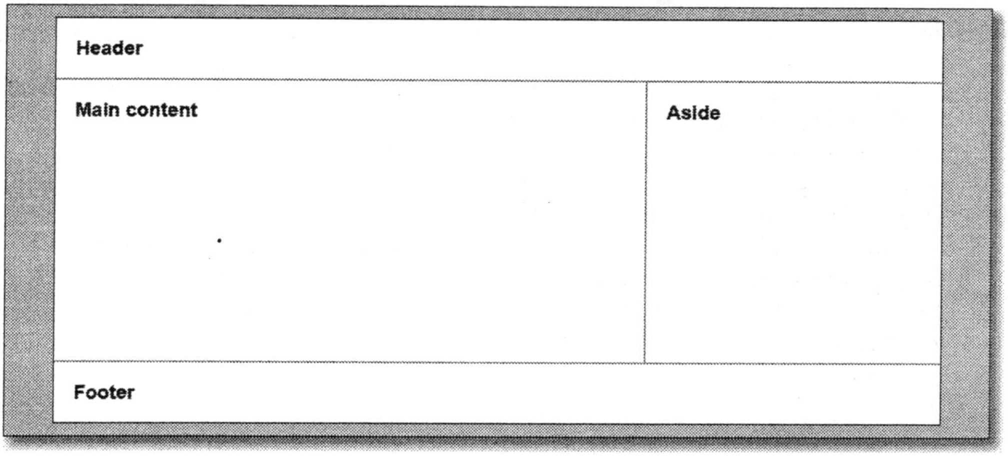

The CSS for the page when both columns are fluid

```
body {
    width: 90%;
    background-color: white;
    margin: 15px auto;
    border: 1px solid black; }
main {
    width: 66%;
    height: 350px;          /* to give the main content some height */
    border-right: 2px solid #ef9c00;
    float: left; }
aside {
    width: 33%;
    float: right; }
```

The CSS for the page when the aside is fixed and the section is fluid

```
body {
    width: 90%;
    background-color: white;
    margin: 15px auto;
    border: 1px solid black; }
main {
    float: left; }
aside {
    height: 350px;          /* to give the aside some height */
    width: 360px;
    border-left: 2px solid #ef9c00;
    float: right; }
```

Description

- The benefit of using fluid column sizes is that the size of the page is adjusted to the resolution of the browser.
- The disadvantage is that changing the size of the columns may affect the typography or the appearance of the page.

Figure 6-3 How to use floating in a 2-column fluid layout

How to use floating in a 3-column, fixed-width layout

Figure 6-4 shows how to take floating to one more level and thus create a 3-column, fixed-width page layout. Here, the width of the body is 964 pixels, which is the sum of the two sidebars, the main content, and the two sidebar borders. Once those widths are set up, the first sidebar is floated to the left. The main content is floated to the left. And the second sidebar is floated to the right.

One of the keys here is getting the widths right. If, for example, you set the body width to 960 pixels instead of 964 pixels, the two sidebars and the main content won't fit into the width of the body. In that case, the main content will flow beneath the left sidebar.

A 3-column web page with fixed-width columns

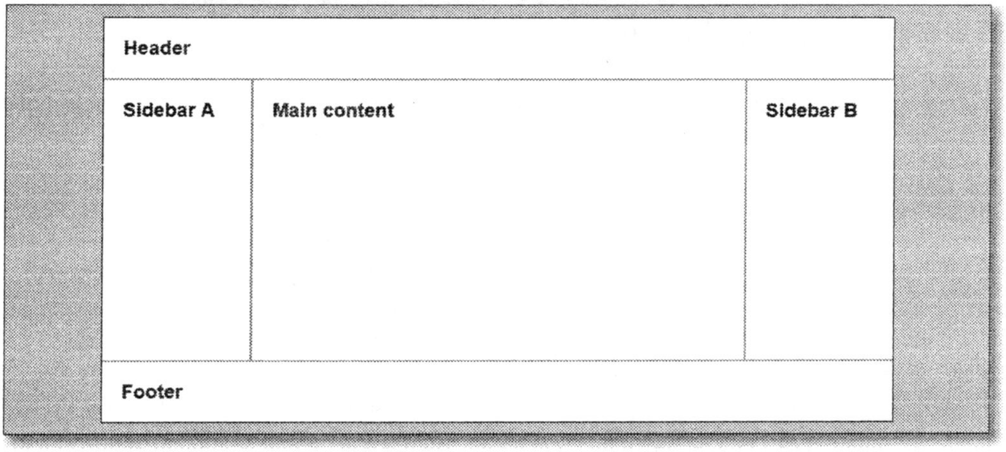

The HTML for the page

```
<body>
    <header><h2>Header</h2></header>
    <aside id="sidebarA"><h2>Sidebar A</h2></aside>
    <main><h2>Main content</h2></main>
    <aside id="sidebarB"><h2>Sidebar B</h2></aside>
    <footer><h2>Footer</h2></footer>
</body>
```

The critical CSS for the page

```
body {
    width: 964px;
    background-color: white;
    margin: 15px auto;
    border: 1px solid black; }
#sidebarA {
    width: 180px;
    height: 350px;     /* to give the sidebar some height for its border */
    float: left;
    border-right: 2px solid #ef9c00; }
main {
    width: 600px;
    float: left; }
#sidebarB {
    width: 180px;
    height: 350px;     /* to give the sidebar some height for its border */
    float: right;
    border-left: 2px solid #ef9c00; }
```

Description

- The first aside is floated to the left; the main content is floated to the left; and the second aside is floated to the right.
- You could get the same result by floating both asides and the main content to the left.

Figure 6-4 How to use floating in a 3-column, fixed-width layout

Two web pages that use a 2-column, fixed-width layout

To show how floating works in a more realistic application, the next topics present two pages of a web site along with their HTML and CSS.

The home page

Figure 6-5 shows the home page for the Town Hall web site. It uses a 2-column, fixed-width layout. Except for the aside, this is the same content that you saw in the page at the end of the last chapter. It's just formatted a little differently.

Note here that instead of using a border to separate the two columns on this page, a background color is applied to the aside. This adds some visual interest to the page, and it saves you from having to set the height of either of the columns.

A home page with a sidebar floated to the right of a section

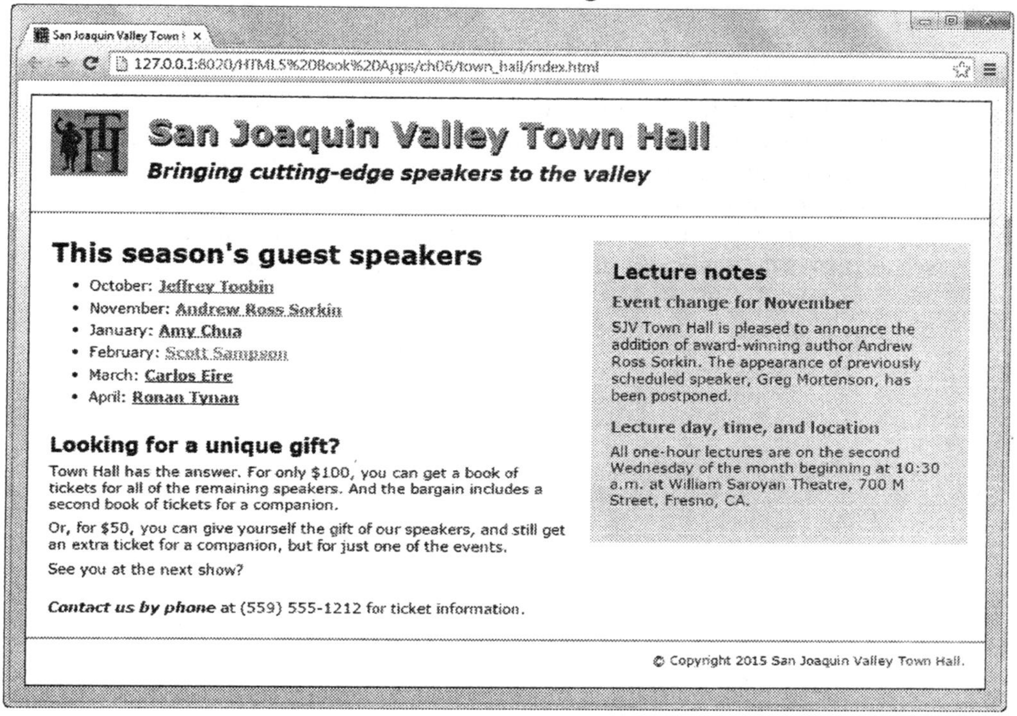

Description

- This web page illustrates a common page layout that includes a header, two columns, and a footer.
- The columns for this page are coded as a section element and an aside element within a main element.
- The columns are created by floating the aside element to the right so the section element that follows it in the HTML flows to its left.
- The image in the heading is floated to the left so it appears to the left of the h2 and h3 elements that follow it.
- A bottom border is applied to the header, and a top border is applied to the footer. The page is formatted so these borders extend to the left and right borders for the body of the page.
- Instead of using a border to separate the two columns, this page uses a background color for the portion of the aside with content. That way, you don't have to worry about which column is longer like you do if you use a border.

Figure 6-5 A 2-column, fixed-width home page

The HTML for the home page

Figure 6-6 presents the HTML for this web page. Here, the only new content is in the aside. Note that the aside is coded before the section. Then, if the aside is floated to the right, the section will flow beside it.

Before looking at the CSS, take a minute to note the use of the HTML5 semantic elements. The header and footer start and end the HTML and the remaining content of the page is coded within a main element. The aside and section provide the content for the two columns. And the nav element within the section marks the navigation list. That helps make this code easy to understand.

The HTML for the home page (index.html)

```
<head>
    .
    <link rel="stylesheet" href="styles/normalize.css">
    <link rel="stylesheet" href="styles/main.css">
</head>
<body>
    <header>
        <img src="images/logo.jpg" alt="Town Hall Logo" width="80">
        <h2>San Joaquin Valley Town Hall</h2>
        <h3>Bringing cutting-edge speakers to the valley</h3>
    </header>
    <main>
        <aside>
            <h2>Lecture notes</h2>
            <h3>Event change for November</h3>
            <p>SJV Town Hall is pleased to announce the addition of award-
               winning author Andrew Ross Sorkin. The appearance of previously
               scheduled speaker, Greg Mortenson, has been postponed.</p>
            <h3>Lecture day, time, and location</h3>
            <p class="news_item">All one-hour lectures are on the second
               Wednesday of the month beginning at 10:30 a.m. at William
               Saroyan Theatre, 700 M Street, Fresno, CA.</p>
        </aside>
        <section>
            <h1>This season's guest speakers</h1>
            <nav>
                <ul>
                    <li>October: <a class="date_passed"
                        href="speakers/toobin.html">Jeffrey Toobin</a></li>
                    .
                    .
                    <li>March: <a href="speakers/eire.html">
                        Carlos Eire</a></li>
                    <li>April: <a href="speakers/tynan.html">
                        Ronan Tynan</a></li>
                </ul>
            </nav>
            <h2>Looking for a unique gift?</h2>
            <p>Town Hall has the answer. For only $100, you can get
               a book of tickets for all of the remaining speakers. And the
               bargain includes a second book of tickets for a companion.</p>
            <p>Or, for $50, you can give yourself the gift of our speakers,
               and still get an extra ticket for a companion, but for just one
               of the events.</p>
            <p>See you at the next show?</p>
            <p id="contact_us"><em>Contact us by phone</em> at (559) 555-1212
               for ticket information.</p>
        </section>
    </main>
    <footer>
        <p>&copy; Copyright 2015 San Joaquin Valley Town Hall.</p>
    </footer>
</body>
</html>
```

Figure 6-6 The HTML for the home page

The CSS for the home page

Figure 6-7 presents the CSS for this web page. Since you've already seen code like this in the earlier figures, you shouldn't have much trouble following it. But here are a few highlights.

First, the width of the body is set to 992 pixels, but the width of the section is set to 535 pixels and the width of the aside is set to 350 pixels, or a total of 885 pixels. The other 107 pixels come from the left and right borders for the body (2 pixels), the left margin for the section (20 pixels), the right padding for the section (25 pixels), the left and right padding for the aside (40 pixels), and the right margin for the aside (20 pixels).

Second, the left margins of the h2 and h3 elements in the header are set to 120 pixels instead of being centered as they were in previous examples. This sets them to the right of the image in the header, which has been floated to the left.

The CSS for the home page (main.css) Page 1

```
/* type selectors */
html {
    background-image: -moz-linear-gradient(to bottom, white 0%, #facd8a 100%);
    background-image: -webkit-linear-gradient(
        to bottom, white 0%, #facd8a 100%);
    background-image: -o-linear-gradient(to bottom, white 0%, #facd8a 100%);
    background-image: linear-gradient(to bottom, white 0%, #facd8a 100%);    }
body {
    font-family: Verdana, Arial, Helvetica, sans-serif;
    font-size: 100%;
    width: 990px;
    background-color: white;
    margin: 15px auto;
    padding: 15px 0;
    border: 1px solid black; } /* no border radius or box shadow */
section, aside, h1, h2, h3, p {
    margin: 0;
    padding: 0; }
section, aside {
    margin-top: 1.5em;
    margin-bottom: 1em; }

a { font-weight: bold; }
a:link { color: #931420; }
a:visited { color: #f2972e; }
a:hover, a:focus { color: blue; }

ul {
    margin-top: 0;
    margin-bottom: 1.5em; }
li {
    font-size: 95%;
    padding-bottom: .35em; }
p {
    font-size: 95%;
    padding-bottom: .5em; }
em { font-weight: bold; }

/* the styles for the header */
header {
    padding-bottom: 2em;
    border-bottom: 2px solid #f2972e; }
header img {
    float: left;
    margin-left: 20px; }
header h2 {
    font-size: 220%;
    color: #f2972e;
    text-shadow: 2px 3px 0 black;
    margin-left: 120px;
    margin-bottom:.25em; }
header h3 {
    font-size: 130%;
    font-style: italic;
    margin-left: 120px; }
```

Figure 6-7 The CSS for the home page (part 1 of 2)

Third, both the aside and section are floated to the right, but you could float the section to the left. This would also work if you didn't float the section at all since the aside comes first in the HTML.

Finally, because both the aside and the section are floated, the footer is cleared so it will appear below both columns. Because both the aside and section are floated to the right, I could have coded the clear property with a value of right. In most cases, though, you'll code this property with a value of both so it doesn't matter how the columns are floated.

At this point, you may be wondering why the left margins of the image in the header and the section and the right margins of the aside and the footer paragraph are set to 20 pixels instead of setting the padding for the body as in chapter 5. The answer is that this allows the borders below the header and above the footer to extend to the left and right edges of the border around the body of the page. This is just another visual element of this page.

The CSS for the home page (main.css)

Page 2

```
/* the styles for the section */
section {
    width: 535px;
    margin-left: 20px;
    padding-right: 25px;
    float: right; }
section h1 {
    font-size: 170%;
    margin-bottom: .35em; }
section h2 {
    font-size: 130%;
    margin-bottom: .35em; }

#contact_us { margin-top: 1em; }
a.date_passed  { color: gray; }

/* the styles for the sidebar */
aside {
    width: 350px;
    float: right;
    padding: 20px;
    background-color: #ffebc6;
    margin-right: 20px; }
aside h2 {
    font-size: 130%;
    padding-bottom: .5em; }
aside h3 {
    font-size: 100%;
    color: #931420;
    padding-bottom: .5em; }
aside p { margin-bottom: .5em; }

/* the styles for the footer */
footer {
    clear: both;
    border-top: 2px solid #f2972e;
    padding-top: .7em; }
footer p {
    font-size: 80%;
    text-align: right;
    margin-right: 20px; }
```

Figure 6-7 The CSS for the home page (part 2 of 2)

The speaker page

Figure 6-8 shows the page that's displayed if you click on the fourth link of the home page. This page has the same header and footer as the home page, and it has a 2-column, fixed-width page layout like the one for the home page.

Unlike the home page, though, this page uses an article for the left column instead of a section. This is consistent with HTML5 semantics since the content is an article about the speaker. Within the article, an image of the speaker is floated to the left of the text.

A speaker page with a sidebar floated to the right of an article

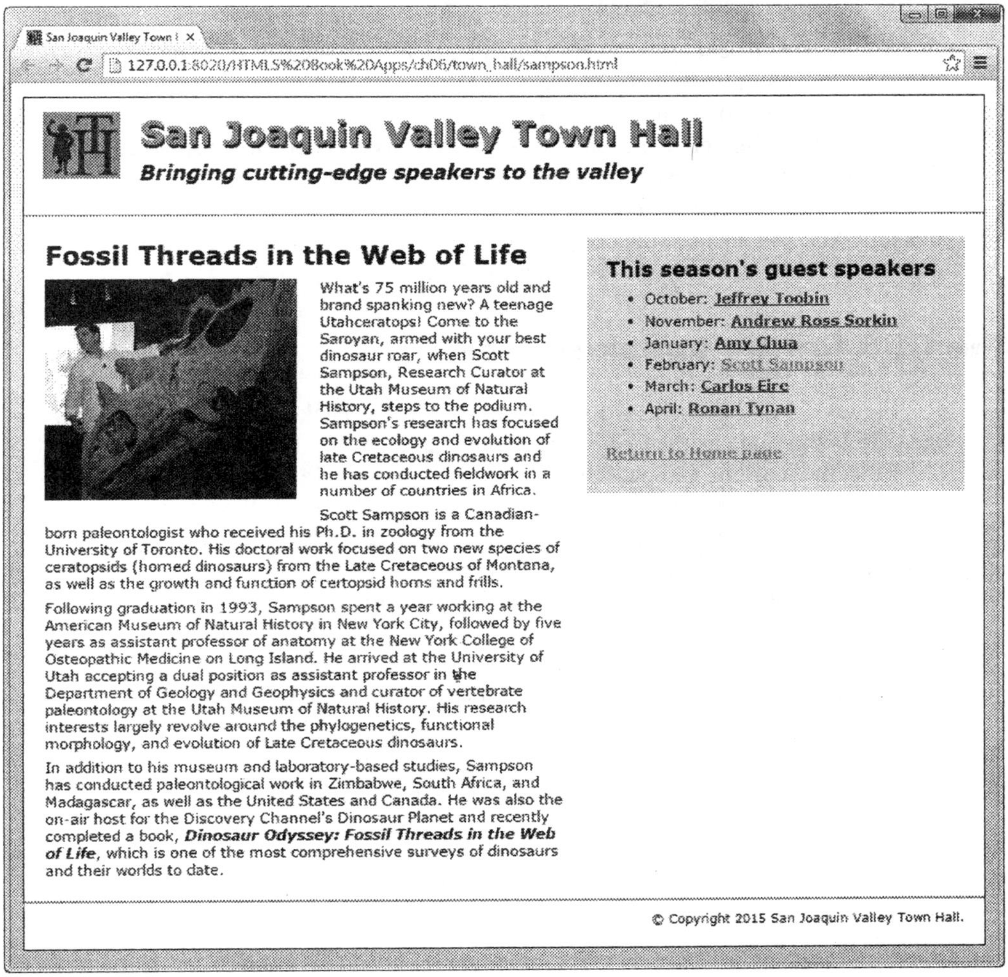

Description

- The columns for this page are coded as an article element and an aside element.
- The columns are created by floating the aside element to the right so the article element that follows it in the HTML flows to its left.
- The image in the article is floated to the left. In the HTML, the image is coded after the h1 element and before the <p> elements that make up the article.
- A background color is applied to the aside to separate it visually from the article.

Figure 6-8 A 2-column, fixed-width speaker page

The HTML for the speaker page

Figure 6-9 presents just the HTML changes for the speaker page. For instance, it doesn't include the header and footer elements because they are the same for the home page and the speaker page.

To start, the link element refers to a different style sheet named speaker.css. This style sheet can be used for all of the speaker pages.

After that, you can see the contents for the aside, which includes a nav element. You can also see the contents for the article, which includes an h1 element, an img element, and several <p> elements.

The CSS for the speaker page

Figure 6-9 also presents the CSS changes for the speaker page. Otherwise, the CSS is the same as the CSS for the home page.

First, the margins and padding are set up for the article and the aside, just as they were for the section and aside of the home page. Then, the article is formatted just like the section of the home page. In addition, though, the img element within the article is floated to the left.

Like the home page, both the aside and article are floated to the right, but you could float the article to the left. This would also work if you didn't float the article at all.

Because the CSS for the home page (main.css) and the CSS for the speaker pages (speaker.css) are so much alike, you could combine the CSS into a single file. Often, though, it's easier to manage the CSS if you keep it in separate files. Then, if you want to modify the CSS for the speaker pages, you don't have to worry about affecting the home page.

The HTML changes for the speaker page (sampson.html)

```
<head>
    .
    <link rel="stylesheet" href="styles/speaker.css">
</head>
<aside>
    <h2>This season's guest speakers</h2>
    <nav>
        <ul>
            <li>October: <a class="date_passed"
                href="speakers/toobin.html">Jeffrey Toobin</a></li>
            .
            .
            <li>April: <a href="speakers/tynan.html">Ronan Tynan</a></li>
        </ul>
        <p><a href="index.html">Return to Home page</a></p>
    </nav>
</aside>
<article>
    <h1>Fossil Threads in the Web of Life</h1>
    <img src="images/sampson_dinosaur.jpg" alt="Scott Sampson" width="260">
    <p>What's 75 million years old and brand spanking new? A teenage
       ...
       ...</p>
    <p>Scott Sampson is a Canadian-born paleontologist who received his
       ...
       ...</p>
    <p>Following graduation in 1993, Sampson spent a year working at the
       ...
       ...</p>
    <p>In addition to his museum and laboratory-based studies, Sampson has
       ...
       ...</p>
</article>
```

The CSS changes for the speaker page (speaker.css)

```
article, aside, h1, h2, p, ul {
    margin: 0;
    padding: 0; }
article, aside {
    margin-top: 1.5em;
    margin-bottom: 1em; }

/* the styles for the article */
article {
    width: 535px;
    margin-left: 20px;
    padding-right: 25px;
    float: right; }
article h1 {
    font-size: 170%;
    margin-bottom: .35em; }
article img {
    float: left;
    margin: 0 1.5em 1em 0; }
```

Figure 6-9 The HTML and CSS for the speaker page

How to use CSS3 to create text columns

So far we've been talking about the columns in a page layout. But CSS3 provides a new feature that makes it easy to create text columns. For instance, you can easily format an article into two or more text columns within a 2- or 3-column page layout.

The CSS3 properties for creating text columns

Figure 6-10 summarizes the properties for creating text columns. For instance, the column-count property automatically formats the text within an article into the number of columns specified. You can use the column-gap property to set the width of the gaps between columns. You can use the column-rule property to set borders within the columns. And you can use the column-span property to cause an element like the heading in this example to span the columns.

Three of these properties are illustrated by the example in this figure. Here, an article is formatted into 3 columns with 35-pixel gaps and 2-pixel rules between the columns. To fit this into this figure, the bottom of the article is truncated, but the entire article is formatted correctly.

The problem with this feature is that only Internet Explorer versions 10 and above support it in its native form. To use it with Chrome, Opera, and Safari, you have to include the properties with the -webkit- prefixes as shown here. And to use it with Firefox, you have to use the -moz- prefix. Note, though, that Firefox doesn't currently support the column-span property even with this prefix. Nevertheless, this is a powerful feature that can easily improve the readability of an article by shortening the line length.

When using this feature, though, you don't want to make the columns too narrow because that can make the text more difficult to read. Also, you don't want to justify the text because that can cause gaps between the words.

The primary CSS3 properties for creating text columns

Property	Description
`column-count`	The number of columns that the text should be divided into.
`column-gap`	The width between the columns. Otherwise, this is set by default.
`column-rule`	Defines a border between columns.
`column-span`	With the value "all", this property can be used to have an element that's a child of an element that's formatted with columns span all of the columns. Not currently supported by Firefox.

3 columns with default-sized gaps

```
article {
    -moz-column-count: 3;
    -webkit-column-count: 3;
    column-count: 3; }
```

3 columns with 35px gaps and 2px rules between the columns

```
article {
    -moz-column-count: 3;
    -webkit-column-count: 3;
    column-count: 3;
    -moz-column-gap: 35px;
    -webkit-column-gap: 35px;
    column-column-gap: 35px;
    -moz-column-rule: 2px solid black;
    -webkit-column-rule: 2px solid black;
    column-rule: 2px solid black; }
```

3 columns with 35px gaps and 2px rules in a browser window

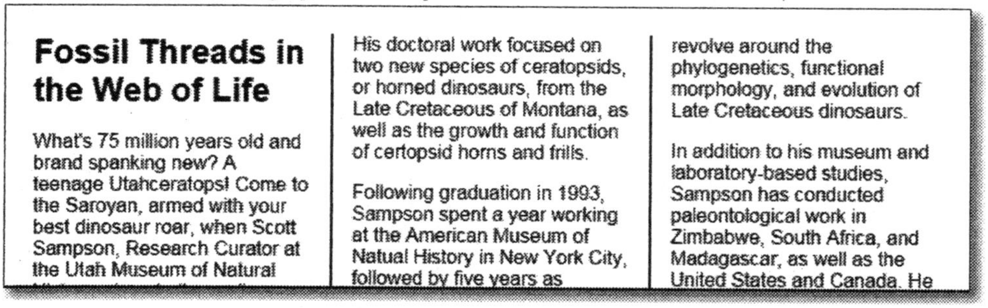

Description

- At this writing, only Internet Explorer versions 10 and above support these properties in their native form. Chrome, Safari, and Opera require the -webkit- prefix. Firefox requires the -moz- prefix, but Firefox doesn't currently support the column-span property.
- If you want the heading of an article to span the columns, you can code the HTML for the heading before the article. Then, you don't have to use the column-span property.
- If the columns are too narrow, an article becomes harder to read.

Figure 6-10 The properties for creating text columns

A 2-column web page with a 2-column article

Figure 6-11 shows how easily this feature can add columns to the article in the speaker page of figure 6-8. It just takes one column-count property, plus the two prefixed versions of it. Then, if a browser doesn't support this property, it just ignores it, so there's no harm done.

Although you might think that you could use the CSS3 column-span property to get the heading to span the columns in this example, that doesn't work. That's because the article that contains the columns is floated, and that somehow interferes with the span. In the future, though, this should work correctly, so you can start using this feature right away. Alternatively, you can code the heading before the article in the HTML.

Incidentally, if you want to float the image that's coded at the start of the text to the right when you use two or more columns, it won't work the way you want. Instead of floating the image in the rightmost column, the browser will float the image in the first column. Although there are ways around this, it's usually best to float the image to the left when you use this feature.

A web page with a two-column article

The CSS for creating the columns

```
article {
    -moz-column-count: 2;
    -webkit-column-count: 2;
    column-count: 2;
}
```

Description

- This shows how easy it is to divide an article in columns.
- If you compare this page with the one in figure 6-8, you can see that this page is easier to read because the lines are shorter, but not too short.
- If a browser doesn't support this feature, the page is displayed as in figure 6-8, which is acceptable.
- If you want the heading in the article to span the columns, you have to code the heading before the article in the HTML. In the future, this should work using the CSS3 column-span property.
- In general, it's best to float an image within the columns area to the left so it will be in the leftmost column. If you float it to the right, the browser will float the image to the right, but in the first column, which usually isn't what you want.

Figure 6-11 A 2-column web page with a 2-column article

How to position elements

Although floating provides an easy way to create pages with two or more columns, you may occasionally need to use other positioning techniques. You'll learn about those techniques in the topics that follow.

Four ways to position an element

To position the elements on a page, you use the properties shown in the first table in figure 6-12. The first property, position, determines the type of positioning that will be used. This property can have four different values as shown in the second table.

The first value, static, is the default. This causes elements to be placed in the normal flow.

The second value, absolute, removes the element from the normal flow and positions it based on the top, bottom, right, and left properties you specify. When you use *absolute positioning*, the element is positioned relative to the closest containing block that is positioned. If no containing block is positioned, the element is positioned relative to the browser window.

The third value, fixed, works like absolute in that the position of the element is specified using the top, bottom, left, and right properties. Instead of being positioned relative to a containing block, however, an element that uses *fixed positioning* is positioned relative to the browser window. That means that the element doesn't move when you scroll through the window.

The fourth value, relative, causes an element to be positioned relative to its normal position in the flow. When you use the top, bottom, left, and right properties with *relative positioning*, they specify the element's offset from its normal position.

One more property you can use to position elements is z-index. This property is useful if an element that you position overlaps another element. In that case, you can use the z-index property to determine which element is on top.

Properties for positioning elements

Property	Description
`position`	A keyword that determines how an element is positioned. See the table below for possible values.
`top, bottom, left, right`	For absolute or fixed positioning, a relative or absolute value that specifies the top, bottom, left, or right position of an element's box. For relative positioning, the top, bottom, left, or right offset of an element's box.
`z-index`	An integer that determines the stack level of an element whose position property is set to absolute, relative, or fixed.

Possible values for the position property

Value	Description
`static`	The element is placed in the normal flow. This is the default.
`absolute`	The element is removed from the flow and is positioned relative to the closest containing block that is also positioned. The position is determined by the top, bottom, left, and right properties.
`fixed`	The element is positioned absolutely relative to the browser window. The position is determined by the top, bottom, left, and right properties.
`relative`	The element is positioned relative to its position in the normal flow. The position is determined by the top, bottom, left, and right properties.

Description

- By default, static positioning is used to position block elements from top to bottom and inline elements from left to right.
- To change the positioning of an element, you can code the position property. In most cases, you also code one or more of the top, bottom, left, and right properties.
- When you use absolute, relative, or fixed positioning for an element, the element can overlap other elements. Then, you can use the z-index property to specify a value that determines the level at which the element is displayed. An element with a higher z-index value is displayed on top of an element with a lower z-index value.

Figure 6-12 Four ways to position an element

How to use absolute positioning

To give you a better idea of how positioning works, figure 6-13 presents an example of absolute positioning. Here, the aside element is positioned absolutely within its containing element, which is the body of the HTML document.

For this to work, the containing element must also be positioned. However, the positioning can be either relative or absolute, and the top, bottom, left, and right properties don't have to be set. Since they aren't set in this example, the body is positioned where it is in the natural flow. In other words, nothing changes. However, because the body is positioned, the elements that it contains can be absolutely positioned within it. In this case, the aside element is positioned 30 pixels from the right side of the body and 50 pixels from the top.

When you use absolute positioning, you typically specify the top or bottom and left or right properties. You also are likely to specify the width or height of the element. However, you can also specify all four of the top, bottom, left, and right properties. Then, the height and width are determined by the difference between the top and bottom and left and right properties.

How to use fixed positioning

Fixed positioning is like absolute positioning except that its positioning is relative to the browser window. So, to change the example in figure 6-13 from absolute positioning to fixed positioning requires just two changes. First, you delete the position property for the body since fixed positioning is relative to the browser window. Second, you change the position property for the aside to fixed.

The benefit of fixed positioning is that the element that's fixed stays there when you scroll down the page. If, for example, the section in this figure was so long that it required scrolling, the aside would stay where it is while the user scrolls.

The HTML for a web page

```
<body>
    <main>
        <h1>Our speakers this season</h1>
        <ul>
            <li>October: <a href="speakers/toobin.html">
                Jeffrey Toobin</a></li>
            <li>November: <a href="speakers/sorkin.html">
                Andrew Ross Sorkin</a></li>
            <li>January: <a href="speakers/chua.html">
                Amy Chua</a></li>
        </ul>
        <p>Please contact us for tickets.</p>
    </main>
    <aside>
        <p><a href="raffle.html">Enter to win a free ticket!</a></p>
    </aside>
</body>
```

The CSS for the web page with absolute positioning

```
p { margin: 0;}
body {
    width: 550px;
    margin: 0 25px 20px;
    border: 1px solid black;
    position: relative; }  /* not needed for fixed positioning */
aside {
    width: 80px;
    padding: 1em;
    border: 1px solid black;
    position: absolute;    /* change to fixed for fixed positioning */
    right: 30px;
    top: 50px; }
```

The web page with absolute positioning in a browser

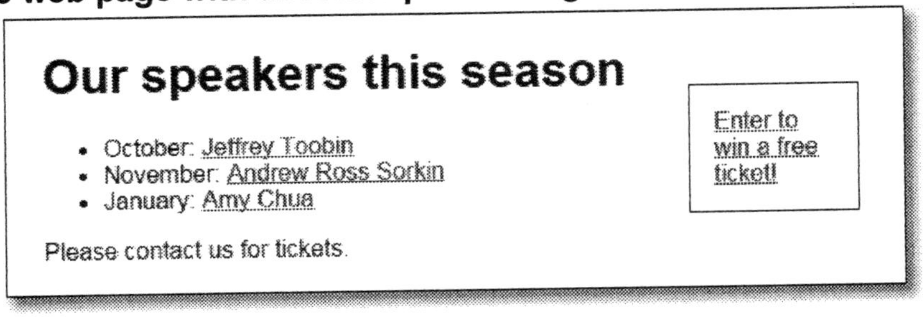

Description

- When you use *absolute positioning*, the remaining elements on the page are positioned as if the element weren't there. As a result, you may need to make room for the positioned element by setting the margins or padding for other elements.
- When you use *fixed positioning* for an element, the positioning applies to the browser window and the element doesn't move even when you scroll.

Figure 6-13 How to use absolute and fixed positioning

A table of contents that uses positioning

Because floating works so well, you won't need to use positioning much. Occasionally, though, it comes in handy.

In figure 6-14, for example, you can see the table of contents for a book that makes good use of positioning. If positioning weren't used, you would have to use a table to display a table of contents like this, which would take more code and be more difficult.

In the HTML for the table of contents, a main element is used as the container for the table of contents. Within this container, h2 elements are used for the sections of the table of contents and h3 elements are used for the chapters. Within the h2 and h3 elements, span elements with "title" as the class name are used to specify the titles of the sections and chapters. And within the h3 elements, span elements with "number" as the class name are used to specify the page numbers of the chapters.

In the CSS for the table of contents, you can see that the h2 and h3 elements are given relative positioning. However, the top, bottom, left, and right properties have been omitted. Because of that, the elements aren't actually offset, but they can be used as containers for absolute positioning. Then, the title and number classes are positioned absolutely within those elements. This indents the titles as shown in the browser display and right aligns the page numbers.

A table of contents that uses absolute positioning

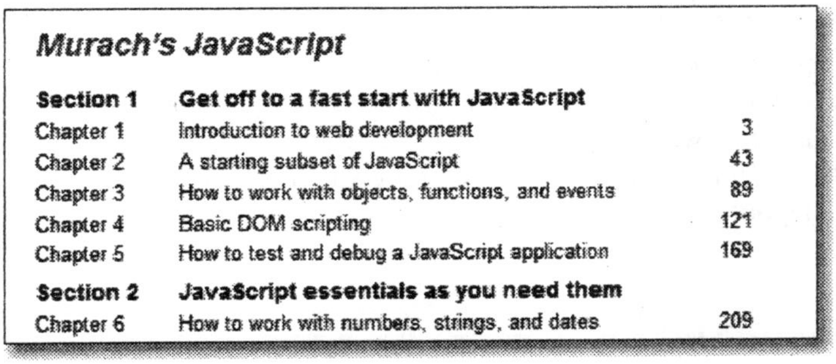

Murach's JavaScript

Section 1	**Get off to a fast start with JavaScript**	
Chapter 1	Introduction to web development	3
Chapter 2	A starting subset of JavaScript	43
Chapter 3	How to work with objects, functions, and events	89
Chapter 4	Basic DOM scripting	121
Chapter 5	How to test and debug a JavaScript application	169
Section 2	**JavaScript essentials as you need them**	
Chapter 6	How to work with numbers, strings, and dates	209

The HTML for the positioned elements

```
<main>
    <h1><i>Murach&rsquo;s JavaScript and DOM Scripting</i></h1>
    <h2>Section 1<span class="title">Introduction to JavaScript
        programming</span></h2>
    <h3>Chapter 1<span class="title">Introduction to web development and
        JavaScript</span><span class="number">3</span></h3>
    <h3>Chapter 2<span class="title">How to code a JavaScript
        application</span><span class="number">43</span></h3>
    ...
    <h2>Section 2<span class="title">JavaScript essentials</span></h2>
    <h3>Chapter 6<span class="title">How to get input and display
        output</span><span class="number">223</span></h3>
    ...
</main>
```

The CSS for the positioned elements

```
main h2 {
    margin: .6em 0 0;
    position: relative; }
main h3 {
    font-weight: normal;
    margin: .3em 0 0;
    position: relative; }
.title {
    position: absolute;
    left: 90px; }
.number {
    position: absolute;
    right: 0; }
```

Description

- To implement absolute positioning, span elements with class names are used to identify the text to be positioned at the left and the page numbers to be positioned at the right.
- The h2 and h3 elements use relative positioning, but no positions are specified. That way, the .title and .number elements that they contain can be positioned relative to the headings.

Figure 6-14 A table of contents that uses positioning

Perspective

Now that you've completed this chapter, you should be able to develop web pages that have headers, footers, and 2- or 3-column layouts. Better yet, you'll be using CSS to do these layouts, which makes these pages easier to create and maintain. In contrast, you'll find that some websites are still using HTML tables to implement page layouts.

Terms

float
fixed layout
fluid layout
absolute positioning
relative positioning
fixed positioning

Summary

- When you use the float property to *float* an element, any elements after the floated element will flow into the space left vacant. To make this work, the floated element has to have a width that's either specified or implied.
- To stop an element from flowing into the space left vacant by a floated element, you can use the clear property.
- In a *fixed layout*, the widths of the columns are set. In a *fluid layout*, the width of the page and the width of at least one column change as the user changes the width of the browser window.
- When you use *absolute positioning* for an element, the remaining elements on the page are positioned as if the element weren't there. Because of that, you may need to make room for positioned elements by adjusting other elements.
- When you use *relative positioning* for an element, the remaining elements leave space for the moved element as if it were still there.
- When you use *fixed positioning* for an element, the element doesn't move in the browser window, even when you scroll.

Exercise 6-1 Enhance the Town Hall home page

In this exercise, you'll enhance the formatting of the Town Hall home page that you formatted in exercise 5-1. When you're through, the page should look like this, but without the Speaker of the Month content:

Open the HTML and CSS files

1. Use your text editor to open the HTML and CSS files that you created for exercise 5-1 or 5-2:

```
c:\html5_css3_2\exercises\town_hall_1\index.html
c:\html5_css3_2\exercises\town_hall_1\styles\main.css
```

Enhance the HTML and CSS to provide for the two columns

2. In the main element of the HTML file, enclose the h2 elements and the elements that follow them up to the h1 element in a section element.

3. Enclose the remaining content of the main element in an aside element. Also, shorten the content of the h1 heading to just "Guest speakers" and change the h1 element to an h2 element now that it's in an aside.
4. Still in the HTML file, add the heading and image for the fourth speaker.
5. In the CSS file, enhance the rule set for the body so the width is 800 pixels. Next, set the width of the section to 525 pixels and float it to the right, and set the width of the aside to 215 pixels and float it to the right. Then, use the clear property in the footer to clear the floating. Last, delete the rule set for the h1 heading. Now, test this. The columns should be starting to take shape.
6. To make this look better, delete the left and right padding for the main element, set the left and bottom padding for the aside to 20 pixels, change the right and left padding for the section to 20 pixels, and set the bottom padding for the section to 20 pixels. Now, test again.
7. To make the CSS easier to read, change the selectors for the main elements so they refer to the section or aside element as appropriate and reorganize these style rules. Be sure to include a rule set for the h2 headings in both the section and aside. Then, test again to be sure you have this right.

Get the headings right

8. Add a rule set for the h3 element in the aside that sets the font size to 105% and the bottom padding to .25 ems.
9. Add a rule set for the img elements in the aside so the bottom padding is set to 1em. Then, test this change.
10. At this point, the page should look good, but it won't include the Speaker of the Month content. Now, make any adjustments, test them in both Chrome and IE, use the developer tools if necessary, and then go on to the next exercise.

Exercise 6-2 Add the Speaker of the Month

In this exercise, you'll add the Speaker of the Month to the home page. Whenever appropriate, test the changes in Chrome.

Enhance the HTML page

1. Copy the content for the speaker of the month from the file named c6_content.txt in the text folder into the HTML file right before the heading for "Our Ticket Packages".
2. Enclose the Speaker of the Month heading in h1 tags, and enclose the rest of the content in an article element.
3. Within the article, enclose the first heading in h2 tags; enclose the second heading (the date and speaker's name) in h3 tags with a <br> tag to provide the line break; and enclose the rest of the text in <p> tags.
4. Add an <a> element within the last paragraph that goes to the sampson.html page in the speakers folder when the user clicks on "Read more." Also, add a non-breaking space and <b> tags so the rest of the line looks right.
5. Add an image element between the h2 and h3 elements in the article, and display the image named sampson_dinosaur.jpg from the images folder.

Enhance the CSS for the home page

6. Add a rule set for the h1 element that sets the font size to 150%, sets the top padding to .5 ems and the bottom padding to .25 ems, and sets the margins to 0. (You need to explicitly set the top and bottom margins of this element to 0 because they're set to .67 ems in the normalize.css style sheet.)
7. Add .5 ems of padding above and below the article. Then, add 2 pixel top and bottom borders to the article with #800000 as the color.
8. Float the image in the article to the right, and set its top, bottom, and left margins so there's adequate space around it. Then, add a 1 pixel, black border to the image so the white in the image doesn't fade into the background.
9. Set the top padding of the h2 element in the article to 0.
10. Set the font size of the h3 element in the article to 105% and set the bottom padding to .25 ems.
11. Make any final adjustments to the margins or padding, use the developer tools if necessary, validate the HTML page, and test in both Chrome and IE.

Exercise 6-3 Add one speaker page

In this exercise, you'll add the page for one speaker. This page will be like the home page, but the speaker information will be in the second column as shown below. As you develop this page, test it in Chrome whenever appropriate.

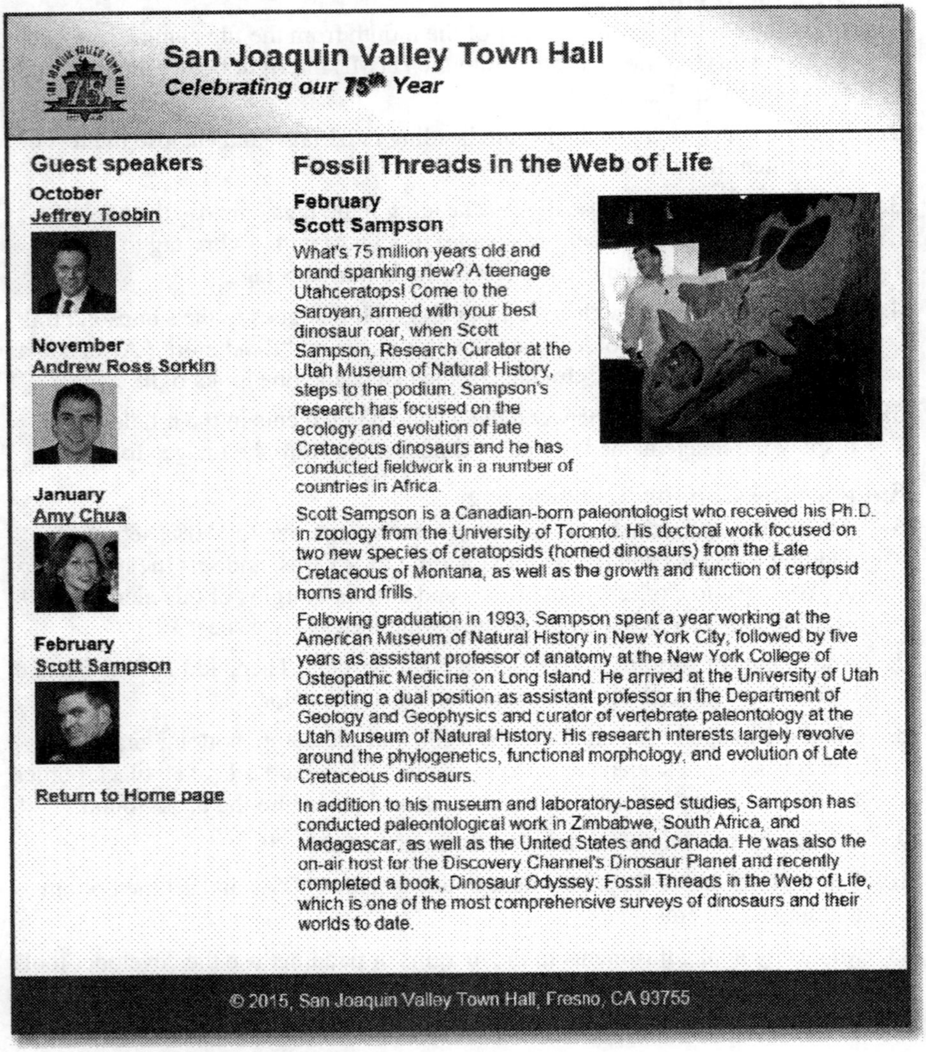

Create the CSS and HTML files for the speaker

1. Copy the index.html file that you've been working with into the speakers folder and name it sampson.html.
2. Copy the main.css file that you've been working with into the styles folder and name it speaker.css.

3. In the head element of the sampson.html file, change the last link element so it refers to the speaker.css file in the styles folder. To do that, you can code a document-relative path like this:

   ```
   ../styles/speaker.css
   ```

   Update the other link elements so they also use relative paths.

Modify the HTML file

4. Update all the image and link references in the header and aside to document-relative paths. Then, at the bottom of the HTML aside element, add a link back to the home page within an h3 element.
5. Delete all of the content from the section in the sampson.html file, but not the section tags. Then, copy the text for the speaker from the c6.sampson.txt file in the text folder into the section of the sampson.html file.
6. Enclose the first heading ("Fossil Threads in the Web of Life") within an h1 element. Then, code an image element after the first heading that displays the sampson_dinosaur.jpg file that's in the images folder.
7. Enclose the rest of the content for the speaker including the image you just added in an article element. Within the article, enclose the first heading (the date and speaker's name) in h2 tags with a <br> tag to provide the line break, and enclose the rest of the text in <p> tags.
8. Validate the file, and fix any errors.

Modify the CSS file

9. If you test the page right now, it should look pretty good. Then, you just need to adjust the styles to get the page to look like the one shown above. For instance, you should delete the borders from the rule set for the article, switch the colors of the h1 and h2 headings in the section, adjust the space between those headings, and reduce the size of the h2 heading.
10. Test all the links to make sure they work correctly. Also, make sure the favicon and all images are displayed correctly.
11. Test the page in IE. Then, if necessary make any corrections, and test again in both Firefox and IE. Now, if you've done everything: "Congratulations!"

7

How to work with lists and links

In chapters 3 and 4, you were introduced to the coding for lists and links. Now, in this chapter, you'll review those skills, and you'll learn the other skills that you may need for working with lists and links.

How to code lists

In the topics that follow, you'll learn the HTML skills that you'll need for working with lists. That includes unordered, ordered, and description lists.

How to code unordered lists

Figure 7-1 presents the two elements for coding an *unordered list*. As you learned in section 1, you use the ul element to create an unordered list, and you use the li element to create each item in the list. This is illustrated in the example in this figure.

In addition to containing text, list items can contain inline elements like links and images. They can also contain block elements like headings, paragraphs, and other lists. For example, the first list item in this figure contains text and a link within a paragraph. Then, the second list item contains only text, but it's divided into two paragraphs. As you can see, the second paragraph is aligned with the first paragraph, but it doesn't have a bullet because it's part of the same list item.

Elements that create unordered lists

Element	Description
ul	Creates an unordered list.
li	Creates a list item for the list.

HTML for an unordered list with text, links, and paragraphs

```
<h1>San Joaquin Valley Town Hall Programs</h1>
<ul>
    <li>
        <p>Join us for a complimentary coffee hour at the
        <a href="saroyan.html">William Saroyan Theatre</a>, 9:15 to 10:15
        a.m. on the day of each lecture. The speakers usually attend this
        very special event.</p>
    </li>
    <li>
        <p>Extend the excitement of Town Hall by purchasing tickets to the
        post-lecture luncheons. This unique opportunity allows you to ask
        more questions of the speakers--plus spend extra time meeting new
        Town Hall friends.</p>
        <p>A limited number of tickets are available. Call (559) 555-1212
        for reservations by the Friday preceding the event.</p>
    </li>
</ul>
```

The list in a web browser

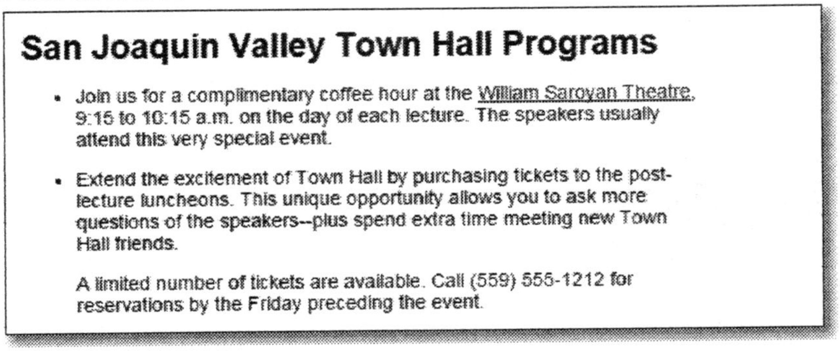

Description

- By default, an *unordered list* is displayed as a bulleted list, but you can change the bullets as shown in figure 7-5.
- An li element typically contains text, but it can also contain other inline elements such as links, as well as block elements such as paragraphs and other lists.

Figure 7-1 How to code unordered lists

How to code ordered lists

If you want to indicate that the items in a list have a sequence like the steps in a procedure, you can use an *ordered list*. To create an ordered list, you use the ol and li elements. These elements are presented in figure 7-2.

The only thing new here is the start attribute of the ol element. You can use this attribute to start a list at a value other than the default. You might want to do that if one list continues from a previous list. For example, this figure shows a procedure that's divided into two parts, and each part is coded as a separate list. Because the first list consists of three items, the start attribute of the second list is set to 4.

Keep in mind if you use the start attribute that it doesn't represent the actual value that's displayed. Instead, it represents the position of the item in the list. When you use decimal values to indicate the sequence of the items in a list as shown here, the position and the value are the same. Later in this chapter, though, you'll learn how to number lists using other values like alphabetic characters. In that case, a start value of 4 would represent the letter "D".

Elements that create ordered lists

Element	Description
`ol`	Creates an ordered list. You can include the start attribute to specify the starting value for the list. The value represents the position in the list. The default is 1.
`li`	Creates a list item for the list.

HTML for an ordered list that continues from another ordered list

```
<h1>How to use the WinZip Self Extractor</h1>
<h2>Before you start the WinZip Self Extractor</h2>
<ol>
    <li>Create a text file that contains the message you want to be
        displayed when the executable starts.</li>
    <li>Create a batch file that copies the exercises, and store it
        in the main folder for the files to be zipped.</li>
    <li>Create the zip file.</li>
</ol>
<h2>How to create an executable file</h2>
<ol start="4">
    <li>Run the WinZip Self Extractor program and click through the first
        three dialog boxes.</li>
    <li>Enter the name of the zip file in the fourth dialog box.</li>
    <li>Click the Next button to test the executable.</li>
</ol>
```

The lists in a web browser

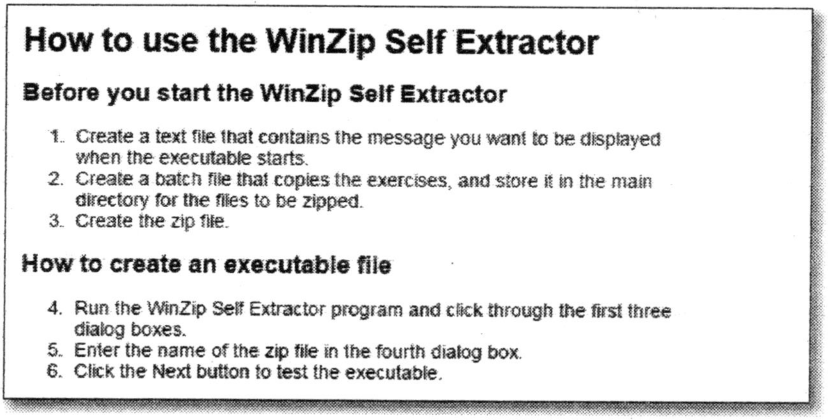

Description

- By default, an *ordered list* is displayed as a numbered list, but you can change that as shown in figure 7-6.
- The start attribute can be used to continue the numbering from one list to another.

Figure 7-2 How to code ordered lists

How to code nested lists

As I mentioned earlier, a list item can contain block elements, including other lists. When you code a list within another list, the lists are referred to as *nested lists*. Figure 7-3 illustrates how nested lists work.

If you look at the HTML in this figure, you'll see that it consists of three lists. The outer list is an unordered list that contains two list items. The first list item defines the first subheading shown in the web browser, along with the three steps that follow it. Then, the second list item defines the second subheading and the remaining steps.

To define the steps, an ordered list is defined within each list item of the unordered list. These lists are coded just like any other ordered list. Because they're nested within other lists, though, they're indented an additional amount.

HTML for ordered lists nested within an unordered list

```
<h1>How to use the WinZip Self Extractor program</h1>
<ul>
    <li>Before you start the WinZip Self Extractor
        <ol>
            <li>Create a text file that contains the message you want
                to be displayed when the executable starts.</li>
            <li>Create a batch file that copies the exercises, and
                store it in the main folder for the files to be zipped.</li>
            <li>Create the zip file.</li>
        </ol>
    </li>
    <li>How to create an executable file
        <ol start="4">
            <li>Run the WinZip Self Extractor program and click through the
                first three dialog boxes.</li>
            <li>Enter the name of the zip file in the fourth dialog
                box.</li>
            <li>Click the Next button to test the executable.</li>
        </ol>
    </li>
</ul>
```

The lists in a web browser

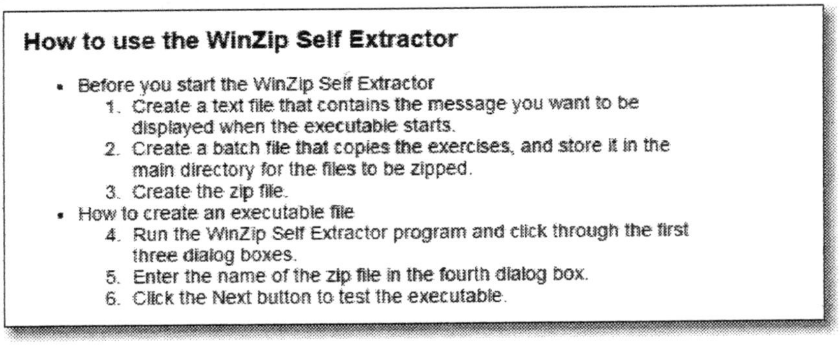

Description

- You can nest lists by coding one list as an item for another list.
- When you nest an unordered list within another list, the default bullet is a circle.

Figure 7-3 How to code nested lists

How to code description lists

In addition to ordered and unordered lists, HTML provides for *description lists*. As the name implies, description lists are typically used to list terms and their descriptions. Figure 7-4 shows how to code description lists.

To code a description list, you use the dl, dt, and dd elements. The dl element creates the description list, the dt element creates the term, and the dd element creates the description for the term. The example in this figure illustrates how this works. Here, the dt and dd elements are coded within the dl element that defines the list. Notice that the dt and dd elements are coded in pairs so there's a description for each term.

When you code a description list, you should know that the dt element can only contain text and inline elements. In contrast, dd elements can also contain block elements. For example, they can contain paragraphs and nested lists.

You should also know that you can code more than one dd element for each dt element. That's useful if you're creating a glossary and a term has more than one meaning. You can also code a single dd element for two or more dt elements. That's useful if you're defining terms that have the same description.

Incidentally, description lists were called *definition lists* in HTML4. The new name implies that a description list can be used for more than just definitions.

Elements that create description lists

Element	Description
dl	Creates a description list that contains pairs of dt and dd elements.
dt	Creates a term in a description list.
dd	Creates a description in a description list.

HTML for a description list

```
<h2>Components of the Internet architecture</h2>
<dl>
    <dt>client</dt>
    <dd>A computer that accesses the web pages of a web application using a
        web browser.</dd>
    <dt>web server</dt>
    <dd>A computer that holds the files for each web application.</dd>
    <dt>local area network (LAN)</dt>
    <dd>A small network of computers that are near each other and can
        communicate with each other over short distances.</dd>
    <dt>wide area network (WAN)</dt>
    <dd>A network that consists of multiple LANs that have been connected
        together over long distances using routers.</dd>
    <dt>Internet exchange point</dt>
    <dd>Large routers that connect WANs together.</dd>
</dl>
```

The list in a web browser

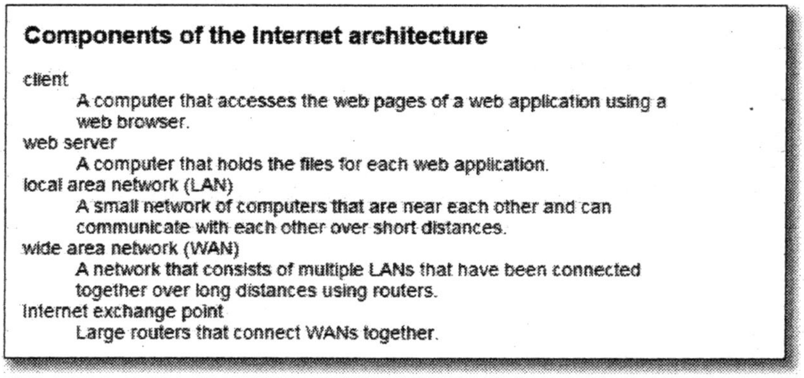

Description

- A *description list* consists of terms and descriptions for those terms. In HTML4, this type of list was called a *definition list*.
- The dt element that creates a term in a description list can only contain text. However, dd elements can contain block elements such as headings and paragraphs.
- You can use one or more dd elements to describe a dt element, and you can describe two or more dt elements with a single dd element.

Figure 7-4 How to code description lists

How to format lists

Once you have a list coded the way you want it, you can format it so it looks the way you want. In most cases, that just means changing the spacing above and below the list and its items. But you can also change the bullets that are used for an unordered list. You can change the numbering system that's used for an ordered list. And you can change the vertical alignment of the items in a list. You'll learn these skills in the topics that follow.

How to change the bullets for an unordered list

To change the bullets for an unordered list, you can use the list-style-type and list-style-image properties shown in the first table in figure 7-5. In most cases, you'll use the list-style-type property to specify one of the values listed in the second table.

By default, a list displays a solid round bullet, but you can specify a value of "circle" to display a circle bullet as shown in the first list in this figure. You can also specify a value of "square" to display a square bullet or "none" if you don't want to display any bullets.

If these predefined bullet types aren't adequate, you can display a custom image before each item in an unordered list. To do that, you start by getting or creating the image that you want to use. For instance, you can get many images that are appropriate for lists from the Internet, often for free or for a small charge. The other alternative is to use a graphics program to create your own image. Once you have the image that you want to use, you use the list-style-image property to specify the URL for the image file, as illustrated by the second example in this figure.

In most cases, you'll code the list-style-type and list-style-image properties for the ul element. Then, this property is inherited by all the items in the list. Another way to do that, though, is to code these properties for the li element.

Properties for formatting unordered lists

Property	Description
`list-style-type`	Determines the type of bullet that's used for the items in the list. See the table below for possible values. The default is disc.
`list-style-image`	The URL for an image that's used as the bullet.

Values for the list-style-type property of an unordered list

Value	Description
`disc`	solid circle
`circle`	hollow circle
`square`	solid square
`none`	no bullet

HTML for two unordered lists

```
<h2>Popular web browsers include</h2>
<ul class="circle">
    <li>Internet Explorer</li>
    <li>Firefox</li>
    <li>Chrome</li>
</ul>
<h2>Prime skills for web developers are</h2>
<ul class="star">
    <li>HTML5 and CSS3</li>
    <li>JavaScript</li>
    <li>PHP</li>
</ul>
```

CSS that changes the bullets

```
ul.circle { list-style-type: circle; }
ul.star { list-style-image: url("../images/star.png"); }
```

The lists in a web browser

Description

- You can change the bullet that's displayed for an unordered list by using the list-style-type property. To display an image for the bullet, use the list-style-image property.

Figure 7-5 How to change the bullets for an unordered list

How to change the numbering system for an ordered list

By default, decimal values are used to number the items in an ordered list. To change that, though, you can use the list-style-type property as shown in figure 7-6. In the example, you can see that "lower-alpha" is used for the value of this property.

Common values for the list-style-type property of an ordered list

Value	Example
decimal	1, 2, 3, 4, 5 ...
decimal-leading-zero	01, 02, 03, 04, 05 ...
lower-alpha	a, b, c, d, e ...
upper-alpha	A, B, C, D, E ...
lower-roman	i, ii, iii, iv, v ...
upper-roman	I, II, III, IV, V ...

HTML for an ordered list

```
<h2>How to create an executable file</h2>
<ol class="lower_alpha">
    <li>Run the WinZip Self Extractor program and click through the first
        three dialog boxes.</li>
    <li>Enter the name of the zip file in the fourth dialog box.</li>
    <li>Click the Next button to test the executable.</li>
</ol>
```

CSS that formats the list

```
ol.lower_alpha { list-style-type: lower-alpha; }
```

The list in a web browser

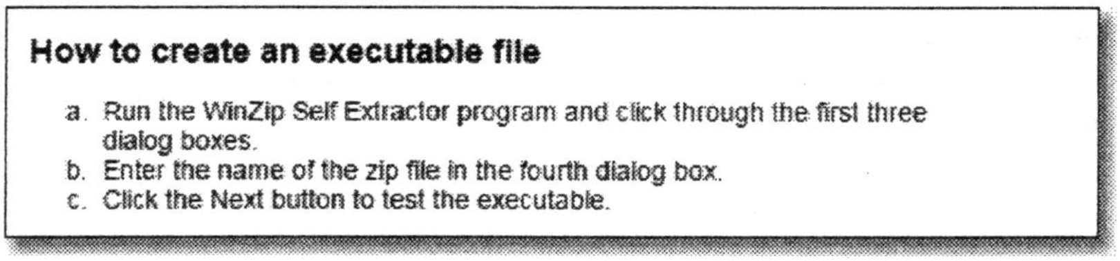

Description

- You can change the numbering system that's used for an ordered list using the list-style-type property. The default is decimal.

Figure 7-6 How to change the numbering system for an ordered list

How to change the alignment of list items

Often, the items in a list will be aligned the way you want them. However, you will usually want to adjust the spacing before and after a list, and you will sometimes want to adjust the spacing before or after the list items. Beyond that, you may want to change the indentation of the items in a list or the amount of space between the bullets or numbers in a list.

In figure 7-7, you can see the HTML and the CSS for a formatted list. In this case, the space between the lines has been adjusted. But more important, the list items have been moved left so the bullets are aligned on the left margin instead of being indented. Also, the space between the bullets and the items has been increased. If you compare this list to the one in figure 7-5, you can see the differences.

In the CSS for the list in this figure, you can see that the margins for the unordered list and its list items have been set to 0. Then, the left padding for the ul element has been set to 1 em. This determines the left alignment of the items in the list. Often, though, you have to experiment with this setting to get the alignment the way you want it.

Similarly, the left padding for the li element is set to .25 ems. This determines the distance between the bullet and the text for an item. Here again, you will often have to experiment with this value to get it the way you want it.

For ordered lists, you can use the same techniques to adjust the indentation and to adjust the space between the number and the text in an item. Remember, though, that the numbers in an ordered list are aligned on the right. So if the numbers vary in width, you have to adjust your values accordingly.

HTML for an unordered list

```
<h2>Popular web browsers</h2>
<ul>
    <li>Chrome</li>
    <li>Internet Explorer</li>
    <li>Firefox</li>
    <li>Safari</li>
    <li>Opera</li>
</ul>
```

CSS that aligns the list items

```
h2, ul, li {
    margin: 0;
    padding: 0;
}
h2 {
    padding-bottom: .25em;
}
ul {
    padding-left: 1em;       /* determines left alignment */
}
li {
    padding-left: .25em;     /* space between bullet and text */
    padding-bottom: .25em;   /* space after line item */
}
```

The list in a web browser

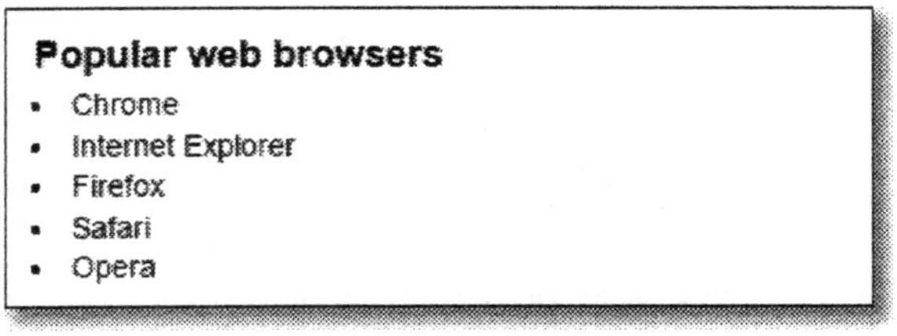

Description

- You can use margins and padding to control the indentation for the items in an ordered or unordered list, and to control the space between the bullets or numbers and the text that follows.
- You can also use margins and padding to remove the indentation from the items in a list as shown above. However, this doesn't work as well with ordered lists because the numbers or letters are aligned at the right.
- You can remove the indentation from the descriptions in a description list by setting the left margin of the descriptions to zero.
- These techniques work best if you specify the padding and margins using ems.

Figure 7-7 How to change the alignment of list items

How to code links

In section 1, you learned how to code and format simple text links that open another web page in the same window. Now, you'll learn other ways to code and use links.

How to link to another page

Figure 7-8 starts by reviewing some of the information that you learned earlier about coding <a> elements that *link* to other pages. Then, it goes on to some new skills.

To start, you code the href attribute so it identifies the page you want the link to display. Then, you code the content that you want to be displayed for the link. The content can be text, an image, or both text and an image.

The first example in this figure illustrates how this works. Here, the first link displays text, and the second link displays an image. Note that when this image is displayed in some older browsers, it will have a border to identify it as a link. In that case, the border is the same color as the underline for a text link. To remove the border, you can use CSS to set the border-style property to "none" or the border-width property to 0. If you use the normalize.css style sheet, it takes care of this for you.

The third link in the first example shows how the title attribute can be used to improve accessibility. Here, the text for the link is just "TOC", but the title attribute says: "Review the complete table of contents". This title is displayed as a tooltip if the mouse hovers over it, and it can also be read by assistive devices. You should also code the title attribute if you include an image-only link.

If the user presses the Tab key while a web page is displayed, the focus is moved from one link or form control to another based on the tab sequence. By default, this *tab order* is the sequence in which the links and controls are coded in the HTML, which is usually what you want. If you need to change that order, though, you can use the tabindex attribute of a link. In the first example in this figure, this attribute is set to zero so that link will be the first one that gets tabbed to.

To set an *access key* for a link, you can code the accesskey attribute. Then, the user can press that key in combination with one or more other keys to activate the link. For example, the accesskey attribute for the first text link in this figure is set to the letter "c". Then, the user can activate the link by pressing a control key plus the shortcut key. For instance, Alt+C (the Alt key and the C key) works in IE, Chrome, and Safari on a Windows system. Alt+Shift+C works in Firefox on a Windows system. And Ctrl+Option+C works in Chrome, Firefox, and Safari on a Mac. For more on both access keys and tab order, see chapter 11.

To indicate what the access key for a link or control is, you normally underline the letter in the text for the control. By default, though, the links are underlined so this won't work. But if you remove the underlining, as shown in the next figure, you can use this technique to identify the shortcut keys.

Four attributes of the <a> element

Attribute	Description
href	A relative or absolute URL that identifies the document a link will display.
title	A description that is displayed as a tooltip. This can clarify where the link is going.
tabindex	Sets the tab order for the links starting with 0. To take a link out of the tab order, code a negative value.
accesskey	Identifies a keyboard key that can be used in combination with other keys to activate the control. The key combination depends on the operating system and browser.

A text link, an image link, and a text link with a title attribute

```
<p>
    <a href="/orders/cart.html" accesskey="c" tabindex="0">Shopping cart</a>
    <a href="/orders/cart.html"><img src="images/cart_animated.gif"
       alt="Shopping cart"></a>
</p>
<p><a href="/books/php_toc.html"
      title="Review the complete table of contents">TOC</a></p>
```

The text and image links in a web browser

Accessibility guidelines

- If the text for a link has to be short, code the title attribute to clarify where the link is going.
- You should also code the title attribute if a link includes an image with no text.

Description

- You use the <a> element to create a *link* that loads another web page. The content of an <a> element can be text, an image, or text and an image.
- The *tab order* is the sequence that the links will be tabbed to when the user presses the Tab key. For more on this, see chapter 11.
- An *access key* is a keystroke combination that can be used to activate a link.

Figure 7-8 How to link to another page

How to format links

Figure 7-9 reviews the formatting skills for links that were introduced in chapter 4. In particular, you can use the pseudo-code selectors to change the default styles for a link.

This figure also shows how to remove the underline for a text link or the border for an image link. To do that, you can set the text-decoration property for a text link or the border-style property for an image link to "none."

In the past, text links were almost always underlined to clearly indicate that the text was a link. Today, though, it's becoming more common to see text links without underlines. What's most important now is that you don't underline text that isn't a link, since that can confuse users.

It's also good to avoid the use of image-only links unless it's clear where the link is going. For instance, most users recognize a shopping cart or shopping bag image because they're common to many sites, but they may not recognize images that are specific to a single site. One exception is using the logo in the header to link to the home page of a site because that's become a common practice.

Common CSS pseudo-classes for formatting links

Name	Description
`:link`	A link that hasn't been visited. Blue is the default color.
`:visited`	A link that has been visited. Purple is the default color.
`:hover`	An element with the mouse hovering over it. Hover has no default color.
`:focus`	An element like a link or form control that has the focus.
`:active`	An element that's currently active. Red is the default color.

The properties for removing underlines and borders

Property	Description
`text-decoration`	To remove the underlining from a link, set this to none.
`border-style`	To remove the border from an image link, set this to none. You can also set the border-width property to 0.

The HTML for three links

```
<ul>
    <li><a href="toobin.html">Jeffrey Toobin</a></li>
    <li><a href="sorkin.html">Andrew Ross Sorkin</a></li>
    <li><a href="chua.html">Amy Chua</a></li>
</ul>
```

The CSS for pseudo-class selectors that apply to the links

```
a:link {
    color: green;
}
a:hover, a:focus {
    text-decoration: none;
    font-size: 125%;
}
```

The links in a web browser with the focus on the third link

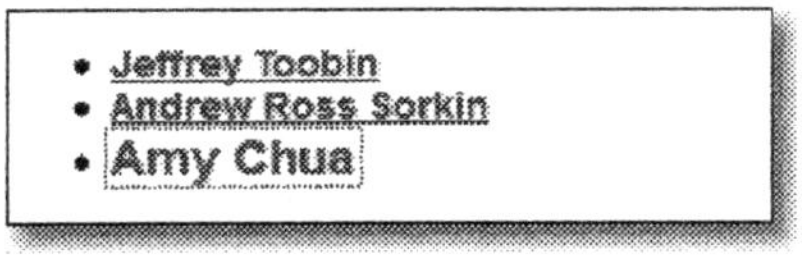

Accessibility guideline

- Apply the same formatting for the :hover and :focus selectors. That way, the formatting is the same whether you hover the mouse over a link or use the keyboard to tab to the link.

Figure 7-9 How to format links

How to use a link to open a new browser window or tab

In most cases, you'll want the page that's loaded by a link to be displayed in the same browser window as the current page. In some cases, though, you may want to open the next page in a new browser window or tab. If, for example, the link loads a page from another website, you may want to display it in a new window or tab.

To open a new browser window or tab, you set the target attribute of the <a> element to "_blank" as shown in figure 7-10. Here, the link opens a page on another website in a new tab.

Whether a new window or a new tab is opened depends upon the browser settings. But you can change that for most browsers. With Firefox, for example, you go to Tools→Options and click on Tabs. With IE, you click the Tools icon at the right side of the address bar, select Internet options, click the Tabs button, and select the appropriate option. Unfortunately, Chrome doesn't provide a way to change this setting using its visual interface. But you can always right-click on the link and choose "Open link in new tab" or "Open link in new window" if it doesn't work the way you want.

Incidentally, the target attribute was deprecated in HTML4. However, it is no longer deprecated in HTML5.

HTML for a link that loads the document in a new window or tab

```
<p>Just go to
   <a href="http://www.html5test.com/" target="_blank">
   the HTML5 testing site</a>. It rates your browser as it loads the
   page and also has data on how well other browsers conform to HTML5.
</p>
```

The HTML in one browser tab

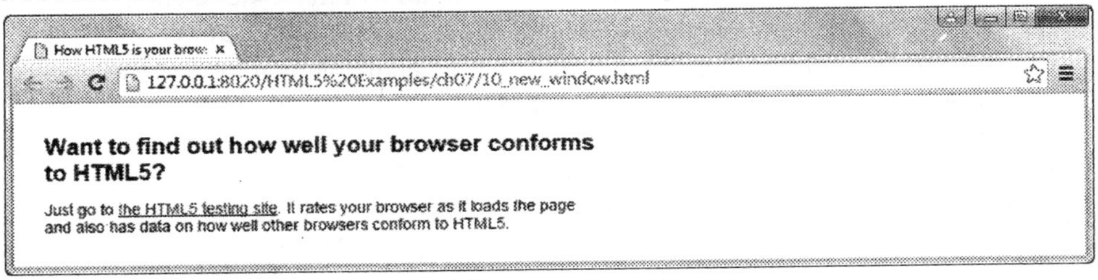

The html5test.com home page in another tab

Description

- You can use the target attribute of the <a> tag to specify where the document referred to in a link should be loaded. To load the document in a new browser window or tab, specify "_blank" for this attribute.
- Whether your browser opens a new window or a new tab for the page depends on your browser settings.

Figure 7-10 How to use a link to open a new browser window or tab

How to create and link to placeholders

Besides displaying another page, you can code links that jump to a location on the same page. To do that, you first create a *placeholder* that identifies the location you want the link to jump to. Then, you code a link that points to that placeholder. This is illustrated in figure 7-11.

To create a placeholder, you code the id attribute within an <a> element at the spot where you want the placeholder. In this figure, the first example shows a placeholder with the id "top" that's coded within an h1 element on the page, and the second example shows a placeholder with the id "reason6" that's coded within an h2 element.

Then, the third group of examples shows two links that jump to those placeholders. To do that, the href attributes of these links use the values of the id attributes for the placeholders, preceded by a pound sign (#). When the user clicks on one of these links, the element that contains the placeholder is displayed.

Placeholders can make it easier for users to navigate through a long web page. For pages like these, it's common to include a placeholder at the top of the page along with navigation links for each section of the page. Then, at the end of each section, it's common to include a link to return to the top of the page.

Although placeholders are typically used for navigating within a single page, they can also be used to go to a location on another page. The last example in this figure shows how this works. Here, the name of the page that contains the placeholder is coded before the value of the placeholder's id attribute. Then, when that page is displayed, it will be positioned at the specified placeholder.

Incidentally, placeholders were called *anchors* in HTML4. But since <a> tags are also known as anchor tags, this could be confusing. In HTML5, the term *placeholder* makes this clearer.

A web page that provides links to topics on the same page

The portion of the page that's displayed when the sixth link is clicked

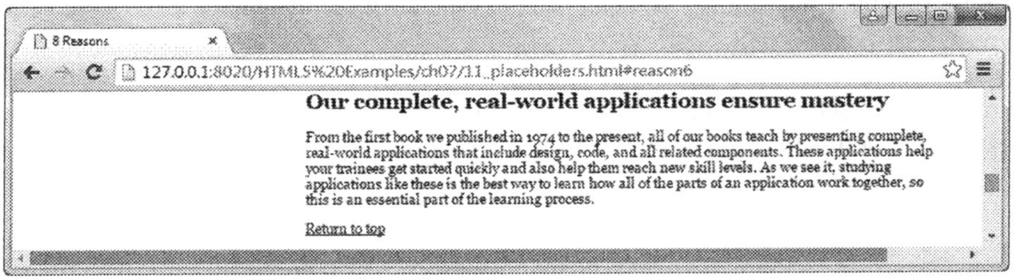

The HTML for the placeholder at the top of the page

```
<h1><a id="top">8 reasons why trainers like our books</a></h1>
```

The HTML for the placeholder for reason 6

```
<h2><a id="reason6">Our complete, real-world applications ensure
mastery</a></h2>
```

Two links that jump to placeholders on the same page

```
<p><a href="#reason6">Complete, real-world applications</a></p>
<p><a href="#top">Return to top</a></p>
```

A link that jumps to a placeholder on this page from another page

```
<a href="8reasons.html#reason6">Complete, real-world applications</a>
```

Description

- To create a *placeholder*, use the id attribute of the <a> tag.
- To jump to a placeholder, code a link with its href attribute set to the value of the id attribute, preceded by the pound sign.
- To jump to a placeholder on another page, code the URL for the page followed by the id for the placeholder.

Figure 7-11 How to create and link to placeholders

How to link to a media file

If the href attribute of an <a> element addresses a media file, the normal behavior of a browser is to try to display or play it using the right program for that type of file. For instance, the first example in figure 7-12 is a link that opens a PDF file in a new browser window or tab. The second example will play an MP3 audio file. And the third example will play a PowerPoint slide show.

This assumes that the browser has the appropriate program or *media player* for the file. In some cases, this will require that the user install the right player or a *plugin* for the right player.

To help a browser identify the type of file that the link addresses, you can code the type attribute. This attribute specifies the *MIME type* for the file. Some of the common MIME types are listed in the first table in this figure, and two of the most popular media players are listed in the second table. To open a PDF for Adobe Reader, for example, you can use the type attribute to specify the MIME type as: application/pdf.

In chapter 12, you'll learn how to add audio and video to your website. For other types of media, though, the <a> element can do a good job of getting the results that you want.

Popular media formats and MIME types

Format	Description	MIME type
PDF	Portable Document Format file	application/pdf
WAV	Waveform audio file	audio/x-wave
MP3	MPEG audio file	audio/mpeg or audio/x-mpeg
MPG/MPEG	MPEG video file	video/mpeg
SWF	ShockWave Flash file	application/x-shockwave-flash

Two of the popular media players

Player	Description
Adobe Reader	Used to display PDF files.
Adobe Flash Player	Commonly used to display Flash animation and videos (SWF).

An HTML link that displays a PDF file in a new window

```
<a href="documents/instructors_summary.pdf"
   type="application/pdf"
   target="_blank">Read the Instructor's Summary<a>
```

The PDF file displayed in a browser

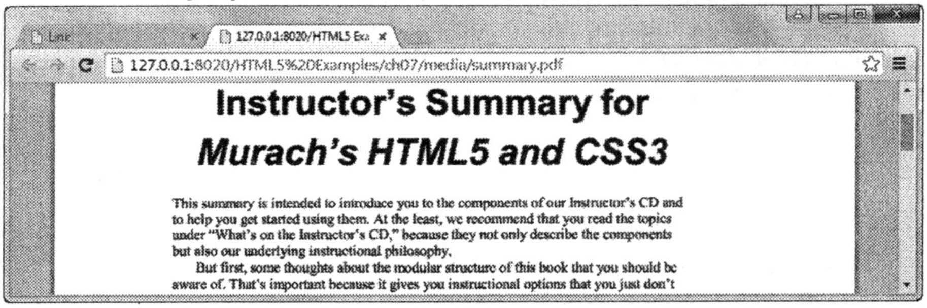

An HTML link that plays an MP3 file

```
<a href="music/twist_away.mp3" type="audio/mpeg">MP3 file</a>
```

An HTML link that plays a PowerPoint slide show

```
<a href="media/chapter_01.pps"
   target="_blank">Review the slides for chapter 1</a>
```

Description

- Special *media players* may be required to play a media file in a browser. Often, media players require browser *plugins* for playing specific types of files.
- When you use the <a> element to display a media file, the file is typically displayed in its own web page and opened in the default player associated with the file type.
- To help the browser determine which player to use, you can include a type attribute on the <a> element to specify a *MIME type* that identifies the type of content.

Figure 7-12 How to link to a media file

How to create email, phone, and Skype links

Figure 7-13 shows how to create three additional types of links. To start, you can use a link to open the user's default email program and start an email message. To do that, you code the href attribute as "mailto:" followed by the email address that the message will be sent to. This is illustrated in the first example in this figure. Here, the email will be sent to support@murach.com. Although this won't work for users who use email services like gmail or yahoo mail instead of the email programs on their computers, those users can at least get the email address from the text that's displayed for the link.

You can also add one or more parameters to an email address to include additional information in the email. To do that, you code a question mark followed by one or more name/value pairs separated by ampersands (&). In the second code example in this figure, for instance, you can see that a copy of the email will be sent to ben@murach.com and the subject will be "Web mail".

In addition to the mailto: prefix that you use to create an email link, you can create other types of links using the prefixes shown in the table in this figure. To create a phone link, for example, you code the tel: prefix followed by the phone number. This type of link is most useful for users who are viewing the website from a mobile device. Then, the device will automatically open its call functionality and attempt to dial the phone number.

To create a Skype link, you code the skype: prefix followed by the name of a registered Skype user. Then, if Skype is installed on the user's computer and that user is registered with Skype, the two users can communicate using Skype.

A web page with links for email, phone, and Skype

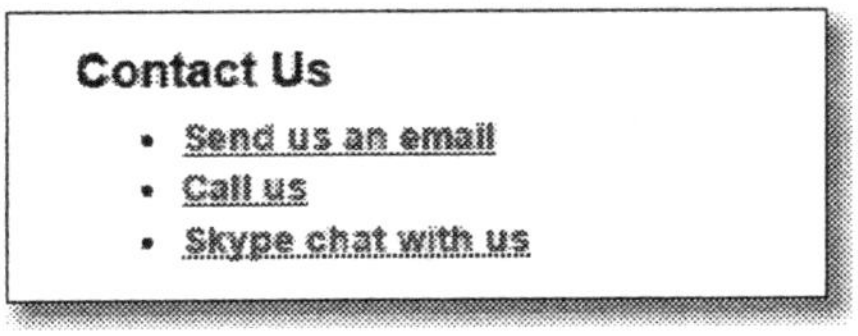

A link that starts an email message

```
<a href="mailto:support@murach.com">Send us an email</a>
```

An email link with a CC address and a subject

```
<a href="mailto:support@murach.com?cc=ben@murach.com"&subject=Web mail>
Send us an email</a>
```

A link that calls a phone number

```
<a href="tel:555-555-5555">Call us</a>
```

A link that starts a Skype session

```
<a href="skype:murachsupport">Skype chat with us</a>
```

Prefixes for coding email, phone, and Skype links

Link type	Prefix
Email	`mailto:`
Phone	`tel:`
Skype	`skype:`

Description

- You can use the <a> element to create several other types of links. To do that, you code the href attribute with the prefix shown above followed by the information that's required by the link.
- To start an email message, you code the email address following the mailto: prefix. You can also populate the subject, cc, bcc, or body fields in the email by coding a question mark after the address followed by one or more name/value pairs separated by ampersands.
- To call a phone number, you code the number following the tel: prefix. This is most useful for mobile devices that provide call functionality.
- To start a Skype session, you code the name of the user you want to contact following the skype: prefix.

Figure 7-13 How to create email, phone, and Skype links

How to create navigation menus

This chapter closes by showing you how to use lists and links in the navigation menus for your web pages. As you will see, the preferred way to do that is to code the <a> elements for the navigation within an unordered list.

How to create a vertical navigation menu

Figure 7-14 shows how to create a vertical *navigation menu*. This is just a vertical list of links. Here, the <a> elements are coded within an unordered list. This is the preferred way to create a navigation menu, because a list is a logical container for the links.

If you look at the CSS for the ul element, you can see that the bullets are removed by the list-style-type property. If you look at the CSS for the li element, you can see that a border is placed around each item and the width of each item is set to 200 pixels. In addition, the margin-bottom property for these elements puts space below them.

The most critical CSS, though, is for the <a> elements. First, the display property of these elements is set to "block". This makes the entire block for each link clickable, not just the text. Then, the padding sets the size of each block. Last, the text-decoration property is used to remove the underlining for the text. This formatting makes the links in the list look like buttons.

Of course, the simple formatting in this example could be improved by making the list items look even more like buttons. For instance, you could round the corners and add shadows. Or, you could add an icon, like an >> icon, to the right side of the link to indicate that it's a link.

To let the users know which page they're on, it's also a good practice to highlight the link that represents the current page. To do that, the HTML in this example uses the "current" class for the third item, and the CSS changes the background color for that class to silver.

A vertical navigation menu

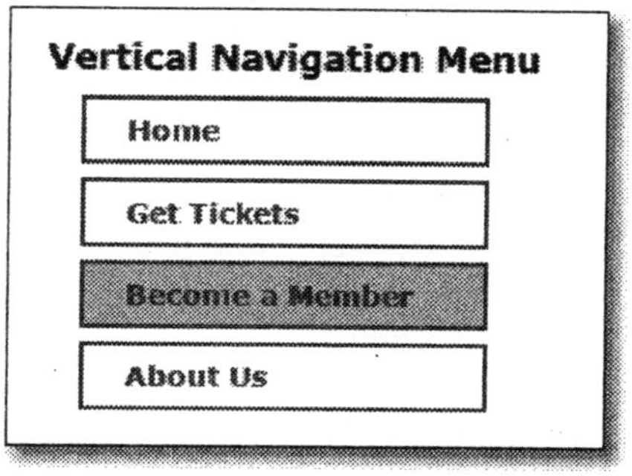

The HTML for the navigation menu

```
<nav id="nav_list">
    <ul>
        <li><a href="index.html">Home</a></li>
        <li><a href="tickets.html">Get Tickets</a></li>
        <li><a href="members.html" class="current">Become a Member</a></li>
        <li><a href="about_us.html">About Us</a></li>
    </ul>
</nav>
```

The CSS for the navigation menu

```
* { margin: 0;
    padding: 0; }
#nav_menu_1 ul {
    list-style-type: none;
    margin-left: 1.25em;
    margin-bottom: 1.5em; }
#nav_menu_1 ul li {
    width: 200px;
    margin-bottom: .5em;
    border: 2px solid blue; }
#nav_menu_1 ul li a {
    display: block;
    padding: .5em 0 .5em 1.5em;
    text-decoration: none;
    font-weight: bold;
    color: blue; }
#nav_menu_1 ul li a.current {
    background-color: silver; }
```

Description

- The HTML for a vertical *navigation menu* is best coded as a series of <a> elements within the li elements of an unordered list.
- To make the entire box for a link clickable, you can set the display property for the <a> elements to block and use padding to provide the space around the links.
- To show the users what page they're on, it's a good practice to highlight the current link. One way to do that is to apply a different background color to it.

Figure 7-14 How to create a vertical navigation menu

How to create a horizontal navigation menu

Figure 7-15 shows how to create a *horizontal navigation menu*, which is commonly referred to as a *navigation bar*. This is a horizontal list of links that often provide the primary navigation for a site. Here again, the <a> elements are coded within an unordered list because that's the preferred way to do this.

The examples in this figure use HTML that's similar to the example in the previous figure. The only difference is that the last <a> element includes the "lastitem" class. I'll explain how this class is used in just a minute.

In the CSS for the first horizontal menu, the bullets are removed from the ul element and the display of the li elements is set to "inline". That displays the links horizontally rather than vertically. In addition, the text for the links is centered in the ul element and top and bottom borders are added to that element. Finally, the link for the current page has its underline (text-decoration) removed.

The CSS for the second menu is somewhat different. Here, the links are displayed horizontally by floating each li element to the left of the previous li element. Then, the text for each <a> element is centered within that element, and the display property for those elements is set to "block" so the entire block for each link will be clickable. To define each block, the width of the <a> elements is set to 175 pixels, padding is added to the top and bottom of the links, and a border is added at the right side of the link. In addition, the background color for each link is set to blue, the text color of the links is set to white, and the underlines are removed from the links.

In this example, the widths of the <a> elements are set so the sum of the widths of those elements plus the widths of the right borders are equal to the page width. Note, though, that it isn't necessary to include a border to the right of the last link. Because of that, the "lastitem" class for that element is used to remove the border.

Of course, you won't always be able to divide the width of the element that contains the navigation menu equally among the links. In that case, you can adjust the width of the last link so the menu extends across the entire width of its parent element.

Two horizontal navigation menus

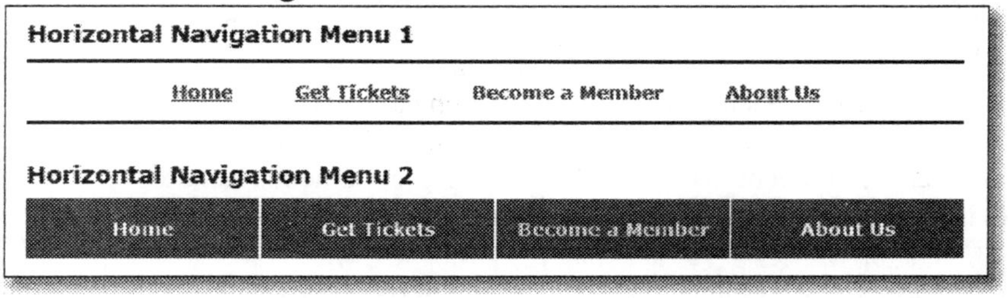

The HTML for the navigation menus

```
<nav id="nav_menu">
    <ul>
        <li><a href="index.html">Home</a></li>
        <li><a href="tickets.html">Get Tickets</a></li>
        <li><a href="members.html" class="current">Become a Member</a></li>
        <li><a href="about_us.html" class="lastitem">About Us</a></li>
    </ul>
</nav>
```

The CSS for the first navigation menu

```
#nav_menu ul {
    list-style-type: none;
    padding: 1em 0;        /* padding above and below li elements */
    text-align: center;
    border-top: 2px solid black;
    border-bottom: 2px solid black; }
#nav_menu ul li {
    display: inline;
    padding: 0 1.5em; }
#nav_menu ul li a {
    font-weight: bold;
    color: blue; }
#nav_menu ul li a.current { text-decoration: none; }
```

The CSS for the second navigation menu

```
#nav_menu ul {  list-style-type: none; }
#nav_menu ul li { float: left; }
#nav_menu ul li a {
    text-align: center;
    display: block;
    width: 175px;
    padding: 1em 0;       /* padding above and below a elements */
    text-decoration: none;
    background-color: blue;
    color: white;
    font-weight: bold;
    border-right: 2px solid white; }
#nav_menu ul li a.lastitem { border-right: none; }
#nav_menu ul li a.current { color: yellow; }
```

Description

- You can code a horizontal navigation menu using an unordered list. You can do that by displaying the li elements inline or by floating the li elements.

Figure 7-15 How to create a horizontal navigation menu

How to create a 2-tier navigation menu

Figure 7-16 shows how to create a *2-tier navigation menu*. In a *multi-tier navigation menu* like this, each item in the navigation bar can contain a submenu with additional items. For example, the About Us item in the navigation bar in this figure contains a submenu with two items. Then, the submenus can drop down from the navigation bar when the user hovers the mouse over an item in the bar.

To create a 2-tier navigation menu, you nest an unordered list within a list item of another unordered list. The HTML in this figure shows how this works. Here, two of the items in the navigation bar contain unordered lists: the Speakers and the About Us items.

Next, this figure shows the CSS that makes the submenus drop down from the navigation bar when the user hovers over an item. To start, all of the ul elements in the nav element have their list-style properties set to none so the bullets are removed and their position properties set to relative so the submenus can be positioned absolutely. Then, the list items in the top-level ul element (#nav_menu ul li) are floated to the left, thus forming the navigation bar.

The third rule set is for the submenus that the HTML contains (#nav_menu ul ul). Here, the display property is set to none so a submenu isn't displayed until the user hovers the mouse over the related item in the navigation bar. In addition, the position property is set to absolute, and the top property is set to 100%. That means that the submenu will be positioned just below the navigation bar (100% from the top of the bar).

The fourth rule set sets the float property for the list items in the submenus (#nav_menu ul ul li) to none. As a result, the list items in the submenus will be displayed vertically instead of horizontally.

Then, the fifth rule set sets the display property for the submenus to block when the user hovers the mouse over a list item in the navigation bar. That displays the drop-down menu for the item.

The last rule set uses the child selector (>) to select just the first ul element in the HTML (the child of the nav element). Then, this selector uses the ::after pseudo-element to add content after the first ul element. To do that, it sets the content property to an empty string so there is some content after the ul element. It uses the display property to make this content a block element. And it uses the clear property to stop the floating of the items in the ul element.

This last rule set is critical to the operation of this 2-tier menu system. Without it, the submenus will float up into the navigation bar, which certainly isn't what you want. So if this rule set is a little cryptic and hard to understand, just copy it into the CSS for your 2-tier menus.

Although this figure doesn't show the CSS for the other formatting of the menus, you'll see that in the next example. In particular, you'll see how the lastitem class is used by the CSS. Often, in a menu structure like this, you need to apply some special formatting to the last item in the navigation bar, so a class attribute named "lastitem" has been coded for the last item in this example.

A 2-tier navigation menu

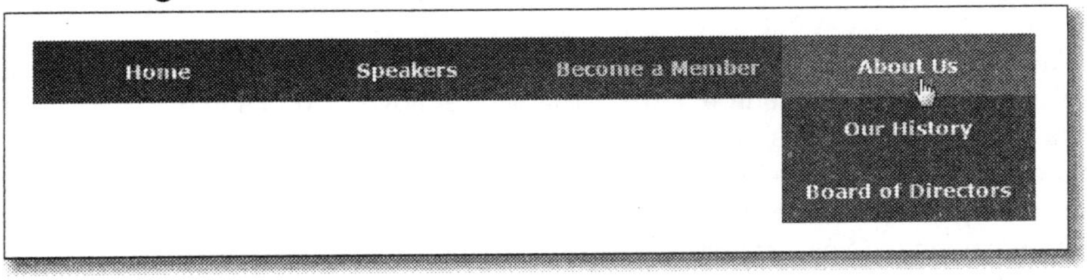

The HTML for the menus

```
<nav id="nav_menu">
    <ul>
        <li><a href="index.html">Home</a></li>
        <li><a href="#">Speakers</a>
            <ul>
                <li><a href="#">Jeffrey Toobin</a></li>
                <li><a href="#">Andrew Ross Sorkin</a></li>
                ...
            </ul>
        </li>
        <li><a href="members.html" class="current">Become a Member</a></li>
        <li class="lastitem"><a href="aboutus.html">About Us</a>
            <ul>
                <li><a href="#">Our History</a></li>
                <li><a href="#">Board of Directors</a></li>
            </ul>
        </li>
    </ul>
</nav>
```

The CSS for the operation of the menus

```
#nav_menu ul {
    list-style: none;            /* Remove bullets from all ul elements */
    position: relative; }        /* So the submenus can be positioned */
#nav_menu ul li { float: left; } /* Display items horizontally */
#nav_menu ul ul {
    display: none;         /* Don't display submenus until hover of li */
    position: absolute;
    top: 100%;             /* Position submenu at bottom of main menu */
}
#nav_menu ul ul li { float: none; }     /* Display submenus vertically */
#nav_menu ul li:hover > ul {            /* Select ul child of li element */
    display: block; }      /* Display submenu on hover of li element */
#nav_menu > ul::after {
    content: "";}          /* Add empty content to the end of the first ul */
    display: block;        /* Display that content as a block element */
    clear: both; }         /* Stop the floating of the li elements */
```

Description

- To create a *multi-tier navigation menu*, you coded unordered lists within the li elements of another unordered list. In other words, you create a nested list as described earlier in this chapter.

Figure 7-16 How to create a 2-tier navigation menu

How to create a 3-tier navigation menu

Figure 7-17 shows a *3-tier navigation menu*. Here, tier 1 is the navigation bar. Tier 2 is the menus that drop down when the user hovers over an item in the navigation bar. And tier 3 is the submenus that are displayed to the left or right of a drop-down menu when the user hovers the mouse over an item in the menu. In this example, the tier-3 menu is displayed when the user hovers over the Scott Sampson item in the Speakers menu.

The HTML for a 3-tier menu like this consists of nested unordered lists. In this figure, you can see unordered lists nested within the Speakers and About Us items in the navigation bar. You can also see nested lists in the Scott Sampson item within the Speakers item and in the Past Speakers item within the About Us item.

Note here that just as in the example for the two-tier navigation menu, a "lastitem" class has been coded for the last list item in the navigation bar. You'll see how this class is used in the CSS in the next figure.

A 3-tier navigation menu

The HTML for the menu

```
<nav id="nav_menu">
    <ul>
        <li><a href="index.html">Home</a></li>
        <li><a href="#">Speakers</a>
            <ul>
                <li><a href="#">Jeffrey Toobin</a></li>
                <li><a href="#">Andrew Ross Sorkin</a></li>
                <li><a href="#">Amy Chua</a></li>
                <li><a href="sampson.html">Scott Sampson</a>
                    <ul>
                        <li><a href="#">September 2010</a></li>
                        <li><a href="#">February 2015</a></li>
                    </ul>
                </li>
                <li><a href="march.html">Carlos Eire</a></li>
                <li><a href="april.html">Roman Tynan</a></li>
            </ul>
        </li>
        <li><a href="members.html" class="current">Become a Member</a></li>
        <li class="lastitem"><a href="aboutus.html">About Us</a>
            <ul>
                <li><a href="#">Our History</a></li>
                <li><a href="#">Board of Directors</a></li>
                <li><a href="#">Past Speakers</a>
                    <ul>
                        <li><a href="#">2014</a></li>
                        <li><a href="#">2013</a></li>
                        <li><a href="#">2012</a></li>
                    </ul>
                </li>
                <li><a href="#">Contact Information</a></li>
            </ul>
        </li>
    </ul>
</nav>
```

Figure 7-17 How to create a 3-tier navigation menu

The CSS for a 3-tier navigation menu

Figure 7-18 presents the CSS for both the operation and formatting of the 3-tier menu. In the operational CSS, the first four rule sets are the same as in the CSS for the 2-tier menu.

Then, the fifth rule set formats all tier-3 submenus so they're displayed to the right of the drop-down menus. To accomplish that, all the submenus are selected (#nav_menu ul ul li ul). Then, the submenus are positioned absolutely, and their left property is set to 100%. That causes each submenu to be displayed on the right side of the drop-down menu, or 100% from the left side. Then, the top property is set to zero, so the submenu will be displayed at the top of the list item in the drop-down menu.

It's important to note that these styles will be applied to all tier-3 submenus, including those for the last item in the navigation bar. If the submenu is displayed to the right of the last item, though, it will extend beyond the body of the page. Because of that, the sixth rule set overrides the fifth rule set so the submenu is displayed to the left of the drop-down menu. To do that, it uses the "lastitem" class to select the unordered list in the drop-down list for the last item in the navigation bar (#nav_menu ul li.lastitem ul li ul). Then, it sets the left property to minus 100% instead of 100%.

The seventh rule set is the one that displays a drop-down menu or submenu when the user hovers the mouse over a list item. Here, the child selector (>) is used so only the submenu for the list item that the mouse is hovering over is displayed. Otherwise, both the drop-down menu and its submenus would be displayed when the mouse hovered over an item in the navigation bar.

Then, the last rule set in the operational CSS is like the last rule set for the 2-tier menu in figure 7-16. It stops the floating of the items in the navigation bar. Otherwise, the items in the nested ul elements would float too.

If you look now at the CSS for formatting the menus, you should be able to understand it without much trouble. But note the highlighted properties.

First, the width of the <a> elements in the list items are set to 176 pixels. That adds up to 704 pixels, but the width of the body (not shown) is set to 706 pixels. To provide for that, the selector for the <a> element in the list item with the "lastitem" class (#nav_menu ul li.lastitem a) overrides the 176 pixels and sets the width to 178 pixels. That way, the four list items add up to 706 pixels and fill out the width of the body.

Incidentally, the CSS for the operation of this menu will also work for a 2-tier navigation menu. In that case, the rule sets for the third tier will be ignored. Or, you can delete them.

The CSS for the operation of the menus

```
#nav_menu ul {
    list-style-type: none;
    position: relative; }    /* So the submenus can be positioned */
#nav_menu ul li { float: left; }
#nav_menu ul ul {
    display: none;           /* Don't display submenu until hover of li */
    position: absolute;
    top: 100%; }
#nav_menu ul ul li {
    float: none;
    position: relative; }
#nav_menu ul ul li ul {
    position: absolute;
    left: 100%;          /* Display submenu to the right of the li element */
    top: 0; }            /* Display submenu at the top of the li element */
#nav_menu ul li.lastitem ul li ul {
    position: absolute;
    left: -100%;         /* Display submenu to the left of the li element */
    top: 0; }            /* Display submenu at the top of the li element /*
#nav_menu ul li:hover > ul {      /* Select ul child of li element */
    display: block; }             /* Display the submenu on hover over li */
#nav_menu > ul::after {
    content: "";
    clear: both;
display: block; }
```

The CSS for formatting the menus

```
#nav_menu ul {
    margin: 0;
    padding: 0; }
#nav_menu ul li a {
    text-align: center;
    display: block;
    width: 176px;
    padding: 1em 0;
    text-decoration: none;
    background-color: blue;
    color: white;
    font-weight: bold; }
#nav_menu ul li.lastitem a {
    width: 178px; }   /* So the navigation bar fills the 706px body width */
#nav_menu ul li a.current {
    color: yellow; }
#nav_menu ul li a:hover, #nav_menu ul li a:focus {
    background-color: gray; }
```

Description

- The CSS for the operation of this 3-tier menu will work for any 3-tier menu like this one. It will also work for a 2-tier menu.
- To add more tiers to a menu system, you continue the logic of the 3-tier menu.

Figure 7-18 The CSS for a 3-tier navigation menu

Perspective

Now that you've completed this chapter, you should have a good perspective on what you can do with lists and links. From this point on, you can use this chapter as a reference whenever you need it.

Terms

unordered list
ordered list
nested list
description list
link
tab order
access key
placeholder
media player
plugin
MIME type
navigation menu
vertical navigation menu
horizontal navigation menu
navigation bar
multi-tier navigation menu

Summary

- An *unordered list* is displayed as a bulleted list, but you can change the bullets with CSS.
- An *ordered list* is displayed as a numbered list, but you can change the types of numbers that are used with CSS.
- A *description list* consists of terms and descriptions.
- You typically code an <a> element to create a *link* that loads another web page. You can use the tabindex attribute of an <a> element to change the *tab order* of a link, and you can use the accesskey attribute to provide an *access key* for activating the link.
- You can use pseudo-code selectors in CSS to change the default colors for links and to change the styles when the mouse hovers over a link.
- You can use the target attribute to load a linked page in a new browser window or tab. This attribute is no longer deprecated in HTML5.
- A *placeholder* is a location on a page that can be linked to. To create a placeholder, you use the id attribute of an <a> element. To go to the placeholder, you specify that id in the href attribute of another <a> element.
- If an <a> element links to a media file, the browser tries to display or play it by using the right *media player*. To help the browser find the right player, you can use the type attribute to specify a *MIME type*.
- You can also use an <a> element to start an email message, call a phone number, or start a Skype session.
- To create a *navigation menu*, you code a series of <a> elements within the li elements of an unordered list. Then, you can use CSS to remove the bullets and to change the display property so the list is displayed horizontally.
- To create a *multi-tier navigation menu*, you code an unordered list within an li element of another unordered list. Then, you can use CSS to position the submenu relative to the main menu, hide the submenu when the page is first displayed, and display the submenu when the mouse hovers over the list item that contains the submenu.

Exercise 7-1 Enhance the Town Hall home page

In this exercise, you'll add a two-tier navigation menu to the Town Hall home page that you worked on in chapter 6. You'll also add a link that plays a video, and you'll enhance the formatting of the list on the page. When you're through, the page should look like this:

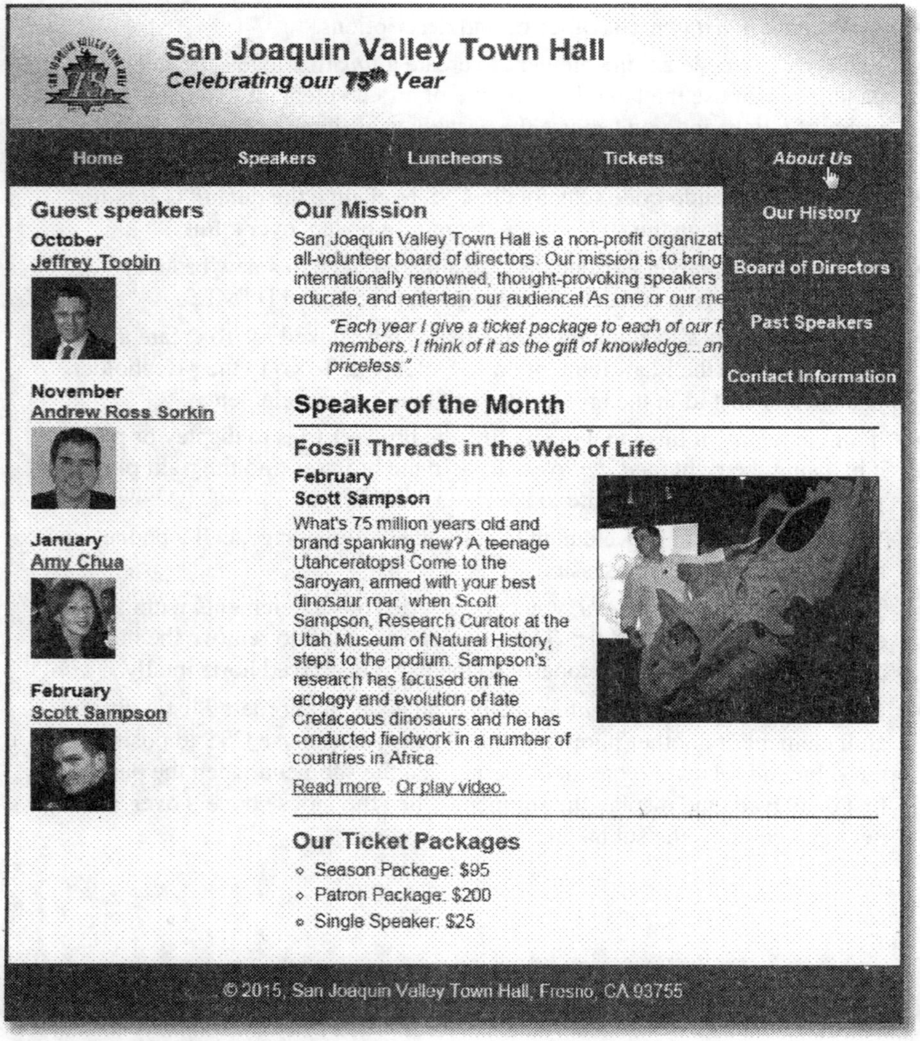

Open the HTML and CSS files for this page

1. Use your text editor to open the index.html and main.css files for the Town Hall website:

```
c:\html5_css3_2\exercises\town_hall_1\index.html
c:\html5_css3_2\exercises\town_hall_1\styles\main.css
```

Add the HTML for the main navigation menu

Use figure 7-16 as a guide as you complete steps 2 through 17.

2. Add a ul element with the id “nav_menu” between the header and main elements.
3. Add the first li element for this list. Then, add an <a> element to this list item with the href attribute set to index.html and the text set to “Home”.
4. Copy the li element you just created and paste it four times to create four more list items. Then, change the text for the links in each list item as shown above and change the href attributes accordingly.
5. Set the class for the first link to “current”.

Add the CSS for the main navigation menu

6. Add a rule set for the ul element of the navigation menu that removes the bullets from the list and sets the margins and padding for the list to 0.
7. Add a rule set for the li elements in the unordered list for the navigation menu that floats the elements to the left so they’re displayed horizontally.
8. Add a rule set for the <a> elements within the li elements that displays these elements as block elements, sets the widths of the elements to 1/5th the width of the body element, and aligns the text for these elements in the center of the block. This rule set should also set the padding above and below the <a> elements to 1 em, remove the underline from the links, set the background color to #800000, set the text color to white, and set the font weight to bold.
9. Add a rule set for the “current” class that sets the text color for that class to yellow. Then, test these changes in Chrome and adjust the CSS until you get it right.

Create and format the submenu

10. Add a ul element within the last li element in the navigation menu. Then, add four li elements with <a> elements that contain the text shown above, but don’t worry about setting the value for the href attribute of these elements.
11. Modify the rule set for the main navigation menu so it uses relative positioning.
12. Add a rule set for the submenu that uses the display property to keep the submenu from being displayed by default. This rule set should also position the submenu absolutely 100% from the top of the main menu.
13. Add a rule set for the list items in the submenu that keeps them from floating so they’re displayed vertically.
14. Add a rule set that causes the submenu to be displayed as a block element when the mouse hovers over the list item that contains the submenu.
15. Test these changes in Chrome. When you point to the About Us menu item, notice that the first item in the submenu is displayed on top of the main menu.

16. Add one more rule set for the ::after pseudo-element of the navigation menu. This rule set should add empty space following the navigation menu, clear the content so it doesn't float, and display the content as a block element.
17. Test the page again. This time, the submenu should be displayed below the main menu.

Play a video

18. At the bottom of the Speaker of the Month copy, change "Or meet us there!" to a link that plays the sampson.swf file in the media folder in a new tab or window. This link should say: "Or play video." Then, test this change.

Change the bullets in the unordered list

19. Change the bullets in the unordered list to circles. Then, test this change.

Validate and test in IE

20. When you've got everything working right, validate the HTML page and test it in IE. If you have any problems, fix them and test again in both Chrome and IE.

Exercise 7-2 Add the navigation menu to the speaker's page

1. Add the navigation menu of exercise 7-1 to the speaker's page for Scott Sampson. To do that, you need to add the HTML for the menu to the file named sampson.html in the speakers folder, and you need to add the CSS for the menu to the file named speaker.css in the styles folder.
2. Test and adjust to get the formatting right if necessary.
3. In the HTML file, make sure the paths in the links for the navigation menu are correct. Because the sampson.html page is in the speakers folder and the index.html page is in the root folder, you'll need to use a document-relative path to go to this page. Also, none of the links in the navigation menu of the sampson.html page should be current.
4. Test to be sure that you can use the link for the Home menu item to return to the home page from the speaker's page. When this works, delete the link at the bottom of the aside that returns to the home page.

8

How to use Responsive Web Design

In the first seven chapters of this book, you've learned how to create and format web pages that will be displayed on desktop computers. Because more and more websites are being accessed on mobile devices, though, it's important to know how to develop pages that adapt to smaller screen sizes. To do that, you can use the principles of Responsive Web Design.

Introduction to Responsive Web Design

In chapter 1, you learned that a website that uses *Responsive Web Design (RWD)* adapts gracefully to the size of the screen where it's displayed while maintaining the overall look-and-feel of the site. Now, you'll learn about the three components that you use to implement a *responsive design*. In addition, you'll learn about some of the ways that you can test a website that uses a responsive design.

The three components of a responsive design

Figure 8-1 describes the three components of a responsive design. To start, a responsive design uses *fluid layouts* rather than fixed layouts. That way, the width of the web page and its structural elements adjust to the size of the screen. In this figure, for example, you can see that the web page always fills 100% of the screen width. In addition, if you reduce the size of the browser window on the desktop, the width of the main content and the sidebar always occupy the same percent of the window.

Although you can use a fluid layout to adjust the widths of the structural elements on a page, you can't use them to adjust the appearance of the page. To do that, you use *media queries*. Media queries let you change the appearance of a page based on conditions, such as the width of the screen. In this figure, for example, you can see that the page looks different on mobile devices than it does on the desktop. That makes it easier to use on these devices.

Finally, a responsive design should use images whose sizes change along with the size of their containing elements. For example, the page shown here uses a *scalable image* for the image in the main content of the page. That way, as the size of the element that contains the main content changes, the size of the image changes.

A website that uses Responsive Web Design

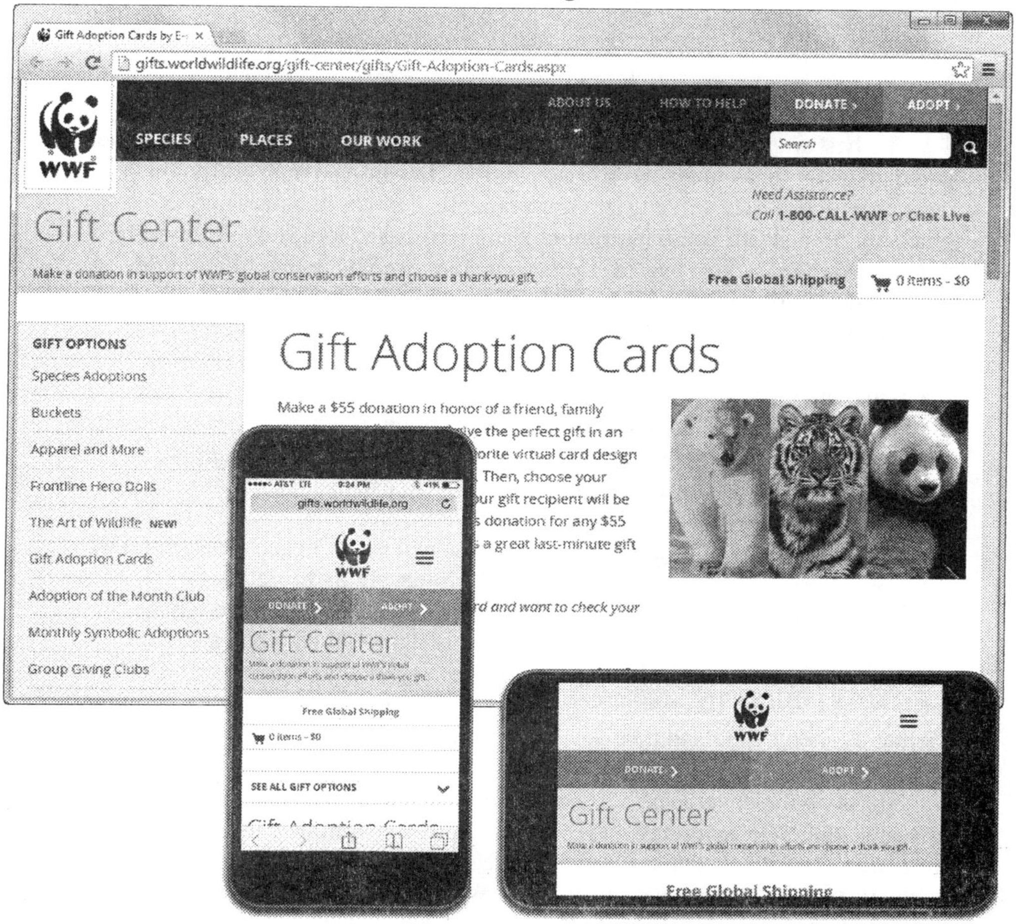

The three components of Responsive Web Design

- You use a *fluid layout* to adjust the width of a web page and its structural elements to the size of the screen.
- You use *media queries* to adjust the appearance of a web page to different device sizes.
- You use *scalable images* so the size of an image is scaled to the size of the element that contains it.

Description

- Websites that are developed using *Responsive Web Design* are designed to adapt gracefully to the size of the screen on which the site is being displayed.

Figure 8-1 The three components of Responsive Web Design

How to test a responsive design

As you develop a website using a responsive design, you'll want to test it in devices of various sizes to be sure it works as expected. Figure 8-2 describes three ways you can do that.

The best way to test a responsive design is to deploy the website to a server and then test it on as many devices as possible. Because so many different devices with different screen sizes are available, though, that may not be practical. So instead, you may want to use a web-based tool such as ProtoFluid that lets you view a web page in the screen sizes used by many different devices.

Another option is to use the device emulators and browser simulators that are available for many of the most popular mobile devices and browsers. To do that, you typically need to download the emulator or simulator from the manufacturer's website so you can run it on your desktop. In a few cases, though, you can run an emulator or simulator online. But before you can do that, you must first deploy the website to a server so it can be accessed online.

A simpler way to test a responsive design is to use the developer tools that are provided by most modern browsers. To access these tools, you display a page in the browser and then right-click on the page and select Inspect Element. You can also press F12 to access these tools in Chrome, IE, and Firefox.

When you access the developer tools, they're typically displayed at the bottom of the browser window as shown in this figure. Then, you can use techniques that are specific to each browser to display the page in various devices. In Chrome, for example, you click the Toggle Device Mode icon in the toolbar as shown here and then select a device from the drop-down list at the top of the window.

Although the developer tools are useful as you're developing a website, they also have their shortcomings. In IE, for example, the options you have to choose from aren't intuitive. And in Firefox, you can't select specific devices. Instead, you have to select from a list of device sizes. Because of that, you should also test your website on all common devices after you've deployed it.

A web page displayed using the developer tools in Chrome

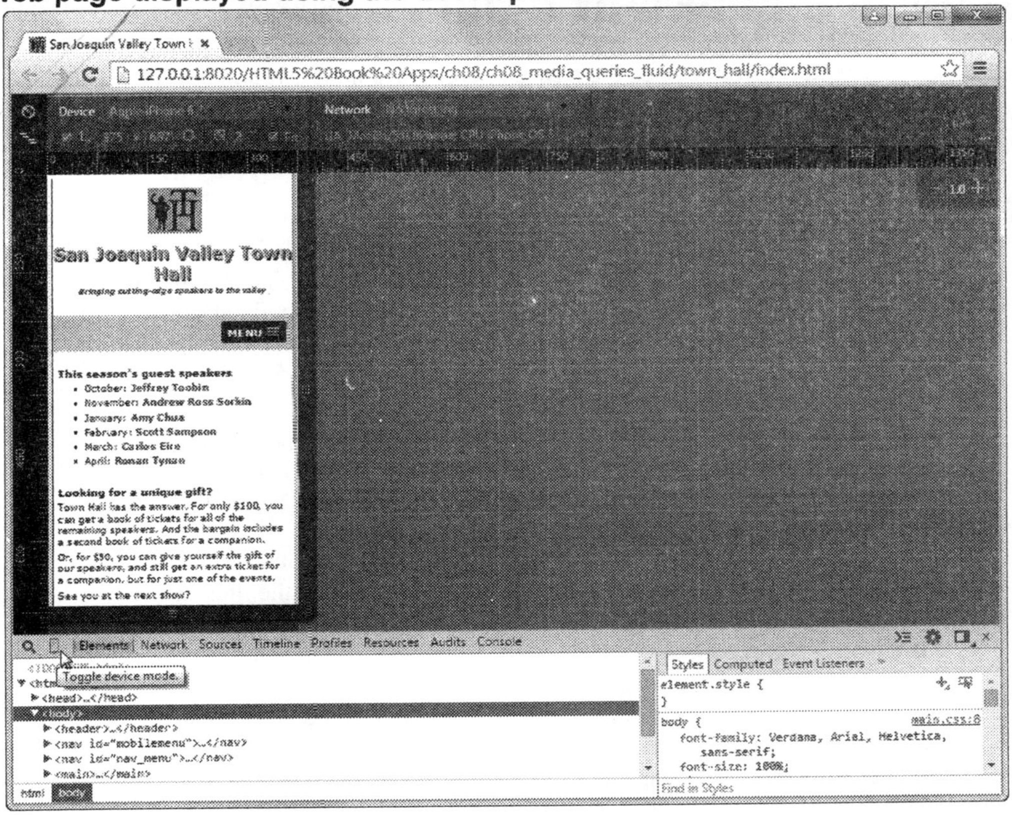

Three ways to test a responsive design

- Deploy your website to a server and then test it on each device or use a web-based tool like ProtoFluid to test it.
- Use device emulators and browser simulators for the various devices and browsers you want to test.
- Use the developer tools provided by most modern browsers.

How to use a browser's developer tools to test a responsive design

- Display the page in a browser and then press F12 or right-click on the page and select Inspect Element to display the developer tools.
- In Chrome or Opera, click the Toggle Device Mode icon near the left side of the developer tools toolbar. Then, select the device you want to emulate from the drop-down list at the top of the page. You can also drag the edges of the screen to create a custom size.
- In IE, click the Emulation tab and then select from the options that are available.
- In Firefox, click the Responsive Design Mode icon near the right side of the developer tools toolbar. Then, select a device size from the drop-down list at the top of the page, or drag the edges of the screen to create a custom size.

Figure 8-2 How to test a responsive design

How to implement a fluid design

In chapter 6, you learned the basics of creating a fluid layout. Now, I'll review those skills and present some additional skills for developing a *fluid design* that uses a fluid layout, relative font sizes, and scalable images.

Fluid layouts vs. fixed layouts

To help you understand how fluid layouts work, figure 8-3 compares them to fixed layouts. Here, you can see the layout of a page with a fixed width of 960 pixels. This page includes a header and a footer that occupy the entire width of the page, along with the main content for the page, which is 600 pixels wide, and a sidebar, which is 360 pixels wide.

When you use fixed widths like this, the width of the page and its structural elements stay the same regardless of the screen size. Because of that, you'll want to use fluid layouts when you develop a responsive design. That's true even if you use media queries, as you'll see later in this chapter.

In contrast to a page that uses a fixed layout, a page that uses a fluid layout adjusts to the size of the screen automatically. For example, the illustration in this figure indicates that the width of the page using a fluid layout is 90%. In other words, the page will fill all but 10% of the screen. Then, the widths of the elements within the page always add up to 100%.

For example, the width of the element that contains the main content is 62.5%, and the width of the sidebar is 37.5%. Note that these percents are relative to the size of the page, not the size of the screen. So in this case, the width of the element that contains the main content is 56.25% of the screen width (.625 x .90), and the width of the sidebar is 33.75% of the screen width (.375 x .90).

A comparison of fixed and fluid widths in a two-column layout

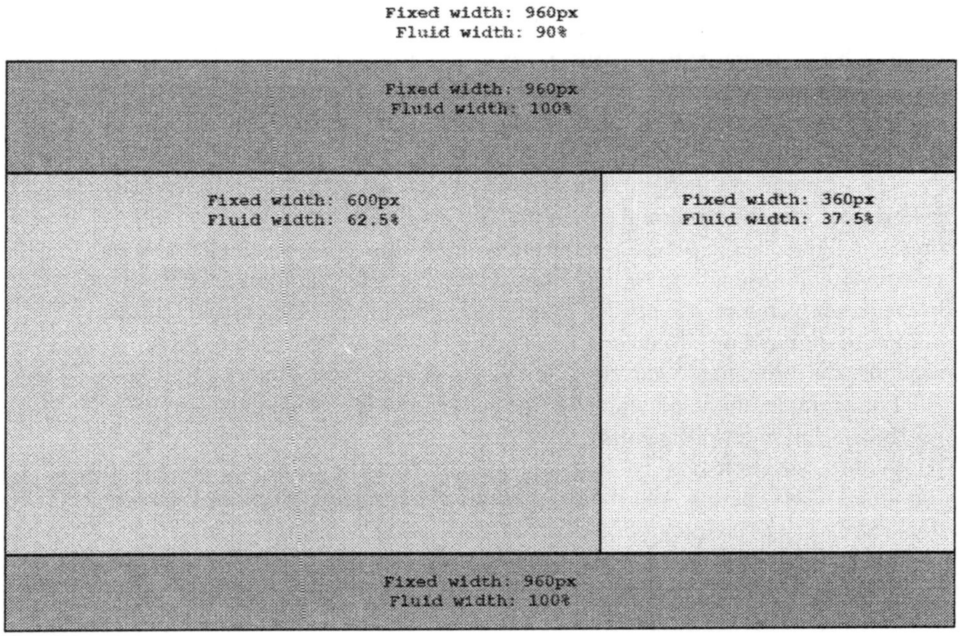

The benefits of using fluid layouts

- Page layouts are proportional to the size of the screen, so they will fill the screen equally at all sizes.
- They are scalable, so when new screen sizes become available in the future, they will automatically adapt to those new sizes.
- They can be used without media queries in some cases, although that's not common.

Description

- A *fixed layout* uses absolute measurements to specify the widths of a page and its main structural elements.
- A *fluid layout* uses percentages to specify the widths of a page and its main structural elements. This meets the challenge of a web page adapting gracefully to all screen sizes, since the layouts are proportional rather than fixed.

Figure 8-3 Fluid layouts vs. fixed layouts

How to convert fixed widths to fluid widths

If you've already developed a web page that uses fixed widths, you'll need to know how to convert the widths in pixels to widths in percents. To do that, you can use the formula shown at the top of figure 8-4. Here, *target* is the width of the element in pixels that you want to convert, and *context* is the width of its containing element in pixels.

The example in this figure illustrates how this formula works. First, the HTML includes the structural elements for a page like the one shown in the previous figure. Then, the CSS shows how the widths of those elements would be converted to use a fluid layout. Note in this example that unlike the example in the previous figure, the header, main, aside, and footer elements all include left and right padding. If you add this padding to the width of the element, though, you'll see that it adds up to the width shown in the previous figure.

For example, the fixed widths of the header and footer elements are 930 pixels plus left and right padding of 15 pixels, for a total of 960 pixels. The fixed width of the main element is 570 pixels plus left and right padding of 15 pixels, for a total of 600 pixels. And the fixed width of the aside element is 330 pixels plus left and right padding of 15 pixels, for a total of 360 pixels.

Because each of these elements is contained within the body element, you calculate its width as a percent by dividing its width in pixels by the width of the body in pixels. Here, the width of each element and its left and right padding is divided by 960 pixels as indicated by the comments on the properties that set the widths and padding for these elements. Remember, though, that the context is always the containing element. So, for example, if the main element in this figure contained additional structural elements, the widths of those elements would be calculated based on the width of the main element, not on the width of the body element.

As you review these calculations, notice that they include all the decimal places from the result. Although you might be tempted to round these results, we don't recommend that. That's because you want these values to reflect the widths of the elements as accurately as possible.

Now, take a look at the two properties that are highlighted for the body element in this figure. As described in the previous figure, the width of the body is set to 90%, which means that the page will always take up 90% of the width of the screen. Although you can set the width to whatever you want, it's typically set between 90% and 100%.

In addition to the width property, the max-width property is set to a fixed width of 1024 pixels. Because of that, the page won't expand beyond this width even if the browser window can accommodate a wider page. This is useful because most fluid pages don't look good when displayed beyond a given width, and many monitors provide for much wider widths.

Although you can specify widths, padding, and margins as percents, you should realize that you can't specify the width of a border as a percent. Because of that, you may sometimes have to adjust the widths of one or more elements within a page if the page contains left or right borders.

A formula for converting pixels to percents

```
target ÷ context x 100 = result
```

The HTML for a page with padding and borders

```
<body>
    <header><p>This is the text for the header.</p></header>
    <main><p>This is the text for the main element.</p></main>
    <aside><p>This is the text for the aside.</p></aside>
    <footer><p>This is the text for the footer.</p></footer>
</body>
```

The CSS for a fluid layout

```
body {
    width: 90%;                           /* changed from 960px */
    max-width: 1024px;                    /* maximum width of page */
    margin: 0 auto;
    border: 2px solid black; }
header {
    width: 96.875%;                       /* 930 ÷ 960 x 100 */
    padding: 15px 1.5625%;                /* 15 ÷ 960 x 100 */
    border-bottom: 2px solid black; }
main {
    width: 59.375%;                       /* 570 ÷ 960 x 100 */
    padding: 15px 1.5625%;                /* 15 ÷ 960 x 100 */
    float: left; }
aside {
    width: 34.375%;                       /* 330 ÷ 960 x 100 */
    padding: 15px 1.5625%;                /* 15 ÷ 960 x 100 */
    float: right; }
footer {
    clear: both;
    width: 96.875%;                       /* 930 ÷ 960 x 100 */
    padding: 15px 1.5625%;                /* 15 ÷ 960 x 100 */
    border-top: 2px solid black; }
```

Description

- To convert the width of an element from pixels to a percent, you divide the width of that element (the target) by the width of its parent element (the context) and then multiply that value by 100.
- The width of the outermost element determines how much of the screen the page occupies. This width is typically set between 90% and 100%.
- In addition to converting the widths of the structural elements on a page to percents, you should convert the left and right margins and padding to percents. However, you can't specify the width of a border using a percent.
- To limit the width of an element, you can use the max-width property. This property is typically used to limit the width of the entire page.

Figure 8-4 How to convert fixed widths to fluid widths

How to size fonts

In chapter 4 of this book, we recommended that you use relative measurements for your font sizes. When you do that, users can vary the sizes by using their browsers.

This is important for responsive design too. That way, the size of the font that's used by an element is relative to the size of the font used by the parent element. So if you want to change the font size that's used by a parent element and all of its child elements, you just need to change the font size for the parent element.

In this book, we've specified relative font sizes as percents, but you can also use ems. If you're working on a website that uses pixels instead, you can easily convert them to percents or ems. Figure 8-5 shows you how.

This figure starts by presenting the HTML for a simple web page. As you can see, this page has the same structure as the one shown in the previous figure, but it contains some additional content.

The CSS that follows shows how the font sizes for this page are calculated in ems. Before I explain how this works, notice that the base font size in the body element is specified as 100% rather than 1em. Although both of these values result in the same font size, we recommend you use a percent for the base font size because an issue can arise in older versions of IE if you use ems.

To calculate a font size in ems, you simply divide the font-size in pixels by 16 since 16 is the default font size for most browsers. For example, the h1 element in this figure has been converted from 28 pixels to 1.75 ems, and the h2 element has been converted from 24 pixels to 1.5em. If you want to use percents instead of pixels, you can just multiply the result by 100.

The HTML for a page with elements that use various font sizes

```
<body>
    <header><h2>San Joaquin Valley Town Hall</h2></header>
    <main>
        <h1>This season's guest speakers</h1>
        <ul>
            <li>October: <a href="speakers/toobin.html">
                Jeffrey Toobin</a></li>
            <li>November: <a href="speakers/sorkin.html">
                Andrew Ross Sorkin</a></li>
            <li>January: <a href="speakers/chua.html">Amy Chua</a></li>
        </ul>
        <p>Please contact us for tickets.</p>
    </main>
    <aside>
      <h3>Lecture day, time, and location</h3>
      <p>All one-hour lectures are on the second Wednesday of the month
         beginning at 10:30 a.m. at William Saroyan Theatre, 700 M Street,
         Fresno, CA.</p>
    </aside>
    <footer>
        <p>&copy; Copyright 2015 San Joaquin Valley Town Hall.</p>
    </footer>
</body>
```

CSS that specifies the font sizes in ems

```
body {
    font-size: 100%;                    /* 16 pixels */
    width: 90%;
    max-width: 1024px;
    margin: 0 auto;
    border: 2px solid black; }
h1 { font-size: 1.75em; }               /* 28 ÷ 16 */
h2 { font-size: 1.5em; }                /* 24 ÷ 16 */
h3 { font-size: 1.125em; }              /* 18 ÷ 16 */
footer p { font-size: .75em; }          /* 12 ÷ 16 */
```

Description

- When you specify the size of a font for a fluid layout, you should use ems or percents.
- When you use ems or percents, the size you specify is relative to the size of the parent element. That makes it easy for you to change the size of an element and all of its children at the same time. This is particularly useful for changing all the font sizes by changing the base font size.
- The default font size for most browsers is 16 pixels. Because of that, you can calculate the font size you want to use in ems by dividing the font size in pixels by 16. To calculate the font size as a percent, multiply the result by 100.
- An issue can arise with older versions of Internet Explorer if you specify the base font size for a page using ems. Because of that, you should use a percent instead.

Figure 8-5 How to size fonts

How to scale images

As the width of an element in a fluid design changes, you'll typically want the width of any images within that element to change as well. In other words, you want the image to scale with the element. Figure 8-6 shows how to create scalable images.

This figure presents part of a web page with a fluid layout that includes a section with a scalable image. To make this image scalable, I removed the height and width attributes from the img element as shown in this figure. Then, I set the max-width property for the image to 100% as shown in the first rule set in this figure. That way, the image will always be as wide as the section that contains it. Of course, an image doesn't always have to have the same width as its containing block. You'll see an example of that later in this chapter.

When you use scalable images, you won't typically want to display an image any larger than its native size. If you do, the quality of the image may be compromised. To limit an image to its native size, you use CSS like that shown in the second rule set in this figure. Here, instead of setting the max-width property to 100%, I set the width property to 100%. That way, the image will still be the same as the width of the containing block. However, I also set the max-width property to 400 pixels, which is the native width of the image. Because of that, the width will never be wider than 400 pixels even if the containing block is wider than 400 pixels.

By the way, some developers also like to set the height property to a value of "auto" when they scale images. That way, the aspect ratio of the height to the width will remain the same regardless of the scale of the image. Because "auto" is the default, though, the height property can be omitted as shown here.

Part of a web page with a fluid layout that includes a scalable image

The HTML for the image

```
<img src="images/students.jpg" alt="Instructor with students">
```

The CSS for the image

```
section img {
    max-width: 100%;
    margin-bottom: .5em;
}
```

CSS that limits the width of the image

```
section img {
    width: 100%;
    max-width: 400px;
    margin-bottom: .5em;
}
```

Description

- To create a scalable image, you remove any height and width attributes from the HTML for the image. In addition, you set the max-width property of the image to a percent of its containing block.
- If you want to limit the size of an image to its native width, you can set the width property to a percent and then set the max-width property to the native width in pixels. That way, the quality of the image will be maintained.

A web page with a fluid design

Figure 8-7 presents a web page that uses a fluid design. This is the speaker page you saw in chapter 6, but with a 3-tier navigation menu like the one you saw in chapter 7. To make this page fluid, I converted the widths of all of the structural elements to percents. For example, the widths of the header, navigation menu, and footer are set to 100% of the body element, and the widths of the article and aside are set to the appropriate percent of the body element. In addition, all of the left and right padding and margins are set to a percent of the body element.

This page also uses scalable images. In this case, the maximum width of the image in the article is set to 100% of the width of the article, so it will always be as wide as the article. Then, the width of the image in the header is set to a percent of the header width, which is the same as the width of the page. In addition, the maximum width of this image is set to the image's native width so its quality will be maintained as the page gets wider. I also set the minimum width of this image. That way, when this page is displayed on a device with a small screen, you'll still be able to tell what the image is. This is often useful for logos and other small images.

Finally, I converted the font sizes for this page to ems. This assumes that the font sizes were originally specified using pixels. If they were specified as percents, they wouldn't need to be converted.

Note that using ems or percents for the font sizes doesn't cause the size of the fonts to change as the width of the page changes. In this figure, for example, you can see the page as it would appear on a Microsoft Surface tablet in portrait orientation. If you compared the font sizes shown here with the font sizes of this page in a desktop browser, you'd see that they're identical. That's why the text in the fourth item in the navigation menu rolls over to a second line. To change the font sizes, you need to use media queries as described next.

You also need to use media queries if you want to change the appearance of the page for different screen widths. As the screen width gets smaller, for example, you'll want to change this two-column layout to a one-column layout. You'll also want to change the navigation menu so it's easier to use on smaller devices.

A page with a fluid layout that includes two scalable images

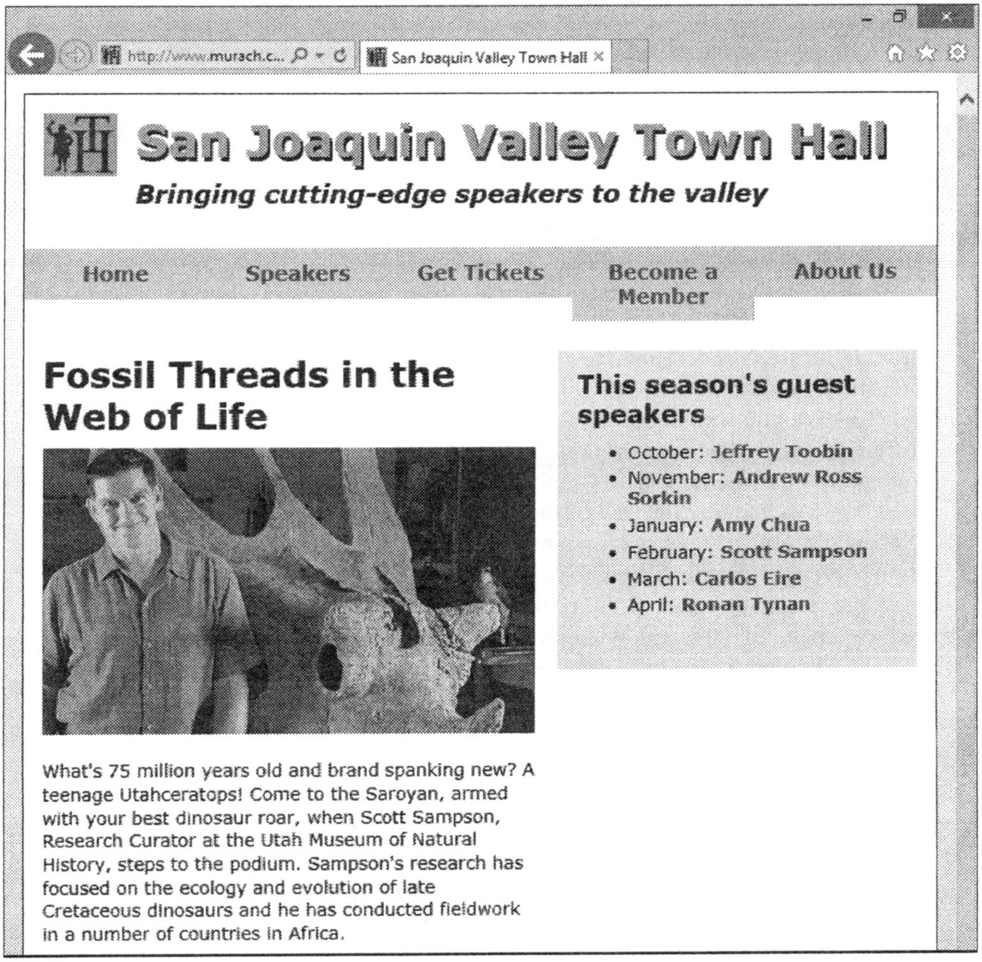

Description

- This web page uses a fluid layout where the widths of the structural elements, margins, and padding are coded as percents. That way, the widths of the elements change as the width of the browser window changes.
- Both of the images on this page are scalable. The logo in the header is scaled so it occupies a percent of the header width, and the image in the article is scaled so it occupies the entire width of the article.
- The font sizes for this page are coded in ems, but these sizes don't change as the width of the browser window changes. To change them, you need to use CSS3 media queries.
- As the width of this page is reduced, it becomes more difficult to use. To fix this, you can use CSS3 media queries.

Figure 8-7 A web page with a fluid design

How to use CSS3 media queries

In the topics that follow, you'll learn how to use media queries to control the appearance of a page in various screen sizes. You'll also learn how to build responsive menus using a jQuery plugin called SlickNav. But first, you'll learn how to control the mobile viewport so it works in conjunction with media queries.

How to control the mobile viewport

When you develop a website that uses Responsive Web Design to provide for various screen sizes, you'll want to be sure it configures the *viewport* appropriately for mobile devices. To do that, you can use the meta element that's presented in figure 8-8.

To start, you should know that the viewport on a mobile browser works differently from the viewport on a desktop browser. On a desktop browser, the viewport is the visible area of the web page. The user can change the size of the viewport by changing the size of the browser window.

In contrast, the viewport on a mobile device can be larger or smaller than the visible area. In this figure, for example, you can see that the first web page is displayed so the entire width of the page is visible. Some mobile browsers reduce a page like this automatically if no meta element is included. In contrast, other mobile browsers don't reduce the page at all, so it extends beyond the visible area of the screen as shown in the second web page in this figure.

When you use media queries, you want to be sure that the web page isn't reduced, since the media queries will adjust the appearance of the page based on the screen size. In other words, you want the page to look like the second one in this figure. To do that, you add a meta element like the one shown in this figure.

Here, the name attribute is set to "viewport" to indicate that the element applies to the viewport. Then, the content attribute specifies the properties for the viewport. The first property, width, indicates that the width of the viewport should be set to the width of the screen in CSS pixels at a zoom factor of 100%. This makes sense if you realize that a CSS pixel isn't always the same as a device pixel. On mobile devices that have high resolutions, for example, one CSS pixel can be equal to two or more device pixels. In addition, if a user zooms into a page, the number of CSS pixels per device pixel increases. At a zoom factor of 200%, for example, each CSS pixel is two device pixels wide and high.

The second property, initial-scale, determines the initial zoom factor, or *scale*, for the viewport. In this case, this scale is set to 1, which represents the default width for the viewport. This is what keeps the browser from scaling the page automatically.

In addition to the width and initial-scale properties, you may want to set some of the other properties that are presented in this figure. Specifically, when you use RWD, you may want to set the user-scalable property to "no" so the user can't zoom in or out of the display. Or, if you want to let the user zoom in or out, you can set the minimum-scale and maximum-scale properties to limit how much the user can zoom.

A web page on a mobile device without and with a meta viewport element

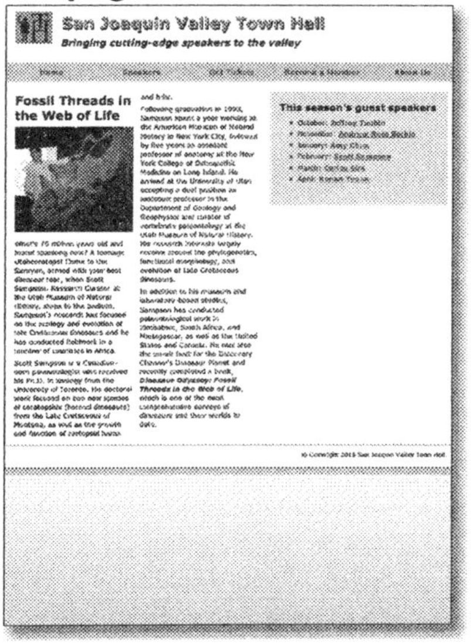

Content properties for viewport metadata

Property	Description
`width`	The logical width of the viewport specified in pixels. You can also use the device-width keyword to indicate that the viewport should be the width of the screen in CSS pixels at a scale of 100%.
`height`	The logical height of the viewport specified in pixels. You can also use the device-height keyword to indicate that the viewport should be the height of the screen in CSS pixels at a scale of 100%.
`initial-scale`	A number that indicates the initial zoom factor that's used to display the page.
`minimum-scale`	A number that indicates the minimum zoom factor for the page.
`maximum-scale`	A number that indicates the maximum zoom factor for the page.
`user-scalable`	Indicates whether the user can zoom in and out of the viewport. Possible values are yes and no.

A meta element that sets viewport properties

```
<meta name="viewport" content="width=device-width, initial-scale=1">
```

Description

- The *viewport* on a mobile device determines the content that's displayed on the screen. It can be larger or smaller than the actual visible area of the screen.
- You use a meta element to control the viewport settings for a device. You add this element within the head element of a page.
- When you use media queries, you should set the width property of the content attribute to "device-width", and you should set the initial-scale property to 1. You can also prevent or limit scaling with the user-scalable, minimum-scale, and maximum-scale properties.

Figure 8-8 How to control the mobile viewport

How to code media queries

Media queries are a CSS3 feature that allows you to write conditional expressions directly within your CSS code. These conditional expressions can be used to query various properties of a device, such as the screen size. Figure 8-9 shows how to code media queries for a responsive design.

At the top of this figure, you can see the basic syntax of a media query. It starts with an *@media selector*, followed by a media type. When you're developing a responsive design, you'll set the media type to "screen" so the media query will only be used if the page is displayed on a screen. You can also precede the media type with the only keyword. Then, if a browser doesn't support media queries, it will only check the media type.

After the media type, you code one or more conditional expressions, where each expression specifies the value of a property. The table in this figure lists some of the common properties for the screen media type. Note that all of these properties can also be prefixed with min- or max-, as shown in the media queries in this figure.

In the first media query, for example, the conditional expression uses the max-width property to check that the width of the viewport is 767 pixels or less. The second media query in this figure includes two conditional expressions. The first one checks that the width of the viewport is 480 pixels or more, and the second one checks that the width of the viewport is 767 pixels or less.

Within each media query, you code the CSS that adjusts the appearance of the web page so it's appropriate for the screen size that's specified by the query. For example, I could use a media query to change the font sizes that are used on a page or to change the layout of a page. You'll see the CSS for a web page that uses media queries like this later in this chapter.

This figure also lists all the desktop browsers that support media queries. This includes all the current versions of all the major browsers. Because of that, you can use any of these browsers to test that the media queries used by a web page work correctly. To do that, you just change the width of the browser window to the width specified by a media query. Then, the styles defined by that media query will be applied. Even if you do that, though, keep in mind that you'll still want to thoroughly test your media queries by using one of the techniques that were presented earlier in this chapter.

Before I go on, you should realize that all the desktop browsers except for Internet Explorer are updated automatically when a new version becomes available. Because of that, you don't need to check what version you have before testing media queries. If you want to use Internet Explorer for testing, though, you need to be sure that you have at least version 9.

The basic syntax of a media query

```
@media [only] media-type [and (expression-1)] [and (expression-2)]... {
    ...styles go here
}
```

Common properties for the screen media type

Property	Description
`width`	The width of the viewport.
`height`	The height of the viewport.
`device-width`	The width of the display area of the device. This is the same as width if the viewport is set as shown in figure 8-8.
`device-height`	The height of the display area of the device.
`orientation`	Landscape or portrait.

A media query that checks that the viewport width is 767 pixels or less

```
@media only screen and (max-width: 767px) {...}
```

A media query that checks that the viewport width is between 480 and 767 pixels

```
@media only screen and (min-width: 480px) and (max-width: 767px) {...}
```

Desktop browsers that support media queries

- Internet Explorer 9 and later
- Firefox 3.6 and later
- Safari 4 and later
- Opera 10 and later
- Chrome 5 and later

Description

- A *media query* is defined by a CSS3 *@media selector*. This selector specifies the media type for the query and, for the screen media type, one or more conditional expressions. If all of the conditions are true, the styles within the media query are applied to the page.
- Each conditional expression can check one of the properties listed above. These properties can also be prefixed with min- or max-.
- The screen size at which a media query is used to change the appearance of a page can be referred to as a *breakpoint*.
- Media queries are supported by all the current versions of all the major desktop browsers. That makes media queries easy to test in those browsers.
- Media queries are also supported by all the current versions of all mobile browsers.
- If you include the only keyword, older browsers that don't support media queries will check the media type but not the conditional expressions.

Figure 8-9 How to code media queries

Common media queries for a responsive design

Figure 8-10 presents some common media queries that are used to implement a responsive design. Before I describe these media queries, you should know that there are two standard techniques for developing the queries you need. First, you can start with the desktop design and then develop media queries that will be applied successively to the next smallest screen size. Second, you can start with the design for the smallest screen size and then develop media queries that will be applied successively to the next largest screen size. This design technique is often referred to as "mobile first design".

If you're developing a new website, the technique you choose may depend on personal preferences. If you're used to designing pages for the desktop, for example, you may want to do that first. But even if you do, you'll want to keep the mobile design in mind from the start. That will make it easier to add the media queries you need for smaller devices later on.

Another consideration is whether your website will be accessed primarily by users on mobile phones or by users on larger devices like tablets and computers. If it will be used primarily by mobile phone users, it makes sense to develop the mobile design first. Then, you can write the media queries for implementing the site on larger devices later.

If you're developing media queries using a desktop down design, your media queries should look something like those shown in the first example in this figure. These media queries check the max-width property, so they apply the styles they contain if a device has a width that's less than or equal to the value that's specified. Here, the first media query is for full-size tablets in portrait orientation (768 to 959 pixels), the second media query is for mobile phones in landscape orientation (480 to 767 pixels), and the third media query is for mobile phones in portrait orientation (479 pixels or less).

In addition to these media queries, you could include a media query for the desktop and tablets in landscape orientation (960 pixels or larger), but these styles are typically coded outside the media queries. You could also include a media query for all mobile phones. Then, that query would contain styles that apply to any mobile phone, and the other two queries for phones would contain styles specific to phones in landscape or portrait orientation.

The second example in this figure shows the media queries that are commonly used for a mobile up design. These queries check for smaller screen widths first by using the min-width property. Because of that, the styles in these media queries are applied if a device has a width that's greater than or equal to the value that's specified. Just as in the first example, you could also code the styles for the smallest device in a media query, but that's not necessary.

It's important to keep in mind that the media queries must be coded in the sequence shown here. That way, the styles in each media query can override the styles in the previous media query if the condition on that media query is satisfied. If you're using desktop down design, for example, and the screen width is between 480 and 767 pixels, the desktop styles will be applied first, followed by the tablet portrait styles, and then the mobile landscape styles. This will make more sense when you see the example at the end of this chapter.

Common media queries for a desktop down design

```
/* tablet landscape and desktop layout (960px or more) */
    ...tablet landscape and desktop styles go here

/* tablet portrait layout (768px to 959px) */
@media only screen and (max-width: 959px) {
    ...tablet portrait styles go here
}

/* mobile landscape layout (480px to 767px) */
@media only screen and (max-width: 767px) {
    ...mobile landscape styles go here
}

/* mobile portrait layout (479px or less) */
@media only screen and (max-width: 479px) {
    ...mobile portrait styles go here
}
```

Common media queries for a mobile up design

```
/* mobile portrait layout (479px or less) */
    ...mobile portrait styles go here

/* mobile landscape layout (480px to 767px) */
@media only screen and (min-width: 480px) {
     ...mobile landscape styles go here
}

/* tablet portrait layout (768px to 959px) */
@media only screen and (min-width: 768px) {
     ...tablet portrait styles go here
}

/* tablet landscape and desktop layout (960px or more) */
@media only screen and (min-width: 960px) {
     ...tablet landscape and desktop styles go here
}
```

Description

- One standard technique for developing the media queries for a responsive design is to start with the queries for larger devices and then work your way down to smaller devices.
- Another standard technique for developing media queries is to develop the design for the smallest mobile devices first and then work your way up to larger devices.
- When you use the techniques shown above, each media query inherits the styles that precede it in the style sheet, including styles that are coded outside of media queries. Then, the media queries can override the inherited styles.
- You can also code the starting set of styles in a media query. For a desktop down design, you would code the styles in a media query that specifies a minimum width of 960 pixels. For a mobile up design, you would code the styles in a media query that specifies a maximum width of 479 pixels.

Figure 8-10 Common media queries for a responsive design

How to build responsive menus with the SlickNav plugin

When you develop a responsive design, you need to provide for menus that can be accessed easily on small mobile devices. One way to do that is to use a jQuery plugin called SlickNav. Figure 8-11 shows how this plugin works.

To use the SlickNav plugin, you start by downloading its Zip file from http://slicknav.com and then unzipping this file. Next, you copy the slicknav.css and jquery.slicknav.min.js files to your website. Then, you include a link element for the .css file, which includes the styles for the plugin, and you include a script element for the .js file, which includes the JavaScript for the plugin.

In addition to the link and script elements for the SlickNav plugin, you must include a script element for the jQuery core library, since this library is used by the SlickNav plugin. Note that this element must be coded before the script element for the plugin. Also note that you can retrieve the jQuery library from the Content Delivery Network (CDN) on the jQuery website by coding the script element as shown here. That way, you don't have to download this library.

Finally, you code a script element that calls the slicknav method within the jQuery ready event handler. To do that, you use a jQuery selector that refers to the id of the standard navigation menu, followed by the method name. Note that this menu must be coded using an unordered list as shown in the previous chapter. You can also code one or more parameters for the slicknav method. Here, the prependTo parameter is used to add the mobile menu to the nav element that has an id of "mobile_menu". Without this parameter, the menu would be added at the beginning of the body element. For a complete list of parameters, see the SlickNav website.

When you use the SlickNav plugin, you must provide a way to display the mobile menu on smaller screens and hide it on larger screens. To do that, you use media queries. If you're using a desktop down design, for example, you'll want to include a rule set in the desktop styles that hides the mobile menu by setting its display property to "none". Then, when you want to display this menu, you set the display property for this menu to "block". In the example in this figure, this is done by using an id selector.

In addition to hiding and displaying the mobile menu, you can change its appearance using classes that are defined in the slicknav.css file. In the next figure, for example, you'll see a mobile menu with a different background color than the one shown here. To find out what classes are available, just display the slicknav.css file.

To use the SlickNav menu, you simply click on the MENU button to display the first level of the menu. Then, you can click an item in the menu to display another page. Or, if a menu item has a submenu, you can click on it to display that submenu. To hide any menus that are displayed, just click the MENU button again.

A multi-tier menu that uses SlickNav

Code for the SlickNav plugin in the head element

```
<link rel="stylesheet" href="styles/slicknav.css">
<script src="https://code.jquery.com/jquery-2.1.3.min.js"></script>
<script src="js/jquery.slicknav.min.js"></script>
<script type="text/javascript">
    $(document).ready(function(){
        $('#nav_menu').slicknav({prependTo:"#mobile_menu"});
    });
</script>
```

HTML for the SlickNav menu and the navigation menu

```
<nav id="mobile_menu"></nav>
<nav id="nav_menu">
    <ul>
        <li><a href="index.html">Home</a></li>
        .
        .
    </ul>
</nav>
```

CSS for the SlickNav menu

```
/* hide the mobile menu */
#mobile_menu { display: none; }
.
.
/* display the mobile menu */
#mobile_menu { display: block; }
```

Description

- To use the SlickNav plugin, download the Zip file from http://slicknav.com. Then, unzip this file and add the slicknav.css and jquery.slicknav.min.js files to your website.
- Before you can use the SlickNav plugin on a web page, you must include a link element for the slicknav.css file and a script element for the jquery.slicknav.min.js file. You must also include a script element for the jQuery core library, and this element must be coded before the script element for the jquery.slicknav.min.js file.
- To use the SlickNav plugin, add a script element with the jQuery code shown above that refers to the element that contains the unordered list for the menu and the element for the mobile menu. Then, use the CSS display property to hide and display the mobile menu depending on the size of the screen.

Figure 8-11 How to build responsive menus with the SlickNav plugin

A web page that uses Responsive Web Design

To complete this chapter, the next three figures present a web page that uses a responsive design. This is the same web page you saw in figure 8-7 that used a fluid layout, but this page also uses media queries.

The design of the web page

Figure 8-12 shows the design of this page on the desktop and in both landscape and portrait orientation on an iPhone 6. The design of this page in portrait orientation on a tablet is identical to the design for the desktop, except that some of the fonts are smaller.

If you compare the appearance of this page in the desktop browser with its appearance in the iPhone in landscape orientation, you'll notice some major differences. To start, everything is smaller on the iPhone, which you would expect. Second, the margin and border have been removed from the page so it can use all of the available screen. Third, the logo is displayed above the text for the header and the logo and text are centered. If you scrolled down to the bottom of the page, you would see that the footer is centered too. Fourth, a SlickNav menu is displayed instead of a standard navigation menu. Fifth, the content is displayed in a single column with the article displayed before the sidebar. And sixth, the image in the article is floated to the left and it's sized so it takes up only a portion of the article width.

You'll also notice one main difference between the appearance of this page in landscape orientation and in portrait orientation on an iPhone. That is, the image in the article is changed back so it once again occupies the full width of the article.

A speaker page in desktop and mobile layouts

Description

- This web page uses a fluid layout and scalable images like the one in figure 8-7.
- This web page also uses media queries to change the appearance of the page depending on the size of the screen where it's displayed.
- The tablet portrait layout for this page is identical to the desktop and tablet landscape layout except that the font sizes are reduced.

The HTML for the web page

Now that you've seen how the speaker page looks, you're ready to see the code that makes it work. Figure 8-13 shows the HTML for the main structural elements of this page.

If you were to compare this code with the code for the same page from chapter 6, you would notice two main differences other than the addition of a navigation manu. First, the widths of the images in the header and the article have been omitted. That way, they can be scaled using CSS. Second, the sequence of the aside and article elements have been switched. That way, the article will be displayed before the aside when the page is displayed in a single column.

Those are the only structural changes to the HTML that are needed to convert this page to a responsive design. Remember, though, that if you're going to use the SlickNav plugin, you also need to add the code that it requires to the HTML. Here, you can see the nav element where the SlickNav menu will be displayed. In addition to this element, you need to include the code in the head element that's shown in figure 8-11.

The HTML for the main structural elements

```
<body>
    <header>
        <img src="images/logo.gif" alt="Town Hall Logo">
        <h2>San Joaquin Valley Town Hall</h2>
        <h3>Bringing cutting-edge speakers to the valley</h3>
    </header>
    <nav id="mobile_menu"></nav>
    <nav id="nav_menu">
        <ul>
            <li><a href="index.html">Home</a></li>
            <li><a href="#">Speakers</a>
                <ul>
                    <li><a href="#">Jeffrey Toobin</a></li>
                    <li><a href="#">Andrew Ross Sorkin</a></li>
                    <li><a href="#">Amy Chua</a></li>
                    <li><a href="sampson.html">Scott Sampson</a>
                        <ul>
                            <li><a href="#">September 2010</a></li>
                            <li><a href="#">Febuary 2015</a></li>
                        </ul>
                    </li>
                    <li><a href="march.html">Carlos Eire</a></li>
                    <li><a href="april.html">Roman Tynan</a></li>
                </ul>
            </li>
            <li><a href="tickets.html">Get Tickets</a></li>
            <li><a href="members.html">Become a Member</a></li>
            <li class="lastitem"><a href="aboutus.html">About Us</a></li>
        </ul>
    </nav>
    <main>
        <article>
            <h1>Fossil Threads in the Web of Life</h1>
            <img src="images/sampson.jpg" alt="Scott Sampson">
            <p>What's 75 million years old and brand spanking new? ... </p>
            .
            .
        </article>
        <aside>
            <h2>This season's guest speakers</h2>
            <nav>
                <ul>
                    <li>October: <a class="date_passed"
                        href="speakers/toobin.html">Jeffrey Toobin</a></li>
                    .
                    .
                    <li>April: <a href="speakers/tynan.html">
                        Ronan Tynan</a></li>
                </ul>
            </nav>
        </aside>
    </main>
    <footer>
      <p>&copy; Copyright 2015 San Joaquin Valley Town Hall.</p>
    </footer>
</body>
```

Figure 8-13 The HTML for the web page

The CSS for the web page

Figure 8-14 shows the changes to the CSS for the speaker page that controls the appearance of the page. Here, I've included a comment for each property that was changed to create a fluid layout to indicate how it was changed. For example, the width property for the body of this page was changed from 990 pixels to 96%, so the page will occupy 96% of the viewport. In addition, I set the max-width property for the body to 1200 pixels so the page won't expand beyond that on a widescreen monitor.

I also converted the widths and left and right margins and padding for all of the structural elements to percents. Because the page was originally defined with a width of 990 pixels, and because most of the structural elements are children of an element that extends the entire width of the page, I calculated the widths for these elements by dividing its width in pixels by 990.

One exception is the Speakers submenu that's displayed below the navigation menu when the mouse hovers over the Speakers list item (#nav_menu ul li:hover ul), which is set to 100% of the width of the Speakers list item. The other exception is the Scott Sampson submenu that's displayed to the right of the Speakers submenu when the mouse hovers over the Scott Sampson list item (#nav_menu ul li:hover ul li:hover ul li), which is set to 100% of the width of the Speakers list. These are two situations where you have to keep the context in mind when you specify a width as a percent. If you need to, you can refresh your memory on how a three-tier menu like this works by referring back to chapter 7.

I also included the width property for elements that extend the entire width of the page. Specifically, I specified a width of 100% for the header, the navigation menu, and the footer. Although this is the default if you don't specify a width, including this property can be helpful documentation.

Next, I converted all of the font sizes to ems. Keep in mind here that I'm assuming that the fonts were originally specified in pixels and not as percents as shown throughout this book. For example, the font size for the <p> element was originally set to 14 pixels, so I calculated its size in ems by dividing that value by 16.

To complete the fluid layout, I made the images scalable. To scale the image in the article, I set its max-width property to 100%. That way, the width of the image will always be the same as the width of the article.

Because I don't want the image in the header to be displayed larger than its native size, I scaled it by setting its width property to a percent and its max-width property to its native width in pixels. In addition, I set the min-width property to half its native width. That way, it won't become so small that you can't tell what it is.

The CSS that controls the appearance of the page Page 1

```
/* standard 960 and above */

/* changes to the styles for the type selectors */
body {
    font-family: Verdana, Arial, Helvetica, sans-serif;
    font-size: 100%;
    width: 96%;                               /* changed from 990 pixels */
    max-width: 1200px;                        /* maximum width of page */
    ...
}
section, article, aside, h1, h2, h3, p {
    margin: 0;
    padding: 0;
}
section, article, aside { margin-bottom: 1em; }
p { font-size: .875em; ... }                  /* 14 ÷ 16 */

/* changes to the styles for the header */
header { width: 100%; ... }                   /* full width of body */
header h2 {
    font-size: 2.25em;                        /* 36 ÷ 16 */
    margin-left: 12.12121%;                   /* 120 ÷ 990 x 100 */
    ...
}
header h3 {
    font-size: 1.25em;                        /* 20 ÷ 16 */
    font-style: italic;
    margin-left: 12.12121%;                   /* 120 ÷ 990 x 100 */
}
header img {
    width: 8.0808%;                           /* 80 ÷ 990 x 100 */
    max-width: 80px;                          /* native size */
    min-width: 40px;                          /* minimum size */
    float: left;
    margin-left: 2.0202%;                     /* 20 ÷ 990 x 100 */
}

/* changes to the styles for the navigation menu */
#nav_menu ul { width: 100%; ... }             /* full width of body */
#nav_menu ul li { width: 20%; ... }           /* 198 ÷ 990 x 100 */
}
#nav_menu ul li:hover ul { width: 100%; }     /* full width of list item */
}
#nav_menu ul li:hover ul li:hover ul li { width: 100%; }
                                              /* full width of list */

/* changes to the styles for the article */
article {
    width: 54.0404%;                          /* 535 ÷ 990 x 100 */
    float: left;
    margin-left: 2.0202%;                     /* 20 ÷ 990 x 100 */
    padding: 1.5em 2.52525% 0 0;              /* 25 ÷ 990 x 100 */

}
article h1 { font-size: 1.625em; ...          /* 26 ÷ 16 */
article img { max-width: 100%; ... }          /* full width of article */
```

Figure 8-14 The CSS for the web page (part 1 of 3)

Finally, I added the media queries that change the appearance of the page for different screens sizes. For a tablet in portrait view, I simply reduced some of the fonts so the elements fit better on the screen. For a mobile phone in landscape view, though, I made a number of changes to the styles to implement the changes to the appearance of the page that you saw in figure 8-12.

First, I changed the display property of the navigation menu to “none” to hide it, and I changed the display property of the mobile menu to “block” to display it. This property is set to “none” in the styles outside the media queries so it’s not displayed on larger screens. I also changed the background-color property of the SlickNav menu using the .slicknav_menu class. Note that I included the !important rule for this property so it will override the property set in the slicknav.css file.

Next, I changed the styles for the body so it will fill the screen. To do that, I set the width to 100%, I removed the margins, and I removed the border.

To display the header as shown in figure 8-12, I removed the floating from the image so it’s displayed above the two headings. I also aligned the text within the header so the image and headings are centered. Then, I reduced the font-sizes for the headings and I adjusted the margins. To change the layout of the footer, I centered and removed the right margin from the paragraph it contains.

The CSS that controls the page layout

Page 2

```
/* changes to the styles for the sidebar */
aside {
    width: 35.35353%;                       /* 350 ÷ 990 x 100 */
    float: left;
    padding: 2.0202%;                       /* 20 ÷ 990 x 100 */
    background-color: #ffebc6;
    margin: 1.5em 2.0202% 0 0;              /* 20 ÷ 990 x 100 */
}
aside h2 { font-size: 1.25em; ... }         /* 20 ÷ 16 */
aside h3 { font-size: 1em; }                /* base font size */
aside li { font-size: .875em; ... }         /* 14 ÷ 16 */

/* changes to the styles for the footer */
footer { width: 100%; ... }                 /* full width of body */
footer p {
    font-size: .75em;                       /* 12 ÷ 16 */
    text-align: right;
    margin-right: 2.0202%;                  /* 20 ÷ 990 x 100 */
}

/* hide the mobile menu initially */
#mobile_menu {
    display: none;
}

/* tablet portrait to standard 960 */
@media only screen and (max-width: 959px) {
    #nav_menu ul li a { font-size: .875em; }          /* 14 ÷ 16 */
    section h1, article h1 { font-size: 1.5em; }      /* 24 ÷ 16 */
    section h2, aside h2 { font-size: 1.125em; }      /* 18 ÷ 16 */
}

/* mobile landscape to tablet portrait */
@media only screen and (max-width: 767px) {
    #nav_menu { display: none; }
    #mobile_menu { display: block; }
    .slicknav_menu { background-color: #facd8a !important; }
    body {
        width: 100%;                        /* full width of screen */
        margin: 0;                          /* no margins */
        border: none;                       /* no border */
    }
    header, footer p { text-align: center; }
    footer p { margin-right: 0; }
    header h2 {
        font-size: 1.625em;                 /* 26 ÷ 16 */
        margin: .4em 0 .25em 0;
    }
    header h3 {
        font-size: 1em;                     /* base font size */
        margin-left: 0;
    }
    header img { float: none; }
```

Figure 8-14 The CSS for the web page (part 2 of 3)

To display the content for the page in a single column, floating is removed from both the article and the aside. In addition, the margins and padding for these elements are adjusted so an equal amount of space is displayed at the left and right sides of the screen. Finally, the widths of these elements are set so they take up the rest of the screen. In other words, the widths of these elements are 100% minus the widths of any margins and padding for the elements.

The styles for the image within the article are also changed so the image floats to the left of the text. The width of this element is set to 50% of the width of the article, and the right margin is set to 2%. That means that the text for the article will take up the remaining 48%.

The media query for a phone in portrait view further reduces some of the fonts. In addition, it changes the image in the article so it takes up the full width of the article again. To do that, it removes the floating from the image, changes its width to 100%, and removes the right margin.

The CSS that controls the page layout

Page 3

```
    article {
        width: 95.9596%;             /* 100 - (2 x 2.0202) for padding */
        float: none;
        margin-right: 2.0202%;       /* 20 ÷ 990 x 100 */
        padding-right: 0;
    }
    article img {
        float: left;
        width: 50%;
        margin-right: 2%;
    }
    aside {
        width: 91.9192%;    /* 100 - (4 x 2.0202) for padding and margins */
        float: none;
        margin: 0 2.0202% 2.0202% 2.0202%;         /* 20 ÷ 990 x 100 */
    }
}

/* mobile portrait to mobile landscape */
@media only screen and (max-width: 479px) {
    header h2 { font-size: 1.375em; }              /* 22 ÷ 16 */
    header h3 { font-size: .8125em; }              /* 13 ÷ 16 */
    p { font-size: .875em; }                       /* 14 ÷ 16 */
    article h1, aside h2 {
        font-size: 1em; }                          /* base font size */
    aside li { font-size: .875em; }                /* 14 ÷ 16 */
}
    article img {
        float: none;
        width: 100%;
        margin-right: 0;
}
    aside h3 { font-size: .9375em; }               /* 15 ÷ 16 */
    footer p { font-size: .6875em; }               /* 11 ÷ 16 */
}
```

Figure 8-14 The CSS for the web page (part 3 of 3)

Perspective

The use of mobile devices has increased dramatically over the past few years. Because of that, it has become important to design websites that are easy to use from these devices. Although that often means more work, this can be a critical aspect of maintaining your presence in the business world.

In this chapter, you learned how to develop websites using Responsive Web Design. With RWD, you use fluid layouts to adjust the width of a page depending on the screen size. You use media queries to adjust the appearance of a page depending on the screen size. And you use scalable images to adjust the size of the images depending on the screen size. With these features, you can develop responsive websites that have the same look-and-feel on desktops, tablets, and smart phones.

Terms

Responsive Web Design (RWD)
responsive design
fluid design
fixed layout
fluid layout
media query
scalable image
viewport
scale
@media selector
breakpoint

Summary

- *Responsive Web Design* refers to a technique that's used to create websites that adapt gracefully to any screen size. A *responsive design* includes fluid layouts, media queries, and scalable images.
- To create a web page with a *fluid layout*, you set the widths of the page and its main structural elements to percents so they increase and decrease depending on the width of the screen.
- To convert the fixed width for an element to a fluid width, you divide the width of the element in pixels by the width of its containing element in pixels and then multiply the result by 100 to get a percent.
- When you develop a responsive design, you should specify font sizes in ems or percents. To convert a font size from pixels to ems, you divide the size by 16 since that's the default size for most browsers. To convert the font size to a percent, you multiply the result of the division by 100.
- To create a *scalable image*, you remove the height and width property from the img element for the image, and you set the max-width property to the percent of its containing block you want it to fill.
- If you want to limit the size of an image to its native size, you can set the width property to a percent and then set the max-width property to the native width in pixels.

- A *media query* is defined by a CSS3 *@media selector* that uses conditional expressions to determine when the styles it contains are applied. You use media queries with RWD to change the appearance of a page for different screen sizes.
- When you use media queries with RWD, you can develop the design for larger devices first and then work your way down to smaller devices. Or, you can develop the design for the smallest device first and then work your way up to larger devices.
- The *viewport* on a mobile device determines the content that's displayed on the screen. When you use media queries, the viewport should be set so the page is displayed at its full size.
- SlickNav is a jQuery plugin that converts a standard navigation menu to a menu that's easier to use on smaller devices.
- An easy way to test a responsive design is to use the developer tools that are provided by most modern browsers. You can also use device emulators and browsers simulators, or you can deploy the website and then test it on various devices or use a web-based tool like ProtoFluid.

Exercise 8-1 Convert the Town Hall home page to use a responsive design

In this exercise, you'll convert the Town Hall home page that you worked on in exercise 7-1 so it uses a fluid layout, scalable images, and media queries. When you're through, the page should look like this in mobile phone portrait and landscape orientations:

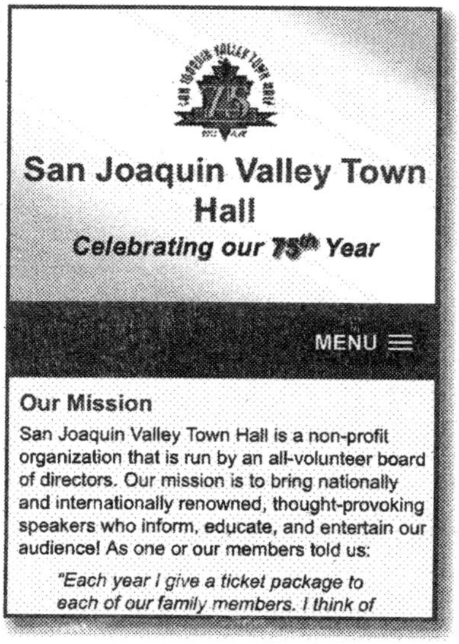

Open the HTML and CSS files for this page

1. Use your text editor to open the index.html and main.css files for the Town Hall website:

```
c:\html5_css3_2\exercises\town_hall_1\index.html
c:\html5_css3_2\exercises\town_hall_1\styles\main.css
```

Add a meta element for the viewport

2. Add a meta element like the one shown in figure 8-8 to the HTML for the page.
3. Display the page in Chrome. Then, size your browser window so it's just wide enough to see all of the page.

Convert the fixed widths to fluid widths

4. Display the CSS file for this page and note that the width of the body is set to 800 pixels. Then, change this width to 99% so there's room for the 3-pixel left and right borders, and change the maximum width to 960 pixels.
5. Change the widths of the section and aside elements and the <a> elements within the unordered list for the main navigation menu to percents by using the formula in figure 8-4. Do the same for the left and right padding for the image in the header, the left and right padding for the section, and the left padding for the aside.
6. Test these changes in Chrome. When you do, you'll notice that changing the widths of the <a> elements doesn't work.
7. Move the style rule that specifies the width of the <a> elements to the rule set for the li elements that contain the <a> elements, and then test the page again. This time, the navigation menu should look the way it did to start.
8. Notice that, unlike when you first displayed this page, it now extends beyond the right side of the browser window. That's because you set the maximum width of the body to 960 pixels, which is 160 pixels wider than the original page. Increase the width of the browser window to see that the width of the page will increase only until it reaches 960 pixels.
9. Now, decrease the width of the browser window until the sidebar no longer fits next to the section to see that the sidebar is now displayed below the section. Although this is generally what you want to happen, the formatting can be greatly improved.
10. Continue decreasing the width of the browser window to see what happens to the article. To improve this, you'll make the image scalable.

Make the image in the article scalable

11. Display the HTML for the page and notice that the img element for the image in the article doesn't contain width or height attributes. Because of that, the image is displayed at its native width of 250 pixels, and the text that flows into the space to its left takes up the rest of the width of the article.

12. Set the max-width property of this image to 40%. In addition, set the min-width property to 150 pixels so the image doesn't get to be too small. Then, test the page.

Add a media query for a tablet in portrait view

13. Code a media query for the screen type that checks that the viewport width is 959 pixels or less. Within this media query, reduce the font size for the h1 element in the section to 135%, and reduce the font size for the h2 elements in the section and aside to 120%.
14. Test this media query. To do that, make the browser window wide enough to see the entire page. Then, reduce the width so it's less than the width of the page. When you do, the size of the h1 and h2 headings in the section and aside should change.

Add a media query for a phone in landscape orientation

15. Code a media query for the screen type that checks that the viewport width is 767 pixels or less. Within this media query, change the image in the header so it doesn't float and center the contents of the header.
16. Test this media query by reducing the width of the browser window until the styles you just coded are applied. Although this looks pretty good, the line length in the section is starting to get too short.
17. Change the section and aside so they don't float. Then, set the right padding for the aside so it's the same as the left padding, and set the widths of the section and aside by subtracting the left and right padding from 100%.
18. Test the page and notice that the image in the article is too big. Fix that by changing the maximum width of the image to 30% and then test again.
19. To improve the formatting for the aside, display the speakers in two columns. To do that, you'll need to add a div around everything in the aside except the h2 element. Then, you can set the -moz-column-count, -webkit-column-count, and column-count properties to 2. Test this change.

Add a media query for a phone in portrait orientation

20. Code a media query for the screen type that checks that the viewport width is 479 pixels or less.
21. Change the base font size to 90%, then test this page. When you reduce the width of the page to less than 480 pixels, all of the font sizes should be reduced. This illustrates the advantage of using relative sizes for fonts.

Add a mobile menu using the SlickNav plugin

22. Use figure 8-11 as a guide to add a link element for the slicknav.css file in the styles folder and a script element for the jquery.slicknav.min.js file in the js folder to the head element of the page. In addition, add a script element for the jQuery core library before the script element for the SlickNav plugin.
23. Add a nav element before the nav element for the navigation menu, and give it an id of "mobile_menu".

24. Add another script element like the one in figure 8-11 that includes the jQuery for calling the slicknav method.
25. Add a rule set outside the media queries that hides the mobile menu. Then, add three rule sets in the media query for a phone in landscape orientation. The first one should hide the standard navigation menu, the second one should display the mobile menu, and the third one should set the background color of the mobile menu to #800000 using the slicknav_menu class.
26. Test this code, and notice that the mobile menu still has its default background color of dark gray. To change that, add an !important rule to the style rule for the background color and test again.

Use the developer tools to test the page

27. With the page still displayed in Chrome, press F12 to display the developer tools in a pane at the bottom of the browser window.
28. Click the Toggle Device Mode icon to display the page in a grid in the top portion of the window that shows the device size. If a message is displayed indicating that you may need to reload the page, go ahead and do that.
29. Select Apple iPhone 6 from the first drop-down list at the top of the window, reloading the page if necessary. The page will be displayed in portrait orientation.
30. Click the Swap Dimensions icon to the right of the dimensions for the iPhone 6 to display the page in landscape orientation.
31. Continue testing to see how the page will be displayed in different devices. When you're done, click the Close button in the upper right corner of the developer tools pane and then close the browser.

Section 2

More HTML and CSS skills as you need them

In section 1, you learned a professional subset of HTML and CSS skills that you can use for building most web pages. Now, in this section, you can add to those skills by learning new skills whenever you need them. To make that possible, each chapter in this section is an independent training module. As a result, you can read these chapters in whatever sequence you prefer.

To start, chapter 9 builds on the skills you learned in section 1 for working with images. Then, the remaining chapters present information on new subjects.

In chapter 10, you'll learn how to code tables that present tabular data. In chapter 11, you'll learn how to code forms using the HTML5 controls and validation features. In chapter 12, you'll learn how to use the HTML5 elements for adding audio and video to your web pages. In chapter 13, you'll learn how to embed fonts in a web page and how to format web pages for printing. And in chapter 14, you'll learn how to use CSS3 transitions, transforms, filters, and animations.

9

How to work with images

In chapter 3, you learned the basic skills for including images on a web page. Now, this chapter will expand upon those skills.

Basic skills for working with images

In the topics that follow, you'll learn the basic skills for working with images. This information will review and expand upon the skills you learned in chapter 3.

Types of images for the Web

Figure 9-1 presents the three types of images you can use on a web page. To start, *JPEG files* are commonly used for photographs and scanned images, because these files can represent millions of colors and they use a type of compression that can display complex images with a small file size.

Although JPEG files lose information when they're compressed, they typically contain high quality images to begin with so this loss of information isn't noticeable on a web page. Similarly, although JPEG files don't support transparency, you usually don't need it for any of the colors in a photograph.

In contrast, *GIF files* are typically used for simple illustrations or logos that require a limited number of colors. Two advantages of storing images in this format are (1) they can be compressed without losing any information, and (2) one of the colors in the image can be transparent.

A GIF file can also contain an *animated image*. An animated image consists of a series of images called *frames*. When you display an animated image, each frame is displayed for a preset amount of time, usually fractions of a second. Because of that, the image appears to be moving. For example, the two globes in this figure are actually two of 30 frames that are stored in the same GIF file. When this file is displayed, the globe appears to be rotating.

Unlike the GIF and JPEG formats, which have been used for years in print materials, *PNG files* were developed specifically for the Web. In particular, this format was developed as a replacement for the GIF format. The PNG advantages over the GIF format include better compression, support for millions of colors, and support for variable transparency.

Image types

Type	Description
JPEG	Typically used for photographs and scanned images because it uses a type of compression that can display complex images with a small file size. A JPEG file can represent millions of colors, loses information when compressed, and doesn't support transparency.
GIF	Typically used for logos, small illustrations such as clip art, and animated images. A GIF file can represent up to 256 colors, doesn't lose information when compressed, and supports transparency on a single color.
PNG	Typically used as a replacement for still GIF images. Compressed PNG files are typically smaller than GIF compressed files, although no information is lost. This format can represent millions of colors and supports transparency on multiple colors. PNG files are supported by all modern browsers, as well as mobile devices.

Typical JPEG images

Typical GIF images

Description

- *JPEG* (Joint Photographic Experts Group) images are commonly used for the photographs and images of a web page. Although information is lost when you compress a JPEG file, the reduced quality of the image usually isn't noticeable.
- *GIF* (Graphic Interchange Format) images are commonly used for logos and small illustrations. They can also be used for *animated images* that contain *frames*.
- The *PNG* (Portable Network Graphics) format was developed specifically for the web as a replacement for GIF files.

Figure 9-1 Types of images for the Web

How to include an image on a page

To include an image on a web page, you use the img element. Figure 9-2 presents the most common attributes of this element. Because you saw these attributes in chapter 3, you shouldn't have any trouble understanding how they work.

The HTML shown in this figure contains two img elements. Although they both display the same image, the first element includes height and width attributes. These attributes should be used to indicate the actual size of the image in pixels, so you shouldn't include any unit of measure when you code them.

When you code them so they represent the actual size of the image, the browser can reserve the correct amount of space for the image as the page is loaded. Then, the browser can reserve the right amount of space for the image and continue rendering the page as it is loaded. This can improve the user experience if a page contains many images.

How to resize an image

If you need to resize an image, figure 9-2 shows how to do that with CSS. Here, the CSS resizes the second image so it's half of its original size. In this example, both the height and width are specified, but if you specify either one, you'll get the same result. That's because the other value will be calculated automatically based on the original proportions of the image.

The trouble with resizing an image is that the image is still downloaded at its full size before it's reduced. The best way to resize an image, then, is to use an image editor to create an image that's the right size. You'll learn more about that later in this chapter.

Before you continue, you should remember that you can also resize an image by making it scalable. You typically do that when you create a web page with a fluid layout, as you learned in chapter 8. Then, the size of the image changes automatically along with the size of the element that contains it. For more information, please see figure 8-6 in chapter 8.

Attributes of the <img> tag

Attribute	Description
`src`	The relative or absolute URL of the image to display. It is required.
`alt`	Alternate text to display in place of the image. It is required.
`height`	The height of the image in pixels.
`width`	The width of the image in pixels.

CSS properties for sizing an image

Property	Description
`height`	A relative or absolute value that specifies the height of the image if the height is different from its original size.
`width`	A relative or absolute value that specifies the width of the image if the width is different from its original size.

The HTML for two images

```
<p><img src="images/students.jpg" alt="teacher and students"
        height="300" width="400">  
   <img id="small" src="images/students.jpg" alt="teacher and students"></p>
```

CSS for resizing the second image

```
#small {
    height: 150px;
    width: 200px; }
```

The images in a web browser

Accessibility guidelines

- For images with useful content, always code an alt attribute that describes the content.
- For images that are used for decoration, code the alt attribute as an empty string.

Description

- Use the height and width attributes of the <img> tag only to specify the size of the existing image. Then, the browser can reserve the right amount of space for the image and continue rendering the page while the image is being loaded.
- To display an image at a size other than its full size, you can use the CSS height and width properties. Better, though, is to use an image editor to correctly size the image.

Figure 9-2 How to include and resize an image

How to align an image vertically

When you include an image on a web page, you may want to align it with the inline elements that surround it. If an image is preceded or followed by text, for example, you may want to align the image with the top, middle, or bottom of the text. To do that, you use the vertical-align property shown in figure 9-3.

To indicate the alignment you want to use, you typically specify one of the keywords listed in this figure. If you specify text-bottom, for example, the image is aligned with the bottom of the adjacent text. In contrast, if you specify bottom, the image is aligned with the bottom of the box that contains the adjacent text.

In most cases, the bottom of the text and the bottom of the box are the same. The exception is if a line height is specified for the box. In that case, the text is centered in the box. Then, if you specify bottom for the image alignment, the image will be aligned at the bottom of the box, which is below the bottom of the text. The top and text-top keywords work the same way.

The middle keyword is useful because it lets you center an image with the surrounding text. This is illustrated in the example in this figure. Here, the HTML includes three paragraphs, each with an image followed by some text. When I didn't specify the vertical alignment for the images, the bottom of each image was aligned with the bottom of the text. When I specified middle for the vertical alignment, the center of each image was aligned with the center of the text.

Note that I specified a right margin for the images for both the aligned and unaligned examples to create space between the images and the text. You can also use padding and borders with images. This works just like it does for block elements.

The property for aligning images vertically

Property	Description
`vertical-align`	A relative or absolute value or a keyword that determines the vertical alignment of an image. See the table below for common keywords.

Common keywords for the vertical-align property

Keyword	Description
`bottom`	Aligns the bottom of the image box with the bottom of the box that contains the adjacent inline elements.
`middle`	Aligns the midpoint of the image box with the midpoint of the containing block.
`top`	Aligns the top of the image box with the top of the box that contains the adjacent in-line elements.
`text-bottom`	Aligns the bottom of the image box with the bottom of the text in the containing block.
`text-top`	Aligns the top of the image box with the top of the text in the containing block.

The HTML for a web page with three images

```
<h2>To order now:</h2>
<p><img src="images/computer.gif" alt="web address">
   <b>Web:</b> www.murach.com</p>
<p><img src="images/telephone.gif" alt="phone">
   <b>Phone:</b> 1-800-221-5528</p>
<p><img src="images/fax.gif" alt="fax">
   <b>Fax:</b> 1-559-440-0963</p>
```

CSS that aligns the images in the middle of the text

```
img {
    vertical-align: middle;
    margin-right: 10px; }
```

The images in a web browser before and after they're aligned

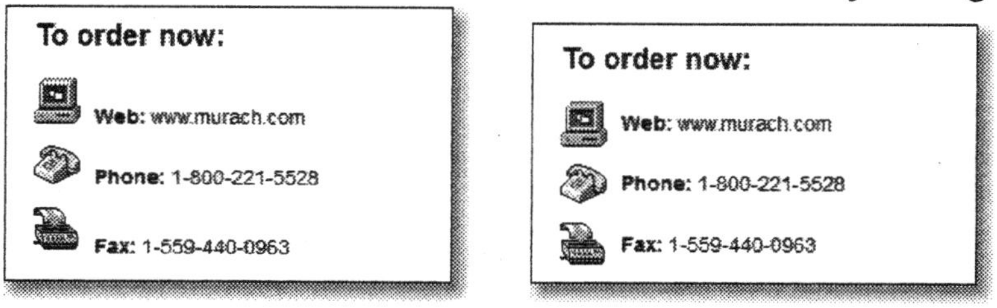

Description

- If you use pixels, points, or ems to specify the value for the vertical-align property, the image is raised if the value is positive and lowered if it's negative. If you specify a percent, the image is raised or lowered based on the percentage of the line height.
- You can use margins, padding, and borders with images just like block elements.

Figure 9-3 How to align an image vertically

How to float an image

In section 1, you learned how to float a logo in a heading and how to float block elements for page layout. Now, figure 9-4 reinforces what you've learned.

At the top of this figure, you can see the two properties for floating images: float and clear. These properties work just like they do for block elements. You use the float property to determine whether the image should be floated to the right or to the left. And you use the clear property to stop an element from floating to the right or left of a floated image.

In the HTML in this figure, you can see that the first element defines an image. This image is followed by an unordered list and a paragraph. In the CSS that follows, you can see that the image is floated to the left. In addition, top and bottom margins are specified for the image to create space between the image and the text that precedes and follows it. In this case, you don't need to specify a right margin for the image because the items in the list are indented by default. Also note that you don't have to specify a width when you float an image. That's because the width can be determined from the actual width of the image.

Finally, notice that the clear property with a value of "left" is specified for the paragraph that follows the list. Because of that, this paragraph won't flow into the space to the right of the image. Instead, the text starts below the image.

The properties for floating images

Property	Description
`float`	A keyword that determines how an image is floated. Possible values are left, right, and none. None is the default.
`clear`	A keyword that determines if an element that follows a floated element flows into the space left by the floated element. Possible values are left, right, both, and none. None is the default.

Some of the HTML for a web page

```
<img src="images/students.jpg" alt="teacher and students">
<ul>
    <li>in college and university MIS programs that focus on providing
        students with practical, real-world experience</li>
    <li>by technical institutes and community colleges that focus on the
        skills that employers are looking for</li>
    <li>in Continuing Ed and Extension programs where the students are
        professionals who are expanding their skills</li>
</ul>
<p id="last">So if your program fits one of those profiles, please take
a look at our books. I&rsquo;m confident you&rsquo;ll discover a new level
of structure, clarity, and relevance that will benefit both you and your
students.</p>
```

CSS that floats the image and clears the last paragraph

```
img {
    float: left;
    margin-top: 15px;
    margin-bottom: 10px; }
#last { clear: left; }
```

The HTML in a web browser

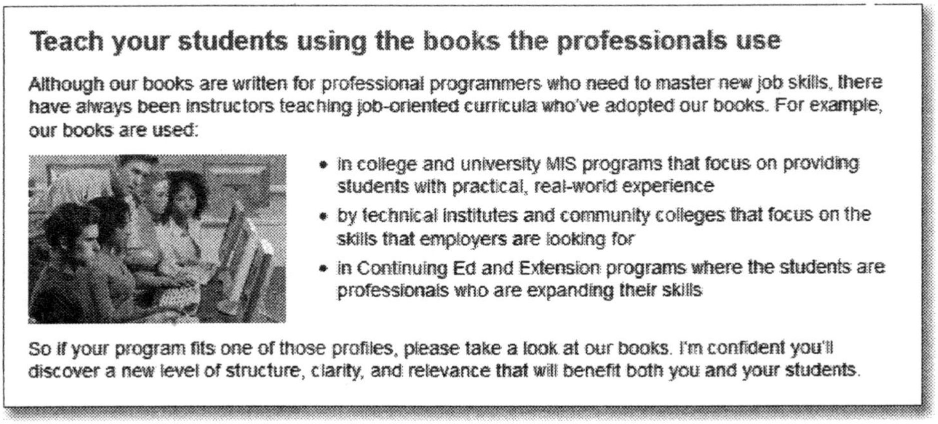

Description

- You can use the same techniques to float an image that you use to float a block element.

Figure 9-4 How to float an image

Advanced skills for working with images

The topics that follow present some advanced skills for working with images. One or more of these may come in handy as you develop web pages that use images.

How to use the HTML5 figure and figcaption elements

The HTML5 figure and figcaption elements can be used with anything that is used as a figure, like an image or table. Because an image is often used as a figure, though, we're presenting these elements in this chapter.

Figure 9-5 shows how to use these elements for an image that's used as a figure. Here, the figure contains one img element plus one figcaption element that provides a caption below the image. Then, the figure is floated within an article, and the image and caption float along with it.

By default, a figcaption element is an inline element, not a block element. As a result, you will usually want to use the CSS display property to change it to a block element. That makes it easier to format the caption. In this example, the figcaption element comes after the image in the HTML so the caption is displayed below the image. But you can change that by coding the figcaption element before the image in the HTML.

Although you can get the same results without using these HTML5 elements, it's better to use these semantic elements. That way, it's easy to tell that the image is used as a figure, and it's easy to tell that the caption applies to the image.

A web page that uses figure and figcaption elements

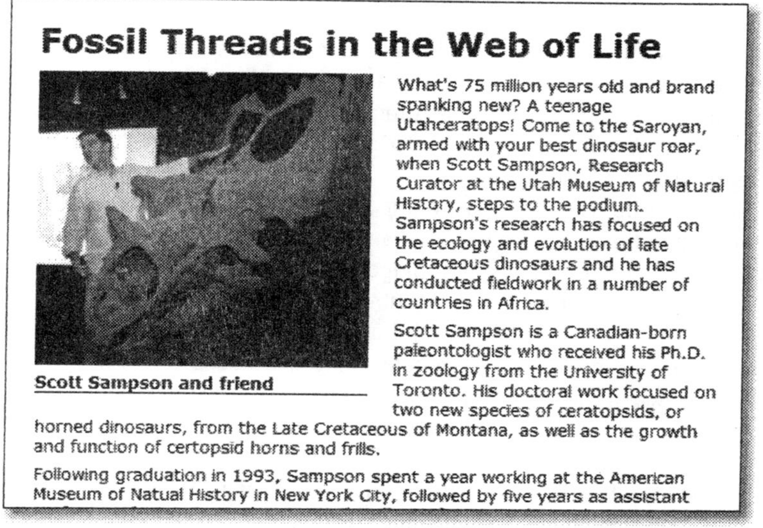

Fossil Threads in the Web of Life

Scott Sampson and friend

What's 75 million years old and brand spanking new? A teenage Utahceratops! Come to the Saroyan, armed with your best dinosaur roar, when Scott Sampson, Research Curator at the Utah Museum of Natural History, steps to the podium. Sampson's research has focused on the ecology and evolution of late Cretaceous dinosaurs and he has conducted fieldwork in a number of countries in Africa.

Scott Sampson is a Canadian-born paleontologist who received his Ph.D. in zoology from the University of Toronto. His doctoral work focused on two new species of ceratopsids, or horned dinosaurs, from the Late Cretaceous of Montana, as well as the growth and function of certopsid horns and frills.

Following graduation in 1993, Sampson spent a year working at the American Museum of Natual History in New York City, followed by five years as assistant

The HTML for the figure and figcaption elements

```
<article>
    <h1>Fossil Threads in the Web of Life</h1>
    <figure>
        <img src="images/sampson_dinosaur.jpg" alt="Scott Sampson">
        <figcaption>Scott Sampson and friend</figcaption>
    </figure>
    <p>What's 75 million years old and brand spanking new? A teenage
    ...
    </p>
</article>
```

The CSS for the figure and figcaption elements

```
figure {
    float: left;
    margin-right: 1.5em; }
figcaption {
    display: block;
    font-weight: bold;
    padding-top: .25em;
    margin-bottom: 1em;
    border-bottom: 1px solid black; }
```

Description

- The figure element can be used as a container for anything that is used as a figure, like an image or a table.
- The figcaption element can be used within a figure to provide a caption that describes the figure, but it is optional. When coded, it can be anywhere within the figure.
- By default, the figcaption element is an inline element so you usually need to change that.

Figure 9-5 How to use the HTML5 figure and figcaption elements

How to work with thumbnails

For some pages, you will want to display images at a small size because you can fit more on the page. However, you will also want to provide a way for the user to display the images at a larger size. For example, many e-commerce pages display small images of their products. Then, the user can click on one of the images to see a larger version of the same image.

When a group of small images is displayed, the images are typically referred to as *thumbnails*. Although this name implies that an image is about the size of a thumbnail, it can be used to refer to any small image.

Figure 9-6 presents an example that uses thumbnails. At the top of this figure, you can see part of a web page with six thumbnails. If you look at the HTML for this page, you can see that the thumbnail images are coded within <a> elements. That way, when the user clicks on an image, the page specified on the href attribute of the <a> element will be displayed. In this case, the page displays a description of the photo along with a larger image.

In this example, the thumbnails are displayed on one web page and the full photos are displayed on separate pages. In other words, a new web page is displayed with a full photo each time a thumbnail is clicked. By using JavaScript, though, you can display the full photos on the same page as the thumbnails by replacing the current photo with a new one each time a thumbnail is clicked. That way, you can greatly reduce the number of web pages that are needed to display a series of photos. In chapter 15, you'll learn more about this JavaScript capability.

Thumbnails in a web page

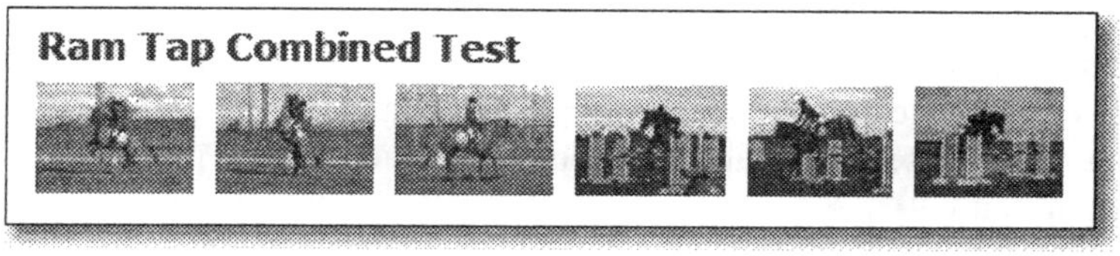

The photo that's displayed when the fifth thumbnail is clicked

The HTML for the page that contains the thumbnails

```
<h3>Ram Tap Combined Test</h3>
<p>
    <a href="p1.html"><img src="thumbnails/t1.jpg" alt="Photo 1"></a>
    <a href="p2.html"><img src="thumbnails/t2.jpg" alt="Photo 2"></a>
    <a href="p3.html"><img src="thumbnails/t3.jpg" alt="Photo 3"></a>
    <a href="p4.html"><img src="thumbnails/t4.jpg" alt="Photo 4"></a>
    <a href="p5.html"><img src="thumbnails/t5.jpg" alt="Photo 5"></a>
    <a href="p6.html"><img src="thumbnails/t6.jpg" alt="Photo 6"></a>
</p>
```

Description

- A *thumbnail* is a small version of an image that can be used to make downloading the image faster and to save space on a web page that contains multiple images.
- To create a thumbnail, you can use an image editor for sizing an image.
- A thumbnail can be used as the image for a link that displays a page with a larger version of the image.
- A larger version of a thumbnail can be displayed on the same page by using JavaScript for an image swap. See chapter 15 for more information.

Figure 9-6 How to work with thumbnails

How to do image rollovers

You may remember from chapter 1 that an image rollover occurs when the mouse hovers over an image and the image is replaced by another image. Although JavaScript is often used for image rollovers, you can do them without JavaScript as shown in figure 9-7.

The HTML in this figure consists of just an h1 and a <p> element within the body element. Also, the <p> element is given an id so CSS can be applied to it. But note that the <p> element is empty. So where is the image for this page?

In the CSS for the <p> element, the first rule set specifies a background image. That displays the image within the element. Then, the second rule set specifies a different background image when the mouse is hovering over the <p> element. That accomplishes the image rollover.

This is a relatively simple technique that you can use for a limited number of image rollovers. But if coding these rule sets gets cumbersome, you can use JavaScript to simplify the process.

The image has been rolled over because the mouse is hovering over it

The HTML for the page

```
<body>
    <h1>Ram Tap Combined Test</h1>
    <p id="image1"></p>
</body>
```

The CSS for the image rollover

```
#image1 {
    background-image: url("h1.jpg");
    width: 434px;
    height: 312px;
}
#image1:hover {
    background-image: url("h2.jpg");
}
```

Description

- An *image rollover* is an image that gets changed when the mouse hovers over it.
- One way to do image rollovers is to use background images and the :hover pseudo-class selector.
- When you use this method, the first background image is applied to a block element like a <p> element. Then, the second background image is displayed when the mouse hovers over it.

Figure 9-7 How to do image rollovers

How to create image maps

You've probably seen web pages that display an image and go to other pages depending on where you click in the image. For example, you might be able to click on a state within a United States map to go to a page with information about that state.

To make this work, you use an *image map* as shown in figure 9-8. Here, the image in the browser consists of pictures of two books. Then, when the Dreamweaver book is clicked, one page is displayed. When the JavaScript and jQuery book is clicked, another page is displayed. Within the image map, each clickable area is called a *hotspot*.

To define an image map, you use the img, map, and area elements. In the usemap attribute of the img element, you code the name of the map element that will be used. In the map element, you code the name that the img element refers to. Then, within the map element, you code one or more area elements that define the hotspots of the map.

The key to defining an area map is coding the area elements. Here, you code the href attribute to specify what page you want to display when the area is clicked. Then, you code the shape attribute to identify the type of shape you want to use for the region. In this example, I used two polygons.

To identify the actual shape and location of an area, you code the coords attribute. The values for this attribute depend on the shape of the area. For rectangular areas, which assumes that the rectangle is vertical, not at an angle, four values are specified. The first two identify the x, y coordinates in pixels of the upper left corner of the area relative to the upper left corner of the image. The second two identify the x, y coordinates in pixels of the lower right corner of the area.

To define a circular region, you specify "circle" for the value of the shape attribute. Then, you specify three values for the coords attribute. The first two values are x, y coordinates for the center of the circle. The third value is the radius of the circle in pixels.

If you want to define a more complex shape than a rectangle or circle, you can specify "poly" for the value of the shape attribute. Then, the coords attribute will consist of a series of x, y coordinates that start in the upper-left corner and travel clockwise around the shape. To identify the shape for the Dreamweaver book, for example, I included six sets of x, y coordinates because part of the book is hidden. To identify the shape for the JavaScript and jQuery book, I only used four sets of coordinates.

To get the coordinates that you need for an image map, you can use an image editor. Then, you just point to the locations in the image and record the coordinates that are shown.

The attribute of the img element that identifies the related map element

Attribute	Description
usemap	Identifies the related map element. The value of this attribute is the value of the name attribute of the map element, preceded by a pound sign (#).

The attribute of the map element that gives it a name

Attribute	Description
name	Provides a name for the map.

The attributes of the area elements that create the image maps

Attribute	Description
href	Specifies a relative or absolute URL that identifies the page that will be displayed when the area is clicked.
shape	A keyword that indicates the type of shape the area represents. Possible keywords are rect, circle, poly, and default, which is the same as rect.
coords	Values that indicate the shape and location of the area. Two sets of x, y coordinates are required for a rectangle to identify the upper left and lower right corners. Three values are required for a circle to identify the x, y coordinates of the center and the radius. Polygonal shapes require a series of x, y coordinates.
alt	Text that's displayed in place of the area if the image can't be displayed.

An image in a web browser with hotspots created by an image map

The HTML for the image and image map

```
<img src="images/html.gif" alt=" Dreamweaver and jQuery books"
     usemap="#books">
<map name="books">
    <area href="Dreamweaver.html" alt="Dreamweaver book" title="Dreamweaver"
        shape="poly" coords="1,19,114,0,122,53,106,143,26,158,24,149">
    <area href="jquery.html" alt="jQuery book" title="jQuery"
        shape="poly" coords="128,21,241,42,218,178,103,159">
</map>
```

Description

- You can use the map and area elements to define an *image map* that provides clickable areas for the image called *hotspots*.
- The coordinates for an area are relative to the upper left corner of the image and are measured in pixels.

Figure 9-8 How to create image maps

Related skills for working with images

At this point, you've learned the HTML and CSS skills that you need for working with images. If someone else is responsible for getting and sizing the images that you use, that may be all you need to know. But if you need to get and size your own images, here are some other skills that you'll need.

When to use an image editor

When you use images on a web page, you want them to be the right size and format. If they aren't that way, you can use an image editor like the one in figure 9-9 to make the adjustments. Today, one of the most popular editors is Adobe Photoshop CC, which is currently available as a monthly subscription for as little as $9.99 per month. Adobe also offers a product called Photoshop Elements that you can purchase for a moderate price. Beyond that, there are many other image editors that range from free to hundreds of dollars. One of the most popular free editors is GIMP, which can be downloaded from the GIMP website.

Because using an image editor goes beyond HTML5 and CSS3, this book doesn't show you how to use one. However, this figure does summarize some of the common uses of an image editor.

The primary use of an image editor is to size the images and save them in the right format so they will load as quickly as possible. In this figure, you can see some of the controls for doing that. Usually, you save an image for the web with a resolution of 72 dpi (dots per inch) because most monitors support that resolution, and lower resolution means faster loading.

By default, an image is displayed on a page only after the entire file has been loaded. In many cases, that's okay. But if a page contains many images, waiting for the page to load can be an unpleasant user experience. One way to improve that is to use an image editor to create *progressive JPEGs*, *interlaced GIFs*, or *interlaced PNGs*. Then, the images will slowly come into view as the page is loaded.

You can also use an image editor to work with an *animated image* like a GIF file that contains *frames*. For instance, you can specify whether the frames are shown only once or repeated. You can also set the timing between the frames.

If an image has a transparent color, you can save it as a GIF or PNG file with *transparency*. To understand how this works, you need to know that an image is always rectangular. This is illustrated by the first starburst example in this figure. Here, the area that's outside the starburst is white, and it isn't transparent. As a result, you can see the white when the image is displayed over a colored background. In contrast, the area outside the second starburst image is also white, but it is transparent. Because of that, you can see the background color behind it.

The second image in this example also uses a *matte*. A matte is useful when a GIF or PNG image with a transparent color is displayed against a colored background. Without a matte, the edges of the image can appear jagged. But if you add a matte that's the same color as the background, it will help the image blend into the background and minimize the jagged edges.

An image editor as it is used to change the size of an image

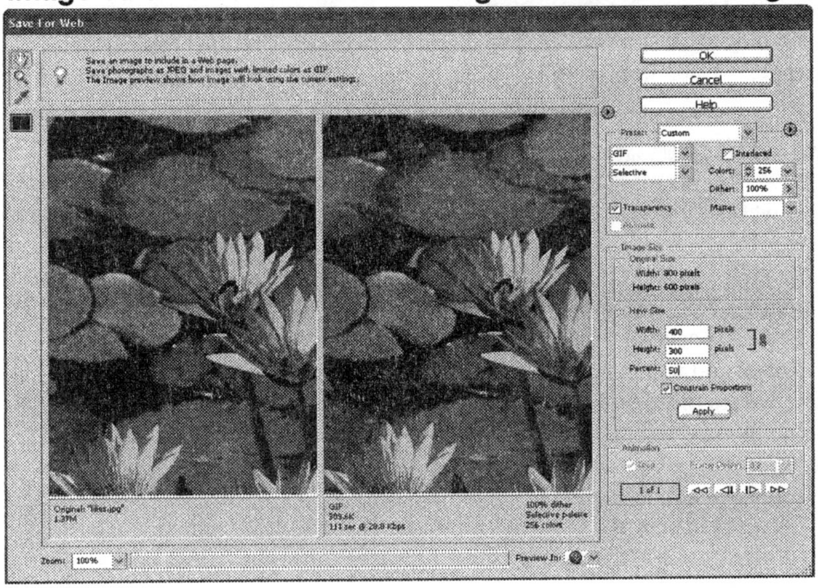

Typical editing operations

- Change the size, image type, or quality of an image.
- Control the animation of an animated GIF file.
- Save an image with transparency or a matte.
- Get the coordinates for an image map.

Three popular image editors

- Adobe Photoshop CC (the industry standard for graphic artists)
- Adobe Photoshop Elements (an inexpensive editor)
- GIMP (a free editor)

An image without transparency and with transparency and a matte

Description

- If an image with *transparency* is displayed over a colored background, the background color will show through the transparent portion of the image.
- If an image with a transparent color is displayed over a colored background, a *matte* of the same color will help the image blend into the background.

Figure 9-9 When to use an image editor

You can also use a matte with a JPEG image. Then, all of the transparent area in the original image is filled with the color you choose. Later, when the image is displayed against a background that's the same color as the matte, the matte area appears to be transparent.

How to get images and icons

For most websites, you'll use your own photos and create most of the graphic images that you use. But sometimes, you may need to get images or icons from another source. The easiest way to do that is to copy or download them from another website.

Figure 9-10 lists several of the most popular websites you can use to get and search for images and icons. For example, www.freefoto.com, openphoto.com, and www.sxc.hu are three of the most popular websites for getting images.

Although you can find many images and icons that are available for free on the Web, most require a Creative Commons license. The types of licenses that are available and the conditions required by these licenses are summarized in this figure. As you can see, all of the licenses require attribution, which means that you must give credit to the author of the image or the website that provided the image. The other license conditions determine how an image can be shared, whether it can be used for commercial purposes, and whether you can derive new images from the existing image.

Stock photos are special images that are typically produced in a studio. For example, the JPEG file in figure 9-4 is a stock photo. You must pay for these types of images, and they can be expensive.

Incidentally, you can also get an image or the link to an image from another site by right-clicking on the image and selecting the appropriate command from the shortcut menu. Then, if you save the link to the image in the href attribute of an <img> tag, your web page will display the image that's actually stored on the other site. This is known as "hot linking" and it is highly discouraged unless you have an agreement with the other site. If, for example, you agree to provide a link to another site and that site agrees to provide a link to your site, this is a quick way to get the images and URLs that you will need.

Creative Commons license conditions for images and icons

Conditions	Description
Attribution	You can use the image and images derived from it as long as you give credit as requested by the author or website providing the image.
Share Alike	You can distribute the image based on the license that governs the original work.
Non-Commercial	You can use the image and images derived from it for non-commercial purposes only.
No Derivative Works	You can use only the original image and not images derived from it.

Creative Commons licenses

- Attribution
- Attribution No Derivatives
- Attribution Non-Commercial Share Alike
- Attribution Share Alike
- Attribution Non-Commercial
- Attribution Non-Commercial No Derivatives

Popular websites for images

- www.sxc.hu
- www.freefoto.com
- www.openphoto.net
- www.google.com/imghp

Popular websites for stock photos

- www.istockphoto.com
- www.gettyimages.com

Popular web sites for icons

- www.glyphicons.com
- www.flaticon.com
- www.iconarchive.com

A popular search engine for stock photos

- www.everystockphoto.com

Description

- Many of the images and icons that are available from the Web are licensed under a Creative Commons license. The license can restrict the use of an image to one or more of the conditions listed above. The most common condition is attribution.
- Stock photos are typically produced in studios and can be purchased for a one-time fee of one dollar to several hundred dollars.
- You can also search for specific images and icons from a generic search engine such as Google.

Figure 9-10 How to get images and icons

How to create favicons

In chapter 3, you learned how to add a *favicon* to a web page. Now, figure 9-11 shows you how to create a favicon. As a refresher, this figure also includes the link element for a favicon. As you can see in the browser display, this favicon is displayed in the tab for the page. It may also be displayed in the address bar and as part of the bookmark for the page.

To start, you should know that a favicon is just a special-purpose icon. Like other icons, a favicon should always be stored in a file with the ico extension. That's because this is the only extension Internet Explorer supports for favicons.

To create a favicon, you can use a program or tool like the ones described in this figure. If you want to create your own icons from scratch, you can purchase a program like Axialis Icon Workshop. Otherwise, you can get one of the free products listed here.

If you're using Photoshop, for example, you can get the free plugin that's available for that program. You can also download a free image converter such as IrfanView from the Internet. Or, you can use an online image converter such as FavIcon from Pics.

Although they can be larger, most favicons are 16 pixels wide and tall. In fact, some image converters will automatically convert the image you specify to 16x16 pixels. That's the case with FavIcon from Pics.

Other image converters will maintain the original size of the image when they create the favicon. When the favicon is displayed on the web page, however, it will be cropped so it's square. That's the case with IrfanView. To make sure a favicon is displayed the way you want, you should make sure the original image is square before you convert it to a favicon.

A web page with a favicon (circled)

The link element in the head section that links to the favicon

```
<link rel="shortcut icon" href="images/favicon.ico">
```

Popular programs and tools for creating favicons

Program/tool	Description
Axialis Icon Workshop	A software product that lets you create, edit, and convert icons. For more information, go to www.axialis.com/iconworkshop/.
Photoshop plugin	Free software that you can use with Photoshop. To download, go to www.telegraphics.com.au/sw/.
IrfanView	A free image converter that you can download from www.irfanview.com.
FavIcon from Pics	A free image converter that you can run online at: www.html-kit.com/favicon/.

Description

- A *favicon* is a small image that appears to the left of the title in the browser's tab for the page. It may also appear to the left of the URL in the browser's address bar, and it may be used in a favorite or bookmark.
- A favicon is typically 16 pixels wide and tall and has the extension ico since that's the only extension currently supported by Internet Explorer for icons.
- You can create an ico file by using an icon editor, a program that converts an image to an ico file, or a web-based converter.

Figure 9-11 How to create favicons

Perspective

Now that you've finished this chapter, you should have all the HTML and CSS skills that you need for developing web pages with images. But if you're going to need to do your own image editing, you'll also need to get an image editor and learn how to use it. At the least, the image editor that you choose should provide for sizing images and changing the image type and quality.

Terms

JPEG file
GIF file
animated image
frame
PNG file
thumbnail
image rollover
image map
hotspot
progressive JPEG
interlaced GIF
interlaced PNG
transparency
matte
favicon

Summary

- The three common formats for images are *JPEG* (for photographs and scanned images), *GIF* (for small illustrations, logos, and animated images), and *PNG* (typically used as a replacement for still GIF images).
- You should use the height and width attributes of an <img> tag only to specify the size of the image, not to resize it. Then, the browser can reserve the right amount of space for the image and continue rendering the page, even if the image is still being loaded.
- You can use CSS to vertically align an image within the block element that contains it. You can also use CSS to float an image.
- The HTML5 figure element can be used to treat an image as a figure that's referred to outside of the figure. The HTML5 figcaption element can be used within a figure element to provide a caption for the figure.
- A *thumbnail* is a small version of an image that is often used as a link to a page that displays a larger version of the image.
- An *image rollover* occurs when the mouse hovers over an image and the image is replaced by another image.
- An *image map* defines the clickable *hotspots* for an image. To define these hotspots, you code map and area elements in the HTML.
- To resize an image so it's the right size for a web page, you can use an image editor like Photoshop CC or Photoshop Elements.
- To reduce the loading time for an image, you can use an image editor to change the image type or quality. To improve the user experience as images load, you can create *progressive JPEGs*, *interlaced GIFs*, and *interlaced PNGs*.
- A GIF file with two or more *frames* is an *animated image*. Then, you can use an image editor to control how that animation works.
- GIF and PNG files support *transparency*. Then, the background color that's behind the image shows through the transparent parts of the image.
- If you use an image editor to specify a *matte* for an image and then set the matte color to the same one that's used for the background color, the image will blend in better with the background.
- The Internet has many sites that offer images, stock photos, and icons that you may want to use for your site.
- A *favicon* is a small image that appears to the left of the title in the browser's tab for the page. It is typically 16 pixels wide and tall and has ico as its extension.

Exercise 9-1 Use a figure on the speaker's page

In this exercise, you'll be working with a second version of the website that you developed for the chapters in section 1 of this book through chapter 7. In this exercise, you'll enhance the speaker page by adding figure and figcaption elements so the page looks like this:

1. Use your text editor to open the HTML and CSS files for this speaker's page, which will be in the exercises/town_hall_2 folder.
2. In the HTML file, enclose the img element at the top of the article in a figure element. Then, add a figcaption element below the img element with the text shown above.
3. In the CSS file, add the rule sets for formatting the figure and figcaption.
4. Test this enhancement in both Chrome and IE.

10

How to work with tables

If you look at the HTML for the websites that are in use today, you'll see that some of them still use tables to control the page layout. As you saw in chapter 6, however, the right way to do that is to use CSS. As a result, you should only use tables to display tabular data. In this chapter, you'll learn how to do that.

Basic HTML skills for coding tables

In the topics that follow, you'll learn the basic skills for coding tables. But first, I want to introduce you to the structure of a table in HTML.

An introduction to tables

Figure 10-1 presents a simple table and points out its various components. To start, a table consists of one or more *rows* and *columns*. As you'll see in the next figure, you define a table by defining its rows. Then, within each row, you define a *cell* for each column.

Within each row, a table can contain two different kinds of cells. *Header cells* identify what's in the columns and rows of a table, and *data cells* contain the actual data of the table. For example, the three cells in the first row of the table in this figure are header cells that identify the contents of the columns. In contrast, the cells in the next four rows are data cells. The last row starts with a header cell that identifies the contents of the cells in that row.

In broad terms, a table starts with a *header* that can consist of one or more rows. Then, the *body* of the table presents the data for the table. Last, the *footer* provides summary data that can consist of one or more rows. For accessibility, a table should also have a caption above or below it that summarizes what's in the table.

A simple table with basic formatting

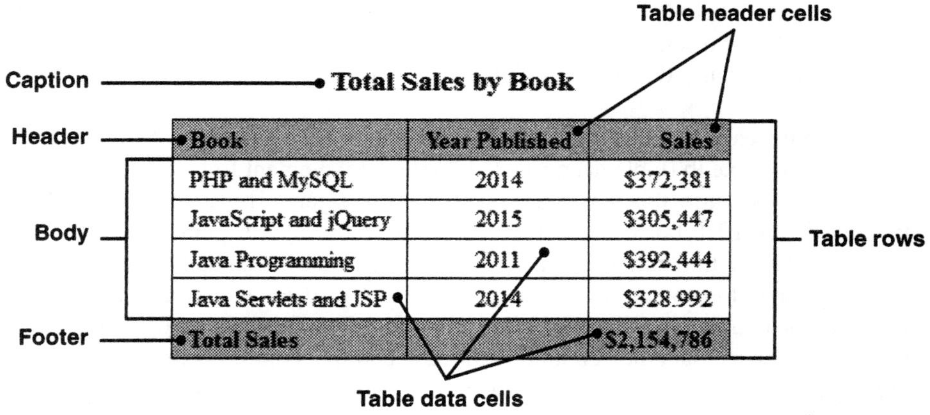

Total Sales by Book

Book	Year Published	Sales
PHP and MySQL	2014	$372,381
JavaScript and jQuery	2015	$305,447
Java Programming	2011	$392,444
Java Servlets and JSP	2014	$328.992
Total Sales		$2,154,786

Description

- A *table* consists of *rows* and *columns* that intersect at *cells.*
- Cells that contain the data of the table are called *data cells.*
- Cells that identify the data in a column or row are called *header cells.*
- The *header* for a table can consist of more than one row, and the *footer* for a table can consist of more than one row.
- The *body* of a table, which contains the data, usually consists of two or more rows.
- Now that CSS can be used for page layout, you should only use tables for tabular data.

Figure 10-1 An introduction to tables

How to create a table

Figure 10-2 presents the four most common elements for coding tables. The table element defines the table itself. Then, you code the other elements within this element.

To define each row in a table, you use the tr (table row) element. Within each row, you code one th (table header) or td (table data) element for each cell in the row. You can see how this works in the table in this figure. This is the same table that's in figure 10-1, but without the formatting. In the last row, note that the first cell is coded as a th element. That's because it identifies the data in the last row.

By default, the content of a header cell is boldfaced and centered in the cell, and the content of a data cell is left-aligned. Also, the width of the cells is determined by the data they contain, with each cell in a column being as wide as the widest cell. You can see how this works in the browser display in this figure. In just a minute, though, you'll learn how to use CSS to format a table. But first, I want to present three additional elements for coding tables.

Common elements for coding tables

Element	Description
`table`	Defines a table. The other elements for the table are coded within this element.
`tr`	Defines a row.
`th`	Defines a header cell within a row.
`td`	Defines a data cell within a row.

The HTML for the table in figure 10-1 before it's formatted

```
<table>
    <tr>
        <th class="left">Book</th>
        <th>Year Published</th>
        <th>Sales</th>
    </tr>
    <tr>
        <td class="left">PHP and MySQL</td>
        <td>2014</td>
        <td>$372,381</td>
    </tr>
    <tr>
        .
        .
    </tr>
    <tr>
        <th class="left">Total Sales</th>
        <td></td>
        <td>$2,154,786</td>
    </tr>
</table>
```

The table in a web browser with no CSS formatting

Book	Year Published	Sales
PHP and MySQL	2014	$372,381
JavaScript and jQuery	2015	$305,447
Java Programming	2011	$392,444
Java Servlets and JSP	2014	$328.992
Total Sales		$2,154,786

Description

- By default, the width of each column in a table is determined automatically based on its content.
- By default, the content of a th element is boldfaced and centered, and the content of a td element is left-aligned.

Figure 10-2 How to create a table

How to add a header and footer

Figure 10-3 presents the elements for grouping rows into headers and footers. It also presents the element for grouping rows in the table body, which you'll typically do when you use a header and footer.

To code a header, you simply code the rows that make up the header between the opening and closing tags of the thead element. Similarly, you code a footer by coding rows within a tfoot element. And you code a body by coding rows within a tbody element.

The example in this figure illustrates how this works. Here, the first row of the table is coded within a thead element, the last row of the table is coded within a tfoot element, and the remaining rows are coded within a tbody element. If you compare the browser display for this table to the one in the previous figure, you'll see that they're identical. The main reason for adding these elements, then, it to make it easier to format the table with CSS. You'll see how that works in the next figure.

The elements for coding the header, body, and footer

Element	Description
thead	Groups one or more rows into a table header.
tbody	Groups the rows between the header and footer into a table body.
tfoot	Groups one or more rows into a table footer.

The HTML for a table with a header, body, and footer

```
<table>
    <thead>
        <tr>
            <th class="left">Book</th>
            <th>Year published</th>
            <th>Total sales</th>
        </tr>
    </thead>
    <tbody>
        <tr>
            <td class="left">PHP and MySQL</td>
            <td>2014</td>
            <td>$372,381</td>
        </tr>
        .
        .
    </tbody>
    <tfoot>
        <tr>
            <th class="left">Total Sales</th>
            <td></td>
            <td>$2,154,786</td>
        </tr>
    </tfoot>
</table>
```

The table in a web browser

Book	Year Published	Sales
PHP and MySQL	2014	$372,381
JavaScript and jQuery	2015	$305,447
Java Programming	2011	$392,444
Java Servlets and JSP	2014	$328,992
Total Sales		$2,154,786

Description

- The thead, tbody, and tfoot elements make it easier to style a table with CSS. See figure 10-4 for details.
- You can code the thead, tbody, and tfoot elements in any sequence and the header will always be displayed first and the footer last.

Figure 10-3 How to add a header and footer

Basic CSS skills for formatting tables

Now that you know the basic skills for coding tables, you're ready to learn the basic skills for formatting tables using CSS.

How to use CSS properties to format a table

Figure 10-4 presents some of the common CSS properties for formatting tables. However, you can also use many of the other CSS properties that you've already learned to format a table.

As you saw in the last two figures, a table doesn't include borders by default (the border around those tables were added by the program that we use for capturing screens). In many cases, though, you'll want to add a border around a table to make it stand out on the page. You may also want to add borders around the cells or rows in a table to help identify the columns and rows.

To do that, you can use any of the border properties you learned about in chapter 5. In the CSS in this figure, for example, the shorthand border property adds a solid black border around the table and around each cell in the table.

By default, a small amount of space is included between the cells of a table. To remove that space, you can set the border-collapse property to a value of "collapse". Then, the borders between adjacent cells will be collapsed to a single border as shown in the first table in this figure. But note that if two adjacent cells have different borders, the most dominant border will be displayed. If one border is wider than the other, for example, the wider border will be displayed.

When you use the padding property with tables, it works similarly to the way it works with the box model. That is, it specifies the amount of space between the contents of a cell and the outer edge of the cell. In this figure, for example, you can see that .2 ems of space has been added above and below the contents of each cell, and .7 ems of space to the left and right of the contents.

To complete the formatting, the CSS left aligns those elements that are in the "left" class. Then, it applies a background color to the header and footer using a selector that includes the thead and tfoot element. And it changes the font weight for the footer to bold. If you look at the HTML in the last figure, you can see how this works. In figure 10-5, though, you'll learn how you can use CSS3 to do this without using classes or ids to identify the elements you want to format.

Common properties for formatting table, tr, th, and td elements

Property	Description
`border-collapse`	A keyword that determines whether space exists between the borders of adjacent cells or the borders are collapsed to a single border between cells. Possible values are collapse and separate. The default is separate.
`border-spacing`	A relative or absolute value that specifies the space between cells when the borders aren't collapsed.
`padding`	The space between the cell contents and the outer edge of the cell.
`text-align`	The horizontal alignment of text.
`vertical-align`	The vertical alignment of text.

The CSS for the table in figure 10-3

```
table {
    border: 1px solid black;
    border-collapse: collapse; }
th, td {
    border: 1px solid black;
    padding: .2em .7em;
    text-align: right; }
th.left, td.left { text-align: left; }
thead, tfoot { background-color: aqua; }
tfoot { font-weight: bold; }
```

The table in a web browser

Book	Year Published	Sales
PHP and MySQL	2014	$372,381
JavaScript and jQuery	2015	$305,447
Java Programming	2011	$392,444
Java Servlets and JSP	2014	$328.992
Total Sales		**$2,154,786**

The table without collapsed borders

Book	Year Published	Sales
PHP and MySQL	2014	$372,381
JavaScript and jQuery	2015	$305,447
Java Programming	2011	$392,444
Java Servlets and JSP	2014	$328.992
Total Sales		**$2,154,786**

Description

- In HTML5, the attributes that were commonly used for formatting tables have been deprecated. As a result, you should use CSS for all table formatting.

Figure 10-4 How to use CSS to format a table

How to use the CSS3 structural pseudo-classes for formatting tables

In chapter 4, you were introduced to a few of the CSS3 pseudo-classes. Now, figure 10-5 presents some of the ones that are especially useful for formatting tables. These classes can be referred to as the *structural pseudo-classes*, because they let you select elements by their structural location. By using these pseudo-classes in your selectors, you can avoid the use of id and class selectors, which simplifies your HTML.

To illustrate, the first example in this figure uses the first-child pseudo-class to select the first th and the first td element in each row. This is a structural pseudo-class that you were introduced in chapter 4. Then, the rule set left aligns the data in these cells. This means that you don't need to use the "left" class that was used in figure 10-4 for formatting.

The second example uses the nth-child selector to select the second th and td element in each row. Then, the rule set centers the heading and data in those cells. The result is that the contents of the cells in the second column of the table are centered.

The last example also uses the nth-child selector to select all even rows in the body of the table. Then, it applies silver as the background color for these rows. If you look at the table of n values in this figure, you can see that the n value could also be coded as 2n to select all even rows or 2n+1 to select all odd rows. If you want to apply a different color to every third row, you can use other combinations of n values to get that result.

The syntax for the CSS3 structural pseudo-class selectors

Syntax	Description
`:nth-child(n)`	nth child of parent
`:nth-last-child(n)`	nth child of parent counting backwards
`:nth-of-type(n)`	nth element of its type within the parent
`:nth-last-of-type(n)`	nth element of its type counting backwards

Typical n values

Value	Meaning
odd	Every odd child or element
even	Every even child or element
n	The nth child or element
2n	Same as even
3n	Every third child or element (3, 6, 9, ...)
2n+1	Same as odd
3n+1	Every third child or element starting with 1 (1, 4, 7, ...)

The CSS3 code for formatting a table without using classes

```
th:first-child, td:first-child {
    text-align: left; }
th:nth-child(2), td:nth-child(2) {
    text-align: center; }
tbody tr:nth-child(even) {
    background-color: silver; }
```

The table in a browser

Book	Year Published	Sales
PHP and MySQL	2014	$372,381
JavaScript and jQuery	2015	$305,447
Java Programming	2011	$392,444
Java Servlets and JSP	2014	$328,992
ASP.NET with Visual Basic	2011	$351,200
ASP.NET with C#	2011	$404,332
Total Sales		$2,154,786

Description

- The CSS3 *structural pseudo-classes* let you format a table without using classes or ids.

Figure 10-5 How to use the CSS3 structural pseudo-classes for formatting tables

Other skills for working with tables

In addition to the skills you've just learned, you may need to use some other skills when working with tables. You'll learn these skills in the remaining topics of this chapter.

How to use the HTML5 figure and figcaption elements with tables

If you read chapter 9, you already know how to treat an image as a figure by using the HTML5 figure and figcaption elements. Now, figure 10-6 shows how to use these elements for a table that's used as a figure. Here, the figure element contains a figcaption element followed by a table element.

By default, a figcaption element is an inline element, not a block element. As a result, you will usually want to use the CSS display property to change it to a block element. That makes it easier to format the caption. In this example, the figcaption element comes before the table in the HTML so the caption is displayed above the table. But you can change that by coding the figcaption element after the table in the HTML.

In the CSS for the table element, you can see that the top and bottom margins are set to 10 pixels, and the right and left margins are set to "auto". As a result, the table is centered within the figure element.

In figure 10-8, you'll see that you can also use the caption element within a table element to provide a caption for a table. In general, though, it's better to use the figure and figcaption elements to present a table. That way, it's easier for a screen reader to tell that the table is used as a figure and that the caption applies to the table.

A table within a figure

Total Sales by Book

Book	Year Published	Sales
PHP and MySQL	2014	$372,381
JavaScript and jQuery	2015	$305,447
Java Programming	2011	$392,444
Java Servlets and JSP	2014	$328,992
ASP.NET with Visual Basic	2011	$351,200
ASP.NET with C#	2011	$404,332
Total Sales		$2,154,786

The HTML for the figure and figcaption elements

```
<figure>
    <figcaption>Total Sales by Book</figcaption>
    <table>
            .
            .
    </table>
</figure>
```

The CSS for the figure and figcaption elements

```
figure, figcaption {
    margin: 0;
    padding: 0; }
figure {
    border: 1px solid black;
    width: 450px;
    padding: 15px; }
figcaption {
    display: block;
    font-weight: bold;
    text-align: center;
    font-size: 120%;
    padding-bottom: .25em; }
table {
    border-collapse: collapse;
    border: 1px solid black;
    margin: 10px auto; }
```

Description

- The figure element can be used as a container for anything that is used as a figure. The figcaption element can be used within a figure to provide a caption that describes the figure, but it is optional. When coded, it can be anywhere within the figure.
- By default, the figcaption element is an inline element.
- Although you can use the HTML caption element to provide a caption for a table, it's better semantically to use the figure and figcaption elements.

Figure 10-6 How to use the HTML5 figure and figcaption elements with tables

How to merge cells in a column or row

For complicated tables, it often makes sense to *merge* some of the cells. This is illustrated in figure 10-7. Here, four cells are merged in the first row so "Sales" spans the last four columns of the table. Also, two cells are merged in the first column, so "Book" is in its own cell.

To merge cells, you use the two attributes of the th and td elements that are summarized in this figure. To merge cells so a cell in a row spans two or more columns, you use the colspan attribute. To merge cells so a cell in a column spans two or more rows, you use the rowspan attribute. The value you use for these attributes indicates the number of cells that will be merged.

The example in this figure illustrates how these attributes work. Here, you can see a table header that consists of two rows and five columns. However, the first header cell spans two rows. As a result, the second row doesn't include a th element for the first column.

Now, take a look at the second header cell in the first row of the header. This cell spans the remaining four columns of the row. As a result, this row includes only two th elements: the one that defines the cell that contains the "Book" heading, and the one that defines the cell that contains the "Sales" heading.

In the CSS for the merged cells, you can see how the CSS3 structural pseudo-classes are used in the selectors. First, the first-child class is used to bottom align "Book" in the merged cell that spans two rows. Second, the nth-child class is used to center "Sales" in the merged cell that spans four columns. Third, the nth-child class is used to right align the th cells within the second row of the table.

Attributes of the <th> and <td> tags for merging cells

Attribute	Description
colspan	Identifies the number of columns that a cell will span. The default is 1.
rowspan	Identifies the number of rows that a cell will span. The default is 1.

A table with merged cells

Book	Sales			
	North	South	West	Total
PHP and MySQL	$55,174	$73,566	$177,784	$306,524
JavaScript and jQuery	$28,775	$24,349	$168,228	$221,352
Java Programming	$27,688	$39,995	$239,968	$307,651
Java Servlets and JSP	$23,082	$24,858	$129,619	$177,559
Sales Totals	$140,775	$165,550	$762,794	$1,069,119

The HTML for the table

```
<table>
    <thead>
        <tr>
            <th rowspan="2">Book</th>
            <th colspan="4">Sales</th>
        </tr>
        <tr>
            <th>North</th>
            <th>South</th>
            <th>West</th>
            <th>Total</th>
        </tr>
    </thead>
    <tbody>
        .
        .
    </tbody>
    <tfoot>
        <tr>
            <th>Sales Totals</th>
            <td>$140,775</td>
            <td>$165,550</td>
            <td>$762,794</td>
            <td>$1,069,119</td>
        </tr>
    </tfoot>
</table>
```

The CSS for the merged cells

```
th:first-child { vertical-align: bottom; }  /* bottom aligns "Book" */
th:nth-child(2) { text-align: center; }     /* centers "Sales" */
tr:nth-child(2) th { text-align: right; }   /* right aligns 2nd row hdgs */
```

Figure 10-7 How to merge cells in a column or row

How to provide for accessibility

Because tables are difficult for visually-impaired users to decipher, HTML provides a few attributes that can improve accessibility. These attributes are summarized in figure 10-8, and they can be read by screen readers.

First, it's important to provide a caption for each table that summarizes what the table contains. To do that, you can use the caption element as shown in this figure or the figure and figcaption elements as shown in figure 10-6.

Second, you can code the headers attribute on a td or th element to identify one or more header cells that the cell is associated with. To identify a header cell, you code the value of the cell's id attribute. In the example in this figure, you can see that an id attribute is coded for each of the three th elements in the table header as well as the th element in the table footer. Then, each of the td elements includes a headers attribute that names the associated th element or elements.

For instance, the headers attribute for the first td element in each row of the body names the header cell that contains the header "Book" because the content of these cells are book names. Similarly, the td element in the footer includes a headers attribute that names two th elements. The first one is for the header cell in the third column of the first row (the one with the heading "Sales"), and the second one is for the header cell in the first column of the last row (the one with the heading "Total Sales").

The last attribute for accessibility is scope. Although you can code this attribute on either a td or th element, it's used most often with the th element. The scope attribute indicates whether a cell is associated with a column, a row, or a group of merged cells in a column. In this figure, for example, this attribute indicates that each of the three th elements in the header row is associated with a column.

Even if you use these attributes, a table can be difficult for a visually-impaired person to interpret. So besides coding these attributes, try to keep your tables simple. That is not only good for the visually-impaired, but also for all the users of your website.

Attributes that can be used for accessibility

Attribute	Description
caption	Describes the contents of the table. The other alternative is to treat the table as a figure and use the figcaption element to describe the table.
headers	Identifies one or more header cells that describe the content of the cell.
scope	A keyword that tells if a cell is associated with a column or row. Common keywords are col and row. You can also use the keyword rowgroup to refer to merged cells.

The HTML for a table that provides for accessibility

```
<table>
<caption>Total sales for books published from 2008 to 2012</caption>
<thead>
    <tr>
        <th id="hdr_book" scope="col">Book</th>
        <th id="hdr_year" scope="col">Year Published</th>
        <th id="hdr_sales" scope="col">Sales</th>
    </tr>
</thead>
<tbody>
    <tr>
        <td headers="hdr_book">PHP and MySQL</td>
        <td headers="hdr_year">2014</td>
        <td headers="hdr_sales">$372,381</td>
    </tr>
    <tr>
        <td headers="hdr_book">JavaScript and jQuery</td>
        <td headers="hdr_year">2015</td>
        <td headers="hdr_sales">$305,447</td>
    </tr>
</tbody>
<tfoot>
    <tr>
        <th id="hdr_total" scope="row">Total Sales</th>
        <td></td>
        <td headers="hdr_sales hdr_total">$2,154,786</td>
    </tr>
</tfoot>
</table>
```

Accessibility guideline

- Use the attributes listed above to make a table more accessible to visually-impaired users who use screen readers.

Figure 10-8 How to provide for accessibility

How to nest tables

In the past, when tables were used for laying out pages, it was common to nest one table within another table. Today, that type of page layout should be replaced by the techniques that you learned in chapter 6.

Occasionally, though, *nested tables* can be useful for presenting tabular data. That's why figure 10-9 shows how nested tables work. Here, the example is a simple table that lists the year-to-date sales by region. For the West and East regions, a single sales amount is displayed. But for the Central region, two sales amounts for two different areas within the region are displayed. To accomplish that, the cell for this region contains another table.

To code a table within another table, you simply code a table element within a td element. Then, you code the other elements of the table within the table element just like you would any other table. In this case, the table consists of two rows, each with two cells, but there's no limit to the size of a nested table or the number of levels of nesting.

In general, though, you shouldn't need to nest tables for two reasons. First, you can get the same result in other ways. Second, it's better to keep your tables simple so it's easier for your users to understand them, especially your visually-impaired users.

A table with another table nested within one of its cells

Region	YTD sales
West	$68,684.34
Central	North $21,223.08 South $41,274.06
East	$72,741.06

The HTML for the table

```
<table id="outer">
    <caption>YTD Sales by Region</caption>
    <tr>
        <th>Region</th>
        <th>YTD sales</th>
    </tr>
    <tr>
        <th>West</th>
        <td>$68,684.34</td>
    </tr>
    <tr>
        <th>Central</th>
        <td>
            <table id="inner">
                <tr>
                    <th>North</th>
                    <td>$21,223.08</td>
                </tr>
                <tr>
                    <th>South</th>
                    <td>$41,274.06</td>
                </tr>
            </table>
        </td>
    </tr>
    <tr>
        <th>East</th>
        <td>$72,741.06</td>
    </tr>
</table>
```

Description

- You can *nest* one table within another table by coding a table element within a td element.
- Nested tables were used frequently when tables were used for page layout. Now that tables should only be used for tabular data, you should rarely need nesting.

Figure 10-9 How to nest tables

How to control wrapping

By default, the content of the cells in a table will *wrap* to two or more lines if you size the browser window so the content can't be displayed on a single line. This is illustrated by the table in the browser at the top of figure 10-10. Here, you can see that the heading in the second column and some of the data in the first column have been wrapped onto two lines.

In some cases, though, you won't want the headings and data to wrap. Then, you can use the white-space property to prevent that from happening. In the CSS in this figure, for example, I coded this property with a value of "nowrap" for the table element. Then, the table appears as in the second browser in this figure. Here, the table is too wide for the window. As a result, the browser displays a horizontal scroll bar so the user can scroll to see the rest of the table.

A table with wrapping

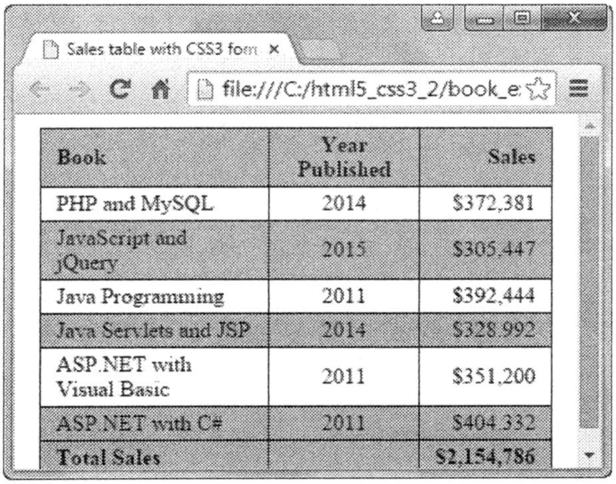

Book	Year Published	Sales
PHP and MySQL	2014	$372,381
JavaScript and jQuery	2015	$305,447
Java Programming	2011	$392,444
Java Servlets and JSP	2014	$328,992
ASP.NET with Visual Basic	2011	$351,200
ASP.NET with C#	2011	$404,332
Total Sales		$2,154,786

A table without wrapping

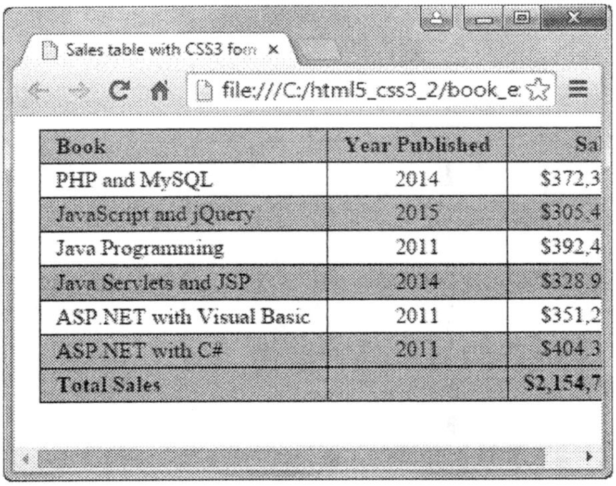

Book	Year Published	Sa
PHP and MySQL	2014	$372,3
JavaScript and jQuery	2015	$305,4
Java Programming	2011	$392,4
Java Servlets and JSP	2014	$328,9
ASP.NET with Visual Basic	2011	$351,2
ASP.NET with C#	2011	$404,3
Total Sales		$2,154,7

The property that stops wrapping

```
table { white-space: nowrap; }
```

Description

- You can use the white-space property to keep table data from wrapping if the table doesn't fit in the browser window. To do that, code the value "nowrap" for this property.
- You can code the white-space property for an entire table or individual cells.

Figure 10-10 How to control wrapping

Perspective

As you've seen in this chapter, it's relatively easy to create and format simple tables. Remember, though, that you should only use tables when you're presenting tabular data. You should be using CSS, not tables, for page layout.

Terms

table
row
column
cell
data cell
header cell
header
footer
body
structural pseudo-class
merged cells
nested tables
wrapped rows

Summary

- A *table* consists of *rows* and *columns* that intersect at *cells*. *Data cells* contain the data of a table. *Header cells* identify the data in a column or row.
- The rows in a table can be grouped into a *header*, a *body*, and a *footer*.
- To define a table in HTML, you use the table, tr, th, and td elements. Then, you can use CSS to apply borders, spacing, fonts, and background colors to these elements.
- If you use the thead, tfoot, and tbody elements to group the rows in a table, it's easier to style the table with CSS.
- You can use the CSS3 *structural pseudo-classes* to format the rows or columns of a table without using id or class selectors.
- The HTML5 figure element can be used to treat a table as a figure. The HTML5 figcaption element can be used within a figure element to provide a caption for the figure.
- To make tables more accessible to visually-impaired users, you can use the HTML attributes that can be read by screen readers.
- You will often want to *merge* two or more cells in a column or row, and you may occasionally want to *nest* one table within another.
- If a table doesn't fit in the browser window, the browser will *wrap* the data so it does fit. If you don't want that, you can use CSS to turn the wrapping off.

Exercise 10-1 Add a table to the luncheons page

In this exercise, you'll enhance the luncheons page by adding a table to it so it looks like the one that follows.

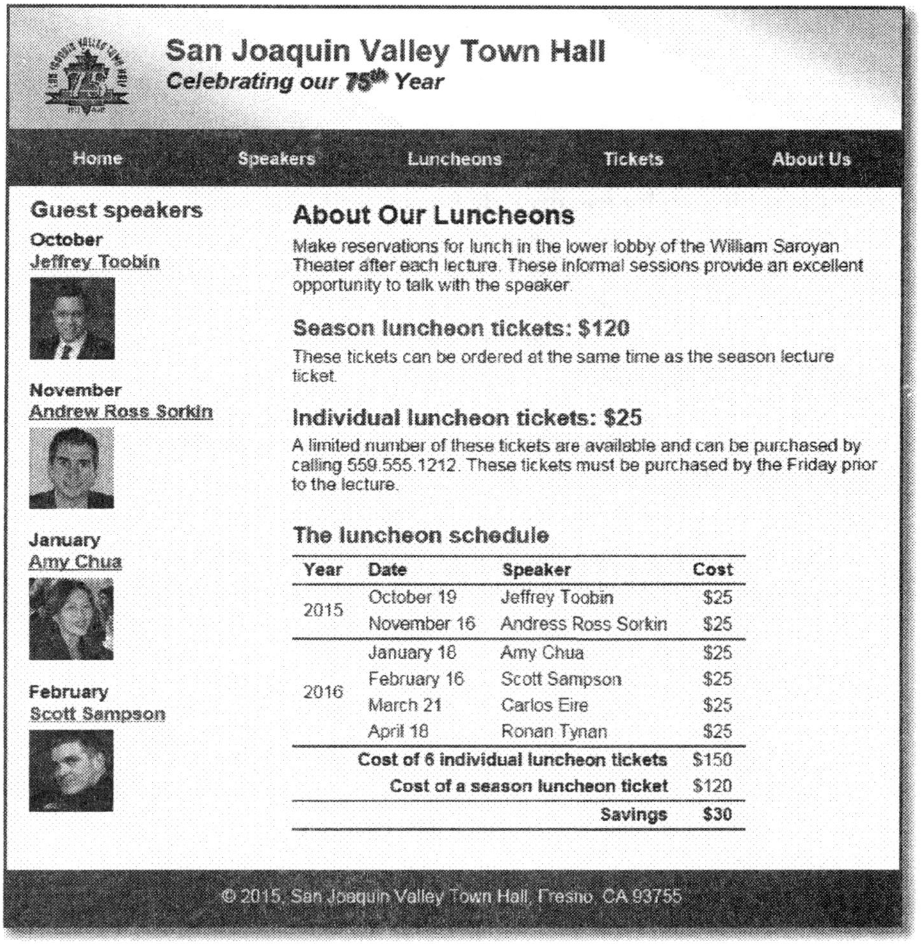

Enter the table into the luncheons.html file

1. Use your text editor to open the luncheon.html page in the town_hall_2 folder. Then, run the page to see that everything but the table is already in the file.
2. Add the table shown above to the page. To start the table, you may want to copy the HTML for one of the tables in the book applications into the file. Then, you can modify that code and add the data for the new table. To quickly add new rows to the table, you can copy and paste earlier rows.
3. Test the page to make sure the contents are all there, even though the table won't be formatted right.

Add the CSS for the table to the main.css file

4. Use your text editor to open the main.css file in the styles folder. To start the code for the table, copy the CSS for one of the tables in the book applications into the file. Then, test to see how the table looks.
5. Modify the CSS so the table looks like the one above. Here, all of the borders and the text in the heading above the table should have #800000 as their color. To do some of the alignment and to add borders to some of the rows, you should use classes.
6. Test and adjust until the table looks the way you want it to.

Treat the table as a figure, provide for accessibility, and experiment

7. Enclose the table within a figure element, and code a figcaption element above the table, but within the figure element. Then, copy the h2 element that says: "The luncheon schedule" into the figcaption element.
8. Test this change. The page should look the same as it did in step 6, except the table will now be centered.
9. Open the developer tools for your browser and review the styles that are applied to the figure element by the normalize style sheet. Then, adjust the CSS so the figure isn't centered.
10. Using figure 10-8 as a guide, add the attributes for user accessibility.
11. Experiment with the CSS3 structural pseudo-classes to see whether you can replace some of your class selectors with pseudo-class selectors.

11

How to work with forms

To create dynamic web pages, you use HTML to create forms that let the user enter data. Then, the user can click on a button to submit the data to a web server for processing.

In this chapter, you'll learn how to code forms and the controls they contain. You'll also learn how to use the HTML5 features for data validation and how to use the HTML5 controls.

How to use forms and controls

A *form* contains one or more *controls* such as text boxes and buttons. In the topics that follow, you'll learn how to create a form and how to add the controls that are currently supported by all browsers to a form. If you already know how to create forms with HTML4, you can skim the topics that follow until you come to the new material on HTML5 validation and controls.

How to create a form

Figure 11-1 shows how to code a form that contains two controls: a text box and a button. To start, you code the form element. On the opening tag for this element, you code the action and method attributes. The action attribute specifies the file on the web server that should be used to process the data when the form is submitted. The method attribute specifies the HTTP method that should be used for sending the form to the web server.

In the example in this figure, the form will be submitted to the server using the HTTP "post" method when the user clicks the Subscribe button. Then, the data in the form will be processed by the code that's stored in the file named subscribe.php.

When you use the post method, the form data is packaged as part of an HTTP request and isn't visible in the browser. Because of that, the submission is more secure than it is when you use the "get" method, but the resulting page can't be bookmarked.

When you use the get method, the form data is sent as part of the URL for the HTTP request. That means that the data is visible and the page can be bookmarked. This is illustrated by the URL in this figure. Here, the URL is followed by a question mark and name/value pairs separated by ampersands. In this case, two values are submitted: the email address that has been entered, and the value of the Submit button. Because browsers and servers limit the amount of data that can be in a URL, you often are forced to use the post method.

Between the opening and closing tags of the form element, you code the controls for the form. In this example, the first input element is for the text box that will receive the user's email address. The second input element displays a button. You'll learn how to code these controls in the next two figures.

But first, this figure summarizes the four attributes that are common to most controls. Here, the type attribute specifies the type of control you want to use, like the button and text types used in this example. In contrast, the name attribute is only required for radio buttons and check boxes (see figure 11-4). Although the name attribute can also be referred to by JavaScript or server-side code, the id attribute is more commonly used for that today. Nevertheless, most of the examples in this chapter include the name attribute.

In contrast, the disabled and readonly attributes are Boolean attributes that you'll use infrequently. The disabled attribute disables a control so the data in the control isn't submitted with the form. And the readonly attribute provides a value that can't be changed but is submitted with the form.

Attributes of the form element

Attribute	Description
`name`	A name that can be referred to by client-side or server-side code.
`action`	The URL of the file that will process the data in the form.
`method`	The HTTP method for submitting the form data. It can be set to either "get" or "post". The default value is "get".
`target`	Where to open the page that's specified in the action attribute. If you specify, _blank, the page is opened in a new window or tab.

Attributes common to most input elements

Attribute	Description
`type`	The type of control like "button", "text", or "checkbox".
`name`	A name that can be referred to by client-side or server-side code.
`disabled`	A Boolean attribute that disables and grays out the control. Then, the control can't receive the focus, the user can't tab to it, and the value isn't submitted with the form.
`readonly`	A Boolean attribute that means a user can't change the control's value. But the control can receive the focus, the user can tab to it, and the value is submitted with the form.

The HTML for a form

```
<form name="email_form" action="subscribe.php" method="post">
    <p>Please enter your e-mail address to subscribe to our newsletter.</p>
    <p>E-Mail: <input type="text" name="email"></p>
    <p><input type="submit" name="submit" value="Subscribe"></p>
</form>
```

The form in a web browser

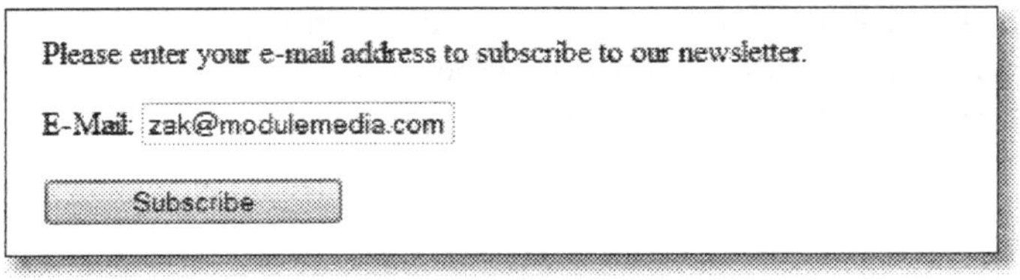

The URL that's used when the form is submitted with the get method

```
subscribe.php?email=zak%40modulemedia.com&submit=Subscribe
```

Description

- A *form* contains one or more *controls* like text boxes, radio buttons, lists, or check boxes that can receive data.
- You should code the name attribute to uniquely identify each form and control. You only need to code the id attribute if you want to use it as a CSS selector.
- When a form is submitted to the server for processing, the data in the controls is sent along with the HTTP request.
- For the get method, the URL is followed by a question mark and name/value pairs that are separated by ampersands. For the post method, the data is hidden.

Figure 11-1 How to create a form

How to use buttons

Figure 11-2 shows five different types of *buttons*. To code the first four, you use the input element as shown in the HTML in this figure.

In the examples, the first button is a generic button, defined by setting the type attribute to "button". When the user clicks this type of button, client-side code is usually run. For instance, JavaScript can be used to validate the data on the form. Then, if the data is valid, the script can submit the form to the server.

The second button is a *submit button*. When it is clicked, the form and its data is submitted to the server for processing. Unlike a generic button, a submit button sends the data to the server automatically without using client-side code.

The third button is a *reset button*. When it is clicked, the values in all of the controls on the form are reset to their default values.

The fourth button is an *image button*. It works like a submit button. The difference is that an image button displays an image rather than text. To specify the URL for the image, you use the src attribute. To specify text if the image can't be displayed, you use the alt attribute. And if you want to size the image, you can set the width and height attributes.

If you don't specify a value attribute for the first three types of buttons, the web browser supplies a default value depending on the button type. For example, the default text for a submit button is usually "Submit", the default text for a reset button is usually "Reset", and the default text for a generic button is usually "Button."

To code the fifth type of button, you use the button element instead of the input element. When you use the button element, you can format the text that's displayed on the button, and you can include elements other than text. In the example in this figure, the img element has been used to add a shopping cart image in front of the "Add to Cart" text for the button. When you use the button element, you still need to set the type attribute so the browser knows how to treat the button when it is clicked by the user.

Attributes of the input element for buttons and for the button element

Attribute	Description
`type`	The type of button. Valid values include "submit", "reset", "button", or "image". The "submit" and "image" types submit the form to the server, the "reset" type resets all fields to their default values, and the "button" type is typically used to run a client-side script.
`value`	The text that's displayed on the button and submitted to the server when the button is clicked.
`src`	For an image button, the relative or absolute URL of the image to display.
`alt`	For an image button, alternate text to display in place of the image.
`height`	For an image button, the height of the button in either pixels or percent.
`width`	For an image button, the width of the button in either pixels or percent.

Four buttons that are created by the input element

```
<input type="button" name="message" value="Alert Me">
<input type="submit" name="checkout" value="Checkout">
<input type="reset" name="resetform" value="Reset">
<input type="image" src="images/submit.jpg" alt="Submit button"
       width="114" height="42">
```

A button that is created by the button element

```
<button type="submit">
    <img src="images/addtocart.png" width="30" height="23"
        alt="Add to Cart">Add to Cart</button>
```

The buttons in a web browser

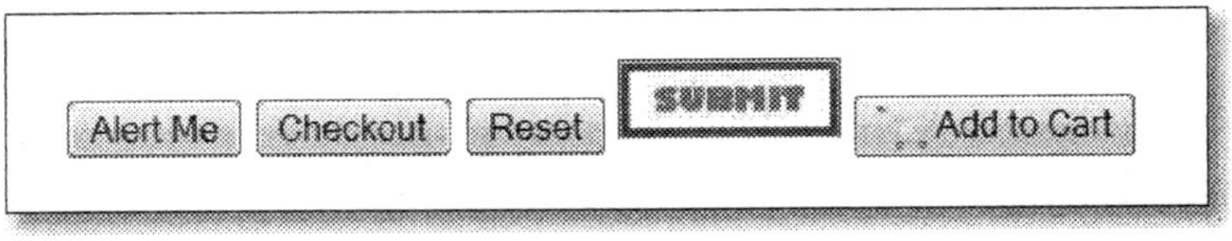

Description

- You can use the input element to create four different types of *buttons*.
- You can also use the button element to create a button. The main difference between the input and button elements is that the input element only allows a button to contain plain text or an image, but the button element allows a button to contain formatted text as well as other HTML elements such as images.
- When you click on a *submit button* for a form (type is "submit"), the form data is sent to the server as part of an HTTP request. When you click on a *reset button* (type is "reset"), the data in all of the fields is reset to the default values.
- You can use the "button" type to perform processing on the client before the form is submitted to the server. For instance, when the user clicks on the button, a client-side script can be run to validate the form data. Then, if the data is valid, the script can submit the form to the server.

Figure 11-2 How to use buttons

How to use text fields

Figure 11-3 shows how to use the input element to create three types of *text fields*, also referred to as *text boxes*. In the example in this figure, the first and second input elements display text fields that accept input from a user. To do that, the type attribute for both elements is set to "text". In addition, the name attribute is set to "quantity" for the first text box and "username" for the second text box.

If you want to put a starting value into a text field, you use the value attribute. For instance, the value attribute for the first text field is set to 1. As a result, this field will contain a value of 1 when the browser displays this page for the first time. Then, the user has the option of changing that value. If the value attribute is omitted, as in the second example, no value is displayed when the text box is displayed for the first time.

The first input element in this figure illustrates the use of the readonly attribute. This Boolean attribute doesn't let the user enter data into the field. However, the field can receive the focus, and the data in the field is submitted with the form. In contrast, the disabled attribute grays out a field, the field can't receive the focus, and the data in the field isn't submitted with the form.

The second input element illustrates the use of the HTML5 autofocus attribute. This instructs the browser to put the focus in the text box when the page is loaded.

The third input element in this figure creates a *password field* that works much like the first two text fields. However, the value in the field is displayed as bullets or asterisks. This improves the security of an application by preventing others from reading a password when a user enters it.

This password field also shows how to use the maxlength attribute. Here, this attribute is set to 6. As a result, the user can enter a maximum of six characters into this field. This is useful if you're working with a database that limits the number of characters that can be stored in a field.

The password field also demonstrates how to use the HTML5 placeholder attribute. Like the value attribute, the placeholder attribute displays text within the control. The difference is that the placeholder text disappears when the focus is moved to the field.

The fourth input element in this figure creates a *hidden field* that works much like the other three text fields. However, this field isn't displayed by the browser. Nevertheless, you can use client-side or server-side code to work with the value that's stored in this field. Because the user can't enter text into a hidden field, you usually code a value attribute for a hidden field.

In these examples, the username and password fields are displayed at their default width. One way to change that is to include the size attribute as shown in the quantity field. A better way, though, is to use CSS, which you can also use to align the controls. You'll learn how to format and align controls later in this chapter.

Attributes of the input element for text fields

Attribute	Description
`type`	The type of text field. Valid values include "text", "password", and "hidden".
`value`	The default value for the field, but the user can change this value. If a reset button is clicked, the field will revert to this value.
`maxlength`	The maximum number of characters that the user can enter in the field.
`size`	The width of the field in characters based on the average character width of the font. However, it's better to use CSS to set the size of a field.
`autofocus`	New to HTML5, a Boolean attribute that tells the browser to set the focus on the field when the page is loaded.
`placeholder`	New to HTML5, this attribute puts a default value or hint in the field. Unlike the value attribute, though, this value is removed when the user's cursor enters the control.

The HTML for text fields

```
Quantity:<input type="text" name="quantity" value="1" size="5"
                readonly><br><br>
Username:<input type="text" name="username" autofocus><br><br>
Password:<input type="password" name="password" maxlength="6"
                placeholder="Enter your password"><br><br>
Hidden:<input type="hidden" name="productid" value="widget">
```

The text fields in a web browser

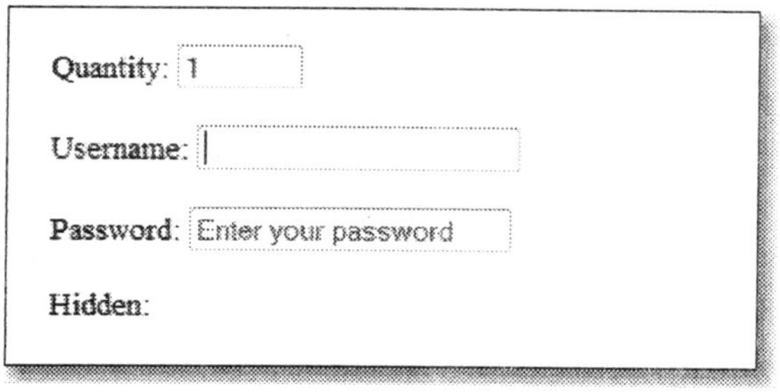

Description

- There are several types of *text fields*. The three most common are text, password, and hidden.
- A normal text field accepts input data from the user. Then, when the form is submitted, the name and value attributes are passed to the server.
- A *password field* also accepts input data that is submitted to the server, but the entry is obscured by bullets or asterisks.
- A *hidden field* has name and value attributes that are sent to the server when the form is submitted, but the field isn't displayed in the browser. However, if you view the source code for the web page, you can see the data for the hidden field.

Figure 11-3 How to use text fields

How to use radio buttons and check boxes

Figure 11-4 shows how to use the input element to code *checkbox fields* and *radio fields*, commonly referred to as *check boxes* and *radio buttons*. Although check boxes work independently of each other, radio buttons are typically set up so the user can select only one radio button from a group of buttons. In the example in this figure, for instance, you can select only one of the three radio buttons. However, you can select or deselect any combination of check boxes.

To create a radio button, you set the type attribute of the input element to "radio". Then, to create a group, you set the name attribute for all of the radio buttons in the group to the same value. In this figure, all three radio buttons have "crust" as their name attribute. That way, the user will only be able to select one of these radio buttons at a time. Note, however, that each of these buttons has a different value attribute. That way, your client-side or server-side code can get the value of the selected button.

To create a check box, you set the type attribute of the input element to "checkbox". Then, you set the name attribute so you can access the control from your client-side and server-side code. When you submit the form to the server, a name/value pair for the check box is submitted only if it's selected.

If you want a check box or radio button to be selected by default, you can code the checked attribute. In this figure, for example, the second radio button has been selected by default.

Attributes of the input element for radio buttons and check boxes

Attribute	Description
`type`	The type of control, either "radio" or "checkbox".
`value`	The value to submit to the server when the control is checked and the form is submitted.
`checked`	A Boolean attribute that causes the control to be checked when the page is loaded. If a reset button is clicked, the control reverts to the checked state.

The HTML for radio buttons and check boxes

```
Crust:<br>
<input type="radio" name="crust" value="thin">Thin Crust<br>
<input type="radio" name="crust" value="deep" checked>Deep Dish<br>
<input type="radio" name="crust" value="hand">Hand Tossed<br><br>
Toppings:<br>
<input type="checkbox" name="topping1" value="pepperoni">Pepperoni<br>
<input type="checkbox" name="topping2" value="mushrooms">Mushrooms<br>
<input type="checkbox" name="topping3" value="olives">Olives
```

The radio buttons and check boxes in a web browser

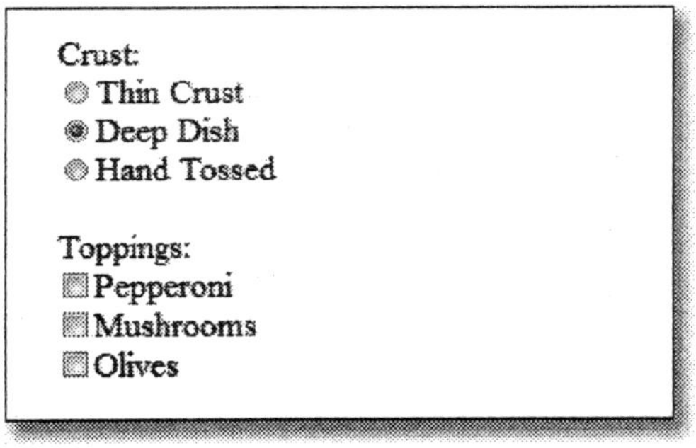

Description

- Only one *radio button* in a group can be selected at one time. The radio buttons in a group must have the same name attribute, but different values.
- *Check boxes* are unrelated, so more than one check box can be checked at the same time.

Figure 11-4 How to use radio buttons and check boxes

How to use drop-down lists

Figure 11-5 shows how to code a *drop-down list*. With a drop-down list, the user can select one option from a list of options. To display the list of options, the user must click the arrow at the right side of the control. In this figure, for example, you can see a drop-down list of sizes after the list is displayed.

To code a drop-down list, you use a select element. For this element, you code the name attribute. Then, between the opening and closing tags, you code two or more option elements that supply the options that are available for the list. For each option element, you code a value attribute. In addition, you supply the text that's displayed in the list for the content of the element. This text is often the same as or similar to the value for the option.

If you want to group the options in a drop-down list, you can code one or more optgroup elements. In this figure, for example, two optgroup elements are used to divide the options that are available into two groups: The New Yorker and The Chicago. To do that, the label attribute specifies the label for each group. Note, however, that the user can't select a group, only the options it contains.

When a drop-down list is first displayed, the first option in the list is selected by default. If that's not what you want, you can code the selected attribute for the option you want to be selected.

Attributes of the optgroup and option elements

Element	Attribute	Description
`optgroup`	`label`	The text that's used to identify a group of options.
`option`	`value`	The value of the selected option that will be sent to the server for processing.
`option`	`selected`	A Boolean attribute that causes the option to be selected when the page is loaded.

The HTML for a drop-down list

```
Style:<br>
<select name="style_and_size">
    <optgroup label="The New Yorker">
        <option value="ny10">10"</option>
        <option value="ny12">12"</option>
        <option value="ny16">16"</option>
    </optgroup>
    <optgroup label="The Chicago">
        <option value="chi10">10"</option>
        <option value="chi12">12"</option>
        <option value="chi16">16"</option>
    </optgroup>
</select>
```

The drop-down list in a web browser when the user clicks on the arrow

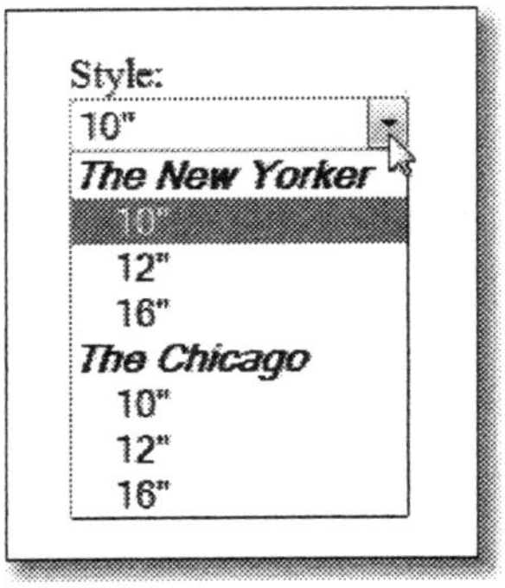

Description

- To create a *drop-down list*, you code a select element that contains option elements.
- To group the options in a list, you can code the options within an optgroup element. However, that isn't required.
- To use a drop-down list, the user clicks the arrow at the right side of the field to display the list, and then clicks on an option to select it. Or, the user can press the Tab key until the focus is on the list, and then press the down arrow to cycle through the options.
- By default, the first option in the list is selected when the page is loaded. To change the default option, code the selected attribute for the option you want to be selected.

Figure 11-5 How to use drop-down lists

How to use list boxes

In addition to drop-down lists, you can code another type of list called a *list box*. A list box differs from a drop-down list in that two or more of its options are always displayed. You can also define a list box so two or more options can be selected at the same time.

Figure 11-6 shows how to code list boxes. To start, you code a select element with a name attribute. You also code the size attribute to indicate the number of options that are displayed at a time. In the example in this figure, the size attribute is set to 4. However, because the list contains seven options, the browser adds a scroll bar to the list.

By default, the user can select only one option from a list box. In some cases, though, it makes sense to let the user select two or more options. To do that, you code the multiple attribute. Then, the user can select multiple options by holding down the Ctrl key in Windows or the Command key in Mac OS and clicking on the options.

Attributes of the select element for list boxes

Attribute	Description
size	The number of items to display in the control. If the value is 1, the control will be a drop-down list. The default value is 1.
multiple	A Boolean attribute that determines whether multiple items can be selected. It is only valid if size is greater than 1.

The HTML for a list box

```
<select name="toppings" size="4" multiple>
    <option value="pepperoni">Pepperoni</option>
    <option value="sausage" selected>Sausage</option>
    <option value="mushrooms">Mushrooms</option>
    <option value="olives">Black olives</option>
    <option value="onions">Onions</option>
    <option value="bacon">Canadian bacon</option>
    <option value="pineapple">Pineapple</option>
</select>
```

The list box in a web browser with a scroll bar

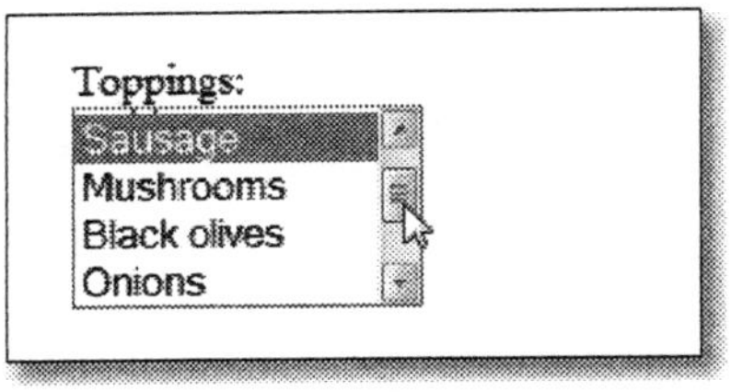

Description

- A *list box* displays the number of options you specify on the size attribute. If the list contains more options than can be displayed at once, a scroll bar is added to the list box.
- By default, only one option can be selected from a list box. To allow two or more selections, include the multiple attribute.
- You use the option element to define the options in a list box, and you can use the optgroup element to define option groups, just as you can with drop-down lists.

Figure 11-6 How to use list boxes

How to use text areas

Figure 11-7 shows how to code a *textarea field*, or just *text area*. Although a text area is similar to a text field, a text area can display multiple lines of text. As the user enters text into a text area, the text is automatically wrapped to the next line when necessary. Or, the user can start a new line by pressing the Enter key. If the user enters more lines than can be displayed at one time, the browser adds a scroll bar to the text area.

To code a text area, you use a textarea element with a name attribute just as you do for other controls. You can also code the initial text for an area by using the value attribute. Or, you can use the placeholder attribute to display text that disappears when the text area receives the focus, as illustrated by the example in this figure.

You can also code the rows attribute to specify the approximate number of visible rows the text area will contain, and you can code the cols attribute to specify the approximate number of columns. Although these attributes were required with HTML4, they are no longer required with HTML5. As a result, it's better to size the area by using CSS.

Attributes of the textarea element

Attribute	Description
`rows`	The approximate number of rows in the text area. Not required in HTML5.
`cols`	The approximate number of columns in the text area. Not required in HTML5.
`wrap`	Specifies how the text should wrap. Possible values include soft and hard, and soft is the default.

The HTML for a text area with default text

```
Comments:<br>
<textarea name="comments"
    placeholder="If you have any comments, please enter them here.">
</textarea>
```

The CSS for the text area

```
textarea {
    height: 5em;
    width: 25em;
    font-family: Arial, Helvetica, sans-serif; }
```

The text area in a web browser

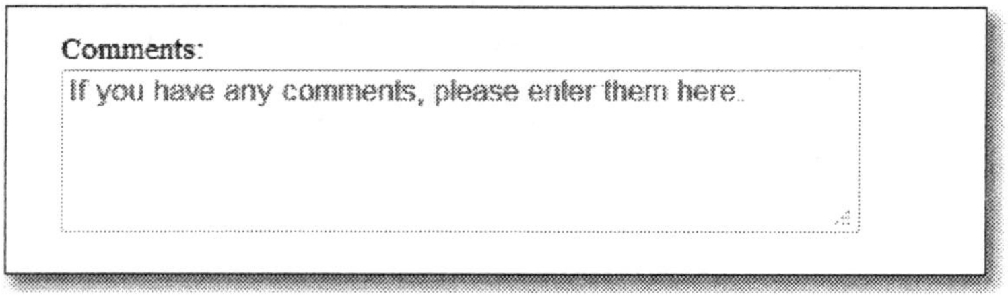

The text area after text has been entered into it

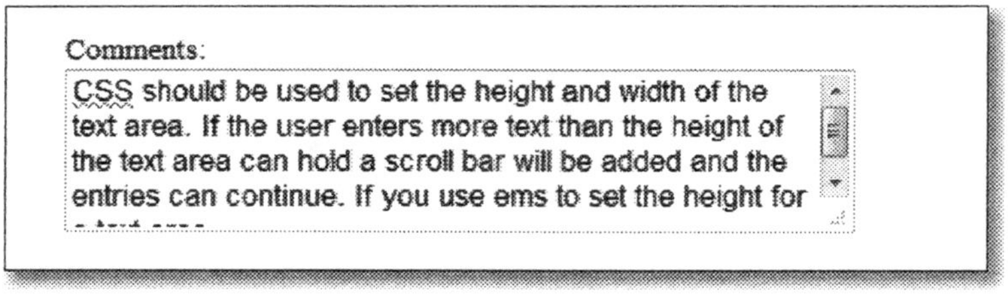

Description

- A *textarea field* (or just *text area*) can be used to get multi-line text entries.
- Any whitespace in the HTML for the content of a text area is shown in the value that's displayed in the browser.
- To set the height and width for a text area, you should use the CSS height and width properties. If you use ems to specify the height, the text area will hold approximately as many lines as ems.
- If you use ems to specify the width, each line in the text area will provide for more characters than ems except for a mono-spaced font. That's because an em is approximately the width of a capital M and most characters are narrower than that.

Figure 11-7 How to use text areas

How to use labels

The first label element in the example in figure 11-8 shows how to use a *label* to display text that identifies the contents of a related text field. To do that, the for attribute of the label element is used to specify the id of the related text field. Thus, the label is associated with the text field. This is a simple but common use of labels that makes it easier to align the controls of a form with CSS. You'll see how this works in figure 11-11.

The other label elements in this example show how labels can be used with radio buttons and check boxes to improve the accessibility of these items. Here again, the for attribute of the label is used to specify the id of a related radio button or check box. If you compare this coding to the coding in figure 11-4, you'll see that the label elements, not the input elements, now provide the text that is displayed after the buttons and check boxes.

When you code radio buttons and check boxes in this way, the user can click on the label text to turn a button or check box on or off. For instance, the mouse pointer in the browser display has clicked on the text for the third radio button to turn it on. This makes the buttons and check boxes more accessible to users who lack the motor control to click on the smaller button or box.

Coding buttons and check boxes this way also makes it easier for assistive devices such as screen readers to read the text associated with a control and tell it to the user. If you don't use labels in this way, the assistive devices have to scan the text around a control and guess which snippet of text is associated with the control.

Attribute of the label element

Attribute	Description
for	Should be set to the id of the related control. Although the id attribute is optional in forms that don't rely on client-side scripting, it is required when using labels and the for attribute.

The HTML for a form with label elements

```
<label for="quantity" id="quantity">Quantity:</label>
<input type="text" name="quantity" id="quantity" value="1" size="5"><br><br>

Crust:<br>
<input type="radio" name="crust" id="crust1" value="thin">
<label for="crust1">Thin Crust</label><br>
<input type="radio" name="crust" id="crust2" value="deep">
<label for="crust2">Deep Dish</label><br>
<input type="radio" name="crust" id="crust3" value="hand">
<label for="crust3">Hand Tossed</label><br><br>

Toppings:<br>
<input type="checkbox" name="topping1" id="topping1" value="pepperoni">
<label for="topping1">Pepperoni</label><br>
<input type="checkbox" name="topping2" id="topping2" value="mushrooms">
<label for="topping2">Mushrooms</label><br>
<input type="checkbox" name="topping3" id="topping3" value="Black Olives">
<label for="topping3">Black Olives</label><br><br>
```

The HTML in a browser as the user clicks on a label to check its box

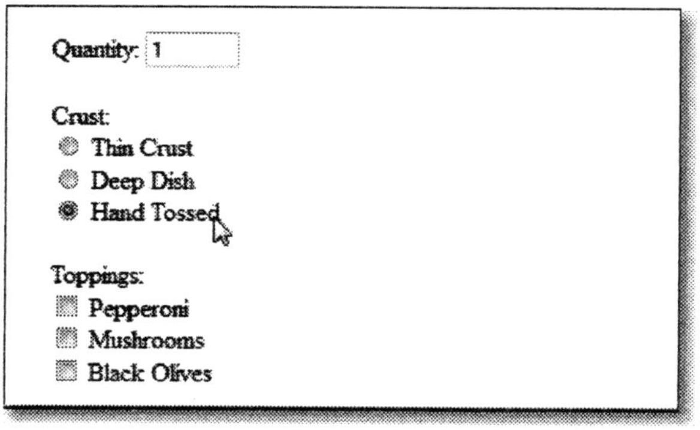

Accessibility guideline

- Use labels with radio buttons and check boxes so the user can click on the label text to select the control that the label is associated with. This also helps assistive devices.

Description

- A *label* is commonly used to identify a related field. However, labels should also be used to improve the accessibility of radio buttons and check boxes.
- Labels also make it easier to align the controls on a web page (see figure 11-11).

Figure 11-8 How to use labels

How to group controls with fieldset and legend elements

In many cases, you'll want to group related controls on a form to make it easy for users to see that they're related. To group controls, you use the fieldset and legend elements as shown in figure 11-9.

To start, you code the fieldset element. Then, you code the legend element right after the opening tag of the fieldset element. The content of this legend element determines the text that's displayed for the group. Then, the controls in the group follow the legend element.

The example in this figure illustrates how this works. Here, two groups are defined: one that contains radio buttons and one that contains check boxes. By default, this code places a thin gray border around the groups, as shown in this figure. To change the appearance of this border, though, you can use CSS.

HTML that uses fieldset and legend elements

```
<form name="order" action="order.php" method="post">
<fieldset>
    <legend>Crust</legend>
    <input type="radio" name="crust" id="crust1" value="thin">
    <label for="crust1">Thin Crust</label><br>
    <input type="radio" name="crust" id="crust2" value="deep">
    <label for="crust2">Deep Dish</label><br>
    <input type="radio" name="crust" id="crust3" value="hand">
    <label for="crust3">Hand Tossed</label>
</fieldset>
<br>
<fieldset>
    <legend>Toppings</legend>
    <input type="checkbox" name="topping1" id="topping1" value="pepperoni">
    <label for="topping1">Pepperoni</label><br>
    <input type="checkbox" name="topping2" id="topping2" value="mushrooms">
    <label for="topping2">Mushrooms</label><br>
    <input type="checkbox" name="topping3" id="topping3" value="olives">
    <label for="topping3">Black Olives</label>
</fieldset>
</form>
```

The elements in a web browser

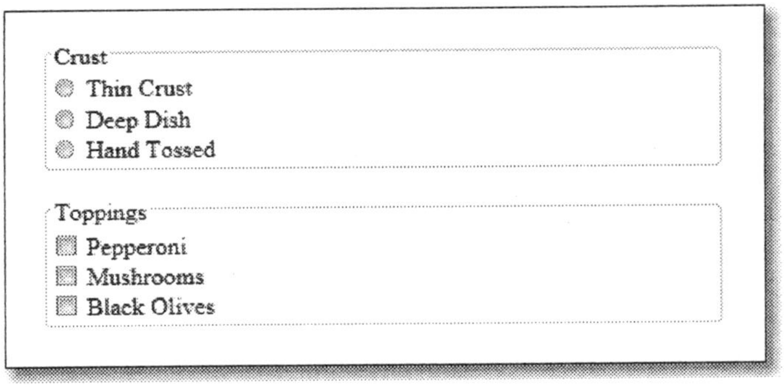

Description

- The fieldset element is used to group controls.
- The legend element can be coded within a fieldset element. It is used to label the group of controls.
- If you want to disable all of the controls within a fieldset element, you can code the disabled attribute for the fieldset element.

Figure 11-9 How to group controls with fieldset and legend elements

How to use a file upload control

Figure 11-10 shows how to use the *file upload control*. This control lets users upload one or more files to your web server. Typically you'll use this control with a server-side programming language such as PHP, which transfers the file or files from the user's computer to the web server. When you code a file upload control, you set the type attribute to "file" and set the name attribute as you would for any other control.

You can also code the accept attribute for a file upload control. This attribute lets you specify the types of files that will be accepted by this control. In the example in this figure, the JPEG and GIF types are specified so the control will only display those types of files when the Browse button is clicked and the files are displayed. If you omit this attribute, all types of files will be displayed.

When using the file upload control, the method attribute of the form should be set to "post". In addition, the enctype attribute of the form should be set to multipart/form-data. This is typically the only time this attribute will be modified within the form element.

Attributes of the input element for a file upload control

Attribute	Description
`accept`	The types of files that are accepted for upload. When the operating system's open dialog box opens, only files of those types will be shown.
`multiple`	A Boolean attribute that lets the user upload more than one file.

The HTML for a file upload control that accepts JPEG and GIF images

```
<form name="upload_form" action="sendemail.php" method="post"
      enctype="multipart/form-data">
    Attach an image:<br>
    <input type="file" name="fileupload" accept="image/jpeg, image/gif">
</form>
```

The file upload control in the Chrome browser

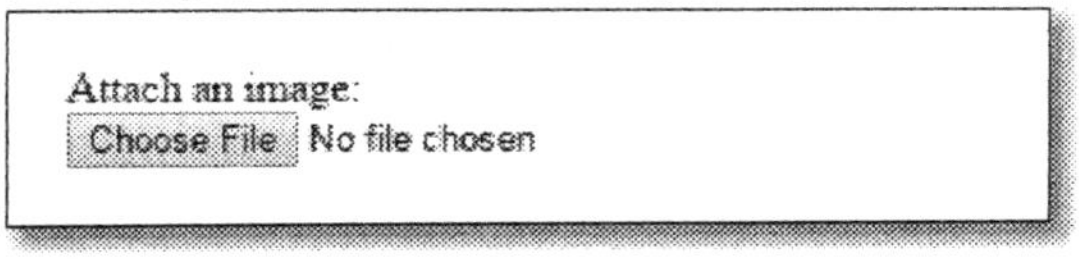

The Windows dialog box that's displayed when Choose File is clicked

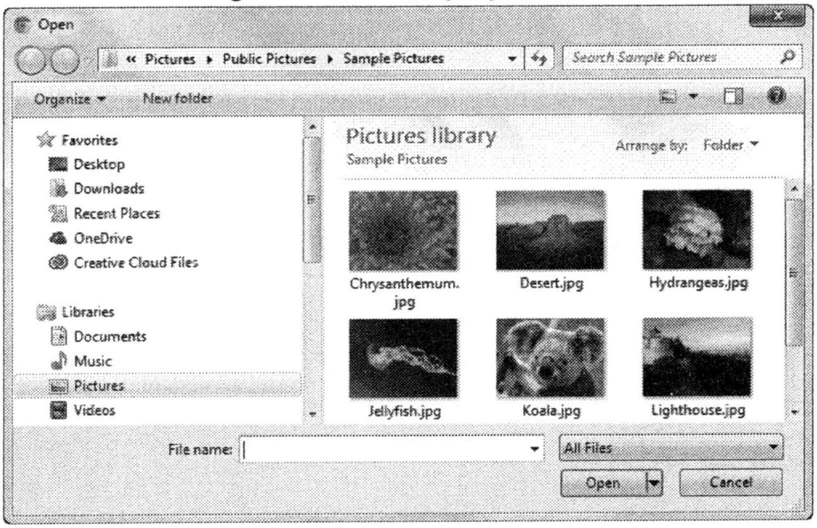

Description

- To create a *file upload control*, code the input element with "file" as the type attribute. This control lets your users select the files they want to upload to your web server.
- In the form element that contains the file upload control, the method attribute must be "post", and you must code the enctype attribute as shown above.
- How the file upload control is implemented varies by browser. For example, the Firefox browser displays a Browse button instead of a Choose File button.

Figure 11-10 How to use a file upload control

Other skills for working with forms

Now that you know how to code forms using common controls, you're ready to learn some other skills for working with forms and controls. In particular, you should know how to use CSS to align and format the controls. You should also know how to set the tab order of the controls on a form and how to assign access keys to the controls. Here again, if you already have these skills, you can skip ahead to the HTML5 features for data validation.

How to align controls

The best way to align controls is to use the technique shown in figure 11-11. Here, the rule set for the labels starts by floating the labels to the left. That causes the labels to be treated like block elements. Then, the rule set sets the width property so all the labels are the same width, and it sets the text-align property so the labels are aligned at the right. This makes the form more readable.

After the rule set for labels, a rule set is coded for the input controls. Here, the margin-left property increases the space between the labels and text boxes to 1 em. Then, the margin-bottom property sets the space after the text boxes to .5 ems.

The last rule set aligns the buttons on the form by adjusting the left margin of just the Register button to 7 ems. To do that, it uses the Register button's id as the selector. This aligns that button with the text boxes above it. Then, the Reset button is 1 em to the right of the Register button because the left margin for all input controls is set to 1 em.

Label, text box, and button controls aligned on a form

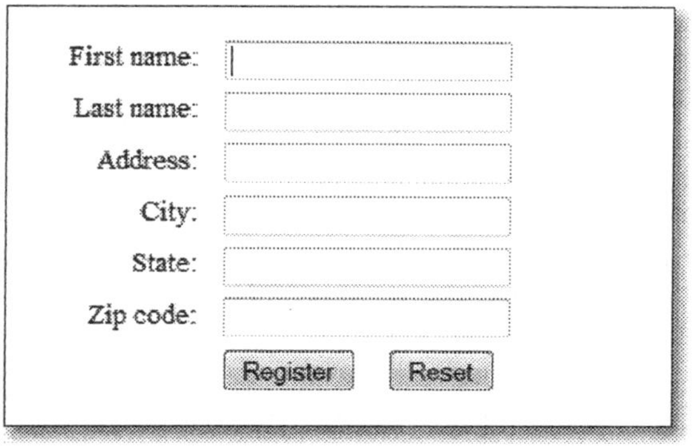

The HTML for the form

```
<label for="firstname">First name:</label>
<input type="text" name="firstname" id="firstname" autofocus><br>
<label for="lastname">Last name:</label>
<input type="text" name="lastname" id="lastname"><br>
<label for="address">Address:</label>
<input type="text" name="address" id="address"><br>
<label for="city">City:</label>
<input type="text" name="city" id="city"><br>
<label for="state">State:</label>
<input type="text" name="state" id="state"><br>
<label for="zip">Zip code:</label>
<input type="text" name="zip" id="zip"><br>
<input type="submit" name="register" id="button" value="Register">
<input type="reset" name="reset" id="reset">
```

The CSS for the controls

```
label {
    float: left;
    width: 5em;
    text-align: right;}
input {
    margin-left: 1em;
    margin-bottom: .5em;}
#button {
    margin-left: 7em;}
```

Description

- If a form includes a series of controls and labels that identify them, you can align the labels by floating them to the left of the controls and setting a width that provides enough space for all the labels. Then, you can set a left margin for the controls to add space between the labels and the controls.
- A series of labels is typically more readable if the labels are aligned at the right.

Figure 11-11 How to align controls

How to format controls

In the last topic, you learned how to use a few of the CSS properties to align the controls on a form. But you can also use CSS properties to format controls. Figure 11-12 shows how this works. The form shown here has the same HTML that's in the previous figure, but with some additional formatting.

First, the font property is used to change the font family and font size for the entire page. This not only affects the label elements but also the text that the user enters into the controls and the font on the buttons.

Second, the color for the labels has been set to navy, and the font weight for the labels has been set to bold. This is done by using a selector for all labels.

Third, the :focus pseudo-class is used to change the appearance of the text box that has the focus. In this case, a 2-pixel solid navy border is added to the text box. You can see that in the first text box in the browser.

Last, both of the buttons have been formatted with a box shadow and a silver background color. To select these buttons, I used a combination of two id selectors: #button and #reset.

The form in figure 11-11 with some additional formatting

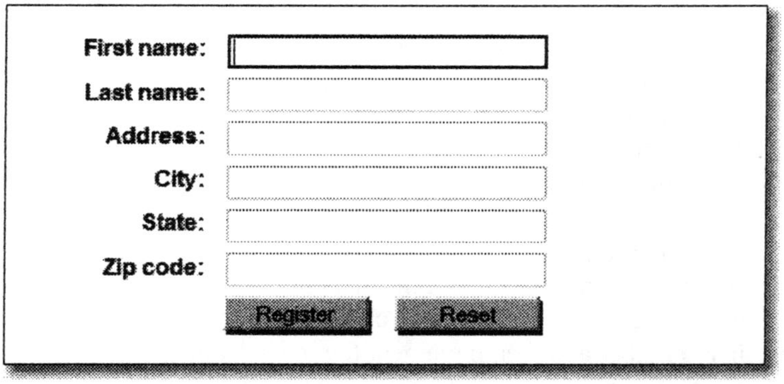

The CSS for the form

```
body {
    font: 90% Arial, Helvetica, sans-serif;
    margin: 20px; }
label {
    color: navy;
    float: left;
    width: 8em;
    font-weight: bold;
    text-align: right;}
input {
    width: 15em;
    margin-left: 1em;
    margin-bottom: .5em;}
input:focus {
    border: 2px solid navy; }
#button, #reset {
    width: 7em;
    box-shadow: 2px 2px 0 navy;
    background-color: silver; }
#button { margin-left: 9.5em; }
```

Description

- You can use many of the properties you learned about in chapters 4 and 5 to format controls.
- You can use the :focus pseudo-class to change the appearance of a control when it has the focus.

Figure 11-12 How to format controls

How to set the tab order and assign access keys

Figure 11-13 shows how to set the tab order of the controls and how to assign access keys to controls. By default, when the user presses the Tab key on a web page, the focus moves from one control to another in the sequence that the controls appear in the HTML, not including labels. This sequence is referred to as the *tab order* of the controls, and it includes the links created by <a> elements.

To change this default tab order, you can code tabindex attributes. To remove a control from the tab order, for example, you assign a negative number to its tabindex attribute. To include a control in the order, you start the tabindex attribute at zero or any positive number and then increment the index by any amount as you add more controls. You can also code the same tabindex value for more than one control. Then, within those controls, the tab order will be the sequence that the controls appear in the HTML.

Controls that aren't assigned a tabindex value will also receive the focus in the sequence that the controls appear in the HTML. These controls will receive the focus after all the controls that are assigned tabindex values. As a result, you usually assign tabindex values to all of the controls on a form if you assign values to any of the controls.

With HTML5, though, you can use the autofocus attribute to put the focus in the control that you want the user to start with. This is often all you need to do to get the tab order the way you want it.

When you work with the tab order, you should be aware of browser variations. That is, when you press the Tab key right after a page is loaded, the focus may move to a browser control like the address bar instead of the first control on the page. In fact, you may have to press the Tab key several times before the focus is moved to the first control. Here again, you can use the autofocus attribute to get around this problem.

When you provide an *access key* for a control, the user can press that key in combination with one or more other keys to move the focus to a control. If the page is displayed in Internet Explorer, for example, the user can move the focus to a control by pressing the Alt key and the access key.

To define an access key for a control, you code the accesskey attribute as shown in this figure. The value of this attribute is the keyboard key you want to use to move the focus to the control. In the first example in this figure, you can see that the accesskey attribute is coded for the three text boxes on the form. The access key for the First name text box is "F", the access key for the Last name text box is "L", and the access key for the Email text box is "E". Here, the letters that are used for the access keys are underlined in the labels that are associated with the controls. This is a common way to identify the access key for a control.

The second example in this figure shows another way to code access keys for controls that have labels associated with them. Here, the accesskey attribute is coded for each of the labels instead of for the text boxes. Then, when the user activates one of these access keys, the focus is moved to the associated text box (the one specified by the for attribute) because labels can't receive the focus.

The attributes for setting the tab order and access keys

Attribute	Description
`tabindex`	To set the tab order for a control, use a value of 0 or more. To take a control out of the tab order, use a negative value like -1.
`accesskey`	A keyboard key that can be pressed in combination with a control key to move the focus to the control.

Three labels with access keys

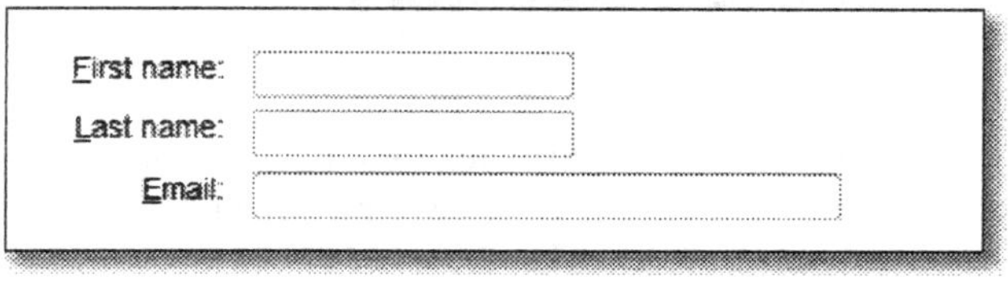

The HTML for the controls

```
<label for="firstname"><u>F</u>irst name:</label>
<input type="text" name="firstname" id="firstname" accesskey="F"><br>
<label for="lastname"><u>L</u>ast name:</label>
<input type="text" name="lastname" id="lastname" accesskey="L"><br>
<label for="email"><u>E</u>mail:</label>
<input type="text" name="email" id="email" accesskey="E">
```

Another way to define the access keys

```
<label for="firstname" accesskey="F"><u>F</u>irst name:</label>
<input type="text" name="firstname" id="firstname"><br>
<label for="lastname" accesskey="L"><u>L</u>ast name:</label>
<input type="text" name="lastname" id="lastname"><br>
<label for="email" accesskey="E"><u>E</u>mail:</label>
<input type="text" name="email" id="email">
```

Accessibility guideline

- Setting a proper tab order and providing access keys improves the accessibility for users who can't use a mouse.

Description

- The *tab order* for a form is the sequence in which the controls receive the focus when the Tab key is pressed. By default, the tab order is the order of the controls in the HTML, not including labels, and most browsers include links in the default tab order.
- *Access keys* are shortcut keys that the user can press to move the focus to specific controls on a form. If you assign an access key to a label, the focus is moved to the control that's associated with the label since labels can't receive the focus.
- To use an access key, you press a control key plus the access key. On a Windows system, use the Alt key for IE, Chrome, Safari, and Opera, and use Alt+Shift for Firefox. On a Mac, use Ctrl+Option for all browsers except IE, which can't be installed on a Mac.

Figure 11-13 How to set the tab order and assign access keys

How to use the HTML5 features for data validation

Now, it's on to the HTML5 features for *data validation*. These features let you validate some of the data that the user enters into a form without using client-side or server-side scripting languages!

The HTML5 attributes and CSS3 selectors for data validation

As figure 11-14 shows, HTML5 provides three attributes for data validation. The autocomplete attribute is on by default in all modern browsers, which means that a browser will use its *auto-completion feature* to display a list of entry options when the user starts the entry for a field. These options will be based on the entries the user has previously made for fields with similar names. If you're using a modern browser, you've probably noticed that your browser does this.

If you don't want the browser to use this feature, you can use the autocomplete attribute to turn it off for an entire form or for one or more fields. For instance, you may want to turn this off for fields that accept credit card numbers. In the example in this figure, this attribute is turned off for the phone field.

In contrast, the required attribute causes the browser to check whether a field is empty before it submits the form for processing. If the field is empty, it displays a message like the one in this figure. The browser also highlights all of the other required fields that are empty when the submit button is clicked. However, the message, how it's displayed, and how the other empty fields are highlighted vary from one browser to another.

If you would like to stop one or more controls from being validated, you can code the novalidate attribute for the form or for the controls. This is illustrated by the address field in the example.

To format required, valid, and invalid fields, you can use the CSS3 pseudo-classes that are listed in this figure. For instance, you can use the :required pseudo-class to format all required fields. If your browser doesn't support these pseudo-classes, you can still format the required fields by using the attribute selector shown in this figure. You'll see these pseudo-classes in action in the web page at the end of this chapter.

The HTML5 attributes for data validation

Attribute	Description
`autocomplete`	Set this attribute to off to tell the browser to disable auto-completion. This can be coded for a form or a control.
`required`	This Boolean attribute indicates that a value is required for a field. If the form is submitted and the field is empty, the browser displays its default error message.
`novalidate`	This Boolean attribute tells the browser that it shouldn't validate the form or control that it is coded for.

HTML that uses the validation attributes

```
Name:     <input type="text" name="name" required><br>
Address: <input type="text" name="address" novalidate><br>
Zip:      <input type="text" name="zip" required><br>
Phone:    <input type="text" name="phone" required autocomplete="off"><br>
<input type="submit" name="submit" value="Submit Survey">
```

The error message and highlighting used by Chrome

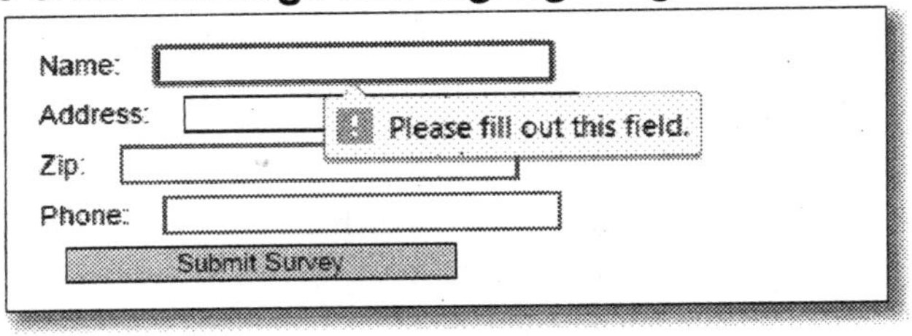

The CSS3 pseudo-classes for required, valid, and invalid fields

```
:required
:valid
:invalid
```

A CSS attribute selector for all controls with the required attribute

```
input[required]
```

Description

- By default, the *auto-completion feature* is on in all modern browsers. That means that the browser will display entry options when the user starts an entry. These options will be based on previous entries for fields with similar names.
- If the required attribute is coded for a field, the browser checks to see whether the field is empty when the form is submitted. If it is, the browser displays its default error message for the field. But what this message says and how it's displayed are browser-dependent.
- At this writing, Chrome, IE, Firefox, and Opera all support these HTML5 attributes, as well as the three CSS3 pseudo-classes shown above.
- To select all the input elements with the required attribute, you can also use the attribute selector shown above.

Figure 11-14 The HTML5 attributes and CSS3 selectors for data validation

How to use regular expressions for data validation

A *regular expression* provides a way to match a user entry against a *pattern* of characters. As a result, regular expressions can be used for validating user entries that have a standard pattern, such as credit card numbers, zip codes, dates, phone numbers, URLs, and more. Regular expressions are supported by many programming languages including JavaScript and PHP, and now regular expressions are supported by HTML5.

As figure 11-15 shows, HTML5 provides a pattern attribute that is used for the regular expression that will be used to validate the entry for the field. In the example, regular expressions are used for the zip code and phone fields. As a result, the user must enter a zip code that has either 5 digits or 5 digits, a hyphen, and 4 more digits. And the phone number must be 3 digits, a hyphen, 3 more digits, another hyphen, and 4 more digits. If these fields don't match those patterns when the user clicks the submit button, an error message is displayed by the browser and the form isn't submitted.

If you code a title attribute for a field that is validated by a regular expression, the value of that attribute is displayed when the mouse hovers over the field. It is also displayed at the end of the browser's standard error message for a field that doesn't match the regular expression. In the example, the browser's standard message is: "Please match the requested format.", which is followed by the value of the title attribute. But here again, the message that's displayed and how it's displayed are browser-dependent.

The trick of course is coding the regular expressions that you need, and that can be difficult. For more information or to find the expressions that you need, you can search the web. Or, you can refer to our JavaScript or PHP book, which gives detailed instructions on how to create regular expressions.

Attributes for using regular expressions

Attribute	Description
`pattern`	Specifies the regular expression that is used to validate the entry.
`title`	Text that is displayed in the tooltip when the mouse hovers over a field. This text is also displayed after the browser's error message.

Patterns for common entries

Used for	Pattern
Password (6+ alphanumeric)	`[a-zA-Z0-9]{6,}`
Zip code (99999 or 99999-9999)	`\d{5}([\-]\d{4})?`
Phone number (999-999-9999)	`\d{3}[\-]\d{3}[\-]\d{4}`
Date (MM/DD/YYYY)	`[01]?\d\/[0-3]\d\/\d{4}`
URL (starting with http:// or https://)	`https?://.+`
Credit card (9999-9999-9999-9999)	`^\d{4}-\d{4}-\d{4}-\d{4}$`

HTML that uses regular expressions

```
Name: <input type="text" name="name" required autofocus><br>
Zip: <input type="text" name="zip" required
    pattern="\d{5}([\-]\d{4})?"
    title="Must be 99999 or 99999-9999"><br>
Phone: <input type="text" name="phone" required
    pattern="\d{3}[\-]\d{3}[\-]\d{4}"
    title="Must be 999-999-9999"><br>
<input type="submit" name="submit" value="Submit Survey">
```

The form in Chrome

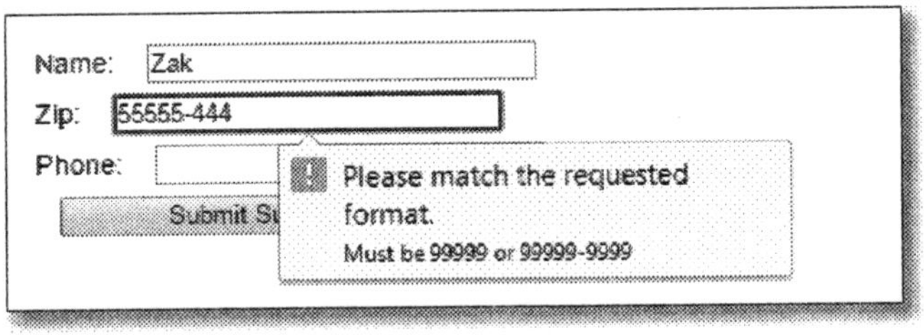

Description

- To use *regular expressions* to validate entries in text fields, you code the expression in the pattern attribute of the control. Then, the user's entry must have the *pattern* that's defined by the regular expression.
- At this writing, Chrome, IE, Firefox, and Opera all support this feature.
- To learn how to code regular expressions, you can search the web or use our JavaScript or PHP book.

Figure 11-15 How to use regular expressions for data validation

How to use a datalist to present entry options

Figure 11-16 shows how you can use the new HTML5 datalist element to provide a *datalist* of entry options for a text field. Here, you can see a datalist that includes four common search engines. Then, the user can select from just these four options. This can assure that the user's entry is valid.

To provide a datalist, you code a datalist element that contains the option elements that define the options in the datalist. For each option element, you code value and label attributes. The value attribute should contain the value you want to be submitted to the server. It may or may not be shown in the datalist, but it's always shown in the text box if the user selects that option. The label is always shown in the list, and it should be a friendly text-based description of the option. In Chrome, for example, the value is shown at the left side of the list and the label is shown at the right side. But in IE, the value isn't shown at all.

To associate a datalist with a text field, you add a list attribute to the field that specifies the id of the datalist element. In the example in this figure, the text field has a list attribute with a value of "links" that is the same as the id attribute of the datalist element.

In addition to the appearance of the datalist, its operation is also browser-dependent. In Chrome, for example, the datalist isn't displayed until the user starts typing in the text field or clicks the down arrow at the right side of the text field. In contrast, the datalist is displayed immediately when the user moves the focus to the text field in IE. Regardless of when the datalist is displayed, once it's displayed the user can either use the mouse to select an option or use the down-arrow key to highlight an option and the Enter key to select it.

Attributes for the option elements within a datalist element

Attribute	Description
value	The value of an option in the datalist. It is left-aligned.
label	The description of the item in the datalist. It is right-aligned.

HTML that uses a datalist element

```
<p>Our company is conducting a survey. Please answer the question below.</p>
<label for="link">What is your preferred search engine:</label>
<input type="url" name="link" id="link" list="links">
<datalist id="links">
    <option value="http://www.google.com/" label="Google">
    <option value="http://www.yahoo.com/" label="Yahoo">
    <option value="http://www.bing.com/" label="Bing">
    <option value="http://www.dogpile.com/" label="Dogpile">
</datalist>
<br><br>
<input type="submit" name="submit" value="Submit Survey">
```

The form in Chrome after the user clicks the down arrow

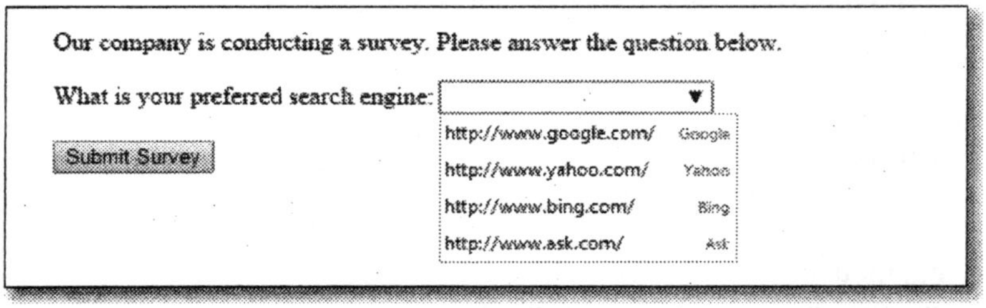

The form in IE after the user moves the focus to the field

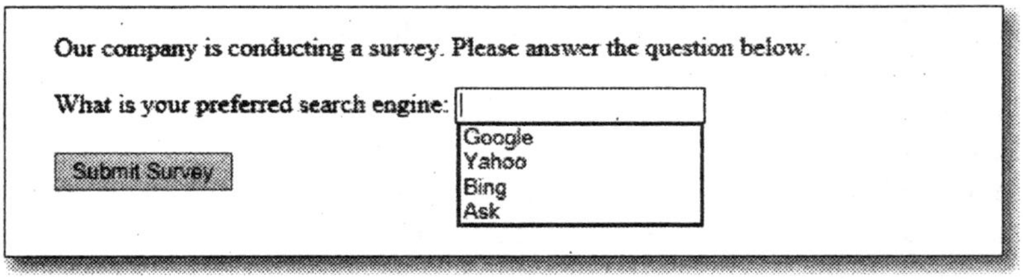

Description

- You can use the HTML5 datalist element to define a *datalist* that appears under a field when a user begins typing in the field. This is similar to the "auto suggest" feature that's used by search engines.
- To associate a control with a datalist, you set the list attribute of the control to the id of the datalist element.
- To define the items in the datalist, you use option elements.
- To select an option, the user can click on it with the mouse or use the Up- and Down-arrow keys to select an option and then press the Enter key.
- At this writing, Chrome, IE, Firefox, and Opera all support this element, but the appearance and operation of this feature is browser-dependent.

Figure 11-16 How to use a datalist to provide entry options

How to use the HTML5 controls

Besides the validation features that you've just learned, HTML5 provides several controls. Some of these do some validation. Some provide better ways to enter data. And all of them are good semantically.

In the topics that follow, you'll learn how to use these controls in a desktop browser. Keep in mind, though that many mobile browsers also provide some support for these controls. When you move the focus to an email control, for example, a keyboard that is optimized for entering email addresses may be displayed. And when you move the focus to a date control, a date-picker widget may be displayed. Because of that, these controls are particularly useful for websites that use RWD as described in chapter 8.

How to use the email, url, and tel controls

Figure 11-17 presents the email, url, and tel controls. To use one, you code an input element with the type attribute set to "email", "url", or "tel". That is good semantically, because the type clearly indicates what type of data the control is for: an email address, a URL, or a telephone number.

Beyond that, a browser that supports the email and url controls will validate the data in the controls when the form is submitted. For instance, the Opera browser in this figure is displaying its error message for an invalid email address. This works the same for a url control.

At this writing, though, validation isn't done for tel fields. That's because the format of telephone numbers can vary so much from one country to another. However, this may change as browsers evolve.

If you experiment with the validation that's done by the browsers that currently support these elements, you'll see that it isn't foolproof for email and url fields. In fact, you can do a better job of validation by using regular expressions. But this too may change as browsers evolve.

If a browser doesn't support these controls, they are treated as text boxes. Since this doesn't cause any problems, you can start using these controls right away. That way, you still get the semantic benefits.

The email, url, and tel controls

Control	Description
`email`	A control for receiving an email address. This implies that the entry will be validated by the browser when the form is submitted.
`url`	A control for receiving a URL. This implies that the entry will be validated by the browser when the form is submitted.
`tel`	A control for receiving a telephone number, but currently this doesn't imply validation because the formats vary from one country to another.

HTML code that uses the email, url, and tel controls

```
<form name="email_form" action="survey.php" method="post">
    <h3>Your information:</h3>
    <label for="email">Your email address:</label>
    <input type="email" name="email" id="email" required><br>
    <label for="link">Your website:</label>
    <input type="url" name="link" id="link" list="links"><br>
    <label for="phone">Your phone number:</label>
    <input type="tel" name="phone" id="phone" required><br><br>
    <input type="submit" name="submit" value="Submit Survey">
</form>
```

The form in Chrome

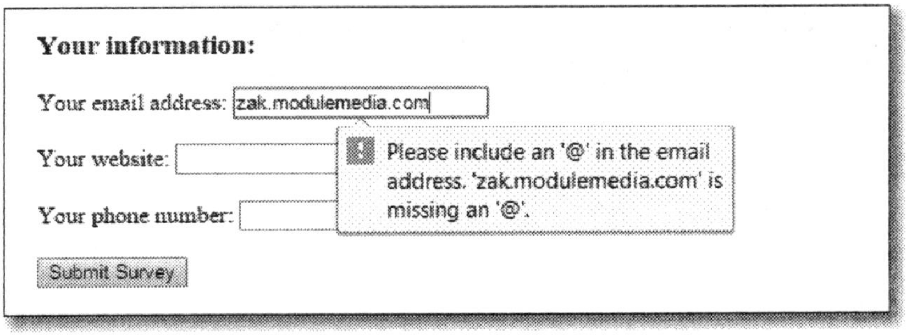

Description

- The HTML5 email, url, and tel controls are designed for email address, URL, and telephone number entries. The first two imply that validation will be done by the browser when the form is submitted, but phone numbers aren't validated.
- It's good to use these controls for semantic reasons because they indicate the type of data each control accepts.
- At this writing, the email and url controls are supported by all browsers except Safari, and the tel control is essentially supported by all browsers since data validation isn't required.
- Here again, the wording of the error messages and the way they're displayed depends upon the browser.

Figure 11-17 How to use the email, url, and tel controls

How to use the number and range controls

Figure 11-18 shows how to use the number and range controls. In browsers that support these controls, the number control is presented as a text box with up and down arrows that can increase or decrease the value in the box. And the range control is presented as a slider that the user can use to increase or decrease the initial value.

When you code these controls, you usually include the min, max, and step attributes. Those attributes set the minimum and maximum values that the control will accept, as well as the amount to increase or decrease the value when a number arrow is clicked or the slider is moved.

The examples in this figure show how this works. Here, the number control has 100 as its minimum value, 1000 as its maximum value, and 100 as the step value when an arrow is clicked. In contrast, the range control has 1 as its minimum value, 5 as its maximum value, and 1 as the step value.

If you code a value attribute for a number control, it will appear in the text box as the starting value. Otherwise, no value is displayed. This is illustrated by the example in this figure. If you code a value attribute for a range control, the slider will be set to that value. Otherwise, it will be set to the middle of the slider.

Here again, if a browser doesn't support these controls, they are treated as text boxes. Since this doesn't cause any problems, you can start using these controls right away. That way, you still get the semantic benefits.

Attributes for the number and range controls

Attribute	Description
`min`	The minimum value that may be entered.
`max`	The maximum value that may be entered.
`step`	The value that the entry is increased or decreased by when the user clicks on the up or down arrow for a number field or moves the slider for a range field.

HTML that uses number and range controls

```
<h3>Your information:</h3>
<form name="test_form" action="test.php" method="get">
    <label for="investment">Monthly investment: </label>
    <input type="number" name="investment" id="investment"
           min="100" max="1000" step="100" value="300"><br><br>
    <label for="book">Rate the book from 1 to 5: </label>
    <input type="range" name="book" id="book"
           min="1" max="5" step="1"><br><br>
    <input type="submit" name="submit" value="Submit Survey">
</form>
```

The form in Chrome

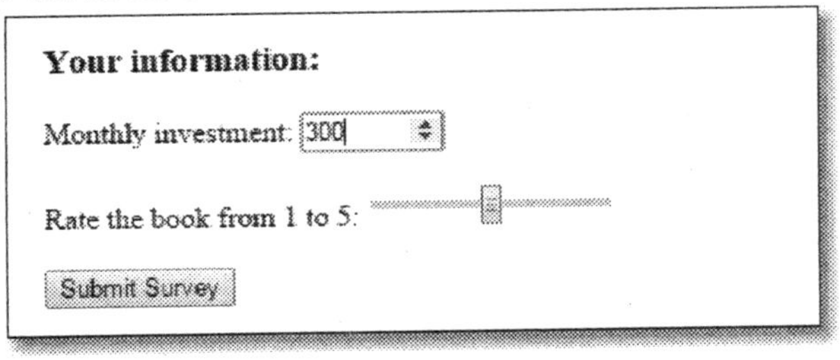

Description

- The HTML5 number and range controls are designed for numeric entries.
- It's good to use these controls for semantic reasons because they indicate the type of data each control accepts.
- In all browsers except for IE, a text box with up and down arrows is rendered for the number control. In IE, a text box is displayed.
- In all browsers, a slider is rendered for the range control.

Figure 11-18 How to use the number and range controls

How to use the date and time controls

Figure 11-19 shows how to use the date and time controls for user entries. When the user clicks on the down arrow for any one of the date types, the calendar is displayed, as shown by the last control in this figure. Then, the user can select the date, month, or week. When the user clicks on the up or down arrow for a time, the time is increased or decreased. (You may have to move the focus to a control or hover the mouse over the control to see these arrows.)

If you study the examples, you can see how to code the input elements for these controls. The only difference between the datetime and the datetime-local types is that datetime is formatted in Coordinated Universal Time, or UTC. This is the time by which the world sets its clocks. In contrast, datetime-local is based on the date and time used by your system's clock.

At this writing, Firefox and Internet Explorer treat these controls as text boxes. Safari adds up and down arrows to the text boxes. And Chrome and Opera provide up and down arrows for some fields and popup calendars for others. Even if they're not fully supported, it's good to use these controls for semantic reasons. And there's no harm done if they're rendered as text boxes.

Attributes for the date and time controls

Attribute	Description
max	The maximum value that may be entered within a date or time field.
min	The minimum value that may be entered within a date or time field.

HTML that uses the date and time controls

```
Date and time:  
    <input type="datetime" name="datetime"><br><br>
Local date and time:  
    <input type="datetime-local" name="datetimelocal"><br><br>
Month:  
    <input type="month" name="month"><br><br>
Week:  
    <input type="week" name="week"><br><br>
Time:  
    <input type="time" name="time"><br><br>
Date:  
    <input type="date" name="date">
```

The controls in Chrome

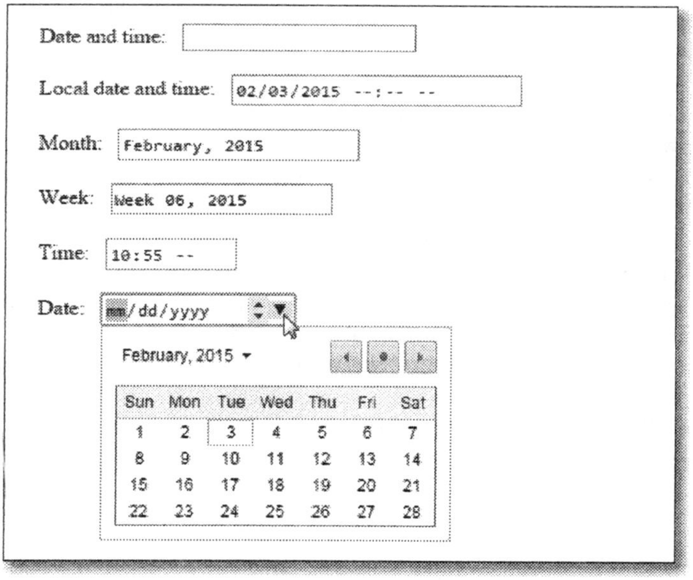

Description

- The HTML5 date, datetime, datetime-local, month, week, and time controls are designed for date and time entries. Here again, it's good to use these controls for semantic reasons.
- At this writing, Firefox and Internet Explorer ignore the date and time elements and render text fields instead, and Safari renders text fields with up and down arrows. In contrast, Chrome and Opera provide good support for all these elements except the local date and time element.

Figure 11-19 How to use the date and time controls

How to use the search control for a search function

Figure 11-20 shows how you can add a search function to a website. To do that, you use the search control along with several hidden fields to create a form that submits the search data to a search engine.

At the top of this figure, you can see the two controls that are needed for a search function: a search element for the search entry and a Search button that submits the search entry to the search engine. This is the standard way to set up the controls for a search function, and this mimics the way Google uses these controls. If you want to vary from this at all, you can use a Go button instead of a Search button, but users expect all search functions to look this way. You should also make the text box large enough for a typical entry.

If you look at the HTML code for the search form, you will see that the form is submitted to www.google.com/search, which is the Google search engine. That's why the results of the search are displayed on the standard Google results page.

In the code for this search form, the first input element is for the search control. Although a text field would also work, the search control is rendered differently in some browsers. For instance, as the Safari browser at the top of this figure shows, the search box is highlighted and has an "x" at the right of the box. This is meant to mimic the look of other Apple products such as the iPad, iPhone, iPod, the Apple website, and more.

To limit the search to www.murach.com, this HTML uses two hidden fields that pass the required data to the Google search engine. To use this HTML for a Google search of your site, you just need to change the value attribute in the two hidden fields to the URL for your website.

The trouble with the standard Google search engine is that sponsored links will be displayed on the results page. That's why it's better to use a search engine that can be customized so it returns results that are appropriate for users of your site. To find a search engine like this, you can search the web for "add search function to website." Some of these search engines are free, and some like Google Site Search charge a nominal fee like $100 a year for a small site.

A search function that uses a search control in the Chrome browser

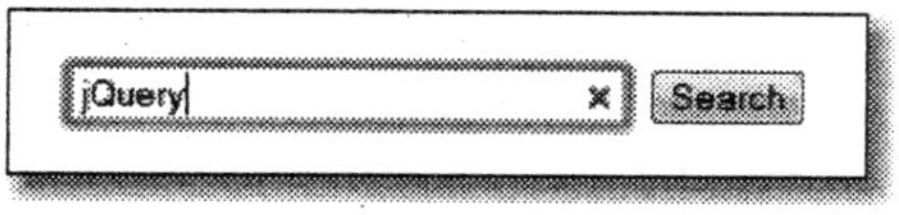

The results of a search when the Google search engine is used

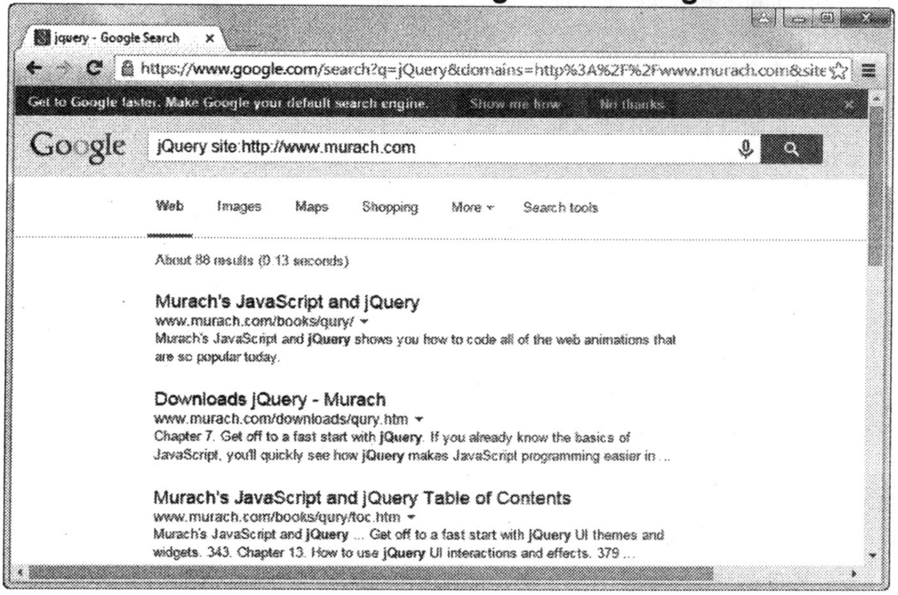

The HTML for using the Google search engine

```
<form method="get" action="http://www.google.com/search">
    <input type="search" name="q" size="30" maxlength="255">
    <input type="hidden" name="domains" value="http://www.murach.com">
    <input type="hidden" name="sitesearch" value="http://www.murach.com">
    <input type="submit" name="search" value="Search">
</form>
```

Description

- To implement a search function, you use an HTML form to submit the search text and other required data to the search engine.
- Within the form for the search function, you can use an input element of the "search" type for the text that's entered. This is good for semantic reasons.
- This control should be followed by a submit button that says Search or Go. The form must also include one hidden field to specify the domain for the search and another one to specify that only that domain should be searched.
- If you use a search engine like Google, you have no control over the search results. If you want to customize the results, you can use a search engine like Google Site Search.
- At this writing, Safari and Chrome are the only browsers that stylize the search control when the user enters data into it. Other browsers treat this control as a text box.

Figure 11-20 How to use the search control for a search function

How to use the color control

Figure 11-21 demonstrates the use of the color control. In browsers that support this control, a box is displayed with the current color in it. The current color is black by default, but you can set it to any color by coding the value attribute. Then, if the user clicks on this box, the color palette for the user's operating system is displayed. Later, when the color selection is submitted to the browser, it is sent as a hexadecimal code.

At present, Chrome, Firefox, and Opera support this control, and the other browsers treat it as a text box. But here again, it's good to use this control for semantic reasons, and there's no harm done if the control is treated as a text box.

Attribute for the color control

Attribute	Description
value	A 6-digit hexadecimal number that indicates the initial color for the control. Must be preceded by the pound sign (#).

The HTML for a color control

```
<label for="firstcolor">Choose your first background color:</label>
<input type="color" name="firstcolor" id="firstcolor" value="#facd8a">
```

The color control in Chrome

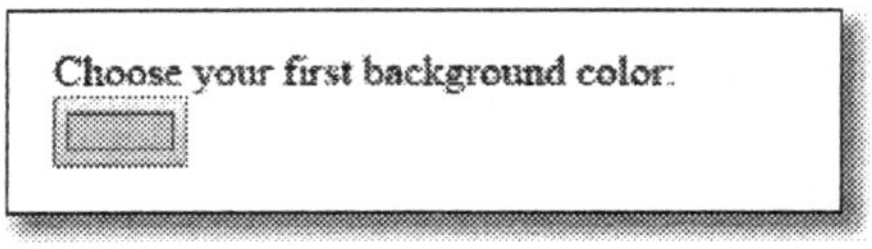

The Windows color palette

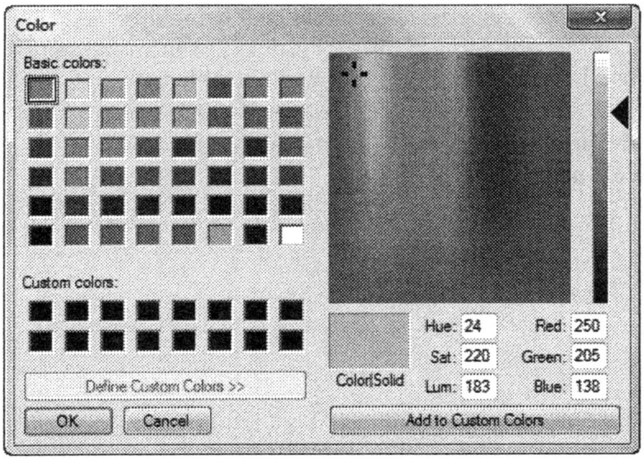

Description

- Use the input element with “color” as its type to let users select a color from the color palette.
- At this writing, Chrome, Firefox, and Opera support this control by displaying a box with the current color. The user can click on this box to display the color palette and then use the controls of this palette to create custom colors.
- When the form is submitted, the hexadecimal value for the selected color is used as the data for the control.
- Other browsers treat the color control as a text box. But here again, using this control is good for semantic reasons.

Figure 11-21 How to use the color control

How to use the output element to display output data

Figure 11-22 shows how to use the output element. Unlike the other controls that you've seen in this chapter, the output element is used to display output data, not to accept input data. To create the output, though, you need to use client-side code like JavaScript or server-side code like PHP.

In the example in this figure, JavaScript is used to add the values in the number controls and display the output in the output element. In this case, I used CSS to add a border to the output element so it's easy to spot. Otherwise, this element wouldn't have a border.

To show which fields the output element is associated with, you can code the for attribute. In this example, this attribute is used to show that the result is derived from the input fields that are named x and y.

Although you could use a label or text box to display the output, using the output element is good for semantic reasons. Also, browsers that don't support it render the output control as a text box. As a result, you can start using this control right now.

If you don't know how to use JavaScript or PHP, you won't be able to provide the code that calculates the result. But as a web designer, you may be asked to provide controls that the programmers for your site can use for their results. In that case, the output element is a good option.

An attribute for the output element

Attribute	Description
`for`	Can be used to associate an output element with one or more form controls.

The HTML for a form that uses an output element

```
<p>Enter numbers in both fields and click the Calculate button.</p>
<form onsubmit="return false">
    <input name="x" type="number" min="100" step="5" value="100"> +
    <input name="y" type="number" min="100" step="5" value="100"><br><br>
    <input type="button" value="Calculate"
        onClick="result.value = parseInt(x.value) + parseInt(y.value)">
    <br><br>
    Total: <output name="result" for="x y"></output>
</form>
```

The form in Chrome with a border around the output element

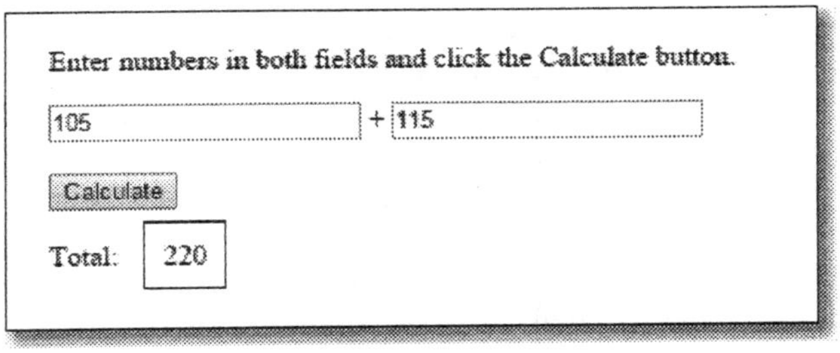

Description

- The output control is designed to display data that is calculated by a client-side or server-side scripting language.
- Although you could use a textbox or label to display the output data, using the output element is better for semantic reasons.
- In this example, JavaScript is used for the onClick event of the Calculate button. This code just adds the values in the number controls that are named x and y. For more on JavaScript, see chapter 15.
- At this writing, IE is the only browser that doesn't support this element.

Figure 11-22 How to use the output element to display output data

How to use the progress and meter elements to display output data

Like the output element, the progress and meter elements are designed for output data that's developed by JavaScript. However, both of these controls present the data in a graphical form as shown in figure 11-23. The default color used in these controls depends on the browser.

To use these elements, you code an id attribute that can be referred to by the JavaScript code. Then, you can code some of the attributes supported by these elements including the high, low, min, max, optimum, and value attributes.

The high and low attributes can be used to define the points at which the progress or meter element's value is considered a high or low point. When the low and high attributes are set for the meter element, the meter color changes from default to yellow when the indicator is either below the low value or above the high value.

The min and max attributes can be used to define the lower and upper limits of the progress or meter elements. Typically, you use 0 to represent 0% for the min attribute of a progress element and 100 to represent 100% for the max attribute because most progress indicators work within that range. In contrast, a meter might work differently. If, for example, a meter element is used to represent a car's speed, 0 will still be the min value, but 140 might be the max value, which represents the maximum speed that the car will go.

You can use the optimum attribute to define the point at which the progress or meter element's value is considered the optimum value. Again, if we use the speedometer in a car as an example, the optimum value might be 65 to represent 65 miles per hour.

The value attribute works the same as it does for most other form controls in that it allows you to define a default value for the progress or meter element. However, JavaScript can be used to change this value.

One reason for using these elements is semantics because they clearly indicate the type of data that will be presented. The other reason is that these elements make it easier to display progress and meter data in a graphical form. And most browsers already support these elements.

Here again, if you don't know how to use JavaScript, you won't be able to provide the code that changes the values in these controls. But as a web designer, you should know how to code these elements so they can be used by the programmers for your site.

Attributes for the progress and meter elements

Attribute	Description
`high`	The point at which the element's value is considered a high point.
`low`	The point at which the element's value is considered a low point.
`min`	The lower limit of the element. Typically, this will be 0 to represent 0%.
`max`	The upper limit of the element.
`optimum`	The point at which the element's value is considered optimum.
`value`	The current value of the element.

The HTML for progress and meter elements

```
<body onLoad="setProgressAndMeter()">
    <h3>Progress Element</h3>
    Progress set by JavaScript on page load:
    <progress id="progressBar" max="100" value="0"></progress>
    <h3>Meter Element</h3>
    Meter set by JavaScript on page load:
    <meter id="meterBar" max="100" value="0" optimum="50" high="60"></meter>
</body>
```

The progress and meter elements in Chrome

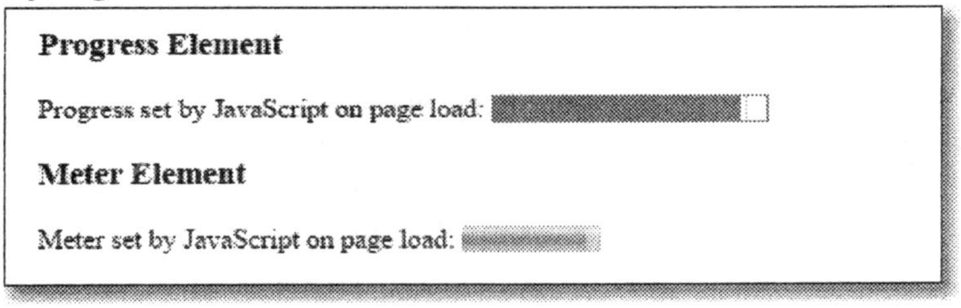

The JavaScript that manipulates the progress and meter elements

```
<script>
    function setProgressAndMeter() {
        var progress = document.getElementById("progressBar");
        setInterval(setProgressAndMeter, 500);
        progress.value += 10;
        var meter = document.getElementById("meterBar");
        setInterval(setProgressAndMeter, 500);
        meter.value += 10;
    };
</script>
```

Description

- These controls are designed to display data in progress bar or meter form. This is good semantically, and these controls also make it easier to display the data graphically.
- In this example, JavaScript is used to update these controls as the page is loaded. For more on JavaScript, see chapter 15.
- At this writing, all browsers except Safari support the progress element, and all browsers except IE and Safari support the meter element.

Figure 11-23 How to use the progress and meter elements to display output data

A web page that uses HTML5 data validation

To show how the HTML5 features for forms can be used in a web page, this chapter ends by presenting a complete example.

The page layout

Figure 11-24 presents a web page that contains a form that uses some of the HTML5 controls. This includes an email control for the email address entry, a date control for the starting date entry, and a number control for the number of tickets entry.

Because this page is displayed in Chrome, which supports these controls, you can click on the down arrow for the date control to display a calendar like the one in figure 11-19. You can also click on the up or down arrow for the number control to change the number of guest tickets.

The CSS for this form, puts a 3-pixel, red border around the required fields and a 1-pixel, black border around the fields that have valid entries. In this example, the first two fields, the address field, the phone field, and the guest tickets field are considered valid.

Because the autofocus attribute is used for the email field, you don't need to change the tab order for this form. But otherwise, the tab order would start with the five links in the navigation menu and continue with the six links in the navigation list in the right sidebar before the focus got to the first field in the form.

A web page in Chrome with a form that uses HTML5 validation

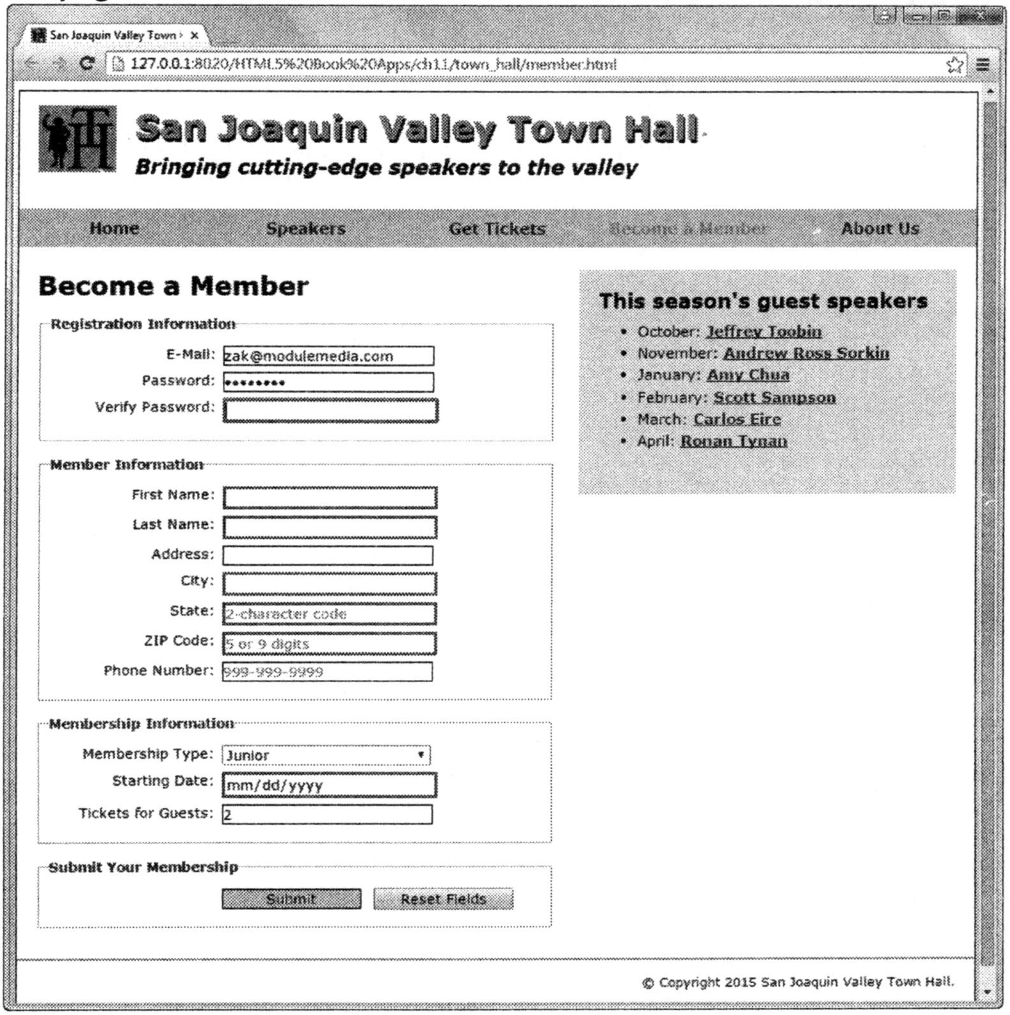

Description

- The form in this web page uses many of the HTML5 controls that were presented in this chapter. Its controls are formatted and aligned with CSS, and the CSS3 pseudo-classes are used to format the required, valid, and invalid fields.
- Form validation is done by using required attributes, regular expressions, and the email, date, and number controls.
- The autofocus attribute is used for the first control in the form so the tab order doesn't need to be changed. Otherwise, the navigation links and sidebar links would come before the form controls in the tab order.
- The placeholder attribute is used in some fields to indicate how the user should enter the data. When the focus moves to the field, the placeholder text is removed.

Figure 11-24 A web page with a form that uses HTML5 validation

The HTML

Figure 11-25 presents most of the HTML for the form within this web page. The rest of the code for this page is like the code that you've seen for this website in earlier chapters.

To help you focus on the HTML5 elements for a form, most of them are highlighted in this figure. For instance, the type attributes for the email, tel, date, and number controls are highlighted. Also, the autofocus and required attributes are highlighted. Last, the pattern and title attributes are highlighted for those fields that use regular expressions for data validation.

If you study this code, you'll see that it doesn't do a complete job of data validation. For instance, there's no way to verify that the second entry of the password is the same as the first entry when you use HTML5.

Similarly, the state field uses the maxlength attribute to limit the entry to two characters, but those characters won't necessarily be a valid state code. In fact, they may not even be letters. You could fix this by using a regular expression that requires two letters, but even then the code may not be valid.

This illustrates some of the limitations of HTML5 data validation. That's why JavaScript is commonly used to do client-side data validation. For instance, JavaScript could check that the second password entry is the same as the first entry. And JavaScript could look up the state entry in a table that contains the 50 state codes that are valid. Then, any entry that isn't in the table would be considered invalid.

Keep in mind, though, that the entries for a form should always be validated by the server-side code too. Like JavaScript, that code can validate data more thoroughly than the HTML5 features. As a result, the data validation on the client doesn't have to be thorough. In fact, the main point of client-side validation is to save some of the round trips that would be required if the validation was only done by the server. And if you use the HTML5 features for data validation, you will certainly save many round trips.

In that context, it's okay to start using the HTML5 features for data validation right now. Then, if a browser doesn't support them, you can rely on the server-side programming for data validation.

The HTML for the form

```
<form action="register_account.html" method="get"
      name="registration_form" id="registration_form">
<fieldset>
    <legend>Registration Information</legend>
    <label for="email">E-Mail:</label>
    <input type="email" name="email" id="email" autofocus required><br>
    <label for="password">Password:</label>
    <input type="password" name="password" id="password" required
           placeholder="At least 6 letters or numbers"
           pattern="[a-zA-Z0-9]{6,}"
           title="Must be at least 6 alphanumeric characters"><br>
    <label for="verify">Verify Password:</label>
    <input type="password" name="verify" id="verify" required><br>
</fieldset>
<fieldset>
    <legend>Member Information</legend>
    <label for="first_name">First Name:</label>
    <input type="text" name="first_name" id="first_name" required><br>
    ...
    ...
    ...
    <label for="state">State:</label>
    <input type="text" name="state" id="state" required maxlength="2"
           placeholder="2-character code"><br>
    <label for="zip">ZIP Code:</label>
    <input type="text" name="zip" id="zip" required
           placeholder="5 or 9 digits"
           pattern="^\d{5}(-\d{4})?$" title="Either 5 or 9 digits"><br>
    <label for="phone">Phone Number:</label>
    <input type="tel" name="phone" id="phone" placeholder="999-999-9999"
           pattern="\d{3}[\-]\d{3}[\-]\d{4}"
           title="Must be 999-999-999 format"><br>
</fieldset>
<fieldset>
    <legend>Membership Information</legend>
    <label for="membership_type">Membership Type:</label>
    <select name="membership_type" id="membership_type">
        <option value="j">Junior</option>
        <option value="r">Regular</option>
        <option value="c">Charter</option>
    </select><br>
    <label for="starting_date">Starting Date:</label>
    <input type="date" name="starting_date" id="starting_date" required><br>
    <label for="tickets">Tickets for Guests:</label>
    <input type="number" name="tickets" id="tickets"
           value="2" min="1" max="4" placeholder="from 1 to 4"><br>
</fieldset>
<fieldset id="buttons">
    <legend>Submit Your Membership</legend>
    <label> </label>
    <input type="submit" id="submit" value="Submit">
    <input type="reset" id="reset" value="Reset Fields"><br>
</fieldset>
</form>
```

Figure 11-25 The HTML for the form

The CSS

Figure 11-26 presents the CSS for the form that's used in the web page. Of most interest is the use of the CSS3 selectors. For instance, the input:required selector is used to put a 3-pixel, red border around required fields in browsers that support the :required pseudo-class. But note that the attribute selector

```
input[required]
```

is also used to apply the red border in any browser that doesn't support that pseudo-class, but does support the required attribute.

You can also see how the :valid and :invalid pseudo-classes are used to format the invalid fields. First, a black border is applied to valid fields, as shown in figure 11-24. Then, the box shadow is removed from invalid fields. This is done specifically for the Firefox browser because it's the only one that applies a box shadow to those fields.

The CSS for the form

```
fieldset {
    margin-top: 1em;
    margin-bottom: 1em;
    padding-top: .5em;
}

legend {
    color: #931420;
    font-weight: bold;
    font-size: 85%;
    margin-bottom: .5em;
}

label, input, select {
    font-size: 90%;
}

label {
    float: left;
    width: 12em;
    text-align: right;
}

input, select {
    width: 15em;
    margin-left: .5em;
    margin-bottom: .5em;
}

input:required, input[required] {
    border: 3px solid red;
}

input:valid {
    border: 1px solid black;
}

input:invalid {
    box-shadow: none;
}

br {
    clear: both;
}

#buttons input {
    width: 10em;
}
```

Figure 11-26 The CSS for the form

Perspective

Now that you've completed this chapter, you should have all the skills you need for creating forms, including forms that use HTML5 controls. You should also be able to use the HTML5 features for data validation.

Remember, though, that you can do a better job of data validation by using JavaScript. You'll see a simple example of how that works in chapter 15. On the other hand, data validation should always be done on the server too, so the client-side data validation doesn't have to be foolproof.

Terms

form
control
button
submit button
reset button
image button
text field
text box
password field
hidden field
check box
radio button
drop-down list
list box
text area
label
file upload control
tab order
access key
data validation
auto-completion feature
regular expression
pattern
datalist

Summary

- A *form* contains one or more *controls* like text boxes, radio buttons, or check boxes that can receive data. When a form is submitted to the server for processing, the data in the controls is sent along with the HTTP request.
- When the get method is used to submit a form, the data is sent as part of the URL for the next web page. When the post method is used, the data is hidden.
- A *submit button* submits the form data to the server when the button is clicked. A *reset button* resets all the data in the form when it is clicked. Buttons can also be used to start client-side scripts when they are clicked.
- The controls that are commonly used within a form are *labels*, *text fields*, *radio buttons*, *check boxes*, *drop-down lists*, *list boxes*, and *text areas*.
- A *text field* is used to get data from a user. A *password field* also gets data from the user, but its data is obscured by bullets or asterisks. A *hidden field* contains data that is sent to the server, but the field isn't displayed on the form.
- A *label* is commonly used to identify a related control. To associate a label with a control, you use the for attribute of the label to specify the id value of the control.
- You can use a *file upload control* to upload a file from the user's system. Then, server-side code is used to store the file on the web server.
- You can use CSS to align controls by floating the labels to the left of the controls. You can also use CSS to format the controls.
- The *tab order* of a form is the order in which the controls receive the focus when the Tab key is pressed. By default, this is the sequence in which the controls are coded in the HTML. To change that, you can use tabindex attributes.
- *Access keys* are shortcut keys that the user can press to move the focus to specific controls on a form. To assign an access key to a control, you use its accesskey attribute. To let the user know that an access key is available, you can underline the access key in the label for the control.
- HTML5 introduced some attributes for *data validation*, and CSS3 introduced some pseudo-classes for formatting required, valid, and invalid fields. The HTML5 attributes for data validation include the required attribute and the pattern attribute that provides for *regular expressions*.
- HTML5 also introduced some input controls including the email, url, tel, number, range, date, time, search, and color controls. These are good semantically because they indicate what types of data the controls accept.
- HTML5 also introduced some output controls that can receive the results of client-side or server-side programming. These include the output, progress, and meter controls.

Exercise 11-1 Create a form for getting tickets

In this exercise, you'll create a form like the one that follows. To do that, you'll start from the HTML and CSS code that is used for the form in the chapter application.

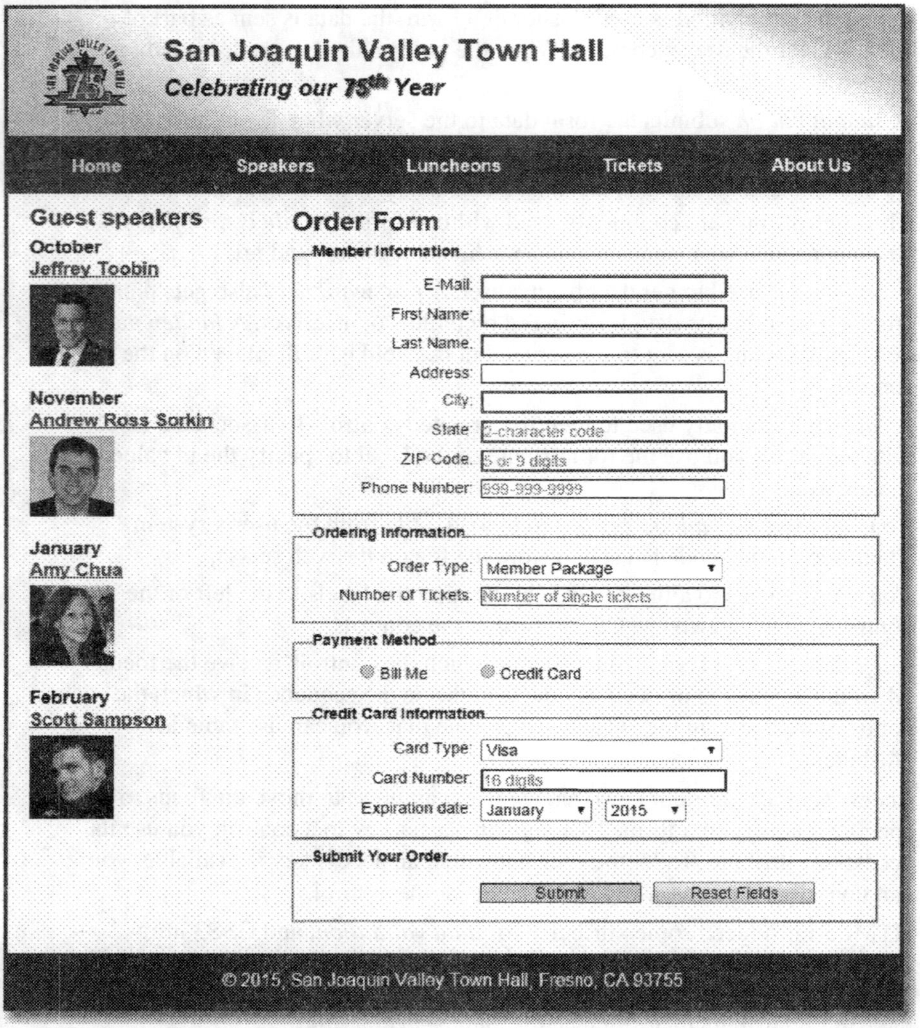

Open the HTML and CSS files

1. Use your text editor to open the HTML and CSS files for the Tickets page:

```
c:\html5_css3_2\exercises\town_hall_2\tickets.html
c:\html5_css3_2\exercises\town_hall_2\styles\tickets.css
```

2. Run the HTML file in Chrome to see that this page contains the form and the formatting that is used in the application at the end of the chapter. Your job is to modify the form and its CSS so the page looks like the one above.

Fix the formatting of the form and test after each change

3. Change the fieldset margins and padding so there is no top margin, the bottom margin is .5em, the top and bottom padding is .5em, and the right and left padding is 1em.
4. Change the legend formatting so the color is black.
5. Change the formatting so the required and the invalid fields have a 2-pixel border with #800000 as the font color, and the valid fields have a 1-pixel black border.

Fix the HTML one fieldset at a time and test after each change

6. In the HTML, change the heading before the form to "Order Form". Then, combine the first two fieldsets, change the legend to "Member Information", and delete the password fields so the first fieldset looks like the one above.
7. In the Membership Information fieldset, change the legend to "Ordering Information" and modify the HTML for the fields. Here, the Order Type list should have these choices: Member Package, Donor Package, and Single Tickets. Also, the Number of Tickets field should be a text field with the placeholder shown above.
8. Add the Payment Method fieldset with two radio buttons, and use the coding method in figure 11-8 so the user can activate the buttons by clicking on the labels. Then, adjust the CSS so the buttons are side by side as shown above.

   One way to do that is to code an id for the fieldset, and then use an id selector to turn off the float for the labels, to set the width of the buttons to "auto", and to set the left margin for the buttons to 3 ems.
9. Add the Credit Card Information fieldset. Here, the Card Type list should have these choices: Visa, MasterCard, and Discover. The Card Number field should have the placeholder shown. The month list should have values from January through December. And the year list should have values from 2015 through 2019.

   To format these lists, you can use id selectors and set the width of the month to 7 ems and the width of the year to 5 ems. To check the validity of the card number, you can use this pattern: \d{16}.
10. For the Submit Your Order fieldset, you just need to change the legend.

Test, validate, and test in other browsers

11. Test the validation that's done by the form by entering combinations of invalid data. Then, enter valid data for all the fields and click the Submit button. This should display a page (register_account.html) that shows the data that has been submitted.
12. Validate the HTML file, and test the form in IE. Then, if you have the time, test the form in Firefox, Opera, and Safari too.

12

How to add audio and video to your website

In this chapter, you'll learn how to add audio and video to your website. As you will see, HTML5 provides audio and video elements that make this easier than before. To make sure that your audio and video will work on older browsers, though, you'll also learn how to use the old elements for delivering audio and video.

An introduction to media on the web

Before I show you how to include media files in a web page, you need to be familiar with the various media types and codes that are used for video and audio. You also need to know what media types and encoders work with the browsers that are used today.

Common media types for video and audio

When most of us think about *media types*, a short list comes to mind: MPEG, AVI, MP3, and maybe even AAC. The reality, though, is that there are dozens of media types for both video and audio. Some of them are summarized in figure 12-1.

These media types are nothing more than containers of information that are used by *media players* to play the content that the types contain. For example, an MPEG file contains a video track, which is what the users see, and one or more audio tracks, which is what the users hear. To keep the video coordinated with the audio, a media type can also contain markers that help the audio sync up with the video. In addition, a media type can contain metadata, such as the title of the video, any still imagery related to the video (cover art), the length of the video, and digital rights management information.

For some media types, a browser will require a *plugin* that plays that type. These plugins are generally released by the player manufacturers. For instance, Apple provides a QuickTime plugin, Windows provides a Windows Media Player plugin, and Adobe provides a Flash Player plugin. If a browser supports a media type without requiring a plugin, you can say that the browser "natively" supports that media type.

Common media types for video

Type	Description
MPEG-4	Commonly found with either an .mp4 or .m4v extension. The MPEG-4 media type is loosely based on Apple's QuickTime (.mov) media type. Although movie trailers on Apple's website are still delivered in the older QuickTime .mov media type, iTunes uses the newer MPEG-4 media type for delivering video.
Flash Video	Commonly found with either the .flv or .f4v extension. Flash Video, developed by Adobe, was the most common media type for delivering video on the web during the last decade.
Ogg	Usually found with the .ogg extension. Ogg is an open-source, open-standard media type currently supported natively by Firefox, Chrome, and Opera. The video stream of an ogg media type is technically referred to as Theora.
WebM	A relatively new file format that is usually found with the .webm extension. WebM is currently supported natively by Chrome, Firefox, and Opera, and Adobe has recently announced that future releases of Flash will also support WebM video.
ASF	The Advanced Systems Format is commonly found with the .asf extension. ASF is a Microsoft proprietary media type and is specifically meant for streaming media. The video stream of an ASF media type is typically Windows Media Video (WMV).
AVI	Audio Video Interleave is commonly found with the .avi extension and is another Microsoft proprietary media type. It is one of the oldest media types and was introduced in 1992 when computer-based video was largely a hope for the future.

Common media types for audio

Type	Description
MP3	MPEG-1 Audio Layer 3, which is commonly known as MP3, is one of the most widely-used media types for audio.
AAC	Advanced Audio Coding or AAC is the format that Apple uses to deliver audio for its iTunes store. AAC was originally designed to deliver better quality audio than MP3.
Ogg	Usually found with the .ogg extension. Ogg is an open-source, open-standard media type currently supported natively by Chrome, Firefox, and Opera. The audio stream of an ogg media type is technically referred to as Vorbis.
WMA	Windows Media Audio or WMA are usually found with the .wma extension. The audio stream of an ASF media type is typically Windows Media Audio.

Description

- A *media type* is a container for several components, including an encoded video track, one or more encoded audio tracks, and metadata.
- To play a media type, a browser requires a *media player* for that type.
- For specific media players, browsers often require special *plugins*. These plugins are generally released by the player manufacturers, and include QuickTime, Windows Media Player, and Adobe Flash Player.
- To say that a browser "natively" supports a media type means that the browser doesn't require a plugin for it.

Figure 12-1 Common media types for video and audio

Video codecs

Within a media type, a video is encoded with a specific type of code. Although there are dozens of different codes used for video, figure 12-2 summarizes the three that are most noteworthy. H.264 is usually mentioned in the same breath as MPEG since it was developed by MPEG in 1993. Theora is the video stream portion of the Ogg media type. And VP8 was originally developed by On2 Technologies (later acquired by Google).

When a media player plays a media type, it has to do the five tasks that are summarized in this figure. Of these tasks, it's the decoding of the video and audio tracks that is the most difficult.

To decode, media players use software components called *codecs*. This name is derived from COmpressor/DECompressor, because video and audio are compressed when they're encoded and decompressed when they're decoded. You can also think of codec as COder/DECoder. Once the codecs have been used to "crack the codes," the media players display a series of images (otherwise known as frames) on the screen.

Video codecs

Codec	Description
`H.264`	Developed by the MPEG group in 1993. The goal of the Movie Picture Experts Group (MPEG) was to provide a single "all inclusive" codec that would support low bandwidth, low-CPU devices (think mobile phones); and high bandwidth, high-CPU devices (think your computer); and everything in between.
`Theora`	Theora is a royalty free codec which can produce video streams that can be embedded in virtually any format. Theora is typically mentioned in the same breath as Ogg.
`VP8`	Originally developed by On2 Technologies (later acquired by Google), VP8 is an open-source, royalty-free encoder.

What a media player does when it plays a video

- Determines the media type that the user is attempting to play.
- Determines whether it has the capability of decoding its video and audio streams.
- Decodes the video and displays it on the screen.
- Decodes the audio and sends it to the speakers.
- Interprets any metadata and makes it available.

Description

- A *codec* (derived from COmpressor/DECompressor or COder/DECoder) is a software component that is used to code and decode the algorithms that are used for a media type.
- A codec also compresses the code so it will load faster in a browser and decompresses the code before it is played.
- Although there are dozens of codecs for video, the three most common are H.264, Theora, and VP8.

Figure 12-2 Video codecs

Audio codecs

Like video, dozens of audio codecs are available. In fact, it's safe to say that there are many more audio codecs than there are video codecs. That's because there's a multi-billion dollar industry that revolves around the delivery of audio via mobile devices, set-top boxes, gaming consoles, smart TVs, and more.

An audio codec is used to decode the audio portion of an audio or video file, convert it to audible waveforms, and send it to the speakers of a system, which convert those waveforms into sound. The biggest difference between video and audio is that audio can store channels that let the sound be delivered to different speakers at the same time.

Most audio files contain two channels, which represent the left and right speakers, but it's common for video media types to have several channels of audio that represent left, right, and center speakers plus speakers in the rear. This is commonly referred to as "surround sound."

Unlike video, where the codecs have different names than their media types, audio codecs often have names that are the same as or similar to their media types. MP3 is one example, which can be played on a dedicated MP3 player or as part of a video track. Another example is AAC, which was adopted by Apple and is currently supported by all of Apple's products, including iTunes, iPhone, and iPad. Similarly, Vorbis is commonly used for the Ogg media types (both audio and video), and Windows Media Audio (WMA) is commonly used for Microsoft's WMA and ASF media types.

Audio codecs

Codec	Description
AAC	AAC is one of the most common media types and is also the encoding standard for the media type. It is currently used on all Apple products, as well as YouTube, Nintendo's DSi, Wii and 3DS, Sony's Playstation 3 and Portable, as well as several mobile devices including phones powered by Sony Ericsson, Nokia, Android, and WebOS.
FLAC	Free Lossless Audio Codec (FLAC) is a free, open-source codec that has seen its popularity increase over the years due in large part to its high compression ratio. Audio files that use FLAC can have their file sizes reduced by up to 60%.
MP3	MPEG-1 Audio Layer 3, commonly known as MP3, is one of the most widely-used media types for audio.
Vorbis	Typically packaged within the .ogg extension and commonly referred to as Ogg Vorbis. Vorbis is a free, open source format that is supported natively by some of the most popular Linux installations as well as Chrome, Firefox, and Opera browsers.
WMA	Windows Media Audio (WMA) is usually found with the .wma extension. The audio stream of an ASF media type is typically Windows Media Audio.

Description

- Although there are more than a dozen codecs for audio, the five most common are those in the table above.
- When you watch a video or listen to audio in your browser, your media player is responsible for interpreting the media type. It is also responsible for decoding the audio so it can direct the sound to the speakers on your device.
- Unlike video codecs, audio codecs often have the same name as their media type or a similar name.

Figure 12-3 Audio codecs

Audio and video support in current browsers

One of the problems when adding audio or video to a website is that there isn't a single combination of audio or video types that will work on all modern browsers as well as older browsers such as Internet Explorer versions prior to version 9. This is shown by the first two tables in figure 12-4.

One solution to this problem is to encode your media in the Flash file format (SWF) and rely on the browser's Flash Player plugin to play your media. Although this has worked well for many years, it presents three problems. First, you're forcing your users to rely on a plugin to view your media. Although it's true that 97% of the users have the Flash plugin installed, this plugin consumes resources and that still leaves 3% who won't be able to play your media.

Second, what about the ever-expanding use of mobile devices such as iPhones that don't support Flash? That segment, which currently represents more than 50% of Internet traffic, is also left out.

Third, the Flash player is unstable in some browsers so it sometimes crashes. This is one of the biggest reasons why the iPhone doesn't support Flash. As you'll see shortly, the HTML5 video and audio elements help eliminate the need for Flash.

The third table in this figure lists some common *MIME types* that you can use to identify the contents of an audio or video file. A MIME type helps a browser determine what player to use to open the file. To refer to an MP3 file, for example, you code "audio/mp3". Or, to refer to an Ogg Theora file, you code "video/ogg". In some cases, you'll also need to include the codecs for a MIME type as shown here.

Audio support in current browsers

Browser	Ogg Vorbis	MP3	AAC	WebM
Chrome	Yes	Yes	Yes	Yes
IE	No	9.0+	No	No
Firefox	Yes	Yes	Yes	Yes
Safari	No	Yes	Yes	No
Opera	Yes	Yes	Yes	Yes

Video support in current browsers

Browser	Ogg Theora	MP4	WebM
Chrome	Yes	Yes	Yes
IE	No	9.0+	No
Firefox	Yes	Yes	Yes
Safari	No	Yes	No
Opera	Yes	Yes	Yes

MIME types for identifying audio and video files

Media type	MIME type	Codec
MP3	`audio/mp3`	
Ogg Vorbis	`audio/ogg`	
WebM	`video/webm`	`theora, vorbis`
Ogg Theora	`video/ogg`	`theora, vorbis`
Flash	`application/x-shockwave-flash`	

Description

- The most common audio types are Ogg Vorbis, MP3, and AAC.
- The most common video types are Ogg Theora, MP4, and WebM.
- Mobile devices such as Apple's iPhone and Google's Android support H.264 video and AAC audio within the MPEG media type.
- A *MIME type* describes the contents of a file and can assist browsers in determining what player to use to open the file. The table above summarizes the MIME types and the codecs that are associated with them.

Figure 12-4 Audio and video support in current browsers

How to encode media

Figure 12-5 shows how easy it is to use software products that can convert a media file from one type to another, like MPEG/AAC to Ogg Theora/Vorbis. A product like this can also convert a raw, uncompressed video or audio file that you've recently captured on a digital video camera into a compressed format that targets one of the codecs.

Although many free and commercial software packages are available for encoding media types, one free product that I like is Miro Video Converter (www.mirovideoconverter.com). It lets you convert a file from just about any media type into the types needed for web applications. Miro Video Converter also supports audio-only formats including MP3 and Ogg as well as formats for mobile devices such as iPhone, Android, and PSP.

To use Miro Video Converter, you just drag the media type that you'd like to convert into the file pane, select the media type/codec that you'd like to target from the drop-down menus, and click the Convert button. Depending on the size of the file, the conversion process will take anywhere from seconds to minutes to hours. When the conversion process is finished, the new media file will be in the default folder for Miro Video Converter. To find out where that folder is, you can click the settings button (the one with the gear on it) and then click the "Show output folder" link in the settings that are displayed.

Other converters that warrant mention are: Apple's iTunes (for audio) and QuickTime Pro (for just about anything); Microsoft's Windows Media Encoder; Adobe's Media Encoder (great for Flash); Firefogg, which is a handy add-in to Firefox and specifically supports the Ogg file format; FFmpeg, which is great for batch encoding; and Handbrake, which is ideally suited for mobile device output and comes as a graphical user interface or command line install.

Miro Video Converter used to convert an MP4 file to an Ogg Theora file

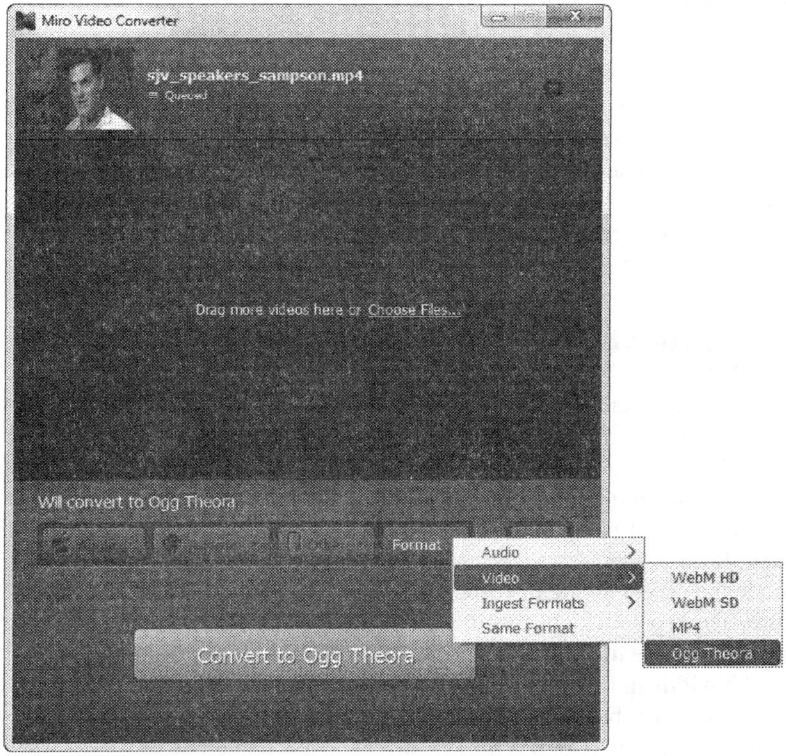

Description

- To encode audio and video files in the formats that you need, you can use one of the many encoders that are currently available, including Miro Video Converter, iTunes, QuickTime, Windows Media Encoder, Adobe Media Encoder, Firefogg, FFmpeg, and Handbrake.
- One encoder that I recommend is Miro Video Converter. It is a free program that lets you convert audio and video from one format to another as well as encode video for the popular media types including Ogg, WebM, and MPEG-4.
- Miro Video Converter also supports mobile devices including iPhone, Android, and PSP.

Figure 12-5 How to encode media

How to add audio and video to a web page

With that as background, you're ready to learn how to add audio and video to your web pages. As you'll see, there are several ways to do that. To start, you'll learn how to use the older HTML elements that are still required by some of the older browsers. Then, you'll learn how to use the HTML5 elements for audio and video. Last, you'll learn how to use a combination of these elements with a twist of Flash to provide the best solution for backward compatibility.

How to use the object and param elements

Figure 12-6 shows how you can use the object element to embed a media type in a web page. For years, this element was the standard element for doing that. When you use the object element, you can include one or more param elements to provide values to the media player that's being used. This has always been one of the advantages of using an object element since this lets you vary the way the media player works.

When you code the object element, you usually code the four attributes listed in this figure. The type attribute specifies the MIME type. The data attribute specifies the URL of the file you want to play. And the width and height attributes specify the width and height of either the media type or the player.

For a Flash file, these attributes apply to the file. For other types of media, they apply to the media player. Also, if a file doesn't have a visual element, you can omit the width and height attributes or set their values to 0. You can use this technique, for example, to play an audio file in the background.

This figure also presents the two attributes of the param element that you're most likely to use. For the name attribute, you specify the name of a parameter for a specific media player. Then, you specify the parameter's value on the value attribute. In the example in this figure, you can see how this works for the autoplay parameter. Here, the autoplay parameter tells the player to start playing the file as soon as the page is loaded.

The parameters that you can use depend on the media player that you're targeting. For a complete list of parameters, you need to review the Internet documentation for the targeted media player.

Of note in this example is that the object element doesn't specify what media player to use. Instead, the player depends on what media player the user has installed and, worse, whether or not that player is capable of playing the media type that's offered by the object element. For this reason, the use of the object element is on the decline and for the most part has been relegated to serving as a "fallback" mechanism that serves up a "safe" media type such as Flash for browsers that don't support the HTML5 video and audio elements.

The object and param elements

Element	Description
`object`	Embeds a media file into a web page.
`param`	Provides parameters to the media player that's used to open a file.

Attributes of the object element

Attribute	Description
`type`	The MIME type of the file.
`data`	The URL of the file.
`width`	The width of the file or the media player that's used.
`height`	The height of the file or the media player that's used.

Attributes of the param element

Attribute	Description
`name`	The name of the parameter. Each media player has its own parameters.
`value`	The value of the parameter.

An object element for playing a Flash file

```
<object type="application/x-shockwave-flash"
        data="media/sjv_anniversary.swf"
        width="400" height="150">
    <param name="autoplay" value="true">
</object>
```

Description

- When you use the object element, you can control the appearance and operation of the media player by coding parameter elements. These elements are standard HTML.
- If you don't specify the MIME type for a file, the file will be opened in the browser's default media player for the media type.
- Because different players accept different parameters, you typically specify the parameters for all the players you want to provide for. Then, if a player doesn't support a parameter, it will ignore it.
- If you don't want to display the interface for a media player, you can omit the width and height attributes or set them to 0.
- Some browsers require a param element that specifies the URL of the file even if the file is identified in the object element.
- The object element is rarely used today thanks in large part to the video and audio elements in HTML5.

Figure 12-6 How to use the object and param elements

How to use the embed element

Another element that is commonly used in existing sites for embedding media files is the embed element. Although this element wasn't supported by previous HTML standards, it was supported by all of the major browsers, and it is now supported by the HTML5 standard. As a result, you should feel free to use it whenever that makes sense.

Figure 12-7 presents some of the most useful attributes of the embed element. As you can see, all of these are the same or similar to the attributes you code on the object element.

In addition to the basic attributes, you can code the parameters for media players as attributes, rather than as separate param elements. For instance, the first example in this figure uses the autoplay attribute to pass a parameter to the default player for an MP3 file that tells the player to start playing the file as soon as the page is loaded.

Here again, these attributes vary depending on the target media player, and you should consult the documentation for the players to find out which media player supports which attributes. In this figure, you can see the URLs for the documentation of some of the common media players. Note, though, that the URL for Windows Media Player displays a page with information about the parameters that can be coded on the param element of an object element. So remember that you can also code these parameters as attributes of the embed element.

Like the object element, you'll notice that the embed element doesn't explicitly specify what player to use. For this reason, the use of the embed element is also on the decline and for the most part has been relegated to the role of serving as a "fallback" mechanism for browsers that don't support the HTML5 video or audio elements.

One exception is the use of the embed element for playing YouTube videos as shown in the second example in this figure. Although you can use the video element to play a YouTube video, it's more complicated than using the embed element. In fact, it requires extensive use of JavaScript code. So for now, it's best to use the embed element.

When you code an embed element for a YouTube video, you'll need to know what URL to code for the src attribute. To find out, you can display the page that contains the video. Then, you can click on the Share link below the video and then on the Embed link to display the iframe element for the video. When I did that for the video in the second example in this figure, for instance, this iframe element was displayed:

```
<iframe width="560" height="315"
        src="https://www.youtube.com/embed/NkfJjWJnl-w"
        frameborder="0" allowfullscreen>
</iframe>
```

Then, I used the value of the src attribute for this element as the value of the src attribute for the embed element. I also used the width and height attributes, but I added some additional height for the video controls.

Attributes of the embed element

Attribute	Description
`type`	The MIME type of the file to be played.
`src`	The URL of the file to be played.
`width`	The width of the file or the media player that's used.
`height`	The height of the file or the media player that's used.

An embed element for playing an MP3 file

```
<embed type="audio/mp3"
       src="media/sjv_welcome.mp3"
       width="300" height="25"
       autoplay="true">
```

An embed element that plays a YouTube video

```
<embed src="https://www.youtube.com/embed/NkfJjWJnl-w"
       width="560" height="349">
```

Websites for information about other attributes

QuickTime attributes

http://support.apple.com/kb/TA26485

Flash attributes

http://kb2.adobe.com/cps/127/tn_12701.html

Windows Media Player attributes

https://msdn.microsoft.com/en-us/library/windows/desktop/dd564581(v=vs.85).aspx

Description

- When you use the embed element, you code all parameters as attributes, not as param elements.
- Although the embed element wasn't part of the HTML4 specification, this element was supported by all major browsers, and now it is included in the HTML5 specification.
- Often, an embed element is easier to code and works better than a comparable object element. That's why the embed element is currently in use on many websites.
- If you don't specify the MIME type for a file, the file will be opened in the browser's default media player for the media format.
- The embed element provides an easy way to display YouTube videos within your web pages.
- The HTML specification lists four standard attributes, but other attributes are supported for specific media players.

Figure 12-7 How to use the embed element

How to use the HTML5 video and audio elements

Figure 12-8 shows how to use the HTML5 video and audio elements to add video and audio to your web pages. In their simplest form, you just add the video and audio elements to a page and code the src attributes that point to the media files to be played. This is illustrated by the first example in this figure.

If you want to set some of the options that these elements support, you can code the other attributes that are summarized in this figure. This is illustrated by the second and third examples. Here, the controls attribute instructs the browser to display a toolbar that displays play, pause, volume, and progress controls. And the autoplay attribute tells the browser to begin playing the media as soon as the page is loaded. In addition, the width and height attributes are used with the video to set the dimensions of the media player in the browser.

Within the video and audio elements in these examples, you can see the source elements that refer to the different media types. Although I included three different media types for video and two different media types for audio, you should realize that isn't usually necessary. That's because, as you saw in figure 12-4, the MP3 and MP4 media types are supported by all modern browsers. So if you have an MP3 or MP4 file available, or if you can convert the file you have to MP3 or MP4 format, that's all you need.

If you do include a source element for a video media type other than MP4, you should realize that you don't typically have to include the type attribute as shown here. That's because most current web browsers are able to determine what media player to use without this attribute. However, it's good to include it so browsers don't have to do that. Note that if you're using Aptana to run the page, you have to include the type attribute so Aptana's built-in server knows what media player to use.

These examples show how the HTML5 audio and video elements can be used to simplify the way that audio and video are added to a web page. To start, this coding will work for all modern browsers. But even better, these elements provide video and audio that is native to all current editions of the major browsers.

That means that you no longer have to worry about whether or not your users have the right player or plugin installed on their browsers. That also means you don't have to worry about whether or not their browsers will crash because of the instabilities of the Flash player. The only problem is that older browsers, specifically versions of Internet Explorer prior to version 9, don't support these elements, but the next topic will show you how to fix that.

Common attributes for the audio and video elements

Attribute	Description
src	The URL of the file to be played.
poster	Supported only by the video element, this attribute provides the path to a static image to be displayed in place of the video file before it is played.
preload	One of three possible values that tell the browser whether to preload any data: none (the default), metadata (only preload metadata like dimensions and track list), or auto (preload the entire media file).
autoplay	Starts playing the media as soon as the web page is loaded in the browser.
loop	Causes the media to repeat playing when it reaches the end.
muted	Supported only by the video element, this attribute causes the video to begin playing (if autoplay is also coded) with the volume muted.
controls	Displays the default control toolbar underneath the audio or video being played.
width	Specifies the width of the media file to be played within the browser.
height	Specifies the height of the media file to be played within the browser.

The attributes for the source element

Attribute	Description
src	The URL of the file to be played.
type	The optional MIME type of the file to be played, including the codec for video files.

The easiest way to add a video or audio element to your web page

```
<video src="media/sjv_speakers_sampson.mp4"></video>
<audio src="media/sjv_welcome.mp3"></audio>
```

A video element for playing MPEG-4, Ogg (Theora), and WebM media types

```
<video id="videoplayer" width="480" height="270" controls autoplay>
    <source src="media/sjv_speakers_sampson.mp4">
    <source src="media/sjv_speakers_sampson.webm"
            type='video/webm; codecs="vp8, vorbis"'>
    <source src="media/sjv_speakers_sampson.ogv"
            type='video/ogg; codecs="theora, vorbis"'>
</video>
```

An audio element for playing MP3 and Ogg (Vorbis) media types

```
<audio id="audioplayer" controls autoplay>
    <source src="media/sjv_welcome.mp3">
    <source src="media/sjv_welcome.ogg">
</audio>
```

Description

- The video and audio elements play the various media types natively within a browser.
- To play a video on any modern browser, all that's needed is a src attribute that refers to an MP4 file. To play audio, all that's needed is a src attribute that refers to an MP3 file.

Aptana warning

- To play a video from Aptana, you also need to include the type attribute.

Figure 12-8 How to use the HTML5 video and audio elements

How to fall back to Flash for backward compatibility

Figure 12-9 shows how to use the HTML5 audio and video elements and still provide backward compatibility with older browsers. The key point here is that you also provide the audio or video as a Flash media type and fall back to that file in browsers that don't support the HTML5 elements. Since a majority of the browsers today support the audio and video elements and since 97% of Internet users have the Flash plugin installed on their browsers, this means that just about everyone will be able to play your media.

As you can see in the first example in figure 12-9, the code for doing this is relatively straightforward. To start, a video element that contains a source element for an MP4 file provides the video for all modern browsers. Then, to provide for backward compatibility, the code nests an object element that refers to a Flash video within the video element. This will work in older IE browsers because they will ignore elements that they don't understand (the video element) and pick up on the nested object element.

After that, a second object element is nested within the first object element. This is like the first object element, but it uses the data attribute instead of the param element to refer to the media type. This will work in older browsers other than IE.

As the second example shows, you use this same approach for audio-only media types. Here, a single source element for an MP3 file is coded within the audio element. Then, a Flash file is used as the fallback mechanism for older browsers.

HTML for playing a video that falls back to Flash

```
<video id="videoplayer" width="480" height="270" controls autoplay>
    <source src="media/sjv_speakers_sampson.mp4">

    <object type="application/x-shockwave-flash" width="480" height="270">
        <param name="movie" value="media/sjv_speakers_sampson.swf">
        <param name="wmode" value="transparent">
        <param name="quality" value="high">
        <!--[if !IE]>-->
            <object type="application/x-shockwave-flash"
                    data="media/sjv_speakers_sampson.swf"
                    width="480" height="270">
                <param name="wmode" value="transparent">
                <param name="quality" value="high">
            </object>
        <!--<![endif]-->
    </object>
</video>
```

HTML for playing an audio that falls back to Flash

```
<audio id="audioplayer" controls>
    <source src="media/sjv_welcome.mp3" type="audio/mp3">

    <object type="application/x-shockwave-flash" width="50" height="50">
        <param name="movie" value="media/sjv_welcome.swf">
        <param name="wmode" value="transparent">
        <param name="quality" value="high">
        <!--[if !IE]>-->
            <object type="application/x-shockwave-flash"
                    data="media/sjv_welcome.swf" width="50" height="50">
                <param name="wmode" value="transparent">
                <param name="quality" value="high">
            </object>
        <!--<![endif]-->
    </object>
</audio>
```

Description

- For browsers that don't support the video and audio elements, you can nest an object element within the video or audio element to play a Flash file.
- This also works for browsers that don't support any of the media types listed within the source elements of the video or audio element.
- If you prefer, you can use an embed element instead of an object element to fall back to Flash.

Aptana warning

- If you use Aptana to run a page that uses an object element within a video element, it won't work correctly. Instead, you'll need to access the page directly from the browser as described in chapter 1.

Figure 12-9 How to fall back to Flash for backward compatibility

A web page that offers both audio and video

Now that you've seen how the object, param, video, and audio elements work, it's time to put it all together into a simple web page that uses these elements.

The page layout

The web page in figure 12-10 starts with a short audio message that welcomes the visitor to the site. Then, it offers a video of one of the speakers who's scheduled to speak. In the embedded video, you can see an image of the speaker that will disappear when the video is played.

A web page that offers both audio and video

Description

- This web page offers both audio and video to the user. The audio is a brief introduction to the speakers. The video is a video of the selected speaker.
- The poster attribute of the video element is used to display a static image in place of the media type when the page is displayed. The poster file will be replaced with the actual video when the user clicks on the play button.
- The control toolbar automatically appears when the page loads and while the video is playing and your cursor is over the video. As you move your cursor off the video, the control toolbar automatically drops off and becomes hidden. Moving your cursor back onto the video causes the control toolbar to reappear.

Aptana warning

- If you use Aptana to run a page that uses an object element within a video element, it won't work correctly. Instead, you'll need to access the page directly from the browser as described in chapter 1.

Figure 12-10 A web page that offers both audio and video

The HTML

Figure 12-11 presents the HTML file for the web page. Here, both the audio and video fall back to Flash in browsers that don't support the audio and video elements. You shouldn't have any trouble following this code because it is so similar to what you saw in figure 12-9.

In the code for the audio element, you might notice the absence of the autoplay attribute. This prevents the browser from automatically playing the sound when the page loads.

In the code for the video element, you might notice the addition of the poster attribute. This displays a static image in place of the video that would otherwise begin playing automatically.

The HTML for a page that uses both audio and video elements

```
<body>
<h1>Welcome to the San Joaquin Valley Town Hall</h1>
<audio id="audioplayer" controls>
    <source src="media/sjv_welcome.mp3" type="audio/mp3">

    <object type="application/x-shockwave-flash" width="50" height="50">
        <param name="movie" value="media/sjv_welcome.swf">
        <param name="wmode" value="transparent">
        <param name="quality" value="high">
        <!--[if !IE]>-->
            <object type="application/x-shockwave-flash"
                    data="media/sjv_welcome.swf" width="50" height="50">
                <param name="wmode" value="transparent">
                <param name="quality" value="high">
            </object>
        <!--<![endif]-->
    </object>
</audio>

<h2>San Joaquin Valley Town Hall welcomes Dr. Scott Sampson</h2>
<p>On February 15, 2012, Dr. Scott Sampson will present a lecture titled
&lsquo;Fossil Threads in the Web of Life&rsquo;<br>In the meantime, you can
see a video of Dr. Sampson below.</p>

<video id="videoplayer" controls width="480" height="270"
       poster="images/poster.png">
    <source src="media/sjv_speakers_sampson.mp4">

    <object type="application/x-shockwave-flash" width="480" height="270">
        <param name="movie" value="media/sjv_speakers_sampson.swf">
        <param name="wmode" value="transparent">
        <param name="quality" value="high">
        <!--[if !IE]>-->
            <object type="application/x-shockwave-flash"
                    data="media/sjv_speakers_sampson.swf"
                    width="480" height="270">
                <param name="wmode" value="transparent">
                <param name="quality" value="high">
            </object>
        <!--<![endif]-->
    </object>
</video>
</body>
```

Figure 12-11 The HTML for the web page

Perspective

Now that you know how to embed media files within your web pages, here's a caution about overusing them. First, remember that media files are often large so web pages that embed media files are likely to load slowly, particularly on systems that have slow Internet connections. Second, remember that users who can't see or hear won't benefit from video or audio. As a result, if the audio and video are essential to the site, you should also provide text versions of the audio and video. So, before you decide to use media files, please be sure that they support the goals of your website and enhance the user experience.

Terms

media type
media player
plugin
codec
MIME type

Summary

- A browser uses a *media player* to play an audio or video *media type* when media are embedded in a web page.
- Some browsers require *plugins* for the media players that play specific media types.
- Audio and video files come in a variety of media types. MPEG, Ogg, and WebM are common types for video, and AAC and MP3 are common types for audio.
- *Codecs* are software components that are used by browsers to decipher the algorithms in a media type.
- A *MIME type* describes the contents of a file and can help a browser determine what media player to use for the file.
- To embed media types in the web page for older browsers, you can either use the object and param elements or the embed element.
- The HTML5 video and audio elements are supported by modern browsers and will play media without the need for special plugins.
- You can nest object or embed elements within video and audio elements to fall back to the Flash media type. This allows you to target older browsers that don't support the HTML5 video and audio elements.

Exercise 12-1 Add video to a speaker's page

In this exercise, you'll add video to a copy of the speaker's page for Scott Sampson. This will show you how easy it is to add video to a page. When you're through, the page should look like the one that follows.

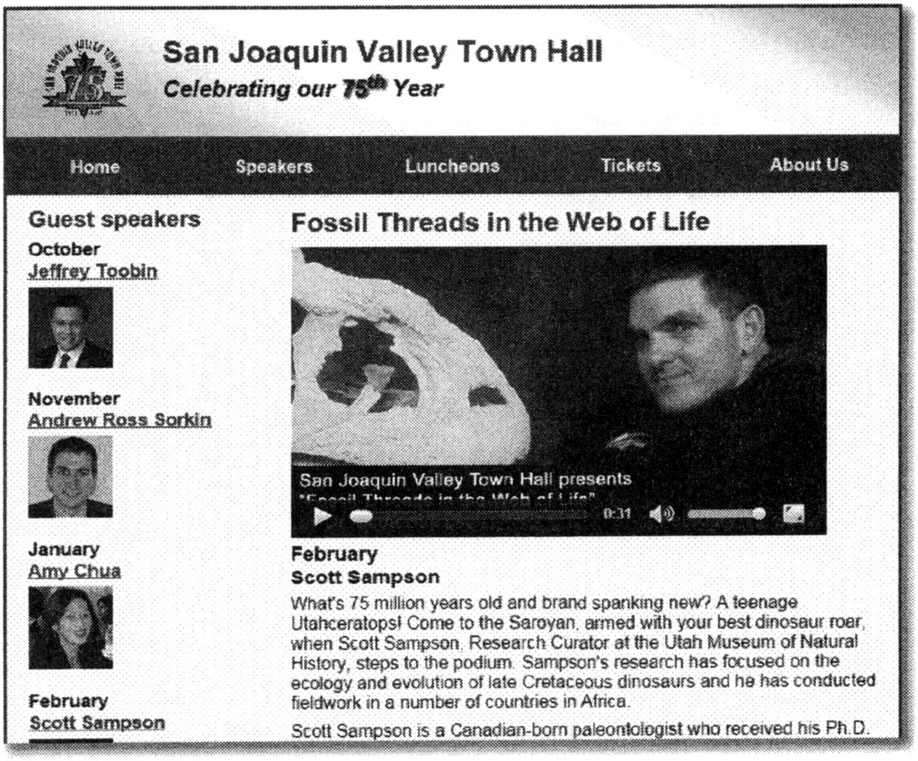

Open the page, copy it, and copy in the HTML for running a video

1. Use your text editor to open this page:
   `c:\html5_css3_2\exercises\town_hall_2\speakers\sampson.html`
2. Make a copy of this page in the same folder, and name it sampson_video.html. If you're using Aptana, you can use the File→Save As command to do that.
3. Open the book application for this chapter, and copy the code for running the video to the clipboard. Then, paste in into the sampson_video.html file so it replaces either the figure element (if your file has one) or the img element.
4. Test the page to see what the result is. But don't run it from Aptana because the video won't work right. Instead, run the page from your browser or file server.

Modify the HTML to get this working right

5. Modify the references to the media files so they point to the right files. To do that, you need to use a document-relative path that goes up one level, and you need to use the right filenames. For instance, the reference in the first source element should be:

   ```
   src="../media/sampson.mp4"
   ```

   To find out what the right filenames are, you can look in the media folder.
6. You also need to modify the reference to the poster file that's in the images folder with a similar document-relative path.
7. Test this page again and it should work. This shows how easy it is to add a video to a page because you'll use the same code each time. Only the references will change.

13

How to work with fonts and printing

In this chapter, you'll first learn how to embed fonts within your pages. That way, you can be sure the fonts are available to every browser. For graphic designers, these font features open up a new range of typographical options.

Then, you'll learn how to control the formatting for a printed web page. If you don't do that, the users can print any web page, but the browser determines how it's printed. Often, that means that unnecessary content is printed or the print is so small that you can barely read it. So if you want to make sure the printed page is readable, this chapter will show you how.

How to embed fonts in a web page

For years, web designers were frustrated by the limited number of fonts that were available for a website. In fact, web pages were limited to the fonts that are available to each browser. That's why the font families throughout this book have been set to a series of fonts like Arial, Helvetica, and sans-serif. Then, each browser uses the first font in the series that's available to it.

But now, you can use a new CSS3 feature to *embed fonts* within your pages. That way, you know the fonts are available to the browser. You can also use third-party services like Google Web Fonts and Adobe Edge Web Fonts to embed fonts within your pages.

How to use the CSS3 @font-face selector to embed fonts

Figure 13-1 shows how to use the CSS3 @font-face selector to embed fonts within your web pages. To start, you look in the folders that are listed in this figure where you'll see that you already have access to many fonts that most browsers don't have access to. Then, you find the font that you want and copy it into one of the folders for your website. In this example, the Windows True Type Font named HARNGTON.TTF has been copied to the root folder of the website.

Once you've copied the font to a folder, you code a CSS rule set for the @font-face selector that names and locates the font. In this example, the font-family property gives the name "Murach" to the font, and the src property points to the file, which is in the same folder as the web page.

After the font has been imported, you can code CSS rule sets that apply the new font to HTML elements. In this example, the second rule set applies the font to h1 elements. To do that, the font-family property is set to the name of the embedded font. Note, however, that a backup font is also specified for this property. This means that the default sans-serif font should be used by browsers that don't support the new @font-face selector. This also means that you can start using this feature right away because it will work on new browsers and won't cause any problems on old browsers.

A heading that uses a font imported with CSS3

The CSS for embedding a font

```
@font-face {
    font-family: Murach;
    src: url("HARNGTON.TTF"); }
```

The CSS for applying the font to an HTML element

```
h1 {
    font-family: Murach, sans-serif; }
```

The HTML for the element that the font is applied to

```
<h1>Murach Books</h1>
```

Where to find the fonts on your computer

On a Windows system

```
C:\Windows\Fonts
```

On a Mac OS system

```
System\Library\Fonts
```

How to import a font

- Copy the file for the font family into a folder for your website.
- In the CSS for the page, code a rule set for the @font-face selector. Use the font-family property to provide a name for the imported font family, and use the src property to locate the font file.

How to apply an imported font to an HTML element

- In the rule set for the HTML element, use the name that you gave the font as the value for the font-family property. Then, list one or more other font families in case the browser doesn't support the CSS3 @font-face selector.

Description

- CSS3 provides an @font-face selector that can be used to import a font family.
- In this example, the file for a True Type Font (TTF) named HARNGTON has been stored in the same folder as the web page.

Figure 13-1 How to use the CSS3 @font-face selector to embed fonts

How to use Google Web Fonts

Figure 13-2 shows how you can use Google Web Fonts to import fonts into your web pages. Google Web Fonts is a free Google service that lets you select fonts from hundreds of different font families. Then, you can use those fonts in your web pages by including a link to a CSS file that Google provides.

To select a font, go to the website for Google Web Fonts and browse through the font families. To help you find the fonts you want, you can filter the fonts that are displayed by using the controls at the left side of the page. To display the styles that are available for a font, you can click the See all styles link. And to get more information about a font, including what each character in the font looks like, you can click on the Pop out link.

When you identify a font that you like, you can click on the Quick-use link to display a page with a four-step procedure for using the font. The first two steps are to select the styles and character sets you want to use. The third step is to add the code that imports the font into your web page. One of these options is to use a link element provided by Google. This is the option that's easiest to use, so it's the one that's used in this figure. The other two options are to use the @import selector or JavaScript code.

The last step is to use the font-family property to apply the font to an HTML element in the page. In the example in this figure, that property is set to "Sorts Mill Gowdy", which is the name of the font that has been imported. Here again, a backup font has been coded for those browsers that don't support this code.

If you want to add more than one font to a page, you can click on the Add to Collection button for each font. This adds the font to the collection pane at the bottom of the window. If you want to see what the fonts you've selected will look like in some randomly generated paragraphs, you can click on the Review button. To use the fonts you've selected, you click the Use button. This displays a page with a four-step procedure like the one for using a single font.

The Google Web Fonts website (www.google.com/fonts)

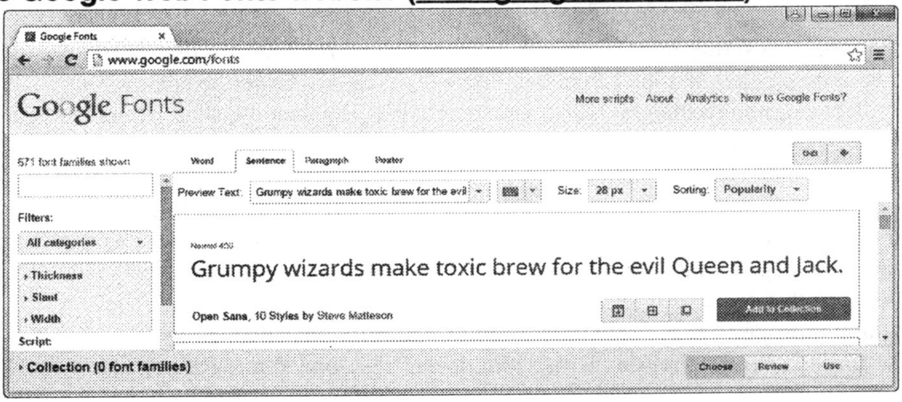

How to select and use Google Web Fonts

- Go to the Google Web Fonts page and browse through the fonts until you find one that you like. You can also filter the fonts that are displayed by using the controls at the left side of the page.
- To select a single font, click the Quick-use button. To select multiple fonts, click the Add to Collection button for each font and then click the Use button in the lower-right corner of the page.
- Complete the four-step procedure for using the fonts, including selecting the styles and character sets you want to use, adding the link element that imports the font to the head section of each web page that will use the font, and using the Google Web Font name as the value for the font-family property of any elements you want to use that font.

A heading that uses a Google Web Font

The CSS for importing a Google Web Font

```
<link href="http://fonts.googleapis.com/css?family=Sorts+Mill+Goudy"
      rel="stylesheet">
```

The CSS for applying the font to an HTML element

```
h1 { font-family: "Sorts Mill Goudy", serif; }
```

The HTML for the element that the font is applied to

```
<h1>Murach Books</h1>
```

Description

- Google Web Fonts is a free Google service that lets you select and use any of the fonts in their current collection of more than 670 font families.
- When you use Google Web Fonts, you should list one or more other font families in case the browser doesn't support the Google font reference.

How to use Adobe Edge Web Fonts

Figure 13-3 shows how you can use Adobe Edge Web Fonts to import fonts into your web pages. Adobe Edge Web Fonts is a free Adobe service that lets you select from more than 500 different fonts. Then, you can use those fonts in your web pages by including script elements for the JavaScript files that import the fonts.

The procedure for getting an Adobe Edge Web Font is quite easy. Just go to their website, select a font, and follow the three-step procedure for using the font in your web pages. In this figure, you can see the script element that's provided in step 2 of this procedure for a font called Alex Brush. You can also see the font-family property that's provided for this font. Here, the cursive font is added to the font list in case the Alex Brush font doesn't get loaded into the page.

The Adobe Edge Web Fonts website (edgewebfonts.adobe.com)

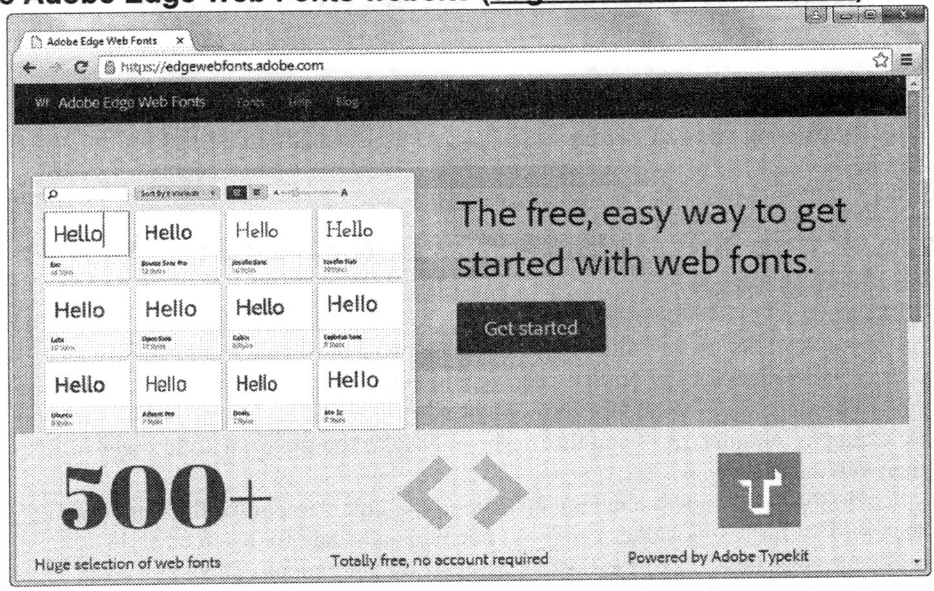

How to select and use Adobe Edge Web fonts

- Go to the Adobe Edge Web Fonts web page, and click "Get started".
- Browse through the fonts until you find one that you like. Then, hover over it and choose the "Select this font" link. That displays a three-step procedure for using the font.
- The first step is to visually verify that you've selected the right font.
- The second step is to copy the script element that's provided so you can paste it into any web page that will use the font. This script element delivers a JavaScript file for the font.
- The third step is to copy the font-family property that's provided so you can use it to apply the font to HTML elements.

A heading that uses a Google Web Font

The link element for importing an Adobe Edge Web font

```
<script src="//use.edgefonts.net/alex-brush.js"></script>
```

The CSS that applies the Adobe Edge Web font to an element

```
h1 { font-family: alex-brush, cursive; }
```

Description

- Adobe Edge Web Fonts is a free Adobe service that lets you use any of the fonts in their current collection of more than 500 fonts. It is powered by Adobe's commercial Typekit engine so the fonts are delivered to your web pages quickly and with minimal downtime.

Figure 13-3 How to use Adobe Edge Web fonts

The skills for formatting printed web pages

To format the printing of a web page, you need to know how to define the styles for printing and you need to know how to use the CSS properties for printing.

How to define the style sheets and rule sets for printed pages

One way to define the rule sets for the printing of a web page is to code a separate style sheet for the printed page. Then, you code the link element for the *print style sheet* after the one for the *screen style sheet*. This is illustrated by the first example in figure 13-4, and this makes it easy to use the print style sheet for other web pages too.

To do that, you code the media attribute in the link element for the print style sheet with "print" as its value. You don't need this attribute for a screen style sheet because screen is assumed when the attribute isn't coded. Then, you code the link element for the print style sheet after the one for the screen style sheet so the rule sets in the print style sheet override the styles in the screen style sheet.

Another way to define the styles for printing is to add a *media query* for the print media type at the end of a screen style sheet. Then, you code the rule sets for printing within that media query. This is similar to coding a media query for Responsive Web Design, and this is illustrated by the second example in this figure.

A third way to provide styles for printing is to use the style element in the head section of the HTML. This is illustrated by the third example in this figure. But if you want to use these styles for other web pages, you have to copy these styles to the HTML of the other pages.

Link elements for separate screen and print style sheets

```
<link rel="stylesheet" href="styles/main.css">
<link rel="stylesheet" href="styles/print.css" media="print">
```

A media query for printing at the end of a screen style sheet

```
@media print {
    body {
        font-family: "Times New Roman", Times, serif;
        background-color: white;
    }
}
```

A style element for printing in the head section of the HTML

```
<style media="print">
    font-family: "Times New Roman", Times, serif;
    background-color: white;
</style>
```

Description

- The default media type for a link element is “screen”, so you don’t have to specify that for a web page that’s going to be displayed by a browser. The media type for a link element that specifies a style sheet for printing a web page is “print”.
- When you provide separate style sheets for screen and print, you usually code the link element for the print style sheet last. That way, the print style sheet just needs to override the screen rules that need to be changed.
- Within a screen style sheet, you can specify rule sets for the printed page by coding @media=“print” followed by the rule sets for the printed page. This *media query* is normally coded after the rule sets for the screen so the print rule sets just need to override the screen rule sets.
- You can also embed a style element within the head section of the HTML that provides rule sets for printing.

Figure 13-4 How to define the style sheets and rule sets for printed pages

Recommendations for print formatting

Figure 13-5 starts by presenting some basic recommendations for formatting printed pages. As you can see, the first three recommendations have to do with changing the fonts so they're more readable. In particular, a serif font should be used for text other than headings because that makes the printed text easier to read (although sans-serif text is more readable on the screen).

The fourth recommendation is to keep the line length of the text to 65 characters or fewer. Beyond that length, the text gets harder and harder to read, and this is a common problem with printed pages. Incidentally, this is also a problem for text pages in the browser, so you should apply this recommendation to your browser pages too.

The fifth recommendation is to remove site navigation. That makes sense because navigation can't be used when the page is printed. You may, however, want to print links that link to other topics to show the reader what is available.

The last recommendation is to remove any images that aren't needed to understand the content of the page. That will make the page print more quickly.

CSS properties for printed pages

Figure 13-5 also shows the CSS properties that you can use to control printing. The one you'll probably use the most is display. Although you can use it to display an inline element as a block element and vice versa, you're most likely to use it to exclude an element such as an image from a page when it's printed. To do that, you set this property to "none".

The remaining properties let you control page breaks. A *page break* is the point at which the printing skips from the bottom of one page to the top of the next page.

The page-break-before and page-break-after properties let you specify whether a page break always occurs before or after an element, may occur before or after an element, or shouldn't occur before or after an element. The page-break-inside property is similar, but it specifies whether a page break can occur within an element. For headings, you will usually want to set the page-break-after property to "avoid" so a heading isn't printed on one page and the text that follows on another page.

When a page break occurs within an element, the orphans and widows properties specify the minimum number of lines that can be printed at the bottom of the current page and the top of the next page. In printing terminology, *orphan* refers to the first line of a paragraph by itself at the bottom of a page, and *widow* refers to the last line of a paragraph by itself at the top of a page. To avoid orphans and widows, which you usually want to do, you can set these properties to 2 or more.

Although some browsers don't support the orphan, widow, and some of the page break properties, that's usually okay. If these properties are ignored, the page breaks will occur where you don't want them, but the users will still be able to read the text.

Recommendations for formatting printed pages

- Change the text color to black and the background color to white.
- Change text other than headings to a serif font to make the text easier to read when printed.
- Use a base font size that's easy to read when printed.
- Keep the line length of the text to 65 characters or fewer.
- Remove site navigation since it can't be used from a printed page.
- Remove as many images as possible, particularly Flash and animated images.

CSS properties for printing

Property	Description
`display`	A keyword that determines how an element is displayed. Common keywords are block, inline, and none.
`page-break-before`	A keyword that determines when a page break is allowed before an element's box. Common keywords are always, auto, and avoid.
`page-break-after`	A keyword that determines when a page break is allowed after an element's box. Common keywords are always, auto, and avoid.
`page-break-inside`	A keyword that determines when a page break is allowed within an element's box. Possible keywords are auto and avoid.
`orphans`	An integer that determines the minimum number of lines within an element that can be printed at the bottom of a page when a page break occurs within the element.
`widows`	An integer that determines the minimum number of lines within an element that can be printed on the next page when a page break occurs within the element.

CSS that uses two of the properties for printing

```
img { display: none; }
h1, h2, h3 { page-break-after: avoid; }
```

Description

- If you don't want an element to be included when a page is printed, you can set its display property to none. Then, no space is allocated for the element's box.
- The auto keyword for the page-break properties indicates that a break may occur, but doesn't have to occur, like it does when you use the always keyword.
- The avoid keyword for the page-break properties tells the browser to avoid a page break if it can.
- Although the widows, orphans, and some of the page break properties aren't supported by all browsers, it's usually okay if they're ignored.

Note

- By default, most browsers don't print background colors, images, and gradients. Users can change an option that controls this when the page is printed, though. Because of that, you should remove any backgrounds you don't want printed.

Figure 13-5 Formatting recommendations and CSS properties for printed pages

A two-column web page with print formatting

To illustrate the use of a style sheet for a printed page, the next three figures present a two-column web page, the HTML that includes the screen and print style sheets, the printed version of the page, and the CSS for the print style sheet.

The web page

Figure 13-6 presents the two-column web page that you studied in chapter 6. However, this web page has been enhanced by a navigation bar and by figure and figcaption elements.

To understand the style sheet for printing that you're going to see in a moment, you shouldn't need to review the HTML for this page. Just keep in mind that the major structural elements in sequence are header, nav, aside, article, and footer.

The links to the style sheets

Figure 13-6 also presents the links for the screen and print style sheets. Note here that the print style sheet comes after the screen style sheet so the print rules override the screen rules for the same elements. If, for example, the print rules for the headings in the header set the font color to black, the printed headings will be in black. However, the other screen rules for headings, like the text shadow and italics will be retained.

A web page with two columns

The link elements in the head section

```
<link rel="stylesheet" href="styles/speaker.css">
<link rel="stylesheet" href="styles/speaker_print.css" media="print">
```

Description

- This is the same page that is presented in chapter 6, plus the navigation bar that was added in chapter 7 and the figure and figcaption elements that were added in chapter 9.
- The main structural elements in sequence are header, nav, aside, article, and footer.
- In the CSS for the article, the CSS3 column-count property is used so the first column contains two text columns.
- Since IE9 doesn't support the column-count property, you won't see two columns of text in that browser.

Figure 13-6 The screen layout for a two-column web page

The printed page

Figure 13-7 shows the print layout for the web page. If you compare this layout with the screen layout, you'll notice a number of differences. For instance, the navigation bar and sidebar are removed. All of these differences are summarized in this figure.

This figure also shows how to preview a page. You can do that by using your browsers Print Preview or Print command. These commands are available from the menu icon in Chrome and Firefox and from the Tools icon in Internet Explorer. For this example, I used Internet Explorer's Print Preview command, which shows the page in preview mode.

Note that the print layout for a page isn't always the same in all browsers. If you previewed the page shown here in Chrome, for example, you'd see that the text in the article isn't displayed in columns and the text in the h2 element in the header doesn't have a shadow. Because features like these are browser dependent, you don't have any control over them.

As a developer, you can make it easier for the user to print a web page by adding a Print button or link to the page. Then, you can use JavaScript to call the browser's print command when the button or link is clicked. You'll learn how to do that in chapter 15. No matter how the page is printed, though, the style sheet for print media is used if one is available.

Incidentally, preview mode is helpful when you're designing a print style sheet because it lets you see the layout without having to print the page. Then, when you have the layout the way you want it, you can print it as a final check that everything is working right.

The layout for the web page in Print Preview mode

Changes to the printed page

- The navigation menu and side aren't printed.
- The headings, text, and borders are set to black.
- The article is wider.
- The font for the text has been changed to a serif font so it's easier to read.

How to preview and print a web page

- To preview a web page, use your browser's Print or Print Preview command. If the browser doesn't have a Print Preview command, its Print command will display the page in preview mode. Then, you can decide whether you want to print it.
- For pages that are likely to be printed, you can make that easier for the user by adding a Print button or link that uses JavaScript to call the browser's print command. You'll learn how to add this feature to a page in chapter 15.

Figure 13-7 The print layout for the web page

The CSS for the print style sheet

Figure 13-8 presents the CSS in the style sheet for the printed web page. As an alternative, these rule sets could be coded in a media query for printing at the end of the screen style sheet.

Either way, the rules sets for printing only need to override the rule sets for the screen. For instance, since the screen rule for the body sets the width to 990 pixels, the print rule for the body needs to override that by setting the width to auto. That way, the body will fill the printed page. Similarly, the width for the article is set to auto.

Incidentally, when you use the margin or padding property to set margins or padding for boxes that will be printed, you may want to use inches (in) as the unit of measure. For instance, you could set the margin of the body to .25in. Note, however, that this value doesn't replace the default margin provided by a browser for printed output. Instead, this value is added to the default margin.

Unfortunately, different browsers can have different default margins. Because of that, it's often best to specify no margin at all, which is the way this is handled in the CSS in this figure.

In this example, the text is printed in two columns so the line length is sure to be under 65 characters. But for single-column text, this may be an issue. Then, you may want to set the width of the element that contains the text.

The style sheet for the printed web page (speaker_print.css)

```
body {
    font-family: "Times New Roman", Times, serif;
    width: auto;
}
h1, h2 {
    font-family: Verdana, Arial, Helvetica, sans-serif;
}
/* the styles for the navigation bar */
#nav_menu {
    display: none;
}
/* the styles for the sidebar */
aside {
    display: none;
}
/* the styles for the article */
article {
    width: auto;
}
/* the styles for the header */
header {
    border-bottom: 2px solid black;
}
header h2 {
    color: black;
    font-size: 180%;
}
header h3 {
    color: black;
    font-size: 120%;
}
/* the styles for the footer */
footer {
    border-top: 2px solid black;
}
```

Description

- All of the rules in the print style sheet override the settings in the style sheet for the screen.
- The width of the body and article are set to auto so they will be as wide as the printed page permits.
- The font-family for the body is set to a serif font, the font-family for the headings is set to a sans-serif font, and the color of the h2 and h3 elements in the header is set to black.
- The display properties for the navigation bar and sidebar are set to none so they aren't included in the printed page.
- The borders for the header and footer are set to black.
- To set margins and padding, you can use *in* (inches) as the unit of measure, which makes sense when you're printing on pages that are 8½ by 11 inches.

Figure 13-8 The CSS for the print style sheet

Perspective

With CSS3, you can easily embed fonts within your pages. You can also use third-party services like Google Web Fonts and Adobe Edge Web Fonts to embed fonts within your pages. Either way, you can be sure that the fonts will be available to all browsers. For graphic designers, these features open up a new range of typographical options.

When it comes to printing, you can use a print style sheet or media query to format the printed page. This makes sense for pages that users are likely to want to print. You may know from experience how frustrating it can be to print a web page that is poorly formatted or barely readable. So if the information on a page is important enough to print, be sure to provide styles that will make it easy to read.

Terms

embed fonts
@font-face selector
print style sheet
screen style sheet
media query
page break
widow
orphan

Summary

- CSS3 provides a new @font-face selector that you can use to *embed fonts* from your libraries into a web page. You can also embed fonts in your web pages by using Google Web Fonts or Adobe Edge Web Fonts.
- If you want to change the way a web page is formatted when it's printed, you can code a separate style sheet for printing. Then, you can use a link element to include the *print style sheet* after the *screen style sheet*. That way, the print styles will override the screen styles.
- Another way to provide the styles for printing is to code a *media query* for printing at the end of the screen style sheet. Here again, the styles for printing will override the styles for the screen.
- CSS provides several properties for printing, including the display property for omitting an element from a web page, several page-break properties for controlling where *page breaks* occur, and orphans and widows properties for avoiding *orphans* and *widows*.
- When you code the CSS for a page that's going to be printed, you should remove site navigation and unnecessary images, use dark print on a white background, and use a serif font for the text in a size and with a line length that's easy to read.

Exercise 13-1 Format the printing for a page

In this exercise, you'll style the printing for the speaker's page for Scott Sampson so it prints like this:

Open the HTML and CSS files for this page

1. Use your text editor to open these pages:

   `c:\html5_css3_2\exercises\town_hall_2\speakers\sampson.html`

   `c:\html5_css3_2\exercises\town_hall_2\styles\speaker.css`

2. Run this page in your browser, and use the Print Preview command to see what it will look like when printed.

Add the styles for printing the page to the style sheet

3. In the style sheet for this page, add a @media print selector to the end of the file, as shown in figure 13-4. Then, add rules sets that do the following:

   Change the font family for the body to Times New Roman, Times, or the default serif font.

   Change the width of the body to "auto", the background color to white, and the border to none.

Turn off the display for the navigation bar and the first heading in the aside.

Set the width of the section to 5 inches and the width of the aside to 2 inches.

Set the right padding for the section and the left padding for the aside to zero.

Now, test these changes in Chrome to see how things are going.

4. Add the other rule sets that are needed to get the print preview to look like the one above, such as:

   Reduce the font size for the h2 elements in the aside to 100%.

   Reduce the font size for the <p> elements in the article and footer to 87.5%.

   Remove the underlines from the <a> elements in the aside and set their color to black.

   Change the top padding for the <p> element in the footer to .75 ems, and add a 3-pixel solid border with the color #931420.

   Now, test these changes. The page should be looking pretty good.

5. Make any final adjustments, and test the page in Chrome one last time.
6. Test the page in IE or Firefox and notice that the sidebar isn't aligned at the left side of the page. To fix that, remove the floating from the aside and test again.

Exercise 13-2 Use a web font

In this exercise, you'll enhance the header of a page with a web font:

1. Use your text editor to open the HTML and CSS files for this page:
```
c:\html5_css3_2\exercises\town_hall_2\speakers\sampson.html
c:\html5_css3_2\exercises\town_hall_2\styles\speaker.css
```
2. Test this page in your browser to see what it looks like.
3. Using figure 13-1 as a guide, choose a web font on your system and copy it into the styles folder.
4. Use CSS3 to apply the font to the h2 element in the header. Be sure to include one or more additional font families in case the browser doesn't support the @font-face selector.

14

How to use CSS3 transitions, transforms, animations, and filters

This chapter introduces you to the CSS3 features for transitions, transforms, animations, and filters. Although none of these features are currently supported by all modern browsers, they will be within a few years. In the meantime, you should at least be aware of what they can do and how you might use them in your web pages.

How to use CSS3 transitions

Transitions let you gradually change one or more of the CSS properties for an element over a specified period of time. As you'll see, transitions let you provide features with CSS3 alone that would otherwise require JavaScript and jQuery. Today, CSS3 transitions are well supported by modern browsers, although you do need to use the -webkit- prefix for Safari.

How to code transitions

Figure 14-1 summarizes the five properties that can be used for transitions. Note, however, that the transition property is the shorthand property for the other four properties. Because using this shorthand property is the easiest way to code most transitions, that's what you'll see in the examples in this chapter.

The first example in this figure uses a transition for the change in two properties that are applied to an h1 element: font-size and color. In the CSS for this transition, the rule set for the h1 selector sets the font-size to 120% and the color to blue. Then, the shorthand transition property provides two sets of values that are separated by a comma.

The first set of values is for the font-size property. It says that the transition should take 2 seconds, use the ease-out *timing function* (or *speed curve*), and wait 1 second before starting. The second set is for the color property. It's the same as the set for the font-size property except it uses the ease-in timing function. This timing function causes the transition to start slowly and end quickly. In contrast, the ease-out timing function causes the transition to start quickly and end slowly.

This rule set is followed by one for the hover pseudo-class for the h1 element. It changes the cursor to the pointer, the font-size to 180%, and the color to red. This means that when the user hovers the mouse over the h1 heading, the two values in the transition are changed. As a result, the transition takes place. You can see this in the before and during views of the heading that are above the code. When the user stops hovering, the transition returns to the original font-size and color settings.

Please note that the heading would change when the mouse hovers over it, even if a transition weren't applied to it. However, the changes would be immediate. What the transition does is provide a gradual change from one set of properties to another that gives the appearance of animation.

The second example in this figure shows the code for a transition with just one property. Note here that the -webkit- prefix is used so this will work with Safari. Note too that if you omit one of the values for the transition property, the default is assumed. In this case, the delay value is omitted so the transition will start right away. If you omit the timing function value, "ease" is assumed. And if you omit the duration function, 0 is assumed, which means that no transition will take place.

The third example in this figure shows how to code the transition property so it applies to all of the property changes for an element. In this case, *all* is used instead of a specific property name.

Properties for working with transitions

Property	Description
`transition`	The shorthand property for setting the properties that follow.
`transition-property`	The CSS property or properties that the transition is for. Use commas to separate multiple CSS properties.
`transition-duration`	The seconds or milliseconds that the transition will take.
`transition-timing-function`	The speed curve of the transition. Values include: ease, linear, ease-in, ease-out, ease-in-out, and cubic-bezier.
`transition-delay`	The seconds or milliseconds before the transition starts.

The syntax for the shorthand transition property

```
transition: [property] [duration] [timing-function] [delay];
```

A transition that occurs when the mouse hovers over a heading

Before the transition

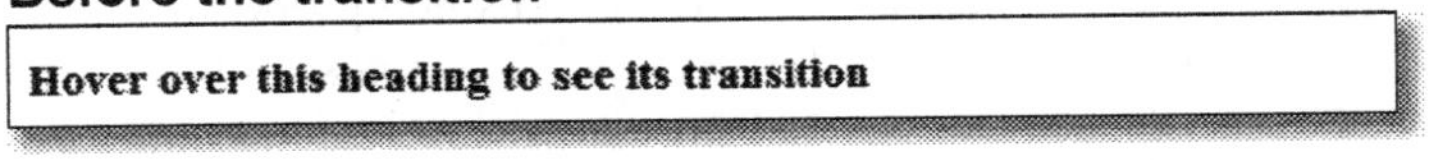

During the transition

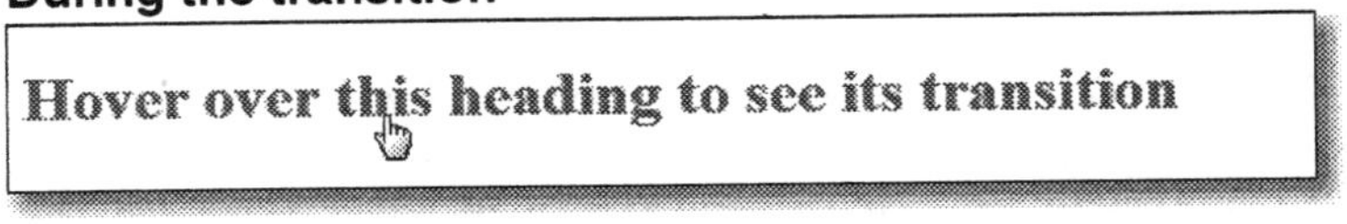

The HTML for the element that will be transitioned

```
<h1>Hover over this heading to see its transition</h1>
```

The CSS for this two-property transition

```
h1 { font-size: 120%;
     color: blue;
     transition: font-size 2s ease-out 1s,
                 color 2s ease-in 1s; }
h1:hover {
    cursor: pointer;
    font-size: 180%;
    color: red; }
```

A transition for one property when the mouse hovers over the heading

```
h1 { font-size: 120%;
     transition: font-size 2s ease-out;
     -webkit-transition: font-size 2s ease-out; }
h1:hover { font-size: 180%; }
```

A transition for all properties when the mouse hovers over the heading

```
transition: all 2s ease-out 1s
```

Description

- A *transition* provides a smooth change from one set of properties to another.
- For Safari, you need to add the -webkit- prefix, as shown in the second example.

Figure 14-1 How to code transitions

How to create an accordion using transitions

Figure 14-2 shows some of the power of CSS3 transitions. Here, transitions are used to create an accordion with three headings and three panels that contain the contents for those headings. When the user clicks on a heading, the related panel gradually opens and any other open panel gradually closes. This is similar to the accordion that you'll see in chapter 16, but without the need for JavaScript, jQuery, and jQuery UI. Instead, this accordion is built with CSS3 alone.

The HTML for this accordion consists of h3 elements for the accordion headings and div elements for the contents of the panels. Note, however, that the headings contain <a> elements that point to the placeholders in the div elements. For example, the href attribute of the first <a> element (#Q1) points to the id of the div element that follows (Q1).

The CSS that makes this accordion work starts with a rule set for the div elements. There, the height property is set to zero, and the transition property takes effect when the height property is changed. It will take 2 seconds for the transition and the transition will use the ease speed curve, which starts and ends slowly but progresses more quickly in between. Because the delay value is omitted, the transition will start right away.

The next rule set, however, is the one that makes this accordion work. It uses the target pseudo-class for the div elements in the accordion. This pseudo-class is activated when the user clicks on an <a> element that refers to a div element. Then, the height of the div element is changed from 0 to 120 pixels. And that starts the transition.

Here again, please note that the panel will be displayed whether or not a transition is applied to the change in height. The transition just makes the change gradual instead of immediate and adds an effect to the opening and closing of the panels.

An accordion created with CSS3 transitions

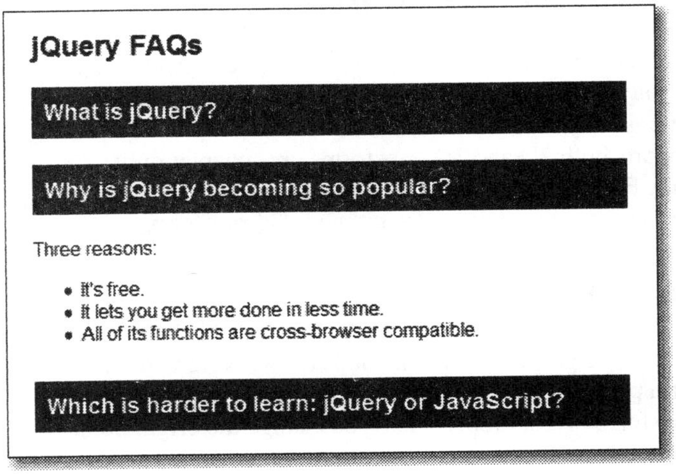

The HTML for the accordion

```
<h1>jQuery FAQs</h1>
<div id="accordion">
    <h3><a href="#Q1">What is jQuery?</a></h3>
    <div id="Q1">Contents for first panel</div>
    <h3><a href="#Q2">Why is jQuery becoming so popular?</a></h3>
    <div id="Q2">Contents for second panel</div>
    <h3><a href="#Q3">Which is harder to learn: ...?</a></h3>
    <div id="Q3">Contents for third panel</div>
</div>
```

The CSS for the transitions

```
#accordion div {
    overflow: hidden;
    height: 0;
    transition: height 2s ease-in-out;
    -webkit-transition: height 2s ease-in-out;
}
#accordion div:target {
    height: 120px;
}
```

Description

- The transition for this accordion occurs when the user clicks on an <a> element. The transition is applied to the change in the height property of the div element.
- To change the height property for the div element, the CSS uses the target pseudo-class. This pseudo-class selects the div element that is the target of the <a> element that has been clicked.
- The rule set for the target selector changes the height property from 0 to 120 pixels. That opens the panel to a size that is large enough for the contents of the panel.

Figure 14-2 How to create an accordion using transitions

How to use CSS3 transforms

Transforms let you rotate, scale, skew, and position HTML elements using CSS code alone. When you combine transforms with transitions, you can create some interesting animations for your HTML elements.

Although CSS3 supports both 2D and 3D transforms, this chapter only introduces 2D transforms. For an introduction to 3D transforms, we recommend David DeSandro's GitHub post at http://desandro.github.io/3dtransforms.

How to code 2D transforms

Figure 14-3 summarizes the properties and methods for working with 2D transforms. The transform property lets you apply one or more transforms to an HTML element. The transform-origin property lets you change the origin point for the transform.

This is illustrated by the example in this figure. Here, two copies of the same image are displayed side by side. Then, when the user hovers the mouse over the image on the right, it is rotated 180 degrees. As a result, it looks like a mirror image of the image on the left. In addition, the origin point has been changed so the rotation takes place from the right side of the second image. That's why there's an empty image space between the first image and the transformed image.

The HTML for this example is just a <p> element that contains two img elements for the same image, but the second one has a class attribute of "image1". Then, the first rule set in the CSS provides a two-second transition for all changes (the default) to the elements in the image1 class. This is followed by a rule set for the hover pseudo-class for the image1 class. It uses the transform property to rotate the image 180 degrees on its Y- axis. But it also uses the transform-origin property to change the origin point for the rotation to the right edge of the image.

Normally, though, the origin point is in the middle of the element that is being transformed. That's 50% or center on the X-axis and 50% or center on the Y-axis. Then, if you use the rotateX or rotateY method with a 360 degree value, the image will rotate in place horizontally or vertically and end up the way it started.

Properties for working with 2D transforms

Property	Description
`transform`	Applies one or more transform methods to the element.
`transform-origin`	Changes the default origin point. The parameters can be percents or keywords like left, center, right and top, center, bottom.

Methods for 2D transforms

Method	Description
`rotate(angle)`	Rotates an element by a specified angle.
`rotateX(angle)`	Rotates an element horizontally.
`rotateY(angle)`	Rotates an element vertically.
`scaleX(value)`	Changes the element's width by scaling horizontally.
`scaleY(value)`	Changes the element's height by scaling vertically.
`scale(x-value,y-value)`	Changes the element's width and height by scaling.
`skewX(angle)`	Skews an element along the X axis.
`skewY(angle)`	Skews an element along the Y axis.
`skew(x-angle,y-angle)`	Skews an element along the X and Y axis.
`translateX(value)`	Moves an element to the right or left.
`translateY(value)`	Moves an element up or down.
`translate(x-value,y-value)`	Moves an element right or left and up or down.
`matrix(a,b,c,d,e,f)`	The 6 parameters are values in a matrix that let you rotate, scale, translate, and skew elements with a single method.

The image on the right has been rotated right with a changed origin

The HTML for the images

```
<p><img src="images/01.jpg" ><img src="images/01.jpg" class="image1"></p>
```

The CSS for the transforms

```
.image1 {
    transition: 2s; }
.image1:hover {
    transform: rotateY(180deg);
    transform-origin: right; }
```

Description

- *Transforms* are often combined with transitions as shown by this example.
- For Safari, you need to use the -webkit- prefix (not shown).

Figure 14-3 How to code 2D transforms

A gallery of images with 2D transforms

Figure 14-4 shows how 8 images will look after various transforms have been applied to them, all with the default origin point. In this case, these transforms are applied when the page is loaded, but you can change that by using the hover pseudo-class to initiate the transforms as in the previous figure. You can also combine that with a transition to provide a gradual change to the transform.

The best way to understand what these transforms can do is experiment with them on your own. You can do that by working with the example for this figure after you finish reading this chapter. It is set up so you can run all the transforms by hovering over the images. Remember that for Safari, you need to add the -webkit- prefix to both the transform and transform-origin properties.

The one method that isn't explained in this chapter is the matrix method. It lets you rotate, scale, translate, and skew elements with a single method by setting the values in a matrix. If you're mathematically inclined and are familiar with matrixes, you can learn more about this method by searching the web.

Images that have 8 different transforms applied to them

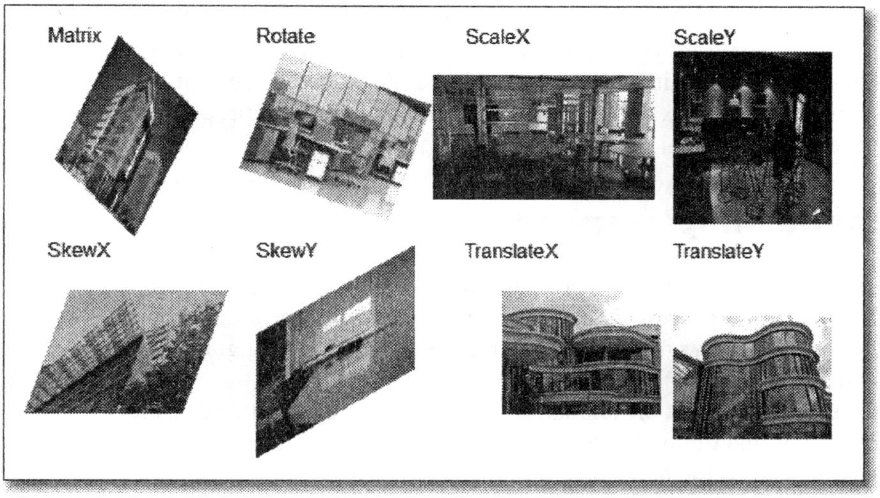

The HTML for the images

```
<ul>
    <li><p>Matrix</p><img src="images/01.jpg" class="image1"></li>
    <li><p>Rotate</p><img src="images/02.jpg" class="image2"></li>
    <li><p>ScaleX</p><img src="images/03.jpg" class="image3"></li>
    <li><p>ScaleY</p><img src="images/04.jpg" class="image4"></li>
    <li><p>SkewX</p><img src="images/05.jpg" class="image5"></li>
    <li><p>SkewY</p><img src="images/06.jpg" class="image6"></li>
    <li><p>TranslateX</p><img src="images/07.jpg" class="image7"></li>
    <li><p>TranslateY</p><img src="images/08.jpg" class="image8"></li>
</ul>
```

The CSS for the 2D transforms

```
.image1 {transform: matrix(0.5,0.5,-0.5,1,0,0);}
.image2 {transform: rotate(20deg);}
.image3 {transform: scaleX(1.4);}
.image4 {transform: scaleY(1.4);}
.image5 {transform: skewX(-20deg);}
.image6 {transform: skewY(-30deg);}
.image7 {transform: translateX(30px);}
.image8 {transform: translateY(20px);}
```

Description

- The 2D transforms in this example are applied when the page is loaded.
- If you want the transforms applied when the mouse hovers over an image, you can use the hover pseudo-class as shown in the previous example with or without a transition.
- For an excellent resource on working with 3D transforms, please visit David DeSandro's GitHub post: http://desandro.github.io/3dtransforms.

Figure 14-4 A gallery of images with 2D transforms

How to use CSS3 animations

CSS3 *animations* let you create frame-based animations that are similar to what you might create with a program like Flash. As you will see, animations can be simple or complex and can animate more than one CSS property at the same time.

How to code simple animations

Figure 14-5 summarizes the primary properties for working with animations. Here, the animation property is the shorthand property for the other six properties, and the animation property is used in the examples in this figure and the next figure.

Of the six values that the animation property can include, the values for duration, delay, and timing function work as they do for a transition. The value for iteration count is the number of times the animation should be run. And the value for direction is the direction in which the animation should be run.

The other value for the animation property is the name of the *@keyframes selector* rule. It's within this rule that you define the *keyframes* for the *animation sequence*. When those keyframes are played, they give the impression of motion.

The example in this figure shows how this works. Here, the left margin for a heading is changed from 20% to 60% and the color is changed from blue to red. As a result, the animation moves the heading from left to right and at the same time changes the color of the heading from blue to red.

In the CSS for this animation, the animation property for the h1 element points to the @keyframes selector named "moveright". It also says that each repetition should take 3 seconds, the start of the animation should be delayed 2 seconds, the animation should keep repeating, and the ease-in-out speed curve should be used. The animation property also says that the direction should alternate, which means the first animation will move from left to right, the second one from right to left, and so on.

The @keyframes selector rule that follows illustrates one way that the keyframes can be defined. Here, you use the from group to set the properties for the first frame and the to group to set the properties for the last frame. Then, the browser recognizes that it needs to fill the "in-between" frames for you. This is known as *tweening*.

Properties for working with animations

Property	Description
`animation`	The shorthand property for setting the properties that follow.
`animation-name`	The name of the @keyframes rule for the keyframe sequence.
`animation-duration`	The seconds or milliseconds that the animation will take.
`animation-delay`	The seconds or milliseconds before the animation starts.
`animation-iteration-count`	Infinite or the number of times the animation should repeat.
`animation-timing-function`	The speed curve of the animation.
`animation-direction`	Use normal, reverse, or alternate to set the direction of the animation.

The syntax for the shorthand animation property

```
animation: [name] [duration] [timing-function] [delay] [iteration-count]
           [direction];
```

A simple animation that moves a heading and changes its color

Starting in blue with a left margin of 20%

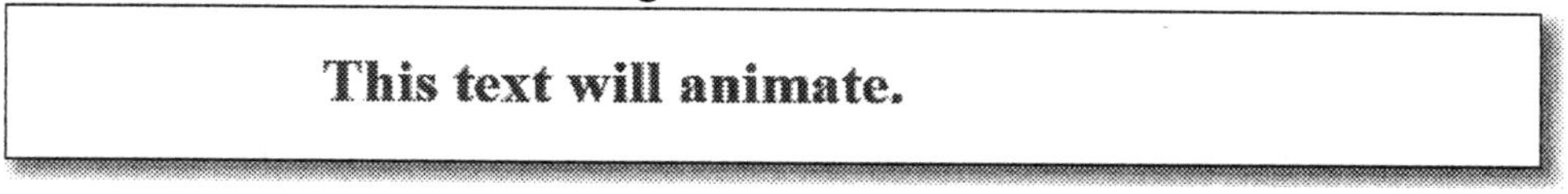

Ending in red with a left margin of 60%

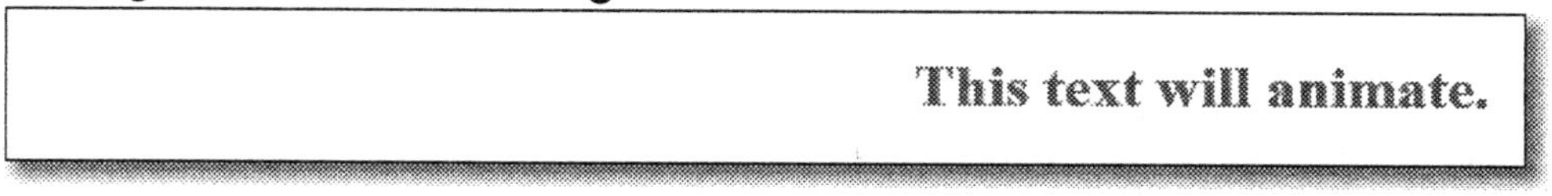

The HTML for the heading

```
<h1>This text will animate.</h1>
```

The CSS for the animation

```
h1 {animation: moveright 3s 2s infinite ease-in-out alternate; }
@keyframes moveright {
    from { margin-left: 20%;
           color: blue; }
    to {   margin-left: 60%;
           color: red; }
}
```

Description

- The animation-name property points to an *@keyframes selector* rule that defines the *keyframes* for a CSS3 *animation*.
- For a simple animation, the keyframes are set automatically, as shown above, but you can define them yourself as shown in the next figure.
- Today, the animation properties work in every modern browser, although you need to add the -webkit- prefix for Chrome, Opera, and Safari.

Figure 14-5 How to code simple animations

How to set the keyframes for a slide show

Figure 14-6 shows how you can set more of the keyframes for an animation and then let the browser do the tweening. This example creates a slide show for five images and captions without the need for JavaScript or jQuery.

The HTML for this slide show is just an unordered list, but each list item contains an h2 element for the caption and an img element for the image. Not shown is the CSS for the formatting of all the elements, but when that formatting is done, all five images are in a row with four of them hidden to the right of the one shown when the page is rendered in the browser.

This figure does show some of the formatting for the ul and li elements. Here, relative positioning is used for the ul element. That way, the keyframes for the animation sequence for that element can also use relative positioning. In addition, the width of the ul element is set to 500% of its containing block so it can accommodate all five images. Finally, the width of each list item is set to 20% of the ul element, or 100% of the ul element's containing block (20% of 500%).

The CSS for the animation is applied to the ul element. This animation uses the @keyframes rule named "slideshow". Unlike the @keyframes rule in the previous figure, this one sets the keyframes for eleven different points in the animation: 0%, 10%, 20%, and so on up to 100%. Here, the starting keyframe sets the left property for relative positioning to 0. This means that the first list item in the unordered list is shown. Then, at the 20% point in the animation, the left property is changed to -100%, which is the width of one list item. This means that the second image slides into place from the right and the first one is hidden. This animation continues until the left property is changed to -400% in the keyframe at the 80% point in the animation, which means that the last image slides into place and stays there until the animation is finished.

Then, because the animation property specifies "alternate" for the direction, the next repetition of the animation reverses the order of the slides so they go from the last to the first. If "normal" had been specified for the direction, the slides would restart from the first keyframe for the next repetition.

To get a better idea of how this works, you can review all of the CSS in the downloaded example for this figure. You can also experiment with the animation property and the keyframe settings.

A slide show animation with captions above the images

The HTML for an unordered list that contains the images and captions

```
<ul>
    <li>
        <h2>Front of Building</h2>
        <img src="images/01.jpg" alt="">
    </li>
    ...
</ul>
```

The CSS for the ul and li elements

```
ul { list-style: none;
     width: 500%;
     position: relative; }
ul li { width: 20%;
        float: left; }
```

The CSS for the animation

```
ul { animation: slideshow 15s infinite alternate; }
@keyframes slideshow {
    0%    {left:    0%;}
    10%   {left:    0%;}
    20%   {left: -100%;}
    30%   {left: -100%;}
    40%   {left: -200%;}
    50%   {left: -200%;}
    60%   {left: -300%;}
    70%   {left: -300%;}
    80%   {left: -400%;}
    90%   {left: -400%;}
    100%  {left: -400%;}
}
```

Description

- This animation works like a jQuery slide show. However, it is done with CSS3 alone.
- For Chrome, Opera, and Safari, you need the -webkit- prefix for the animation property and the @-webkit-keyframes selector for the keyframe rules.

Figure 14-6 How to set the keyframes for a slide show

How to use CSS3 filters

Filters let you change the appearance of images after they have been loaded into the browser without changing the image files. For instance, you can use filters to convert an image to grayscale or to blur an image. The first browser to support filters is Firefox 35, which was released in 2015, but you can expect the other browsers to soon follow suit. In the meantime, you can use the -webkit- prefix for Chrome and Opera.

How to code filters

Figure 14-7 summarizes the filter property and the ten filter methods that it supports. Most of these filter methods accept percent values that can either be expressed as a percent like 50% or a decimal value like .5. But some require degree values, and the drop-shadow method requires a series of values like the box-shadow property does.

The example in this figure shows how to invert an image. Here, the same image is displayed side by side, but the one on the right inverts the colors of the original image when the user hovers the mouse over it. In this case, an 80% inversion is used, but that can range from 0 (no inversion) to 100% (full inversion).

The syntax for adding a filter to an element

```
filter: filtermethod(value);
```

The filter methods

Method	Description
`blur(value)`	Applies a Gaussian blur. The value is in pixels.
`brightness(value)`	Adjusts the brightness, from 0% (black) to 100% (unchanged). Numbers higher than 100% result in a brighter image.
`contrast(value)`	Adjusts the contrast, from 0% (black) to 100% (unchanged).
`drop-shadow(values)`	Adds a drop shadow just as the box-shadow property does.
`grayscale(value)`	Converts the image to grayscale. 100% is completely grayscale, while 0% leaves the image unchanged.
`hue-rotate(angle)`	Adjusts the hue rotation of the image. The angle value is the number of degrees around the color circle that the image will be adjusted.
`invert(value)`	Inverts the colors of the image. 100% is completely inverted, while 0% leaves the image unchanged.
`opacity(value)`	Applies transparency to the image. 0 results in an image that is completely transparent while 1 leaves the image unchanged.
`saturate(value)`	Saturates the image. 0% results in an image that is completely saturated while 100% leaves the image unchanged.
`sepia(value)`	Converts the image to sepia. 100% is completely sepia, while 0% leaves the image unchanged.

An image before and after its colors are inverted

The HTML for the images

```
<li>Original<br><img src="images/01.jpg" alt=""></li>
<li>Inverted<br><img src="images/01.jpg" class="image1" alt=""></li>
```

The CSS for the filter

```
.image1:hover { filter: invert(.80); }
```

Description

- You can use *filters* to change the appearance of an image in the browser.
- Percentage values like 50% can also be expressed as decimal fractions like .5.
- Mozilla's 2015 release of Firefox 35 is the first browser to support the filter property. For Chrome and Opera, you must use the -webkit- prefix.

Figure 14-7 How to use filters

The ten filter methods applied to the same image

Figure 14-8 gives you an example of what an image will look like when each of the ten filters is applied to it. If you're reading this in black and white, of course, it's hard to evaluate some of the differences. So the best way to see what these filters can do is to experiment with them on your own. You can do that by working with the downloaded example for this figure after you finish reading this chapter.

The last example shows how you can apply two filters to the same image. To do that, you code one method after the other without using commas to separate them.

A web page in Chrome with different filters applied to an image

The HTML for the images that will have filters applied

```
<ul>
  <li>Blur<br>          <img src="images/01.jpg" class="image1" alt=""></li>
  <li>Brightness<br>    <img src="images/01.jpg" class="image2" alt=""></li>
  <li>Contrast<br>      <img src="images/01.jpg" class="image3" alt=""></li>
  <li>Drop Shadow<br>   <img src="images/01.jpg" class="image4" alt=""></li>
  <li>Grayscale<br>     <img src="images/01.jpg" class="image5" alt=""></li>
  <li>Hue Rotate<br>    <img src="images/01.jpg" class="image6" alt=""></li>
  <li>Invert<br>        <img src="images/01.jpg" class="image7" alt=""></li>
  <li>Opacity<br>       <img src="images/01.jpg" class="image8" alt=""></li>
  <li>Saturate<br>      <img src="images/01.jpg" class="image9" alt=""></li>
  <li>Sepia/blur<br>    <img src="images/01.jpg" class="image10" alt=""></li>
</ul>
```

The CSS for the filters

```
.image1 { filter: blur(2px); }
.image2 { filter: brightness(50%); }
.image3 { filter: contrast(50%);}
.image4 { filter: drop-shadow(2px 2px 5px #333); }
.image5 { filter: grayscale(50%); }
.image6 { filter: hue-rotate(90deg); }
.image7 { filter: invert(.8); }
.image8 { filter: opacity(.50); }
.image9 { filter: saturate(30%); }
.image10{ filter: sepia(100%) blur(1px); }
```

Description

- This example shows how the 10 filter methods look when applied to the same image. If you download and experiment with this example, you'll get a better idea of what the filters can do.
- The filters in this example are applied when the page is loaded, but you can use the hover pseudo-class to apply them when the mouse hovers over an image. Note, however, that you can't use transitions with filters.

Figure 14-8 The ten filter methods applied to the same image

Perspective

Now that you've been introduced to CSS transitions, transforms, animations, and filters, you should be able to use them in your own web pages. But what should you do with them? If you're looking for ideas, just search the web for examples. For instance, you can find countless examples of transitions and animations that include slide shows, carousels, accordions, and some incredible animations. You can also find plenty of examples for transforms and filters.

But the other question that you need to ask is whether you need these CSS3 features. In chapter 16, for example, you'll learn how to use jQuery UI and jQuery plugins to provide features like slide shows, carousels, and accordions. Often, this is an easier way to provide these features, and they work even better than those you can create with CSS3 transitions and animations. Note, too, that most websites don't use transforms and filters now and may never need them.

Of course, the benefit of using these CSS3 features is that they don't require JavaScript or jQuery. They are also relatively easy to use. Nevertheless, they're likely to play a minor role in your web pages...especially if you keep the focus on usability.

Terms

transition
timing function
speed curve
transform
animation
@keyframes selector
keyframe
animation sequence
tweening
filter

Summary

- When the CSS properties for an HTML element are changed, a CSS3 *transition* provides a smooth change over a specified period of time.
- CSS3 *transforms* let you rotate, scale, skew, and position HTML elements.
- CSS3 *animations* let you create frame-based animations that are similar to what you can create with programs like Flash.
- The CSS3 animation property always points to an *@keyframes selector* rule that defines the *keyframes* that are used in the *animation sequence*. When those keyframes are played, they give the impression of motion.
- CSS3 *filters* let you provide effects like blurring or grayscale to HTML elements like images and backgrounds.

Exercise 14-1 Use transitions, transforms, and animation

In this exercise, you'll have some fun with the CSS3 features that you learned about in this chapter. For instance, you'll animate the four images in the aside when the page is loaded, and you'll rotate the speaker image in the article when the user hovers the mouse over it. When both of those features are in progress, the page will look something like this:

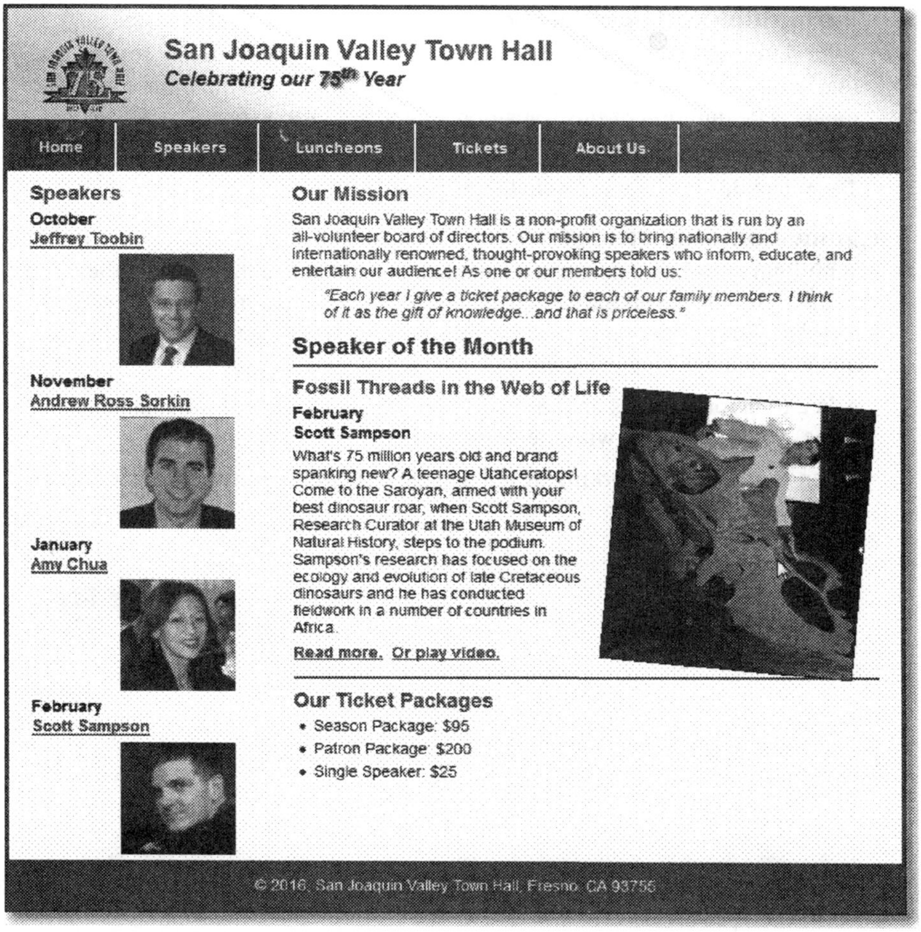

Use a transition

1. Use your text editor to open these pages:

```
c:\html5_css3_2\exercises\town_hall_2\index
c:\html5_css3_2\exercises\town_hall_2\styles\main.css
```

2. With figure 14-1 as a guide, add a transition to the page that moves any of the images in the aside 100 pixels to the right and 20 pixels down when the user hovers the mouse over one of them. The duration of the transition should be 2 seconds. Then, test this change in Firefox and test all of the changes that follow using that browser.
3. Comment out the transition and test this again to see that the movement still works, but there isn't a gradual transition to the new location. Then, uncomment the transition.

Use a transition with a transform

4. With figure 14-3 as a guide, add a transition and a transform that rotates the image in the article by 720 degrees when the user hovers the mouse over the image. The duration of this transition should be 3 seconds.
5. Change the origin of this transform so it is at the upper left of the image. Then, test this change and note the difference.

Use animation with a transform

6. With figure 14-5 as a guide, animate the four images in the aside so they move to the right 100 pixels and down 20 pixels when the page is loaded into the browser. The animation should be delayed 2 seconds, last 3 seconds, be run 4 times, and alternate directions.
7. Add a transform to this animation that increases the size of the image 1.4 times. You can do that with the scale method.
8. When everything is working, test this page in Chrome to see whether everything still works.

Section 3

JavaScript and jQuery for the non-programmer

Sections 1 and 2 of this book present the HTML and CSS skills that you use as you build websites. But a modern website requires more than that. That's why this section presents some of the JavaScript and jQuery skills that you'll need as you develop a website. Although these chapters won't teach you how to write your own JavaScript code, they will teach you how to use code that was written by others to get the results that you want.

In chapter 15, for example, you'll learn how to enhance your web pages by using JavaScript and jQuery to add features like image rollovers, image swaps, and slide shows. In chapter 16, you'll learn how to use jQuery UI and jQuery plugins to add features like accordions, tabs, carousels, and slide shows. And in chapter 17, you'll learn how to use jQuery Mobile to develop separate websites for mobile devices, which is a practical alternative to responsive web design.

15

How to use JavaScript and jQuery to enhance your web pages

In this chapter, you'll learn how you can use JavaScript and jQuery to enhance your web pages. Although you won't learn how to code in JavaScript and jQuery, you will learn the concepts and terms that you need for understanding how JavaScript works. Then, you'll learn how you can use tested JavaScript and jQuery code to get the results you want.

Introduction to JavaScript

In this introduction, you'll learn how JavaScript and DOM scripting work together. This will be an early demonstration of why JavaScript is so important to the modern website.

How JavaScript works

Figure 15-1 presents a diagram that shows how JavaScript fits into the client/server architecture. Here, you can see that the *JavaScript* code is executed in the web browser by the browser's *JavaScript engine*. This is referred to as *client-side processing,* in contrast to the *server-side processing* that's done on the web server. This takes some of the processing burden off the server and makes the application run faster. Today, almost all web browsers have JavaScript enabled so JavaScript applications will run on them.

To illustrate the use of JavaScript code, the example in this figure gets the current date and the current year and inserts both into an HTML document. To do that, the JavaScript code is embedded within script elements in the body of the document. This code is executed when the page is loaded.

You can see the results in the web browser in this figure. In this case, the JavaScript code in the first script element writes the first line into the web page, which includes the current date. And the JavaScript code in the second script element writes the copyright line into the web page, which includes the current year.

How JavaScript fits into the client/server architecture

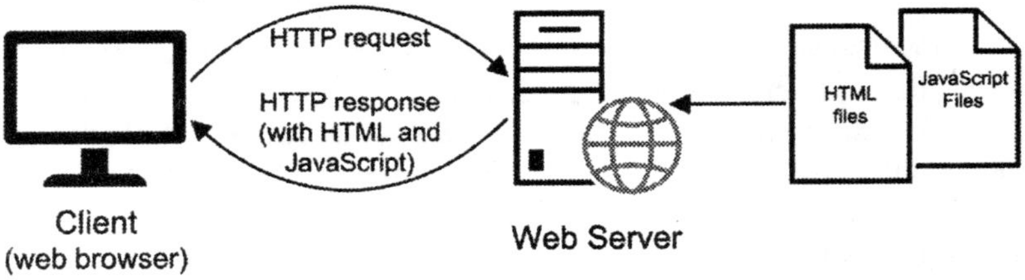

JavaScript in an HTML document that gets the current date and year

```
<p>
    <script>
        var today = new Date();
        document.write("Current date: ");
        document.write(today.toDateString());
    </script>
</p>
<p>
    <script>
        var today = new Date();
        document.write("&copy; ");
        document.write(today.getFullYear());
        document.write(", San Joaquin Valley Town Hall")
    </script>
</p>
```

The HTML in a web browser after the page is loaded

Description

- *JavaScript* is a scripting language that is run by the *JavaScript engine* of a browser. As a result, the work is done on the client, not the server.
- JavaScript can modify the contents of a web page when the page is loaded or in response to a user action.
- In this example, JavaScript inserts the text shown above into the two <p> elements on the page.

Figure 15-1 How JavaScript works

Three ways to include JavaScript in a web page

Figure 15-2 shows how to include JavaScript in an HTML document, or web page. To start, this figure describes two attributes that can be used with the script element. The src attribute specifies the location of the external JavaScript file that should be included in the document. The type attribute specifies that JavaScript is the client-side scripting language.

In HTML5, though, the type attribute can be omitted since JavaScript is assumed to be the scripting language. That's why the type attribute is omitted in the examples that follow. These examples illustrate the three ways that you can include JavaScript in an HTML document.

In the first example, the script element is coded in the head section of an HTML document, and the src attribute identifies an external JavaScript file named set_date.js. This assumes that the external file is in the same folder as the HTML page. If it isn't, you can code the path to the file along with the filename.

In the second example, the script element is again coded in the head section of an HTML document. In this case, though, the JavaScript is embedded in the script element.

In the third example, a script element that contains JavaScript is embedded in the body of an HTML document. As you saw in figure 15-1, a script element like this is replaced by the output of the JavaScript code when the page is loaded.

Two attributes of the script element

Attribute	Description
src	Specifies the location and name of an external JavaScript file.
type	With HTML5, this attribute can be omitted. If you code it, use "text/javascript" for JavaScript code.

A script element in the head section that loads an external JavaScript file

```
<script src="set_date.js"></script>
```

A script element that embeds JavaScript in the head section

```
<head>
    ...
    <script>
        var $ = function (id) {
            return document.getElementById(id);
        }
        window.onload = function() {
            var today = new Date();
            $("date").firstChild.nodeValue =
                "Current date: " + today.toDateString();
        }
    </script>
</head>
```

A script element that embeds JavaScript in the body

```
<p>
    <script>
        var today = new Date();
        document.write("Current date: ");
        document.write(today.toDateString());
    </script>
</p>
```

Description

- You can have more than one script element in a web page. These elements are executed in the order that they appear in the document.
- If a script element in the head section includes an external JavaScript file, the JavaScript in the file runs as if it were coded in the script element.
- If a script element is coded in the body of a document, it is replaced by the output of the JavaScript code.
- The HTML document must be valid before and after all scripts have been executed.

Figure 15-2 Three ways to include JavaScript in a web page

How DOM scripting works

As an HTML page is loaded by the web browser, the *DOM (Document Object Model)* for that page is created in the browser's memory. This DOM is an internal representation of the HTML elements on a web page. In figure 15-3, you can see a simple HTML document and the structure of the DOM for that document.

Here, each element of the page is represented by a *node* in the DOM. The nodes in the DOM have a hierarchical structure based on how the HTML elements are nested inside each other. The DOM starts with the html element and follows the nesting of the elements down to the text that is in each element.

Within the DOM, several types of nodes are used to represent the contents of the web page. HTML elements are stored in *element nodes*, and text is stored in *text nodes*. In this figure, element nodes are shown as ovals, and text nodes are shown as rectangles. Other common node types are *attribute nodes* and *comment nodes*.

What's interesting about this is that JavaScript can be used to modify the nodes in the DOM. Furthermore, whenever a change is made to the DOM, the web browser updates the page in the browser window to reflect that change. This means that you can use JavaScript to modify the contents and appearance of a web page after it has been loaded. This is called *DOM scripting*, and this is what makes JavaScript so powerful.

The code for a web page

```
<!DOCTYPE html>
<html>
<head>
    <title>Join Email List</title>
</head>
<body>
    <h1>Please join our email list</h1>
    <form id="email_form" name="email_form" action="join.html" method="get">
        <label for="email_address">Email Address:</label>
        <input type="text" id="email_address">
        <span id="email_error">*</span>
    </form>
</body>
</html>
```

The DOM for the web page

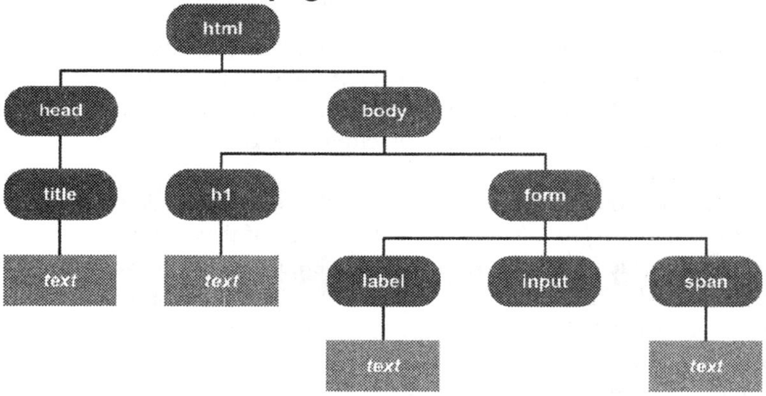

The DOM nodes that you commonly use in DOM scripting

Type	Description
`Element`	An element in the web page. It can have Element, Text, and Comment nodes as child nodes.
`Attr`	An attribute of an element. Although it is attached to an Element node, it isn't considered a child node. It can have a Text node as a child node.
`Text`	The text for an element or attribute. It can't have a child node.

Description

- The *DOM* (*Document Object Model*) is a hierarchical collection of *nodes* in the web browser's memory that represents the current web page.
- The DOM for a web page is built as the page is loaded by the web browser.
- When you use JavaScript to modify the DOM, you are *DOM scripting* or *scripting the DOM.*
- DOM scripting is a powerful capability because when the DOM is changed, the web browser changes the web page to reflect the changes to the DOM.

Figure 15-3 How DOM scripting works

Methods and properties for DOM scripting

To give you some idea of how DOM scripting works, figure 15-4 presents a few of the methods and properties that you can use for DOM scripting. Here, the first table presents two *methods* of the *document object*, which is the object that lets you work with the DOM.

The first method is the getElementById method. It gets the HTML element that's represented by the id attribute that's passed to it within the parentheses. In the first example after the table, you can see how this method is used to get the HTML element (or *object*) that has "rate" as its id attribute. In this case, that element (or the object that represents that element) is stored in a variable (var) named rateBox.

The second method in the first table is the write method, which you've already seen in figures 15-1 and 15-2. It writes whatever is in the parentheses into the body of the document.

The third example after this table is the code for a standard function named $ that uses the getElementById method to get an HTML element. This function can be called by coding just the $ sign followed by a set of parentheses that contains the id attribute of the element that the function should get. You'll see this used in just a moment.

To modify the DOM, though, you need to work with its nodes. To do that, you use the *properties* that are provided by the DOM. Three of these properties are shown in the second table in this figure. The first one gets or sets the value that's in an input element like a text box. The second one gets the Node object for the first child of an element. The third one gets or sets the text for a Text, Comment, or Attribute node.

The first example after this table shows how the value property can be used to get the value that has been entered into a text box. It uses the $ function to get the object for the text box with "email_address" as its id attribute, and it uses the value property to get the value that's in the text box. Then, this value is stored in a variable named emailAddress.

The second example shows how the firstChild and nodeValue properties can be used to set the value for an HTML element with "email_error" as its id attribute. This example uses the $ function to get the HTML element, the firstChild property to get the text node for the element, and the nodeValue property to set the text in that node to "Entry is invalid."

If you're new to programming, this may seem complicated, but you don't need to worry about that. Just take away the concept that JavaScript can script the DOM by using its many methods and properties.

The code for a web page

```
<h1>Please join our email list</h1>
<form id="email_form" name="email_form" action="join.html" method="get">
    <label for="email_address">Email Address:</label>
    <input type="text" id="email_address">
    <span id="email_error">*</span>
</form>
```

Two methods of the document object

Method	Description
getElementById(id)	Gets the HTML element that has the id that's passed to it and returns that element.
write(string)	Writes the string.

Examples of document methods

```
// returns the object for the HTML element
var rateBox = document.getElementById("rate");
// writes a string into the document
document.write("Today is " + today.toDateString());
```

A standard $ function that gets the object for an element by using its id

```
var $ = function (id) {
    return document.getElementById(id);
}
```

Three properties that can be used for scripting the DOM

Property	Description
value	For an input element like a text box, gets or sets the value in the element.
firstChild	Returns a Node object for the first child node of an element.
nodeValue	For a Text, Comment, or Attribute node, gets or sets the text that's stored in the node.

How to get the text of an HTML element with "email_address" as its id

```
var emailAddress = $("email_address").value;
```

How to set the text of an HTML element with "email_error" as its id

```
$("email_error").firstChild.nodeValue = "Entry is invalid.";
```

Description

- The *document object* is the object that lets you work with the Document Object Model (DOM) that represents all of the HTML elements on a page.
- When scripting the DOM, the $ sign is commonly used for a function that uses the getElementById method of the document object to get the element that has the id that's coded in the parentheses.
- The second table above presents just three of the many properties that can be used for scripting the DOM.

Figure 15-4 Methods and properties for DOM scripting

How JavaScript handles events

One other concept that you should be aware of is the way JavaScript handles events. An *event* occurs when an action like loading a web page or clicking on a button occurs. Then, the JavaScript code can respond to the event with code that is called an *event handler*.

The diagram in figure 15-5 describes the event cycle that drives DOM scripting. First, the page is loaded and the event handlers are attached to the events that will be processed. Next, when an event occurs, the appropriate event handler is executed. Then, if the event handler modifies the DOM, the page is immediately updated.

The example in this figure illustrates the use of event handlers. In this case, JavaScript is used to print the page when a Print button is clicked. The JavaScript code in this example consists of the standard $ function, an event handler named printPage that is executed when the user clicks on the button, and an event handler for the onload event of the page.

When the page is loaded, the onload event handler for the onload event sets the onclick event of the button with "printButton" as its id so the printPage function will be called when the button is clicked. Then, when the button is clicked by the user, the printPage event handler is executed. Within that handler, the print method of the window object is used to print the page.

It's worth noting that you don't have to understand this JavaScript code in order to use it. Since the JavaScript is stored in an external file named printPage.js, you start by coding a script element in the head section that includes the file. Then, you set the id attribute of the button that you want to use for printing to "printButton".

If you aren't a programmer, that's the approach you can take for adding JavaScript features to your web pages. And that's the approach that's emphasized in the rest of this chapter and the next chapter.

A web page that prints the current page when the button is clicked

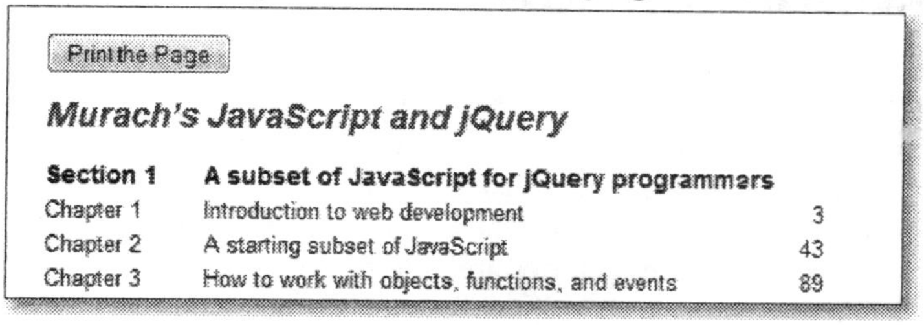

The JavaScript in an external file named printPage.js

```
var $ = function (id) {
    // this function returns the object for the HTML element
    return document.getElementById(id);
}
var printPage = function() {
    // this is the event handler for the click event of the button
    window.print();
}
window.onload = function() {
    // this is the event handler for the onload event
    $("printButton").onclick = printPage;
}
```

The HTML code for the external JavaScript file in the head section

```
<script src="printPage.js"></script>
```

The HTML code for the button in the body section

```
<input type="button" id="printButton" value="Print the Page">
```

The DOM event cycle

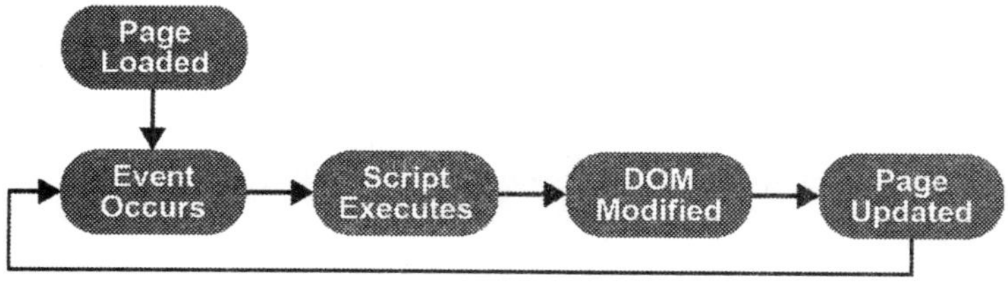

Description

- An *event* occurs when the page is loaded or the user performs an action like clicking on an HTML element.
- The JavaScript code that handles an event is called an *event handler*, and the event handler can script the DOM or use any of the methods of the objects in the DOM.
- In this example, the event handler for the onload event runs when the page is loaded. It sets up the button with "printButton" as its id so the printPage event handler is called when the button is clicked. Then, the printPage handler executes the print method of the window object, which causes the page to print.

Figure 15-5 How JavaScript handles events

The Email List application in JavaScript

If you are interested in the programming side of JavaScript, the next two figures present a simple Email List application. It asks the user to make three entries and then click on the Join our List button. The asterisks to the right of the text boxes for the entries indicate that these entries are required.

When the user clicks on the button, JavaScript checks the entries to make sure they're valid. If they are, the entries are sent to the web server for server-side processing. If they aren't, messages are displayed so the user can correct the entries. This is a common use for JavaScript called *data validation* that saves a trip to the server when the entries are invalid.

The HTML

If you've read chapter 11, you should be familiar with the HTML in figure 15-6. Just note that each entry line on the form consists of a label, input, and span element. Also, each span element starts with an asterisk (*) in it, but DOM scripting will be used to replace that asterisk with an error message if the user makes an invalid entry or with nothing ("") if the entry is valid.

The HTML file in a browser after CSS has been applied to it

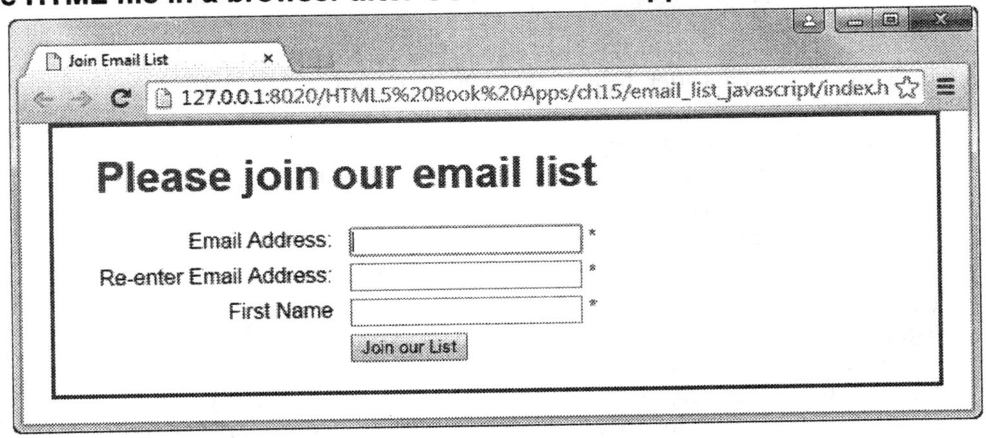

The code for the HTML file named index.html

```
<!DOCTYPE html>
<html>
<head>
    <meta charset="UTF-8">
    <title>Join Email List</title>
    <link rel="stylesheet" href="email_list.css">
    <script src="email_list.js"></script>
</head>
<body>
    <main>
        <h1>Please join our email list</h1>
        <form id="email_form" name="email_form"
              action="join.html" method="get">
            <label for="email_address1">Email Address:</label>
            <input type="text" id="email_address1" name="email_address1">
            <span id="email_address1_error">*</span><br>

            <label for="email_address2">Re-enter Email Address:</label>
            <input type="text" id="email_address2" name="email_address2">
            <span id="email_address2_error">*</span><br>

            <label for="first_name">First Name</label>
            <input type="text" id="first_name" name="first_name">
            <span id="first_name_error">*</span><br>

            <label> </label>
            <input type="button" id="join_list" value="Join our List">
        </form>
    </main>
</body>
</html>
```

Figure 15-6 The HTML for the Email List application

The JavaScript

Figure 15-7 shows how this application looks in a browser if the JavaScript finds any invalid data after the user clicks the Join our List button. Here, you can see that the asterisk after the first text box has been removed because the entry is valid, and error messages are displayed to the right of the entries for the second and third text boxes because the entries aren't valid. In other words, the JavaScript has actually changed the contents of the span elements.

After the browser display, this figure shows the JavaScript for this application. That should give you a better idea of how JavaScript is used. For this book, you don't have to understand this code. But if you're interested, here's a brief description of how it works.

To start, this code consists of three functions: a $ function, a joinList function that is executed when the user clicks on the button, and a function that is run when the page is loaded into the browser. Then, in the joinList function, you can see four if-else statements that provide most of the logic for this application.

Here, you can see that the if-else structures are similar to those in any modern programming language like Java, C#, or PHP. You can also see that declaring a variable (var) and assigning a variable is done in a way that's similar to the way that's done in other programming languages.

What's different about JavaScript are the methods and properties that let you modify the DOM. In this example, you can see how the value property is used to get the values from the text boxes and how the firstChild and nodeValue properties are used to set error messages in the span elements for invalid entries.

The web page in a browser with JavaScript used for data validation

The script element in the HTML file that includes the JavaScript file

```
<script src="email_list.js"></script>
```

The code for the JavaScript file named email_list.js

```
var $ = function (id) {
    return document.getElementById(id);
}
var joinList = function () {
    var emailAddress1 = $("email_address1").value;
    var emailAddress2 = $("email_address2").value;
    var isValid = true;

    if (emailAddress1 == "") {
        $("email_address1_error").firstChild.nodeValue =
            "This field is required.";
        isValid = false;
    } else { $("email_address1_error").firstChild.nodeValue = ""; }

    if (emailAddress1 !== emailAddress2) {
        $("email_address2_error").firstChild.nodeValue =
            "This entry must equal first entry.";
        isValid = false;
    } else { $("email_address2_error").firstChild.nodeValue = ""; }

    if ($("first_name").value == "") {
        $("first_name_error").firstChild.nodeValue =
            "This field is required.";
        isValid = false;
    } else { $("first_name_error").firstChild.nodeValue = ""; }

    if (isValid) {
        // submit the form if all entries are valid
        $("email_form").submit(); }
}
window.onload = function () {
    $("join_list").onclick = joinList;
}
```

Figure 15-7 The JavaScript for the Email List application

Introduction to jQuery

jQuery is a free, open-source, JavaScript library that provides dozens of methods for common web features that make JavaScript programming easier. Beyond that, the jQuery functions are coded and tested for cross-browser compatibility, so they will work in all browsers. Note, however, that starting with version 2.0, jQuery doesn't provide compatibility for IE 6, 7, and 8.

Those are two of the reasons why jQuery is used by more than half of the 10,000 most-visited websites today. And that's why jQuery is commonly used by professional web developers. In fact, you can think of jQuery as one of the four technologies that every web developer should know how to use: HTML, CSS, JavaScript, and jQuery. But don't forget that jQuery is actually JavaScript.

In this introduction, you'll learn how to include jQuery in your applications and how to use its selectors, methods, and event methods. Here again, the goal isn't to teach you how to program with jQuery. It's to give you a better idea of what you can do with jQuery and why you may want to master it.

How to include jQuery in your web pages

If you go to the website that's shown in this figure and go to the download page, you'll find links that let you download the file for the jQuery library in either of two forms: compressed or uncompressed. The compressed version loads quickly into browsers, which is another reason why developers like jQuery. The uncompressed version is for developers who want to study the JavaScript code in the download.

Once you've downloaded the compressed version of jQuery, you can include it in a web page by coding a script element like the first one in this figure. Then, if you store the file on your own computer or a local web server, you'll be able to develop jQuery applications without being connected to the Internet. For production applications, though, you'll need to deploy the file to your Internet web server.

In this script element, the file name includes the version number, but you can use whatever file name you want. However, if the file name doesn't include the version number, it's easy to lose track of which version you're using.

The other way to include the jQuery library in your web applications and the one we recommend is to get the file from a *Content Delivery Network* (*CDN*). A CDN is a web server that hosts open-source software, and the Google, Microsoft, and jQuery websites are CDNs for getting the jQuery libraries. In the second example in this figure, the script element uses the jQuery CDN with a URL that gets version 2.1.3 of jQuery.

The benefit to using a CDN is that you don't have to download the jQuery file. The disadvantage is that you have to be connected to the Internet to use a CDN.

The jQuery website at jQuery.com

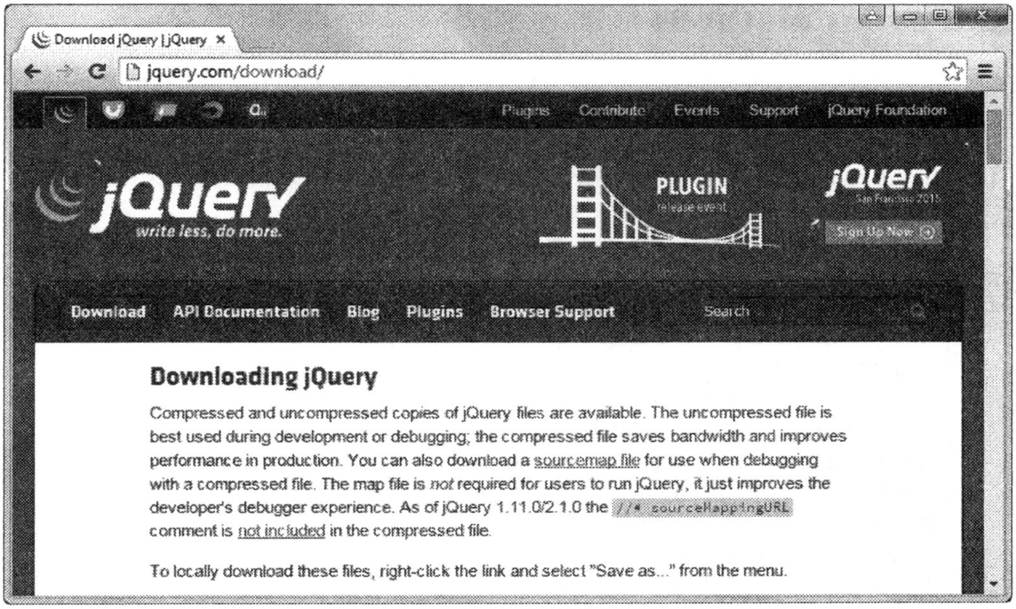

What jQuery offers

- Dozens of methods that make it easier to add JavaScript features to your web pages
- Methods that are tested for cross-browser compatibility

How to include the jQuery file after you've downloaded it to your computer

```
<script src="jquery-2.1.3.js"></script>
```

How to include the jQuery file from a Content Delivery Network (CDN)

```
<script src="http://code.jquery.com/jquery-2.1.3.min.js"></script>
```

Description

- *jQuery* is a free, open-source, JavaScript library that provides methods that make JavaScript programming easier. Today, jQuery is used by more than 50% of the 10,000 most-visited websites, and its popularity is growing rapidly.
- The jQuery download comes in two versions. One version (min) is a compressed version that is relatively small and loads fast. The other version is uncompressed so you can use it to study the JavaScript code in the library.
- If you include the jQuery file from a *Content Delivery Network* (*CDN*), you don't have to provide it from your own server, but then you can't work offline.
- If you download the jQuery file to your system, you can change the filename so it's simpler, but then you may lose track of what version you're using.

Figure 15-8 What jQuery is and how to include it in a web page

How to code jQuery selectors, methods, and event methods

To give you some idea of how jQuery works, figure 15-9 introduces the selectors, methods, and event methods that you can use in your jQuery code. To start, you should know that the $ sign always refers to the jQuery library. Then, in the parentheses after the dollar sign, you code a selector that identifies the HTML element or elements that the jQuery will be applied to.

This is illustrated by the first set of examples in this figure. Here, the first *selector* is a type selector that applies to all h2 elements. The second selector is an id selector that applies to the HTML element with "email_address" as its id. And the third selector is a class selector that applies to all of the elements with "warning" as their class name. This shows how closely the jQuery selectors relate to the CSS selectors, which is another reason why developers like jQuery.

After the selector, you can use the dot syntax to run a jQuery *method* on the HTML element that's referred to by the selector. This is illustrated by the second set of examples in this figure. Here, the first statement uses the val method to get the value in the text box with "email_address" as its id attribute. The second statement uses the text method to set the text that's in an HTML element with "email_address_error" as its id. And the third statement uses the next and text methods to set the text for the sibling element that follows the element with "email_address" as its id. This is a nice simplification over comparable JavaScript code.

The third group of examples shows how to use *event methods*. The first example in this group uses the ready event method. It is executed when the DOM for the entire page has been built. In this example, the alert method of the window object is executed when the ready event occurs.

The ready event method is important because some applications that use the DOM can't be run until the entire DOM has been built. As a result, this event method is a nice improvement over the JavaScript onload event which occurs while the page is being loaded and the DOM is being built.

The second example in this group shows how the click event method can be used to provide an event handler for the click event of all h2 elements. Here again, an alert method is executed when an h2 element is clicked.

The third example combines the ready and click event methods. In this case, the click event method isn't prepared until the ready event has occurred. As a result, the click event method will apply to all of the h2 elements in the DOM.

How to code jQuery selectors

By element type

```
$("h2")
```

By id

```
$("#email_address")
```

By class attribute

```
$(".warning")
```

How to call jQuery methods

How to get the value from a text box

```
var emailAddress = $("#email_address").val();
```

How to set the text in an element

```
$("#email_address_error").text("Email address is required");
```

How to set the text for the next sibling

```
$("#email_address").next().text("Email address is required");
```

How to code jQuery event methods

How to code the ready event method

```
$(document).ready(function() {
    alert("The DOM is ready");
});
```

How to code the click event method for all h2 elements

```
$("h2").click(function() {
    alert("This heading has been clicked");
});
```

How to use the click event method within the ready event method

```
$(document).ready(function() {
    $("h2").click(function() {
        alert("This heading has been clicked");
    }); // end of click event handler
}); // end of ready event handler
```

Description

- When you use jQuery, the dollar sign ($) is used to refer to the jQuery library. Then, you can code jQuery *selectors* by using the CSS syntax within quotation marks within parentheses.
- To call a jQuery *method*, you code a selector, the dot operator, the method name, and any parameters within parentheses. Then, that method is applied to the element or elements that are selected by the selector.
- To code a jQuery event handler, you code a selector, the dot operator, the name of the jQuery *event method*, and a function that handles the event within parentheses.
- The event handler for the ready event method will run any methods that it contains as soon as the DOM is ready, even if the browser is loading images and other content for the page.

Figure 15-9 How to use jQuery selectors, methods, and event methods

The Email List application in jQuery

If you are interested in the programming side of jQuery, you're ready to see how jQuery can be used in the Email List application that you studied in figures 15-6 and 15-7. That will show you how jQuery can simplify coding.

To refresh your memory, figure 15-10 presents the user interface and HTML for the Email List application. To use the application, the user enters text into the first three text boxes and clicks on the Join our List button. Then, the JavaScript validates the entries and displays appropriate error messages if errors are found. If no errors are found, the data in the form is submitted to the web server for processing.

The HTML

In the HTML in this figure, note first the script element that loads jQuery. It is followed by the script element that identifies the file that holds the JavaScript for this application. That sequence is essential because the JavaScript file is going to use the jQuery file.

In the HTML for the form, note that the span elements are adjacent siblings to the input elements for the text boxes. The starting text for each of these span elements is an asterisk that indicates that the text box entry is required. Later, if the JavaScript finds errors in the entries, it displays error messages in these span elements.

Note also that the span elements don't require id attributes as they did for the JavaScript version of this application in figure 15-6. That's because jQuery can change the text in those elements without referring to them by id. In other words, the use of jQuery has simplified the HTML requirements for this application.

The user interface for the Email List application

The HTML

```
<!DOCTYPE html>
<html>
<head>
    <meta charset="UTF-8">
    <title>Join Email List</title>
    <link rel="stylesheet" href="email_list.css">
    <script src="http://code.jquery.com/jquery-2.1.3.min.js"></script>
    <script src="email_list.js"></script>
</head>
<body>
    <main>
        <h1>Please join our email list</h1>
        <form id="email_form" name="email_form"
              action="join.html" method="get">
            <label for="email_address1">Email Address:</label>
            <input type="text" id="email_address1" name="email_address1">
            <span>*</span><br>

            <label for="email_address2">Re-enter Email Address:</label>
            <input type="text" id="email_address2" name="email_address2">
            <span>*</span><br>

            <label for="first_name">First Name:</label>
            <input type="text" id="first_name" name="first_name">
            <span>*</span><br>

            <label> </label>
            <input type="button" id="join_list" value="Join our List">
        </form>
    </main>
</body>
</html>
```

Figure 15-10 The HTML for the Email List application

The jQuery

Figure 15-11 presents the jQuery for this application. This is the code in the email_list.js file that's included by the HTML. Here, all of the jQuery is highlighted. The rest of the code is JavaScript code.

To start, you can see that an event handler for the click event of the Join our List button is coded within the event handler for the ready event. Within the click event handler, the first two statements show how jQuery selectors and the val method can be used to get the values from text boxes.

In the first if statement, you can see how an error message is displayed if the user doesn't enter an email address in the first text box. Here, the next method gets the adjacent sibling for the text box, which is a span element, and then the text method puts an error message in that span element. This changes the DOM, and as soon as it is changed, the error message is displayed in the browser.

The next and text methods are used in similar ways in the next two if statements. Note here that the first if statement starts by checking if no entry was made for the second email address. This is different from the JavaScript code shown in figure 15-7, which just checked if the entry was the same as the first entry. This provides more complete data validation.

Finally, the fourth if statement tests to see whether the isValid variable is still true. If it is, the submit method of the form is issued, which sends the data to the web server.

If you compare this jQuery code to the JavaScript code in figure 15-7, you can see that the jQuery provides some nice simplifications. That's another reason why programmers like jQuery, but that doesn't begin to illustrate the power of jQuery.

The jQuery for the Email List application (email_list.js)

```
$(document).ready(function() {
    $("#join_list").click(function() {
        var emailAddress1 = $("#email_address1").val();
        var emailAddress2 = $("#email_address2").val();
        var isValid = true;

        // validate the first email address
        if (emailAddress1 == "") {
            $("#email_address1").next().text("This field is required.");
            isValid = false;
        } else {
            $("#email_address1").next().text("");
        }

        // validate the second email address
        if (emailAddress2 == "") {
            $("#email_address2").next().text("This field is required.");
            isValid = false;
        } else if (emailAddress1 != emailAddress2) {
            $("#email_address2").next().text(
                "This entry must equal first entry.");
            isValid = false;
        } else {
            $("#email_address2").next().text("");
        }

        // validate the first name entry
        if ($("#first_name").val() == "") {
            $("#first_name").next().text("This field is required.");
            isValid = false;
        }
        else {
            $("#first_name").next().text("");
        }

        // submit the form if all entries are valid
        if (isValid) {
            $("#email_form").submit();
        }
    }); // end click
}); // end ready
```

Figure 15-11 The jQuery for the Email List application

How to use jQuery as a non-progammer

This chapter ends by presenting a few applications that are typically developed with jQuery. However, the jQuery for these applications isn't presented. Instead, the focus is on being able to use these applications without even looking at the jQuery code.

The Image Rollover application

Figure 15-12 presents a typical jQuery application that starts to show the power of jQuery. In short, when the user hovers the mouse pointer over one of the starting images, it is replaced by another image. And when the user moves the mouse pointer out of the image, the original image is again displayed. This is called an *image rollover*.

In case you're interested, this figure presents the jQuery code for this application. Quite complicated, isn't it. But you don't need to understand this code. Since the code is stored in a file named rollovers.js, you just need to code the two script statements that are shown in this figure in the head section of your document.

Then, to use this application, you need to code the HTML the way it's shown in this figure with img elements within the li elements of an unordered list that has "image_rollovers" as its id attribute. You also need to code the src attribute of each img element as the location of the original image and the id attribute as the location of the rollover image. Although this is an unorthodox use of the id attribute, it provides a simple way to implement the image rollovers.

Three images with the middle image rolled over

The JavaScript in the rollovers.js file

```
$(document).ready(function() {
    $("#image_rollovers img").each(function() {
        var oldURL = $(this).attr("src");          // gets the src attribute
        var newURL = $(this).attr("id");           // gets the id attribute
        var rolloverImage = new Image();
        rolloverImage.src = newURL;
        $(this).hover(
            function() {
                $(this).attr("src", newURL);       // sets the src attribute
            },
            function() {
                $(this).attr("src", oldURL);       // sets the src attribute
            }
        );  // end hover
    }); // end each
}); // end ready
```

The script elements for the external files in the head section of the HTML

```
<script src="jquery-2.1.3.js"></script>
<script src="rollovers.js"></script>
```

The HTML for the images

```
<main>
    <h1>Ram Tap Combined Test</h1>
    <ul id="image_rollovers">
        <li><img src="images/h1.jpg" alt="" id="images/h4.jpg"></li>
        <li><img src="images/h2.jpg" alt="" id="images/h5.jpg"></li>
        <li><img src="images/h3.jpg" alt="" id="images/h6.jpg"></li>
    </ul>
</main>
```

Description

- You don't need to understand the code in the rollovers.js file to use it. Just include the jQuery library and the JavaScript file in the head section of the HTML.
- Then, set the id of the ul element to "image _rollovers", and set the src attribute of each image to the starting image, and the id attribute to the rollover image.

Figure 15-12 The Image Rollover application in jQuery

The Image Swap application

Figure 15-13 presents another typical jQuery application that works like this: When the user clicks on one of the thumbnail images at the top of the browser window, the caption and image below the thumbnails are changed. This is called an *image swap*. This time, the jQuery for this application isn't shown.

To use this application, you again need to code the two script elements that are shown in this figure in the head section of your document. Then, you need to code the HTML for the elements as shown in this figure.

Here, img elements are used to display the six thumbnail images. However, these elements are coded within <a> elements so the images are clickable and they can receive the focus. In the <a> elements, the href attributes identify the images to be swapped when the links are clicked, and the title attributes provide the text for the related captions. In this case, both the <a> elements and the img elements are coded within a ul element.

After the ul element, you can see the h2 element for the caption and the img element for the main image on the page. The ids of these elements are highlighted because the jQuery will use those ids as it swaps captions and images into them.

For the motor-impaired, this HTML provides accessibility by coding the img elements for the thumbnails within <a> elements. That way, the user can access the thumbnail links by clicking on the Tab key, and the user can swap the image by pressing the Enter key when a thumbnail has the focus, which starts the click event.

Of note in the CSS for this page is the rule set for the li elements. Their display properties are set to inline so the images go from left to right instead of from top to bottom. Also, the padding on the right of each item is set to 10 pixels to provide space between the images.

The user interface for the Image Swap application

The script elements for the external files in the head section of the HTML

```
<script src="jquery-2.1.3.min.js"></script>
<script src="image_swaps.js"></script>
```

The HTML for the images

```
<main>
    <h1>Ram Tap Combined Test</h1>
    <ul id="image_list">
        <li><a href="images/h1.jpg" title="James Allison: 1-1">
            <img src="thumbnails/t1.jpg" alt=""></a></li>
        <li><a href="images/h2.jpg" title="James Allison: 1-2">
            <img src="thumbnails/t2.jpg" alt=""></a></li>
        ...
        ...
        <li><a href="images/h6.jpg" title="James Allison: 1-6">
            <img src="thumbnails/t6.jpg" alt=""></a></li>
    </ul>
    <h2 id="caption">James Allison 1-1</h2>
    <p><img src="images/h1.jpg" alt="" id="image"></p>
</main>
```

The CSS for the li elements

```
li {padding-right: 10px; display: inline; }
```

Description

- To use this application, set up the HTML as shown above, and set the id of the ul element to "image_list", the id of the h2 element below the ul element to "caption", and the id of the image element below that caption to "image".
- Next, set the href attribute for each <a> element in the unordered list to the large image, and the title attribute to its caption. Then, set the src attribute of each img element in the unordered list to the thumbnail image.

Figure 15-13 The Image Swap application in jQuery

A Slide Show application

Figure 15-14 presents one more example of an application that can be coded with jQuery. This is a Slide Show application that fades the old slide out and the new one in. Also, the slide show stops when the user clicks on the current image and restarts when the user clicks on it again.

To use this application, you code the script elements that are shown in the head section and set up the HTML as shown. In the div element in the HTML, you can see that five img elements provide the slides for the show, and each of these has an alt attribute that provides the caption that is shown above the slide. Note, however, that the slide show will work for as many images as you code in the div element.

Before the div element for the slides, an h2 element is used for the caption of each slide and an img element is used for the slide show. The id attributes for these elements should be "caption" and "slide", and these elements should contain the caption and slide for the first slide in the series. The id for the div element that follows should be "slides".

In the CSS that's shown for this application, the display property of all of the img elements in the div element named "slides" is set to "none". This means that those img elements will be loaded into the browser when the page is loaded, but they won't be displayed.

A Slide Show application with fading out and fading in

The script elements for the external files in the head section of the HTML

```
<script src="jquery-2.1.3.min.js"></script>
<script src="slide_show.js"></script>
```

The HTML for the slide show

```
<section>
    <h1>Fishing Slide Show</h1>
    <h2 id="caption">Casting on the Upper Kings</h2>
    <img id="slide" src="images/casting1.jpg" alt="">
    <div id="slides">
        <img src="images/casting1.jpg" alt="Casting on the Upper Kings">
        <img src="images/casting2.jpg" alt="Casting on the Lower Kings">
        <img src="images/catchrelease.jpg"
             alt="Catch and Release on the Big Horn">
        <img src="images/fish.jpg" alt="Catching on the South Fork">
        <img src="images/lures.jpg" alt="The Lures for Catching">
    </div>
</section>
```

The critical CSS for the slide show

```
#slides img {
    display: none;
}
```

Description

- To use this application, set the ids for the h2 element, the main img element, and the div element to “caption”, “slide”, and “slides”.
- Then, put the images for the slide show in the “slides” div element, and set the alt attribute for each image to the caption that will be displayed in the slide show.

Figure 15-14 The Slide Show application in jQuery

Websites for JavaScript and jQuery code

You can, of course, use any of the JavaScript and jQuery code in the applications that you've just reviewed because the code is available in the downloadable applications for this book. But you should also know that many websites provide JavaScript and jQuery code that you can use in your programs, and much of it is free.

In figure 15-15, for example, you can see a web page that offers free JavaScript code for doing Image Slideshows. This web page is on the Dynamic Drive website, and it's one of my favorite sites for getting JavaScript code. The other is The JavaScript Source website.

To find sites like this, you can search for "free javascript code" or "jquery code examples". Often, these sites provide JavaScript and jQuery for games and special effects that you can easily add to your site. Remember, though, that you don't want to distract the users of your site from doing what you see as the primary goals of your site.

One of the problems with the code that you get from websites like this is that it can be difficult to figure out how to use, especially if you don't understand JavaScript. Another problem is that websites like this often provide code that you embed in your HTML, instead of code that's in separate JavaScript files, and that can make your code more difficult to create, test, and maintain.

With these problems in mind, it still makes sense to search for free JavaScript and jQuery code, especially if you're looking for code that does a specific function. Eventually, though, you should learn how to do your own JavaScript and jQuery programming. That will not only make it easier for you to use the code that you get from JavaScript websites, but it will also let you write your own code if you can't find what you want.

A website that offers free JavaScript code

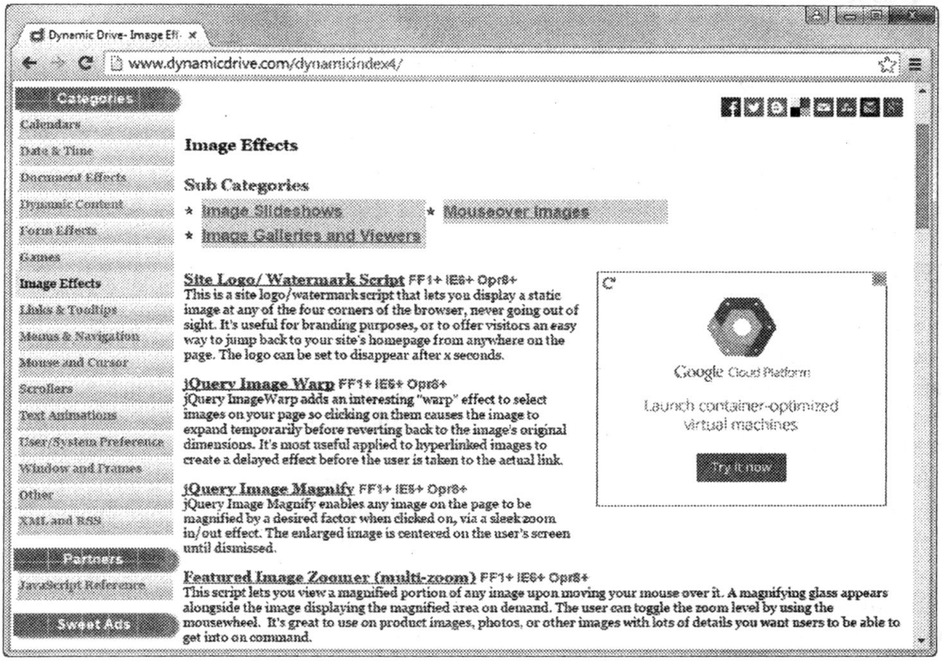

Zak's recommendations for JavaScript websites

- Dynamic Drive (http://www.dynamicdrive.com)
- The JavaScript Source (http://javascript.internet.com)

Description

- Many websites provide JavaScript and jQuery code that you can download or cut-and-paste into your web pages. Most of these sites also provide instructions for using that code.
- To find sites that provide JavaScript code, you can search for terms like "free javascript code" or "jquery code examples".
- These sites often provide code for special effects or games that you can add to your site. Remember, though, to keep your focus on the goals of your website.
- One of the problems with the code that you get from these sites is that it is often hard to figure out how to use it. Another problem is that these sites often provide code that you embed in your HTML, but that can make your code more difficult to create and maintain.

Figure 15-15 Websites for JavaScript and jQuery code

Perspective

Now that you've completed this chapter, you should be able to use tested JavaScript and jQuery code to enhance your web pages. Eventually, though, you should take the time to learn how to do your own programming. That way, you will not only be able to make better use of existing code, but you will also be able to write your own code so it works just the way you want it to. To learn all of that, please consider *Murach's JavaScript and jQuery*.

Terms

JavaScript
JavaScript engine
client-side processing
server-side processing
DOM (Document Object Model)
node
element node
text node
attribute node
comment node
DOM scripting
scripting the DOM
document object
event
event handler
data validation
jQuery
CDN (Content Delivery Network)
jQuery selector
jQuery method
jQuery event method
image rollover
image swap

Summary

- *JavaScript* is a scripting language that is run by the *JavaScript engine* of a browser. As a result, the work is done on the client, not the server, and that takes some of the processing burden off the server.
- To embed JavaScript code or to include JavaScript files in an HTML document, you code a script element. If a script element is coded in the body of a document, it is replaced by the output of the JavaScript code.
- The *DOM* (*Document Object Model*) is a hierarchical collection of *nodes* in the web browser's memory that represents the current web page. The DOM for each page is built as the page is loaded.
- *DOM scripting* is the process of changing the DOM by using JavaScript. When the DOM changes, the browser immediately displays the results of the change.
- An *event* is an action the user performs, like clicking on a button or image. When an event occurs, it can be handled by JavaScript code known as an *event handler*.
- *jQuery* is a JavaScript library that makes JavaScript programming easier. To use jQuery, you code a script element in the head section that either includes a downloaded jQuery file or accesses it through a *Content Delivery Network* (*CDN*).

- When you code statements that use jQuery, you use *selectors* that are like those for CSS. You also use jQuery *methods* and *event methods*.

Exercise 15-1 Enhance a page with JavaScript

In the exercises for this section, you'll be working with a third version of the Town Hall website. In this exercise, you'll make two JavaScript enhancements to the speaker's page for Scott Sampson:

Open the HTML and CSS files for this page

1. Use your text editor to open the HTML file for this page:
   `c:\html5_css3_2\exercises\town_hall_3\speakers\sampson.html`
2. Run the page in your browser to see that it looks like the one above, but without the Print Page button.

Add the Print Page button

3. With figure 15-5 as a guide, add the script element for the external printPage.js file that's in the javascript folder. Then, add the Print Page button to the page at the top of the aside, and be sure to set its id to "printButton".
4. Test this enhancement. If it doesn't work, make sure that you have the script element and the button id coded correctly.
5. When you get this working, note that the formatting of the button isn't the same as above. To fix that, adjust the CSS file for the page, and test again.
6. If you preview the printing for this page, you'll see that the Print Page button will be printed. If you've already read chapter 13 and know how to fix this, adjust the media query for the printed page so the button isn't printed.

Automatically update the year in the footer

7. With figure 15-1 as a guide, use JavaScript to get the current year and put it into the copyright line in the footer. Then, test this change.

Exercise 15-2 Use jQuery for image swaps

In this exercise, you'll enhance a page so it uses jQuery to do image swaps. That page will look like the one below, which is the page that's displayed when you click on the Speakers link in the navigation bar. Then, when the user clicks on a small image, a larger image of that speaker is displayed below the small images.

Open the HTML and CSS files for this page

1. Use your text editor to open the HTML file for this page:
   c:\html5_css3_2\exercises\town_hall_3\image_swaps.html
2. Look in the head section of the HTML file to see that it contains two script elements that load the jQuery library and the JavaScript file for this application. Then, test this page to see that it looks okay, but it doesn't work.

Modify the HTML so the image swaps work

3. Using figure 15-13 as a guide, modify the HTML so it should work. You can assume that the ul element is coded correctly, so the problem is elsewhere.
4. When the image swaps are working, try each one and note that the caption for Amy Chua is incorrect. So there actually is a problem somewhere within the ul element. Now, fix this.

16

How to use jQuery UI and jQuery plugins to enhance your web pages

The easiest way to add common features like accordions, tabs, and carousels to your web pages is to use jQuery UI and jQuery plugins. In this chapter, you'll learn how to do that. As you will see, both of these approaches use the jQuery library that you learned about in the last chapter.

Introduction to jQuery UI

To get you started with jQuery UI, you'll first learn what it is, where to get it, how to download it, and how to add it to your web pages.

What jQuery UI is and where to get it

jQuery UI (User Interface) is a free, open-source, JavaScript library that extends the use of the jQuery library by providing higher-level features that you can use with a minimum of code. To provide those features, the jQuery UI library uses the jQuery library. In fact, you can think of jQuery UI as the official plugin library for jQuery.

Figure 16-1 shows the home page and the URL for the jQuery UI website. That's the site where you can download jQuery UI. The quickest way to do that is to just click on the Stable button in the Quick Downloads box on the right of the page.

This figure also summarizes the four types of features that jQuery UI provides. *Widgets* are features like accordions, tabs, and date pickers. These are the jQuery features that developers use the most, and you'll learn how to use four of the widgets in this chapter.

Themes provide the formatting for widgets, and they are implemented by a CSS style sheet that's part of the jQuery UI download. *Interactions* and *effects* are less-used features, so you won't learn how to use them in this chapter.

The jQuery UI website

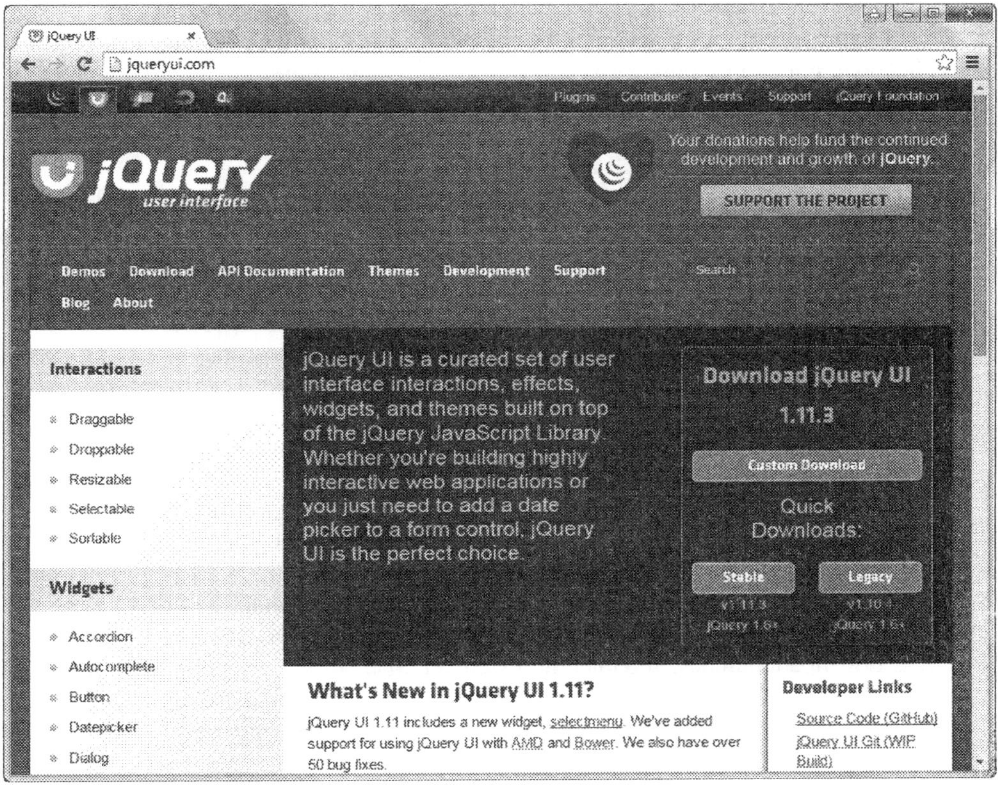

The URL for jQuery UI

`http://jqueryui.com/`

The four types of features provided by jQuery UI

Name	Description
Widgets	Accordions, tabs, date pickers, and more.
Themes	24 predefined themes as well as a ThemeRoller application that lets you create a custom theme. A theme is implemented by a CSS style sheet.
Interactions	Draggable, droppable, resizable, and more.
Effects	Color animations, class transitions, and more.

Description

- *jQuery UI* is a free, open-source, JavaScript library that extends the jQuery library by providing higher-level features. jQuery UI uses jQuery and can be thought of as the official plugin library for jQuery.
- The jQuery UI website can be accessed by the URL above.

Figure 16-1 What jQuery UI is and where to get it

How to download jQuery UI

Figure 16-2 shows how to build a custom jQuery UI download and download it to your computer. When you're learning how to use jQuery UI, though, you can just click the Stable button under Quick Downloads on the right side of the home page that's shown in the previous figure. Then, you can experiment with all of the jQuery UI features.

For production websites, though, it's better to build a custom download that includes only the components that are required. That will reduce the time that it takes to load jQuery UI into a browser. If, for example, you're only going to use a few of the widgets and you're not going to use the Dialog widget, you can uncheck all of the other widgets, the interactions, and the effects. However, if a component like a widget requires other components like interactions or effects, a message will be displayed that lets you know what you need. Then, you can respond accordingly.

In this figure, you can see some of the folders and files that are included in a typical jQuery download. For widgets, you only need the jquery-ui.min.css file, the jquery-ui.min.js file (the jQuery UI library), and the images in the images folder. The min files are compressed versions of the CSS and jQuery UI files, which are smaller than the uncompressed versions.

A jQuery UI download also includes the jQuery library in the external folder, an index.html file that displays a page that demonstrates the features that your download includes, and uncompressed versions of the CSS and jQuery files. You can use these versions if you want to see the code in these files. And you can use the jQuery library file if you haven't already downloaded jQuery and aren't using a CDN to get the jQuery library.

Last, the download includes structure and theme CSS files. However, all of the rule sets for these files are included in the core CSS file. As a result, you don't need these files unless you want to use only the structure or theme rule sets.

How to include jQuery UI in your web pages

To include the jQuery UI CSS and JavaScript files in a web page, you use the link and script elements that are shown in this figure. Here, the link element points to the min version of the CSS file. Then, the first script element points to the CDN address for the jQuery library (it doesn't use the downloaded jQuery file). And the second script element points to the min version of the jQuery UI file. But note that the script element for the jQuery UI file must follow the script element for the jQuery file because jQuery UI uses jQuery.

The last script element either points to the developer's external JavaScript file or it contains the JavaScript code. If the code that's needed is short, it is often embedded within the script element in the HTML document. Otherwise, an external JavaScript file can be used.

The link and script elements in this example assume that the jQuery UI folders and files are kept in the top-level folder that's downloaded. But you can organize the downloaded files in the way that you think is best for your applications. You can see this in the downloaded applications for this chapter.

The primary folders and files in a full jQuery UI download

Name	Type	Compressed size	Pass...	Size
external	File folder			
images	File folder			
index.html	Chrome HTML Document	5 KB	No	31 KB
jquery-ui.css	Cascading Style Sheet Document	10 KB	No	35 KB
jquery-ui.js	JS File	141 KB	No	459 KB
jquery-ui.min.css	Cascading Style Sheet Document	9 KB	No	30 KB
jquery-ui.min.js	JS File	78 KB	No	234 KB

How to build a custom jQuery UI library and download its files

1. From the home page, click the Download link in the navigation bar or the Custom Download button. That will take you to the Download Builder page.
2. Select or deselect the interactions, widgets, and effects until the checked boxes identify the components that you want in your download.
3. If you want to select a theme for the download, use the drop-down list at the bottom of the page. Or, if you want to build a custom theme, click on the link above the list.
4. After you select a theme or design a custom theme, click the Download button to download a zipped folder that contains the jQuery UI files.

How to include the downloaded files in your application

```
<!-- link elements for the jQuery UI stylesheets -->
<link rel="stylesheet" href="/jquery-ui-1.11.2/jquery-ui.min.css">

<!-- the script elements for the jQuery and jQuery UI libraries -->
<script src="http://code.jquery.com/jquery-2.1.3.min.js"></script>
<script src="/jquery-ui-1.11.2/jquery-ui.min.js"></script>

<!-- the script element for your external JavaScript file or your code -->
<script></script>
```

Description

- A jQuery UI download consists of a zip file that contains the CSS files, the images for the theme that has been selected, the jQuery UI files, and an HTML document that demonstrates the components in the download.
- The only folders and files that you have to include in your pages are the images folder and the min (compressed) versions of the first CSS file and the jQuery UI file.
- The external folder in a download includes the jQuery library file.
- The download also includes full and compressed versions of structure and theme CSS files, but you don't need them because the jquery-ui.css and jquery-ui.min.css files include the rule sets in both the structure and theme files.
- When you're building a download for a web page, you can keep the file sizes smaller by selecting just the widgets, interactions, and effects that the web page needs.

Figure 16-2 How to download jQuery UI and include it in your web pages

How to use any jQuery UI widget

The next three figures show how to use four of the widgets in their basic forms. That may be all the information that you need for using these widgets in your own web pages. All of these widgets, however, provide options, events, and methods that go beyond what these figures present. So, if you want to see how else these widgets can be used, you can review the jQuery UI documentation for the widgets, which is excellent.

For instance, figure 16-3 shows how to use the documentation for the Accordion widget. A good way to start is to click on the names of the examples in the right side bar to see how the widget can be used. Then, you can click on the View Source link to see the source code that makes the example work. After that, you can review the options, methods, and events for the widget by clicking on the API Documentation link. (These two links aren't shown here.)

After you're comfortable with the way a widget works, you're ready to implement it on a web page, which you do in three stages. First, you code the link and script elements for jQuery UI in the head element of the HTML as shown in the previous figure. Second, you code the required HTML for the widget. Third, you code the jQuery for running the widget.

Beyond that, though, you must make sure that the jQuery UI images folder and the jQuery CSS file have the relationship shown in this figure. That is that the jQuery CSS file must be at the same level as the images folder because that's where it looks to get the images that it requires.

In the jQuery example in this figure, you can see the general structure for the jQuery code that's required for a widget. First, the code for using the widget is within the ready event handler. Second, a jQuery selector is used to select the HTML element that's used for the widget. Third, the method for running the widget is called. Fourth, any options for the widget are coded within the braces for the method.

The accordion documentation on the jQuery UI website

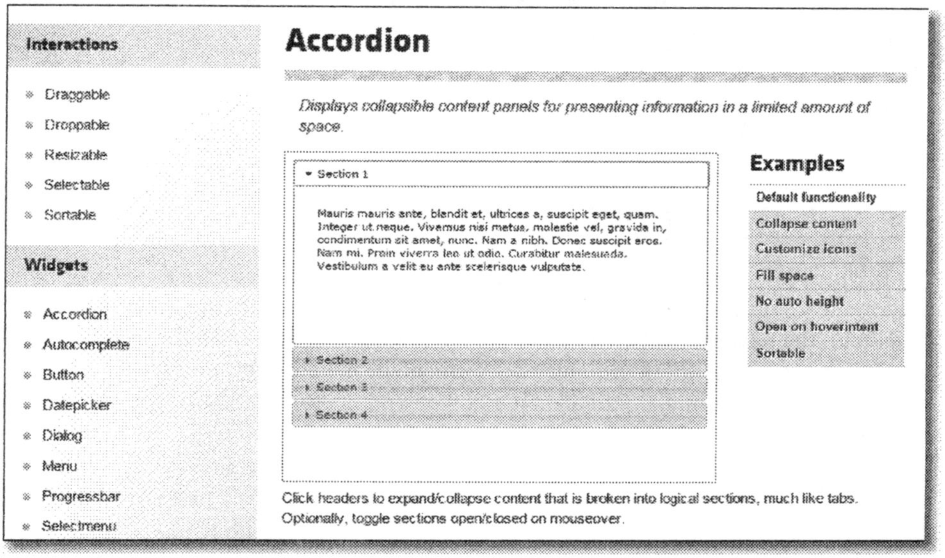

How to use the jQuery UI documentation

- In the left sidebar, click on a widget name to display its documentation.
- In the right sidebar, click on an example name to see a working example, then click on the View Source link to see the code for the example.
- Click the API Documentation link to display information about the widget's options, methods, and events.

The images folder and jquery-ui.min.css relationship that jQuery UI expects

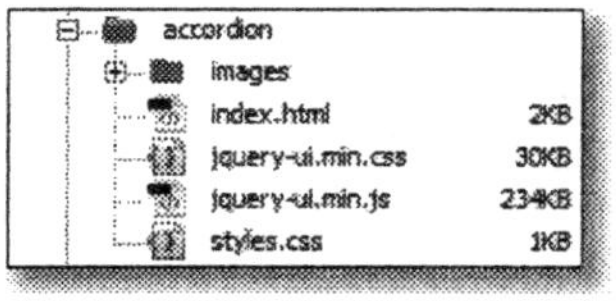

The jQuery for using a widget

```
$(document).ready(function(){
    $("selector").widgetMethod({
        // option settings
    });
});
```

Description

- To use a jQuery UI *widget*, you code the HTML and jQuery for the widget. In the jQuery, you code a selector, the method to be used, and the options.
- For a widget that requires images, jQuery UI expects the CSS file and the images folder to be at the same level.

Figure 16-3 How to use any jQuery UI widget

How to use four of the most popular jQuery UI widgets

In the topics that follow, you'll learn how to use four of the most popular widgets that are currently supported by jQuery UI.

How to use the Accordion widget

Figure 16-4 shows how to use an Accordion widget, which consists of two or more headings and the contents for those headings. By default, an accordion starts with the panel for the first heading displayed, and only one panel can be open at a time. Then, when the user clicks on one of the other headings, the contents for that heading are displayed and the contents for the first heading are hidden.

As the HTML in this figure shows, an Accordion widget consists of a top-level div element that contains one h3 element and one div element for each item in the accordion.

In the jQuery for an accordion, you select the top-level div element of the accordion and call the accordion method with or without options. Often, you'll use this method without options because its defaults work the way you want them to.

In the example in this figure, though, three options are coded. First, the event option changes the event that causes the contents of a heading to be displayed from the "click" to the "mouseover" (hover) event. Second, the heightStyle option is set to "content" so the height of the open panels is based on the height of the content. Third, the collapsible option is set to true, which means that all of the panels can be closed at the same time.

Although the basic formatting for an accordion is done by the CSS style sheet for jQuery UI, you can use your own style sheet to format the contents of a panel. In fact, you usually need to do that when the panel consists of several different types of HTML elements.

Because the jQuery code in this example is typical of the code for all widgets, this is a good time to take a close look at it. As you can see, this code uses parentheses, braces, commas, colons, and semi-colons in a way that can be bewildering to new programmers, and every punctuation mark is required for this code to work.

For that reason, it's usually easiest to copy a block of code like this into your script and modify it for whatever widget you're going to use. In general, you just change the selector for the widget, the method name, and the options. For the options, you code the name of the option before the colon and the value after it, with a comma after every option setting but the last one.

An Accordion widget

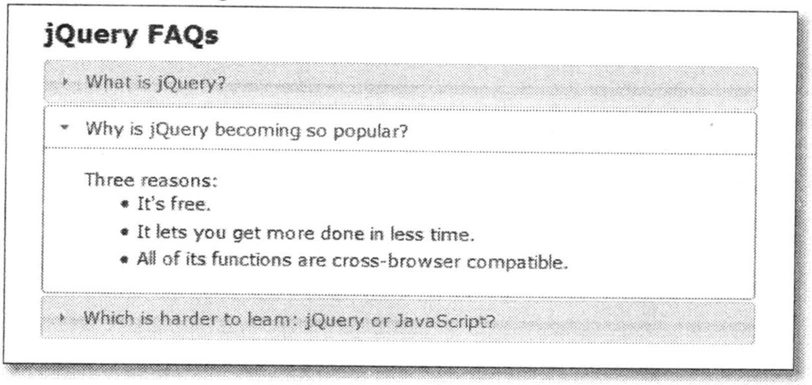

The HTML for the accordion

```
<div id="accordion">
    <h3>What is jQuery?</a>
    <div><!-- the content for the panel --></div>

    <h3>Why is jQuery becoming so popular?</h3>
    <div><!-- the content for the panel --></div>

    <h3>Which is harder to learn: jQuery or JavaScript?</h3>
    <div><!-- the content for the panel --></div>
</div>
```

The jQuery for the accordion

```
$(document).ready(function(){
    $("#accordion").accordion({
        event: "mouseover",
        heightStyle: "content",
        collapsible: true
    });
});
```

Description

- The HTML consists of h3 elements that provide the headers for the panels, followed by div elements that contain the contents for the panels. These elements should be within an outer div element that represents the accordion.
- In the jQuery, the accordion method is used to implement the accordion widget for the div element that represents the accordion.
- By default, a panel is opened when its header is clicked, one panel always has to be open, and all the panels open to the same size. But you can change that by setting options for the accordion method.
- The basic formatting of the accordion is done by the CSS file for jQuery UI, but you can use your style sheet to format the contents within the panels, and you can modify the jQuery UI style sheet to change the appearance of the accordion.

Figure 16-4 How to use the Accordion widget

How to use the Tabs widget

Figure 16-5 shows how to use the Tabs widget. This widget has the same general function as an Accordion widget, but it displays the contents of a panel when the related tab is clicked.

As this figure shows, the HTML for a Tabs widget consists of a top-level div element that represents the widget. Then, this element contains an unordered list that contains the headings for the tabs, followed by one div element for each tab that contains the content of the tab. To relate the tab headings to their respective div elements, the href attributes of the <a> elements within the li elements are set to the ids of the div elements.

To activate a Tabs widget with jQuery, you just select the top-level div element and call the tabs method. Usually, you don't need to set any options because the defaults work the way you want them to. However, you might want to use the event option to change the event for opening a tab from the click event to mouseover, which can work well with tabs.

Here again, the basic formatting for a Tabs widget is done by the CSS style sheet for jQuery UI. However, you can use your own style sheet to format the contents of a panel. In fact, you usually need to do that when the panel consists of several different types of HTML elements.

A Tabs widget

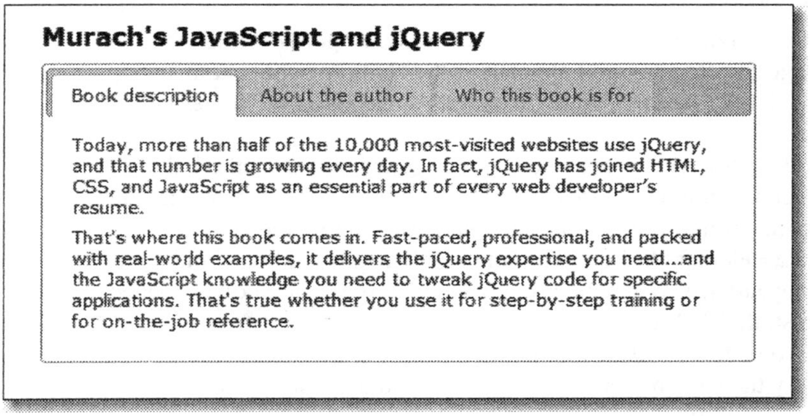

The HTML for the tabs

```
<div id="tabs">
    <ul>
        <li><a href="#tabs-1">Book description</a></li>
        <li><a href="#tabs-2">About the author</a></li>
        <li><a href="#tabs-3">Who this book is for</a></li>
    </ul>
    <div id="tabs-1"><!-- the content --></div>
    <div id="tabs-2"><!-- the content --></div>
    <div id="tabs-3"><!-- the content --></div>
</div>
```

The jQuery for the tabs

```
$(document).ready(function(){
    $("#tabs").tabs();
});
```

Description

- The HTML should consist of a div element that contains an unordered list that represents the tabs, followed by div elements that contain the contents for the tabs.
- The heading for each tab should be in an <a> element within an li element of the list. The href attribute for each tab should point to the id of the div element that contains the contents for the tab.
- In the jQuery, the tabs method is used to implement the Tabs widget for the div element that represents the tabs. By default, a tab is switched to when its header is clicked.
- The basic formatting of the tabs is done by the CSS for jQuery UI, but you can use your own CSS to format the contents within the panels.

How to use the Button and Dialog widgets

Figure 16-6 shows how the Button and Dialog widgets work. The HTML for a Button widget is often an input element of the "button" type, but this widget also works with the "submit", "reset", "radio", and "checkbox" types, and with <a> elements too.

When a Button widget is activated by the jQuery button method, the HTML is converted into a button that uses the jQuery UI theme. Other than that, the button works its normal way. In the example in this figure, the Button widget is coded as an <a> element that contains an img element for a book, and jQuery UI changes its appearance. When the user clicks on it, the dialog box is opened.

In contrast, the HTML for a Dialog widget consists of a div element that contains the contents for the dialog box. The title attribute of this element can be used to specify the heading for the dialog box. And the contents of this element can contain any HTML elements.

When the dialog box is displayed, it is both draggable and resizable. This means that you can drag the box by its title bar, and you can resize the box by dragging the resize handle in the lower right corner. You can also close the box by clicking on the "X" icon in the upper right corner.

To display a Dialog widget with jQuery, you use the dialog method. If, for example, you want to display a dialog box right after a page is ready, you select the div element for the dialog box and call the dialog method. If you want the user to have to close the dialog box before continuing, you can also set the *modal* option to true.

Usually, though, you want to open a dialog box when some event occurs, like clicking on a Button widget. Then, you use the jQuery code that's shown in this figure. First, the button method is called to convert the HTML for the button to a Button widget. Then, an event handler for the click event of the button is set up. Within that event handler, the dialog method of the dialog box is called to display the box. Here, the modal option is set to true so the user has to close the dialog box before proceeding. That's why the page behind the dialog box in this figure is dimmed.

You may also need to use some of the other options for a Dialog widget. If, for example, you want to change the height or width of the dialog box, you can set the height or width option. If you don't want the dialog box to be draggable and resizable, you can set those options to false. You can also use the title option to set the title for a dialog box if you don't want to use the title attribute for that purpose.

Incidentally, the Dialog widget is generally considered to be a nice improvement over the JavaScript technique for opening another window and using it as a dialog box. That's especially true because most browsers have built-in features for blocking popup windows.

A Button widget that activates a Dialog widget

The HTML for the Button and Dialog widgets

```
<a id="book"><img src="images/jquery.jpg" alt="jQuery book"/></a>
<div id="dialog" title="JavaScript and jQuery" style="display:none;">
    <!-- the contents for the dialog box -->
</div>
```

The jQuery for the Button and Dialog widgets

```
$(document).ready(function(){
    $("#book").button();
    $("#book").click(function() {
        $("#dialog").dialog({
            modal: true
        });
    });
});
```

Description

- The HTML for a Button widget can be an input element with any of these type attributes: button, submit, reset, radio, or checkbox. It can also be an <a> element. When activated, jQuery UI styles a Button widget so it looks like a button.
- The HTML for a Dialog widget consists of a div element that contains the contents for the dialog box. The title attribute can be used to provide the heading for the dialog box.
- To prevent the Dialog widget from appearing when the page loads, set its display property to "none".
- In the jQuery, use the button method to activate the Button widget. Then, in the click event handler for the button, use the dialog method to display the Dialog widget.
- jQuery UI provides many options for Dialog widgets. For instance, if the *modal* option is set to true, the box must be closed before the user can proceed. And the width option can be used to change the width of the box from its default of 300 pixels.
- By default, a dialog box is resizable and draggable, but you can change those options by setting them to false.

Figure 16-6 How to use the Button and Dialog widgets

Introduction to jQuery plugins

In this introduction, you'll learn how to find and use jQuery plugins. A *jQuery plugin* is just a jQuery application that does one web task or a set of related web tasks. A plugin makes use of the jQuery library, and most plugins can be used with limited knowledge of JavaScript and jQuery.

How to find jQuery plugins

Figure 16-7 starts with a screen capture that shows the results of a Google search for "jquery plugin rotator". Often, doing a search like this is the best way to find what you're looking for. Note, however, that the search entry includes the word *jquery* because there are other types of plugins.

Another way to find the type of plugin that you're looking for is to go to the URLs for the websites in the table in this figure. The first one is for the jQuery Plugin Repository, which is part of the jQuery website, and the second one is for a site that is only for jQuery plugins.

In contrast, the next three websites are repositories for many types of code, including jQuery plugins. As a result, you must search for jQuery plugins to find what you want on these sites.

In most cases, jQuery plugins are free or are available for a small price or donation. Besides that, jQuery plugins can often be used by non-programmers, and they can save you many hours of development time if you are a JavaScript programmer. For those reasons, it makes sense to look for a plugin whenever you need to add a common function to your website.

This figure also summarizes some of the most useful plugins for displaying images and running slide shows, carousels, and galleries. You'll see three of these illustrated in the pages that follow.

A Google search for a jQuery plugin

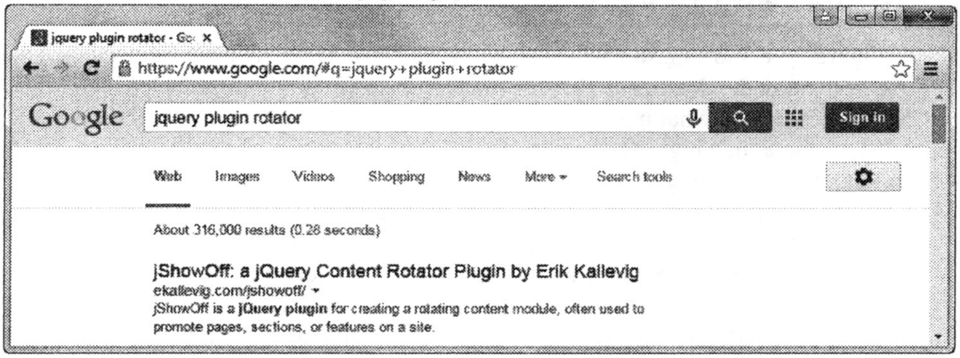

Websites for finding jQuery plugins

Site name	URL
jQuery Plugin Repository	http://plugins.jquery.com
jQuery Plugins	http://www.jqueryplugins.com
Google Code	http://code.google.com
GitHub	https://github.com
Sourceforge	http://sourceforge.net

Popular plugins for displaying images

Lightbox	http://lokeshdhakar.com/projects/lightbox2/
Fancybox	http://fancybox.net
ThickBox	http://jquery.com/demo/thickbox
Shadowbox.js	http://www.shadowbox-js.com

Popular plugins for slide shows, carousels, and galleries

bxSlider	http://bxslider.com
Malsup jQuery Cycle 2	http://jquery.malsup.com/cycle2
jCarousel	http://sorgalla.com/jcarousel
Nivo Slider	http://nivo.dev7studios.com
Galleria	http://galleria.io

Description

- jQuery *plugins* are JavaScript applications that extend the functionality of jQuery. These plugins require the use of the core jQuery library.
- Some of the websites that provide jQuery plugins are listed above. Often, though, you can find what you're looking for by searching the Internet.
- Plugins are available for dozens of web functions like slide shows, carousels, and data validation. In general, if you can find a plugin for doing what you want, that's usually better than writing the jQuery code yourself.

Figure 16-7 How to find jQuery plugins

How to use any jQuery plugin

Figure 16-8 shows how to use any plugin after you find the one you want. First, you study the documentation for the plugin so you know what HTML and CSS it requires and what methods and options it provides. Usually, you'll do this as you evaluate the plugin to see if it does what you want and if its documentation tells you everything you need to know.

Second, you usually download the files for the plugin and save them on your web server. This download is often in the form of a zip file, and it will always include at least one JavaScript file. In addition, it may include CSS or image files that are used by the plugin.

The download may also include two versions of the main JavaScript file for the plugin. If you want to review the code for the file, you can open the full version in your text editor. But the one you should use for your applications is the compressed version, which usually has a name that ends with min.js.

For some plugins, the files are also available from a Content Delivery Network (CDN). If you want to access the files that way, you can record the URLs for the files. Then, you can use those URLs in the link and script elements for the files.

Third, if a plugin requires one or more CSS files, you code the link elements for them in the head element of the HTML. Then, you code the script elements for the JavaScript files for the plugin. Usually, only one JavaScript file is required, but some plugins require more than one.

Fourth, if the download includes a folder for images, you need to make sure the folder has the right structural relationship with the CSS and JavaScript files for the plugin. Otherwise, you may have to adjust the CSS or JavaScript code so it can find the images folder (and you probably don't want to do that).

At this point, you're ready to use the plugin. So, fifth, you code the HTML and CSS for the plugin. And sixth, you code the JavaScript for using the plugin. This can be in an external file or it can be within the head element of the HTML.

This procedure is illustrated by the example in this figure, which uses the bxSlider plugin. Here, the script elements show that the element for the plugin must come after the element for the jQuery library. That's because all jQuery plugins use the jQuery library. As the first caution in this figure points out, not coding these script elements in this sequence is a common error.

The HTML that follows shows the elements that the plugin requires. In particular, the id attribute for the unordered list is set to "slider" so the jQuery code can select that element when it calls the bxSlider method of the plugin. Also, the title attributes for the img elements are set to the captions for the slides.

This is followed by the jQuery code for using this plugin. As you can see, it is like the code for using a jQuery UI widget. Here, the bxSlider method is called as the first statement within the function for the ready method for the document. This method name is followed by a set of braces that contains the code for setting four options for this method.

Before you continue, note the second caution in this figure, which is that some plugins won't work with the latest version of jQuery. So if a plugin doesn't work, you should check its documentation to see what version of jQuery it uses.

General steps for using a plugin within your web pages

1. Study the documentation for the plugin so you know what HTML and CSS it requires as well as what methods and options it provides.
2. If the plugin file or files are available via a Content Delivery Network (CDN) and you want to access them that way, get the URLs for them. Otherwise, download the file or files for the plugin, and save them in one of the folders of your website.
3. In the head element of the HTML for a page that will use the plugin, code the link elements for any CSS files that are required. Also, code the script elements for the JavaScript files that are required. These script elements must be after the one for the jQuery library because all jQuery plugins use that library.
4. If the download for a plugin includes an images folder, make sure the folder has the right structural relationship with both the CSS and JavaScript files for the plugin.
5. Code the HTML and CSS for the page so it is appropriate for the plugin.
6. If necessary, write the jQuery code that uses the methods and options of the plugin.

The script elements for the jQuery library and the bxSlider plugin

```
<!-- the script element for the core jQuery library -->
<script src="http://code.jquery.com/jquery-2.1.3.min.js"></script>
<!-- the script element for the plugin when it has been downloaded -->
<script src="js/jquery.bxSlider.min.js"></script>
```

The HTML for the bxSlider plugin

```
<ul id="slider">
    <li><img src="images/building_01.jpg" alt="" title="Front"></li>
    <li><img src="images/building_02.jpg" alt="" title="Left sideli>
    ...
</ul>
```

The jQuery for using the bxSlider plugin

```
$(document).ready(function(){
    $("#slider").bxSlider({
        minSlides: 2,
        maxSlides: 2,
        slideWidth: 250,
        slideMargin: 10
    });
});
```

Two cautions

- Make sure that you include a script element for jQuery and make sure that the script element for the plugin comes after it. Not doing one or the other is a common error.
- Some plugins won't work with the latest version of jQuery. So if you have any problems with a plugin, check its documentation to see which version of jQuery it requires.

Description

- Some plugins can be accessed via a CDN, but most must be downloaded and stored on your server.

Figure 16-8 How to use any jQuery plugin

How to use three of the most popular plugins

Now, you'll get a close-up view of three of the most useful plugins. This will introduce you to the power of plugins. It will also show you how the procedure in the last figure works with specific plugins.

How to use the Lightbox plugin for images

Figure 16-9 presents the Lightbox plugin. This is a popular plugin that displays a larger version of a thumbnail image when the user clicks the thumbnail image. This image is displayed in a modal dialog box, which means that it must be closed before the user can continue. The image in this box has a thick white border, and it may have a caption below it. The part of the web page that's outside of the dialog box is darkened. To close the dialog box, the user clicks on the "X" in the bottom right corner.

If images are grouped in sets, this plugin not only displays the dialog box for the thumbnail, it also displays the image number and total number of images below the image, as in "Image 3 of 5". Also, when the mouse hovers over the left or right side of an image, previous and next icons are displayed. Then, if the user clicks on an icon, the display is moved to the previous or next image.

As the link and script elements in this example show, this plugin requires both CSS and JavaScript files. These elements use the names of the downloaded files. Remember, though, that the script element for the plugin must come after the script element for the jQuery library.

The download also includes an img folder that contains the images used by the plugin. Here again, you must maintain the proper relationship between the img folder and the JavaScript and CSS files for this plugin.

Next, this figure shows the HTML for using this plugin. Here, img elements that represent the thumbnail images are coded within <a> elements. To make this work, each <a> element must have an href attribute that identifies the related large image and a data-lightbox attribute that activates the Lightbox plugin.

If you're using the Lightbox plugin with independent images, the value of the data-lightbox attribute should be unique for each <a> element. On the other hand, if you're using this plugin with a set of related images as shown here, the value of this attribute should be the same for all <a> elements. The last attribute shown here, data-title, provides a caption for each image.

Once all of that's done, you're done, because you don't have to initiate the Lightbox plugin by calling one of its methods. In other words, no JavaScript code is required. It just works!

A Lightbox after the user has clicked on a thumbnail image to start it

The URL for the Lightbox website

http://lokeshdhakar.com/projects/lightbox2/

The link and script elements for the Lightbox plugin

```
<link href="styles.css" rel="stylesheet">
<link href="css/lightbox.css" rel="stylesheet">
<script src="http://code.jquery.com/jquery-2.1.3.min.js"></script>
<script src="js/lightbox.min.js"></script>
```

The HTML for the images used by the Lightbox plugin

```
<a href="images/building_01.jpg" data-lightbox="vecta" data-title="Front">
    <img src="images/building_01_thumb.jpg" alt=""></a>
<a href="images/building_02.jpg" data-lightbox="vecta" data-title="Left side">
    <img src="images/building_02_thumb.jpg" alt=""></a>
...
```

Description

- The Lightbox plugin can be used to display larger versions of thumbnail images. The Lightbox starts when the user clicks one of the thumbnail images.
- When the user clicks on a thumbnail image within a set of images, the rest of the page is darkened and a larger version of the image is displayed with a counter and a caption. Then, if the mouse pointer moves over the larger image, next or previous icons appear.
- The Lightbox download includes a CSS file, a plugin file, and an img folder that contains an image for loading and images for the close, next, and previous icons.
- The HTML for a Lightbox consists of img elements within <a> elements. The src attributes of the image elements identify the thumbnail images, and the href attributes of the <a> elements identify the larger images.
- The data-lightbox attributes of the <a> elements activate Lightbox. Their values should be unique for independent images but the same for a group of images.
- The data-title attributes of the <a> elements can be used to provide captions.

Figure 16-9 How to use the Lightbox plugin for images

How to use the bxSlider plugin for carousels

Figure 16-10 shows how to use the bxSlider plugin for creating carousels. In this example, this plugin displays two images at a time, it slides from one set of images to the next automatically, it provides captions in the slides, it provides controls below the carousel, and you can move to the next or previous image by clicking on the right or left icon that's displayed.

If you download the JavaScript file for this plugin, the script element can refer to it as shown in this figure. As part of this download, you also get a CSS file and an images folder that contains the images that can be used with this plugin.

One way to set up the HTML for use with this plugin is shown in this figure. Here, img elements are coded within the li elements of an unordered list. Then, the src attributes of the img elements identify the images that are displayed, and the title attributes provide the captions.

To run the bxSlider plugin, you use the jQuery code in this figure. Within the ready function, the selector selects the ul element that contains the slides and executes the bxSlider method.

Within that method, several options are set. The auto option makes the carousel run automatically, the autoControls option puts the controls below the carousel, the captions option causes the title attributes to be used for captions, the minSlides and maxSlides options set the carousel so 2 slides are always displayed, and the slideWidth and slideMargin options set the size of the slides and the space between them.

These options show just some of the capabilities of this plugin. To learn more, you can go to the website for this plugin and review its demos and option summaries.

By the way, if you try to run a page that contains a bxSlider plugin from Aptana, you'll see that the plugin doesn't work. Because of that, you'll need to run the page from outside of Aptana.

When you use this plugin, you will often want to change the location of components like the left and right icons, the captions (which I adjusted for this example), and the controls below the carousel. To do that, you can adjust the styles in the CSS file for this plugin.

If, for example, you want to adjust the location of the left and right icons, like moving them outside of the slider, you can modify the CSS for the bx.next and bx.prev classes. You won't find these classes in the HTML, though, because they're added to the DOM by the plugin. Usually, you'll learn a lot by studying the code in the CSS files for plugins and by making adjustments to that code.

A web page that uses the bxSlider plugin for a carousel

The URL for the bxSlider website

http://bxslider.com

The link and script elements for the bxSlider plugin

```
<link href="styles.css" rel="stylesheet">
<link href="jquery.bxslider.css" rel="stylesheet">
<script src="http://code.jquery.com/jquery-2.1.3.min.js"></script>
<script src="js/jquery.bxSlider.min.js">
```

The HTML for the bxSlider plugin

```
<ul id="slider">
    <li><img src="images/building_01.jpg" alt="" title="Front"></li>
    <li><img src="images/building_02.jpg" alt="" title="Left side"></li>
    ...
</ul>
```

The jQuery for using some of the bxSlider options

```
$(document).ready(function(){
    $("#slider").bxSlider({
        auto: true,
        autoControls: true,
        captions: true,
        minSlides: 2,
        maxSlides: 2,
        slideWidth: 250,
        slideMargin: 10
    });
});
```

Description

- The bxSlider plugin makes it easy to develop a carousel. The HTML is an unordered list with one list item for each slide that contains images or other HTML.
- The bxSlider website provides excellent examples and option summaries.
- If the slide images contain title attributes, the captions option will make them captions.
- The bxSlider download consists of a JavaScript file, a CSS file, and an images folder that contains the images that are used by the plugin.

Figure 16-10 How to use the bxSlider plugin for carousels

How to use the Cycle 2 plugin for slide shows

Figure 16-11 shows how to use the Cycle 2 plugin for slide shows. The easiest way to include this plugin in your web pages is to use the URL for the CDN that's shown in this figure. This plugin doesn't require a CSS file or any images.

The HTML for this plugin works with the children of a selected div element. These children are usually img or div elements. When you use div elements, you can code whatever you want within them, including headings, text, lists, and images. In this example, there is one img element for each slide that's contained within a div element for the slide show. The class attribute for this div element must be set to "cycle-slideshow".

If you don't want to set any options for the slide show, that's all you need. Otherwise, you can set options by coding data-cycle attributes for the main div element. In this example, options are set for the effect (fx) that's used to move from slide to slide, how many milliseconds each slide should be displayed, where the captions should be displayed, and what caption template should be used. Here, the caption option points to the div that has been added after the img elements.

If you go to the Cycle 2 website, you'll find demos that show the many ways that this plugin can be used. You'll also find a complete summary of its options. Incidentally, all of the options can either be set by data-cycle attributes or by jQuery code like that for the bxSlider plugin in the previous figure.

A web page that uses the Cycle 2 plugin for slide shows

The URL for the Cycle 2 website

http://jquery.malsup.com/cycle2/

The elements for the Cycle 2 plugin

```
<script src="http://code.jquery.com/jquery-2.1.3.min.js"></script>
<script src="http://malsup.github.com/jquery.cycle2.js"></script>
```

The HTML for the Cycle 2 plugin

```
<div class="cycle-slideshow"
        data-cycle-fx="scrollHorz"
        data-cycle-timeout="2000"
        data-cycle-caption="#adv-custom-caption"
        data-cycle-caption-template="Slide {{slideNum}}: {{cycleTitle}}" >
    <img src="images/building_01.jpg" alt="" data-cycle-title="Front">
    <img src="images/building_02.jpg" alt="" data-cycle-title="Left side">
    ...
    <!-- empty element for caption -->
    <div id="adv-custom-caption"></div>
</div>
```

Description

- The Cycle 2 plugin treats the children of a div element as the slides. Those children are usually img elements, but they can be div elements that contain both text and images.
- The best way to include this plugin in your web pages is to use the GitHub CDN for it.
- The Cycle 2 website provides excellent demos and summaries that let you enhance a slide show in many ways.
- To set options for a slide show, you can code data-cycle attributes for the div element.
- To provide captions below the slides, you can code data-cycle-title attributes for the img elements, data-cycle-caption attributes for the div element, and an empty div element for the captions below the slides.

Figure 16-11 How to use the Cycle 2 plugin for slide shows

Perspective

Now that you've completed this chapter, you should be able to use some of the popular jQuery UI widgets and jQuery plugins. Of course, you can do a better job of that if you actually understand the JavaScript and jQuery that's used for these features.

So, if you want to do a better job of using widgets and plugins, we recommend *Murach's JavaScript and jQuery*. It will teach you the JavaScript and jQuery skills that you need for using widgets and plugins. It will show you how to use all of the jQuery UI widgets as well as interactions and effects. And it will not only show you how to use jQuery plugins, but also how to create your own.

Terms

jQuery UI (User Interface)	modal
widget	jQuery plugin
theme	

Summary

- *jQuery UI (User Interface)* is a JavaScript library that extends the jQuery library. Since the jQuery UI library uses the jQuery library, the script element for jQuery UI must come after the script element for jQuery.
- Before you download the jQuery UI library, you can build a custom download that can include a custom *theme* for styling the jQuery UI components. This theme is implemented by a CSS style sheet that's part of the download.
- As you build a jQuery UI download, you can select the components for the features that you're going to use, including widgets, interactions, and effects. As you would expect, the fewer components you select, the smaller the jQuery UI file that has to be loaded into the user's browser.
- The most widely-used jQuery UI components are the *widgets*. To use a widget, you code the prescribed HTML for it. Then, in the jQuery, you select the widget and run its primary method, often with one or more options.
- If you need a common function for a web page, chances are that a *jQuery plugin* is already available for it. By using a plugin, you can often save hours of work and do the job even better than you would have done it on your own.
- To access a plugin, you code a script element for it in the head element of the HTML document. This script element must come after the script element for the jQuery library, because all jQuery plugins use that library.
- To use a plugin, you often need to use jQuery code to call its method within the ready event handler for a page. Then, if the plugin requires options, you code the options as part of the method call. For some plugins, though, you just need to code the HTML and the required attributes correctly.

Exercise 16-1 Add an Accordion widget to a page

In this exercise, you'll add an Accordion widget to a page so it looks like this:

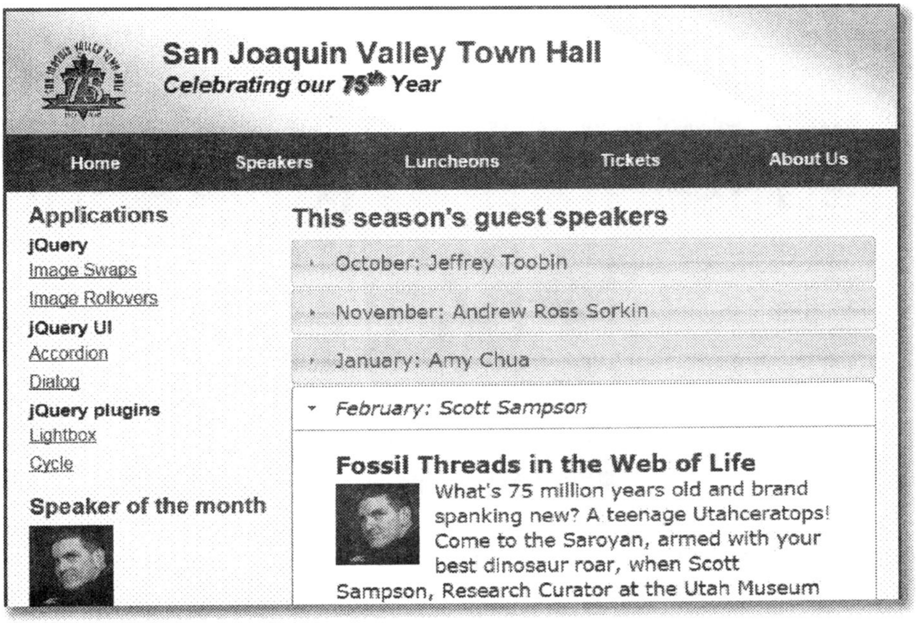

Open and review the HTML for this page

1. Use your text editor to open the HTML file for this page:
   `c:\html5_css3_2\exercises\town_hall_3\speakers\accordion_dialog.html`
2. Review the files in the jquery-ui-1.11.2.custom folder. This is the folder for a custom jQuery UI download. It contains the images folder, the jquery-ui.min.css file for the smoothness theme, and the jquery-ui.min.js file. Then, look at the link and style elements in the accordion_dialog.html file to see that these jQuery UI files have been included for the web page.
3. Note that the last script element contains the jQuery code for implementing the accordion. Then, test this page to see that the accordion works in default mode. That means that an accordion panel is opened when you click on its heading, the height is the same for all panels, and you can't close all of the panels.

Change the way the Accordion works and looks

4. Modify the CSS for this page so any image in an accordion panel will be floated left with appropriate margins as shown above.
5. With figure 16-4 as a guide, modify the script for the accordion so the user can close all of the panels, but note carefully the punctuation that's required.
6. Add the heightStyle option to the accordion with its value set to "content". That way, the size of each accordion panel will depend on its content.
7. Test the page to be sure these changes work.

Exercise 16-2 Use the Cycle 2 plugin for a slide show

In this exercise, you'll enhance a page so it uses the Cycle 2 plugin to run a slide show that displays the speakers. That page will look like this:

Open and review the HTML for this page

1. Use your text editor to open the HTML file for this page:
   c:\html5_css3_2\exercises\town_hall_3\speakers\slideshow.html
2. Review the link and style elements for this page. Note that there isn't a CSS file for the Cycle 2 plugin, and that the script element gets the JavaScript file for the plugin from a CDN. Note too that a second script element gets a cycle2.shuffle JavaScript file from a CDN.
3. Test this page to see that it runs a default Cycle 2 slide show.

Change the way the Slide Show works and looks

4. With figure 16-11 as a guide, add a data-cycle-timeout attribute to the div element to the slide show so each slide is shown for 2 seconds.
5. With figure 16-11 as a guide, add a data-cycle-fx attribute so the shuffle transition is used for the slides. This option requires the use of the cycle2.shuffle.js file that's included by the third script element.
6. Add a data-cycle-pause-on-hover attribute set to a value of "true" so the slide show will pause when the user hovers the mouse over a slide.
7. Go the website for the Cycle 2 plugin, and then go to the demo for providing captions that get their text from the alt attributes of the images. Then, see if you can add the code to the HTML file that will make this work. The caption should be displayed below the images as shown above.
8. Test the page to be sure these changes work.

17

How to use jQuery Mobile to build mobile websites

In chapter 8, you learned how to use Responsive Web Design to provide pages for mobile devices. Now, you'll learn another approach to providing web pages for mobile devices. That is, you'll learn how to build separate websites with native interfaces for mobile devices. To do that, you'll use a jQuery library called jQuery Mobile.

How to work with mobile devices

The topics that follow provide the background that you need for building mobile websites.

How to provide pages for mobile devices

As you learned in chapter 8, the preferred approach to providing web pages for mobile devices is using Responsive Web Design. The trouble is that most large websites were developed before Responsive Web Design became practical. And now that it is practical, the time and expense of converting those websites to Responsive Web Design makes doing that impractical.

As figure 17-1 shows, the common alternative is to develop a separate website for mobile devices that users are redirected to when they access the main site. This is illustrated by the Home pages in this figure. One is for the full version of a site; the other is for the mobile version.

To detect mobile devices and redirect them to the mobile versions of the sites, the full versions of the sites use either client-side or server-side code. For instance, JavaScript or jQuery can be used to do that in the browser, and a scripting language like PHP can be used to do that on the web server. You'll learn more about this in the next figure.

When you use this technique, one common convention for the mobile site name is to precede the domain name for the main site with the letter m followed by a period, or dot. For instance, the name for the mobile version of vectacorp.com would be m.vectacorp.com. A second convention is to store the mobile site in a subdirectory of the main site as in vectacorp.com/mobile.

The good news is that jQuery Mobile makes it easier than ever to create a mobile version of a website. That means that even small companies should now be able to afford mobile versions of their sites. That's one benefit of developing a mobile website instead of re-engineering it with Responsive Web Design.

Another benefit is that you can simplify the content of the main site so it is more appropriate for a mobile device. In other words, you don't need to include all of the content for the main site in the mobile site. Instead, you can remove all the content that doesn't contribute to the usability of the mobile site.

The Home pages for a full website and the mobile version of the site

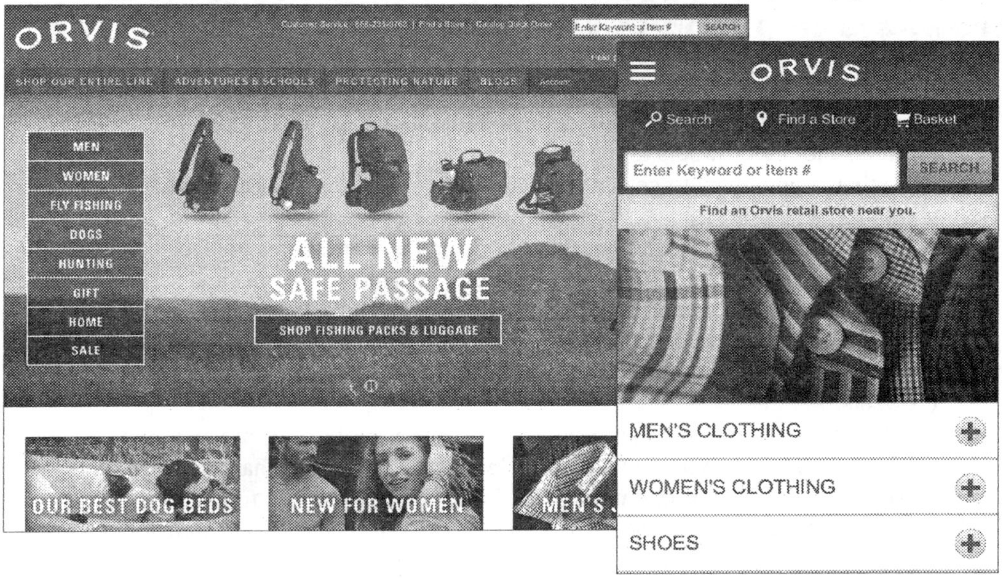

Two ways to provide web pages for a mobile device

- Use Responsive Web Design so the pages of a website will work on devices of all sizes, including mobile devices. This technique is presented in chapter 8.
- Develop a separate mobile version of the website that the user is redirected to when the browser for a mobile device tries to open the web page for the main site.

Two ways to redirect a user to the mobile version of the site

- Use JavaScript or jQuery to detect mobile devices and redirect them to the mobile version of the site.
- Use a server-side scripting language such as PHP to detect mobile devices and redirect them to the mobile version of the site.

The benefits of having a separate website for mobile devices

- It's usually easier and less expensive to develop a separate mobile website than it is to re-engineer an established website with Responsive Web Design.
- The mobile website can be simplified in a way that is appropriate for mobile devices, with less content and fewer pages.

Description

- Today, Responsive Web Design is the preferred way to provide web pages for mobile devices. But if you have a large, established website, converting it to Responsive Web Design is likely to be so time-consuming and expensive that it's impractical.

Figure 17-1 How to provide pages for mobile devices

How to use a JavaScript plugin to redirect mobile browsers to a mobile website

Because there are so many different types of mobile devices and mobile browsers, it would be difficult to code and maintain a JavaScript application that redirects mobile browsers to the mobile version of a website. So when you need to do that, a good way to get started is to look for a plugin that does what you want.

One website that provides scripts for detecting browsers is the Detect Mobile Browsers site shown in figure 17-2. It provides scripts for clients and servers that detect mobile browsers and redirect them to the mobile versions of the sites. As you can see, it provides these scripts in many different languages, including ASP.NET, JSP, PHP, and Python for servers as well as JavaScript and jQuery for browsers.

The procedure in this figure shows how to use the JavaScript version of the application. In brief, you download the JavaScript file, which has a txt extension. Next, you use your editor to modify the URL at the end of the file so it points to your mobile website, rename the file so it has a js instead of a txt extension, and deploy the file to your web server. Then, you code a script element that includes this file in any web page that you want redirected to the mobile site when a mobile browser is detected.

The home page for Detect Mobile Browsers

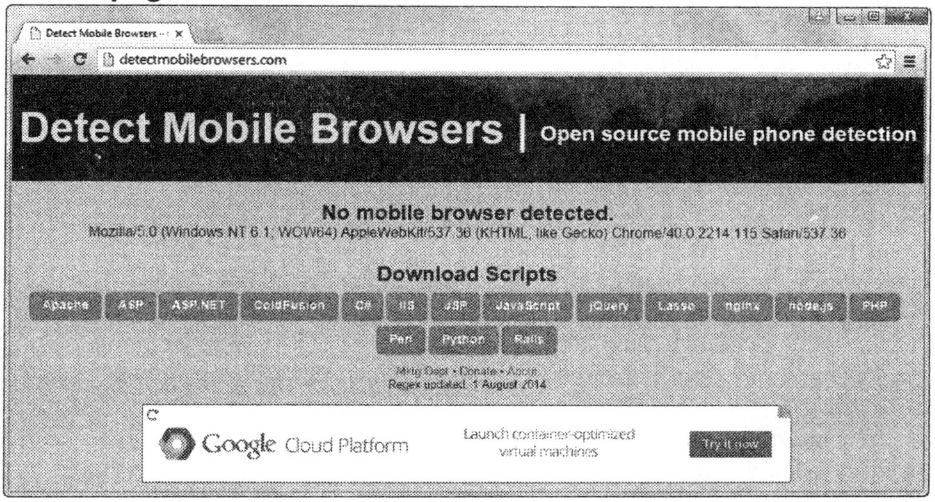

The URL for Detect Mobile Browsers

`http://www.detectmobilebrowser.com`

The end of the code in the downloaded file (detectmobilebrowser.js.txt)

```
...||window.opera,'http://detectmobilebrowser.com/mobile');
```

The end of the code after the URL has been edited

```
...||window.opera,'http://www.vectacorp.com/mobile');
```

The script element for any page that wants to redirect to a mobile site

```
<script src="detectmobilebrowser.js"></script>
```

How to use the JavaScript plugin for mobile browser detection

1. Go to the URL above. Then, click on the JavaScript button under the Download Scripts heading to download a file named detectmobilebrowser.js.txt.
2. Open the file in your text editor, and move the cursor to the end of the JavaScript code, which will include a URL like the one above. Then, change this URL to the path of the mobile site that you want the user redirected to.
3. Save your work, close the file, and rename the file so the .txt extension is removed. Then, deploy the file to your web server.
4. In any web page that you want to redirect to the mobile website, code a script element that refers to the file that you've just deployed.

Description

- The Detect Mobile Browsers website offers many server-side and client-side scripts that will redirect a mobile device from the full version of a site to the mobile version.
- After you modify the URL in the JavaScript plugin so it points to the correct mobile page, you need to provide a script element for it on every page that you want redirected.

Figure 17-2 How to use a JavaScript plugin to redirect users to a mobile website

How to set the viewport properties

When you develop a website for mobile devices, you can use a special meta element that lets you configure a device's *viewport*. You learned how to use this element with Responsive Web Design in chapter 8. But you should also use it if a full website will be displayed on mobile devices or if you're developing a mobile website with jQuery Mobile. Figure 17-3 shows you how.

As you learned in chapter 8, the viewport on a mobile device can be larger or smaller than the visible area of a web page, and it determines how the page content appears in that area. In this figure, for example, you can see that the first web page is displayed without a meta element so almost the entire width of the page is visible. That's because the default width of the viewport for an iPhone like the one shown here is 980 pixels, and the width of the page that's displayed is 990 pixels.

In contrast, the second web page has a viewport meta element that sets the viewport to the width of the device and the scale to .5. This makes the pages of the full website easier to work with on a mobile device.

To configure the viewport, you use a meta element with the name attribute set to "viewport". Then, for the content attribute, you can specify any of the properties that are summarized in this figure to set the dimensions and scaling of the web page within the mobile device.

In practice, though, if the pages you're designing are for mobile devices, you use a viewport meta element like the example in this figure. Here, the viewport is set to the width of the device, and the scale is set to 1.

A web page on an iPhone before and after scaling

No viewport meta element

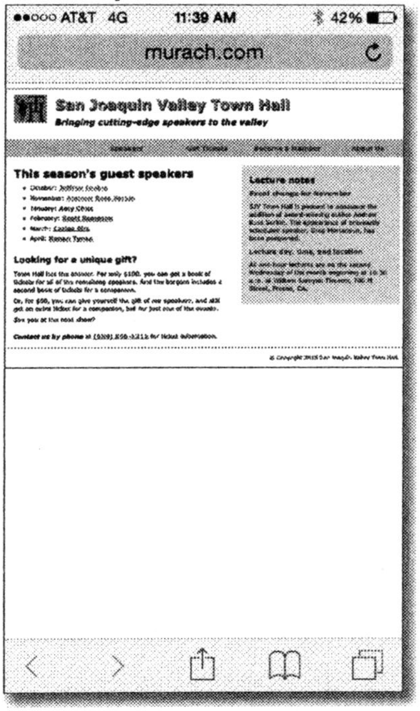

width=device-width, initial-scale=.5

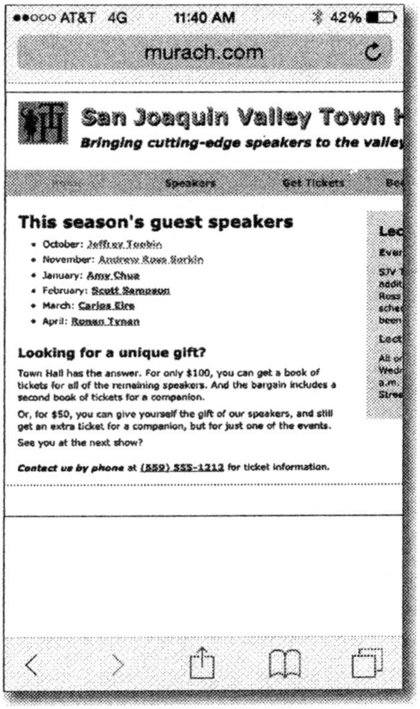

Basic settings for a mobile website

```
<meta name="viewport" content="width=device-width, initial-scale=1">
```

Content properties for viewport metadata

Property	Description
`width`	The width of the viewport in pixels. You can also use the device-width keyword to indicate that the viewport should be as wide as the screen.
`height`	The height of the viewport specified in pixels. You can also use the device-height keyword to indicate that the viewport should be as tall as the screen.
`initial-scale`	A number that indicates the initial zoom factor that's used to display the page.
`minimum-scale`	A number that indicates the minimum zoom factor for the page.
`maximum-scale`	A number that indicates the maximum zoom factor for the page.
`user-scalable`	Indicates whether the user can zoom in and out of the viewport. Possible values are yes and no.

Description

- The *viewport* on a mobile device determines the content that's displayed on the page. It can be larger or smaller than the visible area of the screen.

Figure 17-3 How to set the viewport properties

Guidelines for designing mobile web pages

If you create web pages specifically for mobile devices, you should follow some general guidelines so it's easy for users to work with those pages. Figure 17-4 presents these guidelines.

In general, you want to simplify the layout and content of your pages. This is illustrated by the two pages in this figure. The first shows the home page for the mobile version of a large website. This page consists primarily of links to the major types of products that the site offers. The second page shows a product list after the user has drilled down into the site. If you review the full version of this site, you'll get a better idea of just how much the full version has been simplified.

Guidelines for testing mobile web pages

Figure 17-4 also presents some guidelines for testing mobile web pages. You learned about these techniques in chapter 8, so I'll just summarize them here.

First, you can deploy the page to a web server and then display it on a variety of devices. Because there are so many mobile devices, though, that isn't always possible. In that case, you may want to use a web-based tool such as ProtoFluid that lets you view a web page in different screen sizes.

You can also use the device emulators and browser simulators that are available for many of the mobile devices and browsers. Most of these emulators and simulators must be downloaded to your computer and then run from there. In a few cases, though, you can run the emulator or simulator online. But to do that, you may need to deploy the web page so it can be accessed online. If you use an emulator or a simulator, keep in mind that it may not always provide accurate results, although it should approximate what a page will look like.

As you're developing a website, you can also use the developer tools that are available with Chrome, Firefox, and IE to test web pages. To access these tools, you display a page in the browser and then press F12. When you do, the tools are displayed at the bottom of the browser window. Then, you can use techniques that are specific to each browser to display the page in devices of various sizes. For more information and for an illustration of these tools in Chrome, please see figure 8-2 in chapter 8.

Two pages from the mobile website for www.orvis.com

The Home page

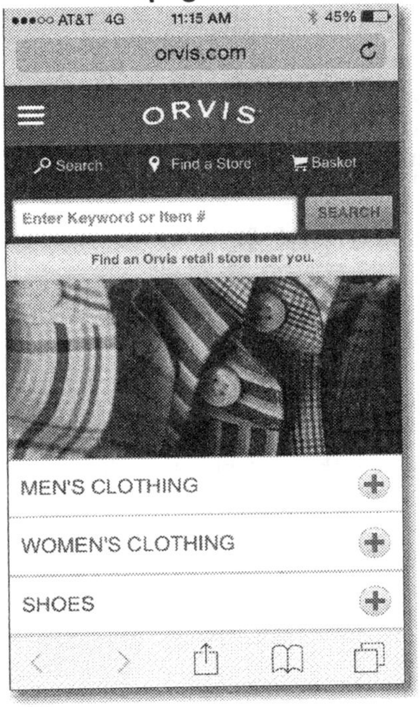

A product list

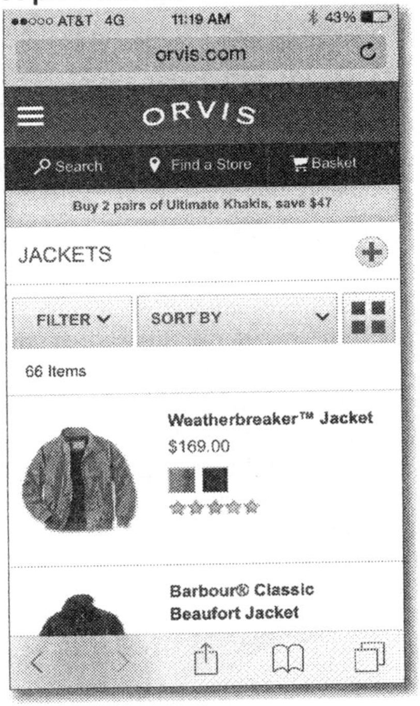

Guidelines for designing mobile web pages

- Keep your layout simple so the focus is on the content. One-column layouts typically work best.
- Include only essential content.
- Keep images small and to a minimum.
- Avoid using Flash. Most mobile devices, including the iPhone, don't support it.
- Include only the essential navigation in the header of the page. The other navigation should be part of the content for the page.
- Make links and other elements large enough that the user can easily manipulate them.
- Use relative measurements so the page looks good regardless of the scale.

Guidelines for testing mobile web pages

- Test all pages on as many different mobile devices and in as many different mobile browsers as possible.
- The best way to test mobile web pages is to deploy them to your web server and test them on the devices themselves.
- When you can't test your pages on the devices themselves, you can use device emulators and browser simulators, web-based tools such as ProtoFluid, or the developer tools that come with Chrome, Firefox, and IE.

Figure 17-4 Guidelines for designing and testing mobile web pages

How to get started with jQuery Mobile

In chapters 15 and 16, you learned how to use jQuery and jQuery UI to enhance your web pages. Now, in this chapter, you'll learn how to use the jQuery Mobile library to develop mobile websites. Although there are other ways to develop mobile websites, we think jQuery Mobile sets a standard that other development methods are going to have a hard time beating.

What jQuery Mobile is and where to get it

As figure 17-5 summarizes, *jQuery Mobile* is a free, open-source, cross-platform, JavaScript library that you can use for developing mobile websites. This library lets you create pages that look and feel like the pages of a native mobile application.

To include jQuery Mobile in your pages, you can download the required JavaScript and CSS libraries from the jQuery Mobile website, deploy them to your web server, and then include them in your mobile web pages. Or, you can use a Content Delivery Network to get the latest versions of the files.

The jQuery Mobile website (www.jquerymobile.com)

The two jQuery libraries that you need

- jQuery
- jQuery Mobile

Description

- *jQuery Mobile* is a free, open-source, JavaScript library that makes it easier to develop websites for mobile devices. It is used in combination with the jQuery library.
- jQuery Mobile lets you store multiple pages in a single HTML file; create dialogs, buttons, and navigation bars; format your pages without coding your own CSS; lay out pages with two columns, collapsible content blocks, and accordions; and much more.
- jQuery Mobile is supported by most devices including iPhone iOS, Android, BlackBerry, Windows Phone, Palm WebOS, and Symbian.
- The jQuery Mobile website features all of the documentation, sample code, and downloads that you need for beginning your work with mobile devices.
- To download jQuery Mobile, go to its website (www.jquerymobile.com). However, you won't need to do that if you include it from a CDN (see figure 17-6).

Figure 17-5 What jQuery Mobile is and where to get it

How to include jQuery Mobile in your web pages

To use jQuery Mobile, you need to include the three files listed at the top of figure 17-6 in your web pages: the jQuery file, the jQuery Mobile file, and the jQuery Mobile CSS style sheet. As this figure shows, there are two ways to do that.

The first way to include the three files is illustrated by the first example in this figure. Here, the link element for the CSS file and the script elements for the jQuery and jQuery Mobile files use a Content Delivery Network. At this writing, Microsoft and jQuery are the only CDNs that you can use for getting the jQuery Mobile library, and this example uses the jQuery CDN.

The benefit to using a CDN is that you don't have to manage the jQuery and jQuery Mobile versions on your server as new ones become available. Instead, you just have to change the version numbers in the link and script elements for these files.

The second way is to download the three files and deploy them on your system or web server. To do that, you download the compressed zip files, extract the files from the zip files, and copy the files to your web server. Then, for each web page that uses jQuery Mobile, you code one link element that includes the CSS file and two script elements that include the jQuery and jQuery Mobile files.

This is illustrated by the second example in this figure. Here, the names for the current versions of the files are retained. Although you can change those names once they're on your server, keeping the downloaded names makes it easy to tell which versions of the files you're using.

No matter which method you use, you must code the script element for jQuery Mobile after the one for jQuery. That's because jQuery Mobile uses the jQuery library.

The three files that you need to include for jQuery Mobile applications

- The jQuery JavaScript file
- The jQuery Mobile JavaScript file
- The jQuery Mobile CSS style sheet

Two ways to include the jQuery files

- Include the files from a Content Delivery Network (CDN) like Microsoft or jQuery.
- Download and deploy the files on your web server. Then, include them from the server.

How to include the jQuery Mobile files from a Content Delivery Network

```
<!-- include the jQuery Mobile stylesheet -->
<link rel="stylesheet"
   href="http://code.jquery.com/mobile/1.4.5/jquery.mobile-1.4.5.min.css">

<!-- include the jQuery and jQuery Mobile JavaScript files -->
<script src=" https://code.jquery.com/jquery-2.1.3.min.js"></script>
<script
   src="https://code.jquery.com/mobile/1.4.5/jquery.mobile-1.4.5.min.js">
</script>
```

How to include the jQuery Mobile files when they're on your web server

```
<!-- include the jQuery Mobile stylesheet -->
<link rel="stylesheet" href="jquery.mobile-1.4.5.min.css">

<!-- include the jQuery and jQuery Mobile JavaScript files -->
<script src="jquery-2.1.3.min.js"></script>
<script src="jquery.mobile-1.4.5.min.css"></script>
```

Description

- To use jQuery, you need to include the three files shown above. The first two are the JavaScript files for jQuery and jQuery Mobile. The third is the CSS file for the jQuery Mobile style sheet.
- jQuery Mobile is continually being improved and enhanced, so check the website often for the latest version.
- At this writing, only Microsoft and jQuery provide Content Delivery Networks (CDNs) that can be used to access the jQuery Mobile files.
- The jQuery and jQuery Mobile filenames always include the version number. At this writing, the latest stable version of jQuery Mobile is 1.4.5.
- If you download and deploy the jQuery files to your system, you can change the filenames so they're simpler. But that way, you can lose track of what versions you're using and when you need to upgrade to newer versions.

Figure 17-6 How to include jQuery Mobile in your web pages

How to create one web page with jQuery Mobile

To give you an idea of how jQuery Mobile works, figure 17-7 shows how to create one web page with it. In the HTML for a page, you use data-role attributes to identify the page, header, and footer components. In contrast, you use the role attribute with a value of "main" to identify the component that will contain the main content for the page. You also assign the class named ui-content to this component.

Note that the technique you use to identify the content component is new in jQuery Mobile 1.4. Previously, you identified this component by coding a data-role attribute with the value "content". Although you can still use the data-role attribute like this, it has been deprecated and will be dropped in a future version of jQuery Mobile. So you should use the role attribute and ui-content class instead.

To define the text that's displayed within the header, you use an h1 element. Similarly, to define the text for the footer, you use an h4 element. In the page that's shown here, you can see how jQuery Mobile automatically formats the header, content, and footer components. Here the text for both the header and footer is centered in bold, dark gray type against a light gray background, while the text for the content is dark gray against an extra light gray background. This is the default styling that's done by jQuery Mobile, and it's similar to the styling for a native iPhone application.

Of course, you can code the HTML for whatever content you need within the header, footer, and content components. You'll see this illustrated in the examples that follow. However, this simple example should give you some idea of how easy it is to code and format a single web page.

A web page that uses jQuery Mobile

The HTML for the mobile web page

```
<div data-role="page">
    <header data-role="header">
        <h1>Header</h1>
    </header>

    <section class="ui-content" role="main">
        <p>The page content</p>
    </section>

    <footer data-role="footer">
        <h4>Footer</h4>
    </footer>
</div>
```

Description

- The HTML for a typical web page that uses jQuery Mobile will contain div, header, section, and footer elements.
- The data-role attribute is used to identify three parts of a mobile web page: the page itself, the header and the footer.
- The text that's displayed in the header should be coded within an h1 element. The text that's displayed in the footer should be coded within an h4 element.
- The role attribute with a value "main" is used to identify the section element that contains the main content for the page. This section should also be assigned to the ui-content class. You can code whatever elements you need within this section.
- The style sheet for jQuery Mobile formats the web page based on the values in the data-role, role, and class attributes.

Figure 17-7 How to create one web page with jQuery Mobile

How to code multiple pages in a single HTML file

In contrast to the way you develop the web pages for a full website, jQuery Mobile lets you create multiple pages in a single HTML file. This is illustrated by figure 17-8. Here, you can see two pages of a site along with the HTML for these pages. What's surprising is that both pages are coded within a single HTML file.

For each page, you code one div element with "page" as the value of the data-role attribute. Then, within each of those div elements, you code the elements for the header, content, and footer of each page. Later, when the HTML file is loaded, the first page in the body of the file is displayed.

To link between the pages in the HTML file, you use placeholders as shown in figure 7-11 of chapter 7. For instance, the <a> element in the first page in this example goes to "#toobin" when the user taps on the h4 or img element that is coded as the content for this link. This refers to the div element with "toobin" as its id attribute, which means that tapping the link takes the reader to the second page in the file.

Although this example shows only two pages, you can code many pages within a single HTML file. Remember, though, that all of the pages along with their images, JavaScript, and CSS files are loaded with the single HTML file. As a result, the load time will become excessive if you store too many pages in a single file. When that happens, you can divide your pages into more than one HTML file.

Two web pages that use jQuery Mobile

The HTML for the two pages in the body of one HTML file

```
<div data-role="page">
    <header data-role="header"><h1>SJV Town Hall</h1></header>
    <section class="ui-content" role="main">
        <h3>This Season's Speakers</h3>
        <a href="#toobin">
            <h4>Jeffrey Toobin<br>October</h4>
            <img src="images/toobin75.jpg" alt="Jeffrey Toobin"></a>
        <!-- THE ELEMENTS FOR THE REST OF THE SPEAKERS -->
    </section>
    <footer data-role="footer"><h4>&copy; 2016</h4></footer>
</div>
<div data-role="page" id="toobin">
    <header data-role="header"><h1>SJV Town Hall</h1></header>
    <section class="ui-content" role="main">
        <h3>The Supreme Nine:<br>Black Robed Secrets</h3>
        <img src="images/toobin_court.cnn.jpg" alt="Jeffrey Toobin">
        <p>Author of the critically acclaimed best seller, <i>The Nine:
        <!-- THE COPY CONTINUES -->
    </section>
    <footer data-role="footer"><h4>&copy; 2016</h4></footer>
</div>
```

Description

- When you use jQuery Mobile, you don't have to develop a separate HTML file for each page. Instead, within the body element of a single HTML file, you code one div element for each page with its data-role attribute set to "page".
- For each div element, you set the id attribute to a placeholder value that can be accessed by the href attributes in the <a> elements of other pages.

Figure 17-8 How to code multiple pages in a single HTML file

How to navigate between pages

The next three figures show how to navigate between the pages of a mobile website when you use jQuery Mobile. That includes the use of dialogs, transitions, buttons, and navigation bars.

How to use dialogs and transitions

Figure 17-9 shows how to create a *dialog* that opens when a link is tapped. To do that, you code the data-dialog attribute with a value of "true" on the div element for the page.

This is different from how you created a dialog with versions of jQuery Mobile before version 1.4. With those versions, you coded the dialog just as you would any page. But in the <a> element that goes to that page, you coded a data-rel attribute with "dialog" as its value. Although you can still use this technique, it has been deprecated and will be dropped in a future version of jQuery Mobile. So you shouldn't use it in new web pages you develop.

When you create a dialog, the jQuery Mobile CSS file formats it as shown in the example in this figure. Here, the dialog doesn't occupy the entire screen, and it's displayed with rounded corners and a drop shadow. In addition, it has an "X" in the header that the user must tap to return to the previous page.

When you code an <a> element that goes to another page or dialog, you can also use the data-transition attribute to specify one of the six *transitions* that are summarized in the table in this figure. Each of these transitions is meant to mimic an effect that a mobile device like an iPhone uses.

A page and a dialog that have the same HTML

The web page

The dialog

The transitions that can be used

Transition	Description
`slide`	The next page slides in from right to left.
`slideup`	The next page slides in from bottom to top.
`slidedown`	The next page slides in from top to bottom.
`pop`	The next page fades in from the middle of the screen.
`fade`	The next page fades into view. This is the default.
`flip`	The next page flips from back to front similar to a playing card being flipped over. This transition isn't supported on some devices.

HTML that causes the page to open as a dialog

```
<div data-role="page" id="toobin" data-dialog="true">
```

HTML that opens the page with the "pop" transition

```
<a href="#toobin" data-transition="pop">
```

Description

- To display a page as a dialog, you include the data-dialog attribute with the value "true" on the div element for the page. To close the dialog, the user taps the X in the header of the box.
- To specify the way a page or a dialog is opened, you can use the data-transition attribute with one of the values in the table above in the <a> element that links to the page. If a device doesn't support the *transition* that you specify, the attribute is ignored.
- The styling for a dialog is done by the jQuery Mobile CSS file.

Figure 17-9 How to use dialogs and transitions

How to create buttons

Figure 17-10 shows how to use buttons to navigate from one page to another. To do that, you just set the data-role attribute for an <a> element to "button", and jQuery Mobile does the rest.

However, you can also set some other attributes for buttons. If, for example, you want two or more buttons to appear side by side, like the first two buttons in this figure, you can set the data-inline attribute to "true".

If you want to add one of the 18 icons that are provided by jQuery Mobile to a button, you also code the data-icon attribute. For instance, the third button in this example uses the "delete" icon, and the fourth button uses the "home" icon. All of these icons look like the icons that you might see within a native mobile application. Incidentally, these icons are not separate files that the page must access. Instead, they are provided by the jQuery Mobile library.

If you want to group two or more buttons horizontally, like the Yes, No, and Maybe buttons in this figure, you can code the <a> elements for the buttons within a div element that has "controlgroup" as its data-role attribute and "horizontal" as its data-type attribute. Or, to group the buttons vertically, you can change the data-type attribute to "vertical".

If you set the data-rel attribute for a button to "back" and the href attribute to the pound symbol (#), the button will return to the page that called it. In other words, the button works like a Back button. This is illustrated by the last button in the content for the page.

The last two buttons show how buttons appear in the footer for a page. Notice in the code for these buttons that, even though the data-inline attribute isn't set to "true", the buttons appear side by side. That's because this is the default for buttons in a footer. Also notice that the class attribute for the footer is set to "ui-bar". That tells jQuery Mobile to put a little more space around the contents of the footer.

A mobile web page that displays buttons

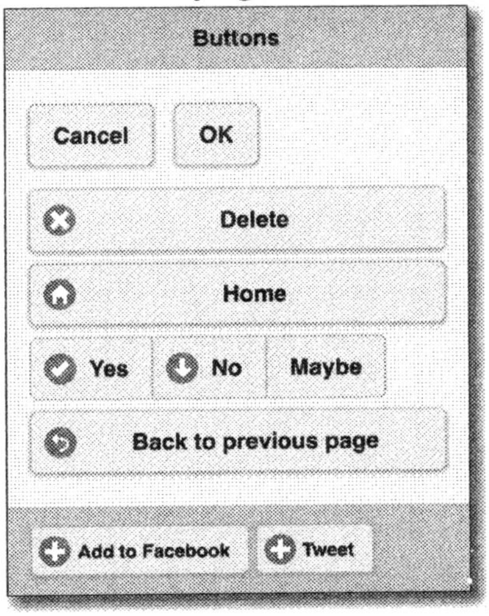

The icons that are provided by jQuery Mobile

delete	arrow-l	arrow-r	arrow-u	arrow-d	search
plus	minus	check	gear	refresh	forward
back	grid	star	alert	info	home

The HTML for the buttons in the section

```
<!-- For inline buttons, set the data-inline attribute to true -->
<a href="#" data-role="button" data-inline="true">Cancel</a>
<a href="#" data-role="button" data-inline="true">OK</a>
<!-- To add an icon to a button, use the data-icon attribute -->
<a href="#" data-role="button" data-icon="delete">Delete</a>
<a href="#" data-role="button" data-icon="home">Home</a>
<!-- To group buttons, use a div element with the attributes that follow -->
<div data-role="controlgroup" data-type="horizontal">
    <a href="#" data-role="button" data-icon="check">Yes</a>
    <a href="#" data-role="button" data-icon="arrow-d">No</a>
    <a href="#" data-role="button">Maybe</a>
</div>
<!-- To code a Back button, set the data-rel attribute to back -->
<a href="#" data-role="button" dat-rel="back" data-icon="back">
    Back to previous page</a>
```

The HTML for the buttons in the footer

```
<footer data-role="footer" class="ui-bar">
    <a href="http://www.facebook.com" data-role="button"
       data-icon="plus">Add to Facebook</a>
    <a href="http://www.twitter.com" data-role="button"
       data-icon="plus">Tweet</a>
</footer>
```

Description

- To add a button to a web page, you code an <a> element with its data-role attribute set to "button".

Figure 17-10 How to create buttons

How to create a navigation bar

Figure 17-11 shows how you can add a *navigation bar* to the header of a web page. To do that, you code a div element with its data-role attribute set to "navbar". Within this element, you code a ul element that contains li elements that contain the <a> elements for the items in the navigation bar. Note, however, that you don't code the data-role attribute for the <a> elements.

By default, all of the items in a navigation bar are displayed with a light gray background and dark gray type. If you want to make one of the items active, though, you can assign the ui-btn-active class to it. Then, the item is displayed with an attractive blue background and white type. This is illustrated by the "Home" item shown here.

A mobile web page with a navigation bar

The HTML for the navigation bar

```
<header data-role="header">
    <h1>SJV Town Hall</h1>
    <div data-role="navbar">
        <ul>
            <li><a href="#home" class="ui-btn-active"
                   data-icon="home">Home</a></li>
            <li><a href="#speakers" data-icon="star">Speakers</a></li>
            <li><a href="#news" data-icon="grid">News</a></li>
        </ul>
    </div>
</header>
```

How to code the HTML for a navigation bar

- Code a div element within the header element. Then, set the data-role attribute for the div element to "navbar".
- Within the div element, code a ul element that contains one li element for each link.
- Within each li element, code an <a> element with an href attribute that uses a placeholder for the page that the link should go to. Then, set the data-icon attribute to the icon of your choosing.
- For the active item in the navigation bar, set the class attribute to "ui-btn-active". Then, this item will be displayed with a blue background and a white font.

Figure 17-11 How to create a navigation bar

How to format content with jQuery Mobile

As you've already seen, jQuery Mobile automatically formats the components of a web page based on its own style sheet. Now, you'll learn more about that, as well as how to adjust the default styling that jQuery Mobile uses.

The default styles that jQuery Mobile uses

Figure 17-12 shows the default styles that jQuery Mobile uses for common HTML elements. For all of its styles, jQuery Mobile relies on the browser's rendering engine so its own styling is minimal. This keeps load times fast and minimizes the overhead that excessive CSS would impose on a page.

As you can see, jQuery Mobile's styling is so effective that you shouldn't need to modify its styling by providing your own CSS style sheet. For instance, the spacing between the items in the unordered list and the formatting of the table are both acceptable the way they are. Also, the dark gray type on the light gray background is consistent with the formatting for native mobile applications.

The default styles for common HTML elements

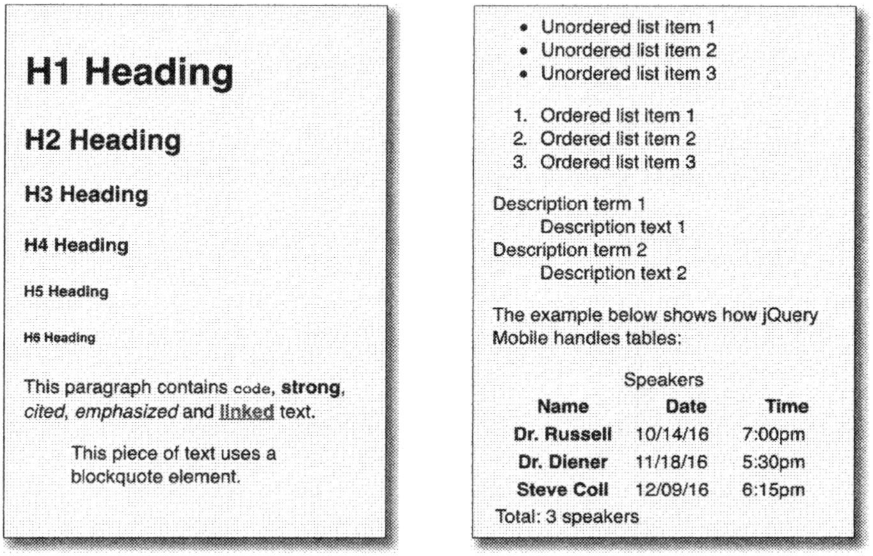

Description

- By default, jQuery Mobile automatically applies styles to the HTML elements for a page. These styles are not only attractive, but also mimic a browser's native styles.
- By default, jQuery Mobile applies a small amount of padding to the left, right, top, and bottom of each mobile page.
- By default, links are slightly larger than normal text. This makes it easier for the user to tap the links.
- By default, links are underlined with blue as the font color.
- Although you can use your own CSS style sheet with a jQuery Mobile application, you should avoid doing that whenever possible.

Figure 17-12 The default styles that jQuery Mobile uses

How to apply themes to HTML elements

The styles that jQuery Mobile uses are provided by its default *theme*, which is meant to mimic the appearance of a native mobile application. This theme includes some global settings, such as the font family, as well as two *swatches*: swatch "a" and swatch "b". These swatches control the color schemes that are used by various elements. Figure 17-13 shows how these theme swatches work.

By default, jQuery Mobile uses swatch "a", which is the swatch you've seen so far in this chapter. You can use one of two techniques to change an element so it uses swatch "b". First, you can code a data-theme attribute with the swatch letter as its value. You can see this in the HTML for the second navigation bar in this figure. Here, the data-theme attribute applies swatch "b" to the header and swatch "a" to the items in the navigation bar. That's why the header appears with white type on a dark gray background.

Before I go on, you should realize that when you apply a swatch to an element, it's inherited by any child elements. For instance, because swatch "b" is coded for the header in the second example, the items in the navigation bar inherit that swatch. To use swatch "a" for those items, then, you must code the data-theme for them.

The other way to apply swatches is to set the class attribute for an element to a class name that indicates a swatch. This is illustrated by the second example after the table. Here, the class attribute is used to apply both the "ui-bar" and "ui-bar-b" classes to a div element. As a result, jQuery Mobile first applies its default styling for a bar to the element and then applies swatch "b" to that styling.

You may be interested to know that versions of jQuery Mobile prior to 1.4 provided five different swatches. Even though these swatches have been simplified and reduced to two basic swatches, you should know that you can modify these swatches and create additional swatches. To do that, you can use the ThemeRoller application that's available from the jQuery Mobile website to roll your own theme. Then, you can download that theme and use it in your mobile website.

Two headers and navigation bars that illustrate the use of theme swatches

Header “a”, bar “b”

Header “b”, bar “a”

The HTML for the second header and navigation bar

```
<header data-role="header" data-theme="b">
    <h1>Solutions</h1>
    <div data-role="navbar">
        <ul>
            <li><a href="#home" data-icon="home"
                   data-theme="a">Home</a></li>
            <li><a href="#solutions" data-icon="star"
                   data-theme="a" class="ui-btn-active">Solutions</a></li>
            <li><a href="#contactus" data-icon="grid"
                   data-theme="a">Contact Us</a></li>
        </ul>
    </div>
</header>
```

Two ways to apply a swatch

By using a data-theme attribute

```
<li><a href="#home" class="ui-btn-active"
       data-icon="home" data-theme="b">Home</a></li>
```

By using a class attribute that indicates the swatch

```
<div class="ui-bar ui-bar-b">...</div>
```

The URL for a page that illustrates the two swatches

```
http://demos.jquerymobile.com/1.4.5/theme-default/
```

Description

- jQuery Mobile includes a default *theme* that consists of global settings, including the font and the corner radius of buttons and boxes, and swatches.
- The two *swatches* that come with the default theme define different color combinations for various elements. In general, swatch “a” (the default) provides a light gray background with a dark gray font, and swatch “b” provides a dark gray background with a white font.
- If you specify a swatch for an element, that swatch is inherited by any child elements. If that’s not what you want, you can specify a different swatch for the child elements as shown above for the second header and navigation bar.

Figure 17-13 How to apply themes to HTML elements

How to use jQuery Mobile for page layout

The last three topics in this chapter show how to use jQuery Mobile for special page layouts.

How to create collapsible content blocks

Figure 17-14 shows how you can display content in *collapsible content blocks*. Then, the user can tap on an item to display (or expand) the content within the block. By default, jQuery Mobile formats these blocks and adds plus and minus signs to them as shown in this figure.

In the code for this feature, you can see that there's one section element for all of the blocks with its class attribute set to "ui-content" and the role attribute set to "main". You can also see that there's one div element for each content block with its data-role attribute set to "collapsible". By default, the content blocks are collapsed when the page is loaded, but you can change that by setting the data-collapsed attribute for one or more blocks to "false".

Within the div element for each content block, you code a heading with the content you want to be displayed when the block is collapsed. In this figure, for instance, an h3 heading is used for this content. Then, any elements that follow this heading aren't displayed until the block is expanded.

A mobile web page with collapsible content blocks

With all blocks collapsed

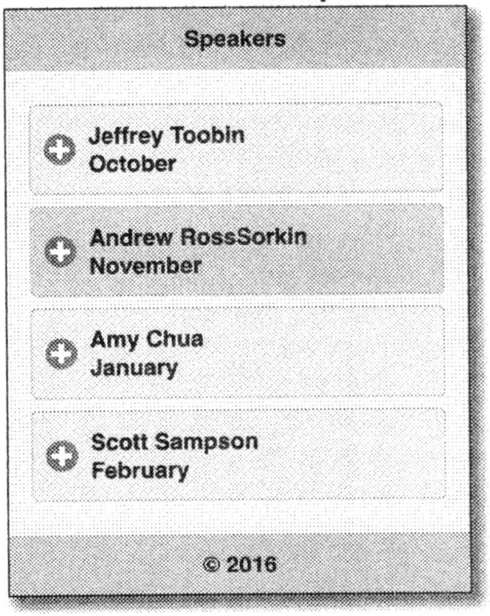

With the second block expanded

The HTML for the collapsible content blocks

```
<section class="ui-content" role="main">
    <div data-role="collapsible">
        <h3>Jeffrey Toobin<br>October</h3>
        <h3>Black Robed Secrets</h3>
        <img src="images/toobin75.jpg" alt="Jeffrey Toobin">
        <p>Author of the critically acclaimed best seller...</p>
    </div>
    <div data-role="collapsible" data-collapsed="false">
        <h3>Andrew RossSorkin<br>November</h3>
        <h3>Too Big to Fail</h3>
        <img src="images/sorkin75.jpg" alt="Andrew Ross Sorkin">
        <p>A leading voice on Wall Street and corporate America...</p>
    </div>
    <!-- THE DIV ELEMENTS FOR THE OTHER CONTENT BLOCKS -->
</section>
```

How to code the HTML for collapsible content blocks

- Code a div element for each content block with the data-role attribute set to "collapsible".
- By default, each content block will be collapsed when the page is displayed. To expand a content block, add the data-collapsed attribute with its value set to "false".
- Within each div element, you can code the HTML for whatever content you want. However, the first element, which contains the content that's displayed when a content block is collapsed, must be a heading.

Description

- More than one *collapsible content block* can be expanded at the same time.
- jQuery Mobile automatically adds the plus and minus icons for the content blocks.

Figure 17-14 How to create collapsible content blocks

How to create an accordion

When you create an *accordion*, you code the content blocks the same way you code the collapsible content blocks of the previous figure. This is illustrated by figure 17-15. However, you code these content blocks within a section or div element that has its data-role attribute set to "collapsible-set".

One difference between an accordion and collapsible content blocks is that jQuery Mobile formats the blocks in the accordion as a unit. You can see this if you compare the example in this page with the one in the previous page. The other difference is that the user can only expand one block at a time in an accordion. So, when one block is expanded, the other block is collapsed.

A mobile web page with an accordion

With all blocks collapsed

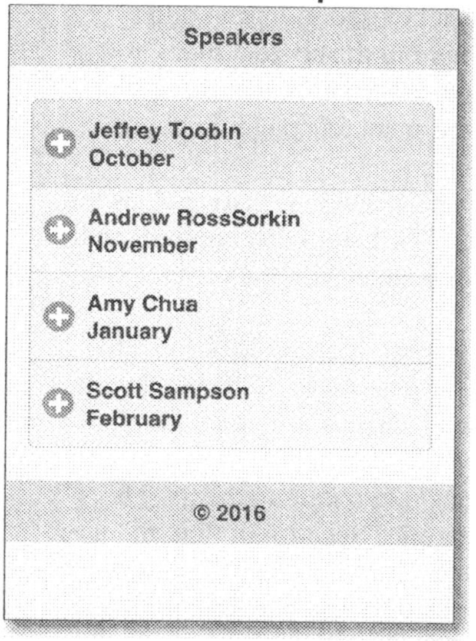

With the first block expanded

The HTML for the accordion

```
<section class="ui-content" role="main">
    <section data-role="collapsible-set">
        <div data-role="collapsible" data-collapsed="false">
            <h3>Jeffrey Toobin<br>October</h3>
            <h3>Black Robed Secrets</h3>
            <img src="images/toobin75.jpg" alt="Jeffrey Toobin">
            <p>Author of the critically acclaimed best seller,
               <i>The Nine: Inside the Secret World of the Supreme
               Court</i>, Jeffrey Toobin brings us the inside story
               of one of America's most mysterious and powerful
               institutions.</p>
        </div>
        <!-- THE DIV ELEMENTS FOR THE OTHER CONTENT BLOCKS -->
    </section>
</section>
```

How to code the HTML for an accordion

- Code a section (or div) element for the accordion within the section for the page and set its data-role attribute to "collapsible-set".
- Code the content blocks the same way you code collapsible content blocks (figure 17-14).

Description

- In contrast to collapsible content blocks, only one block in an *accordion* can be expanded at the same time.
- jQuery Mobile automatically adds the plus and minus icons for the content blocks.

Figure 17-15 How to create an accordion

How to create a list

Figure 17-16 shows how to create a list that can be used to link to other pages. In the first example, the user can tap anywhere in the content block to go to a page that gives more information about the speaker. In the second example, the user can tap on the image or the text to go to the speaker's page, or the user can tap on the gear icon to go to a Buy Tickets page.

To create a list like this, you start with a ul element that has "listview" as the value of its data-role attribute. Then, you code the HTML for each block in an li element. Within each li element, you code an <a> element with the content you want displayed.

In the HTML for the first example, the <a> element in each block links to the page for the speaker. As a result, the user can tap anywhere in the block to go to the speaker's page. In this case, the default icon is used for the link, and that icon is the right arrow.

The content blocks in the second example include two <a> elements. The first one is coded the same way it is in the first example. Because of that, the user can tap the image or text to go to the speaker's page. The second <a> element causes a second column to be added to the list. If the user taps the icon in this column, the page with "buytix" as its id is displayed. This example also uses the data-split-icon attribute to set the icon that's used in this column to a gear, and it uses the data-inset attribute to inset the list as shown in this example.

A mobile web page that displays a list

Using the defaults

With two columns and data-inset="true"

The HTML for the first list (tapping a list item goes to the speaker's page)

```
<section class="ui-content" role="main">
    <ul data-role="listview">
        <li>
            <a href="#toobin">
                <img src="images/toobin75.jpg">
                <p><strong><br>Jeffrey Toobin<br>
                    October</strong></p></a>
        </li>
        <!-- THE LI ELEMENTS FOR THE OTHER CONTENT BLOCKS -->
    </ul>
</section>
```

The HTML for the second list (tapping the gear goes to a Buy Tickets page)

```
<ul data-role="listview" data-split-icon="gear" data-inset="true">
    <li><!-- SAME AS ABOVE -->
        <a href="#buytix">Buy Tickets</a>
    </li>
    <!-- THE LI ELEMENTS FOR THE OTHER CONTENT BLOCKS -->
</ul>
```

How to code the HTML for a list

- Code a ul element with its data-role attribute set to "listview". If you set the data-inset attribute for this element to "true", the list will be inset as in the second example above.
- Within the ul element, code one li element for each item in your list. Within each li element, code an <a> element that links to a page that contains more information about the item. The link can contain text and images.
- To add a column with an icon that goes to a different page when clicked, code another <a> element.

Figure 17-16 How to create a list

A mobile website that uses jQuery Mobile

To show how the features you've just learned work together in a complete website, this chapter ends by presenting several pages of a mobile website that uses jQuery Mobile. This should give you a better idea of how you can use jQuery Mobile to build your own sites.

The layout for the mobile website

Figure 17-17 presents four pages of the mobile version of the Town Hall website. That includes the Home, Speakers, and Contact Us pages, as well as one of the speaker's pages. On all of these pages, you can see the navigation bar that lets the user go from one page to another.

On the Home page, you can see the speaker of the month and the link that will take the user to that speaker's page. This is followed by copy that tells what the website does.

On the Speakers page, the user can tap on any item in the first column of the list to go to the page for that speaker. Or, the user can tap on the gear icon to open a dialog that shows how to buy tickets. Unlike the list in the previous figure, this one doesn't include images so the text is more prominent.

On the Contact Us page, you can see a phone number, an email address, and a Buy Tickets button that includes a gear icon. If the user taps on the phone number, the user's device will try to call that number. If the user taps on the email address, the user's device will try to start an email to that address. And if the user taps on the Buy Tickets button, the Buy Tickets page will be opened as a dialog. This is the same page that's opened when the user taps on the gear icon on the Speakers page.

The page layouts for a mobile website that uses jQuery Mobile

The Home page

The Speakers page

The Scott Sampson page

The Contact Us page

Description

- When the user taps a speaker on the Speakers page, a page for that speaker is opened. When the user taps a gear, a Buy Tickets dialog is opened.
- When the user taps the phone number on the Contact Us page, the device's phone feature will try to call the number. When the user taps the email address, the device's email feature will try to start an email.

Figure 17-17 A mobile website for Town Hall

The HTML for the mobile website

Figure 17-18 presents the primary HTML for this website in three parts. Since this HTML uses the features that you've learned about in this chapter, you should be able to understand it on your own. In case you're interested, though, here are a few highlights.

In the head section in part 1, the viewport metadata specifies a width equal to the device's width and an initial scale of 1. This should work for all mobile devices, including iPhones and Android devices.

In the body section in part 1, you can see the HTML for the Home page of the site. Since this page is first in the file, it is the one that will be displayed when the HTML file is loaded. Like any jQuery Mobile web page, it uses data-role attributes to identify the page, header, and footer components and the role attribute and ui-content class to identify the content component.

This page also includes a navigation bar with three items. Each item specifies a different icon in its data-icon attribute. In addition, each item specifies "b" as its data-theme attribute so it's displayed with a dark gray background and white type. The exception is the first item, which is made the active item by assigning the ui-btn-active class to it. This item has a blue background with white type.

In part 2 of this figure, you can see the code for the Speakers page. This uses a list like the second one in figure 17-16, but without the images and with headings for the text. This list also includes a gear icon that opens the Buy Tickets page using the pop transition when it is tapped. Although you can't tell from the code shown here, this page is opened as a dialog.

In part 3 of this figure, you can see the code for Scott Sampson's page. This page can be reached from the Home page as well as the Speakers page. Then, to return to the previous page, the button at the bottom of this page is coded as a Back button. In other words, it will return to either the Home or the Speakers page based upon which page linked to it.

In part 3, you can also see the code for the Contact Us page. Here, <a> elements are used for the phone number and email address. That's why the device will try to call the phone number when the phone number is tapped and why the device will try to start an email message when the email address is tapped.

This Contact Us page uses a third <a> element for the button at the bottom of the page content. It specifies the gear icon in its data-icon attribute, so the gear appears on the button. It also specifies "b" as its data-theme attribute so the button is dark gray with white type. Note, however, that it doesn't have a data-role attribute that is set to "button". Instead, this <a> element is coded within a div element that has its class set to "ui-bar", and that's what makes the link look like a button.

The HTML for the head section and the Home page

```
<!DOCTYPE HTML>
<html lang="en">
<head>
    <meta charset="utf-8">
    <meta name="viewport" content="width=device-width, initial-scale=1">
    <title>San Joaquin Valley Town Hall</title>
    <link rel="stylesheet"
    href="http://code.jquery.com/mobile/1.4.5/jquery.mobile-1.4.5.min.css">
    <!-- include the jQuery and jQuery Mobile JavaScript files -->
    <script src=" https://code.jquery.com/jquery-2.1.3.min.js"></script>
    <script
        src="https://code.jquery.com/mobile/1.4.5/jquery.mobile-1.4.5.min.js">
    </script>
</head>

<body>
<div data-role="page" id="home">
    <header data-role="header">
        <h1>SJV Town Hall</h1>
        <div data-role="navbar">
            <ul>
                <li><a href="#home" data-icon="home" data-theme="b"
                       class="ui-btn-active">Home</a></li>
                <li><a href="#speakers" data-icon="star"
                       data-theme="b">Speakers</a></li>
                <li><a href="#contact" data-icon="grid"
                       data-theme="b">Contact Us</a></li>
            </ul>
        </div>
    </header>
    <section class="ui-content" role="main">
        <h3>Speaker of the month<br>February</h3>
        <a href="#sampson">
            <img src="images/sampson75.jpg" alt="Scott Sampson">
            <h4>Fossil Threads in the Web of Life<br>Scott Sampson</h4>
        </a>
        <h3>Cutting-edge speakers <br>for 75 years</h3>
        <p>Since 1936, San Joaquin Valley Town Hall has showcased nationally
           and internationally renowned, thought-provoking speakers who
           inform, educate, and entertain our audience.</p>
        <h3>Our History</h3>
        <p>1937: In the town of Hanford, California, Clio Lee Aydelott—a woman
        ...
        ...
    </section>
    <footer data-role="footer">
        <h4>&copy; 2016</h4>
    </footer>
</div>
```

Figure 17-18 The HTML for the mobile website (part 1 of 3)

The HTML for the Speakers page

```
<div data-role="page" id="speakers">
    <header data-role="header">
        <!-- same header and navigation bar that's in the other pages
             but the Speakers button is the active button -->
    </header>

    <section class="ui-content" role="main">
        <h3>This Season's Speakers</h3>
        <ul data-role="listview" data-split-icon="gear" data-inset="true">
            <li>
                <a href="#toobin">
                    <h4>Jeffrey Toobin<br>Black Robed Secrets</h4>
                    <h4>October</h4>
                </a>
                <a href="#buytix" data-transition="pop">Buy Tickets</a>
            </li>
            <li>
                <a href="#sorkin">
                    <h4>Andrew Ross Sorkin<br>Too Big to Fail</h4>
                    <h4>November</h4>
                </a>
                <a href="#buytix" data-transition="pop">Buy Tickets</a>
            </li>
            <li>
                <a href="#chua">
                    <h4>Amy Chua<br>Babylon to Beijing</h4>
                    <h4>January</h4>
                </a>
                <a href="#buytix" data-transition="pop">Buy Tickets</a>
            </li>
            <li>
                <a href="#sampson">
                    <h4>Scott Sampson<br>Fossil Threads <br>
                        in the Web of Life</h4>
                    <h4>February</h4>
                </a>
                <a href="#buytix" data-transition="pop">Buy Tickets</a>
            </li>
            <li>
                ...
                ...
            </li>
        </ul>
    </section>

    <footer data-role="footer">
        <h4>&copy; 2016</h4>
    </footer>
</div>
```

Figure 17-18 The HTML for the mobile website (part 2 of 3)

The HTML for Scott Sampson's page

```
<div data-role="page" id="sampson">
    <header data-role="header">
        <!-- same header and navigation bar that's in the other pages
             but there is no active button -->
    </header>

    <section class="ui-content" role="main">
        <h3>Fossil Threads<br>in the Web of Life</h3>
        <img src="images/sampson_dinosaur.jpg" alt="Scott Sampson">
        <p>What's 75 million years old and brand spanking new? A teenage
            <!—the rest of the copy for this speaker -->
        </p>
        <p><a href="#" data-role="button" data-rel="back" data-theme="b">
           Back to previous page</a>
        </p>
    </section>

    <footer data-role="footer">
        <h4>&copy; 2016</h4>
    </footer>
</div>
```

The HTML for the Contact Us page

```
<div data-role="page" id="contact">
    <header data-role="header">
        <!-- same header and navigation bar that's in the other pages
             but the Contact Us button is the active button -->
    </header>

    <section class="ui-content" role="main" style="text-align:center;">
        <strong>Phone</strong><br>
        <a href="tel:15594442180">559.444.2180</a><br><br>
        <strong>Mail</strong><br>
            San Joaquin Valley Town Hall<br>
            P.O. Box 5149<br>
            Fresno, CA 93755-5149<br><br>
        <strong>Email</strong><br>
        <a href="mailto:valleytownhall@aol.com">valleytownhall@aol.com</a>
        <br><br>
        <div class="ui-bar">
            <a href="#buytix" data-icon="gear" data-theme="b">Buy Tickets</a>
        </div>
    </section>

    <footer data-role="footer">
        <h4>&copy; 2016</h4>
    </footer>
</div>
</body>
</html>
```

Figure 17-18 The HTML for the mobile website (part 3 of 3)

Perspective

Now that you have completed this chapter, you should be able to build mobile websites with jQuery Mobile. You should also realize that jQuery Mobile has made the task of building a mobile website much easier.

Keep in mind, though, that this chapter has presented fewer than half of the features of jQuery Mobile. To learn how to use the other features, you can go to the jQuery Mobile website.

Terms

viewport
jQuery Mobile
dialog
transition
navigation bar
theme
swatch
collapsible content block
accordion

Summary

- When Responsive Web Design is impractical, it makes sense to build a separate website for mobile devices. Then, you can use client-side or server-side code to detect mobile devices and redirect them from your full website to your mobile website.
- The *viewport* on a mobile device determines the content that's displayed. To control how that works, you can code a viewport meta element in the head section of a page.
- *jQuery Mobile* is a JavaScript library that's designed for developing mobile websites. jQuery Mobile uses the jQuery library along with its own CSS file.
- To include the jQuery Mobile and jQuery libraries in a web page, you code script elements in the head section. Because jQuery Mobile uses jQuery, the script element for jQuery Mobile must be coded after the one for jQuery.
- jQuery Mobile lets you code the HTML for many mobile pages in a single HTML file. jQuery Mobile also supports the use of dialogs, transitions, buttons, navigation bars, collapsible content blocks, accordions, and more.
- By default, jQuery Mobile uses a *theme* that provides formatting that relies on a browser's native rendering engine. jQuery Mobile also provides two *swatches* that you can use to adjust the default formatting without using CSS style sheets of your own.

Exercise 17-1 Test and modify the mobile website for Town Hall

In this exercise, you'll first test the mobile version of the Town Hall website that's presented in this chapter. Then, you'll make some modifications to it, like changing the Speakers page so it looks like the one that follows. This should demonstrate how easy it is to build mobile websites when you use jQuery Mobile.

Open and test the mobile website for Town Hall

1. Use your text editor to open this HTML page:
   `c:\html5_css3_2\exercises\town_hall_mobile\index.html`
2. Test this page and the navigation from one page to another within the site. The easiest way to do that is to run the page in Chrome, press F12 to display the developer tools, click the Toggle Device Mode icon near the left side of the toolbar, and then choose a mobile device like iPhone 6. Then, you can use your mouse to "tap" on a link. As you go from page to page, remember that all of the pages come from one HTML file.

3. Click on the image on the home page to go to the page for Scott Sampson, and then click the button at the bottom of that page to return to the home page. Next, click the Speakers button in the navigation bar and then the link for Scott Sampson to go to the page for Scott Sampson. This time, when you click on the button at the bottom of the page, you return to the Speakers page.

Modify the way the pages work and test these changes

4. Review the code for the button on Scott Sampson's page. Then, modify the code so it returns to the Speakers page no matter how the user got there.
5. In the HTML for the Speakers page, delete the second <a> element for each speaker. Then, test this change to see how the Speakers page has changed and how the navigation works.
6. Add the small images of the speakers to the Speakers page as shown in figure 17-16. Then, adjust the formatting for the text so the page looks something like the page above, but don't use CSS to do that. Instead, experiment with HTML elements like the h4, p, and strong elements. Without using CSS, this formatting can be time-consuming.
7. Add a page for Andrew Ross Sorkin that's like the ones for the other speakers. Use "Too Big to Fail" as the heading for the page and follow that with the large image for him, but don't bother adding any content beyond that. Then, test to make sure that this works and that the navigation to and from the page works.

Experiment on your own

8. Experiment with themes. Try using CSS to format the Speakers page. Add a page that uses a table. You'll soon see how quickly you can build a mobile website with jQuery Mobile. Keep in mind, though, that this chapter has presented fewer than half of the jQuery Mobile features.

Section 4

How to design and deploy a website

In section 1, you learned how to use a professional subset of HTML and CSS for building web pages. Now, in the two chapters of this section, you can learn how to design and deploy a website. You can read these chapters any time after you complete the chapters in section 1, and you can read these chapters in whichever sequence you prefer.

In chapter 18, you'll learn how to design the pages for a website. You'll also learn the guidelines that will help you create an effective website. Then, in chapter 19, you'll learn how to deploy your website from your local computer or server to a web server that has Internet access. You'll also learn how to test your website and how to get your website into the major search engines and directories.

18

How to design a website

If you've read section 1, you know how to use HTML and CSS to develop web pages. Now, in this chapter, you'll learn the guidelines and procedures that you need for designing a website. When you complete this chapter, you'll have a much better idea of how to design a website.

Users and usability

Before you design a website, you need to think about who your users are going to be and what they are going to expect. After all, it is your users who are going to determine the success of your website.

What web users want is usability

What do users want when they reach a website? They want to find what they're looking for as quickly and easily as possible. And when they find it, they want to extract the information or do the task as quickly and easily as possible.

How do users use a web page? They don't read it in an orderly way, and they don't like to scroll. Instead, they scan the page to see if they can find what they're looking for or a link to what they're looking for. Often, they click quickly on a link to see if it gives them what they want, and if it doesn't, they click on the Back button to return to where they were. In fact, users click on the Back button more than 30% of the time when they reach a new page.

If the users can't find what they're looking for or get too frustrated, they leave the site. It's that simple. For some websites, more than 50% of first-time visitors to the home page leave without ever going to another page.

In web development terms, what the users want is *usability*. This term refers to how easy it is to use a website, and usability is one of the key factors that determines the effectiveness of a website. If a site is easy to use, it has a chance to be effective. If it isn't easy to use, it probably won't be effective.

Figure 18-1 presents one page of a website that has a high degree of usability, and it presents three guidelines for improving usability. First, you should try to present the critical information for a page "above the fold." This term refers to what's shown on the screen when a new page is displayed, which is analogous to the top half of a newspaper. This reduces the need for scrolling, and gives the page a better chance for success.

Second, you should try to group related items into separate components, and limit the number of components on each page. That will make the page look more manageable and will help people find what they're looking for.

Third, you should adhere to the current conventions for website usability. For instance, clickable links should look like they're clickable and items that aren't clickable shouldn't fool users by looking like they are clickable.

If you look at the website in this figure, you can see that it has implemented these guidelines. All of the critical information is presented above the fold. The page is divided into a header and six other well-defined components, including a set of tabs near the bottom of the page. It's also easy to tell where to click.

Of course, it's relatively easy to build a website like this because it has a small number of products. In contrast, building usability into a large website with dozens of product categories and hundreds of products is a serious challenge.

A website that is easy to use

What website users want

- To find what they're looking for as quickly and easily as possible
- To get the information or do the task that they want to do as quickly and easily as possible.

How website users use a web page

- They scan the page to find what they're looking for or a link to what they're looking for, and they don't like to scroll. If they get frustrated, they leave.
- They often click on links and buttons with the hope of finding what they're looking for, and they frequently click on the Back button when they don't find it.

Three guidelines for improving usability

- Present all of the critical information "above the fold" so the user doesn't have to scroll.
- Group related items into separate components, and limit the number of components on each page.
- Adhere to the current conventions for website usability (see the next figure).

Description

- *Usability* refers to how easy it is to use a website, and usability is a critical requirement for an effective website.

Figure 18-1 What web users want is usability

The current conventions for usability

If you've been using websites for a while, you know that you expect certain aspects of each website to work the same way. For example, you expect underlined text to be a link to another web page, and you expect that something will happen if you click on a button. These are website conventions that make a website easier to use because they work the same on almost all sites.

Figure 18-2 summarizes some of the other conventions that lead to improved usability. By following these conventions, you give the users what they expect, and that makes your website easier to use.

To start, a header usually consists of a logo, tag line, utilities, navigation bar, and search function. As a result, the users look for these items in the header. In the example in this figure, this tag line is below the logo: "Powered by Service." The utilities are in the top border, including "Logout", "My Account", "My Favorites", and "Help". The navigation bar contains links that divide the website into sections. And the search function consists of a text box that's large enough for long entries followed by a Search button. All of these are website conventions, and that's where experienced users look for these components.

The navigation conventions are also critical to the usability of a website. In brief, clickable items should look like they're clickable, and items that aren't clickable shouldn't look like they're clickable. A more recent convention is that clicking on the logo in the header of a page should take you back to the home page.

If you implement all of these conventions on your site, you will be on your way to web usability. But that's just a start. In the rest of this chapter, you'll learn many other ways to improve the usability of a site.

A web page that illustrates some of the current website conventions

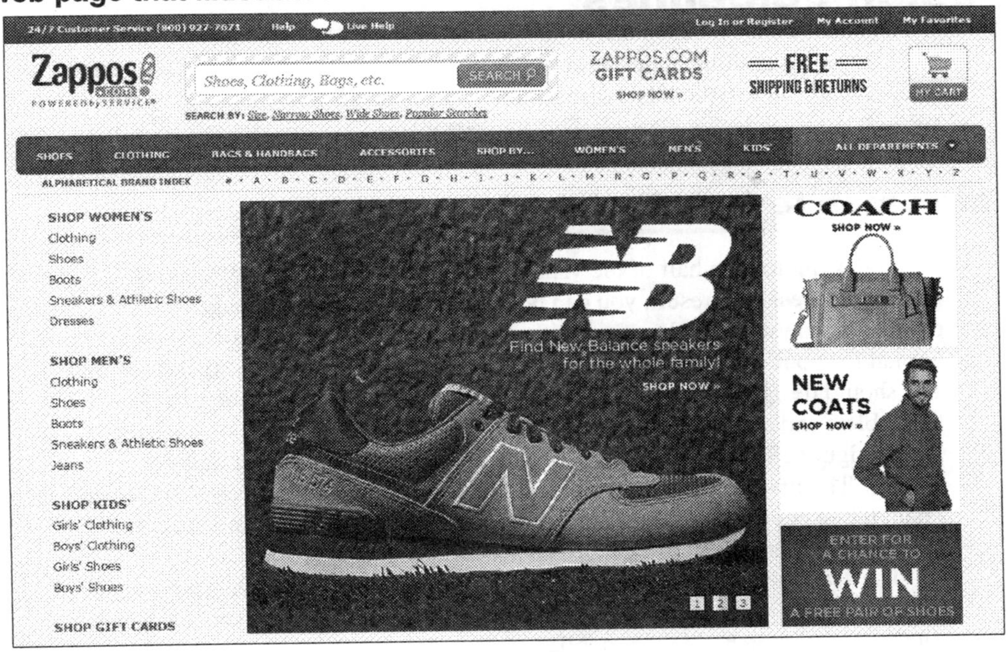

Header conventions

- The header consists of a logo, tag line, utilities, and a navigation bar.
- The tag line identifies what's unique about the website.
- The navigation bar provides links that divide the site into sections.
- The utilities consist of links to useful but not primary information.
- If your site requires a search function, it should be in the header, and it should consist of a large text box for the text followed by a button that's labeled either "Go" or "Search."

Navigation conventions

- Underlined text is always a link.
- Images that are close to short text phrases are clickable.
- A small symbol in front of a text phrase is clickable.
- Short text phrases in columns are clickable.
- If you click on a cart symbol, you go to your shopping cart.
- If you click on the logo in the header, you go to the home page.

Description

- If your website implements the current website conventions, your users will be able to use the same techniques on your site that they use on other sites.

Figure 18-2 The current conventions for usability

Design guidelines

Did you ever think about what makes a good website? Well, a lot of experts have. What follows, then, is a distillation of some of the best thinking on the subject.

Think mobile from the start

Today, more than half of the visitors to a website are likely to be using mobile devices. As a result, you can no longer design your web pages for computer browsers and then deal with mobile devices later on. Instead, you need to plan for your mobile device users from the start. In fact, some experts say that you should design for mobile devices first, and then design for larger devices like tablets and computers.

As figure 18-3 summarizes, there are two ways to provide for mobile devices. The first, as you learned in chapter 8, is to use Responsive Web Design. Then, the pages for large screens also work for mobile devices, and the content for large screens is available to the mobile devices too.

The second way to provide for mobile devices is to build a separate website for them. Then, when users access the full website from mobile devices, they are automatically switched to the mobile website. This is often more practical for large, established websites that would be difficult and expensive to convert to Responsive Web Design. One of the benefits of a separate site for mobile devices is that you can limit the content to what's most needed by mobile users.

When you design the pages for a responsive website, you may want to design the mobile pages first. That's especially true if most of your visitors use mobile devices. Then, you can enhance those designs so they work on large screens too.

The other approach is to design for computer browsers, but make sure that Responsive Web Design can be applied to every page that you design. In this figure, for example, the screen design consists of two columns that can be converted to one column for mobile devices. Also, the navigation bar consists of five links that can be converted to a responsive menu, as you saw in chapter 8.

If you're designing pages for a separate mobile website, the full website is most likely finished and running. Then, you can select the content that is appropriate for the mobile site. This can result in a leaner, more efficient site for mobile users.

So, think mobile from the start or design for mobile users first? To some extent, that depends on how important your mobile users are. But it also depends on your preferences. Since most designers today started by designing for large screens, that's still the predominant approach for designing mobile websites. But even if you don't design for mobile first, you have to think mobile from the start.

The full screen and mobile views of the Town Hall home page

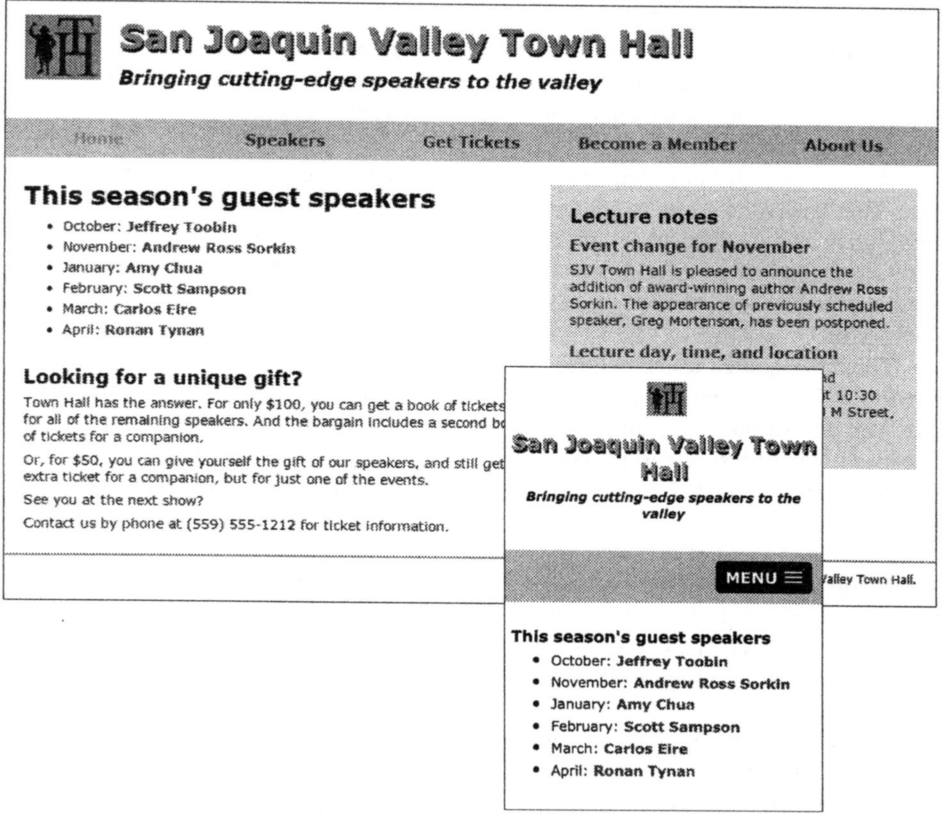

Two ways to provide for mobile devices

- Use Responsive Web Design (see chapter 8)
- Build a separate website for mobile devices (see chapter 17).

Two ways to design the pages for Responsive Web Design

- Design the mobile pages first. Then, expand those designs for larger browsers.
- Design for computer browsers first, but make sure that the designs will work when the pages are displayed on mobile devices.

Description

- By today's standards, the best way to provide for mobile devices is to use Responsive Web Design. However, that isn't always practical for large websites that weren't designed that way. For those sites, a separate mobile site is often a practical alternative.

Figure 18-3 Think mobile from the start

Use the home page to sell the site

Figure 18-4 presents 9 guidelines for the design of a home page. Most important is the first one, which says to emphasize what's different about your site and why it's valuable from the user's point of view. In other words, sell your site to your visitors.

If you're a well-known company with a successful site, this isn't as important. That's why the home pages for the websites of most large companies don't make any special efforts to sell their sites. But if you're developing the website for a small company that still needs to develop a customer base, by all means use the home page to sell the site. That may determine whether or not your site is successful.

The other guidelines should be self-explanatory. For instance, you don't need to welcome users to your site because that space should be used to sell the site. You don't want to include an active link to the home page on the home page because it would just reload the page. You do want to limit the length of the page title to 8 words and 64 characters because it's displayed in the results for search engines. And you do want to use a different design for the home page to set it off from the other pages of the site.

If you look at the home page in this figure, you can see that it tries to sell the site. Its tag line says: "love what you buy." Then, the copy in the top block adds: "We Simplify The Complex" and shows their three-step procedure for doing that. That encourages me to at least try one of their recommendations for a product category.

If you're competing with a known brand like *Consumers Digest*, and most of us are, you obviously need to let people know what you do better, and you need to do that on the home page. Nevertheless, not doing that is a critical failing of most websites.

A home page that tries to sell the site

9 guidelines for developing an effective home page

1. Emphasize what your site offers that's valuable and how your site differs from competing sites.
2. Emphasize the highest priority tasks of your site so users have a clear idea of what they can do.
3. Don't welcome users to your site because that's a waste of space.
4. Group items in the navigation areas so similar items are next to each other.
5. Only use icons for navigation if the users will readily recognize them.
6. Design the home page so it is different from the other pages of the site.
7. Don't include an active link to the home page on the home page.
8. Code the title for the home page as the organization name, followed by a short description, and limit the title to 8 or fewer words and 64 or fewer characters.
9. If your site provides shopping, include a link to the shopping cart on your home page.

Description

- *Homepage Usability* by Jakob Nielsen and Marie Tahir presents 113 guidelines for home pages, plus an analysis of the home pages for 50 websites. Though dated, it is still worth reading.

Figure 18-4 Use the home page to sell the site

Let the users know where they are

As users navigate a site, they like to know where they are. That's why letting the users know where they are is one of the current conventions for website usability. Remember too that many users will reach your site via search engines so they won't arrive at the home page. They have a special need to find out where they are.

As figure 18-5 shows, there are three primary ways to let the users know where they are. First, you should highlight the links that led the user to the current page. Second, the heading for the page should be the same as the link that led to it.

This is illustrated by the first web page in this figure. Here, the Fly Fishing link is highlighted in the navigation bar, which means that the user started there. Then, the Fly Rods and Freshwater Helios Rods are highlighted in the links of the left sidebar (they're red), which means the user first clicked the Fly Rods link followed by the Freshwater Helios Rods link. Last, the heading for the page is "Freshwater Helios Rods", which is the same as the link that led to the page.

The third way to let the users know where they are is to provide *bread-crumbs* that show the path to the page. This is illustrated by the second page in this figure. When you use breadcrumbs, the current convention is to do it just as this website did it, with a symbol like the greater than sign (>) to mark each step in the path.

A product page with the active links highlighted

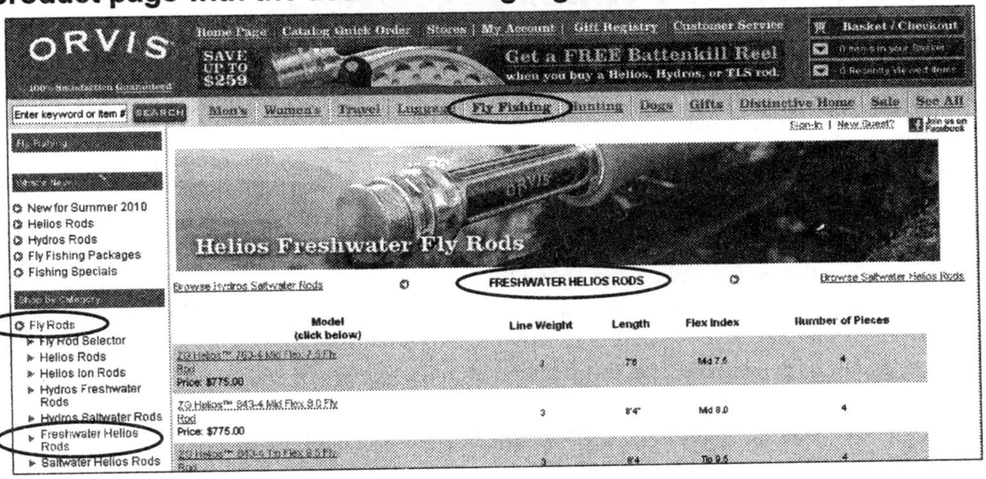

A product page that provides breadcrumbs

How to let the users know where they are

- Highlight the active links.
- The heading for the page should be the same as the link that led to the page.
- Provide breadcrumbs in this format: Homepage > Men > Shoes & Sandals.

Description

- As your site gets more complex, the users are likely to lose track of where they are in the site. But even simple sites should let the users know where they are.

Figure 18-5 Let the users know where they are

Make the best use of web page space

As you design a web page, remember that the part of the page that's above the fold is the most valuable space. As a result, you want to put the most important components of the page in that space. That's why many of the most successful websites have relatively small headers. That way, they have more space for the components that make each page effective.

To emphasize this point, figure 18-6 presents an extreme example of a web page that doesn't get the most out of the space above the fold. In fact, none of the text of the page can be seen above the fold. You have to scroll down for all of the information. Granted that the photos are beautiful (if you're a fly fisher), but does the fish have to show on every page that relates to Bob Cusack's Alaska Lodge? This is a case where the graphics got out of control and diminished the usability of the page.

As you design your pages, remember the three guidelines in this figure. Keep your header relatively small. Prioritize the components that are going to go on the page. And then give the best space to the most important components.

Wasted space on a primary page

Guidelines for the effective use of space

- Keep the header relatively small.
- Prioritize the components for each page.
- Give the most important components the primary locations.

Description

- The most valuable space on each web page is the space above the fold. To get the most from it, you need to prioritize the components on each page and give the best locations to the highest-priority components.

Figure 18-6 Make the best use of web page space

Divide long pages into shorter chunks

Remember that website users don't like to scroll. So a general guideline for web page design is to limit the amount of scrolling to one-and-one-half or two times the height of the browser window. But what if you need to present more information than that?

The best solution is to use *chunking* to divide the content into logical pieces or topics. This is illustrated by the example in figure 18-7. Here, what could be a long page of copy is chunked into smaller topics like "What makes Murach books the best". Then, if the users are interested in the topic, they can click on the MORE button to expand that copy. Below the two topics shown here is an accordion (see chapter 16) that presents "Five more reasons why our customers love our books." So in all, the copy for this page has been broken down into seven topics.

This approach lets the users select the topics that they're interested in so they have more control over their website experience. This makes it easier for the users to find what they're looking for. And this reduces the need for scrolling. How much better this is than forcing the users to scroll through a long page of text trying to find what they're looking for.

A home page that has been chunked

Description

- *Chunking* refers to the division of content into smaller chunks that can be presented on separate web pages or in separate components on the same page. This lets the users select the chunks of information that they're interested in.
- Chunking makes the information more accessible to the user, and reduces the need for scrolling.
- Two JavaScript features that you can use to implement chunking are accordions and tabs (see chapter 16).

Figure 18-7 Divide long pages into shorter chunks

Know the principles of graphics design

If you aren't a graphics designer and you're developing a website, you should at least know the four basic principles of graphics design that are presented in figure 18-8. These principles are in common use on all of the best websites, so it's easy to find examples of their use.

For instance, *alignment* means that aligning related items gives a sense of order to a web page, and all of the examples to this point in this chapter make extensive use of alignment. Similarly, *proximity* means that related items should be close to each other, and all of those examples illustrate this principle too. When proximity is applied to headings, it means that a heading should be closer to the text that follows it than the text that precedes it.

The principle of *repetition* means that you repeat some elements from page to page to give the pages continuity. This is natural for web pages, starting with the header, which is usually the same on all pages. This goes along with *contrast*, which is what draws your eye to a component. For instance, a component with a large heading or a yellow background will draw attention because it stands out from the other components of the page.

The home page in this figure illustrates what happens if you don't obey these principles. Because the principle of proximity isn't obeyed, the headings float above blocks of copy so it looks like the page consists of many small components. Because the contrast of the symbols in the middle of the page (what are they?) draws your eye to them, the user is drawn away from the text that matters. Besides that, the alignment isn't clean so the page looks disorganized.

If you aren't a graphics designer, you don't need to be intimidated by the use of these principles because there are thousands of good examples on the Internet. By copying them, you should be able to develop an attractive and inviting website that delivers a high degree of usability.

But whether or not you're a graphics designer, you should get the typography right. That way, your readers are more likely to read what you've written. In section 1, you were introduced to some of the guidelines for effective typography, but this figure presents them again.

One common problem is text lines that are longer than 65 characters. You'll see this illustrated in the next figure. Some less common problems are using a background image, using a background color that is too dark, centering text, and justifying text.

Also, if you indent the first line of each paragraph, you don't need space between the paragraphs, but you do need space if you don't indent the first lines. Last, you should avoid the use of reverse type (white type on a dark background), especially for text, because it's difficult to read.

A home page that doesn't adhere to the principles of graphics design

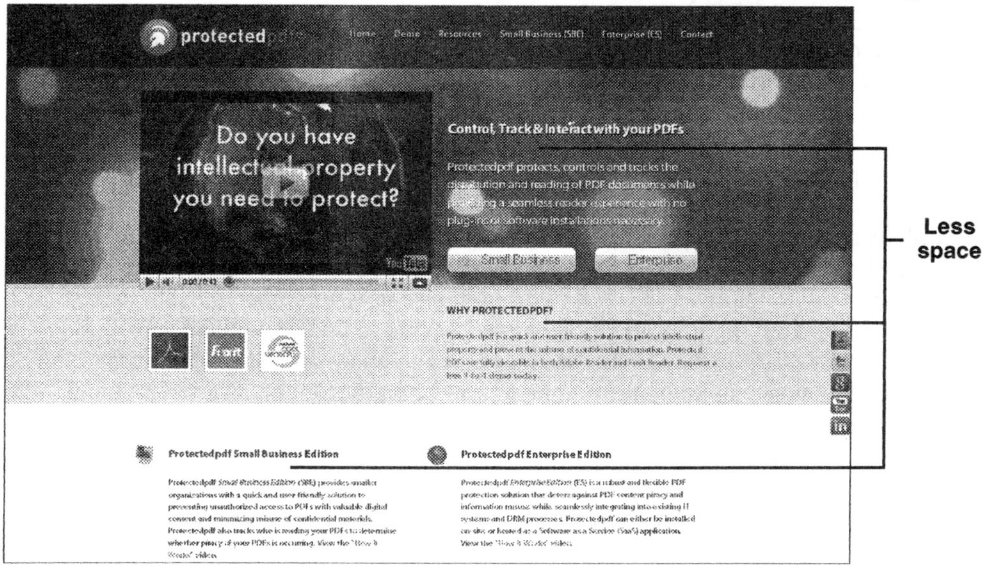

Four principles of graphics design

- *Alignment* means that related items on the page should line up with each other.
- *Proximity* means that related items should be close together.
- *Repetition* means that you should repeat some elements from page to page to give the pages continuity.
- *Contrast* is what draws your eye to the components on a web page. If everything is the same, nothing stands out.

Typographical guidelines

- Limit the line length of paragraphs to 65 characters.
- Use a sans serif font in a size that's large enough for easy reading.
- Show the relationship between a heading and the text that follows by keeping them close.
- Use dark text on a light background, and don't use an image for the background.
- Don't center text and don't justify text.
- If you indent the first lines of paragraphs, you don't need space between the paragraphs.
- Don't use reverse type (white type on a colored background) for text.

Description

- If you aren't a graphics designer, you can at least implement the principles of graphics design and get the typography right.

Figure 18-8 Know the principles of graphics design

Write for the web

Remember how web users use a website. Instead of reading, they skim and scan. They want to get the information that they're looking for as quickly as possible, and they don't want to have to dig through several paragraphs of text for it. That's why writing for a website is so different from writing for the printed page.

In figure 18-9, you can see a block of copy that isn't written for the web, followed by one that is. To present the same information in a way that is more accessible, the second example uses fewer words (135 to 177), which is the quickest way to improve your web writing. It also uses a numbered list to make it easy to find the flight information without having to dig through the text.

If you look through the other web writing guidelines, you'll see that they recommend what we implement in the figures of our books: an inverted pyramid style so the most important items are presented first; headings and subheadings to identify portions of the text; bulleted and numbered lists; tables for tabular information; and no headings with all caps. We do that so you don't have to read all of the text to review the information that you're looking for, and that's also the way web writing should work.

The last guideline is to make the text for all links as explicit as possible. For instance, "Find a job with us" is better than "Jobs", and "Apply for unemployment compensation" is better than "Unemployment". Remember that 30 to 40 percent of a user's clicks are likely to be on the Back button because a link didn't take him where he wanted. The more explicit your links are, the less that will happen.

Incidentally, the first example in this figure also illustrates poor typography. Above all, the text lines are 90 characters long, which makes the text unappealing and difficult to read. To fix that problem, you can increase the font size and shorten the line width, as shown in the second example. In addition, three different font sizes are used in the first four lines of the first example, but the font sizes don't reflect the relative importance of the text.

Writing that isn't for the web (177 words and 1041 characters)

> **The progressive air services you'll use to reach Cusack's Alaska Lodge are a wonderful reflection of your journey into the wilderness. First, you will fly a major jet service from near your home to Anchorage,** Alaska; arriving here, most itineraries will mandate an overnight stay. The next morning you will board a small plane piloted by one of the fine bush pilots of Iliamna Air Taxi (often one of their Pilatus aircraft, a high-flying, very comfortable aircraft), for the transfer between Anchorage and the little village of Iliamna. Upon arriving, Iliamna Air Taxi's Iliamna crew will switch your gear from the mid-sized plane to a smaller, float-equipped Cessna or Beaver, and after a short wait, you will be on the final leg of your adventure, touching down on the lake's surface in front of Bob's lodge a short thirty minutes later. For the remainder of your week, Bob will be your pilot, flying you into amazingly beautiful country in his two small airplanes, giving you a peek into the enormity and grandeur of his corner of Alaska.

The same copy, but written for the web (135 words and 717 characters)

> **The three-part flight to Bob Cusack's Alaska Lodge is a fascinating journey into the Alaskan wilderness**
>
> 1. You take a major jet service from your home to Anchorage, Alaska.
> 2. From Anchorage, you take the Iliamna Air Taxi to the little village of Iliamna. This flight will be piloted by one of the Air Taxi's fine bush pilots in a comfortable plane like the Pilatus.
> 3. In Iliamna, the Air Taxi's crew will switch your bags to a smaller, float plane like a Cessna or a Beaver. Then, after a short wait and a 30 minute flight, you will touch down on beautiful Lake Iliamna in front of Bob's lodge.
>
> For the remainder of your week, Bob will be your pilot as he takes you into the beauty and grandeur of his corner of Alaska.

Web writing guidelines

- Use fewer words.
- Write in inverted pyramid style with the most important information first.
- Use headings and subheadings to identify portions of the text.
- Use bulleted lists and numbered lists to make information more accessible.
- Use tables for tabular information.
- Don't use all caps (all capital letters) for headings. Usually, it's best to capitalize only the first letter in a heading, plus any required capitalization.
- Make the text for all links as explicit as possible.
- Keep the line length to 65 characters or fewer.

Description

- Web users skim and scan; they don't read like book readers do. So when you write for the web, you need to change the way you think about writing.

Figure 18-9 Write for the web

How to design a website

To give you a better idea of how to design a website, the next five figures present a design procedure starting with the lifecycle of a website.

The lifecycle of a website

The diagram at the top of figure 18-10 represents the *lifecycle* of every website. First, you design the website. Then, you implement it. Last, you maintain it, usually for many years. In fact, the cost of maintaining a website is likely to be far more than developing it in the first place. That's why it's so important to develop a website in a way that makes it easier to maintain.

To make a website easier to maintain, you need to implement it with HTML for the content and CSS for the formatting. That's most important, and that's what you've learned to do throughout this book. Beyond that, you should only use tables for tabular information, not for page layout. And you shouldn't use HTML frames, which aren't presented in this book.

Perhaps most important, though, is to take the time to get the design right in the first place and also to get agreement on that design from all who have a vested interest it its success. Then, you should be able to enhance and improve the website with minimal change to what's already in place.

Next, this figure presents a general procedure for designing a website. This procedure will be illustrated by the next four figures, but here's the general idea. Like you would with any design project, step 1 has you define who is going to use the website and what the goals of the website are. In step 2, you develop a site map that summarizes all of the pages of the website and the navigation between those pages. In step 3, you design the critical pages of the website in black and white using sketches or wireframes. And in step 4, you develop full-color illustrations of the designs for the critical pages.

After each step, of course, you get agreement from all who have a vested interest in the success of the site. That doesn't mean that you won't have to back track as you step through the design process, but that should limit it. When you have agreement on the site map and the design of the critical pages, you're ready to start implementing the site.

A general procedure for implementing a site is next in this figure. Here, you start by developing the HTML and CSS templates for the pages of the website. These templates are built off the illustrations for the pages that have already been agreed to. Once they're done, you do the time-consuming work of developing all of the pages. When all of the pages have been tested, you deploy the website to an Internet server, test it, and launch the site, as shown in the next chapter.

The last procedure in this figure is for maintaining a website. In brief, you plan what the changes should be and then design, implement, and test them. If the changes are minimal, that may be all that's needed. But if the changes or enhancements are extensive, this might turn out to be another design project instead of a maintenance project. That's why it's so important to get the design right in the first place.

The lifecycle of a website

How to make a website easier to maintain

- Use HTML for the content and CSS for the page layout and formatting.
- Don't use tables for page layout. Only use tables for tabular information.
- Don't use frames (not presented in this book).
- Get the design right before you start implementing it.

A general procedure for designing a website

1. Define the audience and set the goals for the website.
2. Develop a site map.
3. Sketch or wireframe the critical pages in black and white.
4. Illustrate the critical pages in full color.

A general procedure for implementing a website

1. Develop the HTML and CSS templates for the pages.
2. Develop the web pages.
3. Deploy the site to a web server (see chapter 19).
4. Test and launch the site (see chapter 19).

A general procedure for maintaining a website

1. Plan the changes.
2. Design the changes.
3. Implement the changes.
4. Test and launch the changes.

Description

- The *lifecycle* of all systems including websites is (1) design, (2) implement, and (3) maintain. Often, more time is spent maintaining a website than developing it in the first place.
- As you design a website, you need to get agreement from all reviewers after each design step.

Figure 18-10 The lifecycle of a website

Step 1: Define the audience and set the goals

Step 1 in the procedure for designing a website is to design the audience and set the goals for the site. Figure 18-11 gives an example of that.

This figure starts with a description of a community service organization called Town Hall. Each year, this organization brings six speakers into the local community for lectures. This organization has been doing this for almost 75 years, and the lectures have enlightened and enriched the lives of the organization's members as well as students and non-members who attend the lectures. To balance its budget, this organization also relies on the donations from a core group of donors.

Before you can define the audience and goals of a website, you need to get that type of information. Then, you can draft the definitions of the audience and goals as shown in this figure.

Usually, the *target audience* for a website will consist of more than one type of visitor. In this case, that audience is defined as members, non-members, and donors. And usually there will be more than one goal for the website. Because these definitions will guide the design of the website, it's important to get them right and to get all of the design participants to agree on them.

About Town Hall

- Town Hall is a community service that runs six lectures each year that are available to all of the members of the community.
- The speakers for these lectures come from all over the country and are known experts in their fields.
- After each lecture, a luncheon is held in the same building and the speaker for the day answers questions from the audience.
- Eight days before each lecture, there's a meeting at the local library to discuss the subject of the lecture.
- Students are admitted to these lectures free.
- Town Hall will soon be celebrating its 75th anniversary.

The target audience

- Members of Town Hall
- Prospective members of Town Hall
- Donors and possible donors to Town Hall

The goals of the website

- Provide all of the information that members need for attending the lectures.
- Provide all of the information that non-members need for attending one or more lectures.
- Convince non-members to become members.
- List current donors and encourage people to become donors.

Description

- Like all projects, you start by defining what you're trying to do and who you're going to do it for.
- Before you can define the audience and set the goals for the site, you need to learn about the company or organization that the site represents.
- The people who you want to use your website can be referred to as the *target audience*.

Figure 18-11 Define the audience and set the goals

Step 2: Develop the site map

Step 2 in the design procedure is to develop a *site map*. This is illustrated by the first map in figure 18-12, which is for the Town Hall website that you've been working with throughout this book.

Here, the second level represents the links in the navigation bar for the site: Speakers, Get Tickets, Become a Member, and About Us. This is consistent with the home page shown in figure 18-3. This also shows that there will be multiple speakers that can be accessed by the Speakers link. And it shows that the About Us link in the navigation bar will provide access to four more pages. Because the Town Hall site is simple, the site map is simple too.

The second site map in this figure is more complex because the website it represents is more complex. Here again, the second level represents the links in the navigation bar: Shop Books, About our eBooks, Customer Service, Courseware for Trainers, and About Us. And here again, the boxes below the second level represent the pages that are accessed by each of the buttons in the navigation bar.

The benefit of developing a site map is that it forces you to plan all of the content that the site is going to require as well as the navigation for that content. It also provides a guide for developing the website later on. Although it's tempting to push on to the next steps before you have a thorough site map, that is likely to be counterproductive. If you do the site map right and get agreement from all vested parties, you're on your way to a successful site.

For large sites, of course, the site map gets even more complex. Then, the site map is likely to take several pages. For instance, you can use one page to show the top two levels and maybe the third level for one of the sections of the site, and you can use other pages for the other sections of the site.

A site map for the Town Hall website

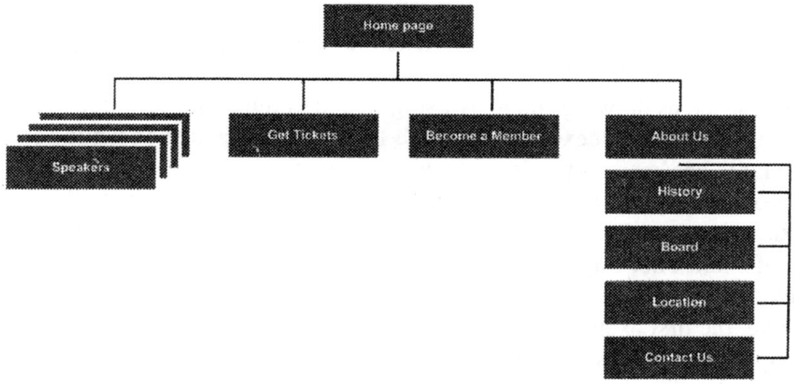

The site map for murach.com

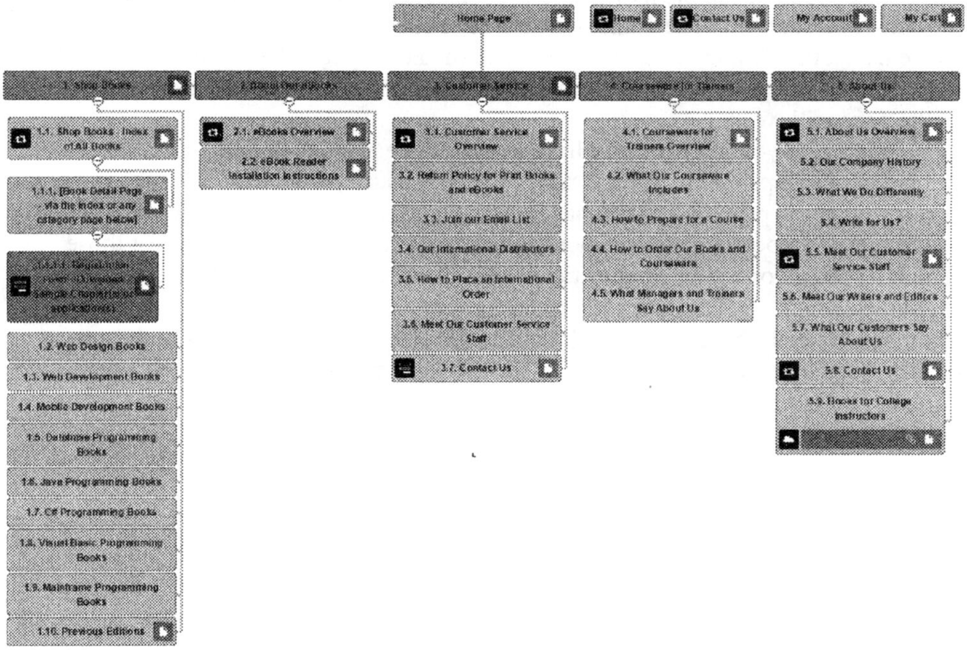

Description

- To document the navigation for a website, you develop a *site map* that shows all of the pages that the website requires.
- In a site map, the second level represents the links in the navigation bar, and the contents below that level represent the pages that are accessed via those links.
- You can develop a site map by using a simple drawing program like Visio or by using one of the free or commercial software products for site maps.

Figure 18-12 Develop the site map

Step 3: Wireframe the critical pages

Step 3 in the design procedure is to *wireframe* the critical pages of the website. Wireframes are sketches or drawings that can be as simple as pencil sketches or as finished as drawings done by using free or commercial software products. For instance, the first example in figure 18-13 is a pencil sketch while the second example has been done with a drawing program.

The intent of a wireframe is to show the layout of a web page, including all of the navigation elements. That's why wireframes are usually done in black and white instead of color. That way, the focus in on what the screens present and how they work, not on what they look like.

In this figure, the first example is a sketch of the Town Hall home page. It shows the navigation bar, the section that presents the main content, and the sidebar that presents news items. For simple websites, a sketch like this can be enough to get the design for a page started.

The second example in this figure is a professional page that was developed with Photoshop CC. The complete wireframe shows the links in the header and the navigation bar, the rotator at the top of the home page, the carousel that presents the best sellers, and so on. This gives the user a much better idea of how the page will work.

Note that you usually don't have to wireframe all of the pages in the site map in this step, just the critical pages. So, you usually start with the home page and one of the primary content pages, like a speakers page for the Town Hall website or a book page for murach.com. Then, when you get approval for those pages, you go on to the other critical pages like the Shopping Cart pages for murach.com.

In general, though, you don't have to wireframe all of the pages in the site map. That's because you can usually base the design for the other pages on the designs for the critical pages.

A sketch of the home page for Town Hall

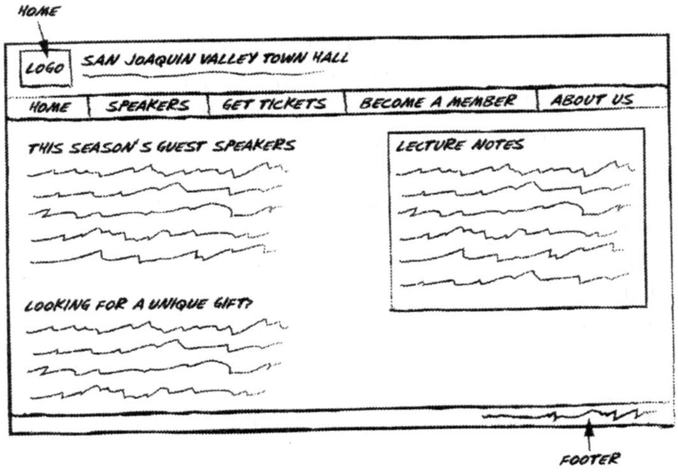

A wireframe for the home page of murach.com

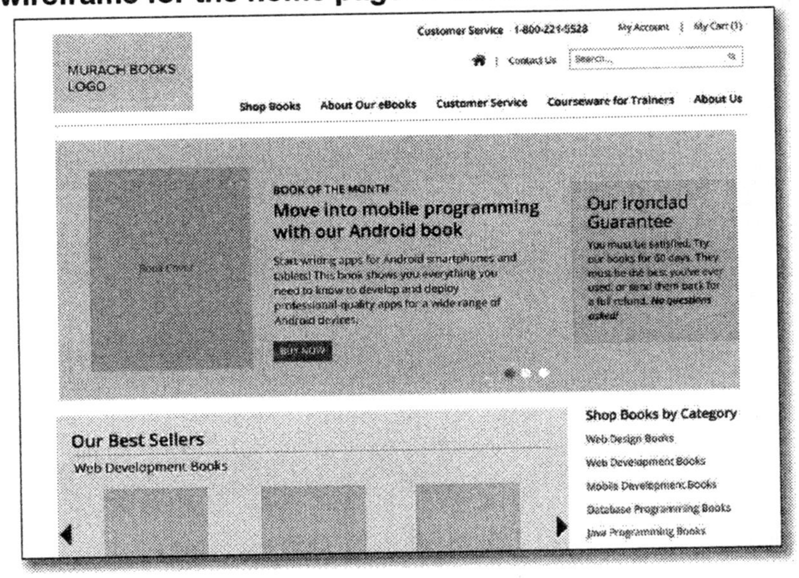

Description

- A *wireframe* is a sketch or drawing done in black and white so the focus is on the components of the page, not how the page looks. A wireframe can be drawn by hand or by using one of the free or commercial software products for wireframes.
- After the site map has been approved, you wireframe the home page and one of the primary content pages. When those are approved, you go on to the other critical pages.
- In general, you don't need to wireframe all of the pages of a website.

Figure 18-13 Wireframe the critical pages

Step 4: Illustrate the critical pages

After you get agreement on the wireframes, step 4 is to develop full-color designs for the critical pages. Usually, these designs are done with a product like Photoshop. But some designers actually build the pages with HTML and CSS. That of course gives them a head start on implementation.

This is illustrated by the examples in figure 18-14. These are the Photoshop illustrations of the home page and Shopping Cart for murach.com. If you compare the home page with the wireframe in the previous figure, you can see that the focus has changed from components to graphics design. Unfortunately, everyone seems to have an opinion when it comes to graphics design, so it can be much harder to get agreement on the full-color designs than the wireframes.

The second example just shows that you need to design all of the critical pages before you start building the web pages. That includes the pages for forms and Shopping Carts, which often have a design that is quite different from all of the other pages.

Here again, you usually don't need to illustrate all of the pages in the site map. Instead, when you get agreement on the designs for the critical pages, you can start building the website.

A Photoshop illustration for the home page of murach.com

A Photoshop illustration for the Shopping Cart

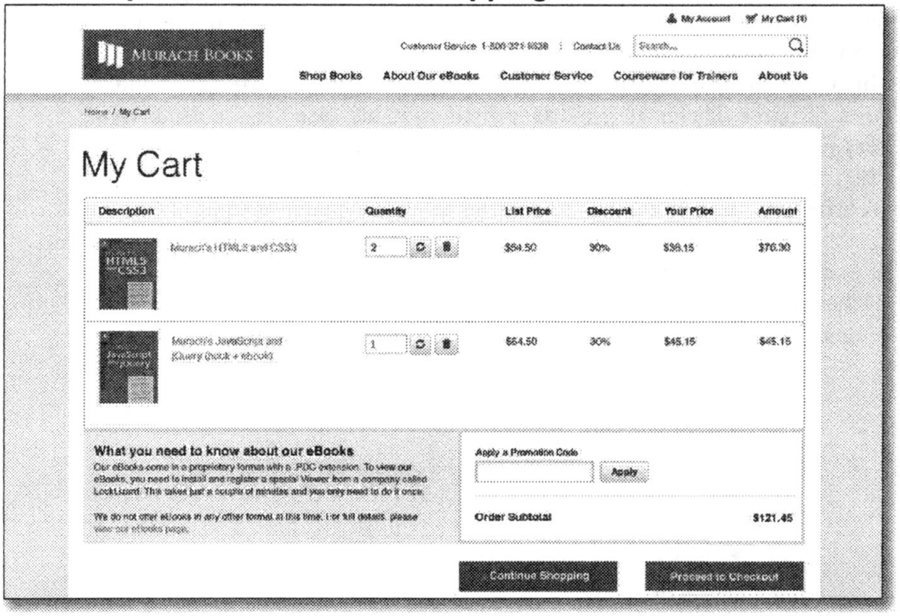

Description

- After the wireframes are approved, you illustrate the critical pages in full color. To do that, most graphics designers use a software product like Photoshop.
- Another alternative is to actually develop the critical pages using HTML and CSS by using a software product like Dreamweaver. That gives you a head start on implementing the pages.

Figure 18-14 Illustrate the critical pages

Other design considerations

At this point, you should have a good idea of how a website is designed. But you should also be aware of a few other design considerations.

Development teams

A large company's website is usually designed and implemented by team members like those that are summarized in figure 18-15. To design the site, a typical team will consist of one or more web designers, one or more writers, a marketing specialist or two, and one or more graphics designers. Then, to implement the website after it has been designed, a typical team will consist of HTML and CSS specialists, client-side programmers, server-side programmers, a database administrator, and a network administrator.

In short, you don't design a website or even a portion of a website by yourself when you work in a large shop. In contrast, a small website may be designed and developed by a single person. In either case, though, you never work alone, unless you're designing your own website. Instead, you review each phase of the design with the people you're working with: your boss, your client, the marketing team, the other members of the design team, or even potential users of the website.

This figure also summarizes the difference between a *web designer* and a *graphics designer*. This is an important distinction because they're usually two different jobs. In short, web designers participate in all phases of web design with the focus on usability. In contrast, graphics designers focus on the aspects of a website that make it look more inviting and manageable so more people will use it.

In practice, then, good graphics design is an essential but relatively small part of the web design process. In fact, the trend is toward simplicity. So if you're designing a small site, don't be afraid to keep it simple.

A large website that is managed by a team

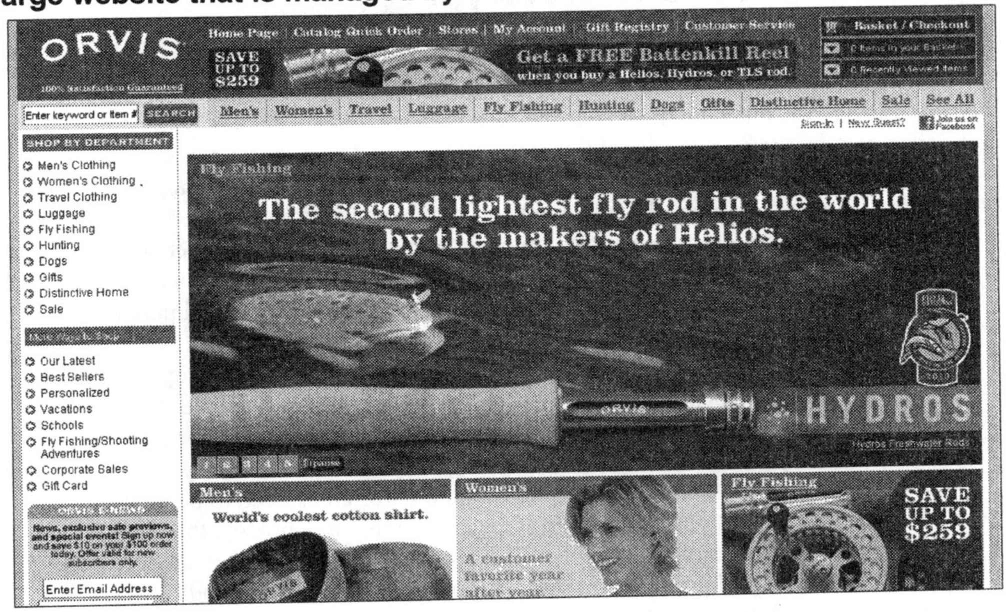

Typical members of a development team

For design

Web designers

Writers

Marketing specialists

Graphics designers

For implementation

HTML and CSS specialists

Client-side programmers

Server-side programmers

Database administrator

Network administrator

Web designers vs. graphics designers

- *Web designers* participate in all phases of web design.
- *Graphics designers* focus on the graphics that make web pages work better and look more inviting.

Description

- In a large company, a website is usually designed and implemented by a team. In a small company, a single person is likely to do everything.
- Unless you're designing your own website, you will be working with others who will review and evaluate your work, such as your boss, marketing specialists, your customer, or potential users.
- *Web designer* is a term that's often confused with *graphics designer*, but graphics design is a relatively small part of web design.

Figure 18-15 The use of development teams

Top-down design and prototyping

For all but the simplest websites, designing a website is a challenging process. To complicate that, your design usually has to please several reviewers so you can't just design the pages and be done with them. That's why the four-step procedure you saw in figure 18-10 usually doesn't work quite that way.

For instance, it would be great if you could develop the site map and be done with it. But that assumes that you know all of the content that's needed for the website, even though some of that content hasn't even been written yet. That also assumes that the people who you're developing the site for have a clear idea how the website should work, even though they often aren't technical people and have no idea what rotators, carousels, accordions, and tabs are.

So instead of a four-step process, the design procedure usually loops through steps 2, 3, and 4. When the reviewers see the wireframes, for example, they are likely to realize that they need more pages, so the site map needs to be adjusted. And when they see the illustrations, they are likely to realize that they didn't understand what the wireframes implied, so the wireframes need to be adjusted. In short, you end up looping through steps 2 through 4 in a process that can easily become frustrating.

With that as background, you should know about the two methods that are presented in figure 18-16. These are proven methods that can help the design process go more smoothly. They have been used for all types of systems for many years, and they work for website projects too.

The first method is *top-down design.* This means that you design the most critical pages of the website first, even though you haven't completed the site map. That way, the reviewers get a much better idea of how the website will work, and that can clear their thinking when they return to the site map and the designs for other pages. For example, the most critical pages in a commercial site are the home page and the product pages. So, if you can get approval for those pages, the design process if off to a good start.

After you get approval for those pages, you continue with the next set of critical pages. For a commercial site, these are typically the Shopping Cart and Checkout pages. And once you get approval for those pages, your design is well on its way to completion.

The second method you should be aware of is *prototyping*. This means that you develop a working model (*prototype*) of the critical web pages early in the design process. Then, the reviewers can actually use the pages to see how they work. That will often raise all sorts of concerns that can be resolved early in the design process when the cost of fixing the problems is relatively inexpensive. If you don't prototype a website, critical issues are likely to be discovered when the pages are implemented, and when they cost a lot more to fix.

Prototyping is usually used in combination with top-down design so the most important pages are prototyped first. Then, other pages can be added to the prototype as the top-down design continues. When the design is complete and approved, the prototype can be built into the actual website or the prototype can be discarded and the website built in a more permanent way.

The prototype for the Shop Books page of murach.com

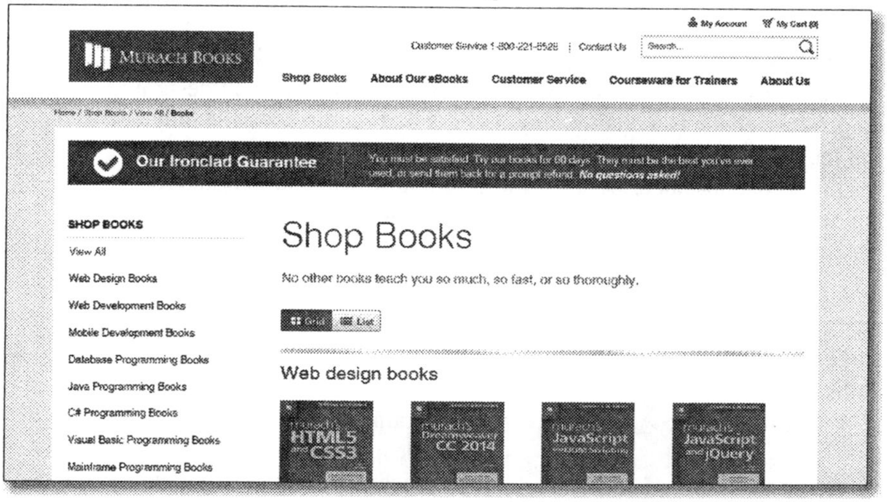

The prototype for one of the book pages

Description

- *Top-down design* means that you start with the most difficult aspects of a website and proceed downwards through the less critical aspects. This implies that you don't have to complete the site map before you wireframe and illustrate each set of critical pages.
- A *prototype* is a working model of a website. This gives reviewers an accurate view of how the web pages will work. The benefit of *prototyping* is that you detect problems early in the development cycle when they cost less to fix. In general, you start by prototyping the critical pages of the site that you've identified through top-down design.

Figure 18-16 Top-down design and prototyping

Perspective

If you apply what you've learned in this chapter, you should be able to design simple websites of your own. But you should also realize that designing and developing a website is a challenging process that requires a wide range of skills. That includes graphics design, HTML and CSS, JavaScript and jQuery, writing for the web, and much more. In short, the more you learn about web design and development, the better your websites will be.

Terms

usability
breadcrumbs
chunking
alignment
proximity
repetition
contrast
lifecycle
target audience
site map
wireframe
web designer
graphics designer
top-down design
prototyping

Summary

- When you design a website, *usability* is the primary issue. That refers to how easy a website is to use, and to a large extent that determines the success of the website. To achieve usability, a website needs to implement the current conventions for website use.
- The home page of a website should be used to sell the site by emphasizing what's different about the site and why users should want to use it.
- To let the users know where they are as they navigate through a site, you can highlight the active links on the page, match the heading on the page to the link that led to it, and use *breadcrumbs*.
- *Chunking* refers to the division of information into topics (chunks) that can be presented on separate web pages or in separate components on a page.
- If you aren't a graphics designer, you should at least know the principles of *alignment*, *proximity*, *repetition*, and *contrast*. You should also know how to make the typography easy to read.
- Writing for the web isn't like writing for print. Instead, web writing should be written in inverted pyramid style, use headings and subheadings, and use bulleted and numbered lists.
- The *lifecycle* of all systems consists of design, implementation, and maintenance. Often, more time and money are spent on the maintenance of a website than on its development.

- When you design a website, you start by defining its *target audience* and goals. Then, those definitions guide you as you develop the site map and design the pages for the site.
- The *site map* identifies all of the pages of the website as well as the links in the navigation bar.
- To plan the designs of the pages for a website, you start with black-and-white *wireframes* so the focus is on function, not appearance. Then, you develop full color illustrations of those pages.
- With few exceptions, you will work with other people on the design of a site. In a large company, the design team may include web designers, writers, marketing specialists, and graphics designers.
- A *web designer* is involved with all aspects of web design. A *graphics designer* focuses on the graphics that make a website look inviting and manageable.
- When you use *top-down* design for a website, you design the most critical pages first, then the next most critical set of pages, and so forth. This implies that you don't have to complete the site map for all of the pages of the site before you design the critical pages. Instead, you work on one set of pages at a time.
- When you *prototype* the critical pages of a website, you develop a working model of those pages. Then, the reviewers can actually run the pages and see how they work. This works in combination with top-down design, and it can resolve misunderstandings early in the design process when they're easier to fix.

19

How to deploy a website on a web server

Once you've developed and tested a website on your local computer, you're just a few steps away from making that website available to anyone in the world who is connected to the Internet. To do that, you just need to transfer the files for your website to a web server that's connected to the Internet.

How to get a web host and domain name

Before you can *deploy* (or *publish*) a website to the Internet, you need to have access to a web server that's connected to the Internet. If you already have access to an Internet web server, you can use that server. Otherwise, you can search the Internet for a web host as described in this topic. If you want to register a domain name for your site, a web host can usually do that for you too.

How to find a web host

Figure 19-1 shows how to find a *web host*, or *web hosting service*. To do that, you can search the web for "web host" or "web hosting service". Then, you can follow the links until you find a web host that has all the features you need. For small websites like the ones presented in this book, you only need a small amount of disk space. For larger websites, you may need more disk space, access to a database server, and a server-side programming language such as PHP, JSP, or ASP.NET.

In addition, most web hosts provide one or more *FTP (File Transfer Protocol)* accounts. This provides a way for you to transfer the files for your website to and from your web host.

Most web hosts charge a monthly fee. For a small website, the price may be as little as $5 per month. Also, some web hosts provide some services for free. If you search the Internet, you'll find a wide range of services and prices.

If you already pay an *Internet Service Provider* (*ISP*) to connect to the Internet, you can check to see if it provides free web hosting as part of its monthly fees. If so, you can check to see if it provides the web hosting features that you need for your website.

When you get a web host, you will receive an *IP address* in this format: 64.46.106.120. You can use this address to access your website. Later, when you get your domain name, you can access your site with either the IP address or the domain name. Internally, the Internet uses IP addresses to address websites, but people use domain names because they're easier to remember.

A web host

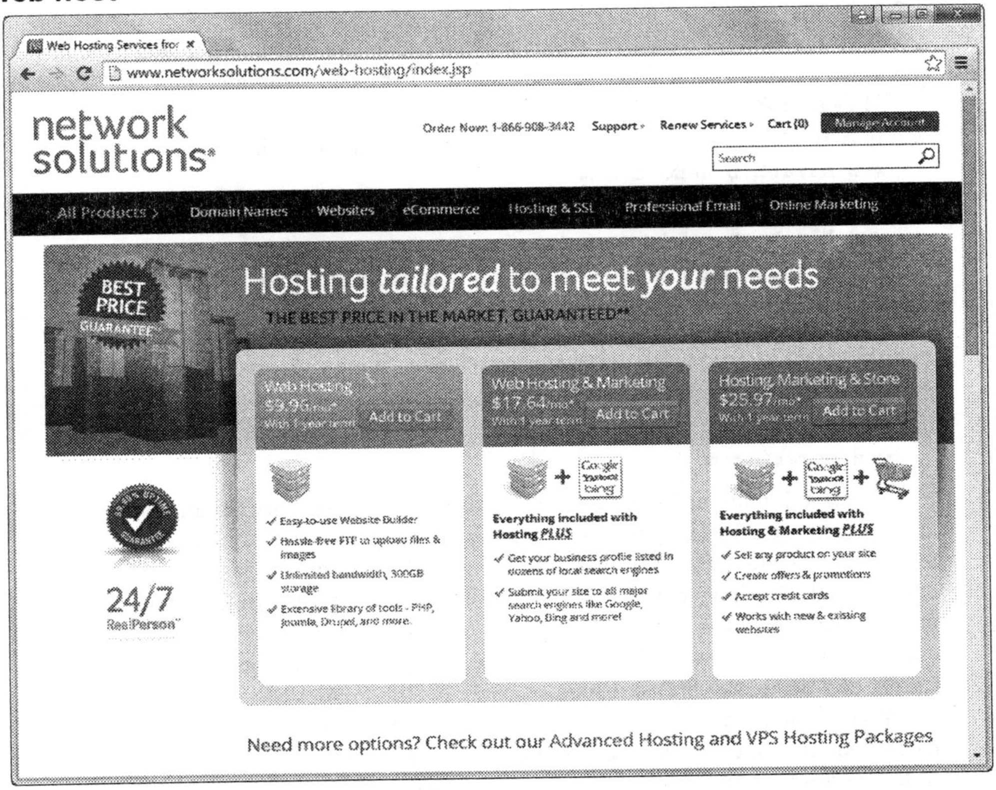

Description

- A *web host*, or *web hosting service*, provides space on a server computer that's connected to the Internet, usually for a monthly fee. You can use a web host to make your website accessible via the Internet.
- *File Transfer Protocol* (*FTP*) allows you to transfer the files for your website to and from your web host.
- To find a web host, search the web for "web host" or "web hosting service". Then, follow the links until you find a web host that has all the features you need.
- An *Internet Service Provider* (*ISP*) often includes free web hosting as part of its monthly fees. As a result, if you have an ISP, you can check to see if it provides the web hosting features that you need for your website.

Figure 19-1 How to find a web host

How to get a domain name

If you're using a web host, you can often use its *domain name* to access your website. For example, if your web hosting company has a domain name of

```
bluehost.com
```

you may be able to access your website using a *subdomain* like this:

```
www.murach.bluehost.com
```

Or, you may be able to access your website using a subfolder like this:

```
www.bluehost.com/murach
```

Either way, the domain name of the web host is included in the URL that's used to access your website.

For most professional websites, you'll want to get your own domain name. That way, you can access your website without including the domain name of the web host in the URL. For example, you can access your website with a URL like this:

```
www.murach.com
```

To get a domain name, you can use a website like Network Solutions, as shown in figure 19-2. But first, you need to decide what extension you want to use for the website. The .com extension was originally intended to be used for commercial websites, .net was intended to be used for networking websites, and .org was intended to be used for other organizations. However, many other extensions are now available, such as those for military (.mil), government (.gov), and business (.biz) websites.

When you use a site like the one shown here, you typically enter one or more domain names. Then, the *domain name registry* is searched to see which of the names is available, and you can choose to purchase any available name for a specific amount of time. If you are using a web host, it may also provide a service like this.

A search for a domain name

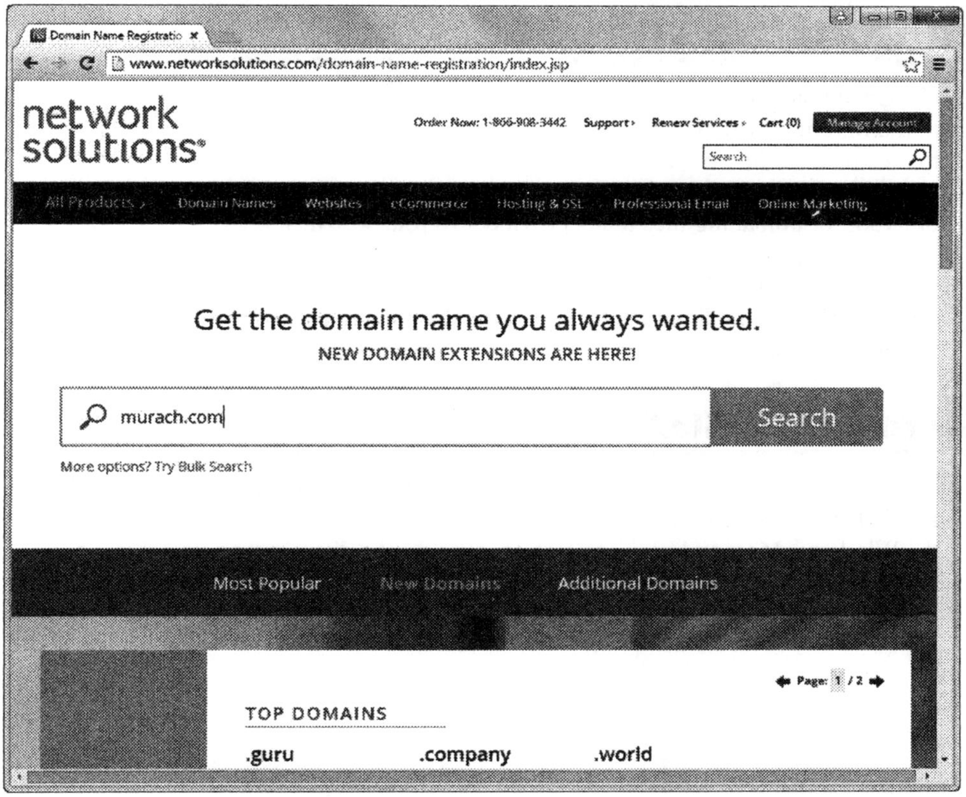

Description

- A *domain name* is a user-friendly name that's used to locate a resource that's connected to the Internet. For example, google.com is a domain name.
- A domain name can have one or more *subdomains*. For example, mail.google.com is a subdomain.
- The .com, .net, and .org extensions are popular endings for domain names. These extensions were originally intended to be used for commercial websites (.com), networking infrastructure websites (.net), and other types of organizations (.org).
- The *domain name registry* is a database of all registered domain names.
- If you are using a web hosting service, you can often use that service to register the domain name for you. To start, you can use your web hosting service to find a domain name that hasn't been registered yet. Then, you can have your web hosting service register that domain name for you.

How to transfer files to and from the web

Once you have a web host and domain name, you can publish your website to the Internet by transferring the files for your website from your local computer to the correct folder on the web host's server. To do that, you can use an FTP client like FileZilla, an IDE like Dreamweaver CC that includes an FTP client, or a tool for uploading files that's provided by your web host.

To give you an idea of how FTP clients work, the next three figures show you how FileZilla Client works. This is a free program that's easy to use. If you're using Aptana Studio 3, though, you may want to use the FTP program that it provides.

How to install FileZilla Client

Figure 19-3 shows how to install FileZilla Client. To do that, go to the FileZilla website and follow the instructions shown there. Since FileZilla runs on the Windows, Mac, and Linux operating systems, the directions for installing it vary depending on your operating system.

An FTP program

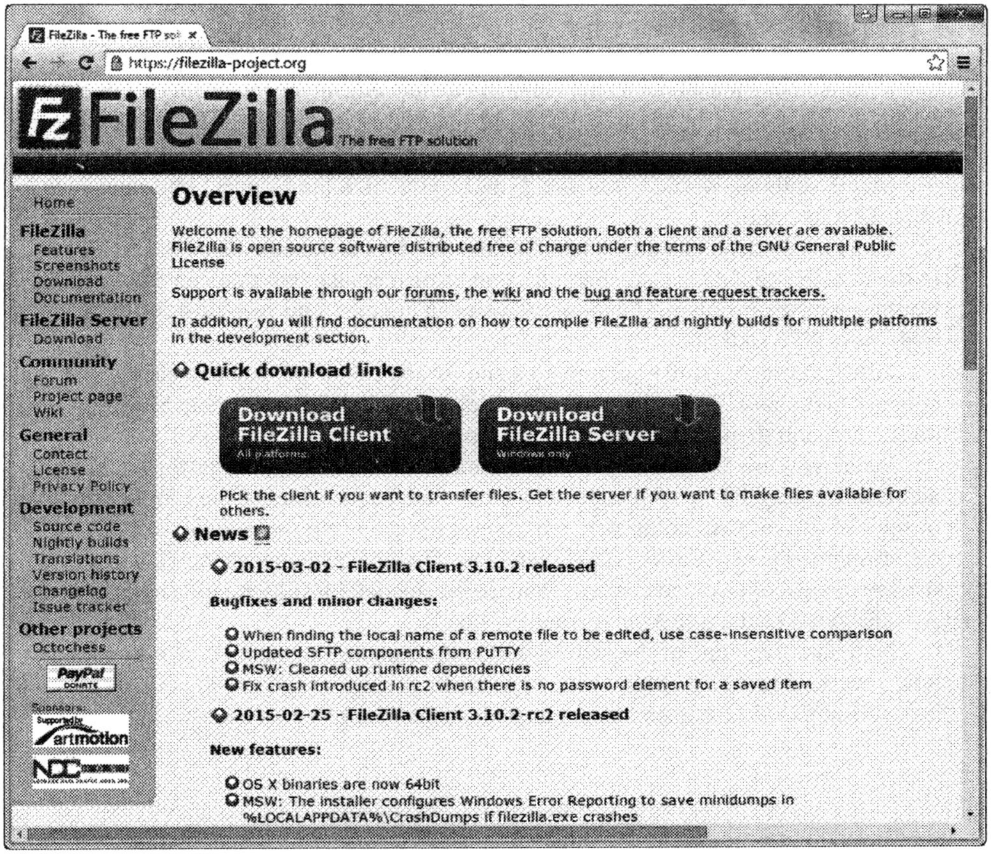

How to install FileZilla Client

1. Go to the FileZilla website (www.filezilla-project.org).
2. Click on the Download FileZilla Client link.
3. Follow the instructions to install the FileZilla Client application on your system.

Description

- FileZilla is a free FTP client application that runs on the Windows, Mac, and Linux operating systems.
- FileZilla supports basic FTP as well as FTP over implicit TLS/SSL (FTPS), FTP over explicit TLS/SSL (FTPES), and SSH File Transfer Protocol (SFTP), which can be used for secure file transfers.

Figure 19-3 How to install the FileZilla FTP client

How to connect to a website on a remote web server

Figure 19-4 shows how to use FileZilla to connect to your website on your web host. To do that the first time, you use the Site Manager dialog box to create the new site and give it a name. Then, you specify the host name, server type, user name, and password for the site. Finally, you click the Connect button to connect to the site.

If the connection is successful, FileZilla displays a window like the one in the next figure. Otherwise, it displays an error message that you can use to troubleshoot the problem. If necessary, you can contact your web host for help with these FTP settings.

After you successfully connect to a site for the first time, you can easily connect to it again. To do that, you just select the site name in the Site Manager dialog box and then click the Connect button.

When you use FileZilla Client, you usually set the default folder for the local and remote sites. For example, you set the default local folder to the root folder of the website on your computer, and you set the default remote folder to the root folder for your website on the web host. That makes it easy to work with the website each time you connect to it. To set the default folder, you use the Advanced tab of the Site Manager dialog box.

Note that the name of the root folder on the remote site varies depending on how your web server is configured. As a result, you may need to ask your web host for help or do some experimenting to set the root folder correctly.

FileZilla's Site Manager dialog box

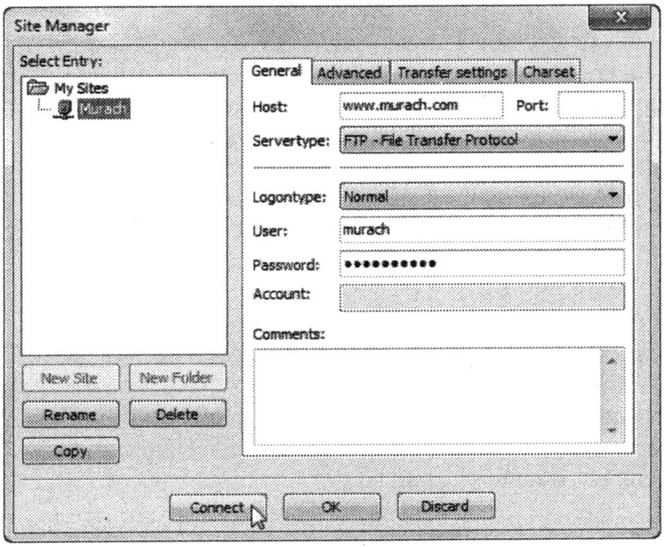

How to connect to a website for the first time

1. Start FileZilla, and then use the File→Site Manager command to display the Site Manager dialog box.
2. Click the New Site button and enter a name for the site.
3. Enter the details needed to connect to the site, including the host name, user name, and password.
4. Click the Connect button to save the connection settings and connect to the site.

How to connect to a website after it has been set up

- Open the Site Manager, click on the site name, and click the Connect button.

How to edit the settings for a website

- Open the Site Manager, click on the site name, edit its settings, and click the OK button.

Description

- For the Server Type option, you typically use FTP. For sensitive data, though, you can use FTP over implicit TLS/SSL (FTPS), FTP over explicit TLS/SSL (FTPES), or SSH File Transfer Protocol (SFTP).
- For the Logon Type option, you typically use Normal. See FileZilla help for a description of the other options.
- To set the default folders for the local and remote sites, use the Advanced tab.

Figure 19-4 How to connect to a website on a remote web server

How to upload and download files

Figure 19-5 shows the FileZilla window after a connection has been made to a remote website. Here, the right pane of the main window shows the folder tree for the remote site, along with the subfolders and files in the selected folder. To display the contents of a subfolder, you can double-click on it, and to move up a level to the parent folder, you can double-click on the first folder (the one that's identified by two dots). You can use the same techniques to work with the files and folders on the local site, which are listed in the left pane of the main window.

To transfer one or more files or folders from your local site to the remote site, you can use the technique described in this figure. This is known as *uploading* files. You can use a similar technique to transfer files from the remote site to your local site, which is known as *downloading* files. Note that before you upload files, you must navigate to the folder on the remote site where you want to store the files. Similarly, before you download files, you must navigate to the folder on the local site where you want to store the files.

FileZilla when it is connected to a web host

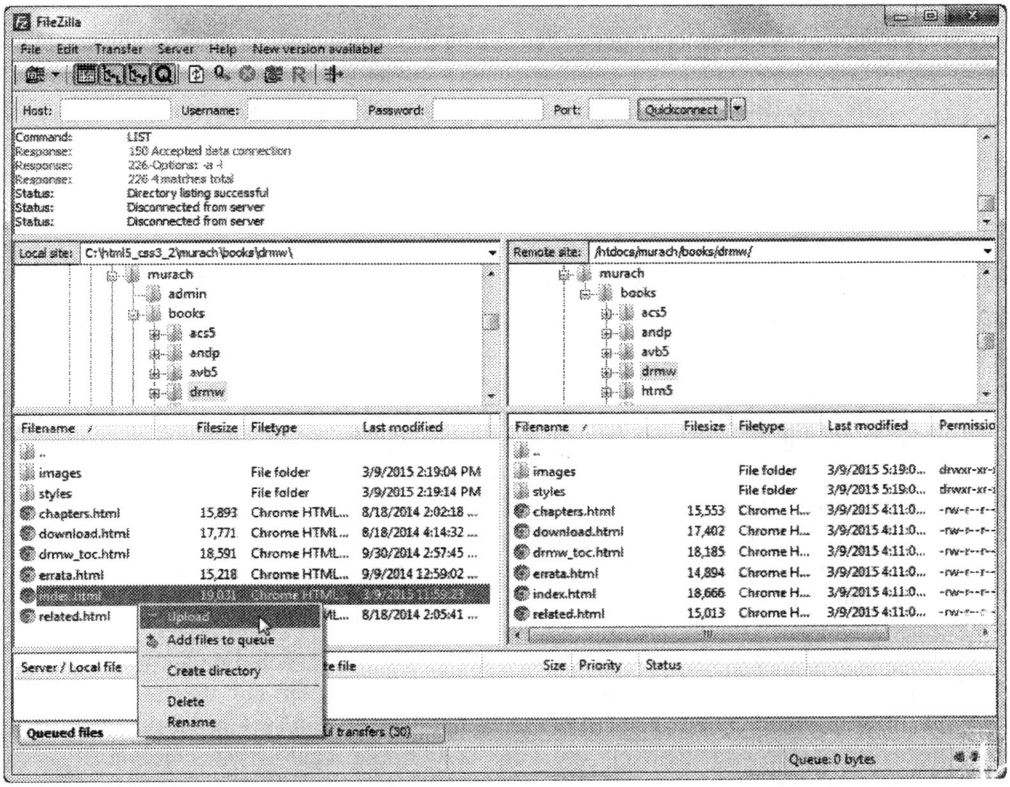

Description

- The top left pane of the main FileZilla window shows the folder structure of the local system, and the top right pane shows the folder structure of the remote system.
- If you select a folder in either folder tree, the subfolders and files in that folder are displayed in the lower pane. Then, you can use that pane to navigate through the folders.
- The folders that are identified by two dots at the top of both lower panes represent the parent folders.
- To *upload* a file or folder from the local site to the remote site, display the folder on the remote site where you want the file or folder uploaded. Then, right-click on the file or folder in the local site and select the Upload command from the resulting menu.
- To *download* a file or folder from the remote site to the local site, display the folder on the local site where you want the file or folder downloaded. Then, right-click on the file or folder in the remote site and select the Download command.
- You can also upload or download multiple files and folders by selecting them and then using the Upload or Download command.

Figure 19-5 How to upload and download files

Four more skills for deploying a website

After you deploy your site to a remote web server, you need to test it. You also need to get your site indexed by the popular search engines so they will deliver people to your site. And you need to analyze you website to maintain its health.

How to test a website that has been uploaded to the web server

Figure 19-6 shows how to test a new web page that has just been uploaded to an existing site. In that case, you need to check all the links that go to it and from it. You also need to check that all its content is there and working correctly, including images, JavaScript features, and jQuery features.

For instance, a web page often links to one or more HTML files, CSS files, and image files. Then, if you forget to upload a supporting file, one of the links won't work correctly. In that case, you can solve the problem by uploading the supporting file.

To test an entire website that has just been uploaded to a web server, you need to methodically review each of the pages on the site, including all of the links to and from each page. The larger the site, the more difficult this is, and the more methodical you need to be. To complicate the task, you need to do this for all of the browsers that your users are likely to use. That includes mobile browsers if your site will be displayed on mobile devices.

Fortunately, a number of automated tools are available that you can use to make sure that a website is working properly. Many of these tools can also be used to maintain the health and effectiveness of a website. You'll learn about some of these tools later in this chapter.

A website on the Internet

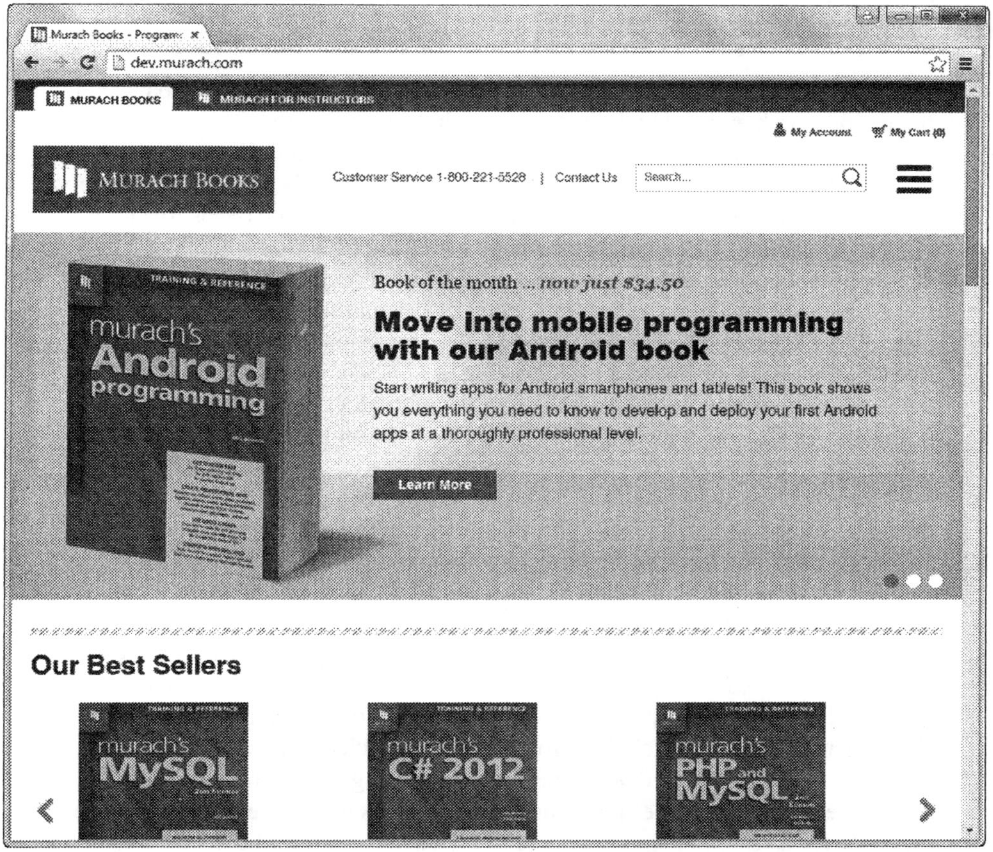

How to test a web page that you've just added to your site

- Start your web browser, go to your home page, and navigate to the new page using every route that your site has for getting there.
- Review the contents for the page, and make sure it's all there and it all works, including the images, JavaScript features, and jQuery features.
- Test all the links on the page to make sure they work correctly.
- Retest the page in all of the other browsers to make sure it works correctly in those browsers too.

How to test a new website

- Methodically review all of the pages and test all of the links, one page at a time.
- Do this for each of the browsers that your users might be using.

Figure 19-6 How to test a website that has been uploaded to the web server

How to get your website into search engines and directories

After you deploy and test your website, you will want to get your pages into the major search engines and directories so they can deliver visitors to your site. To do that, you can go to the URLs in the table in figure 19-7. These URLs take you to submission pages like the Google page shown in this figure. Alternatively, you can search the Internet for "submit site to ..." to locate the pages for these and other search engines and directories, as well as pages that let you submit a site to a number of search engines and directories at once.

At the submission page, you only need to submit the URL of your home page. Then, if your site is linked properly, the search engine's *robot* will "crawl" through the rest of your pages by following the links in your site. As it crawls, the robot will score your pages. Those scores will later determine how high your pages come up in the searches, and of course you want them to come up as high as possible.

The trouble is that the search engines use different algorithms for determining the scores of your pages. For instance, some search engines improve the score of a page if it has links to other sites. Some improve the score if the pages of other websites link to the page. To complicate the process, the search engines change their algorithms from time to time without any notice.

To find out more about the scoring algorithms that are used, you can go to the sites for the search engines or directories that you're submitting your site to. Most of these sites also give advice for optimizing your site for their engines. You can also search the web for information on search engine optimization.

Once you've submitted your website for indexing, you don't have to do it again, even if you've made significant enhancements to the site. That's because the robot for a search engine periodically crawls through all of the sites and indexes the pages again, sometimes with a new algorithm for scoring.

Last, you should be aware that most web hosts offer statistics packages that tell you where your visitors are coming from. You can also buy third-party packages that do that, or you can sign up for a free Google Analytics account (www.google.com/analytics). This data can help you figure out what's working… and what isn't working…so you can make changes that will improve your site.

But what if you don't want a search engine to index some of your pages? And what happens if you delete a page that is still in the index for a search engine? You can find out how to handle those conditions in the next figure.

The URLs for the major search engines and directory

Site name	Site type	Web URL
Google	Search engine	http://www.google.com/addurl/
MSN/Bing	Search engine	http://www.bing.com/webmaster/SubmitSitePage.aspx
DMOZ	Directory	http://www.dmoz.org/add.html

The Google page for submitting your site

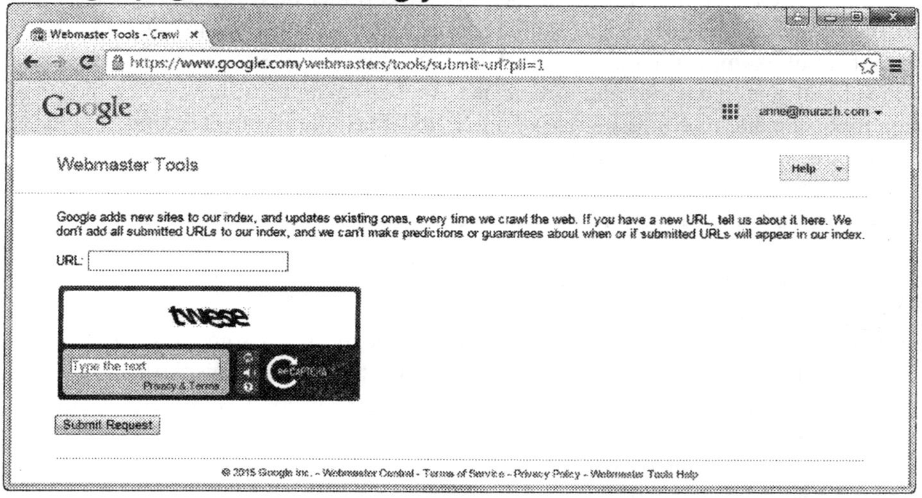

Description

- After you have deployed and tested your site, you will want to get your pages into search engines and directories that can deliver visitors to your site. To submit your site to the two major search engines and the major directory, go to the websites in the table above.
- When you submit your site to a search engine or directory, you only need to provide the URL for your home page. Then, the *robot* (or *spider*) for that engine or directory "crawls" through the pages of your site and indexes them.
- After your site has been indexed the first time, the robot will periodically crawl through your site again to update the index based on the changes that you've made to your site.
- Each search engine or directory has its own algorithms for scoring pages, and those scores determine how high a page will be placed in the search results for specific keywords.
- At the site for each search engine or directory, you can get information that you can use to help your pages do better in the search results.
- Most web hosts offer statistics packages that track which sites and search engines are sending you visitors.

Note

- Yahoo is now part of the Bing network, which means that searches that you run from Yahoo are done with Bing. So you don't have to submit a site to Yahoo separately.

Figure 19-7 How to get your website into search engines and directories

How to control which pages are indexed and visited

For many websites, there are pages and maybe even folders of pages that you don't want indexed. For instance, you usually don't want your shopping cart pages indexed. To stop pages from being indexed, you can use one of the two methods shown in figure 19-8.

First, you can set up a robots.txt file in the root folder of your website that specifies which folders or files to exclude from indexing. This is illustrated by the first set of examples in this figure. Here, the * for user-agent means that it applies to all search engines and directories. As these examples show, you can use a robots.txt file to eliminate one or more folders or files from indexing.

Second, you can code a robots meta tag with the content set to "noindex" and "nofollow". This means that the robot shouldn't index the page, and it also shouldn't follow any of the links on the page as it crawls through the pages of the site.

Now, back to the question of what happens if you delete a page on your website that has already been indexed. Unfortunately, it will still come up in the search results until your site is re-indexed. In the meantime, if somebody clicks on its link, the page won't be found and a 404 error page will be displayed. Since this indicates to the user that your site isn't being properly maintained, you certainly don't want that to happen.

One way to get around this problem is to delete the content from the page, but not the page itself. Then, you can add a refresh meta tag like the one in this figure that will redirect the user to another page. In this tag, the content attribute should be set to zero (0) so the redirection is done right away (no delay). Then, the url attribute should be set to the page that you want the old page to be redirected to.

Unfortunately, the refresh meta tag isn't supported by all browsers, so you need to provide alternatives for it. Since your web server determines how each HTTP request is handled, this is usually handled by server-side code that redirects the request to a current page.

Three robots.txt files

A file that tells all search engines not to index the pages in the cart folder

```
User-agent: *
Disallow: /cart/
```

A file that tells all search engines not to index the pages in two folders

```
User-agent: *
Disallow: /cart/
Disallow: /private/
```

A file that tells all search engines not to index one folder and one file

```
User-agent: *
Disallow: /cart/
Disallow: /backlist/private.html
```

A meta tag that tells a robot not to index a page or follow its links

```
<meta http-equiv="robots" content="noindex, nofollow">
```

A meta tag that redirects the user from a deleted page to a current page

```
<meta http-equiv="refresh" content="0" url="../asp5_cs.html">
```

How to control which pages are indexed

- If you don't want the robot to index the pages in a folder of the site, you can add a text file named robots.txt to the root folder of your website. You can also use this file to specify single pages that you don't want the robot to index.
- Another way to stop a robot from indexing a page is to add a robots meta tag to the page. In the content attribute, "noindex" tells the robot not to index the page and "nofollow" tells the robot not to follow the links on the page.

How to control which pages are visited from the search results

- When you delete a page from your website, it will remain in the index for a search engine until the robot for that engine crawls through your site again, and maybe even longer.
- To prevent users from going to a page that you've deleted before your site is re-indexed, you can delete the content of the page but not the page itself. Then, you can add a refresh meta tag to the page.
- In the refresh meta tag, the content attribute should be 0 so the redirection is done immediately (0 delay), and the url attribute should specify the page that the user should be redirected to.
- Not all browsers support the refresh meta tag, though, so you should provide a server-side alternative to this whenever possible.

Figure 19-8 How to control which pages are indexed and visited

How to maintain a healthy website

Even after a website is deployed to a web server, tested, and ready to be accessed by anyone on the Internet, more can typically be done to improve its effectiveness. For example, you may be able to do more to improve the search rankings for a site or to improve user accessibility. The easiest way to analyze a website and identify the areas that can be improved to keep it healthy is to use tools like the ones listed in figure 19-9.

The most popular tool for analyzing a website is Google Webmaster. This tool is a free, web-based application that you can use to monitor for Google crawl errors, security issues, mobile usability, missing references in the robots.txt file, and more. It can also suggest improvements to the HTML that will help boost search engine rankings. This tool is especially helpful when you integrate it with other Google tools such as Analytics and SiteSearch.

If you're working on a medium to large website, you might want to use a more robust tool such as SiteImprove. SiteImprove is a fee-based application that performs deep crawls of your site and reports back broken links, misspellings, SEO and accessibility issues, and much more. The dashboard for this application is easy-to-use, and the site's customer support is second to none. Unlike the other tools listed in this figure, SiteImprove is costly but well worth it for organizations that depend heavily on their online presence.

Hubspot's Marketing Grader is particularly useful for checking your website's social media marketing effectiveness. It monitors and reports on your website's social media presence, including blog activity, email marketing campaigns, and even mobile responsiveness.

The last three tools listed here—FreeGrader, Nibbler, and Woorank—provide basic checking for accessibility, SEO, user experience, mobile responsiveness, and more. These tools are free to use, and they provide a good starting point when working with site monitoring tools. In general, they will give you an idea of some of the things that you should and shouldn't be doing when building a website.

The Google Webmaster Tools website

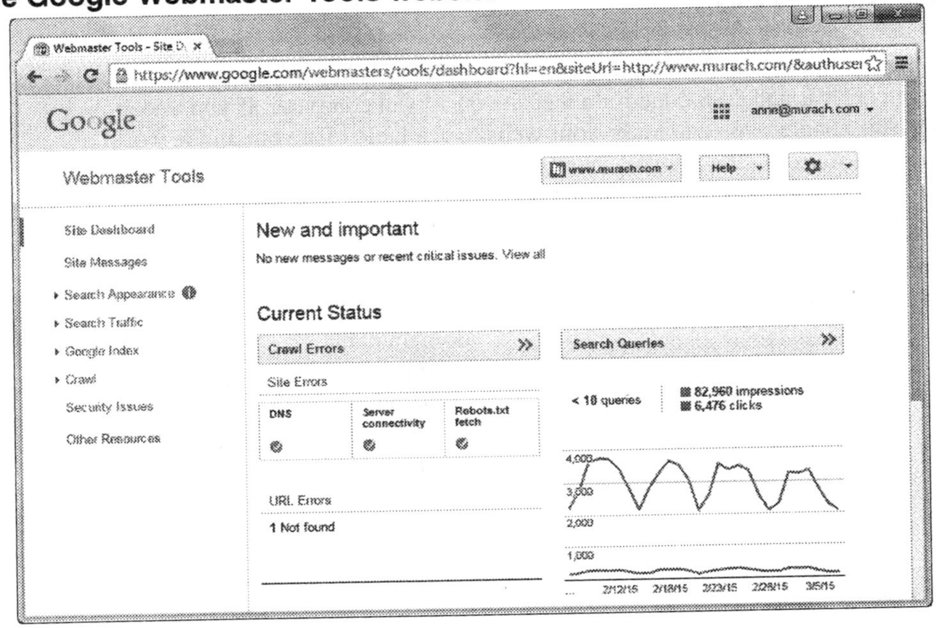

Popular tools for checking the health of a website

Tool	Web URL
Google Webmaster	www.google.com/webmasters/tools/home?hl=en
SiteImprove	www.siteimprove.com
Hubspot's Marketing Grader	marketing.grader.com
FreeGrader	www.freegrader.com
Nibbler	nibbler.silktide.com
Woorank	www.woorank.com

Description

- You can use a number of free and commercial web-based tools to check and maintain the health of your website.
- The most popular tool is Google Webmaster. This free tool analyzes and reports on your site's search appearance, traffic, crawl statistics, security issues, and more.
- SiteImprove is a commercial service that's useful for larger websites. It checks for accessibility and SEO issues, and it will report spelling errors, broken links, site downtime, and more.
- Hubspot's Marketing Grader is a free tool that will report on your website's social media presence, blog activity, email marketing campaigns, and even mobile responsiveness.
- Nibbler, FreeGrader, and Woorank provide free scores on accessibility, user experience, marketing, and technology along with suggestions for improvement.

Figure 19-9 How to maintain a healthy website

Perspective

If you understand the first three sections of this book, you can write and test the HTML and CSS code for a website on a local computer. If you understand this chapter, you can make your website available to anyone in the world who can connect to the Internet. Now, it's up to you to dream up a website that's worth sharing with the world!

Terms

deploy
publish
web host
web hosting service
FTP (File Transfer Protocol)
ISP (Internet Service Provider)
IP address
domain name
subdomain
domain name registry
upload a file
download a file
robot
spider

Summary

- To *deploy* (or *publish*) a website, you can use a *web host*, or *web hosting service*, that will make your website accessible from the Internet.
- You can use *File Transfer Protocol* (*FTP*) to transfer the files for your website to and from your web host.
- An *IP address* uniquely identifies a website, and so does a *domain name*.
- To find a *domain name* for your website, you search the *domain name registry*, which is a database of all registered domain names.
- Once you have a domain name, you can have one or more *subdomains* that address portions of the domain.
- You can use an FTP program to *upload* files from your computer to your Internet web server and to *download* files from your web server to your computer. FileZilla is a free FTP program that runs on the Windows, Mac, and Linux operating systems.
- To test a web page that has been uploaded to the Internet, start your web browser, navigate to the URL for the web page, and click on all links to make sure they work correctly.
- To get your website into a search engine, go to the URL for its submission page. Then, its *robot* (or *spider*) will crawl through your pages and score them for later searches that are based on keywords.
- To stop pages from being indexed by a search engine, you can use a robots.txt file or robots meta tags. To redirect the request for an inactive page on your website to another page, you can use a refresh meta tag.

Appendix A

How to set up your computer for this book

This appendix shows how to install the software that we recommend for editing and testing the web pages and applications for this book. That includes Aptana Studio 3 as the text editor for both Windows and Mac OS users, plus the Chrome and Firefox browsers for both Windows and Mac OS users. This appendix also shows you how to download and install the source code for this book.

As you read these descriptions, please remember that most websites are continually upgraded. As a result, some of the procedures in this appendix may have changed since this book was published. Nevertheless, these procedures should still be good guides to installing the software.

How to install Aptana Studio 3

If you're already comfortable with a text editor that works for editing HTML and CSS, you can continue using it. But otherwise, we recommend that you use Aptana Studio 3. It is a free editor that offers many features, it runs on both Windows and Mac OS systems, and chapter 2 presents a quick tutorial on it that will get you started right.

On a Windows system

Figure A-1 shows how to download and install Aptana Studio 3 on a Windows system.

On a Mac OS system

Figure A-1 also shows how to download and install Aptana Studio 3 on a Mac OS system.

The website address for downloading Aptana Studio 3

http://www.aptana.com/products/studio3/download

How to install Aptana Studio 3 on a Windows system

1. Go to the website address above.
2. Click on the Download Aptana Studio 3 button near the bottom of the page, click on the Save File button in the resulting dialog box, and identify the location where you want the file saved in the Save As dialog box that's displayed.
3. When the Download finishes, use Windows Explorer to find the exe file, and double-click on it to start it.
4. As you step through the wizard that follows, you can accept all of the default settings that are offered.
5. After Aptana Studio 3 is installed, start it. Then, if you don't have a Git application installed on your system, Aptana will ask you if you want it to install a Portable Git application. Accept that option because Aptana won't run without it.

How to install Aptana Studio 3 on a Mac OS X system

1. Go to the website address above.
2. Click on the Customize Your Download button, and select Mac OS X.
3. Click on the Download Aptana Studio 3 button, and click on the Save File button in the resulting dialog box.
4. When the Download finishes, double-click on the dmg file in the Downloads folder to display the Aptana Studio 3 window.
5. Double-click the Aptana Studio 3 Installer folder to start the installation.
6. When the installation is complete, start Aptana Studio 3. Then, if you don't have a Git application installed on your system, Aptana will ask you if you want it to install a Portable Git application. Accept that option because Aptana won't run without it.

Description

- Aptana runs on Windows, Mac, and Linux systems.
- Git is a source code management tool that Aptana requires. If necessary, Aptana will install it for you when you start Aptana for the first time.
- Chapter 2 of this book presents a tutorial that will get you off to a fast start with Aptana.

Figure A-1 How to install Aptana Studio 3 as your text editor

How to install Chrome and Firefox

When you develop web pages and applications, you need to test them on all of the browsers that the users of the application are likely to use. For a commercial application, that usually includes Chrome, Internet Explorer, Firefox, Safari, and Opera. Then, if an application doesn't work on one of those browsers, you need to fix it.

As you do most of the exercises for this book, though, you can test your web pages on just two browsers. Windows users should use Internet Explorer plus Chrome, and Mac OS users should use Safari and Chrome. Then, because Chrome and Safari support most of the HTML5 features, you'll be able to see how these features work.

The first procedure in figure A-2 is for downloading and installing Chrome. As you respond to the dialog boxes for the installer, we recommend that you make Chrome your default browser. Then, you can follow the second procedure in this figure to download and install Firefox so you can use it for any additional testing you want to do. If you want to install Opera or Safari, you can use a similar procedure.

The website address for downloading Chrome

`https://www.google.com/intl/en-US/chrome/browser/`

How to install Chrome

1. Go to the website address above.
2. Click on the Download Chrome button.
3. Review the Google Chrome Terms of Service that are displayed. Then, indicate if you want Chrome to be your default browser and if you want to automatically send usage statistics and crash reports to Google.
4. Click the Accept and Install button.
5. If a dialog box is displayed with a security warning, click the Run button.
6. If you're asked if you want to allow the program to make changes to your computer, click the Yes button.
7. The installer is downloaded and Chrome is installed and started.
8. When the Welcome to Chrome dialog box is displayed asking you to set the default browser, click the Next button and then select a browser.
9. When the Set up Chrome tab is displayed, you can log in using your email address and password so your bookmarks, history, and settings are updated on all the devices where you use Chrome. Or, you can click the "Skip for now" link to skip this step.
10. A tab is displayed with the Google home page.

The website address for downloading Firefox

`http://www.mozilla.com`

How to install Firefox

1. Go to the website address above.
2. Click on the Download Firefox - Free button.
3. Save the exe file to your C drive.
4. Run the exe file and respond to the resulting dialog boxes.

Description

- Because Chrome is the most popular browser today, we suggest that you test all of the exercises that you do for this book in this browser.
- If you have a Windows system, Internet Explorer will already be on it and you should test with it as well.
- If you have a Mac, Safari will already be on it and you should test with it too. You won't be able to install Internet Explorer because it doesn't run on Macs.
- Because Firefox, Safari, and Opera are also popular browsers, you'll want to install them so you can see what level of support they provide for HTML5. To install Safari and Opera, you can use a procedure similar to the one above for installing Firefox.

Figure A-2 How to install Chrome and Firefox

How to install and use the source code for this book

The next two figures show how to install and use the source code for this book. One figure is for Windows users, the other for Mac OS users.

For Windows users

Figure A-3 shows how to install the source code for this book on a Windows system. This includes the source code for the applications in this book, all of the significant examples, the starting files for the exercises, and the solutions for the exercises.

When you finish this procedure, the book applications, examples, exercises, and solutions will be in the four folders that are listed in this figure, but the exercises will also be in the second folder that's shown. Then, when you do the exercises, you use the subfolders and files in this folder:

```
c:\html5_css3_2\exercises
```

but you have backup copies of these subfolders and files in this folder:

```
c:\murach\html5_css3_2\exercises
```

That way, you can restore the files for an exercise by copying the files from the second folder to the first.

As you do the exercises, you may want to copy code from a book application or example into a file that you're working with. That's easy to do because the folders or files for the examples are preceded by the figure numbers that present them. For instance, this file:

```
c:\html5_css3_2\book_examples\ch10\05_table_css3.html
```

is the HTML file that contains the code for the table example in figure 10-5 in chapter 10. And this folder:

```
c:\murach\html5_css3_2\book_examples\ch16\04_accordion
```

is the folder that contains the files for the accordion example that's in figure 16-4 in chapter 16.

If you want to experiment with the code in the book applications or examples, you may want to copy the folders first so the original files won't be changed. For instance, you can copy the book_apps and book_examples folders from this folder:

```
c:\murach\html5_css3_2\
```

to this folder:

```
c:\html5_css3_2\
```

Then, you will have backup copies.

The Murach website

```
www.murach.com
```

The default installation folder for the source code on a Windows system

```
c:\murach\html5_css3_2
```

The Windows folders for the applications, examples, and exercises

```
c:\murach\html5_css3_2\book_apps
c:\murach\html5_css3_2\book_examples
c:\murach\html5_css3_2\exercises
c:\murach\html5_css3_2\solutions
```

The Windows folders for doing the exercises

```
c:\html5_css3_2\exercises\ch02
c:\html5_css3_2\exercises\town_hall_1
c:\html5_css3_2\exercises\town_hall_2
c:\html5_css3_2\exercises\town_hall_3
c:\html5_css3_2\exercises\town_hall_mobile
```

How to download and install the source code on a Windows system

1. Go to www.murach.com, and go to the page for *Murach's HTML5 and CSS3 (Third Edition)*.
2. Scroll down the page until you see the "FREE downloads" tab and then click on it. Then, click the "All book files" link for the self-extracting zip file. This will download a setup file named 3htm_allfiles.exe onto your hard drive.
3. Use Windows Explorer to find the exe file on your hard drive. Then, double-click this file. This installs the source code for the book applications, examples, exercises, and solutions into the folders shown above. After it does this install, the exe file copies the exercises folder to c:\html5_css3_2 so you have two copies of the exercises.

How to restore an exercise file

- Copy it from its subfolder in

  `c:\murach\html5_css3_2\exercises`

  to the corresponding subfolder in

  `c:\html5_css3_2\exercises`

Description

- The exe file that you download stores the exercises in two different folders. That way, you can do the exercises using the files that are stored in one folder, but you have a backup copy in case you want to restore the starting files for an exercise.
- As you do the exercises, you can copy code from the book applications and examples in the book_apps and book_examples folders.
- In the book_examples folder, the prefixes on the files and folders refer to the number of the figure that presents the example.

Figure A-3 How to install the source code for this book on a Windows system

For Mac OS users

Figure A-4 shows how to install the source code for this book on a Mac OS system. This includes the source code for the applications in this book, all of the significant examples, the starting files for the exercises, and the solutions for the exercises.

When you finish this procedure, the book applications, examples, and exercises will be in the four folders that are listed in this figure, but the exercises will also be in the second folder that's shown. Then, when you do the exercises, you use the subfolders and files in this folder:

```
documents\html5_css3_2\exercises
```

but you have backup copies of these subfolders and files in this folder:

```
documents\murach\html5_css3_2\exercises
```

That way, you can restore the files for an exercise by copying the files from the second folder to the first.

As you do the exercises, you may want to copy code from a book application or example into a file that you're working with. That's easy to do because the folders or files for the examples are preceded by the figure numbers that present them. For instance, this file:

```
documents\html5_css3_2\book_examples\ch10\05_table_css3.html
```

is the HTML file that contains the code for the table example in figure 10-5 in chapter 10. And this folder:

```
documents\murach\html5_css3_2\book_examples\ch16\04_accordion
```

is the folder that contains the files for the accordion example that's in figure 16-4 in chapter 16.

If you want to experiment with the code in the book applications or examples, you may want to copy the folders first so the original files won't be changed. For instance, you can copy the book_apps and book_examples folders from this folder:

```
documents\murach\html5_css3_2\
```

to this folder:

```
documents\html5_css3_2\
```

Then, you will have backup copies.

The Murach website

```
www.murach.com
```

The Mac OS folders for the book applications and exercises

```
documents\murach\html5_css3_2\book_apps
documents\murach\html5_css3_2\book_examples
documents\murach\html5_css3_2\exercises
documents\murach\html5_css3_2\solutions
```

The Mac OS folders for doing the exercises

```
documents\html5_css3_2\exercises\ch02
documents\html5_css3_2\exercises\town_hall_1
documents\html5_css3_2\exercises\town_hall_2
documents\html5_css3_2\exercises\town_hall_3
documents\html5_css3_2\exercises\town_hall_mobile
```

How to download and install the source code on a Mac OS system

1. Go to www.murach.com, and go to the page for *Murach's HTML5 and CSS3 (Third Edition).*
2. Scroll down the page until you see the "FREE downloads" tab and then click on it. Then, click the "All book files" link for the regular zip file. This will download a setup file named 3htm_allfiles.zip onto your hard drive.
3. Move this file into the Documents folder of your home folder. Then, use Finder to go to your Documents folder.
4. Double-click the 3htm_allfiles.zip file to extract the folders for the book applications, examples, exercises, and solutions into the folders shown above.
5. To create two copies of the exercises folder, copy this folder

   ```
   documents\murach\html5_css3_2\exercises
   ```

   to

   ```
   documents\html5_css3_2
   ```

How to restore an exercise file

- Copy it from its subfolder in

  ```
  documents\murach\html5_css3_2\exercises
  ```

  to the corresponding subfolder in

  ```
  documents\html5_css3_2\exercises
  ```

Description

- This procedure stores the exercises in two different folders. That way, you do the exercises using the files that are in one folder, but you also have a backup copy.
- As you do the exercises, you can copy code from the book applications and examples in the book_apps and book_examples folders.
- In the book_examples folder, the prefix on a file or folder refers to the number of the figure that presents the example.

Figure A-4 How to install the source code for this book on a Mac OS system

Index

B

C

D

E

F

G

H

I

J

K

L

M

N

O

P

Q

R

S

T

U

V

W

XYZ